CANETTI AND NIETZSCHE

I0895660

SUNY Series, The Margins of Literature
Mihai I. Spariosu, editor

CANETTI AND NIETZSCHE

Theories of Humor in *Die Blendung*

by
Harriet Murphy

State University of New York Press

Published by
State University of New York Press, Albany

© 1997 State University of New York

All rights reserved

Printed in the United States of America

No part of this book may be used or reproduced in any manner whatsoever without written permission. No part of this book may be stored in a retrieval system or transmitted in any form or by any means including electronic, electrostatic, magnetic tape, mechanical, photocopying, recording, or otherwise without the prior permission in writing of the publisher.

For information, address State University of New York Press,
State University Plaza, Albany, NY 12246

Production by Christine Lynch
Marketing by Fran Keneston

Library of Congress Cataloging-in-Publication Data

Murphy, Harriet, 1960-
Canetti and Nietzsche : theories of humor in Die Blendung / by Harriet Murphy.
p. cm. — (SUNY series, the margins of literature)
Includes bibliographical references and index.
ISBN 0-7914-3133-9 (CH : alk. paper). — ISBN 0-7914-3134-7 (PB : alk. paper)
1. Canetti, Elias, 1905-1994 Die Blendung. 2. German wit and humor--History and criticism—Theory, etc. 3. Humorous stories, German--History and criticism. 4. Nietzsche, Friedrich Wilhelm, 1844-1900--Influence. 5. Comic, The, in literature. I. Title. II. Series.
PT2605.A58B5592 1996
833'.912—dc20 95-52246
CIP

10 9 8 7 6 5 4 3 2 1

This book is dedicated to
Sarah and Alexander,
and Timothy and Kate.

CONTENTS

ACKNOWLEDGMENTS

Hanser Verlag, München for extracts from *Die Blendung* (Müchen: Hanser, 1993).

Continuum Books, New York for extracts from *Auto-da-Fé*, translated from the German by C. V. Wedgewood (New York: The Seabury Press, 1979).

The New York Review of Books for the caricature of Canetti by David Levine on the front cover.

I would like to thank John Bayley, formerly of St. Catherine's College, Oxford, for his enthusiasm for this project, when it was discussed for the first time in 1987. I would also like to thank the German Academic Exchange for funding my first research trip to Marbach in the summer of 1989. University College Dublin provided financial assistance for a second research trip to Marbach in the summer of 1990. Herbert Herzmann, of University College Dublin, kindly read the first draft of the first half of this study. His comments and enthusiasm were very welcome. Colleagues in University College Cork were very supportive of my work, as it reached the final stages. T. J. Reiss of New York University kindly put me in touch with Mihai Spariosu, editor of the series "The Margins of Literature," of the University of Georgia. Malcolm Carpenter's Publication Fund at the University of Warwick provided assistance so that the excellent caricature of Elias Canetti, which originally featured in *The New York Review of Books*, could be used on the front cover. My colleagues in the Department of Germanic Studies at the University of Warwick have been particularly supportive of all my work since I joined the Department in 1993. Godfrey Carr must take credit for thinking of the title of this study. Finally, Gregor Dekleva kindly edited the complete manuscript in Vienna in April 1994.

INTRODUCTION

It was not the publication of Canetti's only novel, but the publication of *Masse und Macht* in 1960, which established his international reputation.* It would not be unfair to say that the sociologically topical study of crowds and power was one of the main reasons for the award of the Nobel Prize for Literature in 1981. Indeed, in the academic and popular mind Elias Canetti has become, since 1960 and 1981, virtually synonymous with the assumed concerns of his interdisciplinary study, on the basis of the contribution that study apparently makes to the debate about crowd psychology on the one hand and power on the other. The name Canetti has now become specifically identified with a fierce hatred of power and with the dispassionate ability to anatomize power in its many forms, across geographical, historical, and cultural boundaries. More recently, however, it has been argued that critics have "used" *Masse und Macht* to interpret the works Canetti published before 1960. These have suffered at the hands of that study, and have been seen less on their own terms and more as mere prefigurations of that later "baggy monster" which crosses so many generic and other boundaries. *Die Blendung*, the novel Canetti finally saw published in 1935, when the author was only thirty years old, has, in many cases, been the victim of *Masse und Macht* in precisely this way.

The cultural critic Mihai Spariosu, editor of the series in which *Canetti and Nietzsche: Theories of Humor in Die Blendung* appears, has developed theories of power in his works that are absolutely at variance with Canetti's generally negative thesis about power, as discussed primarily in *Masse und Macht* but also in his essays and the reflections with which he is most often identified. In *Literature, Mimesis and Play* (1982), *Dionysus Reborn* (1989), and *God of Many Names* (1991) Spariosu traces a

*So that this study will be accessible to German and non-German readers, English translations of German quotations from Canetti's novel can be found in the footnotes.

cultural history of power which seems Nietzschean. He stresses its highly positive relationship, in existential terms, with something called play. Spariosu works with the assumption that there is a human instinct for play that has its origins in the will to power or the power principle at the heart of Western civilization. He distinguishes between different phases in Western civilization, stressing the variations there are among the cooperative, rather than the competitive, aspects of power as it manifests itself in what he calls play.

It is now particularly fashionable to promote the playful in literature and the arts generally. The current trend in literary theory and literary criticism, in particular the literary theory and criticism that participates in the movement known as postmodernism, is one that most often, if not exclusively, appeals to critics with loosely leftist leanings. Such critics repeatedly make either stated or unstated claims that playfulness is ideologically subversive of social and political power. This is deemed either intrinsically corrupt or relentlessly destructive of personal power. Their discussions of literary texts that apparently revel in the subversive power of play, make ample use of key terms such as "status quo," "difference," "alterity," "metanarrative," "dialogism," and "the dominant ideology." They make ample use of these terms in the name of "empowering" the individual and rescuing him/her from particular socio-political evils. These are equated with certain stereotypes of race, religion, class, and gender, which are apparently imposed on each individual by society and then psychologically internalized, to result, in extreme cases, in what the Frankfurter Schule has termed "the totalitarian personality." The pressure to conform to such stereotypes is often simply given, with the result that the individual is assured to be a victim, not an author of his/her own destiny.

Set against this group of advocates of the socio-politically subversive nature of play who are motivated by the cause of liberation, are lone voices in the wilderness. A.D. Nuttall, Christopher Prendergast, and Raymond Tallis are united in their assumption that those critics who use a term like "play" or "the free-play of the signifier," or who have provocative things to say about what is meant by their key word, mimesis, in the context of the relationship between literature and life, are pranksters who are a regrettable embarassment to the profession. Nuttall, Prednergast, and Tallis accuse their opponents of a divisive noninterest in the uniqueness of the individual as a member of a wider collective. Their attack has been launched on the strength of their own beliefs in a common humanity and a common human nature, in the universality of human wisdom and values. Their antagonists have been accused of making a virtue of equating particularity and difference with lowest common denominators like race, religion, class, and gender on the strength of a dogmatically held and intellectually spurious point of doctrine about history as the history of oppression by the powerful of the "powerless." In making these kinds of criticisms, the likes of Nuttall et al. seek to reinstate the first principles of traditional liberal humanism, which emphasize what we all have in common, not what is likely to separate us or divide us into antagonistic camps, hostile to our neighbors.

This study of Elias Canetti's single novel is heretical, both in terms of its opposition to some of the tenets of *Die Blendung* criticism, and in its claim that the very motor of *Die Blendung* is a provocative challenge to the dogmatic and the not-so-dogmatic assumptions of the pro-play and anti-play lobbies so prevalent in contemporary "critical" thinking. It claims that it is Nietzsche's theory of great art as something profoundly existential, that is, providing the greatest service to life, developed unsystematically in *Die Geburt der Tragödie*, which best provides the key to an understanding of Canetti's novel. It claims that Canetti's novel is a living, dynamic embodiment of those special kinds of existentially powerful energies that Nietzsche as a philosopher could only ever theorize, even in spite of the amazingly powerful language of his own highly rhetorical prose. Nietzsche's discussion of the qualities that make up great art never ceases to relate those qualities to a unique philosophy of life, already partially developed elsewhere by Schopenhauer, where a competitive struggle to survive is expressed in the desire to affirm the possibility of beautiful, intense life, even in the very face of its pure awfulness, pain, and suffering. This study claims that this very passionate tension lies at the heart of Canetti's novel, a tension that comes across as its compelling drive and its considerable intellectual and emotional power and passion. This power and passion is disciplined, protected, and enhanced by the novel's most characteristic voice, its facetiousness, or heightened sense of play. Its facetiousness assures that the gap between literature and life can be healed by virtue of a spirit which is sociable by nature, preferring the spoken word to the written word, loving energetic and vivacious conversations or exchanges between equals who relish the opportunity to display a kind of originality and brilliance which is infectious, because it encourages us to be brave, daring and imaginative. Facetiousness is thus demanding. The demands are made in the sense of life understood as an invigorating encounter in conversation which heals the wounds of individuation as it affirms our instincts for sociability. These kinds of critical claims have never before been made for this novel, which is why they are tested against a range of theories of humor in culture, on the one hand, and against a detailed textual analysis of the form Canetti's sentences take in his novel, one that demands to be read out loud, to be affirmed as an instrument which can bring people together and make words like society and community actually mean something. The results suggest that the novel's aesthetics are revolutionary in a Nietzschean sense, because they practice the art of affirming life as an intense experience in the present. These results will be particularly amusing, given Canetti's irrational and well-publicized hatred of Nietzsche, which he nowhere developed into a serious engagement with that writer's concerns.

This kind of detailed analysis makes it possible to reflect on the way such revolutionary aesthetics can be thought of as providing a sustained commentary on those currents prevalent in contemporary critical thinking that are either hostile or sympathetic to play. What emerges is the idea that Canetti's novel rejects the first principles of each lobby only because it is intuitively aware of the double bind underlying each position. Canetti's novel is deeply aware of the limitations of the liberal, leftist conviction that it is only socio-political power that is destructive of personal power. He knows that this is often inseparable from a generally hostile outlook, a distrust of the "establishment," a refusal to cooperate with its institutions, and a tendency towards separatism. The novel senses that the limitations of the conservative, traditionalist position are certainly less intellectually spurious, yet it is obvious that the novel's facetiousness is, at the very least, at variance with the deep earnestness of the aspirations of those who hold to the idea that the personal and the social good can be realized within national boundaries, without recourse to hostility to the establishment and without recourse to measures that demand radical action with respect to the establishment. The violent radicalism of the Left is already disciplined by the individual's acceptance of the given, natural order of the world, of pride in the meaningfulness of tradition.

The study argues that Canetti's novel displays its intuitive conviction about the truth of Nietzsche's theories concerning the relationship between life and art in its very vigorous and systematic dedication to a highly challenging kind of play or playfulness, that of facetiousness. This does not recognize any of the first principles of either of the positions briefly outlined above, because it makes huge demands on qualities that so much literature does not even recognize, let alone indulge. The novel makes huge demands on its reader's wits, his receptivity and openness to the potential of the world, his tenacity, his refusal to compromise, his refusal to abandon hope. This is *not* the equivalent of mindless coyness, evasion, or irresponsibility, or of any kind of self-indulgence, rather the reverse. For the novel, in its facetiousness, exudes what is most noticeable and infectious about all idealists, which is that they are driven, first and foremost, by an intense and vital spirit which is vigilant, at all times, about its place, purpose, and mission in the world around. Whereas, however, so many people who regard themselves as idealists limit themselves to certain selective goals, identifying themselves completely with those goals and with often dogmatically held, prescriptive agendas, this novel refuses to identify specific causes: it does not recognize idealism in terms of the letter of the law. The study argues that the facetiousness keeps us alert, so that we learn to worship the value of intensity and commitment, rather than any specific set of ideas. For these reasons *Die Blendung* is rich in the kinds of ideological implication not even dreamed of by those critics currently participating in the play debate. The study is therefore only partially an extension of the very feeble line of thinking in Canetti criticism that has paid homage to Canetti's sense of humor, his black humor, and his skills in the field of the grotesque.

It is often held that facetious writing is less serious than regular serious writing. Thomas Mann's facetious *Lotte in Weimar* is clearly less heavyweight than his other novels, and Henry James' facetious sending up of his own fastidiousness as a writer and thinker, in *The Sacred Fount*, makes that work peripheral and less thought provoking than the concerns of major works like the three last novels. Franz Kafka's *Amerika* likewise constitutes a laconic, relaxed reworking of the intensely paranoid and self-defeating quest motif so prevalent in the rest of his work. Work by Evelyn Waugh or P. G. Wodehouse could be thought of as lightweight, yet only if the satirical edge to the facetiousness with which the decadent upper classes of England are portrayed is disregarded. Whilst the extrovert and sociable qualities of facetious writing are often praised, and whilst the fruitful alliance with a mild form of satire is often acknowledged, it is nonetheless thought that facetious writing is not capable of the intellectually complex or thought-provoking depths typical of the rigorously serious outlook of a work like Thomas Mann's *Der Zauberberg.*

Analysis in this study of the spirit of facetiousness at the heart of *Die Blendung* shows that the novel's facetiousness is exceptionally ambitious in all senses of the word, making it difficult to sustain the equation that relegates facetious writing to the bottom of the pile. This study claims that its facetiousness is an existential challenge, a desire to infuse the world with the kind of overt theatricality that knows that life is an art, a commitment to absolute vigilance at all times, and a creative activity above all else. If this suggests that Canetti equates literature with a purely aesthetic realm, and if this suggests that Canetti has absolutely no interest in the claims of the real world, we are wrong. The highly abstract quality of the novel, with its studied evasion, as this critic sees it, of moral, psychological, social, political, historical, and geographical specificity, let alone complexity, means that it eschews literature's purported purpose—to serve the given world, according to the laws by which the world has revealed and continues to reveal itself, in general. The reductive and obvious crudeness of its own ideas is always self-evident, which is why it will remain an abiding mystery how so many commentators on the work have ended up, parrot-fashion, repeating its vacuous views on scholarship, the masses, and so on. The novel cannot abide note-taking and and smooth paraphrasing, for it despises what these activities give rise to, namely conversations that trade on the monotonously predictable. The novel is, in fact, passionate in its desire to remind us of how our energies can be channelled and focused, to reinvent the world according to the kind of inner vision that is aesthetically and ethically appalled by what the specificity of history and tradition have consistently shown us, namely the relative random chaos of everything, with its promiscuous mix of good and evil. The task is a highly immodest one. If literature does not serve a primarily moral, social, or political function as commentary on certain given, recognizable, geographically and historically specific realities, it emerges, instead, as an activity that is akin to the metaphysical supplement envisaged for it by Nietzsche, where its real "social" function is not criticism of the existing world, but affirmation of the potential for intensity of life credited every creative individual in the whole world at birth, where creativity is understood in the broadest possible sense. According to this new and original interpretation of the novel, Canetti/Nietzsche are obviously violent in their hatred of those particular individuals, like Rousseau, who are responsible for demoting individual responsibility for life on earth, by stressing instead inalienable "rights," where inalienable rights are firstly guaranteed by forces outside the individual, like governments or their agencies, and secondly only equated with vague, emotive conditions. Canetti/Nietzsche reject positivist readings of history as progress, only because its hallmark in the Western world—democracy—has upset a rightful moral/philosophical stress on individual responsibility, in favor of the rights and duties of largely amorphous and anonymous state agencies, which individuals in a democratic age enjoy making fully responsible for individual lives. Canetti's affiliations are like those of Nietzsche, and they lie with a politics of aristocratic radicalism, where radicalism is reserved for the inner vision, for the spirit.

An analysis of the force of the novel's facetiousness, of the absence, in *Die Blendung*, of the kinds of consoling semantic interrelations between sentences that we normally like to think are constituitive of language, meaningfulness, and communication, or non-facetiousness, suggests that we should be talking about this novel metaphorically, as a kind of endless dance. Reaction follows reaction in a virtuoso display of vigilance at work, all of which comes across as a perpetually expressive movement of style. Teleology is instated in place of chaos, as Nietzsche passionately hoped it could be. Words are repeatedly used to deny the past and the already given, in favor of inventiveness and originality, for the narrative rapidly dispenses with any idea we may wish to indulge as objectively true. The shock of the new is the experience of reading each new sentence. This suggests that we are misguided to see *Die Blendung*, above all, as the repository of those ideas for which it is still famed, where it is equated with critical ideas "about" scholarship, madness, the pursuit of secular dreams to do with money, power, and success, ideas about death, the masses, and the forms "Verwandlung" may take. The novel is not primarily a repository of those kinds of ideas, offshoots of the intellect, that normally lie behind words. It does not wish to be appropriated for the discourses of philosophy, psychology, and literary history. Nor does it wish to be appropriated for the kind of readings that make a virtue of its supposed geographical and historical specificity, as a fictional prefiguration of 1939–1945. It does not see itself as the apocalyptic and "visionary" novel that anticipates, to the letter, the horrors of fascism, because it detests the self-serving visions of those literary critics who see literature as the poor man's version of The Book of Revelations. It detests these visions, for the simple reason that the melodramatic, melancholic, or apocalpytic mode more often than not doubles up as a refusal to take responsibility for improving and changing the given, as an abdication of our ability to keep faith with the very best that is possible on earth.

This study argues that the novel's priority is with *the principle of vision*, which is why it has occasionally been seen as ahistorical and timeless. It is idealistic in the extreme in its allegiance to the existential importance of living out a vision, of realizing it and practising it. The novel dictates the general terms that make for a relentless and uncompromising idealism. It is thus compellingly abstract. Again and again in this study attention will be drawn to the character of the constituent part of all writing, namely the sentence. Canetti's sentences make no virtue of the kind of "poetic" writing normally considered to be indicative of literary quality. Canetti, like his hero Stendhal, makes very little use of metaphors, images, similies, alliteration, and so on. Indeed, his language, together with the violent abruptness of his short, sharp, pithy sentences, unite to compel the reader to concentrate, and to abandon his own fantasy, imagination, intellect, melancholy, and rêverie, in short all those experiences which promote solipsism, not genuinely life-giving pleasures, not those personal pleasures that are also socially enhancing pleasures. The suprapersonal quality of the writing forces us to deify our own wills and our intelligence, by fusing together with a collective consciousness that makes no virtue of "difference" as it is being understood today. Instead it makes a virtue of certain sterling moral qualities, those elevated to heroic status only in early Greek civilization. The novel knows about qualities like tenaciousness and excellence for its own sake, ones that can only express themselves if teased into existence by the competitive instinct and drive. It knows that such qualities are deeply common to us all. To tease them into existence presupposes interpersonal skills and social interaction, and leads to the formation of communities united in pursuit of only the very best.

The words that make up sentences in *Die Blendung* wish to be acknowledged as creative forces in the struggle to affirm visions in this world which seems to have no time for them, as sources of power in terms of communication and sociability, specifically intelligence and wit. This view will astonish those critics who maintain that *Die Blendung* contains compelling insights into how communication and sociability break down and then destroy human relationships in society. The sequence of words in the novel does active violence to a reader's desire to impose order and establish common ground at the level of literal ideas. The spirit of facetiousness is capable of destroying the human desire for laws, and law and order, for hierarchy, for stasis, indeed for all forms of the readily identifiable and easily recognizable. The novel actively suppresses the quest for intellectual order and harmony and certain kinds of debilitating emotions and sentiments like rêverie and melancholy, only because it is aware of the socially divisive tendency amongst intellectuals and in intellectual thinking generally, to solitary and solipsistic pleasures and to self-serving, circular "thinking," those self-serving prophecies so prevalent, above all in contemporary literature. It preaches the delights of interaction, of community, of the interpersonal skills that are productive of the goal of personal and social happiness pursued by one of Canetti's heroes, namely Stendhal, in and through the kinds of demands it places on readers as they read. It achieves this because of its astonishingly original attitude toward the sentence, whose vital and highly sociable intelligence manifests itself in the magnificient stress placed on the power and value of living by one's wits, those weapons so capable of making the best of the given, of turning base metals into gold. The reader is asked, again and again, in both a cooperative and competitive way, to use his wits to create new and startling worlds.

The spirit of facetiousness, then, is one that is capable of endorsing the individual as a member of a living, talking, listening community, as a member, therefore, of an ideal kind of humane community. The spirit of facetiousness does not tolerate anything that limits the scope for sociability in the community. In its self-conscious desire to construct the original at every given moment, at the beginning of every new sentence, to demonstrate that it is constructing the world *ex nihilo*, it knows certain truths which are never articulated in words. It knows that art is profoundly artificial, for it is the product of those deepest creative drives summoned up by individuals who possess will power, and who know how to put will power to productive, sociable use. The novel thus forces us to recall Nietzsche, not only in the role assigned art as the way of liberating humanity from a dependence on the known and a way of realizing the deepest creative drives within, but in the corollary quest for the "Umwertung aller Werte," the destruction of the "Geist der Schwere," and the belief in the value of genuinely "freie Geister."

This study therefore concludes that the free spirits posited by *Die Blendung* have no truck with the kind of ideological first principles typical of the pro-play and anti-play lobbies, because they have no prescriptive or descriptive agendas for interpreting the world, let alone changing the world. If those free spirits bypass the political, if they do not appear to believe that the personal is the political, it is not because they wish to dispense with the democratic process or because they wish to deny the value of exploiting the systems that have been set up in its name. Like Stendhal, they accept that democracies have replaced aristocracies and that they affect everyone in society. Like Stendhal, however, they equate democracies with vulgarity for the Nietzschean reasons given above, and because reliance on theories of the world, on the system, or on any system always undermines that naturally dynamic human drive which demands tactics, not ideas, for living in the world. These tactics and strategies are available to individuals who want to achieve things, and who are committed to finding fully effective ways of achieving their goals. Such individuals remain aristocrats at heart, in other words, for they know how to act, they know how to transform the world, on their own terms, and with the confident assistance of other lively minds, sister souls, who also delight in the pleasures of collaboration. They are convinced, in an idealistic kind of way, that there are no genuine obstacles to the pursuit of happiness. In the same way, they are convinced that those who hold to and enjoy publicizing the theory that there are obstacles to the pursuit of happiness are merely creating the perverse climate that will ensure that general sterility, lack of purpose, lack of hope, lack of charity, and lack of good will, in short, lack of faith triumph and hold sway. In the knowledge of the laziness and complacency of human nature, they continue to wage war on the kinds of attitudes that make community living a charade. They despise the debilitating effects of mere sentiment, of melancholy, rêverie, and intellectual knowledge and facts pursued as if they could ever be values in themselves. They are exceptionally demanding. They only tolerate passion. They are acutely aware of the way words can become severed from faith and commitment, of the way they can so easily become vehicles of empty rhetoric. They despise rhetoric, and they despise rhetorical questioning, because they want action, always want proof of the viability of better worlds and better ways of doing things. They are deeply opposed to reactive thinking, because they are deeply proactive by nature. Their capacity for tenacity is unparalleled, inasmuch as they never surrender and never compromise. So the predictable argument whereby any text that revels in the "merely" playful or the gratuitously playful is shallow, irresponsible, or hollow, and thus synonymous with passivity and the non-political or the apolitical, can be ceremoniously put to rest. *Die Blendung* is neither vain nor lazy nor contemptuous enough to retreat into the solipsism of solitary confinement. It also refuses to invest faith in the systems of society or any of the formalized, institutionalized, and well recognized ways of registering protest in a democracy. Instead, its tenacity suggests a very canny ability to negotiate with the complexity of the given. The novel does not recognize the possibility of escapism or retreat, nor some kind of alliance with socio-politically inspired lobbies. It also despises all prescriptive agendas and dogmatic principles, even in spite of the fact it appears to feature a large number of dogmatically inclined individuals and a thoroughly reclusive and thoroughly isolated scholar/intellectual. Its spirit of commitment, manifest in and through the spirit of the words that make up the whole novel, shows up both the self-evident limitations of the agendas and principles of its protagonists as much as the quality of their misplaced passion. It knows that all agendas and principles are limited if they are not driven by the life-enhancing power of an emotionally driven kind of intellectual passion. It senses that even when such agendas are driven by passion, they have an in-built ability to self-destruct, by virtue of the need to repeat key ideas again and again, rather than to be original "*ex nihilo.*" Its sense of commitment is so strong and so comprehensive as to be capable of endorsing a very dazzling notion of civilization, whereby, in the spirit of generosity, cooperation, and affirmation, we systematically seek out and endorse the very best in what we see around us.

In particular, Canetti deconstructs the well-entrenched binary opposition which so many professional intellectuals in the Humanities take for granted, who have been so influenced by the intellectual Left and who are currently powerful in public life. The intellectual Left imitates and perpetuates familiar tunes about power as something outside the self, not within the self, played by the originators of the soft Left in philosophy, like Marx, or the soft Left in literature, like Heinrich Mann, Brecht, and the Avant-Garde in Russia and elsewhere in the early twentieth century. Their simplistic views about power continue to live on, as something intrinsically awful and originating in amorphous sources outside the self, effective only in that it belittles, trivializes, and vanquishes that self, making a victim into a victim and a mere vessel of anonymity. Indeed, it would not be an exaggeration to say that most of the big names in literature in the Federal Republic since 1945, like Enzensberger, Böll, and Grass would be unthinkable without this first premise. Such writers and thinkers all hold firmly to the view that "Macht" is always intrinsically corrupt, always emanating from the socio-political arena and its agencies, always actively capable of destroying the individual powers of individuals, and always destined to turn them into "the undifferentiated masses." They are equally convinced that "Geist" is intrinsically pure, the defining characteristic of an elite of intellectuals whose dominance of the public sphere varies from country to country, yet who are united by the fact that they are opposed to the largely socio-economic or socio-political forms "Macht" takes. Canetti's novel reveals that this set of ideas is shown to be a paralyzing "method" of being in the world, because it is intellectually spurious and socially divisive, responsible for the monotonously repetitive "critiques" of society they are destined, with massive inevitability, to produce. Indeed, the professional intellectual of modern times, created in the wake of the explosion of the Avant-Garde in the early twentieth century, differs from the man of letters of pre-modern times, in that s/he is apparently now part of a separate class outside society, a new class that is definable by virtue of the fact that intellectual knowledge has been acquired, self-consciously, by all its members. These are equally self-conscious about their opposition to traditional symbols of class like wealth, property, and pedigree. Living on the margins of society, then, they produce "critiques" of the society from which they have become detached, critiques for which they and their readers need not be responsible in any fully active way, since to do so would be to destroy the power base they as classless intellectuals apparently constitute, in opposition to mainstream society. For the professional intellectual of modern times, whether as writer or reader, literature has become a pathetic weapon, the institutionalized method of registering criticisms of a "society" it either sees as bankrupt and corrupt, or in which it has no faith, as is evident in the absence of agendas for reform, let alone revolution. Literature in German about Germany offers a particularly acute version of this general problem of nihilism, not surprisingly, given its terrible record, in recent times, of promoting civilized values. For where it is used to produce socio-political critiques it has become complacent, happy to propagate undifferentiated stories about the form "evil" takes in society, which promote ideology, theory, and a general lack of confidence in all things, a passionless nihilism, not faith or hope, still less passion and action, as is evidenced by those dreary classics of post-1945 German literature, now institutionalized on University syllabi, like *Die Ermittlung, Andorra, Biedermann und die Brandstifter, Die verlorene Ehre der Katharina Blum, Bruder Eichmann, Der Stellvertreter, Fürsorgliche Belagerung, Frauen vor einer Flußlandschaft, Schon bist du ein Verfassungsfeind*, and so on. The list is endless, but the problem is the same. Literature, which purports to take a critical look at where "society" has gone wrong, is itself part of the problem, a symptom, not the cure, since it is lost and without direction in terms of radical faith, hope, and commitment. It does not want to provide any genuine leadership, or set the kinds of standards that would be worth pursuing. In the face of the awfulness of the incontrovertible facts of human weakness, as evidenced by German history 1939–1945, and some of the social and political injustices that followed in the complicated history of the Federal Republic post-1945, no alternatives to the reenactments of its disaster scenarios are ever suggested. A series of rather pathetic attempts at scapegoats is made, which either rely very heavily on infantile theories of human nature, or on equally infantile and near-hysterical theories concerning the full-scale corruption of the public system. These can only promote and encourage an anti-social era of suspicion, where it is not possible to have faith in anything. The baby, in short, is thrown out with the bath water. So if we are clearly invited to mourn our awfulness, it is not the kind of mourning the Mitscherlichs wanted in *Die Unfähigkeit zu trauern*, where mourning about the awfulness of the Nazi period is encouraged as a stage on the way back to health. We mourn our awfulness as an end in itself, rather than learn how we can change and progress, still less how it is still possible for people to be responsible for themselves, even in spite of the endless weight of historical evidence against this. In short, it no longer offers guidance or expresses any kind of idealism. Literature has come to express, as such, the present-day mutual resentment and mutual incomprehension typical of the relationship between those institutions responsible for teaching it—the Universities—and society as a whole.

More importantly, however, when exploited as a vessel for "critiques" of the above kind, it is responsible for our not systematically seeking out and endorsing the very best in what we see around us, in a spirit of sympathy, delight, and cooperation with one another. For if there is one thing that this most strange, most demanding, and most challenging of novels knows about, it is love, and love enacted in one of the most original and comprehensive ways ever to be encountered in literature as a whole. Love is about an attitude to life, it is always affirming faith, not propagating despair, misery, self-pity, contempt, and cynicism. This makes the power of the novel as a work of art quite simple. In contrast to Canetti's reputation as an opponent of power, this study is convinced that Canetti *loves* power as the single most important creative principle, as an instrument in the quest to live fully. Further, its power is animated by a profoundly wild, endlessly giving, bountiful spirit, thus "Geist" in the original sense of the word, and not "Geist" in terms of fixed, well-defined ideas. For these reasons, Canetti's novel knows something rather surprising, given Canetti's reputation as a "pure" intellectual. It knows that its own intellectual passion is also the highest form of love, and a kind of love that is more reminiscent of Greek civilization than our modern civilization. Intellectual passion is the highest form of love, precisely because it knows that to emphasize romantic possessiveness, possession, or privacy, least of all heterosexual or homosexual passion, more typical of our modern civilization, is tactically wrong in terms of the wider project of affirming life in the fullest sense. Love and intellectual passion as Canetti's novel practises them have everything to do with a generous social vision of cooperation, in the spirit of delight, between imaginatively vibrant, talking, listening equals, who know that there is something very life-giving about facetiousness. Finally, the kind of love enacted by Canetti's novel is similar to the kind of love preached by Christianity, with the small difference that Canetti's novel is not ashamed to stress the importance of a strong ego, as absolutely vital to the ability to give endlessly, gratuitously, and bountifully, and without a desire for return. Love is synonymous with the ability to recognize, activate, and realize all human potential on earth because all the sentences in the novel, at all times, make equal demands on our ability to talk, and to listen, to give and to receive, to love and be loved.

It is a particular pleasure to offer this study to the community in the wake of Canetti's recent death, on August 14, 1994, when obituaries in the international press once again insisted on seeing him primarily as a man of gravity, a man of ideas, a man of letters, a man of pure intellectual "Geist." In the emphasis that has inevitably been placed on the sober character of his later works, homage has not been paid to those wild and high spirits of his early youth, captured so brilliantly in his only novel, which affirm community as a way of life, for all seasons and for all people. It is my hope that this study can act as that homage.

1

Genesis of the Novel

The official, not to say definitive, version of the genesis of Canetti's single novel is the subject of one of the last chapters of the second part of his autobiography, *Die Fackel im Ohr*, which was published for the first time in 1980. "Der Pavillon der Irren," the first section of "Die Frucht des Feuers: Wien 1929–1931," makes quite clear that in September 1929, when the author was just twenty-four, an epoch had officially come to an end. This was marked by the completion of the thesis in chemistry at the University of Vienna, entitled "Über die Darstellung des Tertiär-butylcarbinols," which Canetti had written to buy time, and which had meant nothing to him. It was also marked by his having achieved the distinction of earning his own living. He had been commissioned to translate into German from the American, works by Upton Sinclair, an author on whom he had already written an article entitled "Upton Sinclair wird 50 Jahre alt."[1] These translations were published as *Leidweg der Liebe* in 1930, *Das Geld schreibt: Eine Studie über die amerikanische Literatur* in 1930, and *Alkohol* in 1932. All were published by the left-wing publishing house in Berlin, Malik.[2] The translation work was also obviously nothing more than a mere pretext, and Canetti soon discovered that his heart was not in this kind of work either (*FO*, 293).[3] Work on *Die Blendung* thus began when Canetti was "free" for the first time, both imaginatively, in terms of the loss of the pressure of having to complete the doctorate, and financially, in terms of the income he now had. But it also began when Canetti was emotionally confused. The writing of *Die Blendung* is often linked up by critics with the background of the decisively disorientating impact a trip to Berlin had had on him, itself the subject of part four of *Die Fackel im Ohr*, called "Das Gedränge der Namen: Berlin 1928." This visit was marked by three encounters. Canetti was introduced to Brecht, Georg Grosz, and Isaak Babel. The encounter with Brecht, in a lively restaurant frequented by intellectuals, had been a humiliating one (*FO*, 253–54). It was an encounter with strictly utilitarian values as these were embodied by a prominent bohemian, who was also an intellectual and an artist. This was a new experience for Canetti. It was at variance with his previous, relatively limited experience of the social side of intellectual life in Vienna, where Canetti had been under the spell of Karl Kraus, whose influence on Canetti as a young student and for quite some years after has been much discussed, both by the author and by critics.[4] What is important is that Kraus had not been bohemian in terms of life style and, in contrast to Brecht, had looked on the business of writing with the reverence and self-consciousness of the convert to a profession felt to be highly exalted. As an orator with a declamatory style of public debate, he had lectured to the young Canetti with considerable theatrical skills. His satirical style of writing was equally provocative. Whether as orator or writer, his persona was well within the tradition inaugurated in the nineteenth century by the Romantics, the belief in the separateness and otherness of the artist figure, whose mission, as a vessel of and for truth, was to propagate that truth to mankind. Brecht, living at large and motivated by largely pragmatic concerns, such as how to stage his plays and whom to employ to act in them, did not project any of the establishment self-consciousness of the artist with which Canetti was already familiar. Brecht thus offended Canetti's innocent reverence for an ideal he had already formulated of the artist as one who, in order to be able to create something worthwhile, *had to* preserve himself from what was clearly felt to be the threat of corruption posed by mixing with the masses. Brecht's identification with the masses, together with his refusal to detach himself from a wider social reality, did not strike a chord with Canetti.

Nevertheless, it was Brecht's generally loveless, impersonal, and exploitative vision that seemed to epitomize the inverse of Canetti's own idealistic feel for the good, the beautiful, and the true, for which values he imagined the artist was destined to fight, as if in a contest (*FO*, 255). This devastating assessment was complicated by respect, bordering on reverence, for Brecht's collection of poems *Die Hauspostille*. This was given the highest accolade when Canetti commented on the personal effects the poems had on him, in terms of their penetrating, charismatic mystique: "Es gab Dinge darunter, die mir durch Mark und Bein gingen" (*FO*, 256). As we know from his other literary criticism, this kind of an effect was generated by only a handful of writers, Büchner, Stendhal, and Kafka amongst them. Comparable to the devastating effect Brecht had on Canetti personally in Berlin, was the effect of Georg Grosz, whom Canetti met in the artist's studio. This encounter was more successful in personal terms, for, whereas Brecht had demolished anything Canetti had ventured to say and dismissed it with contempt, Grosz was less aggressive and more sympathetic. Canetti left the studio with Grosz's series "Ecce-Homo," itself something of a compliment, which he looked at in private. It is interesting to note here that Grosz in his autobiography (published in 1955) does not mention these encounters with Canetti, although he does talk about his encounter with Brecht in Berlin, with Tatlin in the U.S.S.R., with Thomas Mann in New York, indeed his encounters with many other artist figures.[5] The same is incidentally true of Alma Mahler, who also makes no mention of Canetti in her memoirs, despite the fact the two clearly had, according to Canetti's account in his autobiography, quite a lot to do with one another.[6] Nevertheless, the impact of Grosz's art on Canetti, just as literature in the case of Brecht's poems, was emphatic (*FO*, 264). What was devastating about the series was less the satirical force for which Grosz is historically feted, but the mysterious way in which Grosz was able to compel Canetti to assent to his vision, which is to say his capacity to convince observers of the "truth" of his creations. Canetti had mentioned the powerful emotional and intellectual impact of Brecht's poems without in any way being able to suggest, analytically, what it was about them that was capable of generating such an effect, and he does the same here in further comments on the "Ecce-Homo" series. The same apology for the power of art is made with respect to Grosz (*FO*, 264). We have, then, two fine examples of Canetti's capacity to be absolutely dazzled and blinded by art, and dazzled and blinded in a way that defies analysis. Canetti's comments on Brecht's poems and on Grosz's drawings refuse to acknowledge matters relating to content, except in the most perfunctory of ways, as if content were totally irrelevant, and as if imaginative impact were everything. This attitude is consistent with the general approach underlying Canetti's literary criticism, published in essay form as *Der andere Prozeß* (1969), or *Die gespaltene Zukunft* (1972), some of which appear in one volume now as *Das Gewissen der Worte* (1975). The casual reader of these essays cannot fail to notice that substance in literature is rarely taken seriously. In these essays, Canetti insists again and again on the *experiential* nature of contemplation of artistic objects, in particular on the capacity of literature to devastate entirely. For him, interestingly, such effects seem to constitute proof of the intrinsic excellence or merit of the source of the effects. Respect for the intrinsic and objective merits of any given work of art is nothing compared to the subjective effects individual works of art are capable of having on the individual Elias Canetti, a view that will be important for this study's claims about the experiential nature of reading the novel *Die Blendung*.

The experiences of poetry, painting, writers, and artists in Berlin were mingled with equally complicated responses to the quality of sophisticated, urbanized life in Berlin generally. Canetti's friend Ibby, who had introduced him into fashionable intellectual circles, was at ease with the chaos and intensity of life. Canetti was not. His idea was that life was a jungle, with each individual fighting for his own survival, where community and communication become redundant, because each man is on his own: "Es war jeder für sich . . ." (*FO*, 266). In contrast to the unqualified dismissal of Brecht the man and the straightforward approval of Grosz's capacity to take him seriously as an equal, Canetti goes on to endorse Isaak Babel the man unconditionally. His encounter with Babel in Berlin was significant, Canetti tells us, because he met someone who shared his world view. This meant Canetti's generally exalted view about literature and art and his particular views about individual authors. Babel loved Gogol and Stendhal, just as Canetti did. Their approval meant they were both united, in their joint refusal to beautify the world, and their own joint refusal to exploit it (*FO*, 273–74). As if to further defend this approval of Babel's seriousness, we are reminded, at the end of this section, of the acute existential significance of the encounter to Canetti, who records that Berlin would have eaten him alive if he had not met Babel (*FO*, 274).

Canetti's official account of the genesis of *Die Blendung* is one which makes an overt causal link between the general chaos of his imagination, produced by the wealth and variety of the impressions made on him by Berlin, and the production of the novel. The latter is the product of the former, inextricably linked with it. Part of the interest of the account lies in what is said, therefore, about the link between writing and survival, a link that is also vital in Canetti's work generally, particularly in the large section in *Masse und Macht*, entitled "Der Überlebende,"[7] but also in the essay "Macht und Überleben."[8] When Canetti insists on the chaotic dynamism of his imagination after Berlin, emphasizing how it was overwhelmed by impressions made on it, he reminds us that writing *Die Blendung* was an attempt to come to terms with that chaos. *Die Blendung* was the means by which chaos could be grasped in a fully *plastic* way:

> Die eigentliche Tendenz der Dinge war eine *zentrifugale*, sie strebten auseinander, mit größter Geschwindigkeit voneinander weg. Die Wirklichkeit war nicht im Zentrum, wo sie wie an Zügeln alles zusammenhielt, es gab nur noch viele Wirklichkeiten und sie waren außen. Sie waren weit voneinander entfernt, es bestand keine Verbindung zwischen ihnen, wer einen Ausgleich zwischen ihnen herzustellen versuchte, war ein Fälscher. Sehr weit außen, auf einem Kreise, beinahe am Rande der Welt standen wie harte Kristalle die neuen Wirklichkeiten, auf die ich zuging. Als Scheinwerfer waren sie nach innen auf unsere Welt zu richten, um diese mit ihnen abzuleuchten. (*FO*, 294)[9]

This formulation of the function and purpose of writing, partially unpoetic and highly abstract as it is, is not a classic one. It neither directly admits, nor directly denies, the ancient theory of mimesis, the idea that literature *imitates*, or *represents*, or *reproduces*, a given *social* reality, the idea that it must reproduce or be adequate to that given social reality, like a mirror, more often than not in terms of a referential or normative idea of truth and/or wisdom. Equally, however, the account neither directly admits nor denies the possibility of something other than mimesis in literature. Canetti depicts himself as a lone traveller, abandoned, so to speak, in a cosmos full of atoms in perpetual motion, and in a cosmos which has no center. The aggressive, dynamically mobile forces refuse to synthesize themselves into a single whole with a single, unifying meaning. A multiplicity of realities coexist instead, and each one is characterized by its *natural* capacity for autonomy and independence from any other reality, and from any larger whole. The internal dynamism of each individual reality is such, therefore, that there is internal resistance to synthesis. This idea about natural resistance to synthesis is clearly a matter Canetti seems to have established pragmatically, from observation. The dynamism of the cosmos is described as if it corresponded to a state of nature. This is then followed by an article of faith on Canetti's part, concerning the role of human artifice. Canetti moves into the dogmatic mode as he talks about a hypothetical individual. He is categorical that, because there are no links at an internal level, between each of the coexisting realities, ("keine Verbindung," "keinen Ausgleich"), any human attempt to impose either analytic or synthetic links in terms of artifice has to be flatly condemned. Such a person is branded a falsifier, a "Fälscher."

Canetti's condemnation must be interpreted as a statement of respect for what he feels he has established as the truth about the power and energy of chaos: they exist and have to be respected. The nature of the universe is the power and energy of chaos. Canetti's condemnation of the human attempt to impose order on chaos through seeing and constructing links, through acts of culture, emerges as a first principle and single absolute. To impose order on power and energy would be to be unfaithful to the nature of power and dynamism itself. The act of *seeing* links is seen as a heretical act in terms of power and energy. It is a form of denial. In seeing links, power and energy are automatically neutralized, relativized, perhaps even trivialized or denied: and Canetti is, above all, determined to preserve chaos in its natural state. We need, here, to underline the significance of the terms of Canetti's single absolute. The significance concerns the way in which his single absolute doubles up, surreptitiously, as an astonishingly deep hatred of reason. *Canetti identifies reason, analytic or synthetic reason, as an enemy of chaos.*

This idea is, however, complicated by the fact that Canetti goes on to talk about illumination. Canetti uses the verb "ableuchten" and the imagery of spotlights. In what can this new idea of illumination consist, if reason has been ruled out of court from the very beginning? In the first instance, it appears to be difficult to answer this question. The multiple realities around Canetti, it is suggested, can simply be illuminated extravagantly, dramatically, and, above all, artifically. Canetti states that his novel will act as a spotlight. The multiple realities will be illuminated by his novel, they will be illuminated by a work of art, artifice itself, created by a single human being. Given the background examined above, in which Canetti rules out reason, *the multiple realities will be illuminated with a vision, which will do absolutely no violence to the nature of chaos itself*, for the vision will do nothing, at a substantial level, to harm or touch chaos.

This emphasis on vision raised by the idea of the novel as spotlight is, therefore, a violent statement about the power of art, as it is a violent statement about how art must not, need not, and should not, do any violence to what Canetti has decreed is the state of nature, namely the chaos of boundless power and boundless energy. Canetti sees his novel as having the capacity to be as effective as artificial light, not natural light. The novel will be effective like a spotlight, and in being a spotlight, the novel will provide an *alternative* to chaos, in the form of a vision different to, and not dependent on, the extra-textual world of a chaos of multiple realities. The act of creation will have consequences, in that the created object will transform mere multiple realities, *but only on the novel's own terms*, for the novel itself will contain alternative realities, "neue Wirklichkeiten." The created artifact will be transformative, only in that the internal world of the novel will have the power to dazzle and blind, like a spotlight. It will have the power to dazzle and blind, in spite of the existence of chaos. Transformation here clearly does not mean to embellish or to improve upon the given in any shape or form: indeed, there seems to be as great a hatred of beauty as there is of reason. We can see in this how consistent Canetti's first principles are, if we remember now how he valued Isaak Babel's refusal to embellish upon the already given, a view about prose that remained something of a constant throughout Canetti's career (*PM*, 178).[10] Transformation in Canetti's terms means the intellectual act, whereby an absolutely alternative vision, an absolutely autonomous vision, is brought into being. Art is thus autonomous, independent of its human origins, as it is independent of the state of nature, whatever that might be: it is not involved in the business of beautifying or making more palatable the already given.

Yet implicit in the notion of the novel's being a spotlight is some kind of notion of coherence of effect. What will furnish the spotlight with the coherence necessary for vision, if Canetti has already ruled reason and order out of court? We still have no clue whatsoever, given that the above statements of principle about the need to respect the power of power and the corollary of a hatred of reason, offer nothing in terms of substance at the analytical or synthetic level. We merely know at this early stage that the new realities comprising the spotlight will have an orientation in terms of imaginative space. They will be directed at an extra-textual world of dynamically mobile realities, that chaos which is the apparent *modus vivendi* of both author (in Berlin) and, it is assumed, his implied reader. Since the novel-spotlight will illuminate the dynamically mobile realities extravagantly, dramatically, and artifically, as one would expect a spotlight to do, it is possible to conclude here that this illumination will be a manifestation of the formidable power of the novel's own internal realities. We are not talking about content, but the mere brilliant effect of artificial and dazzling light, that created by the power of the human intelligence and creativity behind the creation itself and embodied in that creation. The vocabulary of light-associated words used in the context of the relationship of the novel to an extra-textual reality is, therefore, in a very deep sense, highly misleading. If abstracted from the context just outlined, where Canetti is categorical about the need to exclude synthetic or analytic form imposed on the raw material of chaos, the vocabulary of light-associated words actually raises the possibility of analytic or synthetic interpretation itself. We might be forgiven for assuming that Canetti is, through his central metaphor, when he uses the verb "ableuchten" with the noun "Scheinwerfer," talking about how he proposes to use his novel to throw *metaphorical* light on the world of senseless and meaningless chaos, such as the one he encountered in his social life in Berlin. At first sight, the vocabulary allows us to assume that *Die Blendung* is in a position to provide an *interpretation* of the data of chaos. The vocabulary raises the possibility that the novel will be able to achieve a kind of penetrating through to the *essence* of chaos as *social* experience: it suggests that chaos per se can be understood, that the truth about chaos can be established, in a world of essences beyond time and space.

Yet close analysis of the above passage shows that there is no sign of any kind of reciprocal relationship between the created novel and its extra-textual world. Canetti is rewriting the classic literary metaphor for classic artistic activities. He is not adhering to the convention, whereby the arts exist to throw light on life. He is absolutely defiant that he will not be interpreting a given extra-textual reality. Rather, his created work will be absolute in its refusal to give credit to any kind of given extra-textual reality. Its priority is with the principle of vision. *It will dictate the general terms that make the visionary stance possible. It will not recognize the extra-textual world, except as a hypothesis.* The novel will "merely" have the power of vision detached from particularity—the form of vision not contaminated by content—and the extra-textual reality will not be interpreted, it will be blinded by the power of art.

It is with the contrary view, however, that most critics of *Die Blendung* have worked. They have assumed that the novel's prime interest is with an identifiable socio-political or socio-economic world. They have assumed that Canetti's contract is a mimetic one, in terms of an established social world, and they have consistently endorsed the novel in terms of Canetti's contribution to well-established discourses, of philosophy, psychology, psycho-pathology, cultural history, literary history, and so on. If we pause to examine the commentary on the genesis of the novel again, however, we encounter objections to the theory of mimesis that are absolutely irreconciliable with it. The mimetic theory of interpretative illumination at a synthetic or analytical level is, first and foremost, at variance with the categorical confidence expressed by Canetti that chaos should be respected: it is *not* to be interpreted either synthetically or analytically, but acknowledged to be there in terms of the imaginative orientation of the created novel. As a spotlight, however, even if aimed at a world of chaos acknowledged to exist, Canetti's priority is with the power of art to dazzle, to be brilliant, and to be these things on its own terms.

This argument, which is crucial for an understanding of the new parameters for interpretation of *Die Blendung* proposed by this book, is that the verb and the noun are used for purposes that have resonance only in terms of Nietzsche's well-known view that art is an intensely *metaphysical* activity in the first place, and one that only has status as a *metaphysical* supplement to life in the second. The passage concerning the genesis of the novel just examined is predicated on the Nietzschean assumption that chaos can not be understood, either analytically or synthetically. It is merely given, a cardinal truth that the Nietzschean type neither denies nor tampers with: s/he merely accepts it to be a self-evident truth, which cannot be proved by formal logic, because it is an emotional intuition from the realm of experience. Canetti abolishes the conventional idea of art as a mirror, reflecting back an image already "known" in some way, for he will not be concerned with the known of a readily discernible social world, but with the existence of chaos, with which he will not interfere at all. There will be no kind of *reciprocal* relationship between the work of art and a given, social reality, or a given metaphysical reality, that of the pure anonymity of chaos, power, and energy. Greater power, it is implied, will be concentrated in the individual work of art: it will be effective because of the power that is vision. We move from art as imitation or representation of life at one remove, to art as a Nietzschean enactment of life itself, one that does not need to justify itself as a secondary source of life in any sense, as a reflection on something that has already been identified. Art is not dependent on anything outside itself, it is fully independent.

The significant point about the passage is both the supreme confidence that Canetti expresses in the artist as creator and in the effect the novel can generate, both as a *metaphysical* object within space and, by implication, as a temporal experience within the metaphysical or subjective life of a reader. Canetti does not discuss his novel as if it had either referential or paradigmatic value in terms of truth or wisdom that could be applied in any given *social* world. The terms of the discussion do not raise the possibility that the novel will revert the reader to the already known. On reflection, this metaphysical version is the only option open to an author interested in chaos and respectful of its dynamism as pure energy and capacity to resist the immobility that would be imposed upon it, were analytical or synthetic interpretations to be attempted. The respect for chaos seems to be the open, if tacit, admission of the author's preference for illumination *as dramatic effect only*. Canetti is not interested in the conventional notion of interpretative light being cast on a given subject matter. He is not interested in the idea of illumination as content, but as dramatic effect.

This theory is effectively confirmed by an examination of the second image of the passage, that of the crystal. When Canetti assumes "die neuen Wirklichkeiten" of his novel will have the power of illumination we associate with the spotlight, he defines these "neue Wirklichkeiten" later, where he equates them with pieces of hard crystal. In doing so, he equates the new realities of his novel with the quality of absolute non-mobility, a quality that is the inverse of the energy of perpetual mobility and chaos, the raw material of the world inhabited by both the author and his readers. In suggesting that the new realities in his novel will be like hard pieces of crystal, Canetti accepts that his novel will contain a plurality of realities on the one hand, and that an encounter with them by a reader will be comparable to an encounter with stability. Hard crystal is absolutely static, absolutely impermeable, and absolutely impenetrable. It allows of no traffic with the natural world and is defiant in its rejection of any kind of imposition of force from without.[11]

This seems to be problematic once again, only inasmuch as we have, still, no indication that *Die Blendung* desires to have any claim to a paradigm or to referentially applicable notions of behavioral patterns within a social universe. A reader's encounter with *Die Blendung* will be entirely unlike his encounter with chaos in an extra-textual reality, for the crystal image insists on shape, force, and strength. Canetti is implying here that the world of his novel will be the inverse of the chaos encountered in any given extra-textual world, for his novel is to be form itself, not formlessness. Here Canetti is clearly, albeit covertly, developing a theory of reading. Reading, it is implied by the metaphor of hardness and toughness raised by the idea of the crystal, will be an experience of the truth of the strength and power of human creativity in the face of the truth of chaos. The intervention of Canetti's creativity into chaos is seen as a first existential act, which produces form and clarity, or all those qualitites we associate with the spotlight. This act, which results in the creation of the novel, is to be followed by the reader's experience of what creativity can do when it gives the formless form. Reading will be a reminder that as human beings we are creative in our capacity to resist the destructive aspects of chaos, or the absolute anonymity of chaos, by creating form. The whole novel depends on the existence of chaos. It is a response to chaos, yet it bears and carries the traces of what creativity can achieve, constructively, in spite of chaos. Reading will be an experience of the control of power and energy by form, which makes the idea of a blinding, dazzling spotlight feasible. Reading is not, therefore, about interpretation, but about the experience of what a creative alliance with chaos can reveal: namely that we are stronger than the purely destructive drive inherent in chaos because we can create its inverse, form.

In spite of the fact that Canetti's images talk about his novel as if it were an isolated object in the cosmos, utterly detached from any kind of reciprocal relationship with the extra-textual world, whether it be intellectual engagement with the abstract world of multiple realities or a personalized involvement with the human world of potential readers, the images stress, above all, the *experiential* involvement of the human imagination through the act of reading, and in the above, *existential* terms. The images, theatrical and material as they are, presuppose an audience of individuals, who are all characterized by a creative receptivity to plasticity, above all. We can say that the "vision" of the novel has been reduced to the *effects*, at a creative level, a novel can have on a reader. The novel is not characterized by its causal and interpretative relationship with an extra-textual reality. It is characterized by its direct relationship with individual readers, whose social context, that of chaos, will not be reproduced in the novel, for in its place is form, in the sense of hardness and strength. In so doing, the novel simultaneously assumes, therefore, that all readers are creators, with instincts for plasticity, capable of resisting those destructive aspects of chaos lurking close at hand. The novel posits a particular kind of reader, a reader who is equal to the creative challenge of rising above chaos through the kind of creativity that endows formlessness with absolute form.

The argument, then, about Canetti's puzzling commentary on the genesis of *Die Blendung,* is that the above passage describes, above all, an experience of reading, nothing more. Specifically, the experience of reading will be an experience of an entirely different order to the experience with which the reader is familiar as s/he lives at large, as s/he lives when s/he is not reading. If the novel has the hardness of a crystal, reading it will be an encounter with absolute matter. Significantly, therefore, reading will bring to a halt, for the reader, albeit temporally, the perpetual motion of conflicting sets of realities which is his/her usual form of experience and existence. Reading will provide the reader with *respite* from chaos. In place of chaos, the reader will experience absolute form, the confidence of supreme plasticity. The reader will experience precisely that which ordinary existence at large denies him/her. The passage can be read, therefore, as a doctrinaire vote of confidence in the power of art per se, where power is not the capacity to create or improve upon a given social world, or upon the rational or imaginative skills of a given, articulate, reading public. Canetti will not be playing on the rational or imaginative skills of such a public, since he indicated at an early point that he hated reason, precisely because of its vested interest in imposing order on chaos, an action deemed heretical. Reason imposes order on chaos by building up a network of analytic or synthetic ideas. Reason is the enemy because it has a vested interest in mitigating the truth of chaos. Nowhere does Canetti proclaim any love for reason: on the contrary, he indicates with his reference to the "Fälscher" that he hates it. The above statements are, instead, an expression of confidence in the novelist's power to overwhelm the imagination of the reader, to compel it to submission, to deny it its freedom of movement and independence of thought. This is a denial of the reader as thinker. Such a denial of what many feel to be the noble and ennobling faculties of people generally, is extreme, but it must be understood in terms of Canetti's adoration of plasticity or form. Canetti proposes that he will appeal to a reader's artistic instincts, to his/her sense of plasticity or form. He proclaims an absolute love of form, as he proclaims a love for the human capacity to create form. His reader is one, therefore, who, whilst not a reflective thinker, is, by contrast, a creator in a very particular, Nietzschean sense. His reader is one capable of plasticity, of endowing pure energy, power, and chaos with absolute form, absolute control, absolute mastery.

It appears, therefore, that the passage is more than an idiosyncratic comment on the two theories of mimesis proposed by Aristotle in his *Poetics* and Plato in *The Republic*, which have influenced both the history of philosophy and the history of literary criticism. One of these is the idea that the fabricated world of literature must not be looked at in isolation. There is the strictly *referential* idea of truth, where truth is that which has been created for the purposes of establishing a *correspondence* between words and the things they can properly be used to represent. What is important here for an understanding of Canetti's theory of the novel, is the way in which Plato assumes that truthful statements can be tested or verified as such by determining their "fit" with an outside reality. This is the correspondence theory of truth, a simple adequation between words and things, which has most recently come under attack from post-structuralism.

The other concept of mimesis, equally entrenched, can always be appealed to when language resists or evades such referential treatment. This is the Platonic doctrine of truth as a form of inward revelation, as a writing in the soul that makes itself visible to the mind in a state of receptive wisdom. Such knowledge, as Plato conceived it, would be more authentic than any truth attainable by a mere copying of external reality. Wisdom consists in seeing beyond the world of material objects and events, the world we inhabit whilst we are enslaved to the predominance of sensory perception. There is a higher reality of essences, "forms," or ideas that are locally embodied in the things we perceive but that can only be known, in their essential nature, through a process of inward seeking-after-truth. This is the concept of truth as *aletheia*, as the moment of epiphany or inward "unveiling," vouchsafed to the soul through an exercise of reason transcending all forms of sensory perception. Conservative theories of literature from Aristotle and Plato onwards tend, under the influence of the two theories discussed above, to stress that literature is valid as an activity because of its concern with Truth, in the literal sense of representing what can be registered by the five senses, and in the metaphorical sense of the illumination we associate with wisdom. Literature both *imitates* or *represents* or *reproduces* a given, objective reality "out there" and proposes an illuminating vision of that given, objective reality. The vision will itself, therefore, always partially depend on the substance or data provided by that given, objective reality "out there" in which the author and his/her readers already have a place, but which an author is free to re-present, as befits his/her illuminating vision.

An analysis of the implications of the ideas contained in the above extract from Canetti's autobiography, shows just how strongly, albeit indirectly, Canetti refutes both of the above theories of mimesis. The whole passage points to the *dissolution* of the distinctions on which conservative theories of mimesis tend to be based, namely the distinctions between form and content. The crystal metaphor, in particular, is the vehicle for this radical idea, and is a material object that is brittle, ruthless, uncompromising, hard, and resistant to pressure from without and from within, because of its vicious, unyielding contours. It refracts light, of course, but without in any way indicating that the source of light comes from without: on the contrary, it seduces us into thinking that the light comes from within. As an object, it is capable of deceiving us, quite confidently, into the illusion that the origin and source of light is internal. In choosing the crystal idea and using it as he does in the section quoted above, Canetti's aim is to direct attention away from distinctions between form and content, toward a quality not often discussed in relation to literature, namely the quality of plasticity. This is understood as the nonverbal, intuitive sense communicated to a reader capable of "sensing" the formal control of chaos. Art objects are capable of denying the validity of the world outside their own parameters. They are capable of being so seductively powerful in themselves—like the artificial light of the glistening cluster of crystals, which makes the observer forget that it does owe something to natural light—as to make redundant any need to refer to a world outside their own parameters.

Plasticity is a quality we associate more happily with the visual arts, with sculpture and architecture in particular. Canetti often proclaims his love of Breughel, Bosch, Grünewald, and Michaelangelo: but he has had a particularly close association with sculpture all through his life, with the Austrian, Wotruba, above all his "Zwillingsbruder," on whom he wrote a monograph published in 1955. He also had a close association with the sculptress Anna Mahler and the sculptor Alfred Hrdlicka, who illustrated a few of the scenes in *Die Blendung* and *Hochzeit*, but who is primarily known for his illustrations to *Masse und Macht*. When we mention the quality of plasticity in connection with specific works of sculpture or buildings, we can point to the components that are thought to contain the quality or those components that produce the effect of plasticity on a spectator. We can point, however, only if we believe that plasticity is an intrinsic quality of a created object. If plasticity is, by contrast, an effect, something resembling a feeling, stimulated by an object, but which is really only experienced within the imagination of the individual, it is clearly only partially intrinsic to the created object: it is as intrinsic to the living human subject whose senses have stimulated his/her imagination by a material object. Created objects can stimulate the potential for plasticity which lies latent.

Literary works have no obvious physical contours in the same way that sculptures or works of architecture do, yet, if we understand plasticity in terms of *effects*, there is actually absolutely no reason why literary works should not be capable of generating such responses in precisely the same way as works of sculpture and architecture do. What is important here, however, is not so much that Canetti subscribes to the idea that literary works can achieve a kind of intangible physicality at the level of effect on a reader's imagination. It is more that this stress precludes any sense of the necessity of sustaining any kind of distinction between the parameters of the created art object and the world to which that art object supposedly refers. For the metaphor does not allow for such a distinction: the metaphor insists on the absolute and utter independence of art from life in any shape or form. It is an end in itself. It is important, then, that we see Canetti as a radical theoretician of literature, precisely because the emphasis he wishes to put on the intersubjective encounter between the reader and the art object effectively demotes the claims of the extra-textual world altogether. We are talking about a direct and startling encounter, whereby the novel dazzles a reader's imagination dramatically. Yet Canetti's fascination with the metaphysical effect on the reader's imagination of his novel is one that excludes the capacity of that imagination for critical reflection, or for that poetic moment described by Plato when the imagination, stimulated by a literary work, has the freedom to recognize something already known, but which lies dormant in the soul. The stress on devastating effects shows that Canetti is not interested in using the novel as a means of either furthering a questioning attitude to a given reality in the sense of appealing to a reader's intellect, reason, and imagination, where these can be harnessed to particular ends, or allowing the reader the freedom to enjoy a moment of poetic vision.

Canetti marks himself out as radical in his *cavalier* indifference to the more conventional ends of literature. For formal literary methods, commonly thought to constitute the art or skill of a literary writer, are usually deployed with the precise intention of furthering the cause of interpretation of the given. Effects created by individual literary works, in conservative theories of literature, are generally considered to consist in those well-thought-out analytical positions, implicit in presentation, that ultimately further the relationship of the reader to the world. They further the relationship positively or negatively depending on the author's attitude to that reality, and they do so because they rely on ideas, not words. Canetti's metaphors bespeak his absolute confidence in his own right to use his own imaginative, creative strength and power to overwhelm, compel, and exalt the imagination of the reader. On the one hand, he wishes to deny the value of the intellect as source of reflective consciousness and analytical truths, since he nowhere indicates that the thematic scope of his novel is likely to create social situations, such as conflict, likely to require analysis. The novel has its origins in chaos, yes, but Canetti has been categorical about the need to respect chaos and about the refusal to interpret that chaos. There is no creative engagement with chaos for the principle of respect for chaos precludes the possibility, from the outset, of Canetti's being in a position to examine conflict, or conflict that demands analysis.

On the other hand, Canetti positively celebrates the power of the imagination as something immeasurably creative and capable, above all, of plasticity, or the power of form. In so doing, the metaphors give priority to the direct, unmediated, and intersubjective relationship of *power* between the created literary work and the individual imagination of each individual reader. Now, power, as one of Canetti's systematic preoccupations, is normally identified in his other works as a kind of moral, social, political, or cultural evil, which Canetti wants to criticize. Here, however, the metaphors are resolute in their refusal to let art *service* a given reality, for nowhere does Canetti stress the relationship between created art and the world in time and space "out there." Canetti is surreptitiously making an unusual claim, that art objects can upstage and silence those claims otherwise made on the imagination by something like a social world out there. Art objects are not there to *service* that given social world in any shape or form. They are absolutely pure of such a material aim. The intellect is not only to be silenced, it is not to be called upon, in any way, to further some kind of contract the reader already has with that social world. The rejection of the intellect is comprehensive, since value judgments are held responsible for the view, both that art *must* relate to an already existent world and does service that social world, and that that social world, *as it already is*, is actually worth something. Art that furthers the cause of endorsing the social world is clearly not acceptable. Thus the implicit, violent rejection of a kind of art that would, by appealing to the intellect and reason, merely end up refining, by intellectual and/or analytical means, *the already given.*

Art has to be severed from that world, because Canetti's agenda appears to be a metaphysical one, and not a socio-political one or even a social one. It can do this only if it appeals to different skills, non-rational ones, above all. What is given, in Canetti's terms, is the context of chaos, not the comparative stability and security of an ordered social existence. Canetti's metaphors about writing suggest that he will be writing in such a way as to appeal to a reader's capacity for strength, for power, and for endurance. Art objects should be taken on their own terms, as ends in themselves. They should be taken more seriously than any of the kinds of pressures already exerted on the imagination by the social world already inhabited by the creator and his readers. And they should be ends in themselves, precisely *to deny the social world with its vested interest in order, the inverse of both chaos on the one hand, and artistic form on the other.* They should attempt this for reasons entirely reminiscent of Nietzsche, namely to demonstrate that we are stronger than that social world, and that we are stronger than a greater metaphysical threat, that of falling recklessly into an abyss of absolute chaos.

The issue latent in Canetti's apparently innocent description of the genesis of his novel is one of a high order of generality. The issue to address in life is how to survive, given the real existential threat of chaos. And the answer is not to become more of a thinker, to elevate the status of the already given by reflecting on it. It is not to settle into a space within a relatively stable and ordered social world. It is to become more of a creator in the generalized Nietzschean sense of that word. In becoming either a thinker or a support structure within a social order, the reader is obviously ensured a certain kind of security, but only as something of a passive contemplative within a framework of the already known, itself guaranteed by certain established ideas, of referential value. In becoming a creator, by contrast, the reader is instated as an individual, as a free agent of new imaginings in a dangerous world, where nothing is already known and where all things are possible. The former mode ensures survival with security, with the assistance of variations on the theme of reified, received ideas, whilst the latter mode challenges the individual to survive without security, to unleash and make plastic use of his own power as a creator. The task is to harness all one's creative energies to the goal of imaginative self-creation, to resist defining oneself in terms of the already given. Clearly, Canetti believes the creative capacity for survival on these new terms is latent in all human beings: certain works of art release this potential only by assuming both that it is already there and that it merely needs to be teased into existence (564).[12]

That the novel was to be exploited as a Nietzschean means of injecting plastic form, temporarily, into the ever-mobile, ever-dynamic world of chaos, and not as a means of penetrating through to an understanding of the essence of that chaos, is, however, only partly clear in the extract that follows the quoted section in the autobiography, where Canetti focuses on what the spotlights can achieve: "Sie waren das eigentliche Mittel der Erkenntnis: mit ihnen wäre das Chaos, von dem man erfüllt war, zu durchdringen. Gab es genug solcher Scheinwerfer, waren sie richtig erdacht, so ließe sich das Chaos *auseinandernehmen*. Es durfte nichts ausgelassen werden, man durfte nichts fallenlassen, alle üblichen Tricks der Harmonisierung verursachten Ekel" (*FO*, 295).[13] The spotlights are the means of knowledge, he says, they are the means of penetrating the chaos. Despite the use of the philosophical word "Erkenntnis," which raises the idea inherent in epistemology, namely the issue of knowledge, of how we penetrate things and understand them, we have to reflect on the sense in which Canetti really means knowledge can be attained. One cannot argue from the above that Canetti's intention is to penetrate to the essence of chaos per se. Rather, it seems that his desire is to interrupt the reign of chaos by reducing some of the power of the dynamism of chaos: thus the word "auseinandernehmen." What emerges, later on, is an idea already briefly mentioned, namely the idea of the importance of the writer's respect for the original form of matter: "In Wirklichkeit hatte alles eine Richtung und alles nahm überhand, *Expansion* war eine Haupteigenschaft von Menschen und Dingen, um davon etwas zu fassen, mußte man die Dinge auseinandernehmen. Ein wenig war es so, als hätte man einen Urwald, in dem alles verschlungen durcheinanderwuchs, zu entwirren, jedes Gewächs vom anderen zu lösen, ohne es zu beschädigen oder zu zerstören, es in Spannung für sich zu besehen und weiterwachsen zu lassen, ohne es wieder aus dem Auge zu verlieren" (*FO*, 295).[14]

The startling quality about this passage concerns Canetti's respect for the original form of chaos, which takes precedence over, indeed excludes altogether, a notion of the possibility of penetrating to an analytical understanding of the essence or source of that chaos. In spite of the fact that he uses straightforward vocabulary like "entwirren," Canetti does not suggest that he will be able to make his material yield analytical clarity of the nature of chaos per se. The emphasis is, instead, on two different things altogether. On the one hand, the "temporary" separation of the strands making up the chaos, and on the other, the preservation of the original form of the chaos, for matter encountered is not to be radically realtered in any way, indeed it is not to be altered at all. This amounts to a rejection of analytical vision and an endorsement of the possibility of plasticity as the single means available to creative man in his quest to exert temporary control over chaos, by infusing it with his own, alternative visions. An alliance has to be made with energy.

It is interesting to note here the similarity between Canetti's premises and those of the Presocratic philosophers. Canetti's premises are Greek in origin, and philosophical in a particular way, for the above descriptions resemble the accounts given by the exponents of the school of Presocratic philosophy of the composition of the universe. These first principles are, interestingly, also at the heart of Nietzsche's theories generally speaking, as Moroney has shown in his book: *Nietzsche's Dionysian Aristocratic Culture.*[15] Heraclitus,[16] known as the weeping philosopher, Democritus, the so-called laughing philosopher, and Epicurus all subscribed to the atomic theory that the universe was composed of a chaotic series of atoms, which had come together by chance.[17] Canetti does not make the connection himself in the above official accounts of the genesis of his novel, and he nowhere formally acknowledges that there is any kind of continuity between the first principles of the Presocratic philosophers and his own. It is partly the intention of this study to suggest in what subtle ways the Presocratic theories are mobilized and acted out in Canetti's *Die Blendung.* But before developing such a view about the Greek origins of his novel, it would be useful to record the extent of Canetti's own comments on the significance of Presocratic philosophers to his intellectual development, both at the time of writing the novel and elsewhere.

Canetti's intellectual notebooks are littered with references to Democritus and Heraclitus above all. The attraction to Democritus is philosophical, because of Democritus's sense that the world is composed of a mass of atoms. The attraction to Heraclitus is aesthetic: he is economical in his use of words and, like Stendhal, his thinking is bright.[18] In a discussion with Ruprecht Slavko Baur about *Die Blendung,* published in 1972, Canetti, in characteristic emotive form, stressed that he was merely *fascinated* by early Greek philosophy: "Ich glaube, daß mir außer der frühen griechischen Philosophie überhaupt keine Philosophie soviel bedeutet hat und noch bedeutet wie die chinesische."[19] Elsewhere, he has said that he was working on the Presocratic philosophers when he wrote *Die Blendung*: "Ich vertiefte mich nun in die antiken Historiker, Thukydides ganz besonders, und in die Philosophie der Vorsokratiker," he says in his essay published in 1973, on the composition of the novel.[20] Another, more mysterious comment, from 1984, from *Das Geheimherz der Uhr,* makes a reference in the following terms: "Du führst dich so auf, als hätte es seit Vorsokratikern und Chinesen nichts gegeben."[21]

Canetti's account of the genesis of the characters of his novel is one that continues to show that he was working under the shadow of the Greek school of Presocratic philosophy. The account reads very much like an admission of the way in which human beings resemble atoms in the cosmos, and as such already gives credence to the theory of the relevance of the link with the Preoscratic theory about the composition of the universe:

> Ich scheute davor zurück, ihnen Namen zu geben, sie waren nicht etwa Individuen wie der und jener, den man kannte, jede von ihnen wurde aus ihrem Hauptanliegen heraus erfunden, eben dem, was sie weiter und weiter trieb, fort von den anderen. Sie sollte eine vollkommen eigene Sicht auf die Dinge haben, sie war das Beherrschende ihrer Welt, mit nichts anderem zu vergleichen. Es war von Bedeutung, daß alles in ihrem Sinn durchgehalten war. Die Strenge, mit der alles andere von ihrer Welt ausgeschlossen war, war vielleicht das Wichtigste. Es war ein Strang, den ich aus dem Wirrwarr herausholte, ich wollte ihn pur und unvergeßlich. Er sollte sich einem so einprägen wie ein Don Quijote. Er sollte Dinge denken und sagen, die kein anderer hätte denken oder sagen können. Einen bestimmten Aspekt der Welt sollte er so sehr ausgedrückt haben, daß sie ohne ihn ärmer wäre, ärmer, aber auch verlogener. (*FO*, 297)[22]

Notice how Canetti insists that his characters are not individuals. They are not individuals because they are defined by one characteristic alone, which is the key to the character, and which is really a euphemism for the energetic power that lies within: as atoms they are pure energy which manifests itself, consistently, in terms of one human characteristic. This single characteristic is the motor that positively ensures that each character keeps himself/herself utterly detached from any kind of relationship with any other character. In absolute terms, it ensures his/her uniqueness. In social terms, it ensures that despite physical proximity, no character makes any compromises with any other character, and remains hermetically sealed within his/her own thoroughly unique vision of the world. The vision itself will be uncompromising, just as the rejection of relationships is uncompromising.

If the characters are like the self-contained atoms that move around, and that never unite with other atoms, they are credited with something positively human, which suggests that the atom analogy is not comprehensive. Each one of the eight characters Canetti had in mind, each known by his/her single, defining characteristic ("Wahrheitsmensch," "Phantast," "Fanatiker," "Sammler," "Verschwender," "Tod-Feind," "Schauspieler," "Büchermensch"), is still prone to a recognizably human process: "aber es ging bei ihnen allen um eine bestimmte Art von Wahrheit: die der Übereinstimmung mit sich selbst" (*FO*, 297). This impulse, the idea of a process of synthesis going on within the human personality of each character, mysterious and complicated as it appears here, will be analyzed in later chapters. For the moment, what is important is that we notice how we are leaving the thoroughly neutral world of anonymous atoms, and entering an imaginative world where individuality reigns supreme, as indicated by the names given to the characters, and a world where human processes are at work. As Canetti's account continues, we also enter a world informed by a notion of what constitutes the norm in terms of human behavior and conduct:

> Ein ganzes Jahr war erfüllt von den Entwürfen zu diesen Acht, es war das reichste, das ausschweifendste Jahr meines Lebens. Mir war zumute, als trüge ich mich mit einer "Comédie Humaine," und da die Figuren bis zu einem äußersten Extrem gesteigert und gegeneinander abgeschlossen waren, nannte ich es eine Comédie Humaine an Irren. (*FO*, 299)[23]

To classify the group of characters as mad people is, after all, to admit to a notion of what constitutes the norm in terms of human behavior and conduct. As a form of homage to Balzac, the overall title suggests an ambitious desire to produce a cycle of characters living an existence that could be looked on as a form of comedy. Much has been made of the title, with critics assuming Canetti wanted to present the reader with an image of society as a whole, that Canetti's intentions were roughly interchangeable with those of the great nineteenth-century Realists, all working within the tradition of mimesis outlined above. This may be misleading for a number of reasons, which will be discussed at length later on.

For the moment, it is also vital to bear in mind that this part of Canetti's account of the genesis of his novel presents us with some equally idiosyncratic notions, this time of madness, which are of course vital for an understanding of the last section of *Die Blendung*. According to a letter Canetti wrote to Dieter Dissinger in 1971, the novel was written between Autumn 1930 and the end of August 1931, when he lived opposite an institution for the mad in Steinhof, in Vienna, whose famous church, behind the hospital, was built by Otto Wagner, and whose cupola Canetti could see from his room.[24] According to Canetti's essay on the novel, "Das erste Buch: *Die Blendung*," of 1973, the novel was written between Autumn 1929 and Autumn 1930.[25] This lack of clarity concerning the dates and duration of the writing process apart, what is interesting here is Canetti's attitude toward madness. The presence of those whom society institutionalizes, either permanently because they are incurable, or temporarily, so that they can be rehabilitated, acted as a stimulant on Canetti's imagination. Canetti imagined his own characters living within the institution opposite his flat:

> Als Abschluß schwebte mir vor, daß sie zueinander sprächen. Aus ihrer Abgeschiedenheit heraus würden sie Sätze füreinander finden, und diese, in ihrer Absonderlichkeit, hätten einen ungeheuren *Sinn*. Es schien mir eine Entwürdigung für sie, an Heilung zu denken. Keiner von ihnen sollte in die Belanglosigkeit irgendeines Alltagslebens zurückfinden. Eine Anpassung an uns käme nur ihrer Verringerung gleich, dafür waren sie mir in der Einzigartigkeit ihrer Erfahrungen zu kostbar. Aber von hohem, von unerschöpflichem Wert erschien mir ihre Reaktion aufeinander. Wenn die Inhaber dieser Einzelsprachen einander etwas zu sagen fänden, das für sie sinnvoll würde, so bliebe auch für uns gewöhnliche Menschen, denen die Dignität des Irreseins abging, Hoffnung. (*FO*, 299)[26]

This account contains idiosyncratic notions of madness, in that it does not recognize that the ordinary goal of returning the inmates of such an institution to society, healed of their sufferings or illnesses and fit to lead a more fulfilling and satisfying existence without dependence on medical assistance, is a valid one, medically or otherwise. Madness is not recognized by Canetti to be what it is conventionally thought to be, which is to say a condition requiring medical and imaginative attention, and one from which it would neither be pleasant nor advisable to suffer. Canetti assumes, in this account of how his fictionally mad characters might behave, that there is something superior about being mad. Clearly, Canetti's use of the word is whimsical, in that he nowhere sees madness negatively. Needless to say, he is convinced that each "mad" person literally inhabits a totally individual language. A community of "mad" people seems now to resemble his existential notion of the world as a place where a multiplicity of realities merely coexist, and where organic links between the realities cannot be formed. Madness here then is really the idea of the radically subjective language of each individual. In other words, madness here is an euphemism. It actually stands for the way in which the individual can manage to retain his/her absolute originality: for it is given that each person inhabits his or her original language. This is the existential basis of life. Attempts are made to establish common ground with others: Canetti does not suggest whether and how these experiments might be successful, as he does not suggest how it would be possible for an outsider to judge whether meaningful interchanges have taken place. Madness is, therefore, an imaginatively appealing state to someone, a writer, who is himself not prone to the complaint of madness: it is credited with an aura not commonly thought to pertain. This is not an account, after all, in which Canetti admits to any special sympathy for those actually suffering from the complaint. Madness is not seen in terms of a sickness and in terms of suffering. The significance of these ideas will be discussed when they almost appear to be quoted verbatim in the last sections of *Die Blendung*, those dominated by the psychiatrist, George(s). Meanwhile, this fascination with the original, highly subjective language of hermetically sealed individuals raises some important scientific questions. What objective criteria can be invoked by any outsider, let alone a philosopher of language in an analysis that presumes to deal with something as elusive as meaning? For whom can the language be judged to be meaningful? How can an outsider establish whether a language is meaningful, either to the person who speaks it, or to the person who hears him/her speak it?

It seems more likely that Canetti has a prejudice that whatever is expressed by "mad" people is actually meaningful. And this prejudice is, further, a vote of absolute confidence in, and desire for, a world where absolute originality in human behavior reigns supreme. A vote of confidence, not in a community linked together by individuals and bonds of love, affection, and common experience, but a vote for ruthless individualism and ruthless insularity from the constraints of relationships. Canetti's fascination with language here, obscures the way in which those whom he observes, or imagines he observes, are victims, are suffering. They are actively prevented from entering into relationships with others. It is assumed that his characters are, for the most part, locked into an imaginary world which noone else can penetrate. It is given that those whom he deems to be mad are "Inhaber dieser Einzelsprachen." So, despite possible efforts to find something meaningful, the radically subjective language of each inmate here actively prevents him/her from having the means necessary to establish proper relationships. Even verbal relationships are mere chance possibilities. Despite Canetti's desire that meaningful communication take place, relationships seem fated to be no more than brisk encounters between different discourses. Monologue, or the reign of subjectivity, seems fated to replace dialogue, or the reign of attempted community.

Canetti's discussion of the way in which meaning might be injected into language is difficult. Language may well have meaning in absolute terms, that is to say, in the eyes of an omniscient, God-like figure. But since mortals are not privileged in terms of absolute knowledge of all things, the general "idea" here comes across as indulgent fantasy and speculation. As speculation, the ideas merely reveal Canetti's desire to project a notion of the validity of the utterly unique language onto human beings who are already exceptional anyway, because they have already been cast aside by society, condemned to live in isolation from that society in an institution. Canetti's logic in the rest of the passage depends on these highly specious assumptions. For it is because Canetti assumes, without further debate, that the language spoken might have an incredible kind of meaning, that Canetti considers it undignified to think of subjecting the individuals in question to a healing process. Canetti feels happy and justified in actively sustaining his mad characters in their unique worlds, because he regards ordinary life, the world where a common discourse operates, as banal and insignificant. Canetti does not appear to be aware of the existence of dissenting voices in society outside the institution for the mad, and of the great richness, complexity, and variety of human life outside institutions. He makes a false deduction when he assumes that the existence of one single, common language is responsible for monotony and the absence of originality. After all, he puts it rather strongly when he says: "Keiner von ihnen sollte in die Belanglosigkeit irgendeines Alltagslebens zurückfinden." It is possible to conclude that Canetti's fascination with the unique voice is at least partially dependent on his reductive prejudice against "ordinary" life, for this is referred to in devastatingly dismissive terms, and made to be thoroughly uniform and barren, without richness and variety.

Since these idiosyncratic views are also present, often almost verbatim, in the novel, where they become the basis of George's own theories about madness in his psychiatrist's hospital, it is important that we see through Canetti's apparent love of the extraordinary and rejection of ordinary life as banal and unpoetic. Behind Canetti's theories is a theory of exploitation: here of the suffering of others for private purposes, for in a quite literal sense their circumstances only have status inasmuch as they act as pure imaginative stimulant. Individual sufferers lose all their humanity as individuals and are material for Canetti's fantasy. This must be seen as suspicious. Canetti fails to accept common humanity, and to recognize that all human subjects are, in Kant's terms, ends, not means. His account is, then, despite its harmless tone, the crass transformation of other subjects into mere objects, who, whilst they act as stimulants to a solitary spectator, find themselves deprived of their claim on that solitary spectator's potential humanity, let alone his practical capacity to help alleviate their circumstances, let alone their right to a kind of subjectivity that is empowering in their own personal terms.

This complicated foray into "madness," or Canetti's idiosyncratic series of whimsical ideas on the "meaningfulness" of madness indicate, once again, the extent to which Canetti's fictional human beings resemble atoms. Each mad individual is resolutely and hermetically sealed within his/her own discourse, with genuine contact a mere question of chance. Canetti insists on the possibility of human beings being capable of a skill, that of communication with one another, that of generating meaning, *yet his theory is only a theory*. He does not experiment with his theories here, or subject his whimsical theories to experiment. Neither does he subject the theory to any thorough analytical scrutiny.

Die Fackel im Ohr also indicates that the physical disabilities of Canetti's friend Thomas Marek were important to the genesis of the novel, in terms of the above foray into the relationship between "illness" and existence. Marek's disabilities meant he was something of an outcast, institutionalized in his wheelchair, so to speak. The meeting and friendship with Thomas Marek are the subject of "Fehltritte" (*FO*, 323–35). Thomas Marek was an intellectual and a cripple, whose physical condition had partly contributed to his not being able to form relationships with women, a disadvantage with which, although in comic form, Peter Kien is striken. One of Marek's teachers arranged for him to lose his virginity, and thereafter girls would come to visit him in his flat: he became very successful, and had charming seductive powers, which culminated in his having a long-term relationship with a female doctor, who originally visited him to treat him for a cold. Canetti admired the man generally, because he attempted to take control over all of his disabilities in a way that commanded respect and approval (*FO*, 337). The visits to Thomas Marek coincided with a phase in the genesis of the novel when Canetti felt certain that each of his eight figures would be the centerpiece of a separate novel. This changed into a conviction that he would write a single novel with one central figure. The link between the central character and Thomas Marek is underlined, in the sense that Canetti seems to have carried over into his novel the quality of determination and will power that characterized Thomas Marek (*FO*, 340).

Another important point made in the narrative of the genesis of the novel concerns the impact of the fire in the Palace of Justice in Vienna on the July 15, 1927, which event Canetti related to Thomas Marek as it had happened when he, Canetti, had witnessed it. Thomas Marek was not frightened by the story; on the contrary, he was stimulated by it and laughed heartily, "ein stürmisches Gelächter" (*FO*, 341). This moment gave Canetti the idea of fire, and shortly thereafter "Büchermensch" dominated his imagination. Canetti felt that he sighted his "Büchermensch" once in a Café, Café Pucher in Vienna, to the left of a cactus shop: "Er war so abwesend, wie er dürr war, ohne die Stacheln der Kakteen hätte man nicht auf ihn geachtet, er bestand aus Stacheln. . . . So hatte ich Brand gefunden und er ließ mich nicht los. Ich hatte mir einen Kaktus in den Leib gepflanzt und er wuchs nun entschlossen und unbekümmert weiter" (*FO*, 343). Since *Die Blendung* concludes with a fire and with a lusty laugh, we shall be looking at how Canetti reworks this when we look at the novel in greater detail in later chapters.

Finally, we must look at the impact made on Canetti by literary writers with whom he was familiar when he came to write *Die Blendung*:

> Im Jahr der Ausschweifungen war Gogol, den ich auf das höchste bewunderte, mein Meister gewesen. In seiner Schule hatte ich mich der Freiheit der Erfindung hingegeben, die Lust daran verlor ich auch später nicht, als ich mich um anderes bemühte. Jetzt aber, im Jahr der Konzentration, als es mir um Klarheit und Dichte zu tun war, um eine schlackenlose Durchsichtigkeit, wie in Bernstein, hielt ich mich an ein Vorbild, das ich nicht weniger bewunderte: Stendhals "Rot und Schwarz."

> Täglich, bevor ich mit dem Schreiben begann, las ich einige Seiten daraus und wiederholte so, was er selber getan hatte, mit einem anderen Vorbild, dem berühmten neuen Gesetzbuch seiner Tage. (*FO*, 343)[27]

Gogol gave him "die Freiheit der Erfindung," therefore, and Stendhal the intellectual precision and clarity that are clearly the hallmarks of his *Le Rouge et le Noir*. Canetti has paid tribute to Stendhal in much of his work, both in an interview published in the newspaper *Die Welt am Sonntag* in 1963, entitled "Stendhal war meine Bibel" ("Stendhal was my bible"),[28] in his essay "Dialog mit dem grausamen Partner" in 1965, and in his notebooks 1942–1985. In the essay of 1965, for instance, Stendhal is classified as one of the fast thinkers, one of the fast writers rigorously open to the world. Canetti completes the observation with a comparison with Kafka that makes clear how Canetti sees Stendhal as a primarily happy writer and thinker. Of Kafka he writes: "Er gehört aber zu den Langsamen, wie Stendhal zu den Raschen. Es sind die Raschen, die dazu neigen, ihr Leben als glücklich zu empfinden. So ist Stendhals Werk in die Farbe des Glücks getaucht, Kafkas in die der Ohnmacht".[29] In two entries from Canetti's notebooks, from 1971, reprinted in *Die Provinz des Menschen*, Canetti comments, approvingly, on Stendhal's attitude toward death, on his love of geographical specificity, on his love of "Verwandlung," which is to say, as far as the theme of death and "Verwandlung" are concerned, on two areas he and Stendhal have in common. He also comments that Stendhal divided up his world in *La vie de Henri Brulard* into people he liked and people he disliked, a habit prevalent throughout all of Canetti's "critical" work. Stendhal's habit is supported, in Canetti's view, by a general nobility of outlook and a sense of the uniqueness of each person (*PM*, 293–94). A more sober entry from 1973, which appears in *Das Geheimherz der Uhr*, sees Canetti record his love once again: "Ich erkenne mich in seiner Freiheit und seiner unmäßigen Liebe für Menschen," also saying, more wistfully, that he sees Stendhal as something of a better version of himself "eine Art besseres Ich, das ich nie, keinen Augenblick je wirklich sein werde." Canetti states a page later that "Stendhal belebt mich zu jeder Zeit, in jeder Verfassung."[30] A single entry from 1982 quotes Stendhal in French, a comment made to Balzac: "Si je ne suis pas clair, tout mon monde est anéanti."[31]

Canetti's comments on Gogol are less stimulating. In 1945, an entry in his notebooks, reprinted in *Die Provinz des Menschen*, suggests that Gogol lost his nerve in life and went to the dogs (*PM*, 79).[32] In *Das Geheimherz der Uhr*, Gogol is inspiring: "Das Belebende Gogols ist seine Herzlosigkeit. Sie ist so groß wie seine Angst. Er verhöhnt, um ihr zu entkommen, doch seine Angst schläft nie."[33] This study as a whole will be investigating the way in which both Gogol and Stendhal are imaginatively present throughout *Die Blendung*.

Canetti's character Brand was later christened Kant, and the novel was christened *Kant fängt Feuer* in 1931, yet the reason for the change of name, and in particular for the change to the name of one of the central philosophers in Continental thought, receives no comment. Instead, Canetti tells us of the next metamorphosis, of Kant's name into Kien, which in English means pinewood:

> Aus Kant wurde Kien, die Entzündbarkeit der Welt, deren Bedrohung ich fühlte, blieb im Namen der Hauptfigur erhalten. Der Schmerz aber steigerte sich zum Titel *Die Blendung*. Er bewahrte, für niemand erkennbar, die Erinnerung an Simsons Blendung, der ich auch heute nicht abzuschwören wage. (*FO*, 344)[34]

This notion of the threat and the potential inflammability of the world is expanded upon in the 1973 essay on the genesis of the novel, to which we have already referred:

> Eines Tages kam mir der Gedanke, daß die Welt nicht mehr so darzustellen war wie in früheren Romanen, sozusagen vom Standpunkt *eines* Schriftstellers aus, die Welt war *zerfallen*, und nur wenn man den Mut hatte, sie in ihrer Zerfallenheit zu zeigen, war es noch möglich, eine wahrhafte Vorstellung von ihr zu geben. Das bedeutete aber nicht, daß man sich an ein chaotisches Buch zu machen hätte, in dem nichts mehr zu verstehen war, im Gegenteil, man mußte mit strengster Konsequenz extreme Individuen erfinden, so wie die, aus denen die Welt ja auch bestand, und diese auf die Spitze getriebenen Individuen in ihrer Geschiedenheit nebeneinanderstellen. (*GW*, 249)

In this extract, we return to a way of discussing the novel that emphasizes the contract between the author and the established world "out there," as if the theory of mimesis were one

Canetti took unquestioningly for granted. This is clear from the way in which Canetti still talks about "die Welt," from the way in which he uses the verb "darstellen," and from the way in which he talks of the idea of "die wahrhafte Vorstellung." The idea of imitation or representation of a given, objective, extra-textual reality figures very prominently, in contrast to the sections examined above. The *means* a writer uses to represent the secular world "out there" are, however, simply going to have to be modified to accommodate a change that Canetti believes has taken place in historical time. Both passages cited above show that Canetti believed, at the time of writing, that the world was vulnerable to destruction and that this was a new development in world history. This is put in straightforward terms, when he talks about the "Entzündbarkeit" of the world, about "Zerfall," and when he talks of a still-unspecified threat he intuitively felt to be alive in the world.[35] It is interesting that these statements make no use of recent history. They do not mention politics or personalities or movements, whether in Austria or Germany, let alone in Europe generally. They are utterly devoid of concrete references and retain, as a result, a worrying kind of general mystique, with which a genuinely historically oriented critic should not be satisfied. They serve the purpose, nevertheless, in spite of appearances to the contrary, of discreetly promoting Canetti's own view of himself as a serious commentator, prophet of doom, or eschatologist. Nonetheless, in relying on this posture, Canetti is *complicit* with a world already in decline.

The second extract mentions the "Zerfallenheit" of the world, again in suitably vague terms that make no references to contemporary realities. The idea of collapse here, of which Canetti is utterly convinced, is one that must be respected, he insists, in fictional representations of the world. Defending an assumed objection that his work would inevitably be a description of chaos, if the notion of collapse were imitated faithfully in his imaginative construct of the world "out there," Canetti insists that his novel would contain the vestiges of some sort of "order," because it would be peopled by extreme individualists, set alongside one another. This suggests that although the fabric of the world would be represented in the throes of collapse, the fictional characters populating such a world would have such strong contours that they would succeed in seducing the reader into thinking that the chaos or decline or collapse was not absolute or irrevocable. Once again, Canetti does not deny the idea of the atomic theory of the Presocratic philosophers. The world is a dynamically active one, in which atoms encounter one another by chance. But here a new term enters the argument, namely that of the Nietzschean concept of resistance. The dynamism can be halted, temporarily, so to speak, by the forceful impact made on the imagination of the reader by vigorously well-defined human characters, inhabitants of a chaotic world. Personality, then, is credited with a power, the power of resistance, a power that mitigates the full impact of chaos.

In spite of an attempt to instate himself as something of a historical commentator, we soon realize that Canetti's preference is for the human capacity for resistance to absolute chaos, rather than for an analytical understanding of those social, economic, or political forces responsible for the form history takes at any particular moment in time. We do *not* have any real confidence from the above that Canetti is interested in ultimate causes and their analysis. Chaos is a backdrop he takes for granted, only so that he can show up the human capacity to survive in spite of its presence. The importance of certain writers to the writing of *Die Blendung* is also expanded upon in the same essay, where Canetti reflects further on his ideal of askesis, which he had found so appealing in his encounter with Thomas Marek (*GW*, 250). Stendhal and Kafka are credited with having achieved an absolute in their prose style, the absolute of banishing all signs of anything non-intellectual. They have denied the existence of sentiment, certainly the cheap kind that he felt dominated contemporary Viennese literature, about which Canetti is superbly disparaging. Canetti is obviously thinking of Bahr and Werfel here. The latter he hated for his operatic social behavior and love of operatic sentiment in his writings, as one learns from the autobiography generally. Of course, much as this account is appealing, it is quite obvious that Stendhal's language does not reflect or embody, "accurately," what he really values, because whilst it is so superbly rational, it always manages to allude to a world of emotions and sentiment, although obviously not the cheap variety.[36] Canetti's endorsement of Kafka's *Die Verwandlung*, as if this work were an embodiment of "Strenge," is also questionable, for it could be argued that there is even a mood of self-pity in the story, unique by the standards set by Kafka in his fiction generally. Since this mood also permeates the whole story, it necessarily dissipates any of the muscular strength we associate with the word "Strenge."[37] Nevertheless,

Canetti clearly intends us to read his novel in terms of a particular kind of style, a style that is competitive for the reader, that does not allow him/her to relax or indulge in what is felt to be the luxury of reflection or rêverie or cheap sentiment, for reading is going to be "erbarmungslos." Reading is to be a punishing experience. The point is made again when Canetti proudly admits to the discipline imposed on his imagination by the postcards of Michaelangelo's and Grünewald's works that surrounded him as he wrote (*GW*, 251).

Before concluding, it would be appropriate to indicate the way in which critics have consistently overlooked the clues to Canetti's metaphysical agenda that litter the various accounts of the genesis of the novel. They have, instead, focused on those passages that lend themselves to the notion of the novel as social commentary, and to the view that Canetti's aesthetics are firmly within the ancient tradition of mimesis. In the quotation from *Die Fackel im Ohr* examined above, for instance, Canetti clearly does make a point about the rank confusion of life in Berlin, insisting that nobody knew how to communicate with one another. In the essay on Karl Kraus, "Karl Kraus: Schule des Widerstands," Canetti maintains that he learned from Kraus the truth of noncommunication (*GW*,48). Such ideas have been exploited by critics to prove the truth that in *Die Blendung* is carried out a thoroughgoing analysis of how communication in society fails. The point, at this stage, is merely to indicate how interesting it is that the attention granted such ideas is way in excess of the substantially more demanding and radical theory about the novel that has been examined thoroughly in this chapter. This prioritizes the metaphysical role and function of art, even in spite of the few indications given by Canetti that he was interested in the farce of social life. The points that have been made in this chapter are intended to clarify Canetti's idiosyncratic theory of literature, one that can only be understood in terms of Nietzsche's theories about the relationship between art and life. We have stressed the surprising way in which Canetti's theory, on balance, seems to ignore a notion of literature as mimetic, for missing is a thorough sense of the way in which a literary world might imply some kind of *social* contract with its readership, based on a common sense of lived experience. We have attempted to draw attention to the fascination with and respect for chaos, a *metaphysical* interest by contrast, with a basis in Presocratic philosophy. The obsession with chaos is interesting to Canetti as a challenge. It is a challenge to his non-rational powers, his plastic skills above all, for nowhere do we have any belief in the way analytic or synthetic reason can be used to construct ideas and impose order: this use of artifice was condemned unequivocally.

We shall shortly be expanding on the idea that chaos represents a challenge to the individual's plastic skills, by revealing that the terms of such a challenge have particular resonance in the great Greek tradition known as *agon*. Agon is the characteristic mode of life in Ancient Greek civilization, where all is either a competition or a contest between two individuals. We have already seen how chaos, in Canetti's narrative of how it was he came to write *Die Blendung*, is a *competitive* challenge to the creative powers of a potential creator. We saw how Canetti's assumption is that there is something inherently agonistic about creativity in the face of chaos. Chaos stimulates, agonistically, the creative drive toward form. The drive associated with agon in turn continues to ensure that we remain adequate to the challenge, that of endowing chaos with plastic form.

In contrast to Canetti's reputation as an opponent of power, *Die Blendung* defines power positively. It is defined as intellectual strength and rigor, devoid of analytical or intellectual content, since Canetti indicated at an early point that reason constituted the enemy, only inasmuch as it was capable of depriving power of power. Most importantly, however, this positive belief in power is not power over someone or something else, a theory that would obviously support exploitation for material gain, but power as a contained tension, never deployed for material gain. Rather it is a means of prolonging life, a way of showing that it is possible to assume responsibility for the shape of one's own destiny. We can also conclude that Canetti's theory of power is one that also positively hates anything that threatens to deprive it of its own internal momentum. Sentiment, it is suggested in the references to the inspiring giants who influenced his style, Grünewald, Michaelangelo, and Stendhal, is the second most important enemy of power. Sentiment has to be banished so the struggle to prove the existence of chaos and the power of creativity in the face of chaos can begin.

Aesthetics, then, according to Canetti, are really metaphysics. Aesthetics serve no obvious secular or social ends. They appear to serve metaphysical ends in terms of the high demands they place on the skills of a solitary reader, but only as a training for the best way to survive. They are not a training in solipsism and loneliness. Canetti's metaphysics aim to maximize the potential of existence in the here and now. They stress the Nietzschean struggle for absolute command over each individual moment, where the means already is the end, where *style* is everything. Supremacy in any absolute sense, as an end in itself, is not even entertained, because supremacy can only be achieved by and through reason. Reason always masquerades as an intellectual or analytical *position imposing itself on the moment.* As such, it is implied, when the intellect serves the secular world, the challenge of chaos disappears from sight. Since all analytical, contemplative "positions" have a natural tendency toward the inverse of chaos, namely fixity and reification, they further the obliteration of the drama of the moment. As such, ideas or intellectual positions destroy what chaos can highlight, namely the challenge of temporality and the drama of the moment. Ideas are inimical to chaos.

Style devoid of ideas and as a means of survival in the face of the threat of its inverse, destruction, is, in contrast to any fixed analytical or intellectual position, a mobile attitude of openess, a creative expression of the need to control chaos through form. In doing so, it is equal to the challenge of chaos, for it does nothing to deny the existence of chaos. We are not talking here about the differences between Tolstoy's style and Flaubert's style, where the very obviously personal use of language or style of each author can never be separated from his views about how people live. Canetti means style in an absolute sense, and as an existential attitude, thus style *tout court.* And we are talking about style *tout court* because Canetti has banished from his stage the very private and personal ideas at the level of content that make it possible for us to entertain the truth of the statement: this is Flaubert's style and not Tolstoy's style. The fact that his own use of language is so massively impersonal supports the broader metaphysical aims.

In this respect, it would be appropriate to end this first chapter with a refreshing reminder of the agonistic link between writing, power, and survival, which is so important, generally speaking, in Canetti's life. As is well known, Thomas Mann returned Canetti's manuscript very soon after Canetti submitted it to him in October 1931, after he had completed the novel. Mann had not read it.[38] Although cast down to begin with, Canetti began by reading it aloud to small groups of friends. The novel began its life as a tool of communication between friends. It continued, nevertheless, to be refused by a number of publishers, and was published for the first time, much later, in 1935. There was, therefore, considerable resistance to his novel. This had, however, a creative, agonistic effect on Canetti personally: "Jede Absage bestärkte mich in der Sicherheit, daß dieses Buch später leben würde" (*GW*, 232).[39]

2

The Reception of *Die Blendung*: The Critical Reputation of the Novel

We can continue this study of Canetti's only novel with a thematic survey of the general currents in criticism. This is fascinating in itself. As is well known, circumstances in the German-speaking world in 1935 did not conspire to make dissemination, let alone reception, of the work easy. 1935 was the year of the Nürnberg race laws, when the novel was first published by Herbert Reichner Verlag in Vienna, Leipzig, and Zürich. The novel also suffered again in 1948, this time from the effects of the Second World War, when the novel was reissued by Willi Weismann Verlag in Munich. It was not until the extended German version was published, in 1963, that the novel was taken seriously by German critics in the German-speaking world.[40] It had been successfully published, meanwhile, in 1946 by Johnathan Cape, in London, in an English translation by Veronica Wedgewood, entitled *Auto-da-Fé*. The same translation was published the next year in the United States by Alfred Knopf, but with the title *The Tower of Babel*. It had also won its first prize in France in 1949—the "Prix International," for the best foreign novel—after the publication in the same year of the French translation, by Paul Attex, called *La Tour de Babel*. This had appeared with the publisher B. Arthaud. According to Bensel's bibliography of works by and on Canetti, which appeared in 1989, the novel is now available in twenty-two different languages.[41] This makes *Die Blendung* internationally the best known of all of Canetti's works. *Die gerettete Zunge* is "only" available in thirteen languages, *Die Stimmen von Marrakesch* in twelve, *Masse und Macht* in ten, *Die Provinz des Menschen* in nine, *Der andere Prozeß* in eight, *Die Fackel im Ohr* and *Der Ohrenzeuge* in six, *Das Augenspiel* in three and *Das Gewissen der Worte* in two.

There seems to be little point in working through what has been said about this novel from a purely chronological point of view, since the wealth of material at hand in the secondary literature would merely make the reader confused. It is, therefore, the purpose of this chapter to break down and examine what might be called the prominent currents in *Die Blendung* criticism generally. What is immediately striking about the wealth of secondary literature that relates to *Die Blendung* in particular is the ambitious quality of the criticism itself. Indeed, a whole range of disciplines of thought has been brought to bear on analyses of the novel, in each case appropriating it for a specific, well-established discourse. These discourses have ranged from philosophy, philosophy of language, psychoanalysis, psychology, the theory of the masses, history, cultural history, economics, the history of European literature, the history of Viennese literature, to, more recently, the discourse related to narratology.

Philosophy has been well represented by those critics who maintain that in *Die Blendung* Canetti has specifically taken up a stand against the metaphysics and epistemology of Continental philosophers of the Western world like Descartes, Berkeley, and Kant. The first title of the novel was, after all, *Kant fängt Feuer*, stating, not suggesting, that Peter Kien was Kant himself. At a simple level, the novel's title and the titles of its three sections ("Ein Kopf ohne Welt," "Kopflose Welt," and "Welt im Kopf") would suggest that it deals with either the problem of dualism associated with Descartes, or the problem of transcendental idealism associated with Kant, or the problem of dogmatic idealism associated with Berkeley. The connection with Berkeley is sustained locally in the text when Peter Kien appears to quote Berkeley approvingly, in what is an actual misquotation of the Latin "esse is percipi." In *Die Blendung* this appears as "esse percipi" first, and then as "Sein ist Wahrgenommenwerden."[42] Raymond Furness's brief characterization of the novel is not untypical when he invokes, implicitly, both Berkeley and the discipline of psychoanalysis: he talks about Musil, Broch, and Canetti as sharing a common interest in the dangers of what he calls "solipsistic paranoia": "all three writers show man blinded to reality by his infinite powers of self-delusion."[43] The novelist Salman Rushdie also sees Peter Kien primarily as a solipsist because of his supposedly inward concerns with learning.[44] The novelist Siegfried Lenz has made the same point in his brief article, which appears in a book of essays whose title also relies on the popular assumption that scholars/academics live in ivory towers and have no knowledge of "reality."[45]

One of the most exciting studies of the novel, however, is a Ph.D. dissertation by Marilyn Smith Lovett, entitled "Fire in the

Library: Paranoia and Schizophrenia as models of linguistic crisis in Elias Canetti's *Die Blendung*."[46] This starts with the assumption that Canetti's novel is a study of the crisis of the fixity of the epistemological and psychological subject established by Enlightenment philosophers (Kant) and their forerunners (Descartes), as this is expressed in the psychoanalytic phenomena of paranoia and schizophrenia. Working with Adorno's idea of the "totalitarian personality," she places these psychoanalytic phenomena in intellectual history and the history of philosophy. Indeed, there is something of a predominance of references to psychoanalysis in critical thinking on the novel, much of it dominated by Freud, as Hennighaus's reading is, with its psychoanalytic interpretation of Kien's behaviour in the light of Freud's Oedipus complex theory.[47] Peter Kien's behavior and the behavior of Therese, Fischerle, and Benedikt Pfaff is frequently referred to in terms of abuse of norms of behavior. Canetti is credited with having invested his characters with all the attributes of non-normalcy, as if such attributes *subverted* a kind of reality, that of normalcy, which Canetti and his audience know and can take for granted. Such readings make Canetti and his audience *estranged* from Canetti's characters, whose perverse, subversive behavior of non-normalcy is denounced, as if Canetti and his audience were uniquely positioned, from their vantage point of sanity and normalcy, to reject the characters as perverts or subversives. These are seen as objects, as representatives of the Other. This tendency is often expressed in studies of the novel that insist that its subject is that of madness *tout court*. Roman Karst, for instance, entitles his article on the novel "A study in insanity."[48] J. M. Paul's article is called "Rationalität und Wahnsinn in Canettis Roman *Die Blendung*."[49] Edward Thomson talks in his article of the "changing image of madness" in Canetti's novel.[50] Walter Sokel's article is entitled "The ambiguity of madness: Elias Canetti's novel *Die Blendung*."[51]

Although Canetti has tried to distance himself from the determinist thinking of Freud, Freud is nevertheless frequently cited as an appropriate point of reference in the above kind of "normalcy" debate, as already indicated. Again and again, the highly publicized theories about the Oedipus complex, the death instinct, the behavior of the masses, repression, and so on feature as terms of reference in interpretations of the novel.[52] Peter Kien's general behavior, and his suicide in particular, is seen as living proof of Freud's theory of repression, or of the problems associated with dualistic views of human nature.[53] The other "debt" to Freud, another debt specifically challenged by Canetti, is the Freudian doctrine of the "Todestrieb," which many critics believe to be alive in Peter Kien personally, especially when he takes his own life.[54] Finally, there is the little-discussed but equally significant view, referred to briefly by Kristie Foell, that Canetti actively *parodies* Freud.[55] According to this view, Canetti refuses to take Freud's extraordinarily violent notions of causality seriously: he wants to detach himself from the psychologist by standing his ideas on their head. This is obviously the case in the conclusion to a brief, but hilariously lumpy account of a supposedly meaningful dream in the novel, in "Konfuzius, ein Ehestifter," to be discussed later: "Aus alledem hatte der Schlaf einen Traum gebraut" (DB, 41): a lighthearted dig at Freud's *Traumdeutung*.

Alternatively, the frequency of misogyny as a subject of conversation in the latter parts of the novel is cited as proof that characters have lost all sense of normality and are prone to the perversions associated with paranoia. Misogyny tends, however, in such analyses, to be neutralized as an issue, in favor of the generalized view that we are merely examining paranoia.[56] It is interesting here, for instance, that few female or feminist critics have been drawn to the novel. It is, nevertheless, easy to assume that Kien is, like many male artists and thinkers of turn-of-the-century Vienna, Karl Kraus, Klimt, Kokoschka, and Schiele included, a living example of the cruel misogyny valorized by Weininger in his "study," *Geschlecht und Charakter* (1903), whose cultural influence on turn-of-the-century Vienna has been much discussed by cultural critics like Carl Schorske, Nike Wagner, and Jacques le Rider.[57] We have in *Die Blendung* criticism the occasional references to the work of Otto Weininger, the influence of which Canetti felt in Vienna himself, as he reports the long-term effects of its publication in *Die Fackel im Ohr*.[58]

Elfriede Pöder maintains, in this connection, that Canetti makes fun of Weininger's theories, detaching himself thereby from the common currency they had, at the time of writing, in Vienna. She claims that they are being *parodied* by Canetti in such a way as to suggest that the author thinks they are not worth taking seriously. The satirical attitude toward Weininger is achieved by overexaggerating Weininger *ad absurdum* as far as the portrait of the representative of man, Peter Kien, is concerned, and also by attributing all the worst kinds of characteristics, normally ascribed by Weininger to women, to Kien.[59] What Weininger sees as the male characteristics of vanity, self-consciousness, desire for fame, are supplemented in Peter Kien by Weininger's female characteristics, namely lack of self-consciousness, a capacity to learn, a discontinuous memory. More recently, Johannes Pankau has maintained that in *Die Blendung* Canetti is quite consciously working with Weininger's concepts. Pankau, however, takes the longer view that in the novel is also hidden proof of Canetti's own fears about the complete impossibility of heterosexual relations and fears of "das Wesen der Frau."[60] Both Pöder and Pankau fail, interestingly, to confront the issue of whether Canetti's Therese is a misogynist portrait in the spirit of Weininger: and they both fail to comment on the theory of misogyny that is raised as a subject for discussion in the last section of the novel. For Jacques le Rider, too, *Die Blendung* as a whole is merely a generalized exploration of the consequences of Kien's autistic withdrawal from the world, which can only result in misogyny in the tradition of Weininger. Therese is a pure embodiment of instinct, while Kien is a pure embodiment of intellect.[61] A more elaborate investigation of the response to Weininger can be found in Kristie Foell's full-length study on the topic.[62]

Since references to the "masses" color the conversations at the end of the novel between George(s) and his brother Peter, it is not surprising that Canetti's work has been linked to theories concerning the behavior of the masses.[63] In this connection, critics have suggested that Canetti's investigations are continuous, in spirit if not to the letter, with a tradition originally established by Gustav Le Bon's treatise, *La Psychologie de la Foule*, which had appeared in 1895, Freud's writing on the subject, *Massenpsychologie und Ich-Analyse*, which had come out in 1921, Ortega y Gasset's study entitled *The Revolt of the Masses*, published in 1930, and Wilhelm Reich's *Die Massenpsychologie des Faschismus* of 1933. Canetti's insights expressed in *Die Blendung* have inevitably been linked up with other of his own insights, in particular those in his own theoretical work of 1960, *Masse und Macht*, which the author has always considered to be his most important work. David Darby believes that the successful publication of the third edition of *Die Blendung*, in 1963, following as it did the successful publication of *Masse und Macht*, in 1960, is directly attributable to *Masse und Macht*, as it is the reason why *Masse und Macht* figures so prominently as the interpretative key to *Die Blendung*.[64] After the publication of *Die Blendung*, and in the wake of the Second World War, the interest in the masses has taken a much more concrete, historical form than it had in either Le Bon, Freud, Canetti, Ortega y Gasset, or Wilhelm Reich. There have been serious studies of the relationship between the masses and fascism by literary writers such as Hermann Broch, for instance, with whom Canetti discussed his own theories. Broch published his ideas between 1938 and 1948 in article form. In 1979, these appeared in one volume as *Massenwahntheorie*. Alternatively, psychologists/psychoanalysts like Erich Fromm, with *The Anatomy of Human Destructiveness* of 1974, have turned to the same theme, as have historians like Hannah Arendt, in her provocative *The Origins of Totalitarianism* of 1951.

Canetti has rejected Freud's theories concerning the psychology of the masses, paranoia, and the so-called death instinct, in a conversation with Ruprecht Slavko Baur, already cited, published in 1972. Canetti rejects Freud's *Massenpsychologie und Ich-Analyse* in typically devastating fashion, refusing to justify his dismissal: "Ich halte seinen Erklärungsversuch für wirklich unzulänglich."[65] In response to Freud's theory that all paranoia is suppressed homosexuality, Canetti makes the point: "Das kann manchmal Paranoia erklären, darf aber nicht verallgemeinert werden."[66] In response to Freud's theory of the death instinct: "Ich glaube nicht an die Existenz eines Todestriebes."[67]

Lovett saw the paranoia and schizophrenia in terms of problems associated with language. In this she is not alone. Canetti has been credited with a critical understanding of the problems at the heart of a specific discipline within philosophy proper, namely the philosophy of language. His interests have been related both to the investigations of the Bohemian-born Fritz Mauthner (1849–1923), whose work *Beiträge zu einer Kritik der Sprache* (1901–1903) is occasionally cited. They have also been related to the investigations of the Viennese Wittgenstein (1889–1951), who, indeed, mentions Mauthner's work in his *Tractatus logico-philosophicus* of 1922. Lovett makes much of this kind of climate, as does George Steiner, in his cursory glance at the "language revolution" going on in Vienna between ca. 1900 and 1925, in which *Die Blendung* is mentioned, namely his essay "The Language Animal," published in *Extraterritorial* in 1972.[68] Finally, Laurence Arthur Gretsky, in another fascinating Ph.D. dissertation, entitled "Sprachverzerrung und Sprachüberwindung als Themen in Elias Canettis Roman *Die Blendung*," sets his analysis of what he maintains is the breakdown of language studied by the novel, against the same kind of climate. He cites both Mauthner and Wittgenstein to support the same theory, that Canetti was intuitively in tune with the spirit of the two theoretical enquirers.[69] So Gretsky, Steiner, and Lovett are united in their assumption that Canetti had his fingers on the intellectual pulse of Europe, as far as the debate on language was concerned.

Since, inevitably, the issue of language is also the issue of communication, critics have responded with considerable enthusiasm to the question of whether or not characters succeed in making an impact on one another. The majority of critics believe that communication has broken down irrevocably, and that dialogue is a mere charade. It is the received wisdom that all dialogue is really monologue, since characters are so hermetically sealed within their own mutually exclusive worlds. Characters speak past one another, without in any way being able to penetrate through to each other's value systems. Bridges between value systems are simply not made. There is no successfully applied rhetoric of persuasion or cognition in dialogue between characters, because individual characters are already locked inside their own hermetically sealed fantasy worlds.[70] Peter Jansen's article, however, raises tentative questions as to the function of what he perceives to be the genuine comedy arising from speech in the novel.[71] His point is that if there is comedy, it is at the expense of characters in the novel and for the amusement of the reader alone. According to such a scenario, characters are exploited for the "higher" purpose of bringing the relief with which we associate laughter to individual readers of the novel.

This brings us back to the link with Vienna, which continues to be exploited in a number of different ways. Related to the theoretical considerations on the nature and scope of language by Mauthner and Wittgenstein is the tradition, prominent in Viennese drama above all, that is acutely aware of the power, vitality, and limits of the spoken word as it relates to the intelligence and social vision of the speaker. This distinguished tradition of aggressivity, which finds its expression in satire in Viennese literature, has always been a theatrical one. It has been invoked again and again, to the extent that a genealogy has been constructed in which Canetti is the heir to the traditions inaugurated by Nestroy

(1801–1862), taken up by Schnitzler, and maintained by the man who "discovered" Nestroy, Karl Kraus (1874–1936).[72] Gretsky's dissertation as a whole insists on seeing Canetti's novel in this tradition. He analyzes dialogue in the novel to reveal the structures of chaos and strategies of non-meaning inherent in the spoken word. He, in contrast to Jansen, sees Canetti as skilled in his virtually scientific analysis of those structures that reveal the pitfalls of language. He thus credits Canetti with a "higher" purpose than that of simply entertaining a readership. Language, or, more precisely, the abuse of language "tells" us something about the human mind and how it can be perverted from normality or reality.

Alternatively, Canetti has been seen in terms of the poetically expressed, highly melancholy vision of the problem of existence in the modern world caused by an absolute loss of confidence in the capacity of language to represent what we wish it to represent. This idea was perhaps first expressed by another Austrian associated with Vienna, Hugo von Hofmannsthal (1874–1929), in his *Brief des Lord Chandos* of 1901, where Chandos accounts for his failure to produce written, literary works in terms of a loss of faith in the unity of existence. This crisis of language, of thought, and of existence, is, as is well known, not fixed. Lord Chandos discovers a capacity to be moved in human terms that are edifying. The experience of being moved positively casts aside as unnecessary both written and spoken language. The sudden realization of the redundancy of language is not a bleak experience. It is accompanied by an understanding of the primacy of emotion and intuition. The experience of being moved by phenomena in the world is a kind of ecstasy, which is momentary, and which is reminiscent of the heights reached by the mystics. This leads to an understanding of what he comes to recognize are considerable privileges. His diagnosis and intuition of a solution to the problem of existence and the crisis of language may only partially suit analysis of *Die Blendung*. Yet it is necessary to rehearse the contents of Chandos's letter to draw attention to the current in criticism, understated as it is, that believes that Canetti's novel concludes with a moment of insight comparable to the moment of insight experienced by Lord Chandos.

Critics are by no means united in what they think about the suicide of Peter Kien. As mentioned above, determinist theories of psychology see the suicide as inevitable, as the logical act of someone who has denied whole areas of experience for such a long time, or as concrete proof that human beings are motivated by a "Todestrieb." There are those, however, who maintain that the suicide is shot through with absolute insights into Kien's own life and into existence per se, reminiscent of the ephiphanies we associate with Lord Chandos. As already mentioned, Canetti himself believed that a synthesizing process was going on in his fictional characters (they were moving towards an "Übereinstimmung"). This has undoubtedly encouraged this particular trend.[73] Nevertheless, interpreting Kien's suicide in terms of the *Brief des Lord Chandos* is problematic to say the least, because Kien, unlike Chandos, ends his life voluntarily. So his insight(s), even if absolute, is/are relativized by the way in which Kien feels it no longer possible to apply these to his own life and attempts, quite practically, to correct the mistakes of the past in the name of the possibility of an improved quality of life. Alternatively, critics see in the character of George(s) a vessel who expresses visionary insights into Peter Kien's existence and/or existence per se, to the extent that he has mystical visions like Chandos does or is the author of epiphanies, like Stephen Hero.[74] It is interesting to note here that Canetti has publicly declared his independence of Hugo von Hofmannsthal. In what reads as a statement, he distances himself from both Hofmannsthal and von Doderer, maintaining that he has not been influenced by either.[75]

Another trend within the secondary literature insists on using some of the above kinds of insights to place the novel in terms of those general intellectual or cultural histories of Western Europe, by liberal humanists, that see twentieth-century Europe in the throes of an inevitable and irrevocable decline, with causes both complicated and various. The general thesis is unambiguous: the decline of the West is inseparable from and synonymous with the demise of liberal humanism. This kind of an enquiry has seen the novel in terms of the publications of prominent right-wing Europeans like Jacob Burckhardt (1818–1897), in his *Griechische Kulturgeschichte* (1898–1902), and Oswald Spengler (1880–1936), in his *Der Untergang des Abendlandes* (1918–1922). As it happens, Canetti mentions, in *Die Fackel im Ohr*, that he and Thomas Marek used to discuss Burckhardt during the period of the runup to the writing of *Die Blendung*, and that Burckhardt's *Griechische Kulturgeschichte* was of cardinal importance to him, which is interesting in light of what has briefly been suggested about *Die Blendung* and *agon*, since

Burckhardt is obliged to make much of this motor in Greek Civilization.[76] At another point in his career, Canetti makes a point of recording his debt to Burckhardt. In *Das Geheimherz der Uhr*, the debt is huge (*GU*, 8).

Martin Bollacher's interpretations are set against the above, generalizing kind of historical background. He stresses the general presence of chaos in the novel. The world is collapsing yet human beings can resist the impulse to chaos by initiating change within themselves, thus his emphasis on the term "Verwandlung."[77] Man is capable of resistance. Peter Kien simply fails in his attempt to resist and transform himself.

Burckhardt and Spengler's theories of decline, published before Canetti's novel, are clearly substantially different from those contained in another significant investigation into the possible causes of the same movement of decline. In 1947, Horkheimer and Adorno published *Die Dialektik der Aufklärung*. This has been linked with *Die Blendung* by Lovett, for instance, because all three authors apparently believe in the category of the "totalitarian" model of the mind's relationship to the world established by the Enlightenment (Kant) and its forerunners (Descartes). In their case, the assumptions about what is possible in human terms, and, specifically, the "rights of man" over nature and over his environment, are seen to be at the heart of the Enlightenment project. They have created the conditions that can delude man into thinking he has absolute power over everything. This leads to his capacity to destroy himself and others. In 1962 interview with Canetti, Adorno told the author that he felt that *Die Dialektik der Aufklärung* had explored the human drive toward self-preservation as something potentially demonic. Adorno felt that, in this respect, he had something in common with Canetti's interest in the same human drive. Canetti cordially acknowledged the logic of the comparison.[78] Horkheimer and Adorno, as philosophers working in the tradition of the Frankfurter Schule, clearly construct something resembling a myth in *Die Dialektik der Aufklärung*, specifically to account for the concrete atrocities of Second World War fascism.[79] It is itself heavily dependent on determinist theories of psychology, but like Burckhardt and Spengler, uses intellectual/cultural history to sustain a particular theory.

Indeed, the desire to see Canetti's novel in terms, not of vague theories concerning the general decline of the whole continent, but of the concrete, definitively historical and political realities of Europe between 1939–1945, is a strong one. Dagmar Lorenz thinks that Kien is like Hitler, maintaining that the world depicted in the novel corresponds to the totalitarianism of Deutsch-Österreich in the thirties and forties. Stefan Kaszynski thinks the whole of Canetti's work is significant because of its implicit opposition to the Hitler phenomenon.[80] Richard Lawson has argued that Benedikt Pfaff is a fictional prefiguration of Nazi power.[81] Walter Sokel argues in his article, already mentioned, that the title of the last chapter of *Die Blendung*, "Der rote Hahn," evokes the revolutionary association of the *Florian Geyer Lied*, of Peasant Wars' memory, which song served as a symbol of total revolt. Its leader was a model for both the extreme Left and the extreme Right in Germany and Austria at the time the novel was completed. Walter Sokel also argues that Kien's burning of his library provides an adumbration of the contemporary Nazi bonfires of books on May 10, 1933.[82] Curtius' thesis, which is interesting for other reasons, is one that also claims that *Die Blendung* offers us a critique of fascism, because of its direct link with book burning. Curtius also looks at sexuality and language and sees in both a prefiguration of fascist attitudes.[83] Others protest that the understanding of totalitarianism is so acute that the novel could only have been written by someone who had firsthand experience of totalitarianism, a view that is not borne out by Canetti's autobiography, in which it is obvious Canetti lived a very secluded life indeed and was very sheltered, for the most part, from persecution.[84] Nevertheless, as an interpretation it underlines the love of literary critics for literature as secular prophecy.

More recently, but still in the same vein, Gerald Stieg has argued that *Die Blendung* is a symbolic investigation into the problem of "Vergangenheitsbewältigung" in Austria. He singles out, in particular, the country's desire to repress and ban from scrutiny the real significance of the events of the day discussed by Canetti in *Die Fackel im Ohr*, namely July 15, 1927. This was the day when workers were shot dead on the streets of Vienna, when all they were doing was protesting against an unfair judgment of the supreme court in Vienna.[85] Stieg has claimed that Canetti possesses a well-developed "Sinn für politische Voraussicht."[86] Urs Jenny mentions, *en passant*, and quite exceptionally given the general view, that the novel is "ahistorisch."[87] This exceptional view notwithstanding, the consensus amongst critics with a historico-political bias holds that Canetti had an intuitive understanding of the phenomenon that later became history. Their claim is that a novel first published in 1935 has validity, so to speak, because it anticipates the history we associate with 1939–1945. Its capacity to anticipate history is sinister for those who classify its vision as utterly apocalyptic.[88]

We are already familiar with the argument that says that Canetti's novel is a study of degenerate forms of individualism, where philosophy, psychoanalysis, intellectual/cultural history have been cited to support the view. The argument has gone some way toward providing some kind of narrative that provides us with causes, *crucially deemed to be extra-textual in origin*, to explain (away) the phenomenon of degeneracy itself *within the text*. Another trend in the secondary literature works within this same "determinist" framework. It suggests that human existence in *Die Blendung* is degenerate only because Canetti wanted to be faithful to a social fabric *outside the novel* that he felt had already been corrupted, this time by right-wing, capitalist, or free market economics. This simplistic argument maintains that the socio-economic climate associated with capitalism is one that inevitably subordinates everything to commerce and turns human beings into nothing more than entirely reified objects, whose capacity for feeling becomes entirely dead. Such arguments hope to show how the infrastructure of society at the level of its socio-economic fabric can easily become internalized to form a superstructure within the human personality that itself only further alienates man from his environment.

The East German Marxist, Annemarie Auer, takes a different view in her 1969 introduction to the East German edition of the novel, and in her article "Ein Genie und sein Sonderling—Elias Canetti und *Die Blendung*."[89] She has criticized the novel for not situating people in terms of socio-economic theories, maintaining that the background is too abstract.[90] Mechthild Curtius in detail in the full-length study *Kritik der Verdinglichung in Canettis Roman Die Blendung* promotes the theory, by contrast, that *Die Blendung* is an anatomy of the anti-humanism implicit in capitalism, and he stresses, using his strongly Freudian lense, that the key interpretative words in any analysis of *Die Blendung* have to be "Verdinglichung" and "Entfremdung." Dieter Dissinger's book *Vereinzelung und Massenwahn: Elias Canettis Roman Die Blendung* develops these ideas further, maintaining that the climate of capitalism is partially responsible for the absolute isolation of the individual in society. He explores, therefore, the social implications of the same kind of economic climate. As a result of that climate, individuals become marked by their absolute greed, and by their lack of love and their failure in terms of creating meaningful relationships, to the extent that the novel contains, in his opinion, a panorama of a totally dehumanized society. Dissinger's key words are "Vereinzelung" and "Massenwahn."

More simply, the novel is associated with theories of character. Not surprisingly, since these have always been the linchpin of much critical analysis of the novel generally. Peter Kien is, in this tradition, a study of a certain kind of intellectual, a sinologist, whose rigorous indifference to anything other than his scholarly pursuits is a comment on the danger inherent in promoting the value of the intellect to the exclusion of all else. Pursuit of this goal makes him ruthless with respect to other people. He regards his marriage as an obstacle to his goal. He is, therefore, a study of a megalomaniac. His pursuit of his ideal of absolute social isolation and privacy, so that he can carry on with his scholarly and non-material pursuits, is seen to compromise a human being's capacity to take others seriously, and, above all, to respect as equal their rights to self-determination.

Therese is a study of the frustrated sex-kitten whose disappointment with the slavery, with which she equates her marriage to Peter Kien, culminates in her grandiose materialist ambitions, which know no bounds, and which make her ruthless in her pursuit of her material goals. She wants Peter Kien's money, and she wants to seduce the man from whom she buys furniture. So she wants freedom and public success. So she too is a kind of megalomaniac. Fischerle does not differ from her. He, too, is motivated by the desire to escape the subordination and dependence imposed by a heterosexual relationship. Like Therese, Fischerle wants to achieve financial independence and success in the public world as an acclaimed chess player. This common denominator of a flight from a heterosexual relationship has resulted, for instance, in the view, admirably expressed by Gerald Stieg, that *Die Blendung* as a whole is about marriage. Stieg maintains that the only real marriage is the marriage of Kien with his books in the fire in his library at the very end of the novel—itself, according to Stieg, proof of the triumph of the mass over individuality: "Es handelt sich um eine monströse Fabel über die unmöglich gewordene Hochzeit" (177).

Benedikt Pfaff is also defined by his use and abuse of power. As a sexual pervert whose sadism leads him into an incestuous involvement with his daughter, he appears to be quite simply degenerate. In his job, however, he is like Therese and Fischerle. The pursuit of material gain and success is the single driving force motivating him. All three characters appear to be equally ruthless in that they pay no heed to anything resembling an objective standard of good and evil. They are all utterly indifferent to the rights of others to self-determination. In their terms, all is permitted and all is sanctioned in the name of money, and power, and social success: deceit, trickery, robbery, and theft feature regularly as the means by which the three attempt to pursue their secular ends.

Whatever their methods, therefore, all four characters have something to say about the classic topics of freedom, money, sex, and power. Unlike the other three central characters in the novel, Peter Kien's goal draws attention to itself only because it is explicitly non-material. He is interested only in knowledge, and in books where knowledge can be found. Ruthlessness never manifests itself, in Peter Kien, in wilful acts of malice, deceit, trickery, or theft: it is only manifest in the drive that animates his desire for freedom from the constraints imposed by traffic with other people. He is, therefore, in contrast to Therese, Benedikt Pfaff, and Fischerle, always absolutely innocent of the secular ills or evils with which they are associated. He appears to be the character, however, whom all three abuse in the name of their goals. He, unlike the other three, draws attention to himself because he is an object of abuse, a victim of people who are more worldly wise than he is.

It should now be quite obvious that in every single one of each of the above critical accounts of Canetti's novel, an extra-textual reality figures very prominently. It figures, we can conclude, because each critic wishes to establish what can be called a metanarrative, pregnant with notions of authentic origins, which is held up to the reading public as a kind of consoling image to account for various kinds of failure supposedly dealt with or examined by the text, *Die Blendung*. The implications of metanarrative as a construct have, in the last fifteen years, been investigated by those working within both philosophy and literary theory. Thomas Docherty maintains that there are highly divisive implications to metanarrative, following Jean-Francois Lyotard's rejection of metanarrative (52).[91] The critics mentioned above have also clearly expressed support for Canetti as an institutionalized author, both in the sense that he was discussed as if his greatness did not need to be defended, and in the sense of the regular appeal made to prestigious, established modes of interpretation and discourse. As such, they are party to what self-styled radical critics like Docherty would maintain are ideological positions, the significance of which it would be useful to ponder here, since the influence of self-styled radical critics, like Docherty, is so powerful today in the academy.

For the sake of argument, we can assume that the likely objections of such self-styled radical critics to the particular use of metanarrative by commentators of *Die Blendung* would consist in further additions to Lyotard's own problems with metanarrative. We can assume that the objections would, for the sake of argument, read along the following lines:

1. The extra-textual reality is invoked by critics in a particular way: in the name of the transcendental signified, Truth, where the meaning and intent of Canetti's project coincide. The ultimate truth about Canetti's text lies in a world beyond time and space, a metaphysical world of fixed essences where the transcendental values of reason and order reside in peace. This world provides the perspective through which the world supposedly "described" in *Die Blendung* is evaluated. The degeneracy of the world in the text is interpreted in terms of what that world could be. The degeneracy is examined from the perspective of the ideal values of reason and order. These are actively *privileged* over and above the world of deficient values that supposedly makes up *Die Blendung*.
2. This extra-textual reality is discussed, therefore, either as if it had greater ontological presence than the ontological presence of Canetti's text, or as if it needed to be taken into consideration in order to supplement the deficient ontological presence of Canetti's text. Canetti's text is seen in terms of a wider context or chain of signification. This wider context is really what infuses the text with meaning, giving it a conceptual, univocal unity it would not otherwise have: the origins of that unity are located in either historical, socio-economic, philosophical, or psychoanalytical realities or discourses.
3. The disciplines of philosophy, psychoanalysis, and economics were invoked, as were certain (male) philosophers of language, certain (male) cultural/intellectual historians, and certain (male) Viennese dramatists and poets, to assist analysis of *Die*

Blendung, as if "tradition," not to say "the canon," were the principle defining feature of *Die Blendung*. *Die Blendung* is linked up with its author in terms that suggest that Canetti is primarily interesting for the way in which he has exploited the novel to publish findings made as a result of private "dialogues" held with other authors of previously published literary texts or instigators of already established traditions of thought or modes of enquiry.

4. Readings that insist on the "tradition" and the "canon" have ideological implications in that they simultaneously promote both the *institution* of the canon and the *institution* of the author. Accounts of the novel, in promoting the institution of the author and the institution of the canon express, therefore, a commitment to those hierarchically organized societies where institutions have such status and where, in the exercise of power with which institutions are associated, there are clear assumptions, inherently non-democratic by nature, about the inherent superiority of certain individuals.
5. Hierarchically organized society in the West has always, historically, been patriarchal. Patriarchy perpetuates the sexist assumptions on which such societies are theologically based, namely those of monotheism. A belief in hierarchy goes hand in hand with the material "privileging" of man above woman, in terms of rights and exercise of power. It goes hand in hand with the institution of heterosexuality, which freezes this inequality, as it privileges heterosexuality over and above any other kind of sexuality. In monotheist/patriarchal countries in the West, society has always been proud of the special place allocated the institution of the male author, the modern-day equivalent of Plato's "philosopher king," whose exalted position allows him to develop the notion that the word can be exploited for the possible influence it might have on the lives of the imaginatively and intellectually inferior "masses" "out there." He is the secular messiah who continues the work of the original messiah in bringing Truth to the ignorant. The institution of the male author in patriarchal society, if understood historically, exploits gender to the advantage of the male. He has been allowed to make a social impact, whereas woman has, until comparatively recently, been denied material access to the domain of writing and publishing. The institution of the male author privileges the male, but also perpetuates abuse of the female and others

who find themselves allocated minority status. It furthers the continued non-recognition of the need for equal rights.

6. The hidden, socio-political agenda of many of the readings of the text can be seen in the delight with which the supposed absence of law and order in the social world of *Die Blendung* is condemned. Accounts of the novel discussed above talked about both in hallowed terms. Since, historically, right-wing forms of government tend to put law and order high on the political agenda, this enthusiasm amounts to a principled appreciation of, and commitment to, the policies associated with right-wing forms of government.
7. Many of the readings of the novel perpetuate the spirit of bourgeois liberal humanism. The clear approval of those well-demarcated ideas with which liberal humanism has always been associated, namely the good, the beautiful, and the true, the very idea of the unified subject and its quest for fulfillment, underlies much analysis of *Die Blendung.* Again and again, the critics examined above have assumed, in the tradition of a kind of mimesis that sees literature as imitating a given social world, that we readers recognize ourselves mostly in some highly negative way in the mirror that is the text *Die Blendung.* The moment of *anagnorisis*, or recognition, as Terence Cave would have it, is celebrated as central to the experience of reading.[92] Canetti's characters are "condemned" for the way in which they supposedly fail to live up to the fixed "ideal" of what constitutes the good, the beautiful, and the true in terms of human conduct and the human personality. *Canetti's characters are to be understood negatively, in terms of what they are not.*
8. The notion of the norm so heavily impregnates criticism of the novel that reception of the novel endorses, generally, what has become known in Lacan and elsewhere as the symbolic order. For whether the point of view is metaphysical, socio-economic, political, or liberal, a reign of fixities credited with the status of universal, transcendental essences is endorsed by critics. The symbolic order always creates the "minority." It creates the minority because it believes that its preferences are right, in an absolute sense. The majority compose the symbolic order and are types. The minority is composed of individuals, recalcitrant and unique perversions of what is right, in an absolute sense. The symbolic order thus creates the minority only to denounce it as subversive.

The minority then has to be actively suppressed, put beyond the law, deported into exile, or publicly punished for failing to support or practice what the symbolic order believes should be permitted. The symbolic order creates the other only to destroy it.

9. It is not surprising, therefore, that the novel has occasionally been seen as an allegory (a view with which Canetti is himself not happy).[93] Allegory as a mode has always been exploited by the kinds of writers who have an absolute belief in the Platonic distinction between the world of appearances and the world of essences. Allegory is predicated on the absolute distinction between appearances and essences, the latter deemed superior and the point of reference according to which everything has to be "evaluated." As a term used by critics, the word, allegory, also assists critical classification of literary works generally. To see Canetti's novel as a type of literature is to believe in the category type. The notion of the type is conveniently and crucially vital to the whole idea of the symbolic order and the repression with which the symbolic order can be associated.[94]
10. In absorbing Canetti into the canon in the above kind of way, critics have assumed that they enjoy a certain kind of relationship with *their* readership. They talk about the novel in terms that show they assume readers share their own ideological assumptions. *Die Blendung* is interesting because it provides all of us, so to speak, with an anatomy of those subversive forces that can disrupt our/the symbolic order and threaten its preservation in time and space. Canetti is credited with being a guardian or representative of establishment order and stability, since his analysis is thought to have been motivated by an apparently acute awareness of how order and stability can be undermined. This guardianship of the establishment is mimicked by sympathetic critics of *Die Blendung* in their particular (unconscious) use of the terms outlined in points 1–9 generally, and in the way in which they assume that readers are willing supporters of the establishment too.

Whilst this last point will suffice to open up the terms of the critical debate centering around *Die Blendung,* we should pause for a moment and simply bear in mind the above, generalizing paraphrase of the kind of objections likely to be made by self-styled, radical, contemporary critics to the first principles of the main critics of the novel with which this chapter has been concerned so far. The above kind of objections will be looked at in another context in a later chapter, when we shall turn to a commentary on, and assessment of, the intellectual and other credentials of what the above constitutes by now, namely the new critical orthodoxy in the academy. Whilst such an excursion may interest only some readers, the point is both to query the credentials in themselves, and to test whether *Die Blendung* is yet another of the kind of works that can be appropriated to speak either in favor of or against the above type of apparently subversive ideological principles.

The last point in the list, however, brings us to another contemporary issue, much discussed in literary theory today, namely that of the implied status and character of a reader in any given text. The status of the reader within the analyses of *Die Blendung* examined in this chapter is limited, in the sense that the reader is "discussed" by the critics as if, on entering voluntarily into a contract with *Die Blendung*, the reader surrendered himself/herself to Canetti's authority, and to his value judgments, or to insights into his presumed extra-textual interests. Envisioned as such, however, we should be clear that the contract is clearly not a real contract between equals, but a relationship of dependence, for the reader is the last link in a long chain. Tradition, or the canon or some kind of extra-textual reality, provides the terms that Canetti exploits to provide his reader with some kind of commentary on his sources. The reader's status is further limited by the assumption inherent in the chain, namely that the dependence on the authority of the author and on the author's value judgments or insights is likely to sustain his/her fixed identity within the extra-textual reality s/he inhabits when not reading. The reader is thus ontologically inferior to Canetti, and Canetti inevitably ontologically superior to his reader. The ontological status of the reader is further relativized by the fact that s/he is being exploited and made to serve a further purpose, that of furthering the preservation of the given social and political status quo, that which guarantees the reign of order that Canetti's novel supposedly defends, either implicitly or explicitly.

What will be interesting for the new interpretation of the novel that this study proposes, is the way in which this kind of a contract positively denies the freedom, imagination, and subjectivity of the reader, only as these are felt to be incapable of being harnessed, in Nietzschean fashion, to the creation of *alternative* worlds. The freedom, imagination, and subjectivity, or the creative resources each individual reader has, are actively repressed in those readings of the text mentioned above, which focus so intensely on intellectual ideas as ways of understanding *Die Blendung*. The reader is Canetti's victim, so to speak, and Canetti is endowed with the right to deliver an undisturbed monologue to a passive audience. As a godlike figure, Canetti is authorized to present his audience with something felt to resemble objective truth. An author is allowed the luxury of an association with objective truth which he interprets: he is thoroughly unique as a result. A reader is not allowed a first-hand encounter with objective truth and is condemned to copy or imitate someone else's version of it. A reader is not unique. S/he is a parasite.

Thomas Docherty's by now equally orthodox challenge to the supposed orthodoxies informing "conservative" literary criticism of the novel proposes a counter to this apparently repressive attitude toward the reader. With the assistance of the contributions to the whole area of the status of the reader in fiction already made by seminal works by Wolfgang Iser (*Der implizite Leser: Kommunikationsformen des Romans von Bunyan bis Beckett* of 1972, in particular), and by Roland Barthes (*Le Plaisir du Texte* of 1973, in particular), Docherty proposes a definition and endorsement of the assumptions concerning the status of the reader, on which genuinely postmodern fiction is supposedly based.[95] The chief assault on the orthodoxies informing conservative literary criticism of the novel consists in the way in which Docherty, following Iser and Barthes, stresses the *experiential* nature of reading. In his interpretation, Docherty makes the reader of a text the author of a text, not the author who wrote the text. This well-known idea of the supposed "death" of the author and "birth" of the reader is not without problems, especially for feminists, who read this sovereign indifference to authorship as one of the masks behind which phallocentrism hides its fictions: the action of authorizing the end of naming the author is a refusal to distinguish between male authors and female authors, which is apparently another way of proclaiming the end of woman without consulting her. Only those who can take signature and voice for granted can of course afford to deny its significance: it is also, as an act, in part an attempt to deny the politics of both the writing and reading of texts, which, if taken seriously, always raises issues concerning power—above all, who has it and who has not, for whom it works and for whom it does not.[96] It neutralizes all this and merely instates the view that reading is a metaphysical activity, only an intersubjective encounter, without implication in terms of the material.

The death of the author and the birth of the reader does not, in Docherty's theory, mean that texts are devoid of "meaning," whether singular or plural. The creation of meaning is considered vital, and an experience of multiple possibilities. The experiential nature of reading is crucially defined by the way in which the reader does not relate, statically, so to speak, to the single essence of a character in fiction, but is "forced" to enter dynamically into the multiplicity of experiences that make up the life of a character in a text, who has to have a name, but whose experiences are not necessarily informed by an overwhelmingly univocal logic (86). An important aspect of the intense stress on the potential for actuality inherent in the experience of reading modernist and postmodernist novels is the emphasis on a new attitude toward time (198). The kind of characters who populate modernist and postmodernist fiction are themselves infused with a new sense of time. The reader is in a position to recognize the vitality of the perpetual present (212). Docherty posits a new kind of desire in his proposed theory of character and motivation in modernist and postmodernist fiction. This goes beyond desire termed erotic or thanatic. Both erotic and thanatic desire are considered to lead to stasis. They are pertinent to the "needy" character who is looking for compensation and who reifies those who fulfill his/her needs. Docherty's theory of character and motivation in modernist and postmodernist fiction is infused by the fully liberating experience of the kind of desire that is motivated, not by personal gain and the ultimate satisfaction of needs, but by the spirit of Agape (225). The desire that is motivated by the spirit of Agape is a privileged and superior one, since it frees the reader from need and the inevitably exploitative drive behind need. It encourages the reader to recognize his/her subjectivity and respect for the subjectivity of others (230). Reading reveals the hidden potential of existence and experience (243).

In terms of literary history, Docherty argues that modernists such as Flaubert, Eliot, Yeats, Pound, James, Joyce, Lawrence, Proust, and Woolf were the first writers not to want to paint static selves, but to "paint the passage of the self through time." The idea of "realism" was thus redefined in keeping with a shift from broadly objective to more "psychological" or inward criteria.

Postmodernist novelists, he argues, like Margaret Atwood, Barthelme, late Calvino, Angela Carter, Fowles, Pynchon, Salman Rushdie, and Vonnegut, are as interested in the dynamism of subjectivity. They differ in that they accept that reality is made. It is a cultural construct. It is not found in nature. In order to make the point that fiction is constructed, they draw overt attention to their own fictive devices. These are not disguised. They do not try to pass off their narratives as chunks of real-life experience. Postmodernist narratives apparently challenge, subvert, or, paradoxically, exploit the conventions of narrative technique. This tactic obviously involves a high degree of self-conscious contrivance and a manipulative stance outside and above the story-line flow of events. Postmodernist novelists also dispense with the notion that literature can give us a privileged view, whether of the world outside the book or of the mind's interior workings. Finally, postmodernist novelists like to reflect what they think is typical in late twentieth-century living, the experience of incoherence. They are inclined to see the subjective world as more radically dynamic and more potentially incoherent. They thus use fragments, discontinuity, and self-contradiction in their characters. The reader's task therefore becomes a more creative one. S/he is obliged to create, when reading, multiple selves to accommodate the necessary breadth of a character s/he experiences when reading fiction.

All of the above must lead, it is held, to a rejection of the conservative stress on absolute essences and a recognition, in its place, of the potentially infinite number of moments of being that might make up experience (268). Docherty's position is useful here as we come to review the way in which Canetti's novel has been placed in literary history. It will also be useful for this study as a whole, in that the arguments to be developed about the kind of reader posited by Canetti's novel will point to the limitations of Docherty's endorsement of postmodernist fiction as the only kind of fiction capable of doing justice to his personal belief in full subjectivity and full desire, and his equally vague belief in a reader's breadth and depth of experience.

We saw how Canetti's own account of the genesis of the novel only partly talked about the novel in terms that seemed to see it as bound by a mimetic contract to the given, objective world "out there." Those references present in the narrative of the genesis of the novel, together with his well publicized preferences for nineteenth-century novelists like Stendhal and Gogol, have been overly exploited by critics, and have, of course, furthered the cause of his association with conservative theories of literature, with the realist novel in particular, and with the view that the novel contains a commentary on a given social world. We saw, however, that even though Canetti conceded elsewhere that the modern world had changed, and that a novelist needed new techniques in order to be adequate to the task of mimetically imitating or representing that new world, he nowhere alluded to the substance of those historical changes, as he nowhere alluded to what those new techniques might be. He also failed to indicate where he sees himself in terms of European literary history. He nowhere indicates whether he sees himself as part of a community of writers with common interests, as one, for instance, of the already well-established and well-known group of modernist novelists in Europe who *were* overtly concerned with the whole area of experimentation with new techniques, precisely because they had comparatively new ideas about the nature of human interiority, rather than because they felt obliged to change their techniques to comment on or accommodate a changing historical world out there, so to speak.

It is, of course, tempting to link *Die Blendung* with seminal works of modernism in fiction such as Richardson's *Pilgrimage* (1915–1938), Joyce's *Ulysses* (1922), Svevo's *La Conscienza di Zeno* (1923), Proust's *A La Recherche du Temps Perdu* (1917–1927), Musil's *Der Mann ohne Eigenschaften* Book I (1930), and Broch's *Die Schlafwandler* (1930–1932), and with the works of Virginia Woolf, Dos Passos, Alfred Döblin, Kafka, and Beckett, to name just a few. It is tempting to do this, chiefly because of the historical proximity of Canetti's 1935 text to these now canonical texts and novelists. Yet the above novelists broke with tradition inasmuch as they wanted to experiment with and explore themes and techniques that were only "new" relative to the literary history in which all the above novelists clearly have their origins.

It is also tempting to link up Canetti with this "group" because of Canetti's much publicized and personal fascination with two professional twentieth-century novelists writing in German, Musil and Broch, and because of the problematic statements made by Canetti concerning the need for "new methods" mentioned in the last chapter. It seems obvious, however, that *Die Blendung* stands alone as far as the above "group" of novelists is concerned, on a number of counts.[97] It makes sense to group the above novelists together, because of their common fascination with interiority and subjectivity, with *feeling* temporality at the sensational, emotional, intellectual, and sexual level, as Judith Ryan has suggested in her recent book *The Vanishing Subject.*[98] It was clearly this thematic interest that dictated the need for an exploitation of a variety of narrative techniques never attempted before by novelists *on the same scale.* They succeeded, as a result of the frequency of exploitation of techniques of psycho-narration, narrated monologue, and quoted monologue, in celebrating and exploring the imaginative, and at times superbly lyrical, potential of the internal life of the individual, as well as the thinking, speculative peregrinations of the intellectually alive. The sense of the infinite space of the mind is endorsed to the extent that the capacity of the imagination and intellect to "lead one astray" emerges as only a minor aspect of the larger enterprise.

These are novels that are not primarily dominated by the spirit of satire, but, for the most part, by a loving voluptousness and a desire for rêverie and reflection. The mood of *Die Blendung* is, fairly obviously, entirely different. It is chiefly driven by a powerful, savage, even brutal momentum. Further, this momentum seems to deny both its readers and its characters the time necessary for reflection, let alone rêverie or nostalgia. Such emotions are banished from the novel altogether. In truly Nietzschean fashion, there appears to be no looking back, only looking forward. The reader is not allowed to *savor* or enjoy the moment. There are absolutely no lyrical passages. Serious intellectual exchanges, which only arise in the latter part of the novel, are manifestly questionable in content, as will become clear in Chapter Eight. The forays into "Verwandlung" or organic growth seem to be problematic and specious, as will be made clear.

Virtually unique amongst interpretations of the novel is David Darby's excellent assessment of *Die Blendung*, originally presented as a dissertation entitled "Studies of Disintegration: Narrative Strategies in Elias Canetti's *Die Blendung.*" This appeared in 1988 and is now available as a book.[99] Darby characterizes the novel as a postmodernist work *avant la lettre.* It is a postmodernist work because, in keeping with Docherty's points, the scope and range of the novel's "plot" and of its "characters" simply can not be paraphrased. To paraphrase is to do violence to the novel. As we have seen, this violence was manifest in the way in which the majority of critics wanted to reduce it, and to interpret it in the light of one meaning or one theory. Darby's interpretation works within this framework. Yet the particular value of his findings lies in the fact that his interpretation is based on a thorough understanding of the implications of narratology, in terms of the issue of authority. His interpretation goes a long way toward correcting the almighty stress on simplistic notions of causality proposed by the authors of the assessments paraphrased above, for it is predicated on an acceptance of the fact that the critic's task is the vigilant seeking-out of the blindspots or moments of self-contradiction *inside* texts, where the tension between rhetoric and logic, between what the text manifestly means to say and what it is nonetheless constrained to mean, is examined *as if the tension were meaningful in itself.*

Darby also sees *Die Blendung* in terms of other literary voices that speak, and that are very much alive, inasmuch as they echo Canetti's own enjoyment of literature. This fascination with intertextuality, or with Canetti's overt allusions to literary texts, is not, in Darby's hands, an invitation to the open-ended textual free play that casts aside rigorous protocols of reading. Darby notices the frequency of certain allusions and strategies and attempts to investigate the implications of these. His contention is that there is a tension throughout the novel between order and the process of disintegration, and that the effect of this on the reader is comic. This tension is created in the narrative by the problematic exploitation of techniques that tend toward an authoritative endorsement of thought and action and techniques or strategies that tend toward a relativization of such authoritative endorsements. His investigation of the narrative techniques used by Canetti in the novel shows that the work is as dynamically experimental as that of the modernists, in that character-based focalization is the dominant mode of presenting figural consciousness in the narration. The regular use of the technique of narrated monologue is the dominant mode in large sections of the novel. Sections of omniscient third-person narration are heavily animated, because of the *stylistic contagion of the narrator's language by elements of the linguistic code of a story-level figure.* Darby means by stylistic contagion the idea that both characters and narrator mimic or imitate one another's voice and style. Darby also maintains that, whereas the technique of narrated monologue in novels by the great modernist novelists mentioned above served the purpose of a thoroughly unskeptical investigation into the paths of thought made through the mind by the thinking individual, it is quite clear that the effect generated by Canetti's exploitation of the technique of narrated monologue on the reader is problematic as well as comic, inasmuch as the technique is supplemented by consonant psycho-narration, where we are given intimate access to the private thought processes of individual characters. This is problematic because there is regularly no clearly identified line between the two techniques, and there are often obvious contradictions or discontinuities between the ideas expressed in sections governed by the technique of narrated monologue and those expressed in sections governed by the technique of psycho-narration. There is, in effect, an active confusion between authoritative and non-authoritative perspectives throughout the novel. The narration, in tending to oscillate unpredictably and indeterminately between diegetic narration and the more, although not completely, mimetic mode of third-person discourse termed narrated monologue, makes the reader epistemologically and ontologically unsure of himself/herself. The techniques have a disquieting impact on the reader, in particular on his/her desire to know absolutely what actions and what thoughts of a character are actively being endorsed by the narrative.[100]

Darby's thesis is, however, interesting for other reasons. Although he is able to give good examples of the way in which the reader's ontological security is undermined by the assaults made on it by conflicting points of view, he is also convincing when he is able to prove how large sections of the novel are animated by a quite wicked sense of *parody* of virtually all of the sacred concepts of plot, character, and meaning associated with the novel in the realist tradition. His analysis of the section "Privateigentum" in Part Two of the novel shows how brilliantly Canetti subverts the whole process of detection associated with establishment law and order. The forensic enquiry is, in fact, a grotesque send-up of the norms associated with it. As such, Darby suggests that the novel deserves to be seen as a precursor of the "nouveau roman," since Robbe-Grillet in *Le Voyeur* and Butor in *L'Emploi du Temps* enjoy making a mockery of the search for truth associated with the detective process, in order to make a point about the apparent silliness of the pretentions of classic realist fiction generally.

Another excellent study that is exclusively preoccupied with the implications of Canetti's narratological techniques is Hans-Jakob Werlen's dissertation, which appeared in 1988, entitled

"Narrative Strategies in Elias Canetti's *Die Blendung* and *Masse und Macht*."[101] Werlen argues that the exertion of narrative control at the beginning of the novel is reminiscent of the realist novel and raises the question whether *Die Blendung* fulfills its modernist potential. As the detached voice is, however, more and more replaced by the competing perspectives of the various protagonists, he maintains that a polyphonic perspectivism, a quality of genuinely modernist fiction, comes to characterize the novel as a whole. This is used, however, to express the work's thematic preoccupation with the impossibility of communication between characters. Werlen argues, however, that the ambivalence of the competing alternatives, especially toward the end of the novel, serves another purpose. Since the ambivalence is never overcome, the reader's ontological freedom remains intact. S/he is not allowed the luxury of unlocking the key to the mysteries of the psychology of the masses, of the character of George(s) and the character of his asylum. His/her critical faculties are stimulated but not satisfied: the critical independence of the reader is, as a result, respected, making Canetti into a thoroughly humanist author.

At the very least, both these thoroughly new interpretations of the novel insist on the dynamism of the reader's involvement in the text, even if this dynamic involvement has problematic implications. A smaller minority of critics has also expressed some awareness of the possible dynamism of the novel and the possible dynamism of the reader's involvement in that novel as an *experience*. This small group has suggested that the dynamism of the novel lies not in its architecture as a work of fiction but in its liveliness. There have been passing comments on this quality, and, more interestingly, on the novel's comic energy. Yet, in 1984, Herbert Göpfert, the Munich publisher of Canetti's works, was still justifiably able to complain that Canetti's *sense of humor* had not been adequately researched as a separate area.[102] Timid statements to the effect that the novel is funny have been made by some of the most well-known critics of the novel. Jacob Isaacs, an English critic, is a good example of what is common in criticism of the novel. His view is an extraordinarily ambitious one, that in the novel there is comic invention on a grand Satanic scale. Yet this is not investigated in any detail.[103] The same, equally suggestive, view is also left uninvestigated by another English critic, Walter Allan. For him, the novel is "ferociously funny, rich in character, irony and that unflagging exuberance of invention which is a sign of the great comic writer."[104] Yet another English critic, Anthony Thwaite, in a review of the novel, maintained that it was a "tedious, elaborate, repetitive, arbitrary bore." He conceeded, however, that there was undoubted power in the writing, and "some superb invention, some ingenious and comic set pieces."[105] Another English critic, David Turner, maintains that Canetti has considerable gifts as a comic writer. Canetti provokes irresistible laughter, but this is often accompanied by a chill horror.[106] Another of the early reviewers of the novel, the French critic Marcel Brion, commented that Canetti's attitude toward his assumed readership was similar to that of Stendhal, whose happy few, Brion concludes, will be struck by the novel's poetic combination of seriousness and gaiety: ". . . son aspect bouffon, d'un sérieux et d'une gravité qui retiendront la sympathie du lecteur attentif."[107]

The most systematic study so far of the comedy in *Die Blendung* has been attempted by Peter Jansen, in the article already cited. He systematizes the types of comedy available in the novel, distinguishing between "metonymische Komik," "normativ gebundene Komik," "anthropologisch fundierte Komik," "Komik der Naivität," "Komik der Inkompetenz," "Komik der Fixiertheit," and "Komik des Zufalls." These types of comedy serve a purpose, since they cast light on the inability of characters to use language successfully as an instrument of communication: they have revealing things to say, therefore, about the general chaos in which characters live. Comedy is functional in terms of Canetti's theory of communication.

Dagmar Barnouw, whose critical work on Canetti is well known, once mentions that the worlds of both Peter Kien and Georges Kien are horrible and comical, stressing that this combination might have been the result of Canetti's fascination with Gogol.[108] The point that Canetti's humor is black and anarchic, like Gogol's, has also been made by Mühlberger.[109] Idris Parry believes that the humor is tainted: it is "savagely pathetic."[110] According to Peter Russell, the novel "is at times very funny, although always in a savage sense: the humour is black."[111] For Dissinger, the humor is merely "knisternd."[112] For Jenny, the characters are merely "komisch."[113] For Sebald, the cutting off of Fischerle's hunchback in the novel is "entsetzlich komisch."[114] For Roberts, the comedy is generally "erbarmunglos."[115] For Curtius, commenting on the prevalence of oxymoron in language in the novel, that which is funny simply has to serve a higher, material purpose. There is no such thing as gratuitous humor in the novel.[116] For Piel, the novel's comic qualities are irritating because actions and characters in the novel are horrible.[117] Werlen's case about the freedom of the reader was in part dependent on his assumption that the anarchic humor of the novel prevented the reader from identifying with any one point of view. We have already seen how Darby maintained that the discrepancy between order and disintegration produced an effect which was comic.

The energy of the novel has also been saluted, albeit timidly as well. The quality of "Spannung" has been perceived by Ferber,[118] and by Hermann Hesse more generally.[119] Waldinger, too, maintains that actions in the novel are exciting.[120] Mühlberger maintains that one reads the Balzacian comedy of the novel as a whole with general excitement.[121] Thomas Mann, when he did read the novel, commented on its high spirits, in an eloquent appraisal: "Ich bin aufrichtig angetan und freudig beeindruckt von seiner krausen Fülle, dem Debordierenden seiner Phantasie, der gewissen erbitterten Großartigkeit seines Wurfes, seiner dichterischen Unerschrockenheit, seiner Traurigkeit und seinem Übermut."[122] Broch felt something similar in 1933: "Vielleicht wird Canettis Schaffen mit zunehmender Zeit auch naturnäher werden: vorderhand ist die Landschaft seiner Dichtung reine, beinahe abstrakte Seelenlandschaft. Damit ist aber nicht gesagt, daß seine Gestalten naturentfernt seien. Sie sind vielmehr von intensiver, von intensivster, ja beinahe von dämonischer Lebenserfülltheit."[123] Accordingly, it would now be appropriate to turn to the theory of humor, to refresh our memories as to how humor in literature is recognizable and what it can achieve. The foray into the theory of humor will be a prelude to a later, involved attempt to account for some of the cursory references to the liveliness of *Die Blendung* just mentioned.

3

Agon's Carnival: Laughter and Play in *Die Blendung* (1) or "Alle Guten Dinge Lachen"

The theory of laughter insists, not surprisingly, that laughter must be defined as an effect, for it is the *vocalization* of pleasure. Theories account for this phenomenon in two principal ways. They either stress the psychological mechanisms at work within the personality, set in motion by some kind of external catalyst, or they centre on systematizing those external catalysts, those kinds of incidents, actions, and words most likely to stimulate the psychological mechanisms that result in laughter. The *causes* of vocalization of pleasure depend, crucially, therefore, on an interaction between the personality and the world outside the personality. This *intersubjective* process is a *donnée*, which shows that the real "causes" of the phenomenon of laughter are multiple, not single. They have to be seen as both internal and external to the personality.[124]

Historically, comedy has had a hard time relative to the apparently more pretentious and serious genre of tragedy. Plato proscribed comedy in *The Republic*, because it apparently inspired a real weakness in the audience.[125] Plato also wanted to ban tragedy from the ideal state for the same reason. Historically, it was Aristotle, in his *Poetics*, who first theorized comedy as a literary *genre* of the drama. He did so in a way that allocated the comedy, a potential source of laughter, to a negative position within a hierarchy of literary genres. "Comedy, as we have said, is a representation of inferior people, not indeed in the full sense of the word bad, but the laughable is a species of the base or ugly."[126] He went on to define the comedy in terms of what it was not. It is inferior, as drama, to tragedy, in that it "only" deals in an amusing way with ordinary characters in rather everyday situations, offering an audience inferior emotions like light relief and pleasure. It allows individuals to luxuriate in a sense that they are superior to the acts of banality or stupidity enacted on stage by characters who are only pursuing happiness, and encountering and surmounting obstacles. In that the laughter provoked has no higher purpose than that of relief, it is, as an emotion, intrinsically inferior to the emotion of morally edifying catharsis provoked by the actions of those noble characters who appear, suffer, and endure in tragedies.

This relegation of comedy in drama to a "lower" level was sustained historically for a considerable period of time. More recent centuries have dissolved Aristotle's patronizing distinction, and comedy has flourished as a serious, autonomous subgenre within the drama, on a par with tragedy. Aristotle and Plato, together with Hobbes and Bergson, are also exemplars of the so-called superiority theory, the psychological theory that believes that laughter is an expression of the ego's desire for supremacy.[127] Hobbes formulated the notion of the possible ego-inflation and vanity of the person who laughs at somebody else's misfortune, in a classic statement published in 1651. A *sensation* of superiority accompanies the vocalization of pleasure in laughter. This has a basis in Hobbes's thoroughly cynical view of human nature, for laughter is seen as an existential means of sustaining one's own desperate need to survive, itself a need driven by a sense of one's own inferiority in life: "*Sudden glory* is the passion which maketh those *grimaces* called LAUGHTER; and is caused either by some sudden act of their own, that pleaseth them; or, by the apprehension of some formed thing in another, by comparison whereof they suddenly applaud themselves. And it is incident most to them that are conscious of the fewest abilities in themselves; who are forced to keep themselves in their own favour by observing the imperfections of other men."[128]

Kant is the font for the incongruity theories, which stress the "sudden" aspect of laughter rather than the "glory" one might feel at the sense of superiority it induces. Kant's stress on the way in which laughter interrupts the determinism of time is an important one, since it introduces us to the notion of freedom from constraint. Elsewhere, laughter is defined as an "affectation arising from the sudden transformation of a strained expectation into nothing": it is thus characterized in terms of its effects. Laughter brings relief after the strain of expectation and is a semi-physical sensation. Bergson modifies the concept of superiority with that of incongruity in *Le Rire* (1912). Life and man are informed by a vital force which is essentially vigorous, flexible, and alive. Any stiffening or rigidity, mental or physical, is considered to be contrary to this natural force and hence deathly, and is corrected by ridicule. To the degree that man is a machine, by appearing to be mechanical, repetitive, or unable to adjust, he becomes funny. Release from restraint and discharge of tension are Freud's means of explaining jokes in his full-length work on the subject, *Der Witz und seine Beziehung zum Unbewußten* of 1905. An economy of psychic expenditure is what makes up the inhibition with which formal jokes are to be associated. Civilization rests on repression, and humor touches strain points and triggers laughter, which is a temporary flash of the energy that has previously been used to enforce the repression. According to Freud, the most common repressed bases for humor are sex and aggression. So energy spent in the pleasure of laughter is an aspect of the negative energy of repression.

Baudelaire's view is different, in the essay entitled "De l'Essence du Rire."[129] He concentrates on how, in general, one has to be a spectator in order to laugh in the first place, and his example shows that he shares with Hobbes the idea that one laughs, principally, at another's misfortune: "Le comique, la puissance du rire est dans le rieur et nullement dans l'objet du rire. Ce n'est point l'homme qui tombe qui rit de sa propre chute, à moins qu'il ne soit un philosophe, un homme qui ait acquis, par habitude, la force de se dédoubler rapidement et d'assister comme spectateur désinteressé aux phenomènes de son *moi*. Mais le cas est rare" (251).[130] The man who does laugh at himself as he falls over, however, is exceptional, and to be differentiated from the man who laughs as somebody else falls over. The former is more likely than not a kind of artist/philosopher who has acquired a skill, and whose skill is to be able to duplicate himself, to be simultaneously both actor and witness to his own performance, to develop a relationship within consciousness between two imaginary selves. This is an ideal mode of existence in Baudelaire's terms. Using language, duplication becomes the formal acknowledgment of the fact that one lives in an empirical world in a state of inauthenticity. This is a form of irony, Baudelaire's "comique absolu," which has to be differentiated from the "comique significatif," itself characterized by a relationship *between* two separate individuals, an intersubjective relationship. This is opposed to the *self-reflexive consciousness* that characterizes the person who has attained a higher level of consciousness altogether and whose skill is that of the "comique absolu." Using language, the "philosophe" mentioned above splits the subject into an empirical self, immersed in the world, and a self that becomes like a sign in its attempt at self-definition. The dialectic of self-destruction and self-invention characterizes the ironic mind. It is an endless process that leads to no synthesis. It is a display of mind dominated by artifice, happily and self-consciously alienated from anything resembling a state of nature.

In De Man's essay collection *Blindness and Insight*, the essay "The rhetoric of temporality" discusses Baudelaire's essay on laughter.[131] The discussion is a prelude to his by now famous interpretation of the essence of irony: "More clearly even than allegory, the rhetorical mode of irony takes us back to the predicament of the conscious subject; this consciousness is clearly an unhappy one that strives to move beyond and outside itself" (222). Such comments on the significance of irony are relevant to this brief survey of definitions of laughter and comedy, in that they take us away from ideas discussed above of how particular incidents provoke the vocalization of pleasure known as laughter. Those so-called intersubjective definitions of comedy that Baudelaire found so inferior give way to a new possibility: prose generally can enshrine something resembling the spirit of comedy—what the psychologists mentioned above have talked about as the actions or words that provoke the release of tension in a spectator—*as a tension*. Such a tension will probably not produce the release of tension caused by laughter. It will, instead, sustain a particular kind of existential irony. Although De Man uses the word irony to characterize this degree of self-consciousness, there is no reason why a link with theoreticians of comedy and laughter should not be established, on the grounds that an intuitive or analytical sense of the presence of a kind of *incongruity* has always been felt to be at the heart of comedy and laughter. De Man clearly feels that ironic prose has a self-conscious awareness of the incongruity of projecting a discourse into the void. When De Man ends his essay with the comment that *La Chartreuse de Parme* is the allegory of irony, he shows that particular kinds of novels are capable of sustaining irony over a period of time.[132] We are no longer dealing, therefore, with the kinds of intersubjective encounters with self-contained scenes in a play or in life, for instance, that might conspire to produce the release of tension thought to be at the heart of laughter. Further, De Man sees his version of irony as particularly appropriate to the experience of the isolated individual in a hostile universe, the experience of "modern man," as it were. Irony abandons the division of time into the past, present, and future: it resists the pressure associated with linear time, of forcing all individual moments into a unifying metanarrative that would furnish them all with meaning:"Irony is a synchronic structure, while allegory appears as a successive mode capable of engendering duration as the illusion of a continuity that it knows to be illusionary . . . irony comes closer to the pattern of factual experience as a succession of violated moments lived by a divided self. Essentially the mode of the present, it knows neither memory nor prefigurative duration, whereas allegory exists entirely within an ideal time that is never here and now but always a past or an endless future" (226).

Neil Schaffer, a modern theoretician of laughter, in *The Art of Laughter*,[133] together with another modern theoretician of laughter, Arthur Koestler, in *The Act of Creation*,[134] look at laughter more sympathetically than either Aristotle, Hobbes, Kant, Bergson, or Baudelaire. Both suggest that it must be linked with the sense of freedom that it brings to the person who laughs. Their views do not contribute to an understanding of the causal theories of laughter put forward by psychologists. They achieve something more subtle, in that they insist on the link between laughter and that of general well-being. The act of laughing, an expression of pleasure, brings with it long-term aftereffects in the form of freedom and well-being, because it is provoked by incidents in which there is a sudden irrelevance or dissolution of the laws of determinism with which rationality, morality, and work are associated. As such, it provides a kind of relief that De Man's ironic narratives cannot provide, because irony refuses to collapse certain laws of existence. De Man's irony sustains them, whilst laughter, according to Schaffer, is a realization of the way in which certain laws of existence can suddenly be made to dissolve: "All laughter is the result of the apprehension of an incongruity within a ludicrous context which I have described as a state of mind from which rationality, morality and work have been temporarily excluded" (38).

For Koestler, laughter is an automatic, involuntary reflex, unique in that it serves no apparent biological purpose. It is a kind of luxury reflex which has a utilitarian function, to provide temporary relief from utilitarian pressures. Laughter is inherently unintellectual, for it is *emotion, deserted by thought*. He attributes to it an existential significance, in that it is capable of defeating habit by originality. It is, thus, *a creative act*, which connects previously unrelated dimensions of experience and enables one to attain a higher level of mental evolution. So both these theories look at laughter sympathetically and holistically in terms of benefits to the whole personality. Laughter is thought to be creative in itself, even ideal, and able to initiate the individual into a world free of laws, free of the material. This soft line on laughter is one taken up by Stendhal, Canetti's hero: in his essay "Le Rire" of 1823, which, interestingly, given the massive dearth of amusing literature in German, begins with the view: "Il me semble que l'on fait plus de plaisanteries à Paris pendant une seule soirée que dans toute l'Allemagne en un mois" (63).[135] Laughter, Stendhal argues, is knowing about the pain of pursuing happiness, generally speaking. Stendhal also argues that there has to be clarity of thought in prose destined to create mirth, and that surprise is a crucial element in laughter—the "imprévu." The sense of absurdity one often feels when one laughs is one Stendhal associates with a delicious pleasure: it makes one feel full of gaiety.

Both Schaffer's and Koestler's ideas can be linked to a well-established cultural theory of *play* developed both by Bakhtin and by Huizinga, in his *Homo Ludens*. The contention here is that in *Die Blendung* is both displayed and enacted a specifically agonistic spirit of play, in the Nietzschean tradition. Only at times, and not consistently, does the Nietzschean sense of play provoke that release of tension caused by physical laughing, an ideal release from the material world. The claim is that in *Die Blendung* is to be found a particularly successful alliance of Homo Ridens with Homo Ludens. Before developing this thesis, however, it would be appropriate to remember that to date, critics have only casually alluded to the presence of comedy, laughter, and play in *Die Blendung*, as indicated at the end of the last chapter. Significant about the limited critical space dedicated to these aspects of the novel is the disturbing absence of comparative observations linking comedy, laughter, or humor in the novel to either the theory of comedy, laughter, or humor, or the practice of comedy, laughter, or play in either literature or life. Any references have had mere footnote status in overall studies of the novel.

We can now look at those few critics who have situated *Die Blendung* in terms of a cultural theory of play. Roger Hillman is exceptional in this respect. He has suggested that Bakhtin's idea of the carnival has resonance in *Die Blendung* as a whole.[136] David Darby is exceptional, too, for having singled out Huizinga's *Homo Ludens* as relevant to the debate on the comic energy of *Die Blendung*. Richard Sheppard has suggested quite recently that the apparent ignorance of Bakhtin's theories in literary criticism in German can be accounted for by the absence of translations into German of Bakhtin's works. This is a factual inaccuracy in itself.[137] In his article, "Upstairs-Downstairs—Some reflections on German Literature in the Light of Bakhtin's theory of carnival,"[138] he discusses carnival as an event as it is represented in works of literature in German, as for instance the carnival scene in Köln in *Die verlorene Ehre der Katharina Blum*. He is not, as a result of this narrow focus, in a position to include Canetti's *Die Blendung* in what appears to be a fairly serious attempt at a comprehensive survey of the event as theme in twentieth-century literature. *Die Blendung* contains no carnival scenes as events.

Bakhtin's and Huizinga's theories have some resonance in Schiller's idea of the "Spieltrieb," discussed in the fourteenth letter of his *Über die ästhetische Erziehung des Menschen* of 1795. Schiller explores there how individual works of art can help to achieve a holistic balance within the personality as a whole, by kindling the personality's capacity for play:"Der sinniche Trieb will, daß Veränderung sey, daß die Zeit einen Inhalt habe; der Formtrieb will, daß die Zeit aufgehoben, daß keine Veränderung sey. Derjenige Trieb also, in welchem beyde verbunden wirken, (es sey mir einstweilen, bis ich diese Benennung gerechtfertigt haben werde, vergönnt, ihn Spieltrieb zu nennen) der Spieltrieb also würde dahin gerichtet seyn, die Zeit in der Zeit aufzuheben, Werden mit absolutem Seyn, Veränderung mit Identität zu vereinbaren."[139] Here again, however, although this text is in German and one of the most prominent in German aesthetics generally, a possible link between Schiller and Canetti has not been made by literary critics of Canetti's novel writing in German. Irmgard Kowatzki, for instance, has recently investigated Schiller's notion of the "Spieltrieb" in literature in German generally, but has restricted her study to Schiller, Heine, Hofmannsthal, and Benn.[140]

In Bakhtin's *Rabelais and His World*, Bakhtin develops his theory of carnival as an event in medieval life, an event in selected literary works, and as a way of writing.[141] The carnival is primarily interesting because it dissolves the inequality that dominates life in society. It does not acknowledge any distinction between actors and spectators:"As opposed to the official feast, one might say that carnival celebrated temporary liberation from the prevailing truth and from the established order; it marked the suspension of all hierarchical rank, privileges, norms and prohibitions. Carnival was the true feast of time, the feast of becoming, change, and renewal. It was hostile to all that was immortalized and completed" (10). In writers like Molière, Voltaire, Diderot, and Swift, the carnival form exercises a similar function:"to consecrate inventive freedom, to permit the combination of a variety of different elements and their rapprochement, to liberate from the prevailing point of view of the world, from conventions and established truths, from clichés, from all that is hundrum and universally accepted. This carnival spirit offers the chance to have a new outlook on the world, to realize the relative nature of all that exists, and to enter a completely new order of things" (34). Citing Hippocrates, Aristotle, and Lucian, Bakhtin concentrates on an idea mentioned above by Schaeffer, namely that of the healing and regenerative powers of laughter and how laughter is essentially linked to the ultimate philosophical questions concerning "the regulation of life": "The serious aspects of class culture are official and authoritarian; they are combined with violence, prohibitions, limitations and always contain an element of fear and of intimidation. These elements prevailed in the Middle Ages. Laughter, on the contrary, overcomes fear, for it knows no inhibitions, no limitations. Its idiom is never used by violence and authority" (90).

Laughter, characteristic of the mood of the carnival, is seen, therefore, as a highly effective way of undermining authority and power: it is subversive in social/political/cultural terms. Whether Bakhtin discusses the ritual of the carnival in medieval life or the way in which it is incorporated into specific literary texts, as the prevailing spirit of those literary texts, the power of the laughter associated with the carnival is understood in ideological terms, in terms of its aggressivity with respect to power structures, whose capacity to reify life, energy, and creativity is given. Laughter is an ideological challenge to the prevailing ideology. This is understood to be hostile to or inimical to the reign of laughter, only because it is inimical to the view that the individual has a right to feel powerful.

Bakhtin's endorsement of the liberating powers released in and by the carnival, and his understanding of the ideological significance of these energies, has not always been shared by more recent critics, even those with a clear interest in challenges to "ideological hegemony." Their objections are serious and interesting. Juliet Mitchell, a feminist critic, for instance, maintains that any kind of ludic play merely sets aside all the pressures on the individual exercised by the particular power structure of patriarchy.[142] The carnival only disrupts in terms of the law: it is set up by the law as its own ludic space. It is thus totally devoid of the aggressive ideological substance attributed to it by Bakhtin. Ludic play can achieve, at best, a temporary relief from pressures that the individual still seems willing to accept and not to challenge. Another feminist critic, Patricia Yaeger, is also partly worried by the practice of ludic play in feminist writing, in the sense that play neutralizes the problem of power by hiding power, thus trivializing it: it can implicate women in patriarchy. She also notes that male critics tend to overlook playfulness in feminist writing, assuming that playfulness means lack of seriousness. For this reason, she advocates the need to theorize play in women's writing, so that it does not get overlooked. She ends with an endorsement of playfulness in women's writings in terms of the title of her book, and in doing so partly contradicts her own fears. Nevertheless, play is dangerous, and is assumed to be something that questions the ideology that makes it necessary: it is attractive to women who want to take risks, who are "honey mad."[143]

Umberto Eco, too, does not see the carnival in positive terms. His view is that it denies freedom and liberation.[144] Timothy Reiss, in *The Uncertainty of Analysis*, in a section entitled "Carnival's illusionary place and the process of Order," also argues against the view that the carnival offers any kind of serious dialogue with power.[145] It offers the individual the opportunity to take time off from pressures that, in Reiss' opinion, have to be confronted directly if change within the system is to be effected or brought about, a goal he considers to be necessary in human life. Both Mitchell and Reiss, as representatives of the intellectual Left, share skepticism about the carnival, therefore, only inasmuch as it fails to have a respectable kind of political agenda seriously aimed at challenging the status quo within society. Finally, Peter Stallybrass and Allon White, in *The Politics and Poetics of Transgression*, also conclude that the freedom associated with the carnival and with carnival writing is limited, in the sense that it offers temporary respite from power structures that can never be undermined entirely.[146]

In his *Homo Ludens*, Huizinga stresses the vital existential significance of the ritual of play in culture, in the same terms used by Schaffer.[147] Playing furnishes the individual with an opportunity to use his/her own wits in such a way that his/her own freedom is expressed and experienced. It also furnishes the individual with the opportunity of undermining the reign of absolute determinism outside the personality, for this can be interrupted, albeit temporarily: "Play only becomes possible, thinkable and understandable when an influx of *mind* breaks down the absolute determinism of the cosmos" (3). It is also significant as a cultural or social ritual inasmuch as it is obvious that those who choose to play do so *freely*, of their own free will. It is, further, as a voluntary activity, because of its link with pleasure, a particularly persuasive statement to the effect that freedom is something that has to be expressed in order to be enjoyed. This suggests that playing calls into question the influential view held by eighteenth-century philosophers in particular, that freedom is an inalienable *right*. The notion of play suggests that freedom is something one must *deserve and earn*. It is something of which one becomes worthy when one proves, *by example*, that one is worthy. It is something one *experiences* in play. It is associated with acting and doing, not passive being: "First and foremost, then, all play is a voluntary activity. Play to order is no longer play: it could at best be but a forcible imitation of it. By this quality of freedom alone, play marks itself off from the course of the natural process. It is something added thereto and spread out over it like a flowering, an ornament, a garment. Obviously, freedom must be understood here in the wider sense that leaves untouched the philosophical problem of determinism" (7). Laying stress on its disinterestedness, the point Huizinga makes about all forms of play in culture is that they have to be devoid of purpose, they have to be gratuitous. Any action taken in the name of play must begin and end in itself. The outcome must not contribute to the necessary life-processes of the group. Objectively speaking, therefore, the result of the game is unimportant and a matter of indifference.

According to Huizinga, the competitive instinct motivates the desire for play in the first place, and this culminates in subjective or non-material gain, in the sense that those who win feel pride or some such private emotion. As such, the benefit of play is to be seen primarily in the way in which players develop their own, internal strength of character: they dedicate themselves to competition as a process and a way of life. In drawing such conclusions, Huizinga does not align himself with those "cynical" theoreticians of laughing mentioned above, in that he does not see this mechanism as something unattractive. Culturally speaking, according to Huizinga, *agonistic activities* show up the competitive impulse, and they dominate the whole of Greek and Roman civilization. Public contests in all areas of life, education, sport, the arts, and work, for instance, were set up to teach people to channel their aggressivity into outrivalling their neighbours in a spirit of sympathy. The primacy of play in those cultures was beneficial inasmuch as it was a training in strength of character: thus, envy was not regarded as hostile, since to the Greeks it was a matter of personal pride to outclass their rivals, and to burn with ambition was thought to be great and noble. Huizinga sees those civilizations in which play has a primary importance as civilizations in the archaic phase: "As a civilization becomes more complex, more variegated and more overladen, and as the technique of production and social life itself become more finely organized, the old cultural soil is gradually smothered under a rank layer of ideas, systems of thought and knowledge, doctrines, rules and regulations, moralities and conventions which have all lost touch with play. Civilization, we then say, has grown more serious; it assigns only a secondary place to playing. The heroic period is over, and the agonistic phase, too, seems a thing of the past" (75). Huizinga's conclusion is that the play element in culture has been on the wane ever since the eighteenth century, when he believed it was in full flower. He ends with a reminder of the high premium placed on play as a way of living by Plato in his *Laws*, which again stresses the benefits of play in terms of strength of character. In Plato's *Laws*, the Athenian visitor states how best to conduct oneself in life, or, as he puts it more poetically, "I am really laying the keels of the vessels by due consideration of the question by what means or manner of life we shall make our voyage over the sea of time to best purpose," and "Why, I mean we should keep our seriousness for serious things and not waste it on trifles, and that, while God is the real goal of all beneficent serious endeavour, man, as we said before, has been constructed as a toy for God, and this is, in fact, the finest thing about him. All of us, then, men and women alike, must fall in with our role and spend life in making our play as perfect as possible."[148]

The notion of agon is currently being revived in literary and cultural criticism. A high-profile publication by Harold Bloom is an indication of this. Bloom's *Agon: Towards a Theory of Revisionism* was published in 1982.[149] It sees revisionism as a manifestation of the spirit of agon: "Revisionism, as Nietzsche said of every spirit, unfolds itself, *only in fighting*. The spirit portrays itself as agonistic, as contesting for supremacy, with other spirits, with anteriority, and finally with every earlier version of itself. Burckhardt, Nietzsche, Huizinga are the cultural theorists of the agonistic spirit, from the Greeks and the Hebrews onwards, but Freud is the prophet of agon and of its ambivalences" (viii). A more recent work, by William Fitzgerald, *Agonistic Poetry: The Pindaric Mode in Pindar, Horace, Hölderlin, and the English Ode*,[150] published in 1987, also endorses Bloom's definition of the spirit of agon in the poetry of the above mentioned poets. Equally, it is the subject of Michael Lloyd's recent study of Euripides, *The Agon in Euripides*, where Lloyd looks at those set speeches in the plays that are conflicts between two individuals.[151] The fashionable contemporary theorist Lyotard's works, *La Condition Postmoderne, Le Différend*, and *Just Gaming* in particular, also celebrate *agon*, both in terms of style and content, and specifically in the sense that the so-called free play of the signifier is subversive of metanarrative, and destructive of authority.[152]

As we can see from the above, Bloom cites Nietzsche, and the text he, Fitzgerald, and Lyotard have in mind has been quoted again and again by those interested in agon. Nietzsche's texts, *Der Florentinische Tractat über Homer und Hesiod, ihr Geschlecht und ihren Wettkampf*, of 1870 and 1873, and *Homers Wettkampf*, of 1872, are works in which Nietzsche develops his own theory of culture.[153] Nietzsche praises the all-embracing dedication to the common goal of doing justice to life in the present, typical of Greek culture: he does so in the august tradition of German Romantics, like Hölderlin, for instance. Whereas Hölderlin, however, regretted the withdrawal of the Greek Gods and their absence in a generally godless modern world, as is the case in "Brot und Wein," Nietzsche continues to be inspired by their example. Nietzsche valued the Greeks for their rejection of exclusiveness. His celebration of the Nietzschean in Greek culture informs his survey, throughout the works generally, of the Romantics. Nietzsche argues that the Romantics are opposed to the values promoted by Greek culture, in their love, not of a community of strong, proud individuals dedicated to common goals, but of the solitary individual, his exclusiveness and sense of his self as absolute. This solipsistic individualism gives rise to the existentially debilitating evils of self-love, melancholy, and nostalgia. These are singled out as evils of the day and are hated for the way they rendered unlikely the possibility of self-overcoming and the capacity of the individual to do justice to the present.[154] Play has acquired a status in Nietzsche's revaluation of Greek civilization: play is a way of living. It has ontological status. Moroney, indeed, talks about Nietzsche's ludic ontology, carefully showing how this is elaborated under the influence of the Presocratic philosopher Heraclitus.[155]

Mihai Spariosu, editor of the series "The Margins of Literature," in which this study appears, has made an extensive study of play in culture. His *Literature, Mimesis and Play: Essays in Literary Theory* is another example, like Bloom's, of the centrality of the concept of agon in literary criticism and cultural analysis today.[156] He sees agon as the principle at the heart of imaginative life generally speaking. In the rise, over time, of the status of literature compared to other discourses (such as Philosophy, Religion, Economics, Law, Ethics, Religion), he sees the rise of *aesthetic* fictions (which do not contend for the status of truth or knowledge and enjoy neutrality) over and above *practical* fictions (which aspire to knowledge and truth). This is proof, he maintains, of the existence of a power principle which is at the heart of Western civilization. Agon sets the contest in motion by contesting the relationship of mimesis to truth. Spariosu's work is also interesting here because he points out that the Homeric concept of *arete* (meaning virtue/excellence or prowess in battle) emphasizes the competitive rather than cooperative nature of play as contest or agon. Spariosu reminds us that the word, arete, has the same etymological root as *aristoi*: players are in fact the best types of people. This is obviously the notion that Moroney has brought out so successfully in his book on Nietzsche: an aristocrat is a skilled player, not, as is more commonly thought, someone who is blue-blooded.[157] Lastly, and interestingly, in terms of what has been said about Canetti's love of the Presocratics, Spariosu has the following to say: "The Homeric concept of play as an irrational, spontaneous movement also appears as a philosophical first principle in such atomists as Leucippus, Democritus, and, later on, in Epicurus and the Roman Lucretius."[158]

Huizinga's interest in play was limited to his fascination with particular forms of play, namely those that display the competitive spirit associated with agon. Since the publication of Huizinga's seminal work, Roger Caillois has written *Man, Play and Games*,[159] which expands the forms of play by suggesting that there is greater variety. If *agon* is the desire to win by one's merits, with a high degree of self-reliance, *alea* is the submission of one's will to chance, the anxious and passive anticipation of what might happen (such as in gambling, when one waits to see where the wheel will stop). The desire to assume a strange personality is another form of play: *mimicry* involves one's imagining that one is somebody else. The pursuit of vertigo, finally, known as *ilinx*, is the wish to escape from the tyranny of the ordinary altogether. The game of chess here involves both the use of one's own wits and a certain amount of submission to chance.[160]

Now, we know that Canetti read Burckhardt's *Griechische Kulturgeschichte* as he was writing *Die Blendung*. Burckhardt's survey of Greek culture stresses what he felt was the agonistic mentality at the heart of many of its activities. He also stressed how the cynics and stoics, whose theories are acknowledged by Canetti generally, and many of whose proponents are mentioned by name by Peter Kien in the novel, had no interest whatsoever in affairs of state, which is to say in the world of public affairs, of society. In what follows, we shall be investigating where *Die Blendung* stands as far as a possible relationship is concerned between what might be called that principle of agon outlined above, the competitive contest between two individuals, which in Greek culture was practised by the individual for personal reasons, and the status of that same individual in terms of the body politic as a whole, in particular his response to its power structures. The many queries raised by critics looking more skeptically at the ideological power of agon, such as Mitchell and Reiss, can thus be investigated more thoroughly. We will also be looking critically at those writers who have endorsed the ideologically subversive power of agon, such as Lyotard. Finally and most importantly, we shall be examining whether the grand ontological potential and ambition of Nietzsche with respect to play has been fulfilled by *Die Blendung*.

But before doing so we must first pause to reflect how the spirit of agon might manifest itself in a created literary artifact, in writing. If the spirit of agon is to be imitated in prose, it would have to be enacted by a very special kind of writing. To be worthy of the name, one can assume that at its best, such writing would consist of a large number of short sentences, perpetually contesting with one another as equals, perpetually prolonging the contest by inventing new ways of keeping the contest going. The contest would obviously not be for ultimate supremacy. To contend for ultimate supremacy would be to raise the possibility of a conclusion to the contest. To do this would be to move out of the agonistic mode. This idea of narrative puts a huge pressure on individual sentences. It casts sentences as strong, muscular, and war-like, able to sustain the illusion of perpetual battle.

Now, individual sentences and individual words have always fascinated Canetti, as is clear from the prominence of the title of the set of literary essays, *Das Gewissen der Worte*. In *Die Provinz des Menschen*, Canetti proclaims his respect for words:"Ihre Integrität ist mir beinahe heilig. Es widerstrebt mir, sie zu zerschneiden, und selbst ihre älteren Formen, solche, die wirklich gebraucht wurden, flößen mir Scheu ein, ich lasse mich mit ihnen nicht gern auf heillose Abenteuer ein. Das Unheimliche, das *in* den Worten enthalten ist, ihr Herz, will ich ihnen nicht herausreißen wie ein mexikanischer Opferpriester: diese blutigen Manieren sind mir verhaßt" (*PM*, 104). In the same notebooks, in an entry from 1955, Canetti makes a statement reminiscent of the hatred of beautification, a view also expressed in his commentary on the genesis of his novel: "An den Verwalter der Worte, wer immer er sei: Gib mir dunkle Worte und gib mir klare Worte, aber ich will keine Blumen, den Duft behalte dir selbst. Ich will Worte, die nicht abfallen, Worte, die nicht verblühen. Ich will Dornen und Wurzeln und selten, sehr selten, ein durchscheinendes Blatt, aber andere Worte will ich nicht, die verteile an Reiche" (*PM*, 167). This puritanical attitude to words is clear from his essay on Karl Kraus of 1965, "Schule des Widerstands," where Canetti comments on the muscular strength of Kraus's own sentences in words that sum up an agonistic sentence: "Aus diesen wie zyklopische Festungen gefügten Sätzen, die immer genau ineinanderpaßten, schoß es plötzlich Blitze, nicht harmlose, nicht erleuchtende, auch nicht Theaterblitze, sondern tödliche."[161] Again, in the same essay, the Kraus sentence is a world of its own: "Alle Bau-Gelüste, an denen Schriftsteller reich sein sollen, erschöpfen sich bei Karl Kraus im einzelnen Satz. Seine Sorge gilt diesem; er sei unantastbar, keine Lücke, keine Ritze, kein falsches Komma—Satz um Satz, Stück um Stück fügt sich zu einer Chinesischen Mauer."[162] In *Das Geheimherz der Uhr*, in an entry from 1974, Canetti pays further tribute to the muscularity of the Karl Kraus sentence. We remember how insistent Canetti was, in the account of the genesis of his novel, on the quality of "Strenge": Canetti talks of the "Panzersprache" of *Die letzten Tage der Menschheit*:

> Sie hat mich erfaßt und gestärkt, sie hat mir Knochen wiedergegeben, die ich in meiner Totenstarre vergessen hatte, endlich erlebe ich wieder, was mir vor 50 und 45 Jahren geschah: die innere Gliederung und Härtung durch Karl Kraus. Es gehört dazu die Gliederung dieser Sätze selbst, die Unerbittlichkeit ihrer Längen, ihre Zahllosigkeit, die Unabsehbarkeit, das Fehlen eines Gesamtziels, jeder Satz ist sich selber Ziel, und wichtig ist nur, daß man ihre Gleichmäßigkeit so lange auf sich einwirken läßt, wie es einem möglich ist, ihre Erregung zu fühlen. Es scheint, daß man besser dazu imstande ist aus einer eigenen Erregung heraus, welchen Charakter immer sie habe. Man kann die Panzersätze des Karl Kraus nicht kalt lesen. Man kann sie auch nicht als prüfender Intellekt lesen. Der neugierige Geist ist leicht, wirkliches Wissen gewinnt sich nur auf Flügeln, es ist nicht möglich, durch Karl Kraus zu Wissen zu gelangen. Wissen ist ihm gleichgültig, da es sich nicht verdammen läßt. Karl Kraus gibt einem Durchschauungen und wenn man sie in seiner Erregung erlebt, stärkt er die Wucht in einem gegen das, *was man nicht will.* (*GU*, 25)

These quotations serve to show how Canetti's theory about words is one that, although it makes no reference to agon itself, supports and endorses agonistic writing. For each sentence in a genuinely agonistic narrative has the responsibility of setting out, in its own original way, to prove that it is capable of responding to a challenge, not to the ultimate authority of the next sentence, but to its own creative capacity to respond and stimulate the next sentence to further displays of brilliance and skill. This has to involve a rejection of sentiment, color, embellishment, for to use words for decorative purposes is a way of denying the momentum necessary to agonistic writing. Each sentence is cast as absolute, self-sufficient, and original. It is thus able to stimulate the next to express such skills itself.

If agonistic prose worthy of the name emphasizes competing, one can further assume that agonistic narrative will be devoid of concepts, will have denied the validity of all analytical or synthetic reasoning altogether. For in order to integrate concepts into narrative, and to express an intellectual view, time and space are needed in the form of a number of sentences formalized in a particular order; and the formulation of such a power block would rob individual sentences of their capacity to compete with one another, precisely by endowing that block with the power that is antagonistic to agon, namely supremacy. Ideas, after all, depend on definition, and are in themselves unlikely to further the cause of agon since they normally have a vested interest in seeing themselves preferred to others. Concepts are inimical to agon, as are long, wandering, self-involved sentences. Resistance to ideas can be embodied in short sentences if they do not relate to one another semantically. Endowed with minimal semantic interrelations those short sentences will proclaim a love of and a delight in individual words. Agonistic prose in its ideal form would thus be composed of very short sentences, since short sentences obviously increase the number of acts in which skill is displayed. Short, brittle sentences perpetually jostling with one another also imply sympathy and respect. For if skill is displayed, not with a view to conquest, a point is being made about absolute respect for the absolute autonomy of the other. Agonistic prose creates the imaginative space, in other words, that recognizes, protects and enhances autonomy.

We have moved, therefore, to a consideration of the status of the reader, implied by agonistic writing. What kind of reader is assumed by the prose defined above? Agonistic prose inevitably addresses itself to the reader's "Spieltrieb," which it ignites and provokes, as it assumes that the reader is another competitive player. The reader's intersubjective encounter with the individual sentences that make up an extended, agonistic narrative is a highly creative one. The encounter calls on the reader to produce the text in a Nietzschean way. The reader is forced to start from scratch at every single moment in the narrative, at the beginning of every new sentence. Such an intersubjective encounter is competitive, for reading agonistic prose make heavy demands on the wits and stamina of the reader, above all. Agonistic prose consists of enough sufficiently shocking moments for the reader to feel competitive in the first place. Importantly, the perpetual shock of the ever-new, the ever-original, can only be achieved *at the expense of those consoling semantic connections* that tend to be made by non-agonistic prose. In the attention given to sections from *Die Blendung* that now follow, we shall try to show how the prose of the novel is defiant in its hatred of semantics and formal logic, itself absolutely vital for the construction of concepts, which are themselves inimical to the reign of agon, to the reign of style in the Nietzschean mode. Close attention will be paid to words, because these seem to be much more powerful than ideas in the narrative. We will be indicating how the sentences that make up *Die Blendung* form a tribute to Karl Kraus as he is constructed in the excerpts quoted above. Before doing so, however, we can close with a few comments on Canetti's own experience of agonistic interchanges, as these feature in the autobiography.

Talking of the influence of his intellectually demanding mother on his childhood in Zürich, Canetti commented: "Sie erwartete Antworten auf der Stelle" (*GZ*, 241).[163] This mental agility was a feature of his other friendships. In *Die Fackel im Ohr*, Canetti talks of his friend Fredl and his buddhism, mentioning how the atmosphere in which they all lived was one colored by intellectual gamesmanship: "In dieser Umgebung, wo alles auf intellektuelle Diskussion angelegt war, die sich in Form des Wettbewerbs zwischen je zwei jungen Männern abspielte, wo eine Meinung so lange galt, als sie mit Witz und Schlagkraft vertreten wurde, in dieser Umgebung, die keine wissenschaftlichen Ansprüche stellte, wo es auf die Geläufigkeit, Wendigkeit und Variabilität des *Sprechens* ankam . . ." (*FO*, 77). In *Das Augenspiel*, Canetti actually mentions the word "das Agonale" for the first time, in a discussion of Musil: "Sie zeugte für das, was ich später so stark als das *Agonale* an Musil empfand. Er *maß* sich an anderen, auch eine Vorlesung war für ihn wie bei den Griechen ein Wettkampf" (*AS*, 190).[164]

The very first chapter of *Die Blendung*, "Der Spaziergang," does not, on first or even second reading, present itself as source material for laughter in the spirit of agon or the spirit of the carnival. The formal dialogue with which the novel begins, between Peter Kien and a young boy, is aggressively resistant to the openness of access, on which a reader's capacity to laugh depends. The dialogue suggests, in fact, that an individual can be locked within his/her own imagination and that s/he can defiantly refuse, either to compromise or adapt. Kien urges the young boy to share his love of books by manipulating him, in a studied way, to make statements that bear out *his* prejudice that books are the only things in the world to be taken seriously. As readers, we find ourselves not able to enter into the spirit of this kind of strategy, because Kien appears to be exploiting a young minor who is not in a position to respond on equal terms or to fight back in kind. Kien's obsession with books is, thereafter, shown to be actively devoid of substance. This further distances the reader from him. In spite of the fact that he is billed as a sinologist and a polyglot with an international reputation as a scholar, he is actually characterized by an obsession with owning books, not by his subtlety of thought with respect to the contents of individual books he owns. In the first chapter the fixation on the world of the intellect, such as it already is, is always relativized. It is relativized in one place by the way in which Kien makes a virtue of his being anti-social or asocial, and by his assumption that the rest of the world is corrupt because of a fascination with the physical (football, love, work). The opposition mind-body, an absolute one, hides a further, divisive opposition, that of the isolated intellectual (characterized by a dedication to the non-physical) as someone who is opposed to "the masses," because of their corrupt association with all things linked with the body. Although not quite a misanthrope and not quite a total fraud as a scholar/intellectual, it is to be remembered that Kien's "appreciation" of mankind is limited to his belief that everyone else in the world is capable of stupidity: for this reason, he keeps a journal entitled "Dummheiten" in which he inscribes examples of stupidity that he has encountered on his rare walks around town, possibly like Kant in Königsberg.[165]

It would seem that the first chapter succeeds in distancing the reader from the events, actions and thoughts narrated. Yet Kien, if neither positively appealing nor hopelessly unsympathetic, does succeed in compelling our attention because of his clearly individualistic qualities. They are arresting, even shocking enough in themselves, because they are so extreme, with the result that the reader does not feel inclined to apply sympathy or disdain. This slightly clumsy atmosphere changes radically at the beginning of chapter two, in "Das Geheimnis," where a flashback allows us to understand the background to the presence of Kien's housekeeper, Therese, in his flat. Kien had put an advertisement in the paper eight years ago that read: "Gelehrter mit Bibliothek von ungewöhnlicher Größe sucht verantwortungsbewußte Haushälterin. Nur charaktervollste Persönlichkeiten wollen sich melden. Gesindel fliegt die Treppe hinunter. Gehalt Nebensache" (*DB*, 25).[166]

There is here, by contrast, clear, concrete, and uncomplicated subversion of the clear, concrete, and uncomplicated conventions that govern public advertising in newspapers. This is different, therefore, as a moment in the narration of the novel so far, to the dialogue, interior monologue, and narrative commentary that made up the presentation of Peter Kien in the first chapter. The above extract is absolutely original as a series of sentences. They clearly love jostling with one another, not for absolute supremacy, but in order to keep a chain reaction going. As a series of sentences, we can note, with this particular example, the absolute rejection of semantic interrelations between sentences. Everyone has some kind of image of how a scholar/intellectual behaves, and subjective variations on the theme will have influenced the way in which readers receive Kien throughout the first chapter. Here, by contrast, an incontrovertible reference point is invoked and simply stood on its head, bypassing, in the process, the problem or issue of the subjectivity of reading. The advertisement subverts the convention that serious jobs need serious candidates with objectively professional credentials. Here, training is irrelevant and personality is all you need. The advertisement is also a positive offense against the convention that an advertisement be detached and colorless in its presentation of a job description. "Gesindel fliegt die Treppe hinunter" expresses what normally remains an unspoken convention, that unserious candidates for a job will simply be thrown away. The advertisement finally inverts the set convention that one works in order to earn decent money.

The narrative of events and thoughts described in chapter one can be interpreted according to some fairly flexible standard of *plausibility* in literature or life. This advertisement, however, is utterly implausible by those same fairly flexible standards, and reads as the signal that "norms" are suddenly either redundant or irrelevant. Peter Kien compelled us as a character generally and rather diffusely throughout chapter one. This advertisement is compelling in a different way: it is abruptly compelling in itself, because it stands conventions on their head. It turns out to be compelling, retrospectively so to speak, in the manifestly non-logical effect it has on Therese when she reads it. Therese's reaction to the advertisement is hilarious, in that it defies any serious expectations a reader might have of how people behave when seriously looking for a job: "Der Ton imponierte ihr; das war ein Mann. Es schmeichelte ihr, sich als charaktervollste Persönlichkeit vorzustellen. Sie sah das Gesindel die Treppe herunterfliegen und freute sich aufrichtig darüber. Keinen Augenblick lang befürchtete sie, selbst als Gesindel behandelt zu werden" (*DB*, 25).[167] Therese wants to apply for the job because she assumes that she is not riffraff, that she is personally superior to the category of person "riffraff." She assumes that she has it within her power to present herself as highly personable. The advertisement has an effect on her only because she sees it as a challenge which she believes she can pull off. *Significantly, the interview is the challenge, not the job itself.* She feels the advertisement flatters her capacity to rise to the occasion in an interview of absolute originality. It stimulates her agonistic skills. Her response above shows that she is *not* motivated by a desire for long-term gain in the form of the financial security that would come her way were she to get the job.

Now, Kien did not seriously intend the advertisement to have this kind of effect: he seriously believed in two categories, that of personality, and that of riffraff. He seriously believed that people would simply recognize both, intellectually, as legitimate categories and then either apply or not for the job. Therese's response shows that she has not responded to the advertisement in purely intellectual terms. Her reason does not simply tell her that there are two categories. Something much more profound is stimulated in her, namely her capacity to act, her "Spieltrieb." She believes, in contrast to Kien, that action/conduct/behavior can be improvised. She believes that a part can be acted out so that the truth about the categories can be *proven* in time and space. She is deeply aware, then, of the way in which one has to *invent* oneself in life, to create oneself at every step of the way. Her response shows that she has pronounced competitive instincts. She is an opportunist who enjoys an opportunity to shine. These two qualities, together with her manifest non-interest in long-term material advantage, suggest she cannot be credited at this stage with some intrinsic essence of character. Although Therese's theatrical reaction to the advertisement shows that she is already justified in being in the ontologically superior category of personality raised by Kien, and although it is clear that her personality is *already* theatrically pronounced enough to give readers confidence that she will rise to the occasion and continue to prove she has personality in an interview, the significance of the advertisement and Therese's reaction to it can not be understood in terms of theories of human character. We normally understand incidents in novels in terms of a relationship between character and motive, and thus as some comment on how a sense of psychological coherence can animate the personality and give it some kind of purpose. Yet Therese's reaction to the advertisement gives us absolutely no idea of what kind of person Therese is. She is someone who is always "becoming," because she is an actress by nature who nowhere indicates, either directly or indirectly, what her ultimate aims or goals are.

The link between the advertisement and Therese's reaction to it must be understood as something that positively *privileges* the reader. The narrative emphasizes disinterested play, yet not primarily as a quality of character of a particular individual. It emphasizes disinterested play as the spirit that both animates individual characters in the narrative *and* infuses the narrative as a whole. Exposure to Kien and Therese so far has been an exposure to a series of triumphant celebrations of assertive being, as ends in themselves, devoid of the notion of the ultimate goal or the ultimate purpose with which we associate motive in human character. Yet disinterested play has been sustained by all other aspects of the narrative as well, particularly in the narrative commentary between sections of dialogue. For this reason, it would be totally wrong to suggest that the stress on the gratuitous moments of disinterested play encountered so far in the narrative is exclusively associated with individual characters. This is what Darby meant when he said that much of the narrative is contagiously colored by the speaking "voice" of a character, the issue of mimicry, in other words.

What is being stressed by example by the narrative, therefore, is always the capacity for play, not the player or the "character" responsible for the play. The narrative is composed of a variety of what could be described as playful voices, the polyphony of voices that Bakhtin argues sometimes fill a novel.[168] An example of a different kind of playful "voice" to the human voice using the spoken word in public dialogue was the advertisement. The rest of this chapter and indeed subsequent chapters in this study will show by example how the narrative as a whole uses a polyphony of voices to sustain a performance of disinterested play in perpetual motion and in the agonistic mode.

Conservative novelists who insist on the intrinsic link between character and motive exploit linear time in such a way as to show up that so-called intrinsic link. Henry James's rhetorical statement in the essay "The Art of Fiction," to the effect that character and incident are beautifully and inextricably linked, needs to be quoted here as a reminder, for his view was influential and still is: "What is character but the determination of incident? what is incident but the illustration of character?" (55).[169] A narrative is punctured by incidents that allow characters to reveal motives that express desires in the present for absent, but anticipated, satisfactions in the future. In constructing such a narrative, a novelist reveals that s/he adheres to a belief in a teleological philosophy of existence. Every action expresses meaning in itself and a series of actions contributes to the overall sense of the "meaningful" essence of a person's character. Meaning is intrinsic to action as purpose is intrinsic to existence. Canetti has made a public contribution to this debate in *Das Augenspiel*, stressing that his concern in *Die Blendung* was with the creation of figures, not characters, and stressing that he was influenced by Gogol in this respect (*AS*, 40). To date only Adrian Stevens has taken up Canetti's lead.[170] Needless to say, the majority of critics talk about Peter Kien, Therese, Fischerle, and Benedikt Pfaff as if they were characters. In the course of this study, reference will be made to both terms, to character and figure, on the grounds that this critic feels that the vitality of the sentences dedicated to either Peter Kien, Therese, Fischerle, or Benedikt Pfaff is such as to make a strict separation of the terms impossible. We should, nevertheless, also bear in mind the qualification made above about the extraordinarily suprapersonal quality of the prose Canetti uses.

The possibilities open to a novelist who rejects the conservative theory of narration and its underlying conservative philosophy of existence are varied. On the one hand, if each incident in a novel has no causal link with, or relation to, any other incident in the novel, precisely because characters are not credited with any motives or purposes with respect to the future, representation of character might appear chaotic. Character in experimental novels based on the idea that there is no ultimate purpose and no such thing as meaning, might appear as Docherty described it, which is to say in terms of moments of being in a vacuum, and without any meaning. The experience of reading experimental novels could plausibly be argued to be, in some sense, an exercise for the reader in experiencing the fragility and vulnerability of existence."Character" would always be a relatively fragile and vulnerable construct, even if the spirit of the character were intense in itself.

If a novelist rejects a conservative theory of narration, s/he is clearly not simply left to opt for the latter alternative. S/he does not only have to either inject characters with a momentary intensity of being or present them as already defeated by the challenge of life, thought to be without intrinsic purpose. It follows, however, from the rejection of the conservative theory of narration and the philosophical assumptions on which it is based, that the novel is liberated from a conservative fixation on character and motive altogether. The novel becomes the sum-total of its many individual units, individual sentences, that are either linked together at a deep semantic level or semantically severed from one another entirely. Its constituent parts are no longer human characters whose "essences" or "moments of being" are created and understood by the reader after a lapse of time, and as a result of an effort made by the reader to abstract him-self/herself from the narrative proper. If character is demoted altogether, either in the conservative sense, where it is identified with individual human beings who are vessels of meaning, or in the experimental sense, where the individual is a vessel of being, it follows that the sentence is less likely to be a source of meaning.

It follows from such a rejection of absolutes that the individual sentence is theoretically open to being endowed with character, in particular theatrical character. The individual sentence has to be given a *character* of its own if it is to sustain an audience at some level. Meaning will be exchanged for the dynamism that can be sustained for the duration of an individual sentence, only to expire so that a new sentence or unit of dynamism can come into being. The individual sentence becomes the whole or unit which it is the reader's task to appreciate. If it is not a source of meaning in the absolute sense, if it does not produce a kind of idea that could be absorbed by an already established disourse, its own potential will be released, namely its theatrical character, which will become prominent. This change in priorities is one that will require that a reader enjoy rather than understand the sentence. As *the* constituent part of the novel as a whole the sentence is clearly also liberated to "be" a disinterested moment of play. The narrative becomes composed of a series of moments of disinterested play, and the individual sentence one voice among many other voices.

It can be shown that this highly original theory of the way in which a novelist can sustain his/her reader's interest is applied to brilliant effect to *Die Blendung*. It is, as a theory, in part original because it clearly suggests that the reader will not need to exercise his/her intellectual/analytical skills when reading. It suggests that the reader will be required to use his/her stamina, since every new sentence will be a challenge. Since thought and meaning are not allowed to figure, let alone coincide, all that will be required of the reader is a capacity to concentrate. Reading will not be an exercise in acquiring meaning or reflecting on "truth" or a variety of "truths," but an exercise in sharpening one's wits and improving one's stamina. As units of self-contained experience in themselves, which, when placed side by side, resist those semantic interrelations which the character-motive link automatically gives them, such sentences relate to one another at a purely non-semantic level. It can be argued that what Canetti does in *Die Blendung* is to inject a spirit, rather than ideas, into individual sentences, animating self-contained sentences with theatricality itself, a self-conscious delight at having unconditional faith in the future.

If it can be shown that *Die Blendung* is constructed in this way, it presents us with a highly self-conscious and, indeed, overwhelming counter-argument to the very legitimate and plausible objections concerning the desire for meaning and purpose always voiced by the conservatives, who either find experimental novels disturbing or turn so venomously on the so-called fatuousness of the idea of the free play of the signifier, of post-structuralist criticism generally, Derrida and Lyotard in particular. Tony Nuttall, Christopher Prendergast, and Raymond Tallis, to name but three prominent voices, are all aghast, for some quite brilliant reasons, at the possibility that the contract between reader and text guaranteed by mimesis is being carelessly jettisoned by a fashionable movement, and on ultimately questionable grounds.[171] Their general objection to the rejection of mimesis in favor of the so-called free play of the signifier is an objection motivated by the desire to show off the superiority of mimetic literature and its apparently sound intellectual and human credentials. None of the three critics pauses to reflect imaginatively on the serious intellectual pretentions of playful literature. Play is simply the enemy. It becomes necessary, therefore, to begin by defending play in literature theoretically first, and here without recourse to the involved arguments of the post-structuralists.

It does not and cannot necessarily follow that an interest in play has to exclude any seriousness about the conduct of life. But Tony Nuttall, Christopher Prendergast, and Raymond Tallis have identified play as the enemy of mainstream European liberal humanism. It is felt to be intellectually bankrupt in its apparently vacuous, and humiliating, acceptance of the nothingness of life without purpose or higher meaning, as an oblique statement of a profound nihilism, a jettisoning of the very serious business of thinking and reflecting critically on the way we live, a ruining of the sacred truths *in its cavalier hatred of epistemological and ontological security.* Such arguments can only be countered by the example of a narrative where play is taken seriously in the first place, and where play is not synonymous with intellectual bankruptcy, where the critical instincts are in effect shown to be actually kept alert and stimulated by the sense of play.

Disinterested play, the kind of play we find in *Die Blendung*, is animated by something like a theatrical spirit of *faith in the future*. It is arguable that most people accept privately that this attitude of confidence in the future or commitment to the future is the basis of any contract likely to provide a platform for critique and the likelihood of change in society, the ultimate value of mimetic literature in Prendergast's view.[172] This investment in the future does not just rescue the novel from the charge of nihilism associated with play. As an *enactment*, as opposed to an *imitation*, of the principle of play inherent in agon, *Die Blendung* is also a positive libertarian statement of faith in life per se. It does not prescribe the kinds of life styles, or lives, worth imitating. It knows that what is important is not what you do but how you do it, and it insists that you have to do it with absolute commitment. *Die Blendung* is, therefore, not a prescriptive statement in favor of affirmation of a particular kind of philosophy of life, but a spiritual one, in favor of affirmation of life as a general outlook.

This theory can begin to be understood if we turn to look at how the narrative moves on *after* Therese's formulation of pleasure at the prospect of her interview, her début in public examined above. In the actual interview, Kien presents Therese with a list of tasks: "'Ihr Pflichtenkreis,' sagte er ernst und trocken. 'Täglich wird ein Zimmer von oben bis unten gestaubt. Am vierten Tag sind Sie fertig. Am fünften beginnen Sie wieder mit dem ersten. Können Sie das übernehmen?'" (*DB*,26) Therese relies on two statements: "Ordnung muß sein" and "Ich bin so frei," when responding to her prospective employer. As such, her contributions are absolutely devoid of any overt signs of personality in the grand sense, although the coy precision of the two just cited is formidably personable in its own way. Peter Kien issues her a series of orders. He does not ask her questions or set up a genuine dialogue. We must conclude, therefore, that the exchanges are manifestly insubstantial in themselves. In not including a scene in which Kien subjects Therese to the tests with which we might associate the person who is seriously worried about the quality of a potential employee, and in presenting her with a list of her tasks as a *fait accompli*, as if she had already got the job, Canetti proves that he does not want to take the conventional idea of the search for an employee very seriously. By the same token, in not including a scene in which Therese is granted the opportunity to present herself as personable in the grand sense, Canetti proves that he does not want to endorse personality in the grand sense too seriously. But it is more than this. The giving of the job to Therese when she has explicitly done nothing to warrant this choice/decision does not "show" that Kien is a fool or that Therese is a gold-digger. Although the event happens for no objective "reason" *within* the linear flow of the narrative, Kien and Therese have positively succeeded in sustaining our attention because a certain kind of stylishness has animated their various performances. Their performances were stylish inasmuch as they were animated by an affirmative and assertive spirit. Their performances are not evidence that both are objectively foolish or greedy. They cannot be classified according to such standards, because the exuberance of their verbal contributions when they are in control or center-stage is so compelling.

Canetti has clearly, in so doing, manipulated the narrative to argue two very important and interrelated points. He argues, negatively so to speak, that a referential or transcendental level of reality outside the text simply does not exist. Objective truth and experience are relatively insignificant. He argues, positively so to speak, that stylish performance in public, where stylish performance means affirmative speaking, can be invigorating enough in its own right to sustain the attention of those who are listening. But he also argues that speaking can be invigorating in its own right, only if and when verbal contributions are not delivered in such a way as to exert positive pressure on other potential speakers or manipulate other potential speakers to respond in kind. It is only invigorating if each contributor takes responsibility for what s/he wants to say without attempting to manipulate others to share a given point of view. Speaking is, after all, quite obviously *not* integrated into the narrative in such a way as to promote dialogue. It is not integrated to promote dialogue so that the above ideological points are given a certain kind of humorous prominence.[173]

This is not a valorization of the monologue, nor a valorization of the rhetorical force associated with the orator or demagogue who might actually believe that his audience is composed of intellectually inferior subordinates. Nor is it a patronizing or bored form of indifference to the possibility of invigorating dialogue or exchanges of note and of substance. Nor does it necessarily mean that trivia or meaninglessness as such is valorized. Neither is it a comment on the kind of vacuous conversation one comes across at social gatherings. Finally, and above all, the above cannot be read as evidence that individuals in the text are hermetically sealed within their own imaginative worlds, and incapable of communicating with other human beings, a heretical view indeed given the near-consensus there is amongst *Die Blendung* critics that in this novel is presented a thoroughgoing analysis of the human cost of failure in terms of meaningful communication.

The spoken contributions here are void of substantial meaning and are delivered with affirmative enthusiasm, such that they paradoxically draw our attention, on reflection, to some very sophisticated theories of talk indeed. They draw our attention to the very kinds of conversation likely to generate tolerance at large, to promote both community and communication. The interesting combination of positive meaninglessness and powerful positive energy draws attention to a space that is always left untarnished throughout the novel, the distance that is necessary if real respect for the absolute autonomy of others is to be enshrined in social intercourse. For in excluding meaningful exchanges from the narrative, the narrative affirms a number of unusual ideological points. Firstly, that there is such a thing as the ritual or the democratic formality of allowing people to speak in turn. Secondly, that the individual has a desire to make a contribution and thus a "right" to make a contribution. Thirdly, that it is much more important to stress the right of the individual to make a contribution than to evaluate the contribution itself—thus, in *Die Blendung*, the obvious point that a contribution is *never* either refuted or positively endorsed by another speaker in the course of any "conversation." Fourthly, that there will always be a certain kind of approval of the capacity of an individual character, and an individual sentence, to inject confidence, authority, and faith into the contributions s/he makes.

The narrative, in equating teleology with an attitude of faith, seems to be saying that no one person has any right to impose specific views. This is a way of arguing that your right to speak must take precedence over your ability to present a particular point of view. Most importantly, this is a way of arguing that one must not approach a subject, or come to a conversation, with *preconceived* ideas. The play of ideas that comes from taking part in a conversation where no one person has a right to dominate and provide meaningful ideas is in fact likely to generate really worthwhile thought. *The narrative draws attention to this ideal in its systematic exclusion of the ideal at the level of the literal content of words, and in its systematic inclusion of the spirit of play most likely to ensure that genuine dialogue be able to exist in the first place.* In so doing, it also lays the foundations for the respect that is necessary if substantial exchanges are to take place. We are, as readers of *Die Blendung*, being schooled in this sophisticated theory of conversation, specifically inasmuch as *we* are *not* allowed to test out any preconceived ideas of how a character might behave when we read the interview or any other section of the novel. By the end of the interview nothing has been proven. We are not allowed to luxuriate in the feeling of power and strength that often comes when people think that they already have as much knowledge of motives and characters as they need. We are not allowed to luxuriate in the feeling that we no longer need to be vigilant. After all, Therese gets the job, in narrative terms, only because she is given the job.

Character has been demoted altogether as a legitimate construct by this event alone. Canetti has explicitly not engineered an interview in which either character puts anything to the test. For instance, in making Therese positively ask about money at the end of the interview, Canetti does not refute those expectations of character raised by the narrative at an earlier stage. In making Kien reply in a way that explicitly contradicts the stress on the insignificance of salary made by the advertisement earlier on, and in allowing Therese to have as much money as she wants, Canetti stresses his desire to transform all material into an amusing narrative. This is amusing in large part for us because it does not take itself seriously, and is perpetually alive with a sense of free or disinterested play. Neither character shows any interest in voicing the world view with which s/he had been associated before. In not engineering those "experiences" that would have shown off that world view to effect, Canetti makes it absolutely clear that he is simply not interested in making either of his characters conform to expectations of behavior that they themselves had raised at an earlier point. He is interested in making *his narrative* a form of disinterested play that demands of the reader the vigilance and humility necessary to the view that always assumes that nothing has been won, and that everything has yet to be won. The narrative is a characterization, by example, of the virtue of critical openness.

By the end of the "interview," therefore, we can say that the "interview" is a travesty in itself of what interviews are commonly thought to be if measured by those fairly flexible standards of plausibility that operate in our minds when reading, no matter how willing we are to surrender ourselves wholeheartedly to the imaginative world of the novel we are reading. We can say that it has defied the expectations Kien had of a potential employee, thus demoting intentionality. It has defied the expectations set up by Therese when she seemed to plan at home her strategy for presenting herself as exceptionally personable, thus also demoting intentionality. It has proven by example that character is superbly resistant to meaning. Those "characters" called Kien and Therese are not meaningful in terms of what they want. They are in fact centers of assertive energy, or beings animated by the desire to live fully in the present. Exposure to Kien and Therese in the course of the interview does not help us to build up a picture of who these individuals "are." The interview tells us nothing more about them. They are not people with a range of qualities.

From this, we should conclude that Canetti respects human beings. He refuses to allow fictional people to be exploited in any way, and for any apparently higher purpose. The attitude that a person is a particular quality or collection of qualities is a reductive, repressive attitude. It trains people to erect obstacles to potentially exciting encounters, for it trains people to assume that everything is a foregone conclusion. It actively kills energy, because preconceived ideas concerning somebody's essential character suffocate a natural spirit for play. So whilst events in the novel take place in time in an order, *no one thing positively leads to another in any strictly logical way*. This must be understood as wilful refutation of the reader's expectations by the author. It should also be understood as a way of making the following, major existential points: that it is folly to expect that life adhere to or conform to incontrovertible laws of logic (outside time and space), whether of character, of human purpose, or of human existence; that the absolute purposelessness that follows from the collapsing of these old laws of logic is no reason to despair; that this new law of absolute purposelessness has been instated in the text at a primary level in the sense that linear time has only been allowed to prevail in the most perfunctory of ways. It is present only inasmuch as one thing takes place after another in time. This all opens up existential possibilities, because if those laws outside time and space that normally furnish a narrative with logic are dispensed with, a spirit of theatricality is born, can even reign supreme.

Clearly, to those critics who have so enthusiastically written about the failure of communication, dialogue has to be of the prosaic kind: it has to be obviously fluent at the level of an intellectual exchange of information, and at the level of sympathy for, and emotional understanding of, the unspoken purposes of speakers. This is loading the dice in a way that is fairly unimaginative, since it rules out of court play, above all, and it rules out of court the mysterious and unspoken depths of the spirit of play as a form of communication between two self-conscious players, aware of their skills. Canetti's is a knowing familiarity with a sophisticated and highly civilized notion of a different kind altogether, namely that talk is a pretext for nonverbal things such as respect for, love of, and endorsement of the other's spirit of play.

Artless theatrical behavior is expressed by and in the sentences that make up the general narrative of the interview, as it is expressed in the spaces between those sentences. The text is not an invigorating spectator sport for the reader. When we read it, we practice theatricality as a performance art ourselves. In doing so, we, as the named individuals Kien and Therese, are turned from named, fixed individuals into actors or actresses on the stage of life. We are turned into protagonists: we lose our consciousness of our selves as isolated beings and participate in a social feast. The sacred distinction between literature and life is thereby collapsed. Canetti's refutation of those "mimetic" expectations about words, language, and communication collapses all versions of purpose, yet is not achieved by his specifically singling out and then debasing any particular form of purpose, whether of character, or of motive, or of existence per se. To single out character or motive and debase either or both would be the strategy of the satirist, and Canetti's reputation is, in some quarters, that of a satirist. Canetti's refutation of the reader's expectations of the kind of sacred laws mentioned above does not throw us readers into a void of despair and does not make us feel that character or motive constitute debased kinds of currency. One of the reasons why in this study Canetti will not be categorized as a satirist, has to do with the way Canetti refuses to attach himself to concrete, historical specifics and attack them in a wilfully destructive way, as Swift and Voltaire do.

Instead, Canetti ensures that his readers do not have to adopt the stance of the oppositional fighter to identifiable social evils, by ensuring that his pleasure is, in the course of the interview, satisfied in a different way precisely because something *unexpected*, something *surprising*, happens, something we positively did not expect to happen. Unusual connections, as Koestler argued, are often what cause humor, that release of physical energy that often expresses itself in physical laughter. One cannot claim, in some prescriptive way, that any of the examples of sentences from *Die Blendung* already examined necessarily have to provoke laughter in the reader. This may happen, depending on the capacity for laughter already built into any given reader, of course. The value of the excursion into the psychology of humor embarked upon at the beginning of this chapter lies in the way in which theories stressed the importance of tension, in particular its diffusion in laughter, which was thought to bring *freedom from* certain pressures, to collapse laws that would otherwise pertain. Laughter was valued by the psychologists of humor examined above for the way in which it brought a positive benefit to the individual in the sense of destroying fear and piety before objects deemed to be serious in more ordinary circumstances. It brought temporary respite from power structures.

This critic has laughed out loud many a time reading *Die Blendung*. It has also been established (unscientifically) that this is the case, generally speaking, amongst so-called unprofessional readers. Yet no one laughs the whole time. One does not have the feeling that Canetti is trying to suspend time in some way. The argument developing here is one that will reveal that laughter, which neither I nor Canetti is in a position to prescribe anyway, while it is often a response to an individual clash between two individual sentences, is *secondary* to that agonistic drive toward the future already discussed. The agonistic drive of the narrative preserves a certain kind of tension. It does not dissolve tension, and thus has more in common with the ideas of Baudelaire and De Man on self-reflexive consciousness, or cosmic irony in particular, than with those of the psychologists who stressed laughter in terms of relief. It is probably what Hesse and Ferber meant when they mentioned the quality of "Spannung" in the novel.

Finally, and above all, the significance of the systematic insistence on the agonistic mode lies in the way in which such a mode assumes, not that one is capable of being free from, but that the creative capacity for expression is one that it is always *possible* to stimulate and endow with form: one is always free *to be* creative. Freedom is not a right, neither is it a privilege, neither is it something you experience when you momentarily turn your back on power structures that are otherwise fully considered to be there and to be powerful: it is the exhiliration of realizing that you are always free to be creative. It looks squarely at the future, and it always creates that imaginative space necessary for further play. In place of the almighty stress on *having* rights or privileges, so characteristic of our culture, as Erich Fromm would no doubt see it, on escaping from *having to have* material pressures, Canetti seems to be saying loud and clear that the point is that it is always possible to take responsibility for life, by being creative.[174] So we can now begin to argue against those critics examined above who were worried about the impotence of ludic play, those who maintained that ludic play could not be ideologically subversive. To entertain such a view is to assume that ideology corrupts, that so-called instrumental reason, as Foucault and Horkheimer would have it, works insidiously to undermine our capacity for genuinely free and empowering action. Canetti is not saying, "Be creative *in opposition* to that which is already given in the secular world," as do Bakhtin and all those critics who see the power of the secular world at work in a way that is destructive of the individual. Instead of opposing the power of the secular world, Canetti is saying, "Imagine it's not even there in the first place!" By an act of imagination it is possible, he seems to be saying, to be creative, to *create ex nihilo.*

There is a huge difference between the two positions. Those who start with the assumption that the world out there is powerful, and does intrude into the imaginative world of the individual, compromising his/her status as a free agent, are at odds with Canetti's position, which wishes, in full consciousness, to start out with the denial of that world, in the full knowledge that this is a significant act in terms of the power individuals gain as a result of this act of denial. Ideologically speaking, Canetti's premise translates into a strategy for survival on competitive terms. According to this view, Canetti's writing requires of the individual vigilant, hard work, requires that the individual produce his text at every single moment: it thus imitates the need for vigilance in the extra-textual world. Here we are not talking about the reader as author of the text in the vague way described by Docherty: Canetti's readers have to work very hard when they read, because of the canny way in which Canetti preserves a tension. Those theories of humor examined above, by contrast, and those critics who were worried about the impotence of ludic play, were persuaded that the *work* had *already* been done, by the *writer* of a scene deemed funny. The laughing person is merely a spectator, apparently freed of the need to be creative himself/herself. S/he could just take time off and have a good laugh *at* something. Canetti's theory, a fully democratic one by contrast, is that there is no distinction between actors and spectators. We should all be actors and players, he is saying, and no one should pause to become a spectator and luxuriate in the sense of the "false" freedom provided by the dissolution of tension which is laughter. When we do laugh, we laugh with the spirit of the sentence, and since this sentence has not allowed us to construct any kind of analytical ideas, there is nothing to laugh at. It might seem weird to be suggesting this, when we have been examining an interview scene, a scene that obviously has some resonance in terms of the already given, and as a ritual associated with the power of institutions in the secular world. But Canetti has reinvented the interview, has effectively destroyed its claim to be a power structure only working in the interests of those who already have power concentrated in their hands, such as interviewers. We are pleased, and not disappointed, by the end of the interview, because we have learned to realize that the human capacity for self-invention *ex nihilo* is stronger than we knew. The theatrical character of the individual sentences spoken by Therese and by Kien throughout the interview suggest that personality can defy the possible power of institutions, since personality reveals itself to be creative *ex nihilo*. This power, injected so categorically into those individual sentences that made up the dialogue of the interview, was theatrical, and it was the theatricality that sustained those sentences.

We cannot say that the theatricality is sustained at a secondary level in the sentences that are then provided by the narrator, those sentences that appear to frame the primary dialogue. The theatricality of those sentences happens to be of the same order as the theatricality of the sentences that make up public speech. Theatricality is thus sustained throughout the narrative generally. The narrative puts on a performance of theatricality. Theatricality is not incidental to some major incident in which characters display their qualities as characters. It is the substance of the narrative. Again, this is admirably described by what Darby calls the spirit of contagion. The general quality of exuberance and theatricality, or delight in the *imprévu*, is much more important than the notion of the so-called logic of character, indeed of character per se. The spirit of the feast is far more important than the individual protagonists in that feast. They contribute to the feast, but the feast, in order to be a feast, depends on the participation of more voices than those that can be housed within two individual characters.

Die Blendung teaches us an interesting lesson in this respect. Characters, who act as if they have no motives with respect to the future and who have no *genuine sense of purpose* with respect to the future, succeed in injecting the energy we associate with purpose into everything and anything they say in the present. "Ordnung muß sein," for instance, is exemplary in this respect. As a sentence, the sentence is abrupt, unconditional, and beautifully meaningless. Yet it is delivered *as if* it were a richly meaningful statement. The energy of abruptness and unconditionality is harnessed to a particular goal, that of obvious meaninglessness. This combination finds itself repeated in all other sentences in the surrounding text, not just those spoken by Therese and by Kien, but in those sentences that purport to deal with what goes on when the spoken voice does not dominate. Canetti has *not* relied on the teleological force that comes from the conservative notion of motive, commonly thought to endow character and action with meaning. Neither does his novel have teleological momentum because characters have experiences of moments of being as ends in themselves. Nevertheless, *Die Blendung* seems to be driven by an intense teleological motor. What has already been said should have made clear that this teleological momentum has nothing in common with those teleological metanarratives constructed by critics. The teleological momentum can be accounted for, if one reflects on the character of individual sentences in the novel. Each one is given an intensely well-defined character of its own. As Therese's sentence, "Ordnung muß sein," showed, however, there is a distinction that must be made between the spirit of the statement and the content of the statement. The spirit is the spirit of assertiveness and of affirmation. Yet the statement reveals nothing in terms of a conventional expectation that meaning, in order to be meaning, must be pretentious in some way. Her statement is one of the great platitudes, which contributes nothing to the desire or search for meaning. The character of the sentence is its formidable positive energy. Its causal effect on the proceedings cannot be measured, since it does not contain any thought or idea that could be "used" by someone keen to participate in some kind of discussion or conversation. The effect of what she says has to be limited because her sentence is positively not a repository of meaning in the pretentious sense. We can say here that the character of the sentence serves a purpose only in that it communicates a sense of theatricality, and *to the reader, not to characters within the empirical text*. It achieves nothing, in the sense that it positively refuses to allow itself to be absorbed into some metanarrative of meaning: it is resistant to exploitation for gain. We will find now that the novel is not primarily sustained by individual characters. It is primarily sustained by the drive in each individual sentence. It is this unique marriage that saves the novel from falling into the abyss of total relativity or nihilism, that option always open to novelists who do not accept a conservative theory of narration and its correspondingly conservative philosophy of existence, even when they are capable of injecting assertiveness into the moments of being of character as such. It is this unique marriage that prevents readers from suffering from the radical ontological insecurity with which some experimental theories of narration have come to be associated.

If we return now to the nature of the link between the advertisement, Therese's reaction to it, and the "interview" that ensues, we can see that the logic that links the three together is the logic of absolute non-logic. It is the logic of the chain reaction. In place of the conventional "telos" that animates human utterances and actions in the conventional novel, and that governs the wider context within which those human utterances and actions take place, where action in the present undertaken by a character has to be associated with the pursuit of future gain (commonly known as the motive, whether conscious or subconscious), every human utterance in *Die Blendung* is only a reaction in the present to something that somebody else has just said or done. In *Die Blendung*, therefore, the future does not determine the future in any specific sense: but confidence in the future gives confidence in the present.

The theatricality of the advertisement and Therese's reaction also read, therefore, as deliciously "self-conscious" performances of purposelessness, which we enact ourselves when we read the novel. Indeed, all the sentences that make up the novel seem to need, quite desperately, to be read out loud. That disjunction between reader and text, which is normally effected by a novelist when s/he consciously uses a particularly alien kind of obviously poetic or obviously literary language in his/her text, does not apply here. Canetti's language is nearly void of all the professional literary tropes, such as metaphor, symbol, and oxymoron, taken from formal rhetoric. His language is not the language one feels one's way into, savors in one's imagination, and deconstructs in order to discover the original "meaning" behind the range of literary tropes so common in obviously literary novels. Canetti's language is the language of the word spoken out loud, not for rhetorical effect, not because of a desire to convince an audience to accept a particular point of view, but to show up a commitment to a highly sociable mode of existence, in which everything conspires to create the world of disinterested play in a thoroughly sociable context. The reader is an ear witness and a speaker. The reader is not a listener and a private thinker.

As suggested above, this theory is based on the positive suppression of linear time. We will find that all individual sentences in the novel constitute something of a challenge to time itself. The present moment becomes the sentence and this is exploited vigorously as if it deserved to be taken seriously on its own terms, as a single moment, dissociated from linear time altogether, with all that that dissociation means in terms of its obvious rejection of the greedy and selfish notion of pursuing long-term ends, and only ever agreeing to do things for what one might get out of them, in material terms.

Although we have only spoken about the advertisement and its effects so far, it can be shown that it is not just individual reactions or individual actions that espouse what is obviously beginning to emerge as something of a provocative philosophy of life, a highly challenging reworking of the ancient Greek view of hedonism. Every single sentence in the novel is itself theatrically aware of what it means to put on a purposeful performance in the full knowledge that existential purposefulness is a waste of time. The particular character of the moment in Canetti's novel is the particular character of each individual sentence. Each single sentence, because of its extreme aggressivity and because of its artful wilfulness devoid of true purpose, reads as a kind of homage to the individualistic notion of intelligent pleasure which places performance at a premium and casts any kind of interest in reward or long-term gain firmly aside, as if it were vulgar to a degree.

This philosophy got off to a bad start in the novel, where Peter Kien's words in chapter one were too full of intent harnessed to purpose and gain. He positively wanted to win over the young boy to his vision of life. The incidents above with the advertisement and with Therese show how delightful the playing out of this philosophy is *as a highly serious game* with certain fairly strict rules. This will become clearer as we look at the general style of writing of chapter two as a whole, an example of which will suffice here to open up the terms of the argument:

> Therese hatte sich gerade bemüht, in den gestärkten Rock, mit dem sie ihre Toilette beschloß, hineinzufinden, als der Lärm begann. Sie erschrak zu Tode, band sich den Rock provisorisch fest und glitt eilig an die Tür des Arbeitzimmers. "Um's Himmels willen," klagte sie, eine Flöte, "was ist geschehen?" Sie klopfte erst schüchtern, dann immer lauter. Da sie keine Antwort bekam, suchte sie zu öffnen, vergeblich. Sie glitt von Tür zu Tür. Im letzten Zimmer hörte sie ihn selbst, wie er zornig rief. Hier hämmerte sie mit aller Kraft. "Ruhe!" schrie er böse, so böse war er noch nie. Halb aufgebracht, halb resigniert ließ sie die harten Hände auf den harten Rock sinken und erstarrte zu einer Holzpuppe. "So ein Unglück!" flüsterte sie, "so ein Unglück!" und stand, mehr aus Gewohnheit, noch da, als er öffnete. (*DB*, 31)[175]

In the above passage, Therese reacts to the noise coming from Kien's library. Similar to those sentences cited above in the advertisement, in Therese's reaction to the advertisement, and in the interview itself, the sentences that make up this paragraph are short, abrupt, and unconditional. They are superbly unliterary, and they refuse absolutely, as did those cited above, to be absorbed or harmonize into a metanarrative beyond their own confines. There is no musicality in this kind of prose, for instance, and there is certainly no kind of lyricism. Like his hero Stendhal, Canetti clearly tries to aspire to some level of absolute rationality in his prose. He writes with the systematic authority of someone who believes that the world can be broken down into small units of absolute and incontrovertible form. But what is the nature of this rationality, and in what sense can one say that the paragraph is composed of units of reason? The paragraph is composed of affirmative statements which tell us what Therese did physically in response to the stimulant sound. Emotions appear to be the subject of the passage. Sentences attribute emotions to Therese. She was shocked to death by the sound in the first instance, glides down the corridor as if she were in a hurry, laments what is happening by resorting to one of her small array of superb platitudes, is timid when she knocks on the door, is resigned, etc. But are these responses taken *seriously* as genuine emotions of fear and fright? The style of writing prevents the reader from entering sympathetically or empathetically into a possible mood or emotion of fear and fright, because the attributed reactions of fear and fright are talked about as if they were detached, executive actions that take place one after the other with no pause for the experience of fear or fright itself. The list of reactions does not read as a re-creation of any of the suppleness and flexibility with which we associate something as intangible as a feeling. If this is the case, must we accuse Canetti of failing to take emotions seriously, or must we see the above as a kind of malicious satire on the stupidity of such emotions in the first place? Or more ambitiously, as critics have already done, must we see this kind of writing as an attempt at imitating "mimetically" what it is like to act as a human automaton? The manifest disjunction between what is being said and that absent level (here, of emotion) to which what is said is supposed to refer us, is so totally obvious that the tension results in the reader's finding himself or herself obliged to laugh. The tension is an overtly comic one which is not fuelled by some kind of animus with respect to the emotions, but by its own delight at its own ability to sustain the tension of tension as an end in itself.

We have above another wonderful example of that exhilarating marriage between positive intent and absolute meaninglessness, that marriage which is necessary if the text is to be received as disinterested play. After all, in the sentences that make up the above paragraph there is considerable energy throughout, the energy of unconditional absolutism, the energy one tends to want to associate with conviction and faith and purpose. Yet it is injected into sentences that, when analyzed, prevent us from believing that some level of meaning has been reached beyond the immediate. Energy is injected into sentences as if they contained meaningful essences. Yet analysis of the potential essence or meaning of a sentence reveals that there is absolute meaninglessness. The sentences refuse to really acknowledge that the experience of fear is a genuine one, that the experience of fear is something that genuinely exists and can genuinely be imitated. Finally, there is the delight at not allowing anything meaningful to actually happen. After all, Therese reacts, but her reactions do not lead to any meaningful action.

In a passage a little further on, Canetti exploits tension in a way that, if not representative of the narrative as a whole, is enough of a feature of the narrative to warrant particular attention. Canetti's fascination with the single voice of the text causes him, for instance, to slip from one tense into another without formal justification in terms of character:

> Wenn er fiel und sich was tat, war das Laster zu Ende. Thereseens Arm hob sich, er ließ sich nicht mehr meistern; er griff nach ihrem Ohr und zupfte es kräftig. Mit beiden Augen glotzte sie auf den gefährdeten Herrn. Als seine Füße den dicken Teppich erreichten, atmete sie auf. Die Bücher sind ein Schwindel. Das Richtige kommt erst. Sie kennt die Bibliothek genau, aber Laster macht erfinderisch. Es gibt Opium, es gibt Morphium, es gibt Kokain, wer kann sich das alles merken? Sie läßt sich nichts weismachen. Hinter den Büchern steckt es. Warum zum Beispiel geht er nie quer durch das Zimmer? Er steht bei der Leiter und will was vom Regal genau gegenüber. Er könnte es sich einfach holen, aber nein, er geht immer schön an der Wand entlang. Mit der schweren Tasche unterm Arm macht er den großen Umweg. Hinter den Büchern steckt es. Den Mörder zieht es an die Mordstelle. Jetzt ist die Tasche voll. Es geht nichts mehr hinein, sie kennt die Tasche, sie staubt sie täglich aus. Jetzt muß was geschehen. Es ist doch nicht schon sieben? Wenn es sieben ist, geht er weg. Aber wo ist es sieben? Es darf nicht sieben sein.
>
> Frech und sicher beugt sie den Oberkörper vor, stemmt die Arme in die Seiten, spitzt die flachen Ohren und reißt die schmalen Augen gierig auf. Er packt die Tasche an zwei Enden und legt sie fest auf den Teppich. Sein Gesicht sieht stolz aus. Er bückt sich und bleibt gebückt. Sie ist in Schweiß gebadet und zittert am ganzen Körper. Die Tränen kommen ihr, also doch unterm Teppich. Sie hat sich's gleich gedacht. Wie man so dumm sein kann. Er richtet sich auf, knackst mit den Knochen

> und spuckt aus. Oder hat er nur "so" gesagt? Er greift nach der Tasche, nimmt einen Band heraus und führt ihn langsam an seinen Platz zurück. Dasselbe macht er mit allen andern. (*DB*, 33)[176]

At the beginning of this passage Canetti uses the preterite, in a sentence that qualifies as narrated monologue. Therese is thinking to herself about the possible consequences of a fall of Kien's in the library. We then pass to another of those sentences in which a physical action is recorded as if it were an executive decision. She scratches her ear and then glares at her boss. Thereafter the tense of narration changes to the present. Again and again in the novel when this slipping into a different tense takes place, the effect is to increase the dramatic pace of the narration. It is not a literary technique exploited for mimetic reasons, which is to say, to comment on the pace of the imagination of the character to whom the ideas are credited. Clearly, here the ideas from "Die Bücher sind ein Schwindel" onwards, are those of Therese. They do have to be attributed to a specific character, yet the individual sentences are so absolute in their own right that, reading them, one soon forgets that they are the thoughts of one particular character. One reads them as a series of thoughts, period. One finds oneself absorbed by their own dynamism to the extent that one merges with their spirit and suspends one's belief, in the process, in those supposedly holistic constructs, such as character.

Interestingly, this passage is hardly a training in ontological insecurity. Superficially, we appear to be "adopting" Therese's perspective as she speculates that a crime has taken place on the premises. But this is, again, hardly a serious imitation of what it feels like to be fearful in the face of genuine evidence that something criminal has happened. Canetti refuses to allow us the luxury of starting with genuine evidence, as he refuses to grant us the attendant luxury of being allowed to construct a convincing series of reasons to account for the phenomenon of the crime. At no point are we allowed to feel that there is a genuine point of departure for these suppositions, which could be invoked as some kind of reference point. So what we begin to do is merge with the spirit of Therese's observations, which is the spirit of anticipation, theatrically experienced. It becomes necessary to part company, therefore, with those critics who see the above as evidence of Therese's madness, of her capacity to allow her fantasy to dominate her personality to the exclusion of all else. The tense change is justified only because Canetti privileges dramatic narration over character. This kind of slipping is not a problem in terms of the reader's ontological insecurity. On the contrary, one is contagiously taken by the spirit of play, and feels ontologically very secure.

The momentum of the above is, after all, highly amusing because it is *laconic* to a degree, a rare achievement in prose, generally speaking. Canetti's prose is not the prose of panic and fear. It is far too accurate, far too slow, and far too level-headed. A state of tension is, yes, brilliantly maintained, but it is not the tension of the emotions of genuine fear and panic. The momentum is never allowed to increase in pace or get out of control, for instance. And incidents continually puncture any sign that a goal is in sight, in terms of truth or knowledge or decisive action. For instance, what is the point of Therese's scratching her ear at the beginning of the paragraph? What is the point of her glaring at her boss? What is the point of her suddenly remembering that it is almost seven o'clock? In fact, absolutely nothing of import is actually happening. Even when, once again, Canetti tries to suggest that the emotion is intense or intensifying, something interrupts the potential drama: the best laconic example in the above passage concerns her sweating and trembling and crying: "Sie ist in Schweiß gebadet und zittert am ganzen Körper. Die Tränen kommen ihr, also doch unterm Teppich" (*DB*, 33). Kien is supposedly looking under the carpet and it is her relief that he has located something that suddenly calls to a halt the anxiety implied by tears. By the end of the chapter, we are no clearer as to what on earth has been going on. The reason for this is quite straightforward. Nothing has been going on. There is an absolute disjunction between the spirit of the sentences that make up the above passage and the potential for referential meaning commonly credited to language. The character of each sentence is assertive. Yet sentence after sentence resists integration into the kind of larger whole that would infuse each sentence with meaning. The sentences are devoid of consoling semantic interrelations. Nothing is happening, nothing is being achieved, nobody wants to achieve or do anything. And nobody tries to do or achieve anything, either. As readers we are participating in the construction of illusion, of a subjective fiction, and we are doing this in the heroic, Nietzschean tradition, in the full knowledge that living in the "as if" mode does not mean that I have to be able to prove why it is I have chosen to do things this particular way and not that. The equation in the tradition of mimesis that the "as if" mode has to be able to justify itself in terms of the already given, in terms of the material, is one that is actively refuted. The "as if" mode justifies itself in terms of effects on the subjective individual's internal strength and his/her capacity to survive given that strength, which is to say on his/her own terms.

4

Agon's Carnival: Laughter and Play in *Die Blendung* (2)

In the last chapter, we began to see how it is possible to interpret Canetti's theatrically inflated narrative as radical, because of its implied attack, albeit oblique, on the need for those pretentious world views common to literature, religion, philosophy, and all the major disciplines. The world views obliquely targeted are all heavily dependent on Big Ideas, on referentiality to what self-styled radicals like to call the absent, Transcendental Signified, the so-called metaphysics of self-presence described by Derrida. We were unable to locate any kind of level of reality/meaning/seriousness beyond the individual sentences we considered, because a gap between each sentence had been created by the conscious refusal to use/exploit words to create meaningful semantic interrelations between sentences. The sentences, consistently animated not by an idea or ideas, but by the spirit of theatricality itself, thus achieved prominence as individual units on their own terms. The effect created by this unusual combination of factors was one that proclaimed, with joy, the death of metanarrative, as it also practised, and protected, the openness of space needed for any kind of respectful, effective, and enjoyable communication between speakers in a hypothetical extra-textual world. This betrays Canetti's thorough idealism about the way in which human beings can relate to one another in the community.

The empirical world of the text was limited, in material terms, to an acceptance of an easily recognizable bourgeois world. Characters in the narrative inhabit a world made up of some of the more "ordinary" rituals of bourgeois life, namely those of buying books, putting advertisements in newspapers, reading newspapers, applying for and then getting a job. These rituals were referred to, and incorporated into the narrative, but not in such a way as to suggest that they were "meaningful," since the rituals were subverted.

Evidently, Canetti does not wish to be classified as a metaphysical satirist, since the above "attack" on referentiality was not the primary subject of the narrative. The primary subject of the narrative was a particularly theatrical use of a conceptually non-referential language made up of a series of words. Individual sentences were signs that did not refer meaningfully to a meaningful, absent signifié. Canetti seemed positively fascinated by the way in which individual sentences could be given a character and a *voice* of their own, addressed to the reader in such a way as to make him/her feel compelled to read on, feel propelled forward. If dialogue between characters and the "dialogue" between any one sentence in the novel and the one that either preceeds it or follows it is not infused with a genuine rhetoric of cognition or persuasion, we have, instead, a veritable polyphony of voices. On the one hand, the polyphony of voices could be interpreted as evidence of Canetti's conservative attachment to an anthropomorphic concern, namely the whole idea of the Speaking Subject, as Julia Kristeva would have it.[177] The polyphony of voices does not require of the reader that s/he begin to develop some kind of static or dynamic relationship with a character or with characters in the narrative (these being the only two options considered by Docherty). The polyphony of voices asks that s/he enjoy the experience of not having to reflect on Truth or any kind of static essence. It asks, instead, that we learn to respect, appreciate, and, above all, participate in the art of perpetual disinterested play. This would suggest that Canetti is not a destructive anarchist who has ruined all the sacred truths, but a highly skilled subversive of a different kind and order to the subversives praised by Bakhtin and Stallybrass, for example. To focus on the ideological differences between Canetti and Bakhtin and Stallybrass, we should simply bear in mind the ideological framework within which Bakhtin and his latter-day followers work, with their stress on the ideologically subversive nature of "dialogism."

Up until now, Canetti has been associated with the dialogic principle only by those who see in his *Aufzeichnungen* evidence of the importance to the intellectual thinker who deals in concepts and thought of "talking" to oneself. Canetti obviously concurs in this view of the intellectual, for his own article, "Dialog mit dem grausamen Partner" (1965), shows how much he relishes the exercise, as it were, of keeping himself imaginatively alive by challenging himself about his own ideas.[178] Both critics and Canetti himself, therefore, have only identified the dialogic principle with intellectual thinking and thus abstract Ideas. The dialogic principle as Bakhtin understands it has been misused, one could argue, by Stefan Kaszynski, in "Dialog und Poetik," to instate the quality of the notebooks.[179] Can the principle of dialogism usefully be extended to his only novel?

At first sight the theatricality already identified continues to be sustained in the scenes in *Die Blendung* with which this chapter will be concerned, namely those centered on the bourgeois rituals of courtship, marriage, and adultery. Once again, however, we find that the rituals are not instated seriously in the text, as if Canetti were concerned to raise their status in some way. They produce considerable laughter, inasmuch as virtually all the bourgeois conventions concerning these rituals are stood on their head. In the first place, for instance, Canetti nowhere suggests that either love or sexual desire or both lie behind the attempt by Peter Kien to conquer Therese and marry her. Courtship is reduced to a private moment, when, on his own in the library, Kien reflects on Therese's careful handling of one of his books. This results in the following, clearly chance, public address to Therese:

> "Sie sind eine nette Person."
>
> "Ich muß doch einmal schau'un, was Sie für mich ausgesucht haben," sagte sie, ihre Mundwinkel reichten schon hart bis an die Ohren. Sie schlug das Buch auf, las laut: "Die Hosen . . . ," unterbrach sich und wurde nicht rot. Ihr Gesicht bedeckte sich mit einem leichten Schweiß.
>
> "Aber ich bitt' Sie, Herr Professor!" rief sie und entglitt im schleunigsten Triumph in die Küche.
>
> Während der folgenden Tage bemühte sich Kien, in seine alte Konzentration zurückzufinden. Auch er kannte Augenblicke, in denen er seiner buchstäblichen Leistungen müde wurde und die heimliche Lust verspürte, für länger, als es ihm sein Charakter gestattete, unter Menschen zu gehen. (*DB*, 43)[180]

The book in question was referred to earlier on as *Die Hosen des Herrn von Bredow* (41). As it happens, this has referential value, since the book was written by a Willibald Alexis in 1846.[181] Kien's attitude to the book is not an intellectual one, not because the title does not suggest that the contents will be intellectual, but because he used to lend it to his chums at school and it got dirty as a result. It is because Therese handled it with such loving care that Kien was suddenly encouraged to regard her "as a person."

In the above passage, Canetti shows how he is not interested in exploiting a clearly eccentric piece of historical data concerning a book his readership will doubtless never have heard of, to any kind of effect. The mileage he gets out of including such a title is neither historical nor intellectual. The scene is also not used to show up something meaningful about Therese's "character." Instead, Canetti creates a dynamic atmosphere for the reader which allows him/her to laugh at the dynamics of sexual attraction, without either satirically debasing those dynamics or positively endorsing them. He achieves this effect by not allowing the two "protagonists" to confront one another as they well might have to in any "serious" literary study of the phenomenon of attraction. Impeccable formality is adhered to by Peter Kien in his opening gambit, as it is adhered to by Therese in her reply. Having read out only some of the title, Therese is described, once she has stopped reading, negatively. She does not blush. In other words, Canetti is playing, in a puritan as oppposed to a genuinely salacious kind of way, with the reader's expectation that she might blush because her imagination had been stimulated by the title to reflect on the crudely sexual. That she positively sweats instead instates her, quite positively, as a sexual being. Yet her flamboyant departure as she mutters yet another of her small selection of meaningless platitudes, tells us that Canetti has no interest in turning the potential for a sexual or intimate encounter into a serious intimate encounter.

It becomes apparent in what follows that there is a clear discrepancy between the responses of Therese to the encounter and Kien's response to the encounter, which suggests that there is some misogyny on the part of Canetti in this relatively theatrical "account" of courtship. Whilst Therese is clearly sexualized in a highly unattractive way, as an object, by the sentence that says she is sweating, Kien is defined rather more romantically. His "surrender" to the potential for an encounter is contextualized. With an oblique reference to Zarathustra, Canetti presents Kien as pleasingly heroic. He has been unconditionally dedicated to the life of the mind to the exclusion of any serious human involvements. Suddenly he feels the desire to be humanized or socialized, which experience woman is chosen to provide. That Canetti takes Kien more seriously in this respect, as in all other respects, is apparent in what follows in the text, which is a further investigation of his sudden impulse, at the age of sixty, to join humanity. This culminates, after a few words with his friend Confucius, during which he reflects on the relevance of some of his adages to his present situation, in the following private formulation, in what some have interpreted to be a highly reductive expression of the value of marriage and proof of the degree of Kien's absolute alienation from himself, nature, and society: "Ich werde sie heiraten! Sie ist das beste Mittel, um meine Bibliothek in Ordnung zu halten" (*DB*, 47). ("I will marry her! She is the heaven-sent instrument for preserving my library" [*AdF*, 42]). Obviously, critics like Curtius and Dissinger have taken statements like these seriously, at face value, and have assumed that we are getting to know how a character like Peter Kien suffers from personality disorders. They are offended by this statement because the formulation offends their (extra-textual) assumptions about the meaning of marriage. Those assumptions would insist on mutual love, mutual respect for the other as an individual person, mutual support, the idea that a human being is not a means but an end. Kien resolutely refuses to accept the legitimacy of any of these notions, since he equates marriage with the preservation of his beloved library. It seems, however, that it is unfair to accuse Kien of "failure" here. It would be unfair to use the above statement to support an interpretation of the novel that stresses that it is one of a series of incidents in which everything is reduced to the lowest common denominator, and where everything is exploited to sustain the defenses of a vulnerable ego. It would only be possible if one could show that all preceeding forty-seven pages of the narrative had contained incidents or actions clearly infused by a spirit of bourgeois liberal humanism.

The scenes examined in the last chapter already showed how difficult it was to take characters by the name of Kien and Therese seriously as characters. The narrative refused to make a distinction between character and action, because it privileged narration over and above causal links between character and action. The same can be said again here in reply to those who would condemn Kien. We are as far as ever from believing that Kien is a real person who might exist in an extra-textual world. We are still far from believing in the value of norms. We are as removed from the possibility of invoking an extra-textual standard of normality, only because the narrative has refused to allow us to abandon its own power and control of the reader's imagination, to reflect on normative behaviour in an extra-textual world. It prevents us from taking time off in this way by continually diverting us with ever-more suprising information and by compelling our attention to take the narrative, not an extra-textual world, seriously. In the above, it is diverting us with the manifest non-logic of a decision, taken in isolation, that has its origins in something as humorously meaningless as Therese's wrapping up a dirty book in a couple of covers. Canetti knows full well that we can enjoy the fun he is having, playing with a sacred ritual and standing it on its head.

Whilst the formulation of the decision to marry is funny because its origins are manifestly funny, it is also funny within the linear narrative, because there has been no courtship and no friendship. It is another of those incidents in the narration that is not linked up with any other incident in the narrative by the causality imposed on narrative when novelists seriously explore personality. The decision is presented as a *fait accompli* when Therese has not as yet been asked. When she is asked, she is not asked as a result of a seductive speech carefully designed to lead her to acquiescence. This kind of causality is not apparent. Once again, we become aware that linear time in the narrative is only there in the most perfunctory of ways. Things take place as events, which is to say, one event follows another. Yet there is no *internal* logic that links the events one to another. After he has formulated his decision and thanked Confucius for his assistance, Kien storms into the kitchen:

> Kien hatte keine Zeit, ihm für diese letzte Aufmunterung zu danken. Er stürzte vor die Küche und griff heftig nach der Tür. Die Klinke brach ab. Therese saß vor ihrem Kissen und stellte sich lesend. Als sie spürte, daß er schon hinter ihr stand, erhob sie sich und gab den Blick auf sein Buch frei. Der Eindruck des vorigen Gesprächs war ihr nicht entgangen. Drum hielt sie wieder auf Seite 3. Er zögerte einen Augenblick, wußte nicht, was er sagen sollte, und blickte auf seine Hände. Da bemerkte er die abgebrochene Türklinke; wütend warf er sie zu Boden. Dann stellte er sich steif vor sie hin und sagte: "Geben Sie mir Ihre Hand!" Therese hauchte: "Aber ich bitt' Sie!" und streckte sie ihm hin. Jetzt kommt die Verführung, dachte sie und begann am ganzen Leibe zu schwitzen. "Aber nein," sagte Kien, er meinte die Hand nicht wörtlich, "ich will Sie heiraten!" Eine so rasche Entscheidung hatte Therese nicht erwartet. Sie warf den erschütterten Kopf auf die andere Seite herum und entgegnete stolz und gegen das Stottern ankämpfend: "Ich bin so frei!" (*DB*, 48)[182]

Once again, the effect on the reader of the above scene is comic, because the preamble to the proposal is so manifestly unseductive. Canetti's language refuses to adapt, as it had refused to adapt in other scenes examined so far, to mimic the rhythms of the emotions. But it is more than this. The series of short, sharp, brittle sentences is a report of a series of actions or events, all of which conspire to prevent the atmosphere from modulating into an emotionally suggestive one. When Therese thought she was about to see evidence of a crime in Kien's library, the language of the sentences that reported on her emotions refused to take those emotions seriously. They were merely subjected to comic effect. Here, when mutuality or reciprocity might be possible, everything conspires to keep the two separate, not because in some normative sense Therese and Kien are being presented to us as deficient in the skills necessary to induce mutuality or reciprocity, but because Canetti wants to prolong theatricality as the spirit of the narrative as a whole. He refuses to allow the narrative to be broken down into so-called constituent semantic parts by introducing the surprise. So the doorhandle has to break off as he walks into the kitchen. He is furious, *not* loving. Therese is credited with a desire for abduction, *not* marriage. Therese relies on two platitudes from her small collection of platitudes, and Kien relies on three peremptory statements.

Therese's "Ich bin so frei!," that meaningless statement with which she is associated throughout the novel as a whole, brings to an end the chapter, "Konfuzius, ein Ehestifter," examined above. At the beginning of "Die Muschel" the marriage takes place, although the text has refused to incorporate an incident instating marriage as a mutual decision between consenting adults.[183] The marriage is a civil event, not taken seriously in its own right by the narrative:

> Die Trauung ging in aller Stille vor sich. Als Zeugen fungierten ein alter Dienstmann, der aus seinem zerbrochenen Leib letzte kleine Leistungen schlug, und ein fideler Schuster, der, jeder eigenen Trauung mit List entwischt, sich fremde für sein versoffenes Leben gern ansah. Feinere Kunden bat er inständig um eine baldige Heirat ihrer Töchter und Söhne. Für den Wert früher Ehen fand er überzeugende Worte. "Liegen die Kinder erst beieinander, no so kommen auch gleich die Enkel. Jetzt schaun Sie, daß die Enkel auch bald heiraten, das gibt dann Urenkel." Zum Schluß verwies er auf seinen guten Anzug, der

> ihm eine x-beliebige Anwesenheit erlaube. Vor besseren Ehen lasse er ihn auswärts bügeln, bei gewöhnlichen bügle er ihn selbst zu Hause. Um eines flehte er, um rechtzeitigen Bescheid. War er schon lange nicht mehr dabeigewesen, so bot er, von Natur aus ein langsamer Arbeiter, prompte Reparaturen gratis an. Versprechen, die sich auf diesen Bereich bezogen, hielt er, sonst unverläßlich, pünktlich ein und forderte wirklich einen geringen Preis. Kinder, die so entartet waren, gegen den Willen ihrer Eltern heimlich zu heiraten, aber nicht entartet genug, um auf die Trauung zu verzichten, meist Mädchen, pflegten sich seiner zuweilen zu bedienen. Die Geschwätzigkeit selbst, war er hierin verschwiegen. Nicht durch die leiseste Andeutung verriet er sich, wenn er ahnungslosen Müttern breit und pompös von der Trauung ihrer eigenen Töchter erzählte. Bevor er sich in sein "Ideal," wie er es nannte, begab, hängte er an die Tür der Werkstatt ein mächtiges Schild. Da las man in krausen, kohlschwarzen Buchstaben: "Bin bei einem Bedürfnis. Komme vielleicht. Der Unterzeichnete: Hubert Beredinger." (*DB*, 49)[184]

Generally speaking, the above reads as a forthright refusal to take the convention of marriage seriously. The civil event of marriage is witnessed by a pair of eccentrics, again, not characters introduced into the narrative to raise the tone or provide some new perspectives, but to further the cause of surprise so necessary to the narrative. "Ein alter Dienstmann" is not given any formal introduction: he is merely a body close to disintegration. Is this the expressionist reduction of human beings to single characteristics? Hardly. A justification for his details cannot be found. Positively, however, the detail concerning the incapacitated body of one of the witnesses adds something to the narrative, inasmuch as it deflates any air of expectation raised by the idea of marriage, not to cause disappointment in the reader but to school him/her in the art of the unexpected.

The same has to be said of the "Schuster." Details that relate to him do not encourage us to think of him as a character. Rather, they read as a series of invented and very theatrical possibilities. Why would he mischievously always miss his own marriage? This is left unanswered, in terms of psychology, and in all other terms. And when the narrative appears to be providing us with genuine information, we realize we are reflecting on stupidity or impossibility. For instance, it is stated that the "Schuster" promotes early marriages to his more elevated customers. This statement is followed by what appears to be an explanation of the prejudice in favor of early marriages for the well-bred. Yet it is a statement of the obvious, of the likely consequences of marriage. There is no intrinsic justification for the early marriage as an end in itself. Instead, the "Schuster" has provided us with material that will make us laugh here at the coy/salacious/oblique reference to sex and its consequences. The focus on the "character" of the "Schuster" continues in the next passage:

> Er war der erste, der von Theresens Glück erfuhr. Er zweifelte so lange an der Wahrheit ihrer Worte, bis sie ihn beleidigt aufs Standesamt lud. Als es geschehen war, folgten die Zeugen dem Paar auf die Straße. Der Dienstmann nahm sein Entgelt mit krummem Dank entgegen. Gratulationen murmelnd entfernte er sich. ". . . mich wieder brauchen . . . ," klang es Kiens in den Ohren. Noch zehn Schritt weit weg war der leere Mund voller Eifer. Hubert Beredinger aber war bitter enttäuscht. Um so eine Trauung stand er nicht an. Er hatte seinen Anzug zum Bügeln gegeben, der Bräutigam war wie am Werktag erschienen, mit schiefen Sohlen, das Gewand zerschlissen, ohne Lust und Liebe, statt der Braut sah er immer die Akten an. Das "Ja" sagte er als hätte er danke gesagt, nachher bot er der Schachtel keinen Arm und der Kuß, von dem der Schuster wochenlang lebte—ein fremder Kuß gab ihm für zwanzig eigene aus—, der Kuß, für den er was springen ließ, der Kuß, der als Bedürfnis vor der Werkstatt hing, der öffentliche Kuß, dem ein Beamter zusah, der Kuß in Ehren, der Kuß auf ewig, der Kuß, der Kuß fand überhaupt nicht statt. Beim Abschied verweigerte der Schuster seine Hand. Seine Kränkung verbarg er hinter einem gehässigen Grinsen. "Einen Moment bitte," kicherte er, wie ein Photograph, Kiens zögerten. Da beugte er sich plötzlich nieder zu einer Frau, zupfte sie am Kinn, sagte laut "Gu-gu" und prüfte lüstern ihre vollen Formen. (*DB*, 49–50)[185]

The focus is on the mood of Hubert Beredinger, and not on the feelings or experiences of either Therese or Peter Kien, despite the fact it is their civil wedding. The ceremony is reduced to the utmost insignificance and banality by the use of the neutral "es." What is recorded by the narrative is the inverse of pomp and circumstance. It is the disappointment of the man Hubert Beredinger at the low sartorial standards of Kien. This parody of the marriage ceremony modulates in to what appears to be a humorous moment of near lyrical helplessness. This is another example of the way in which narration is privileged in the novel, over and above the conservative device of the point of view, on which the paragraph cited above only *seems* to depend. For the word "der Kuß" is repeated a total of nine times, in what appears to be a crescendo that promises to lead to a climax, only to fall on its feet, so to speak. This is not a clumsy foray into the possibility of seducing the reader into thinking that another ritual associated with marriage is about to take place. It is another example of the delight the narrative takes in what it assumes is its right to modulate into what ever "mood" it wishes, whenever it wishes. That the kiss which does not take place is, after all, a point that the narrator makes. It is then followed by what appears to be an event in the empirical world, namely Beredinger's feeling up a female passer-by. From signs of love that do not take place, we move to "acts" of lust that do take place.

But what level of seriousness is achieved by this action by Beredinger, after what came over as a ludic moment of free play in the linear flow of the narrative? Mechthild Curtius has quoted the passage looked at above to make a "normalcy" point about the character of Hubert Beredinger. He is a voyeur. The fact that the kiss does not take place "bedeutet für ihn eine bittere Frustration und Kränkung."[186] This is an excellent example of the way in which literary criticism is so deeply colored by a certain assumption that literature must relate to life. It is proof of how such ideology leads to major errors of interpretation. It would only be possible to categorize Beredinger as a voyeur if the narrative had made clear that Beredinger had no right to be present. He would be a voyeur if he were snooping on a pair of lovers who were alone and wanting to enjoy their privacy and intimacy. This is a public ceremony in the street. Further, as is so often the case in the novel, an event that is anticipated (as in Therese's assumption that a crime had taken place in Peter Kien's library) "ends up" not taking place. One can talk, perhaps, about Beredinger's anticipation of a romantic moment. It seems, however, that as the next "moment" within the narration is an incident which is recorded as it happens, with Beredinger going on to feel up a passer-by in such a manifestly unaggressive way (and in fact, by mimetic standards, in such a thoroughly implausible way) that the character Beredinger becomes elusive and without an essence of character. The term, voyeur, fixes him in a way which the narrative refutes, both in terms of events recorded and in terms of the obvious disjunction between the possible autoeroticism of his desire that the couple kiss and his sudden transformation into a hopelessly implausible sexual aggressor. If

"Gu-gu," as an opening gambit of someone supposedly suffering from sexual disorders, is an indicator of sexual disorders. . . . The final point about Curtius' argument here is that the effect of the "Gu-gu" opening gambit on the woman who is being touched is quite evidently *not* investigated. If Canetti were seriously interested in the psychoanalytic phenomenon of voyeurism, he would, at the very least, have to show his credentials by examining those unfortunate enough to be the victim of the strategies of "the voyeur." That the narrative does not want us either to fix Beredinger as a "character" with an "essence of character" or to see him as a series of mutually incompatible identities seems obvious if one allows oneself to reflect on the series of thoroughly miscellaneous "observations" that make up the above passage, on the way in which the events do not conspire to lead us anywhere, and on the way in which it allows itself to modulate into different moods, whenever it feels it would like to. Narration is privileged for the pleasure of the reader. We have, thus, what Liewerscheidt has called a mere "Geist der Erzählung" instead.[187] This is particularly clear when we realize that the effect of the "Gu-gu" opening gambit is registered by Peter Kien alone. Peter Kien reacts to Beredinger's "crude" allusion to sex. Beredinger's action is interesting, in narrative terms, only because it stimulates Peter Kien's imagination. As such, Canetti shows his cavalier disregard for the "intrinsic" meaning of Beredinger's action.

The consequences of Beredinger's action on Peter Kien's psyche are examined in some detail when the couple leaves the scene of the wedding ceremony to board a tram:

> Wie sollte man dieses scheue, zurückhaltende Wesen behandeln? Sie war nicht mehr jung und nahm das Leben sehr ernst. Die Frau ihr gegenüber, sicher viel jünger, hatte bereits vier Kinder, sie noch keines. "Kinder kommen zuletzt." Das klang sehr klar, aber was meinte sie wirklich damit? Sie wollte vielleicht keine Kinder; er auch nicht. Er hatte nie an Kinder gedacht. Wozu sagte sie das? Vielleicht hielt sie ihn für einen unsittlichen Mann. Sie kannte sein Leben. Seit acht Jahren war sie mit seinen Gewohnheiten vertraut. Sie wußte, daß er Charakter hatte. Ging er denn nachts je aus? Hatte ihn je eine Frau besucht, auch für eine Viertelstunde nur? Als sie damals bei ihm den Dienst antrat, hatte er ihr ausdrücklich erklärt, daß er Besuche, männliche oder weibliche, von Säuglingen angefangen bis zu Greisen, prinzipiell nicht empfange. Sie solle jedermann wegschicken. "Ich habe nie Zeit!" Das waren seine eigenen

> Worte. Welcher Teufel war in sie gefahren? Der haltlose Schuster vielleicht. Sie war ein naives, unschuldiges Geschöpf, wie hätte sie sonst, bei ihrer Unbildung, zu Büchern eine solche Liebe gefaßt? Aber der schmutzige Kerl hatte zu drastisch gespielt. Seine Bewegungen waren deutlich, ein Kind, selbst ohne zu wissen, warum er das treibt, hätte begriffen, daß er eine Frau berührte. Solche Leute, die sogar auf offener Straße ihre Beherrschung verlieren, gehören in geschlossene Anstalten. Sie bringen fleißige Menschen auf häßliche Gedanken. Fleißig ist sie. Der Schuster hat sie infiziert. Wie käme sie sonst zu den Kindern? Es ist nicht ausgeschlossen, daß sie davon gehört hat. Frauen reden viel untereinander. Sie muß eine Geburt gesehen haben, in einer früheren Stellung. Was wäre dabei, wenn sie alles wüßte. Besser, als man hätte sie selbst aufzuklären. Eine gewisse Verschämtheit liegt in ihrem Blick, bei ihrem Alter wirkt das beinahe komisch. (*DB*, 52)[188]

Once again, the perspective of the passage is Peter Kien's, yet once again, as in the case of all examples of point of view narration studied so far, the narration is so marked by its own determination to turn the substance of that point of view into theatricality as an end in itself, that its autonomy rides slipshod over the conservative idea that point of view narration must function to make an outlook unique to a particular individual. The sacred bourgeois idea at the heart of liberal humanism, that an individual is the author of his/her unique outlook, is dissolved in favor of the depersonalized spirit of theatricality itself, which privileges the reader, not characters in a fictional world. The "voice of theatricality" exploited "by" Therese, Beredinger, and Peter Kien is one that makes no concessions to gender; makes no concessions to the idea of uniqueness and character; makes it impossible to suggest, as a result, that there is a hierarchy of characters in this novel, that there are primary and secondary characters.

By association, Peter Kien is confronted with the reality of sex. How much of what follows could, in spite of the claim just made for the ideologically pure credentials of play, be said to be evidence that Peter Kien is a misogynist and/or that Canetti is a misogynist?[189] Peter Kien is proud that his life has not been dominated by sex and that it has been marked by his asocial dedication to scholarship. He identifies himself with the intellect and with a systematic disregard for anything likely to undermine his dedication to the intellect. Woman, in the form of Therese, is totally ignorant, intellectually, *and* vulnerable to being "infected," as it were, by the "concept" of sex, because women are socialized, unlike men. They learn about sex when they spend time wittering away with other women. Further, they have it on their minds, are coy and slightly ashamed about it, and are laughable to be still interested when they are old (Therese, Peter Kien knows, is fifty-eight).

It seems that the above passage, when analyzed, does force the reader to think of misogyny, and thus partially undermines the claim that the narrative of *Die Blendung* is, in the investment it makes in theatricality or the spirit of play, beautifully resistant to Big Ideas. The above partially allows us to think of misogyny, because there are clearcut gender specific notions about what makes a man a man, and what makes a woman a woman. Further, woman is clearly more trivial than man, because she is unintellectual and interested only in sex. Such polarized views of sexual difference, and such trivializing views about women, clearly had currency at the time of writing the novel, inasmuch as Vienna was very familiar with Weininger's *Geschlecht und Charakter*. At first sight, therefore, one could simply say that Canetti is working within the highly reductive tradition of sexual "difference" we associate with Weininger.

What is also obvious about the tone of the above scenes is that there is an absolute refusal of both *sentiment*, *melodrama*, and *idolatry*. There is a resistance to a definition of "the feminine." There is no "das ewig-Weibliche zieht uns hinan"; no "l'éternel féminin"; no association of woman and evil; no passive worshipping at the shrine of woman's supposed otherness; and virgins are not really virgins! The three damaging attitudes to woman, those of sentiment, melodrama, or idolatry, are more common in culture generally speaking than Canetti's brand of trivialization, and have obviously been the subject of much feminist deconstruction of the representation of woman in culture. The heretical view one could perhaps develop about Canetti's representation of woman in *Die Blendung*, an issue that might have attracted the attention of the feminists but has not, is that there is some insecurity about how seriously the reductive equation with which Canetti works in general should be taken, either when Therese is center stage, or when other women make their brief appearances later. This can be proved by the range of moods Canetti uses in those incidents in the novel featuring women. The range includes parody, satire, comedy, all of which point to detachment on Canetti's part from the stereotype. Otherwise there is wholehearted, often savage endorsement of the stereotype itself, indicating complicity on Canetti's part with the negative stereotype.

By contrast, when we examine the central episodes, like the one considered above, a totally different spirit takes over. This succeeds in erasing the scope for the endorsement of stereotype because of the self-conscious theatricality of the scene as a whole. But what are we supposed to do with the knowledge that the theatricality needs the material of gender stereotyping? Is the question really appropriate? One might claim, again heretically, that the above scene is, funnily enough, shot through with a spirit of *affection* and respect for the separateness and absolute autonomy of other persons, in spite of appearances to the contrary. Canetti moves beyond gender stereotyping altogether, not by savagely standing the stereotypes on their heads, but by inventing a new spirit that does not know of vulgarity of this kind: the spirit of inflated theatricality as an end in itself, one that cannot do violence. The fact that Peter Kien reflects on the ideas prompted by Beredinger's coarse physical response to a passer-by, for instance, shows he is conscious of sex, first of all, so Canetti allows Kien to deconstruct his own theory that men are purely intellectual. This puts him on a par with Therese, not above her. The account cannot be said to lead to an essentialist definition of woman in terms of sexuality, which would make it a damning, misogynist account, neither does it lead to an essentialist definition of woman, because sexuality is not part of "her" nature, nor part of "his" nature. Peter Kien is reminded of its existence/potentiality by a concrete incident, that of Beredinger's groping a female passer-by, and Therese is told of its existence/potentiality by a friend. Both Peter Kien and Therese are equal in the above passage inasmuch as they are presented as living beyond a state of "nature." Random chance has introduced the "concept" of sex into both their lives. After all, one must bear in mind that neither married because of either love or sexual desire, although Therese was said to be interested in being abducted in the passage examined earlier. Both sexual desire and love have been systematically excluded as potential motives for the event of marriage. They have also been systematically excluded from the above scene after the marriage, in such a way as to suggest that neither has integrated sexual desire into the personality. So the above episode, which began as a virtuous and self-congratulatory set of statements that seemed to privilege the male as beyond sex, and the female as interested in sex imaginatively, if not practically, actually achieves something else. A tacit admission is made of the inevitability of a heterosexual encounter for which both are inadequately prepared. It thus makes both Peter Kien and Therese equal in terms of what "lies ahead." The end of the passage quoted above is also marked by a certain amount of relief on Peter's part that Therese knows, theoretically, about the existence of sex as an activity, because she has probably seen a birth whilst working in another household. As such the comic dimension on the whole issue of their "relationship" is sustained. The above episode is, then, an affectionate acknowledgment of fear about sex due to inexperience.

Peter Kien does not "talk about" Therese in the above passage as if he liked "her." The "Geist der Erzählung" takes over instead, and it is this that is shot through with something more progressive. It is shot through with an acceptance of the autonomy of the other, not in the unsophisticated sense that Therese is a woman and Peter Kien a man, but in the sense that she is there as another human being. This would make Canetti more progressive than some critics have suggested, generally speaking, not just in terms of sexual politics. Certainly, it is quite obvious that the references to Therese frequently remind us that she is not intellectual, but this is not held against her, nor is it written into the spirit of her "character." It is useful material, given the need to sustain a sense of play, and it is a sense of play that knows already that the oblique references to a Small Idea or a Big Idea such as "woman's nature" are not to be taken seriously. In the end, Canetti's inflated theatricality rides slipshod over point of view; and the depersonalized spirit is instead sustained by a mood of love/respect per se.

It thus seems possible to counter the charge levelled against Canetti, that there is deep misogyny in his work. It also has to be pointed out that all characters in the novel are identified with a few characteristics. More importantly, Therese is every much an equal of Peter Kien, Fischerle, and Benedikt Pfaff in terms of power of personality. Yet Therese is the only major female character in the novel and she gets abandoned violently at a later stage in the novel. This suggests that on balance women are disposable and that one can live without them in the community. Therese also gets abandoned at a time when a simple equation takes over, the equation that women are decent men's girlfriends, who live only for men and sex: Fischerle's woman for instance, George(s)'s various wives for instance. There are numerous passing references to the stereotype, which perhaps indicates a value judgment on the part of the author, a view that women are not to be taken seriously except when they can service male sexuality. The last phase of the novel then instates misogyny at a theoretical level, at a point when Peter Kien and George(s) talk about woman as a necessary and disposable evil. These problems will be examined in a later chapter. It is possible to argue, on the basis of the above, however, that at the time of writing Canetti did not have any settled experience of women, that he knew perhaps one woman properly (the Therese equivalent), and that this type was one who partly represented a threat to male autonomy and intellectuality at the domestic level. That the single serious woman character in the novel is surrounded by a very large number of vocal males, also suggests that at the time of writing, Canetti's life was still about men and about talking, in spite of the formidable presence of a very powerful woman close at hand. Meanwhile, one might pause to reflect on some apparently softer male novelists, like Fontane and Goethe, whose "love" of woman is nonetheless a "love" of her inability to be independent, of her victim status in cultural terms, as it is a love of her utility value in terms of male sexuality. One might think about the ugly aggression of Günter Grass, who has to his credit a scene featuring a gang rape in *Die Blechtrommel*, as if it did not require commentary, and whose restless, inane, infantile, and pointless inventions of "femininity" in *Der Butt* make her nothing more or less than a lifeless icon.[190] One should also bear in mind Kate Millett's study of four male novelists, D.H. Lawrence, Norman Mailer, Henry Miller, and Jean Genet, in *Sexual Politics*.[191] Millett shows how what appears to be an attractive attitude toward women is nothing more than a flamboyant demonstration of phallic aggression, violent hatred of anything other than the male self. Aggression with respect to women is not instated at a primary level in Canetti's text. It is not enacted in full-length scenes or episodes, even surreptiously, even when this appears to be the case, as in Benedikt's apparent sadistic incestual exploitation of his wife and daughter. Benedikt Pfaff does no real violence to her and feels no active hatred toward her at a concrete level, if the reader experiences the spirit of the sentences that use the words associated with sadism as facetious. The idea of woman as something more trivial than man is kept alive, but loosely, and only at various *moments* in the novel. There is a substantial difference between the two positions, which should be borne in mind, as we enter this minefield.

The episode after the wedding in the tram is a prelude to another central episode in the novel, namely the wedding night. Here again Canetti is playful:

> Endlich standen sie in der Wohnung. Therese öffnete die Tür zu seinem Schlafzimmer und wies ihn hinein. "Ich komm' gleich," sagte sie, und ließ ihn allein zurück.
>
> Er blickte sich um und atmete auf, aus einem Zuchthaus in die Freiheit entlassen.
>
> Ja, das ist seine Heimat. Hier kann ihm nichts geschehn. Er lächelt bei der Vorstellung, daß ihm hier was geschehen könnte. Er vermeidet es, in die Richtung des Schlafdiwans zu sehen. Jeder Mensch braucht eine Heimat, nicht eine, wie primitive Faustpatrioten sie verstehn, auch keine Religion, matten Vorgeschmack einer Heimat im Jenseits, nein, eine Heimat, die Boden, Arbeit, Freunde, Erholung und geistigen Fassungsraum zu einem natürlichen, wohlgeordneten Ganzen, zu einem eigenen Kosmos zusammenschließt. Die beste Definition der Heimat ist Bibliothek. Frauen hält man am klügsten von seiner Heimat fern. Entschließt man sich doch, eine aufzunehmen, so trachte man, sie der Heimat erst völlig zu assimilieren, so wie er es getan hat. In acht langen, stillen, zähen Jahren haben die Bücher für ihn die Unterwerfung dieser Frau besorgt. Er persönlich hat keinen Finger dazu gerührt. Seine Freunde haben die Frau in seinem Namen erobert. Sicher läßt sich viel gegen die Frauen sagen, nur ein Narr heiratet ohne Probezeit. *Er* war so klug, bis zu seinem vierzigsten Lebensjahr zu warten. Diese achtjährige Probezeit soll ihm ein anderer nachmachen. Was kommen mußte, ist allmählich herangereift. Herr seines Schicksals ist der Mensch allein. Wenn man es genau bedenkt, hat ihm nur noch eine Frau gefehlt. Er ist kein Lebemann—bei "Lebemann" sieht er seinen Bruder Georg, den Frauenarzt, vor sich—, er ist alles, nur kein Lebemann. Aber die schweren Träume der letzten Zeit dürften mit seinem übertrieben strengen Leben zusammenhängen. Das wird jetzt anders. (*DB*, 57)[192]

The return to the flat sees the narrative modulate into a highly skilfully stage-managed episode, which is deeply amusing. And here there is even the faint suggestion of a feminist agenda. Therese makes the relevant initiatives in what is supposed to be the seduction scene. She does so in an authoritative and peremptory way, despite the fact she is supposed to be inexperienced. Canetti does not go for the crass reversal of roles with the woman simply being the aggressor and the man being coyly passive. The whole scene is a send-up of seduction itself. This comes as something of a pleasant shock. The unexpected forces us to dispense with conservative notions of the static essence of character, in favor of the pure pleasure that is the reader's at participation in the unexpected. The modulation from the preterite into the present once again serves to make more immediate the kinds of thoughts that pass through Kien's head as he assesses what has happened to him. His coy refusal to look in the direction of the bed shows he is still prey to the fear examined, at what is inevitable. Once again the passage seems to be affectionately at the expense of Peter Kien's wild idea that he could live without company. Is the account of his asocial paradise one that is misogynist? It is certainly an account of the privilege of a world that is without women, but it is also, rather importantly, one that is without men. Peter Kien does not privilege either sex, because gender is not an issue, because human beings are not an issue. He considers human beings unnecessary, not because he is a misanthrope, but because he is passionately attached to his books.

There is much of *Le Rouge et le Noir* here. Books are his friends, as they are always the friends of Stendhal's preferred characters like Julien Sorel, Mathilde de la Mole, Fabrice, and Lucien. They had, up until this point, guaranteed that the reluctant admission of a human being into his isolated paradise, his library, would not intrude into his privacy. It would be useful to bear in mind that to a critic like Curtius, whose interpretative framework is Freudian, books have to be *substitutes* for people, they cannot be loved as if they were as full of spirit as people are.[193] Obviously words such as "unterwerfen" and "erobern" are strong, but one could regard this as theatrical overstatement, which merely renders laughably humorous and amusing Peter Kien's assumption that the inanimate (his friends, the books in his library) have secured his freedom from the intrusions to be associated with real human beings, rather than evidence that woman is a necessary evil whose services are primarily sexual. Obviously the books cannot, in any realistic way, have really achieved something as dynamic as the silence of Therese. Anyway, further theatricality is alive in this passage when we realise that the "relationship" with Therese developed independently of the existence of these books. In actual, empirical fact, they have none of the power that Kien confidently ascribes to them.

Further theatricality is also alive in that Peter Kien is trying to turn the inevitable into a personal achievement, an agonistic trick. Again, we know that Therese impressed him, against his will as it were, so it is comical that Kien relies on what reads as a Greek-style (Protagoras inspired) adage to the effect that man is the author of his own destiny. "Herr seines Schicksals ist der Mensch allein" is the name which Edgar Piel has given to his article on the novel, an article written in the belief that Peter Kien is a deluded man about himself and the world from beginning to end.[194] Once again, one could argue that the disjunction between Kien's theory about himself and the actual practice of his life is so obvious to the reader that it produces laughter. The disjunction, because it has been treated with such overt theatricality, does not warrant the condemnation that critics express who are motivated by an interest in the "normal" in life and in the "normative" in literature. The disjunction is something that Canetti appears to love for what it is, the essence of the illusion. And illusions sustain and create life in the Nietzschean sense.

What makes this account laughable, in the best sense of the word, is not that it is hostile to womankind or to the deluded, arrogant, overly intellectual scholar type. It is not that it wishes to "show" how deluded Peter Kien is in a world of illusions that are wrong in themselves, nor that it wishes to endorse the crass stereotype whereby if a woman is not a virgin, she is a voracious sexual predator/whore. The narrative is privileged, once again, for the pleasure of the reader, and the pleasure consists in the above being the comedy of the inevitable, lovingly prolonged by Canetti in the full knowledge that the inevitable can be delayed for as long as he sees fit. Delay tactics are there in the opposition between Peter Kien's virtuous self-satisfaction that he has had a reasonable run-in with Therese and the type "Lebemann," the kind of man, like his brother, who dabbles with women. The change in his life is already happening and promises to be beneficial.

Using the present tense once again to highlight the immediacy of what is happening, Therese makes her theatrical appearance in the bedroom, as wife and potential lover, in full confidence, as if she were already sexually experienced:

> "Jetzt bin ich da."
>
> Er dreht sich um. Sie steht auf der Schwelle zum Nebenzimmer, in einem blendend weißen Unterrock, der mit breiten

> Spitzen besetzt ist. Aufs Blau, die Gefahr, hat er zuerst geblickt. Er gleitet erschreckt an der Gestalt hinauf: ihre Bluse hat sie anbehalten. Gott sei Dank. Der Rock ist weg. Jetzt brauch' ich nichts zu zerdrücken. Ist das anständig? So ein Glück. Ich hätt' mich geschämt. Wie kann sie das tun. Ich hätte gesagt: Leg' ihn weg. Das hätt' ich nicht können. So selbstverständlich steht sie da. Wir müssen uns schon sehr lange kennen. Natürlich, meine Frau. Bei jeder Ehe. Woher sie das weiß. Sie war in Stellung. Bei einem Ehepaar. Hat alles mit angesehen. Wie die Tiere. Die finden das Richtige, von selbst. Sie hat keine Bücher im Kopf.
>
> Therese nähert sich mit wiegenden Hüften. Sie gleitet nicht, sie watschelt. Das Gleiten kommt also nur vom gestärkten Rock. Sie sagt freudig: "So nachdenklich? Ja, die Mannsbilder!" Sie krümmt den kleinen Finger, droht und zeigt mit ihm auf den Diwan. Ich muß auch hingehn, denkt er, und steht schon, er weiß nicht wie, neben ihr. Was soll er jetzt tun—auf die Bücher hinlegen? Er schlottert vor Angst, er betet zu den Büchern, der letzten Schranke. Therese fängt seinen Blick, sie bückt sich und fegt mit einem umfassenden Schlag des linken Armes sämtliche Bücher zu Boden. Er macht eine hilflose Bewegung, zu ihnen hin, er will aufschreien, Entsetzen schnürt ihm die Kehle zu, er schluckt und bringt keinen Laut hervor. Ein furchtbarer Haß steigt langsam hoch: das hat sie gewagt. Die Bücher!
>
> Therese zieht sich den Unterrock aus, faltet ihn besorgt zusammen und legt ihn auf die Bücher am Boden. Dann macht sich's auf dem Diwan bequem, krümmt den kleinen Finger, grinst und sagt: "So!"
>
> Kien stürzt in langen Sätzen aus dem Zimmer, sperrt sich ins Klosett, dem einzigen bücherfreien Raum der Wohnung ein, zieht sich an diesem Ort mechanisch die Hosen herunter, setzt sich aufs Brett und weint wie ein kleines Kind. (*DB*, 59–60)[195]

The reliance on purposeful inflation in the above is hilarious, not only inasmuch as Peter Kien is still amazed that Therese should have clues as to how to proceed, but inasmuch as there is a manifest disjunction between Therese's confidence about her intentions and desires and Kien's state of mind. The escape to the loo on Peter Kien's part, when faced with the actuality of Therese's interest in an encounter, does not seem to warrant discussion of the normative idea of Kien's being impotent or primarily frightened of sex. The escape, along with the ideas passing through Kien's head before he flees the room, are the means of sustaining the reader in a state of expectation of the unexpected, for the highly sophisticated reasons discussed in the preceding chapter. Predictably, Gretzky, not alive to the comedy/theatricality of the scene above, concludes, for instance, that the reliance on speaking and language in the novel generally replaces action, and sexual initiatives in particular.[196]

Hereafter, the narrative participates in what is the fun of prolonging the fun of prolonging the fun, at the very idea that something that "ought" to have happened has not happened. Sex is referred to in Therese's mind as "das große Ereignis," the great event. It is kept high in the reader's mind as the two self-consciously sleep apart. Therese then wants to buy a new bed anyway, because the one that is there in the flat is "unanständig," indecent. In the course of her reflections on her anticipation of "das große Ereignis," she remembers how she had been courted as a young girl, and the ensuing fight she had with her mother:

> "Eine Stiefmutter bist, ja, das bist!" schrei ich. Bis zu ihrem Tod hat sie geglaubt, der Mann hat mir meine Jungfernehre geraubt. Dabei ist es gar nicht wahr. Ich bin eine anständige Person und hab' mit keinem Menschen noch was gehabt. Ja, wenn man sich nicht wehren täte, hätt' man zehn an jedem Finger. Aber was macht man dann? Es wird ja alles von Tag zu Tag teurer. Die Kartoffeln kosten bereits das Doppelte. Kein Mensch weiß, wohin das noch führt. Da mach' ich nicht mit. Jetzt bin ich verheiratet und ein einsames Alter steht mir bevor . . . (*DB*, 66)[197]

Just as Kien had been proud of his celibacy, so Therese is proud of her virginity. There is a qualitative difference between the two "positions" however. The narrative turns Therese's virtuous feelings about her having maintained her virginity into a comedy, in roughly the same way it had turned Peter Kien's virtuous feelings about his celibate life into a comedy. Therese quite positively likes to feel as if her virginity has been under threat, as Peter Kien felt that his celibacy had been ensured by the books. Her reflective feelings on her new situation at the end of the above quoted passage show that she has, reluctantly and sadly, come to terms with what has not happened and is keen to ensure her own material future, whereas Peter Kien has come to terms with the necessity of abandoning celibacy in a way that was indulgent.

In the course of her attempt to buy a new piece of furniture for the flat, she establishes a "relationship" with the salesman in question. In narrative terms, as a result, she is transformed from being a relatively theatrical person to a highly theatrical person:

Sie schlug die Richtung nach jenem interessanten Verkäufer ein. Da es bereits ein Uhr war, beeilte sie sich sehr, um vor der Mittagssperre hinzukommen. Sie erregte Aufsehen; unter allden Männern in Hosen und Frauen in kurzen Röcken war sie die einzige, deren Beine, unter dem blauen gestärkten Rock, der bis zu den Füßen reichte, heimlich funktionierten. Es geht auch mit Gleiten, wurde allgemein festgestellt. Es ging sogar gut, denn sie überholte alle. Therese spürte die Blicke der Menschen. Wie dreißig, dachte sie und begann vor Freude und Eile zu schwitzen. Es kostete sie Mühe, den Kopf ruhig zu halten. Sie setzte ein bewundertes Lächeln auf. Von den Ohren, breiten Schwingen, getragen, flogen die Augen zum Himmel empor und ließen sich in einem billigen Schlafzimmer nieder. Therese, ein spitzenbesetzter Engel, machte es sich darin bequem. Und doch war sie nicht aus den Wolken gefallen, als sie plötzlich vor dem bewußten Laden stand. Ihr stolzes Lächeln verwandelte sich in ein freudiges Grinsen. Sie trat ein und glitt auf den jungen Menschen zu, wobei sie die Hüften so heftig wiegte, daß der weitgespannte Rock in Wallungen geriet.

"Da bin ich wieder!" sagte sie bescheiden.

"Küss' die Hand, Gnädigste, welche unerwartete Ehre! Was führt Sie zu uns, Gnädigste, wenn ich fragen darf?"

"Ein Schlafzimmer. Sie wissen doch."

"Das hab' ich mir gleich gedacht, Gnädigste. Für zwei natürlich, wenn ich so sagen darf."

"Aber ich bitt' Sie, Sie dürfen alles." Er schüttelte tief betrübt den Kopf.

"O nein, ich nicht, Gnädigste. Bin ich der Glückliche? Mich hätten Gnädigste garantiert nicht geheiratet. Ein armer Angestellter."

"Warum. Man kann nie wissen. Arme Leute sind auch Menschen. Ich bin nicht fürs Stolze."

"Daran erkennt man das goldene Herz, Gnädigste. Der Herr Gemahl sind zu beneiden."

"Aber ich bitt' Sie, wie sind die Männer heutzutage!"

"Gnädigste wollen doch nicht sagen . . . ," der interessante Mensch zog die Brauen erstaunt hoch. Eine feuchte Hundeschnauze waren seine beiden Augen, und er rieb sie an ihr.

"Die glauben ja, man ist ihr Dienstbot'. Dabei zahlen sie einem nichts. Ein Dienstbot' kriegt gezahlt."

"Dafür werden sich Gnädigste jetzt ein schönes Schlafzimmer aussuchen. Darf ich bitten! Exzellente Primaware, ich hab' gewußt, daß Gnädigste wiederkommen und hab' es eigens für Gnädigste reserviert. Wir hätten es schon sechsmal verkaufen können, Hand aufs Herz! Der Herr Gemahl werden sich freuen. Gnädigste kommen nach Hause, küss' die Hand, Liebling, sagen

> der Herr Gemahl. Guten Tag, Liebling, sagen Gnädigste, ich hab' ein Schlafzimmer für uns, Liebling—Sie verstehen mich, Gnädigste, so sagen *Sie*, und setzen sich dem Herrn Gemahl auf den Schoß. Sie entschuldigen schon, Gnädigste, ich spreche, wie mir der Schnabel gewachsen ist, aber da kann kein Mann widerstehen, das gibt es auf der ganzen Welt nicht, auch ein Herr Gemahl nicht. Wenn ich verheiratet wäre, ich sag' nicht mit Ihnen, Gnädigste, wie komm' ich armer Angestellter dazu, ich sag' mit einer Frau, ich sag' sogar mit einer alten Frau, sagen wir vierzig—ja, das können Sie sich gar nicht vorstellen, Gnädigste!" (*DB*, 80–82)[198]

Once again, what is point of view narration is autonomous narration or theatrically inflated animation, which exceeds any genuinely plausible, mimetic view of how "one" might behave. This is not a rhetorical technique to make us feel what Therese might genuinely have done. It is the autonomy of what Liewerscheidt has called the "Geist der Erzählung," so here we have a consciously inflated vision of Therese as she walks into town. The narrative plays with the idea of someone seeing herself as an infinitely attractive sex kitten, only because the idea is funny in its own right. The idea is not taken seriously; to do so would be to endorse it and to herald in the era of fixities, those things so inimical to agon.

Typically for a narrative that is wilfully set against mimesis of any kind, no attempt is made to endorse or refute this theatrically inflated animation in such a way as to make it clear to the reader whether the vision is objectively true, as the expression of an individual subject. For instance, there is nothing on all those men Therese maintains find her infinitely attractive, and who are watching her as she walks. We are not seeing that she is attractive through the eyes of someone who does find her attractive. Neither is there an obvious disjunction between how Therese feels she is and how others feels she is. The narrative does not refute her view that she is infinitely attractive by showing us how she is not attractive through the eyes of someone who feels she is not attractive. The narrative is absolutely stripped of the kind of context that would encourage us to believe she is at the center of an empirical world peopled by other individuals and other imaginations capable of influential value judgments. As a result, we are not in a position to say that what she feels about herself is wrong, which would be to judge the illusion itself as negative, as proof of the extent to which she is cut off from some kind of "normative" reality.

This refusal to contextualize is the Nietzschean way of assuming that because life is merely and only an aesthetic phenomenon, there are only a series of subjective fictions, which it is no one's right to subject to any critical scrutiny. When the world is only an aesthetic phenomenon, there are no ethical absolutes that can be invoked to measure or evaluate them. Canetti's Nietzschean perspectivism is his particularly original use of point of view narration, which has literally become severed from its Speaking Subject. The perspectivism further functions to make bold the point that the illusions or fictions of individual subjects have a purely functional role in terms of allowing the individual to construct a means of negotiating the world. One has to, in constructing what is a fiction, invent, *to live in the as if mode*, as Vaihinger would have it.[199] Vaihinger's work on Nietzsche stresses Nietzsche's attempt to dissociate fiction from its supposedly causal alliance with reality, to construct fiction as action, as an auxiliary construct used to negotiate reality (12). An unusal pronouncement of Canetti on fiction, partially recognizes all of this, when Canetti introduces a moral dimension: "Mir ist jede Fiktion echt, die die Lebenden in ihren Verhalten zu *einander* bessert."[200]

In *Die Blendung* there is no evaluation of the spirit that animates any character and constitutes his/her fiction, since neither narrator at the level of the diegetic material, nor characters at the level of the mimetic material, respond reflectively to one another. Sentences, more than characters, react to one another, only in the sense that they attempt to imitate the spirit of contesting. Because of the stress on the voice in each sentence, Canetti endorses the immense loquaciousness of the human imagination. This should also be read as a tribute to Stendhal again, for whom the world was not populated with things, as it is in Balzac, but with discourses.[201] It is a statement in favor of the human potential for community at the level of talk, which in no way touches on the issue of the substance of what is being thought and/or spoken. Canetti can be seen to be giving the potential for loquaciousness a huge vote of confidence, discreetly aware that, as a Nietzschean, it is not appropriate to pass judgment on the substance of that loquaciousness, on its "quality," for instance.

In novels like *Watt*, *Murphy*, and *The Trilogy*, Beckett works with the disjunction between the life of the mind and the life of the body as both inhabit an empirical world peopled by other individuals and other imaginations. He explores it in such a way as to suggest that the independence of the mind from the body is an incontrovertible absolute. The mind and the imagination are prisoners within the body. In Canetti's novel, the lives of the figures who people its world consist of dialogue, to a lesser extent, and uninterrupted narrated monologue, to a greater extent. In those instances when dialogue or narrated monologue is not dominant, the loquaciousness of those sections continues to be imitated, to the extent that the narrative as a whole participates in promoting the voice. The reliance on theatrical animation of the liveliness of the human mind is achieved without our feeling any of the melancholy or frustration felt by Beckett's characters. These are marked by their *consciousness* that their minds are imprisoned within their bodies. Beckett's Cartesian dualism is not there in Canetti's novel, inasmuch as Canetti's characters are animated by delight at the infinite loquaciousness of the human mind. This is enforced unconditionally, and ideologically, as it were, by Canetti's narrative techniques, in particular by his "refusal" to subject the loquaciousness of the human mind and imagination to any restraints, from within or without. It is as if Canetti does not want to admit that there are or could be or should be restraints placed on the dynamism of the human mind and imagination. Canetti's absolutism is as intense as Beckett's; but they are at opposed ends of the spectrum. They are separated from one another, despite their common belief in the status of the mind and the imagination and in the undisputed power of the mind and imagination. They are separated from one another, indeed are polarized, in terms of the presence of a feeling of happiness and pleasure in Canetti, and the absence of such feelings in Beckett. A mood of happiness and pleasure is at the heart of Canetti's novel, because Canetti does not see the mind/body issue as an issue, whereas the melancholy and frustration that is in Beckett's novels, despite the anarchic humor and despite the comedy, has its origins in the "traditional" or mainstream view of Cartesian dualism, that the body and the mind are separate.

This suggestion, that the mind/body issue has no resonance in Canetti, will strike some as absurd, given the high-profile status of the critical view that Peter Kien is disembodied intellect in particular, and given the various subtitles of the novel itself: "Ein Kopf ohne Welt," "kopflose Welt," and "Welt im Kopf." My mention earlier of the dionysian quality of the momentum of Canetti's novel was an indication of the way in which this novel can be seen as beyond the conventional dualism of much Continental philosophical and literary thinking. This "normative" view would be that when the spirit of the body has absolute confidence it thereby dissolves any "natural" tendency towards dualism, not in the sense of an arrogant refusal to acknowledge anything other than the spirit, but because the spirit is already the spirit of the body. It has already permeated it, and dissolved the potential for dualism as a consequence. Canetti's novel appears to be the equivalent in literature of this "normative" view, inasmuch as it refuses to acknowledge that the body has any life "of its own," refuses to acknowledge that it is independent. The mind is the body and the body is the mind. This intensity is, of course, far removed from any of the facile and mindless *mere* worshipping of the body, such as that displayed by Gilles Deleuze in his call for "rhizomes" and the "corps sans organes."[202] Neither is it in the tradition of French surrealist poets, for instance, who think they are terribly radical for singing the praises of "desire," as in Apollinaire's "Zone" or Breton's "L'Union libre," to take two simple examples.

It does this by excluding references to sex as an experience of the body, as we have just seen, but it also excludes references to food, unlike the carnival in Rabelais, for instance, when sex and food are privileged. In doing this, Canetti is not saying that either food or sex are trivial; he is saying two things. They are nothing as *material* events—he would despise pornography in all its forms—and they are always only *potentially* significant if conceived of in the spirit of *imaginative* experiences. Once again, the systematic exclusion of meaningful sex is similar to the systematic exclusion of meaningful dialogue: and in both cases a point is made, "elsewhere," about the imaginative space necessary for meaningfulness, for ideal ways of living. The text is, meanwhile, practising meaningfulness in the way in which it is dedicated to the rigorous imaginative involvement of the reader, the agonistic fighting that presupposes that life, in a very general sense, is meaningful only if the imagination is both mobilized and engaged enough to create it. *Die Blendung* also achieves something sophisticated in the vexed area of the body/soul debate in another, more simple, way, by effectively deconstructing the crippling category of the norm, in terms of a related area, which also holds such sway over the human imagination, namely the way the body appears, the way the body can be seen. Peter Kien's gauntness is extreme, the text tells us. We know that Peter Kien looks like Don Quixote, since he is described as tall and thin.[203] We also know that Therese wears a stiff, blue skirt and that her ears are not symmetrical. We know that Fischerle is a hunchback and a dwarf, with a "Jewish" nose that dominates his face. We know that the man who cuts off his hunchback is himself hardly "normal." He is simply called the blindman. We know that Benedikt Pfaff has flamboyant red hair. Is this plain and simple synecdoche, the substitution of a part for the whole, or is there something more ambitious going on? All the above "details" about the human appearance of characters within the novel have caused critics to see Canetti in terms of a fascination with the unusual and grotesque in human appearance typical of Breughel and Goya (two of Canetti's favorite artists, as it happens) and even Dante.[204] David Roberts, for instance, sees Fischerle as a fascinating *caricature* of a Jew.[205] This is a view which Ritchie Robertson has partially corrected.[206] The case of Fischerle is particularly interesting, as will become clear in the next chapter, but both Roberts and Robertson write in a way that shows that they accept that in the novel there is, in some sense, an interrogation of normative standards, which they assume lies behind Canetti's inventions. The fact that they dwell on Fischerle's so-called "Jewish" identity is an indication of their adherence to notions of type, with which norms tend to be associated. For those who see the range of characters as merely grotesque, the point still holds. One can only talk confidently about the "reality" of the grotesque if one has a very clear idea of what constitutes the norm.

An alternative view would be that details concerning Peter Kien's appearance that remind one of the literary character Don Quixote are an obvious sign of respect for a purely literary figure. The second, more original, example, that of Therese, appears to make a concession to the physical and to the body. Yet her skirt only has the status of an uncomplicated fact. It is Therese. It is not as if, for instance, the blueness of the skirt interests Canetti. Neither could one argue that he is interested in how skirts comes to be stiff. It is easy, in the same way, to disagree with those psychoanalytical interpretations that see Peter Kien's apparent reaction to it as proof of his sexual insecurity. Equally, Canetti's interest in the unusual in the form of Fischerle's hunchbank, his *very* brief reference to the fact Fischerle knows he is a Jew, his introduction of the blindman, and the virtual identification of Benedikt Pfaff with his red hair, none of these is handled in such a way as to endorse the extraordinary in terms of physique. Critics regularly forget (rather conveniently) that Fischerle's so-called Jewishness is something exploited knowingly, or agonistically, by Fischerle himself, that is to say for opportunistic reasons. There is also a hilarious diffusion of all the paranoid tension that surrounds the use of the word Jew in discourse generally, in the scene when the "issue" is raised in "Zum idealen Himmel."[207] Given that Fischerle sets out to make use of his Jewishness, it could stand for anything, and should not be interpreted as some attempt on Canetti's part to interrogate "the problem of being a Jew in society," an imaginative project damned from the start anyway, for such formulations are expressions of racism in themselves. In this sense, it is possible to argue, heretically again, that the novel does not actively recognize the "issue" of Jewishness. When it is raised, it is a brief excuse for a piece of facetiousness, in which Canetti deconstructs the paranoia prevalent in society concerning Jews and Jewishness, by refusing to take its source seriously. Canetti thus has the single represented Jew in the story act in a challenging manner, as an aggressor, not as a victim.

The physicality of Peter Kien and the physicality of Therese's skirt, the physicality of Fischerle, the blindman as blindman, and Benedikt Pfaff as crazy because of his red hair, all these facts are totally irrelevant. They are not made meaningful in themselves by the narrative. In all cases, the drawing to one's attention of the extraordinary is a sign to the reader to be ready for the extraordinary and, furthermore, to enjoy the extraordinary. They are not signs of the extraordinary in themselves, however. Canetti prevents them from being associated with static "essence" or "meaning" only because he is convincingly able to allow each character to be animated by the power of personality. The spirit of the mind and body is riotously strong and pays no heed to the body. It is a form of defiance in itself that the body is irrelevant as such as an end in itself. The power of personality alive in each one of the characters is strong enough, therefore, that it forces one to deconstruct all assumptions about oddity clearly raised by the self-consciously clumsy dwelling on the "oddity" of the contours of a body. Again, the disjunction between visually "odd" looks and the quality of life that animates either Peter Kien, Therese, Fischerle, or Pfaff is gaping. Canetti is positively deconstructing that tendency in human beings to assume that the outside of a person tells us something about the inside of a person, that there is any kind of continuity between the two.[208]

Mechthild Curtius has, in this sense, perpetrated a real error here in maintaining, for instance, that Therese's skirt becomes a symbol of the failure of the capacity for a sexual relationship: "Fügt man alles zusammen, Kiens wie Thereses Ersatzhandlungen am jeweiligen Fetisch "Buch" und "Rock," so durchschaut man die Handlung dieses Einverleibens des Buchpenis in den Schoß des Rockes als Ersatz-kopulation."[209] This normative reading, which exploits both of the inanimate things which are most closely associated with Peter Kien and Therese, assumes that there is a normative perspective on events or non-events in the novel that can be read through its symbols. It is to play the binary game of assuming that there are distinctions between appearances and essences, between texts and worlds outside texts, and so on. In both cases, the book and the skirt are what one should perhaps call mock symbols, inasmuch as they do not mean anything constant in narrative terms. The books mean everything to Peter Kien, and are respected by Therese and Fischerle. The skirt means something to Therese when she wears it, as it helps to make her feel infinitely attractive. It is also what "characterizes" Therese in Peter Kien's eyes. As such, both the book and the skirt are instrumental, at best, merely fused with the meanings individual characters wish to give them. These meanings vary. To say that they are symbols is to privilege them over and above the individual perspective of the characters in the text. It is to construct an extra-textual reality where meanings are to be found, detached from the individual psyche, and where meanings are allowed to be timeless and constant.

There is, however, a very respectable history of physiognomy in literature, with its very prominent, romantic idea that the eyes and the body are the windows of the soul. Canetti shows how distant he is from it, and how essentially trivializing and dangerous it is in itself, in his refusal to attribute meaning to physique and those things that disguise or accentuate physique. Canetti cannot be accused of taking part in the ideologically highly suspect endorsement of the human body as the truth about the state of the human soul, popular in particular with the late Romantics and the Expressionists. His choice of features is so extreme as to be a form of absolute defiance of normative standards of "classical beauty," is also his way of showing up the imaginative and intellectual emptiness or shallowness that underlies any kind of positive endorsement of looks, whether classical or not. The introduction of characters into the narrative who do appear to have quirks by normative standards of "classical beauty" seems to be part and parcel of an understated attack on this by-now popular ideology.

Canetti is not like Thomas Mann, for instance, whose interest in physiognomy is ideologically extremely suspect. What appears to be mere art deco fascination with the exterior quirks of human appearance in *Buddenbrooks* or *Tristan* or *Unordnung und frühes Leid* often reads like an anticipation of the criteria invoked by the Nazis for sending people to the concentration camps. Thomas Mann's love of the aryan as the norm bespeaks more than just an appreciation of the notion of a pure race. The aryan is used as a standard by which others are judged, quite mercilessly and ruthlessly. Mann's is more than a self-complacency about his own racist love for a particular type. It can translate into more than a dismissive attitude toward those whose "looks" are unusual in some way, as is proven by the fact that "deviant"-looking types were transported to the concentration camps.

Canetti is interested in endorsing the spirit, the power of personality, that which is invisible, not visible. The dialogue between Therese and the man in the shop is, for instance, a comic masterpiece in its own right in terms of that spirit of play that animates the scene from beginning to end. It is not interesting because in any mimetic sense it "tells" us something about obsequiousness or sexual innuendo. The scene knows that its self-consciously tangential "relationship" to "real life" is a virtue, in terms of courage and confidence. How could anything like the above passage ever actually take place . . . ? It could never actually take place because *the sense of timing* that infuses the passage is near perfect. It is artistic, and speaks of the control exercised by Canetti in creating his work. The execution of the sentences reads like an act of defiance with respect to the chaos and clumsiness of (extra-textual) everyday life.

The sales technique of the salesman is quite brilliant:

> "Ich beschwöre Sie, Gnädigste, vergessen Sie nicht die Hauptsache! Wie man den Herrn Gemahl bettet, genauso revanchiert er sich. Liegen der Herr Gemahl gut, da können Sie mit ihm machen, was Sie wollen. Glauben Sie mir, Gnädigste. Das Eheglück geht nicht bloß durch den Magen, das Eheglück geht durch die Möbel, ganz eminent durch das Schlafzimmer, aber ich möchte sagen prominent durch die Betten, durch die Ehebetten sozusagen. Verstehn Sie mich, liebe Gnädigste, der Herr

Gemahl sind auch nur ein Mensch. Er kann die schönste Gnädigste besitzen, die Gnädigste in den blühendsten Jahren, was hat er davon, wenn er schlecht schläft? Schläft er schlecht, so ist er schlecht gelaunt. Schläft er gut, no, dann rückt er auch gern näher. Ich will Ihnen was sagen, Gnädigste, mir können Gnädigste was glauben, ich versteh was vom Geschäft, 12 Jahre bin ich in der Branche tätig, 8 Jahre steh ich hier auf demselben Fleck, was nützen die Hüften, wenn das Bett schlecht ist? Der Mann pfeift auf die schönsten Hüften. Auch wenn er ein Herr Gemahl ist. Gnädigste können orientalische Bauchtänze aufführen, Gnädigste können Ihrer Schönheit den letzten Schliff anlegen und sich ausgezogen vor ihn hinstellen, nackt sozusagen—ich garantiere Ihnen dafür, daß es nichts nützt, wenn der Herr Gemahl schlecht gelaunt ist, nicht einmal bei Ihnen, meine sehr verehrte Gnädigste, und das will etwas heißen! Wissen Sie, was der Herr Gemahl tun, gesetzt den Fall, Gnädigste sind alt und schlecht—das Bett mein' ich, der Herr Gemahl fliegen aus und suchen sich bessere Betten aus. Und was glauben Sie, was für Betten? Betten von unserer Firma. Ich könnte Ihnen Anerkennungsschreiben zeigen, meine schönste Gnädigste, von Gnädigsten wie Sie. Sie würden staunen über die glücklichen Ehen, die wir stolz auf unserem ruhigen Gewissen haben. Bei uns gibt es keine Scheidungen. Scheidungen kennen wir nicht. Wir tun, was wir können und die Herrschaften sind zufrieden. Am meisten rate ich Ihnen zu dieser Garnitur, Gnädigste. Gut sind alle, dafür garantiere ich Ihnen, Gnädigste, aber diese hier lege ich Ihnen ganz besonders an ihr goldenes Herz, meine liebe Gnädigste!" (*DB*, 82–83)[210]

So in terms of the idea that Canetti enjoys subverting the empirically incontrovertible rituals of everyday bourgeois life, the above is exemplary. Sex has not taken place in marriage, and Therese is being given tips on inducing excitement by a salesman who believes that the article, bed, is what makes or breaks a marriage. If, meanwhile, the actual marriage between Therese and Peter Kien is an active "Kriegszustand," it is important that when Therese returns to Herr Grob in the shop, the narrative does not read like an extract from a mainstream, nineteenth-century novel of adultery. In other words, although the action of pursuing another man constitutes, technically, evidence that Therese is vulnerable to adultery, the spirit of the sections of the narrative that animate her pursuit of an alternative is so theatrical that Canetti shows he does not accept the "category," adultery. There is no distinction in terms of style of writing when we deal with what most "bourgeois" writers would feel to be a "serious" issue.

The narrative does not allow Therese to pursue Herr Grob with any real seriousness of intent. As a result, she is not associated with will power or acts of will. Again, contrary to the sexism latent in many of the bourgeois studies of adultery, Therese is not primarily either an object of her own desire or the object of someone else's. She is an equal participant in the competitive game of existence, whose skills of improvisation come to her aid whenever Canetti sees fit to animate a scene that shows these skills off to effect:

> Sie ladet den Menschen ein und um Dank wird er frech. Hat sie vielleicht was von ihm wollen? Sie hat das nicht nötig, fremden Männern nachzurennen. Sie ist eine verheiratete Frau. Sie ist kein Dienstbot', der mit jedem Mann geht.
>
> Im Gasthaus hat er erst die Speisekarte genommen, gefragt, was er uns bestellen soll. Sie war so dumm und hat darauf gesagt: "Aber zahlen tu ich." Was der sich alles bestellt hat. Sie würde sich ja jetzt noch vor den Leuten schämen. Er hat geschworen, er ist ein besserer Mensch. Es ist ihm auch nicht an der Wiege gesungen worden, daß er ein armer Angestellter sein muß. Sie hat ihn getröstet. (*DB*, 102)[211]
>
> Bevor er mit dem zweiten Schnitzel anfängt, nimmt er ihre Hand und sagt: "Das ist die Hand, die mir zu meinem Glück verhelfen wird."
>
> Dabei kitzelt er sie. So schön kitzeln kann der Mensch. Das hat ihr noch niemand gesagt, daß sie ein Glück ist. Und ob sie sich beteiligen möchte an seinem Geschäft?
>
> Woher er denn auf einmal das Geld dazu hat?
>
> Da hat er gelacht und gesagt: das Kapital gibt ihm seine Geliebte.
>
> Sie spürt, wie sie einen roten Kopf kriegt vor Wut. Wozu er eine Geliebte, wenn sie da ist, sie ist auch noch ein Mensch!
>
> Wie alt die Geliebte ist? hat sie gefragt.
>
> Dreißig, hat er gesagt.
>
> Ob sie schön ist? hat sie gefragt.
>
> Die Schönste von allen, hat er gesagt.
>
> Da hat sie ein Bild von der Geliebten sehen wollen.
>
> "Gleich, bitte sehr, auch damit kann ich dienen." Auf einmal steckt er ihr den Finger in den Mund, so einen schönen, dicken Finger hat er, und sagt: "Das ist sie!"
>
> Wie sie drauf nichts antwortet, zupft er sie am Kinn, so ein zudringlicher Mensch, macht unterm Tisch was mit seinem Bein, drückt fest, tut man das, und schaut ihr in den Mund

> und sagt: er ist in einem glücklichen Liebestaumel und wann er die prachtvollen Hüften ausprobieren darf. Sie soll sich auf ihn verlassen. Er versteht was vom Geschäft. Bei ihm geht nichts verloren. (*DB*, 102–3)[212]

The tension that sustains the above scenes is a comic one. The classic adulteress would actually relish the "dangerous" elements of an encounter in a restaurant. Therese's attitude of surprise that Herr Grob consumes all that is put in front of him is responsible for diffusing the tension of danger that tends to get associated with the illicit. Her "defense" of herself to herself that she is "anständig," despite the fact the scene is set in a restaurant, where she is with someone who is not her husband, could hardly be read in "mimetic" terms. Of course it is plausible for someone to want something deemed illicit but to be prey to doubts at the last minute. But the narrative makes no concessions to the kinds of emotions associated with failure of will.

Therese's self-possession, or her will to live, is as pronounced as the self-possession of Herr Grob. In this respect the encounter is an encounter between equals, not because they treat each other as equals, but because the spirit of theatricality that animates the dialogue and narrated monologue acknowledges the will to live, indeed pays tribute to it. Therese's thoughts as she reflects on the encounter are not an exercise in self-deception, but a theatrical animation of the very idea of being "bourgeois." The dialogue between Therese and Herr Grob is an equally theatrical animation of the difference between a "bourgeois" kind of pride and an opportunist skirt-chaser. The animation of bourgeois pride is as full-blooded as the animation of Herr Grob's opportunism, and in both cases bourgeois pride and opportunism are mere pretexts. For instance, the disjunction between what Therese is doing and the category of bourgeois respectability is as gaping as the disjunction between what Herr Grob is saying and doing and the category of the opportunist seducer. In the latter case, Herr Grob makes the obscene gesture about his girl friend before asking Therese outright when he can show her a good time. As tactics these can hardly compel the imaginative consent of the reader to the category "seducer."[213] Since both "outlooks" are lovingly depicted, Canetti shows how he is able to value and enjoy what it is that makes people have character, which is nerve and verve. From an extra-textual point of view a further implication of the above comedy concerns the way in which Canetti distances himself from the category of the illicit. He promotes play as something licit, once again, and as an experience *for* the reader, not as part of the experience of any one character in the novel. Characters in the text are only important inasmuch as they can be manipulated to produce this effect on the reader.

Curtius' view about Therese's "involvement" with Herr Grob, generally speaking, is a pessimistic one altogether, and is based on the view that there is *no* disjunction between words/concepts and deeds in the novel as a whole: "Die lange Szene aus dem Roman *Die Blendung* zeigte die Warenwerbung als das, was sie ist: die letzte Möglichkeit einer entfremdeten Sexualität, vollendete Umkehrung der Rollen Ware und Kommunikation. Die Sexualität ist Ware geworden, die Ware versucht im Bewußtsein der Individuen an ihre Stelle zu treten."[214] This view is shared by Michel-François Demet, whose idea in his article is that there is a relationship between repressed sexuality and the instinct to murder, in references to blood throughout the novel.[215]

It is possible to argue here, in conclusion, that the sections of the novel that loosely refer us to extra-textual phenomena like love, sex, marriage, and adultery, are as animated by the spirit of theatricality as sections examined in the last chapters. The spirit of theatricality deconstructs the "traditional" meaning of ideas related to society and social living, like seduction and bourgeois pride, ideas that are loosely called up by the scenes examined. However, the scenes do not allow the reader to construct the two ideas as reified concepts. They allow the reader, positively, to participate fully in the spirit of theatricality, which renders them silly as constructs.

It would be appropriate, here, however, to point out how distant Canetti is from turn-of-the-century decadent thinking about love, sex, marriage, adultery, and the relationship of women to these areas of human experience. Turn-of-the-century decadent thinking is highly conceptual. Canetti makes rather timid gestures toward the contributions of Schiele, Klimt, Kokoschka, et al. to the woman question. Schorske, Timms,[216] Wagner,[217] Frank Field,[218] Jacques le Rider,[219] and many others, have all drawn a map that shows that the literati, the painters, and the theoreticians of human behaviour in Vienna at the turn of the century were deeply implicated in a binary method of thinking about women that was reductive in the extreme. As Bram Dijkstra has argued, they are idols of perversity, fantasies of feminine evil:

and as fantasies, as objects of desire, they rob woman of any possibility of subjectivity, of subjecthood, for they are based on the assumption that woman is not a subject.[220] They take the binary method of thinking seriously. Canetti is, for the most part, detached from such a method of thinking, both in the way in which he nervously fails to endorse it at a very serious level, and in the way in which he invents and instates more humane values altogether like agility, mobility, theatricality, and openness in and through language. He preaches a new kind of subjectivity, in contrast to the reified, fixed concentration on stillness common to visual images generally and to the images of women by Klimt, Kokoschka, and Schiele in particular.

Therese does not make a "refreshing" contrast to the misogynist ideas of womanhood promoted by Kraus and Weininger, or to the compromising images of womanhood promoted by Klimt, Kokoschka, Schiele, et al. Canetti must be credited with a highly progressive achievement by the standards of world literature and painting generally, inasmuch as Therese is not seen in terms of sexuality. Neither is Peter Kien and neither are the others, incredible though this may seem, inasmuch as Benedikt Pfaff goes down in the secondary literature as a sadist, or a sexual pervert specializing in incest. What animates Therese's actions and thoughts is what animates the text generally, and all other characters who appear within the text. It is a gratuitous spirit, which is the spirit of play, not for gain, but as an end in itself. For Canetti detaches sexuality by refusing to take it seriously as a goal. He does not make it a motivating force. Canetti also refuses to take sexual possession seriously as an event in the linear flow of the narrative, unlike Schnitzler in *Reigen* for instance. We have already seen that it was not what brought either Peter Kien or Therese into the registry office. When Therese goes back to the shop where she originally bought a bed, and when Herr Grob is suddenly with Therese in a restaurant, it is not sexual desire that has got them there. Indeed, motive is demoted altogether, and we find that events take place one after another in terms of the linear narrative, with no one thing leading to another in any deeply causal sense. Reaction takes precedence over action. Canetti makes no concessions to the view prevalent in Vienna at the turn of the century because of the work of Freud, that the sex drive is something intrinsic to human nature. Canetti clearly states elsewhere that he did believe in the sex drive. As far as his novel is concerned, however, he clearly thinks that the idea is not worth anything on its own terms, and certainly not worth stressing on its own terms. He implies, by contrast, that it is from the imagination that power emanates.[221] This is an insight that could be regarded as liberating as far as human relations in life are concerned, since it takes the whole emphasis away from possession and/or ownership, stressing that the origins of the reciprocity and mutuality necessary for play lie in the quality of the imagination of the individual. This insight also suggests that play is something deeply artificial, not a natural instinct that has to be refined through experience and application. The view that needs to be thought about here is that the text as a whole, with its thorough emphasis on play from beginning to end, is responsible for drawing attention to a view which Canetti is able to suggest only because sexuality as a motive has been detached entirely from individual characters in the text. The sustained interest in play between sentences, in play in scenes, in the gaping disjunction between the tired concepts and ideas with which we all live and the way Canetti rewrites them in practice in his novel, gives *Die Blendung* a formidable agility. This agility has, surprisingly, a very rare kind of eroticism about it. Yet the eroticism is very puritanical, as it is one that does not like easy pleasures. It also refuses to mention any of the words or concepts with which eroticism tends to be more readily associated, like love and sex. It refuses to use these words or turn them into extra-textual concepts that can be applied, as it were, to give textual scenes meaning. It does this because there is a "natural" love and appreciation of infinite play, and partly because, more ambitiously, Canetti presumably believes that love is resistant to description, because it constitutes a mode of being. Love is an attitude and part of an outlook that infuses everything with evidence, proof of its existence within. To say that love and sex as words and events between selected individuals are absent from the text in any primary sense is to state the obvious. Love is absolutely absent in primary terms. Sex is occasionally referred to in bleak terms as a *fait accompli.* Yet the spirit of theatricality which is the dynamism of the novel, and which is the novel's principled refusal to commit a single act of violence against the assumed dignity of individual sentences, and thus persons, is one that, despite all its slapstick, flamboyant qualities, to a very large extent preaches a highly unique theory of love, by the standards of world literature generally.

As Denis de Rougemont and Singer have shown, love in literature has always been imagined as that which can be watched by spectators. Love is a way couples in books and, by extension, on the screen, in pictures, and at large, have of communicating.[222] We acknowledge this particular method of communicating when "looking" at the various well-known gestures we associate with the rituals culture defines as love, gestures with which Canetti's hero Stendhal was obsessed in his *De l'Amour*, where the focus is primarily on the mere moments of falling in love, what Stendhal called "cristallisation," the birth of the relationship with the loved one. Canetti is absolutely original in the way he rejects love as spectacle, as the self-conscious acting out of rituals and conventions or postures devised by culture and acceptable to culture. He is particularly violent about equating love with falling in love, which he rejects altogether. He proclaims, by contrast, that love is an attitude of mind and being, a way of living out an extremely powerful and imaginative kind of closeness. This view does have extra-textual implications as far as eroticism, not "sexuality," is concerned, only because, as already suggested, in promoting play as something endless, the non-material, the non-visible, is stressed. Canetti's eroticism is only something non-material because it is equated with a sense of play, which emanates from the imagination and which makes contact only with other imaginations. Had Canetti wanted to focus more seriously on sex as goal, motive, and event, he could not have written in the agonistic mode. He would have had to write in the mimetic mode, where it is necessary to corroborate things at the level of the material, of the tangible and visible, thereby promoting the material. Again, it is hilarious that an arch-materialist like Freud is invoked so regularly by critics of the novel in support of their interpretations of the novel, since the whole mode of *Die Blendung* is one that is quite violently opposed to causality, that which insists on the material and always gives it precedence over the imaginary. To someone like Stephen Heath, in *The Sexual Fix*, the huge number of discourses about sex that talk "about sexuality" as if it was something you did or had, are a sign not just of the flagging imagination, but of the distance we are from feeling, generally speaking.[223] *Die Blendung* is the novel Heath should have read to write a more hopeful book, because it proclaims so grandly how banal it is to think in the mimetic mode, and because it knows that to counter the potential evil of the material it is necessary to move into a different mode altogether. If the novel's sense of play and eroticism is recognized, this will have the consequence of throwing light on the overt autoerotic and often misogynist basis of so much literature by men that imagines the pleasure of sex with a woman, or imagines heterosexual love. It would obscure those novels by male novelists apparently credited with being progressive for dealing with sexuality, that apparent taboo, such as D.H. Lawrence, the so-called high priest of love. It may even throw light on the limitations of the apparently radical *Ulysses*, with the lyrical/sensual delights of Molly Bloom's soliloquy, the male fantasy of the woman with a nicely insatiable appetite. It would call into question the apparently skillful gestures of the lover/writer as he taps out rhythms on his lover's body, as Goethe does in the fifth of the "Römische Elegien," a poem some critics believe is an erotic poem. Whether Canetti's eroticism is "phallic," and therefore not politically correct, is a matter we can now attempt to investigate.

Phallic desire and phallic eroticism have been identified as the enemy by feminism, not just in the primary sense discussed above, which is to say where heterosexuality at the level of encounter and experience is enacted, but at the secondary level, which is to say at the level of the linguistic rhythm of any text. Phallic desire and eroticism at the level of rhythm are apparently expressed in a certain love of force. The feminists maintain that any text that believes in reason, as it is expressed in character, plot, and the closure of each text, any text that believes in architecture, order, organization, and teleology, believes in the subordination of women and of the feminine at the hands of men, because reason has been the tool, the feminists argue, by which, historically, men have been "empowered" and women "disempowered."

Hélène Cixous, in both her theoretical piece, "le Rire de la Méduse,"[224] and in her own practice as an imaginative writer, in *Le Livre de Promethea*, for instance,[225] and Monique Wittig, in *Les Guérillères*,[226] are obviously advocating "l'écriture féminine," or "weibliches Schreiben." They do this not just by extending the flexibilities of language as we all know it, but by writing in a way that denies the validity of boundaries, ends, moments of absolute power, and moments of submission. This is supposedly a political act, which releases and proclaims the power of what is supposedly essentially "feminine." Feminine is identified with desire in a broader sense than has hitherto been the case amongst primarily male writers, and feminine desire defines itself as that which is endlessly lyrically expressive, never desiring ends, inventive in its vested interest in never bringing "jouissance" to a conclusion. What does *Die Blendung* have to say about the very terms of this debate?

Before attempting to answer this vital question we should indicate where the above comments, generally speaking, stand in relation to the secondary literature on *Die Blendung*. Werner Helwig is one of the few to mention eroticism in any connection with *Die Blendung*. In a review of the novel published in 1963, he speaks of the way in which eros has been banished entirely from the language of the novel, as if this were a real achievement.[227] We have already seen how proudly Canetti spoke of his desire to achieve the same kind of puritanism of language he felt was there in *Le Rouge et le Noir*. The language of Canetti's novel makes no concessions to ornament, to image, metaphor, and symbol, to seductions at the level of surface. The language is pared down almost to an extreme, reminiscent of the kind of puritanism of Loos's theories about architecture, which were so well received by Kraus, as it is reminsicent of the language of Wittgenstein's *Tractatus* and house in Vienna.[228] Loos felt ornament should be banished because it was dishonest and repressive. Canetti's language is not lyrical or expressive, as Cixous and Wittig would wish. In Canetti's novel, however, the non-attention to surface seductions and langorous rhythms expresses a different view, that avoidance of the surface intensifies the spirit and, by extension, the erotic spirit. The spirit has to reign supreme.

Every single sentence of Canetti's vivacious and loquacious novel always assumes the presence of an intimate (the reader) who is always already there and always already disposed to intimacy, who loves in principle, as it were, *already*, for whom love is an attitude of mind. The violently close alliance between two imaginations—the imagination of the text and the imagination of the reader who reads that text—is an alliance at a very deep level, that of a kind of drive, a dionysian rhythm, a rhythm of erotic power. The eroticism of this novel is not something the novel wants to keep to itself because it might be timid, brash, or fearful. It is something already shared. It is not the cultivated autoeroticism of the hermetically sealed solitary (male). *Die Blendung* is writing that assumes community and thus affirms it.

Canetti is unique in this, it would seem, on account of his refusal to exploit the purely aural rhythms of language. Language becomes a tool of intimacy, yet without transforming it aurally, or otherwise, into an overtly self-regarding or stylized kind of language, as both Cixous and Wittig seem to do in their painful attempts to "invent" "new" "intimacy," and to challenge "received" ways of thinking. Canetti assumes, in the way he writes, that his reader is an absolute equal, who is above histrionics. Canetti also refuses to promote himself as an entertainer of a passive audience, as Kraus did. He has put himself at the disposal of his text, as it were, and effaces himself behind a universal spirit of love. Reading the text becomes an exercise in pleasure for his reader, because every single part of the text conspires to produce a kind of pleasure that is not essentially intellectual, by any means, despite the intellectual stamina one needs to read *Die Blendung*. The novel is infused with a gay spirit of hilarity which produces general well being, as opposed to specific "satisfactions." The reader collaborates with the text to discover that his/her capacity for pleasure is infinite.

John Berger, in *Ways of Seeing*, argues that men are and women appear.[229] The feminist Luce Irigaray, in her seminal work, *Speculum de l'autre femme*, argues that woman is measured according to her specular attractiveness on the free market, where she is, anyway, an object of exchange between men.[230] The notion of the woman as the object of sight is of course now central to feminism generally, as it is to film theory. It is also now a problem in theory, generally speaking, as is clear from the sexist question posed by a feminist film theorist, E. Ann Kaplan, in her essay, *Is the Gaze male?*[231] Fredric Jameson, influenced by a different line of argument about seeing, more closely associated with Jean Baudrillard, has taken seeing to its logical conclusion in *Signatures of the Visible* and elsewhere.[232] He has maintained that all seeing is a form of pornography, since when one lingers lovingly on something, an object, its status as a reified object increases the longer one lingers lovingly over it.[233] Further, our postmodern or late capitalist society is one in which the prevalence of mass culture, culture characterized by sight, has succeeded in abolishing the modernist separation of art from the masses. Everything has been aestheticized in a mass cultural way, and we are no longer in a position to launch any critique of our problems, in the tradition of the Frankfurter Schule, to distinguish between what might be life-enhancing and what not.

In other, again highly sophisticated, ways, Canetti is progressive here. Not only is the traditional "object" of sight, woman, in the form of Therese, not seriously "seen" in the text by other characters: no one is seen. She is, more importantly, as active as a force of personality as the other male characters in the novel. She is as personable as Kien. We shall see in the next chapter that she is as personable as Benedikt Pfaff and Fischerle. In primary terms, she is never allowed to be the object of someone else's desire, just as Benedikt Pfaff, Fischerle, and Kien are not the objects of anybody else's desire. When desire between individuals seems to be the theme, we have seen how Canetti diffuses any progress toward conquest, by denying motive and instating the spirit of play, which can speak through individual subjects. This could be interpreted as primary evidence of Canetti's recognition of the equality of the sexes, and, in the second instance, as a recognition of the absolute autonomy of all people, irrespective of sex, and, above all, irrespective of theories of gender. Each character has an aura of absolute otherness that is splendid and, despite the oddity of the claim, extraordinarily charismatic.

But Canetti could be seen to be beyond seeing, generally speaking, in another sense, to which we have alluded already once. The novel's clear priority is with speaking (characters and the narrator are always speaking) and hearing (the reader is always listening to the voice of the characters who speak). For the text stresses the absolute equality and absolute necessity of both hearing and listening, *in absolutely equal measure*. The novel is the living embodiment of civilization conceived as a dialogue, based on an awareness of the equality of both listening and speaking, both themselves animated by the spirit of love. This stress on hearing can be read as homage to Kraus: the section of the autobiography that examines the spell cast on Canetti by Kraus is called "Die Schule des Hörens," and the title of the second volume continually stresses the debt to the great man's rhetorical skills as an orator and to his formidable awareness of the sounds of words: *Die Fackel im Ohr*. And of course Canetti pays tribute to sound in other titles, in *Der Ohrenzeuge* and in *Die Stimmen von Marrakesch*, for instance, just as he also proclaims the body in *Die gerettete Zunge* and *Das Augenspiel*. Here, it is interesting to note that Susan Sontag has stressed the emphasis on hearing in Canetti. Needless to say, her view also has to serve some function. The stress on listening is evidence of Canetti's dependence on listening in Hebraic culture. Sontag argues that it sets him apart from Greek culture, which, she maintains, is characterized by an emphasis on seeing.[234]

Contemporary reflections on the essence of postmodernism, influenced by Baudrillard, who believes that the symbol of First World culture is the television, grapple with the problem and implications of contemporary society's dependence on watching in absolute passivity, as indicated by the reference to Frederic Jameson above. In connection with this, Thomas Docherty in *After Theory*, following a lead taken by Lyotard in *Just Gaming*, has drawn out the distinctions between seeing and listening, arguing in detail why listening is ideologically superior to seeing.[235] Listening is preferable to seeing, because it should lead to a respect for all discourses and thus create what the intellectual Left likes, namely the utopia of a genuinely pluralist society. It is capable of achieving these aims because it is inherently temporal, diachronic, while the visual is spatial and synchronic. It is more likely to promote action, even political action, than seeing. This becomes Docherty's general belief in the so-called ethics of "*alterity*," the free celebration of heterogenous "difference," those two watchwords in postmodernism at the moment, which are receiving so much attention, and to which we can respond in later chapters.

My point here, in mentioning the contemporary "critique" of seeing, is not to endorse Canetti's novel in the terms of that debate. On the contrary, Canetti denies sight altogether in a way that neither Baudrillard, Jameson, Irigaray, nor any of the others can or want to. They hold on to the material; they need it. Canetti is violent and passionate by contrast, both in denying sight and in proclaiming talk and sound. He is free from the source of what, yes, *may be* a debilitating disease, in a way the critics mentioned above, for all their critical protestations of the evil, in essays in which there is an ever-increasing proliferation of information concerning where you can find the evil, are not. Indeed, their desperate affirmation of the awfulness of seeing shows the extent to which they are hostage to the enemy. It is also what prevents them from entertaining viable alternatives, except of course in terms of a Big Idea. Docherty is exemplary in this respect, for his is a utopia that remains clinically abstract. Theory, in the end, one could deduce, prefers the theory of new practices rather than the practices themselves. And theory is incapable of turning itself into practice of any kind, because of its unconscious, vested interest in prolonging debates at a merely theoretical level. This is presumably why the debate is being perpetuated by academics who seem keen, not to train people to think, but to indoctrinate them, in particular to encourage them to mimic their own extraordinarily simplistic and undiscriminating theories.

For the moment, I would like to conclude this chapter with a tribute to Barbara Meili's study of Canetti's novel, *Erinnerung und Vision: Der lebensgeschichtliche Hintergrund von Elias Canettis Roman Die Blendung*, which was first published in 1985.[236] This makes a wonderful, and highly refreshing, change to the extraordinarily turgid quality of most *Die Blendung* criticism, most of which constitutes exceptionally unenjoyable reading for the professional critic. We alluded in Chapter One to Canetti's personal background at the time of writing the novel. Meili takes a much longer view than the one proposed that this chapter about the personal history present in *Die Blendung*. Her sensitive hypotheses are very convincing, none of which one could argue about, as it were, in a court of law, because they are suppositions. She looks at the emotional experiences, in terms of relationships between people, of Canetti's life generally, as described by the man himself in his autobiography. She sees, in most characters in the novel, forms of tribute, colored by love, to concrete characters with whom Canetti was more than familiar. This is a useful corrective to mainstream criticism of the novel, inasmuch as it also identifies love as crucial, despite its non-evidence at the primary level in the text. Meili does not identify love as the spirit of the text as a whole; she works within the more fixed framework that love requires for its existence two named, concrete individuals, and is something experienced privately between two people. The spirit of love is, in terms of the ideas of this chapter, and by contrast, depersonalized. It does not fall into the trap of assuming it will reserve itself for the future, for the one who is worthy of the gift. It is always already both aristocratic and democratic. It despises the bourgeois, and it despises the institution of the couple, for it believes in a community of equals bound together not by law or duty, but by the desire to affirm community by means of a flamboyant, sociable, and bountiful spirit of theatricality. It is both aristocratic and democratic, because it assumes that all people are *capable* of cooperation, and because it links up with Homer's idea of the aristocrat as someone who is powerful, not someone born with blue blood. There is no credence given to the view that there are only *some* people in the world, and further, that that minority, to add insult to injury, is only *worthy* of cooperation.

So where does the above put *Die Blendung* in terms of the debate about politically correct kinds of desire and eroticism? The central weakness of the positions taken up by the protagonists in the debate in feminism paraphrased above, is obvious. Feminism imagines and practices a kind of deconstruction that assumes its ideological origins about the subordination of women are beyond doubt and yet continues to assume a binary opposition. It invents a new one, and this time evil is equated with the masculine and good with the feminine. In other words, it commits the crime of instating more, alternative, monolithic structures. This has been clearly identified by commentators as the problem of essentialism.[237]

But even if one casts aside the political apparatus surrounding writing and reading, and simply takes Wittig and Cixous, to name but two examples, on their own terms, what marks out their writing as better or superior or "empowering," from any point of view? Their weakness is substantial. It consists of an ignorance of detail, of the small thing, of the concrete, intentional no doubt, but problematic, and it consists of the resultant failure to be inventive about the future, as a strategy and an attitude of open commitment. Put in other words, there is no interest in negotiation, in cooperation with others. The creation of desire as an end in itself is not just a refusal in terms of life, it is also a refusal to negotiate with complexity at any level. For desire can never be a strategy for living, if by living one accepts the necessity of having to negotiate obstacles set up by others. The enthusiasm for desire thus doubles up as a refusal to negotiate with, or to enter into an alliance with, the concrete and relatively complicated facts of human existence. As such, it advocates indifference as far as the resolution of issues is concerned, or separatism *tout court*. The writing on the wings of desire, the poems of love in prose, superficially appealing as they may seem at first, also become, after a while, another kind of autoeroticism, of desire on its own, solitary and without community. Whereas male novelists in the past might have hidden their capacity to commune with themselves under a complex web of apparent sociability—inventing characters with personalities meeting other characters with personalities—our two examples of practitioners of "l'écriture féminine" do not even invent character in the obvious way. They dispense with it entirely, yet they are as lonely as their male antagonists.

Cixous, in "le Rire de la Méduse," preached the importance of releasing the libido from its chains. My answer to the question raised above is that *Die Blendung* knows intuitively about the danger of focusing too materially on gender and desire as if they were ends in themselves. By and large, it does away with both, because it knows, deeply, that men and women (and the libido) are absolutely nothing without the imagination. If the imagination is to be given any kind of new lease of life, it has to be encouraged to invent new connections, to see new connections *between the ordinary things, amongst the ordinary things* that we all take for granted, to learn to invest everything with a spirit that assumes already that everything is significant. Thus Canetti's dependence on a loosely bourgeois world is a way of saying that it is necessary to start with the empirical world of ordinary bourgeois reality and take it from there, and, more importantly, use pyrotechnics with respect to language and theatricality, to transform the facts of ordinary bourgeois reality with which we all have to cope at some level on a daily basis. Canetti also indicates, by implication, what kind of disposition, what kind of agility of mind is necessary, if one is going to be able to negotiate genuine complexity, not evade it completely as if it were not relevant. Whether deployed for purely aesthetic or ethical reasons, words, not ideas, are our salvation. The preference for the open-ended quest for agility and hilarity in exchanges is certainly based on a desire to exercise one's wits, and to participate in frivolity and facetiousness. This is not an attempt to downgrade the complexities of ethical reasoning, but to suggest that the spirit of love might itself be a serious answer to issues of ethical reasoning, since, as an attitude, it is likely to produce justice and respect. The first sentence of Canetti's essay on "Macht und Überleben" reads: "Zu den unheimlichsten Phänomenen menschlicher Geistesgeschichte gehört das Ausweichen vor dem Konkreten."[238]

Neither Cixous nor the feminists is likely to take up *Die Blendung*, and indeed, not one feminist has taken up either a positive or negative position with respect to Canetti's novel. They are not likely to do so because there is too much hostility now to writing by men, to writing that is mental, and because there is too strong a belief in the feminine as something superior and as that which is, broadly speaking, only endlessly lyrical: clearly *Die Blendung* is endlessly mental and not even remotely lyrical. Yet the feminist project runs the risk of becoming bankrupt, for even where it is limited to retrieval of lost woman writers, and not just to deconstructing the representation of woman in writings by men, there seems to be no escape from patriarchy. Patriarchy destroys women both literally and figuratively: this is the message. Sensitive to women as George Eliot, Edith Wharton, and Elizabeth Bowen are, and as so many sophisticated women critics are, Eliot's, Wharton's, and Bowen's exceptional women are, after all, exceptional women by the standards of patriarchy. When such women rebel, the independent-minded, those who refuse to market themselves on the terms formulated for them by patriarchy, are still imagined by Bowen, Eliot, and Wharton as victims of patriarchy.

Die Blendung does not know, by contrast, about failure in this absolute sense. It does not know about it because it is imaginatively dedicated to refusing categories altogether, as it is imaginatively dedicated to faith in the future: and it has this faith because it believes in words, not ideas. It was T.S. Eliot who said this about Henry James, that his mind was so fine it was incapable of taking ideas seriously. This is true only in a relative sense, however. Relative to Thomas Hardy and Dickens and George Eliot, Henry James lives experience at a much, much more intense level than his forebears: the reflective consciousness in Henry James is concrete, because it is lived out, it is not expressed in theoretical ideas as these may be personified in characters or discussed by a garrulous narrator. Yet underlying all James's studies of intensity as an experience are, nevertheless, theories about conduct, flexible and non-prescriptive as these are. Canetti's open-minded commitment to the concrete constitutes a more passionate belief in the value of intelligence and the way intelligence can help us invent practical strategies for living in a spirit of faith, and acceptance, and appreciation of other selves in the community. His belief in intelligence is, then, a belief in the importance of asking practical questions in such a way as to increase the likelihood of finding answers and solutions to those questions. It is not a belief in asking endlessly rhetorical questions, which lead to practical and emotional indifference to real problems. Canetti does not believe in a coercively formulated agenda, but in the openness that is likely to lead to justice: the recognition of the points of view of all concerned, and the assistance and enthusiasm that will encourage those points of view to be realities, not merely ideas.

As an indication of the extent to which this position is alien to mainstream criticism of the novel, it would be useful to bear in mind how critics who read with a view to seeing how the world is represented in the text, how its plot and character refer to concepts and ideas, express what it is they think the novel is about, what it displays to such advantage. Claudio Magris might have been any number of critics when he argued that Canetti's novel had an intuitive, and radical, understanding of how awful life is without love (267–68).[239] Canetti is, in fact, one of the very few who knows about love, probably because he is not fascinated by, nor preocuupied with, projecting fantasies onto people, thereby reifying them and fixing the terms within which they are expected to behave. The spirit of agonistic play, by contrast, is one that enacts in the present, as it projects for the future, an imaginative space for a democratic community peopled by aristocrats in the aesthetic sense. Such a community is one within which individuals can collaborate with other individuals, as players, as lovers of, and worshippers of, each human being's capacity for creating pleasure as a mutual experience. It is a community whose sound basis believes that no one has the right to violate the absolute autonomy of the individual, to do violence to that autonomy.

It is this idealism, we can now conclude, and the systematic dedication to the practice of this idealism, that makes it rather obvious that Canetti has very little in common with the kind of apparently radical, apparently subversive postures of Bahktin and his followers. Canetti's idealism is not prepared to accept any one of the tenets of cultural critics of a loosely leftist persuasion. These work with the idea that social, political, and moral life on earth is destructive of the power of the individual. This set of first principles has its origins in their belief that power only operates in and through institutions and always to the detriment of individuals. Their theory is that freedom can only be realized by attacking the social manifestations of power outside the self, by defining oneself by opposing those social manifestations of power outside the self. For Canetti, such a first principle is already a sell-out. Its terms are only dubious because they inevitably result in a kind of affirmation of the possible intrusiveness of power structures outside the individual, and because they can lead to real complacency in terms of those personal initiatives that will lead to life-enhancing experiences for the individual and protect him from the frustration of defeat in the face of the intractability of monolithic power structures in the world. Canetti's first principle is that the priority has to be with the real, creative power within the personality, at each individual's disposal. It is the only power he is prepared to recognize and use. Whilst the Left predictably denounces as practically impotent or apolitical this kind of non-recognition of power structures in politics, society, and culture, Canetti's reply, in the form of the very motor of *Die Blendung*, provides a coherent and ruthless assessment of the bankruptcy, the complacency, the intellectual confusions and dead ends of the leftist world view.

5

Dionysus Dissolves Fixity and Form: "Frohlockender Wahnsinn" in *Die Blendung*

Marcel Brion mentioned in his French review of 1949, in his comparison of *Die Blendung* with Kafka's novels, that Canetti's novel had a kind of freedom not to be found in Kafka: "Il témoigne d'un certain goût de la virtuosité, d'un esprit de jeu, totalement absents l'un et l'autre de l'oeuvre de Kafka . . ."[240] John Bayley is also appreciative of this playfulness. He comments on the sheer mental, magical, and dynamic quality of the language.[241] We have talked about play in the last chapters: now we can show how playfulness takes over when the attention is on the figure Fischerle, and when a number of figures are brought together, exceptionally by the standards of this novel, in the sections running up to "Privateigentum" in the second part of the novel, known as "Kopflose Welt."

It does not seem appropriate to draw a substantial distinction between play and playfulness, but playfulness seems to have more ease about it than "straight" play, as it were. It is also far less intensely competitive than the drive that seemed to animate most of the early sections of the novel examined so far. Playfulness, as it is exploited when Fischerle is himself animated and later throughout the whole of the chapter "Privateigentum," has a lightness of touch that is near-lyrical, in this most apparently unlyrical of novels. The modulation from a mood of play into a mood of playfulness is only achieved because the dynamism of the narrative becomes more leisurely. The narrative throughout these middle sections is as riddled with personality as those sections already discussed: yet the angularity, dryness, and abruptness of the interchanges between Kien and Therese and Therese and Herr Grob, and the abruptness of the narrated monologue attributed to either Therese or Kien, gives way to a kind of talking that is more relaxed in itself, one that involves a number of characters who are themselves more leisurely than either Therese or Kien.

The constituent parts of the middle sections are, however, also ever ready to proliferate and multiply, and in this the middle sections are intrinsically different from the earlier sections already discussed. At a superficial level, this proliferation, or endless capacity of the narrative to sustain imaginative invention, is obvious inasmuch as the middle sections of the novel are, as intimated above, at once both more sociable in tone and more social. Besides Peter Kien, who is a constant throughout, there are a wide range of new figures, all of whom have very individualized contributions to make. Fischerle and Benedikt Pfaff make their first appearances, as do the four figures associated with Fischerle who make up his support group of thieves, known respectively as "der schlaflose Hausierer," "der Kanalräumer," "der Blinde," and "die Fischerin." In the chapter "Privateigentum," a masterpiece of theatricality which is sustained by a quite beautiful elegance, a veritable stage is present on which character after character makes his/her appearance, to give a set speech: the cast is led by the "Kommandant," but also includes Therese, Peter Kien, "Der Gedächtniskünstler," and Benedikt Pfaff. It is noticeable that Fischerle is absent at this point. The middle sections of the novel also see the spoken word used in specifically social contexts, as against its use in, say, the solitary flat of Peter Kien: there is the pub/"brothel" "Zum idealen Himmel," from which Fischerle and his wife operate, and into which Peter Kien walks after he has been thrown out of his own flat. There is the police station where "Privateigentum" is set: there is the pawn shop, there are hotels, there are tailors, etc. Speaking out loud in public, if itself less aggressive and peremptory than the speaking out loud we have already encountered, is accompanied by an emphasis on the set speech, or extended spoken narrative, in which an absolute mockery is consistently made of virtually all of the cardinal rules of rhetoric associated with public speaking, namely those of cognition and persuasion. A series of ideas is specifically not held together by any kind of formal logic. Instead, as we shall see, non-sense, no less, is raised to dazzling heights. Such moments become the key/critical/crucial moments in the narration, and nowhere more so than in "Privateigentum," where figure after figure takes it in turn to present an account to an audience, and an account that is always wantonly whimsical and carelessly dismissive of Truth, Beauty, and/or Goodness.

"Action," such as it is, continues to be irrelevant, only inasmuch as the gap between what is promised in words and what is done is kept as wide as ever. At a superficial level, this is obvious inasmuch as the huge amounts of money that are supposedly exchanged, and that are talked about frequently, are never featured in the action. The possible "plausible" consequences of laying one's hands on large amounts of cash, such as glee at possessing such amounts and glee at what money can buy in the world at large, are also excluded from the action. *Money is a hypothesis*, literally, and a token gesture toward motivation, nothing more. It is really no more than a mere pretext for Canetti's display of his capacity to amuse his readers, by teasing them in all sorts of ways, in this case to tease them at the very least about material notions of gain. This view, about the role of money in the narrative, is of course heretical by the standards of the secondary literature, which generally assumes that money is taken very seriously as motive by Canetti and that the characters Fischerle and Therese are seriously interested in it.[242] This view depends on the assumption that Canetti has convinced us that his novel is about characters in the first instance, and thus about what they might want out of life. In the last chapter, the suggestion was made that it would be more appropriate to see the narrative as an aesthetic construct that emphasizes the activity of constructing an illusion at the expense of belief in certain other illusions, like, for instance, the illusion of the holistic construct of character and motive. Its refusal to invest faith in anything outside its own creative capacity to begin again *ex nihilo* was a refusal to accept metanarrative in any form, shape, or size.

This gap between what is promised in words and what is actually done is particulary wide with respect to the two figures who dominate in "Kopflose Welt," namely Fischerle and Kien. In the case of Fischerle, this is obvious in his relationship with the future, when he *will be* chess champion of the world, something that he believes and attempts to "realize" by continuing to talk only about the goal, not the means by which he can gain that goal. Indeed, the narrative never sees fit to render actual an attempt to realize the much-discussed goal. It is obvious in Peter Kien's relationship with the past and the future. In his account in "Privateigentum" of the "death" and "murder" of Therese, Peter Kien talks as if he believed he was responsible for Therese's demise. The reader knows that his story does not correspond to anything established by the narrative, not least because Therese is standing beside him in the police station as he makes this speech. This gap is also clear from what he says he *will have to say*, as he anticipates a future scene in which he has to defend his action of murder in court. Yet the narrative also does not see fit to invent such a scene. It never takes place within the narrative as a whole. These two are only the most obvious examples of the way in which Canetti continues not to bother to follow "motive" through to its "logical" conclusion, to the extent that one feels obliged to argue that he is making a mockery of teleology per se again.

It is this premise that underlines what appears to be "plot," disguised "beneath" a very generous and indulgent form of gratuitous playfulness. This makes ample use of gloriously obvious gaps, only so that the art of perpetual invention as a technique and skill can be laid bare in all its splendor, and as a principle. The above examples also contribute to the feeling that the narrative is extending itself in a leisurely, almost lyrical way. There is a particular kind of anticipation induced in the reader that is never satisfied, one that lingers on as the reader never knows whether the narrative will really be able to establish that Fischerle is the world chess champion, that Peter Kien is the murderer of Therese.

This is to fly in the face of mainstream criticism of the novel here, inasmuch as Peter Kien and Fischerle are usually seen negatively as wrong/deficient/inadequate/deluded in their "perception" of themselves and of the "world" in which they live. Mainstream criticism would see the arrangement of the text in terms of how it breaks down and exposes the so-called hermetically sealed world view of each individual character, as this intransigence specifically excludes that character from meaningful communication in society. Fischerle is blind to the fact that he is not capable of being a world champion in chess, and Kien is blind to the fact that he is technically ignorant of murder. Both would be seen as realistic portraits of "what it is like" to be trapped in one's imagination. Such readings mean that the reader looks on both as rather unfortunate victims of their own imaginations. The argument here, by contrast, is that the figures Kien and Fischerle are elements within a narrative that, in its entirety, continues to tease the reader, cheerfully and strategically, into a sense of delight at the infinite range of possibilities of which the imagination is capable. It does this in part by making Fischerle and Kien positively endearing, and *endearingly* inventive, when both set about telling their respective stories, or their *fairy tales*, concerning murder or victory on the chess board in international terms to anonymous audiences various. The reader feels well-disposed toward figures so wantonly whimsical in their stories, simply because their narratives are outrageous enough in their own right, and transparently ignorant of, and indifferent to, objective truth, whether intra-textually or extra-textually. Individual figures, whilst exerting considerable seductive power over the reader, continue to be submerged by the narrative as a whole.

The narrative as a whole, not individual figures embedded in that narrative, continues to turn itself into the real subject of this novel. It achieves this in this section of the novel by using a slightly different narrative strategy to that which appears in the first four chapters of *Die Blendung* already examined. The narrative strategy exploited exhaustively throughout the middle sections of the novel consists of a special relationship, that between the primary scenes and the narrative within which those scenes are embedded. In narratological terms, this could be described as the relationship between the parts of the narrative involved in "showing" and the parts of the narrative involved in "telling" (Wayne Booth's famous terms), or, in slightly more sophisticated terms, the relationship between "mimesis" and "diegesis."[243] The relationship between apparently primary and apparently secondary material in the narrative can be characterized relatively easily. The diegetic material, or the material that surrounds what appears in dialogue form (or monologue spoken in public to witnesses), *itself positively reacts to* the contributions made endearingly by endearing characters. It is part of the chain reaction idea we have already developed. The consequence of this strategy, which is systematically sustained, is that it serves the purpose of privileging and pleasing the reader.

In "Kopflose Welt," for instance, the narrative can be seen to make positive use of the contributions made by Fischerle and Kien in two particular ways. It makes positive use of those contributions either by endorsing their contents uncritically or by refusing to refute those contents critically, either immediately or retrospectively, which is to say in terms of the arrangement/development of the plot. The fairy-tale-like, whimsical contributions ultimately only help, because of the use made of them by the diegetic material in which the fairy tales are embedded, to serve the "higher" purpose of privileging the reader. S/he is the only one capable of appreciating the strategy being deployed. The diegetic material presents those spoken contributions actively to readers, as if they were nothing less than the "object" of the diegetic material's love. They are loved in their own right as absolutely different, which is to say they respect them by not calling into question what is said, and by not commenting analytically on what is said. They are left as they are, loved in the sense that their existence and their quality are formally acknowledged.

The narrative as a whole asks readers, as a result, to appreciate how sentences and passages are capable of loving one another in this idiosyncratic way, which is to say without the support of, or reference to, any kind of extra-textual, and indeed intra-textual, "reality." The narrative as a whole, asks us, more ambitiously, to understand how it is already in the process of spinning an illusion, of constructing an illusion. It is not spinning a specific illusion and attaching it to an individual personality to endorse that personality, as mainstream criticism of the novel would have us believe. It is saying that the skill of perpetual invention is necessary to the competitive business of spinning illusions. It must also be saying that the material most suited to the art of learning to spin illusions has to be intrinsically non-serious. Material does not have to have a "utilitarian" function in any extra-textual or intra-textual sense. It does not have to love what already exists outside the imagination or inside the imagination, because to make a kind of alliance with a known point of reference is to defy the challenge of spinning the illusion, by creating the new and original. What is important for this is the spirit of affirmation, the emotional, intellectual, and psychological energy one invests in speaking a series of original sentences, as if speaking were a valuable sociable activity capable of affirming others, as well as the self. Put in other words, the sheer and magnificent uselessness of the "plot" at this particular moment, which is to say the absence of scenes that might wrench Fischerle and Kien from what appear to be their posts outside time and space, is a way of endorsing the overall activity of the narrative as a whole at this stage, which is a creative activity, *the essence of art, that of spinning an illusion over an empty void.* The fact that we laugh, the effect produced by the arrangement of Canetti's chosen material, leads us to believe that Canetti, who is by no means original in this philosophy of existence, cannot be classified as tragic in his vision.[244] The consistent *absence of gravity* seems to suggest this quite persuasively.

There are distinct echoes of Nietzsche here in a number of different ways.[245] Most obviously, in the sense that one can read Canetti's novel in terms of Nietzsche's critique of metaphysics, his attack on the tradition of Idealism in Western philosophy with its assumption that there is a distinction between appearances and reality and that the world behind appearances is the superior world. Nothing in Canetti's text refers to any Big Idea outside its own parameters. There is no such thing as Truth, whether conceived of as single, univocal, or plural and polyvalent, and Truth is not referential. There are no Essences for Canetti as there are no Essences for Nietzsche. The so-called symbolic order is not there, and in its place we seem to have a delight in what self-styled radicals believe is the semiotic. Instead, because life is nothing *in itself*, it is only an aesthetic illusion, "daß nur als ästhetisches Phänomen das Dasein der Welt gerechtfertigt ist," as it is in *Die Geburt der Tragödie*. The energy that is liberated as a result of the rejection of the fixity of perception imposed by Idealist philosophies is one that has to be harnessed to the future, where the present is affirmed as a creative act by the spirit of willing. History as something of the past and something that contributes to the present is negated. The will to power is the only force. Importantly, this much discussed feature of Nietzsche's work as it is applied sympathetically in Canetti's novel does not want or covet or seek power in material terms, merely to affirm the creative power of shaping an eternal present. The eternal return is not repetition of the same but transmutation to eliminate all half-willing. The world created is one that is beyond good and evil. It is a world for Nietzsche's free spirits. Nietzsche's condemnation of everything that is fixed, canonical, and binding, because it is hostile to life, is the view that, interestingly, raises laughter and the dance to dazzling heights. Tarmo Kunnas, in his *Nietzsches Lachen*, reminds us that Nietzsche credits laughter with an existential significance previously not granted it.[246]

These are the activities that turn people from passivity and fixity into genuinely free spirits. No longer is the stress on "Sein" but on "Werden." The distinction between either the tragic vision or the comic vision (into which categories literary critics love to force so much of literature) is dissolved in favor of a vision that apprehends life in a way that mysteriously acknowledges the possibility of both, acknowledging both by way of a tension that is not abandoned. Knowledge of the tension between the two has to be denied and *forgotten*, however, by dreaming, by clothing the terror, pain, and suffering caused by consciousness. One has to escape into a metaphor, as if the metaphor were the truth. In this ability to enchant himself, to discharge Dionsyian insights in Apollonian images, lies man's ability to outstrip himself, to act rather than merely contemplate, and to become rather than be.

It is because of the strange continuity between aspects of Nietzsche and *Die Blendung* that we are now going to move the parameters of the interpretation developed so far, by showing how *Die Blendung* is the novel Nietzsche should have written, given his theories. Canetti translates the theories developed by Nietzsche into actuality, in the sense that *Die Blendung* is a synthesized amalgam of some of the most life enhancing of Nietzsche's insights, collected from the miscellaneous context of Nietzsche's entire opus. Whereas in Nietzsche's entire opus the central precepts are often developed in a thoroughly abrupt and unsystematic way, *Die Blendung enacts* Nietzsche's existential philosophy, a philosophy that Nietzsche maintained again and again was something by which one had to live, not something that remained purely intellectual, yet another contribution to the history of ideas. *Die Blendung* enacts his ideas triumphantly and systematically, and with the kind of emotional mobility, commitment, and steadiness that are clearly not a feature of Nietzsche's method of self-expression. Harold Alderman has this to say about what the link is between laughter and existence as it is developed by Nietzsche in *Also sprach Zarathustra*:

> The over-all structure of the metaphysical comedy at which Zarathustra laughs is now clear: through fear we pretend to be what we are not—absolute, certain, eternal. Through fear we insist that our most illustory pretentions be taken as reality itself. Only this human comedy says, in effect, by lying insistently can we take ourselves seriously enough to accept ourselves. But this apparent seriousness is really only a solemn evasion: unable to accept the light, temporal character of our creations we weigh them down with pretensions to eternality, universality, and absoluteness. Thus it is that the lightest of all things—human creation—is inflicted with the spirit of gravity and becomes, through revenge, too heavy to bear. And thus it is that human thought, the thought of a dancing child playing seriously by himself, becomes transformed into a grotesque heavy thing which we use to hide from ourselves. But this

> absurd metamorphosis merits our laughter. It is the metamorphosis of a finite being pretending to be eternal. Zarathustra's laughter is then a form of criticism which silences and liberates . . . (54)[247]

Canetti's narrative as a whole is this performance. The novel knows that life is only a performance art. The substance of that performance art is relatively insignificant. It is form that indicates whether or not one knows that life is a performance art. That art is the art of spinning an illusion, of working at the necessity of continuing to construct an illusion. This activity has no other function than to show that is answering the challenge of existence. The illusion has no claim to anything resembling absolute truth in itself. The past is always forgotten, in Canetti's novel, in the sense that the prehistory of the characters in the novel is not really presented to the reader in any great detail. When it is presented, it is done in such a way as to suggest that the spirit infusing each personality has always been as mobile as it is. Nietzsche is present in the idea stimulated by *Die Blendung* as a whole, namely that rich and noble souls (the "Übermensch") have to expend themselves prodigally, almost indifferently, in a series of gratuitous acts. Canetti's narrative as a whole, not just individual characters who are presented as ahistorical anyway, is infused by this spirit of prodigality and gratuitousness, a spirit that it very rarely abandons.[248]

Nietzsche's view, contra Decartes et al., was that the individual consciousness and subjectivity had neither ontological nor epistemological status. They had both given rise to the evil of a banal form of individuation, that of feeling alone, being trapped by the constraints placed on action by the Church and State. The Will was capable of liberating people from this prison house and it was, for Nietzsche, a metaphysical entity, the only thing credited with status in his thinking, but without either ontological or epistemological status. It was a source of power in the game of resistance to reductive powers asserted on the individual from without, not something individual, not an instrument of personal dealings or the psychological attribute of a strong-willed person, as it is in, say, Schiller's *Maria Stuart*. It is a force, referred to rather mysteriously as the Primal One, which longs to manifest itself to dissolve the consciousness I have of being me and of being different from everybody else. This process of liberation from the constraints of selfhood and individuation is the experience of reading *Die Blendung.* It is achieved in and through the narrative of *Die Blendung* as a whole, in the sense that the novel does not wish to be read as a display of Canetti's individual will, but is, instead, Will at its most impersonal, in perpetual motion.

The cult of personality to which the notion of the "Übermensch" unfortunately gives rise is one that Canetti's narrative as a whole nowhere endorses. No single individual in the novel achieves an aura and mystique that compel submission of the reader's will. A single spirit, that of theatricality, consistently succeeds in making a mockery of any desire for individuation, by turning all individuals in the narrative into players of a single social game. The presence of Nietzsche can be felt in the way in which the narrative as a whole does not allow for gravity of any kind, least of all for the gravity we associate with the Big Ideas of Plato, Kant, and Descartes. Nietzsche's explicit call for the destruction of the spirit of gravity ("der Geist der Schwere") seems to have been answered very vigorously by Canetti's novel, yet in a way which is much more cool, phlegmatic, and laconic than anything ever attempted in the vein by Nietzsche himself. Big Ideas are not present in Canetti's novel, and figures neither embody Big Ideas nor seem concerned to acquire them.

What is radical, amongst many things, about this, is that in doing so Canetti shows an *indifference* to the cultural, historical, religious, and philosophical framework within which the West has largely worked. Canetti does not take up a position with respect to the Church and the State and the traditions within Western philosophy and social life in Europe, as Nietzsche had done. Nowhere are these institutions and traditions seriously represented in his narrative in a primary sense, as they are in, say, *Katz und Maus, Candide, Gulliver's Travels.* To have done so would have been the gesture of the satirist, at the very least. Canetti has the reputation of a satirist, despite the fact that he ignores altogether the kinds of targets mainstream satirists take for granted. In doing so he suggests, more strongly than Nietzsche and rather grandly, compared to Nietzsche, that they are not only not worthy of our attention, but uninteresting in their own right.

Canetti fulfills Nietzsche's belief that one has to be offensive about life, not defensive. In a *defensive* mind, we erect barriers between ourselves and the hostile reality of a world without meaning, and conventional philosophy, theology, religion, education, and politics assist in this dependence on the already institutionalized and established. In an *offensive*, Dionysian state of mind, we attack these barriers to gain immunity from the effects of nihilism. We enter the nihilistic abyss in order to combat its effects, and we do this by using its own devices. Canetti is different from Nietzsche only in that, in going on the offensive, he refuses absolutely to testify to the intrusions into the subjective imagination of the individual of the State, of the Church, or of the body of knowledge that we all inherit. The offensive drive of the novel in the Nietzschean mode is partly responsible for Broch's view that the novel is singularly abstract. If we compare it to seminal, modernist novels, for instance, where the city is very popular, like Döblin's *Berlin Alexanderplatz*, Dos Passos's *Manhattan Transfer*, and Joyce's *Ulysses*, Canetti is not even prepared to name the city in which the fictional road Ehrlichstraße might be found. It is, to those who know the "Zahnwehchristus" figure in the Stefansdom in Vienna, which features in the first book of *Die Blendung*, obviously Vienna, yet the point here is that Canetti refuses geographical specificity. He wants to banish the already known so that the imagination has a chance to taste its own power for a change. This refusal to acknowledge geography is matched by Canetti's refusal to acknowledge history, as is clear if we read *Die Blendung* alongside seminal works on the complex social, political, and economic history of Austria and Germany, like those by Andics, Carr, Macartney, Garscha, and Zöllner.[249] If there are allusions to social, political, and economic history in Canetti's novel, they are either thin on the ground, incredibly abstract, or simplistic enough to be grabbed at by the kinds of literary critics who are happy to make both the institution of literature and the institution of the critic serve the ends of prophecy, so that novels are just the layman's alternative to the Book of the Apocalypse. Well after the event, critics can then sit around and pat themselves on the back, as they discover that literature affirms how awful History was and is, gloating in the knowledge of the prophet: "I told you so!" So, whereas some people might say that Therese's statement "die Kartoffeln sind zu teuer" is an allusion to the gross economic instability of 1929 and thereabouts, others may suggest that its repeated use in the novel is a strategy that wants to do active violence to the kinds of mindset that adore contemplating (at a safe distance) Causality at work.

Those critics who have tried to appropriate *Die Blendung* for the discourse of history have always done so in a deeply problematic and reductive way. History is nothing more than deeply determinist kinds of psychology/pathology writ large. It is nothing more than the embodiment of a universalist paradigm about how human beings "always are": nature is culture and vice versa. Of course, it goes without saying that the instalment of such paradigms always doubles up as a refusal to instigate change. Universalist paradigms are incapable of *naming* what are the specific reasons/causes for any given phenomenon. They do not want to know about particulars. This eschewal of the particulars that constitute experience is obscured by the confident belief that history is merely a series of protagonists who have individual stories, all of which apparently testify to the "truth" of human nature. It is indicative of the principled weakness of those critics who have adopted *Die Blendung* for history, that *Die Blendung* has been made, not to enact real history of which the author had first hand experience, as Stendhal always did, but something far more spurious, *to anticipate* the totalitarianism associated with the rise of fascism. This is the worshipping of the role of the modern writer as "philosopher king" or prophet. The problem with it is that it advocates the complete alienation of literature from life, as it encourages complacency and passivity as an attitude to real problems that need to be negotiated, not ignored. The writer merely presides over a world deemed already bankrupt and beyond repair, with which decline he has to be complicit if he is merely enacting it. Finally, the attempt by critics to procure *Die Blendung* for history indicates a negative attitude to literature, that literature is not, nor can it be, self-sufficient. It can be dignified, by contrast, by its status as commentary.

Canetti does not use time or place in any overtly historical way. He does not use specific dates, he does not make reference to the body politic in any overt way, and he does not name specific places. If we turn to Stendhal and history and compare *Die Blendung* with the history in any of Stendhal's novels, we can see how Canetti's hero, by contrast, acts as a chronicler who uses dates and recognizable, historically proven movements and ideas relevant to the Restoration in France, in *le Rouge et le Noir*, above all. He does this because he works with the imaginatively flexible view that culture partly constructs nature, and because he more firmly believes in society and community in the ordinary sense of the word than Canetti does. It should be clear from what has been said about *Die Blendung* that Canetti does not accept society in the broader sense, nor the body politic. Yet *Die Blendung* implies that the world can be composed of individuals, who themselves either live in their own highly loquacious imaginations or enjoy civilized agonistic combat in public amongst friends, which is to say in small communities of equals. My argument is that Canetti's two strategies of evasion of place and time, strategies alien to Stendhal's love of place and time, strategies of excluding the named at the level of geography and history/politics, have been misunderstood. They can, however, be seen to serve a Nietzschean purpose that *is* empowering.

Canetti's narrative is a living embodiment of a near-ideal marriage of Apollo and Dionysus, the two central characters of Nietzsche's *Die Geburt der Tragödie*. It is this marriage that constructs *possibility* as an open position, an open agenda. Nietzsche argued that the unchallenged rule of Apollo, or the reliance of the already institutionalized and established, results in rigidity, oppression, repression. Yet without the Apollonian capacity to dream the dream of Parnassus, man cannot live. The dynamic image-making power can be a gift of Apollo and Dionysus only if it is a living synthesis of form and movement, structure and process. Dionysus stops the fixed images of Apollo from becoming frozen into concepts or Big Ideas. Hypostatization of Apollo or Dionysus is destructive of humanity, for humanity can exist only on the boundary line that divides the realms. Nietzsche is present in this sense in *Die Blendung*, in that it is the dynamic drive associated with Dionysus, whom Nietzsche worshipped because he was the ultimate creator/destroyer, that provides the power necessary to keep on constructing the illusion that life is only an aesthetic illusion. This itself can only be realized by Apollonian acts of will. The will is that which resists the "conservative" impulse to rely on fixity and form, the already familiar, the already known, the already *institutionalized*.

The claim here is that Dionysus rules supreme in the novel, in the sense that the "connections" made by the narrative are nothing in themselves in any strictly logical sense. Attention is drawn to what sustains an appearance of purpose, namely the drive and verve of the delivery of sentences, not the "meaning" of the sentences in themselves. Like Nietzsche, who valued the investment of the individual's depersonalized will in the future, Canetti's novel compels the reader in the present by the conviction that teleology is a matter of the future. It is not the gloss one puts on the past when one wants to show that every phenomenon has logical, ultimate causes, which is the more conventional form teleology takes, especially in novels. Nietzsche's philosophy of the future is followed to the letter by Canetti, in the sense that the narrative as a whole and all the characters embedded in that narrative live out life in the present with a commitment that is so dynamic as to imply that it is confidence in the future that is driving everything forward. The momentum of Canetti's novel is sustained by this confidence, with the exception of the problematic chapters at the end of the third part, where Big Ideas feature rather prominently. These will be looked at separately.

Just as Canetti has no truck with any of the Romanticism of Nietzsche, expressed by his occasional worshipping of single, elite individuals who are rebels, challenging the status quo (the "Übermensch" in the guise of the flamboyant Christ-like figure Zarathustra), he has no truck with the world view that might be produced by such an individual, and that would encourage him/her to luxuriate in his/her being that solitary, elite individual. The two are inextricably linked. There is obviously Nietzschean-style perspectivism of a more respectable kind in *Die Blendung* inasmuch as Peter Kien, Therese, Fischerle, Benedikt Pfaff, and George(s) are all memorably individualistic and riddled enough with character to linger for years in the reader's imagination—so perspectivism, or the right of the individual to create his/her own fictions, is enshrined as a principle in the narrative. But the ultimate status of each of those figures in the narrative as a whole is relative to the way in which the substance of their highly individual perspectives or illusions about life furnishes that narrative as a whole with a reason to carry on prolonging the fun of theatricality per se, the ultimate illusion. The narrative as a whole has greater significance than any individual figure or feature of it. In so doing, Canetti makes it clear that art is not an imitation of nature. Rather, art can explore the possibility of getting beyond the isolation of perspectivism, by positing a community of happy and free spirits endlessly helping one another to prolong the fun of having fun, by reacting or responding, at the level of mimicry, to the spirit of theatricality in words, not the letter of those words themselves. Art is *a metaphysical supplement*, raised up beside nature to overcome it, wherein man forgets the past in order to be, existentially, in the present, in the fullest sense, ever-resistant to any kind of Idea that will impose permanent order or fixity.

The diegetic material of Canetti's novel imitates the theatricality of the mimetic material so a *dance* can continue, and so the reader can learn the art of respecting the autonomy of each individual, of realizing that everything is a matter of opinion, that all human beings have points of view in the largest sense of the word, and that no one point of view has any greater or lesser status than any other. Canetti goes one step further than Nietzsche inasmuch as his narrative shows, by example, how life is a dance of endearingly meaningless opinions, where style is of far greater importance than content. The existential significance of the dance, in other words, is as a valuable way of life. This has been examined recently by Georg Stauth and Bryan Turner, in *Nietzsches' Dance: Resentment, Reciprocity and Resistance in Social Life.*[250]

In *Die Blendung*, we find that the authors of specific, albeit meaningless, opinions, are not given any status, and the opinions themselves are suspended, as it were, in a dance-like trance, as if to say that the best thing any one of us can do is play a game with the material that is provided by countless, loquacious voices, expressing opinions. The thing that should be avoided is to latch on to any one view, to either endorse it above all others or endorse its author above all others. To do one or the other is to lapse into the dangerous game of the personality cult, to substitute a game in which one person (a performer) becomes an object of "desire," with the desiring subject a mere passive spectator—a relationship based on inequality. In the dance, by contrast, each person is a performer, who can lose his/her sense of himself/herself in and through dancing. Spectating is redundant. The tyranny of individualism is continually being broken by the rejection of form implicit in the movement that is the dance—Canetti's individual sentences do not relate together at a deep semantic level, but they bristle with energy and respect one another by refusing to comment on or correct one another. They use one another, only to prolong the pleasure of entertainment for all—they react to one another by imitating one another. This is mimicry. Mimicry, which Roger Caillois felt was another of the forms of play neglected by Huizinga, rules supreme. The narrator's function in *Die Blendung* is ludic, not ethical. All of which suggests that the narrative of *Die Blendung* acts as the powerful celebration of the loss of individuation and its pains which Nietzsche associated with the chorus in Greek tragedy in *Die Geburt der Tragödie*.

We can perhaps see in this a rewriting of Schnitzler's *Reigen*. The dance of death which is *Reigen* is kept moving by sexual desire. It is sexual desire that makes a mockery of any of the distinctions (social and otherwise) that allow people to assume that there is order and a "natural" hierarchy within society. The determinism is profound and undercuts any of what is clearly felt to be the individual's "vanity" or hubris of assuming that the individual has any rights. The dance of *Die Blendung* does not allow for the dissolution of autonomy. It celebrates absolute differences between people, because what keeps the dance going is not sexual desire, which can, but does not have to, destroy autonomy, but the spoken word. The spoken word does no violence to other people, if it is not exploited for the purposes of persuasion or cognition. It cannot destroy if used in a non-exploitative way; in fact, it can preserve. Even though it is always partially allied to individualized characters, the arrangement of conversations in the narrative is such as to draw attention to the way the absolute otherness of each individual can be protected. "Selfhood" or "the individual subject" is not celebrated as it is in "*Bildungsromane*," or indeed in most novels featuring a single central character whose internal growth and development is taken seriously, and where contacts with other people are largely significant in terms of what they bring that central character, making secondary characters satellites of the central character, used to shed light on that singular, solitary, central figure. The arrangement, or relationship of the diegetic material to the mimetic material, in *Die Blendung* levels everything out, by implying that conversations in public can be exhilarating if everyone takes his turn, and if everyone makes a point of "mimicry," of "reacting to" and not "commenting on" the contents of any statement. This is not the individualized discussion that comes with analysis, but the natural exuberance of facetiousness, where nothing is taken seriously, only to preserve intact the very conditions that make real seriousness both possible and productive.

Canetti's text, as is theoretically the case with any human creation in the broadest sense, whether consciously artistic or not, does not, however, read like a chance or accidental bringing together of different elements. There is none of the complete nonsense, that associated with the so-called "automatic" writing of the Surrealists where connections between sentences simply do not exist, neither is there the fun-loving, anarchic nonsense of the Dadaists: some *Die Blendung* critics in France have explored this view more positively.[251] Equally, sections of the novel are unlikely to find their way into anthologies of Nonsense writing. Linear progression without semantic interrelation between sentences is there in surrealist writing, as it is in *Die Blendung*. Yet the sentences in *Die Blendung* have the kind of verve of purpose that *sustains* us even though matters of import fail to dominate, where surrealist writing, once understood, becomes rather sterile. Further, Canetti's self-consciousness, or the formidable control exerted over the material by his intelligence, which either intuitively or consciously sets out to validate the existential, not human, potential of the individual reader in a Nietzschean way, is evident in the way that everything is in a particular place. Every detail appears to have been personally assigned a particular place in the text by the master himself, not so that we can marvel at his creation, as it were, but so that we can marvel at how Canetti has subordinated himself to increasing our own capacity for pleasure, for release from constraint. We can marvel at the absolute confidence Canetti expresses in our intelligence, stamina, and imagination as *sources of the power that keeps a dance moving*. Confidence is not invested in the imagination as a source of the specific and individual, since Canetti does not feed his readers with the kind of material (Big or Small Ideas) that would give us passive, imaginative nourishment, the opportunity to reflect and "be" in private. His sentences serve to sharpen our wits so that our own performances in public will be more stylish. His is a commitment to the Greek idea of a community peopled by competitive individuals.

Canetti can also be seen to reverse some of the principles of the Presocratic atomists. His text is composed of highly defined sentences that are bursting with energy, just as the cosmos is composed of atoms bursting with energy. Yet the hand of God is everpresent throughout Canetti's text, as it is not in the chance explosion that produced the cosmos, and as it is not in the feeling Canetti describes, in *Die Fackel im Ohr*, that he had when he went to Berlin, of a world composed of hermetically sealed people bumping against one another in meaningless succession. Sentences do follow one another in rapid succession: yet the mimicry prevents the series from seeming meaningless in a way that, whilst semantically vacant, is imaginatively powerful for the vital stress it puts on the creativity of theatricality as a mode of existence. In this respect, Canetti detaches himself from the Presocratic atomists and shows himself to be an unusual kind of humanist. He is a radical individualist in the confidence he expresses in the power of the imagination of the individual to be phenomenally successful in terms of the performance art of interacting in society. The individual is the measure of all things, as Protagoras, the Presocratic philosopher, has it, and the individual is capable of absolutely anything, yet only inasmuch as he can be an agent of Nietzsche's philosophy of deindividualized affirmation. When philosophy is a kind of theatre of self-enactment, style is everything.

The existential significance of creative engagement is something Canetti believed in passionately, and it is nowhere more apparent than in his highly sympathetic commentary on Wotruba's sculptures, published in 1955, entitled *Fritz Wotruba*.[252] It is also the subject of the sections in the autobiography that deal with Canetti's personal relationship to this sculptor. In both the monograph and these sections of the autobiography, the intervention of the human will into the void of atoms is characterized in a way that is near-desperate, the reverse side, possibly, of the view about intervention into chaos that is embodied by *Die Blendung*. Wotruba was felt to be a sister soul, and a companion in what Canetti describes as the fight to *defy* chaos agonistically, by producing artistic form of huge strength, energy, and power. The passages looking at Wotruba imply that a spectator of any of his works might be overcome by a sense of his/her own impotence when faced with this single artist's success in his personal battle. Rather than encourage the spectator to rejoice that man/woman is the measure of all things, that s/he is godlike in his omnipotence, the command over form in Wotruba's sculptures renders the spectator impotent, since his/her powers, by comparison, look rather feeble. Needless to say, the atavism or violence of Canetti's own descriptions of Wotruba at work is astonishing. Canetti and Wotruba share Zarathustra's claim: "Ich sage euch: man muß noch Chaos in sich haben, um einen tanzenden Stern gebären zu können. Ich sage euch: ihr habt noch Chaos in euch."

Canetti's relationship to sculpture is an interesting one and has not had the attention it deserves. Suffice to say here that it is privileged of the art forms of the visual arts, not only in that Canetti decided to write a book about one particular Austrian sculptor, Wotruba, but in the way in which he has continued to associate himself with sculpture as a particular art form. His friendship with Wotruba was followed later by a less intense "acquaintanceship" with Hrdlicka, Wotruba's pupil, about whom

Elias Canetti has written because Hrdlicka illustrated a few of the scenes from *Die Blendung*, and *Hochzeit*, and produced a cycle of illustrations for *Masse und Macht*. Hrdlicka's own sculptures are in the heroic tradition of Wotruba.[253] Sculpture also features again in *Das Augenspiel*, where Canetti talks about his romantic friendship with Anna Mahler, the daughter of Gustav and Alma Mahler, who was herself a sculptress and pupil of Wotruba, and whose work is also marked by its concessions to the heroic tradition.[254]

Before we go on to look at sections in the novel where the narrative strategy of a very idiosyncratic notion of love is played out, it would be appropriate to take a look at one of the critical terms that has gained a fair amount of credence with critics and has been used in connection with this novel and the three plays. It needs clarification. It is the idea of the "acoustic mask," which has interested Curtius, Gretsky, and Honegger, amongst others.[255] In an interview with Manfred Durzak, Canetti admits that his love of language was something he partially inherited from Kraus. Love of language included love of the nuances of the language spoken throughout Vienna, of dialect in particular, the kind of language that is the subject of *Die letzten Tage der Menschheit*, and of many of Nestroy's plays, themselves enthusiastically improvised by Kraus in his readings of the plays that Canetti heard. Canetti and Durzak both use the term "akustische Masken" and talk about "eine bestimmte Theorie der sprachlichen Mimesis" in the interview.[256] The mimesis is clearly felt to consist of the fact that the speech of characters in plays and Canetti's novel is partly based on a particular kind of language that has geographical specificity, namely "Wienerisch." Both Durzak, to a greater extent, and Canetti, to a lesser extent, see the continuity between the world of the text and the world of Vienna, in terms of language, as a kind of virtue. To a certain extent, it gives Canetti's work a kind of credibility. Although neither Durzak nor Canetti explains what is meant by the mask, Canetti concludes this section of the interview with the claim that his characters are interchangeable with their acoustic masks. The term conjures up an idea of sound, above all. It also conjures up an idea of a possible distinction between the way one speaks in public and the way one is whenever the mask drops, so to speak. In Canetti's view, however, what characterizes *Die Blendung* is the extent to which what is said effectively dissolves the distinction between appearance and so-called reality, for the presentation of self is self: his figures simply *are* masks. Critics, however, have tended to exploit the term "acoustic mask" in a different way. They have inevitably stressed the continuity between the language spoken by characters in *Die Blendung* and the language spoken by the lower classes in Vienna proper. But this is of subordinate importance, according to these critics. What the use of language by character in the novel achieves is something different. It provides us with some kind of commentary on what "happens" when/if communication between people breaks down because language has been corrupted, either from within or from without. People no longer know how to exploit it to effect. They are victims of language, as opposed to knowing manipulators of it. Concepts that may appear to have some kind of intelligent position in a sentence are, in fact, there to show us how removed the speaker is from any kind of analytical understanding of the topic about which s/he presumes to know.

It is this kind of "normative" argument that has led to the widespread view that the novel is a satire, and a satire of language and communication in the tradition of Viennese satire, or the drama associated with Nestroy, Schnitzler, and Kraus. This view is helped by the fact that Canetti has made serious pronouncements on satire himself, maintaining on one occasion that Kraus is the greatest satirist.[257] An extract from the notebooks of 1967 is also a good example (*PM*, 256).

Although the terms Augustan Satire, Menippean Satire, and, to a certain extent, Apocalyptic Satire, are familiar in criticism, because of Northrop Frye's famous typology, they are not used with respect to this novel, and for reasons that need clarifying so that the accuracy of the established view can be tested. The last term, Apocalyptic Satire, used by Edward Timms in his book on Karl Kraus, might constitute something of an exception, for to some critics Canetti's novel is shot through with the spirit of the apocalypse, inasmuch as everything about its characters and plot points to destruction as inevitable.

In *The Augustan Vision*, Pat Rogers states that the Augustan Age can be defined in terms of dates (it lasted from 1688 to 1760) and geography (it refers to either British or Anglo-Irish writers).[258] She feels that it is appropriate to talk about the "Augustan Vision" because there is some kind of common solidarity concerning first principles that is shared by all writers, irrespective of their media: "That the Augustans sought order is no bar to appreciation, for so did most ages prior to our own. What distinguishes this quest in the period we are considering is the presupposition that order will be found, not in some mystic oneness or totality, but in a graded scale or tiered progression. Indeed, the Great Chain of Being, which clanks its way monotonously throughout the history of ideas, is but the ontological expression of something far more deeply interfused in all Augustan life. Its thesis—that the universe comprised a regular continuum of created life, from a tiny insect up to the angels—has seemed unsatisfactory, both to the intellect and the imagination, in subsequent years. But to men and women of the time it was more than a scheme of classification, a biological variant of the periodic table; it was a testimony to the plenitude of creation and to the wisdom of the creator. It described how the universe was, and at the same time provided a moral justification for that set of conditions" (27–28).

In a chapter entitled "The Dress of Thought," she argues that the stress on decorum, on the idea of thought being elaborately clad, was part and parcel of a specific outlook, which distinguished itself from the immediacy of seventeenth-century thinking and writing. The idea that the writer contemplated a reality from which s/he was detached, and a reality that could be contemplated precisely because it was so clad: "Augustan poetics, for instance, is largely based on a grammar of contemplation and response, with epithets more important than verbs: man witnesses something (often spatial arrangements), where the seventeenth-century poet had felt himself part of an elaborate cosmic dance" (46).

Whereas one could argue that all authors in the Augustan period were experimental, relative to the seventeenth century, it is important to note that they, together with those who appear to be radically experimental by our "modern" standards (as is obviously the case in the works of, say, the Anglo-Irish Swift and Sterne), never go so far as to jettison the order associated with the establishment or the guarantors of certain virtues of living, such as the established church, which was supported by the two clerics Swift and Sterne anyway. Talking of *A Tale of a Tub*, Pat Rogers makes the following points about Swift's apparent concessions to the whimsical and lawless: "Swift was a great enough artist to allow wild 'digression' a place in his scheme, and thus to jettison the tame symmetries of orthodox Augustan decorum. But digression is no more allowed to prevail than was conventional story-telling. If there are passages of obscure metaphysical foolery, there are also lucid and easy-going anecdotes. If the sensible pieties of Anglican dogma emerge a little soiled, so assuredly do the ostensible targets—puritan enthusiasm and papist authoritarianism. The *Tale* lives dangerously, but it is not an existentialist manifesto in favour of living to the extreme. Here we come on a central paradox regarding Swift. He liked to employ conventional forms to convey violent ideas, and radical vehicles to get across conformist views" (188).

Finally, the Augustans are known for their memorable/ornamental use of language and for their preoccupation with normative ways of seeing and living, thought to be universally applicable. If such writers finally endorse the idea that metaphysical and secular order are attainable realities, if certain corrections are made to inadequate ways of perceiving and living, they do not promote any radical break with establishment order, or any real belief in rank individualism. Even those most individualistic of writers and thinkers, Swift and Sterne, communicate a feeling of inadequacy at their own brilliant virtuosity, a kind of melancholy that what they are doing is in some way useless, which undermines the apparent confidence about the original and individualistic enacted by the use of language in their texts. So satire in the age of Augustan prose is not the kind of satire that really undermines the world as it is. It attacks it to suggest that it needs to be improved, not abandoned as corrupt.

Highet,[259] Seidel,[260] Petro,[261] and Palmeri[262] have focused on satire in prose throughout the ages and have made some interesting points about its focus. Satires tend to rely on the episodic structure associated with the drama. The stance of a satirist is often prophetic. Satires attack discernible, historically authentic particulars, in the form of named individuals, groups, institutions, customs, beliefs, and ideas. The satiric target has a model, an ideal counterpart, a norm, from which the satiric target is an aberration. The norm is what actually makes the satire satiric. Its commonest subjects are subjects of a high order of generality: what is human nature? what is original sin? what is perfectibility? what is the significance of the garden of Eden story in the Bible? what is the authority of the Bible? what authority does the Church have? and what authority does the state have? These issues are explored outside the established order of the institutions endowed with authority in society, whose laws and traditions are subverted in individual satires in prose. Thus the frequency of the errant traveller, the journey (often around the world), the experiences of utopias, the fascination with low places and high places, the awareness of illegitimacy, both in terms of birth and in terms of behavior. Perversions of human nature, stupidity, new forms of slavery, and lack of love are all looked at from the vantage point of what could be, for there is a prescriptive drive. European satirists in prose, such as De Sade and Voltaire, explore these issues. They are possibly amongst the most radical in their absolute rejection of nature as something innate, their rejection of any kind of authority except that which can be exercised by the individual who accepts responsibility for his/her own destiny or his/her own nature: both destiny and nature are constructs. Establishment sources of authority are rejected out of hand and, in the case of the '*conte philosophique*' *Candide*, a rank individualism is prescribed for each individual who opts to live outside the orbit of society because society is too restrictive and repressive. The memorable maxim, "Il faut cultiver son jardin," is to have utilitarian applicability, as far as conduct in the present is concerned, to all who are prepared to accept the wisdom of detaching themselves from official society and official authority and living according to individualistic notions of their own.

In all of the passages in *Die Blendung* examined so far we noticed that we were only superficially dealing with what could be called scenes. What took precedence was Canetti's positive desire to prolong the reader's pleasure, a pleasure that could be experienced only because the text seemed eminently theatrical. This mood was never brought to a standstill, let alone an abrupt standstill, to the extent that it seems unfair to speak of the episodic structure we associate with the mode of argument of the drama (exploited by prose writers like Voltaire et al. for the purpose of promoting certain new ideas), and to speak of scenes that serve particular ideological "purposes."

Swift, De Sade, and Voltaire also rely very heavily in their scenes on a kind of overstatement and hyperbole and use of caricature that is theatrical, yet only so that the extra-textual reality to which these scenes refer can be thrown into a challenging kind of analytic relief. Theatricality is not an end in itself. Those normative satires with which Swift, De Sade, and Voltaire are associated positively aim at the elimination of the difference between what is and what should be, because normative satires are essentially ameliorative in intent. Irony in them is normative and exists only by virtue of the difference between what is and what should be. It is not the idea of cosmic irony described by De Man.

The ameliorative intention is, in my unorthodox view, missing in Canetti's novel, inasmuch as the behavior of Therese and Peter Kien examined so far was compelling enough in its own right, the authorial control over the narrative as a whole so formidable as to prevent the reader's taking time off to construct any kind of extra-textual reality. We have had some excellent examples of the sustaining of tension, as described by De Man, where tension served the purpose of pleasing the reader: its function was not to endorse certain extra-textual norms.

Menippean Satire, with which Bakhtin was so preoccupied, belongs to a different period in the history of literature than Augustan satire. It is a spirit that is at the heart of Lucian and Petronius. It owes its name to the Greek cynic Menippus, a slave from Sinope on the Black Sea living in the first half of the third century, B.C. He bought his freedom and came to Thebes, where he studied to become a Cynic philosopher. As we have seen, Bakhtin includes Rabelais as an example of a writer whose works are colored by the spirit of Menippean Satire, because Rabelais, like Lucian and Petronius, loved including conversations or dialogues in his novels that celebrated intellectual arguing as an end in itself, raising to the level of an ideal the so-called dialogic principle, with all of its ideological appeal in terms of its apparent recognition of the legitimacy of the plurality of discourses that can exist independent of official authority.

In a recent book by Patrick O'Neill, entitled *The Comedy of Entropy: Humour, Narrative, Reading*, the author opens up the terms of the above kind of debate, and the terms of the debate on play, by suggesting that there are, in principle, two kinds of humor in literature.[263] There is the humor of order, and the humor of entropy or disorder. Entropy, from the greek *entrope*, meaning a turning toward, is a measure of the degree of disorder in a system, especially the universe. In the humor of order, sympathetic humor tends to celebrate order and assume that norms are unthreatened. Derisive humor in the humor of order rejects disorder to defend norms. In the humor of entropy, by contrast, anomic humor rejects order and abandons norms altogether. Parodic humor celebrates disorder and parodies norms. So whereas Swift, De Sade, and Voltaire use satire, irony, and parody for the purposes of changing the extra-textual world, writers associated with entropy rely as heavily on satire, irony, and parody, but as ends in themselves, which help to further the cause of pluralism, not the kind of normality that would obliterate it. Patrick O'Neill's examples are interesting. Handke's *Die Hornissen* is used as an example of entropic parody, Grass's *Die Blechtrommel* is an example of entropic satire, and Kafka's *Der Prozeß* is an example of entropic irony. Canetti does not get a mention, although it should be obvious now that he nowhere endorses institutions associated with the so-called regulation of human behavior, or the norms on which such institutions depend.

The claim here, in response to O'Neill, is that Canetti has an extraordinarily highly developed, and intuitive, sense of the entropic nature of the universe. His literary creation differs, however, from that of Handke, Grass, and Kafka, inasmuch as he refuses categorically to imitate disorder and to reflect it in his literary creation. He shows by example, instead, how chaos can be controlled temporarily by a sense of form. His novel is phenomenally controlled and becomes a plastic work of art, both because of his highly developed sense of Apollonian form, which gives him a plastic confidence in the future, his sense of cosmic irony, and because of the Dionysian drive for perpetual change and movement—that spirit of agonistic play. Again, it is interesting to note here, given that we are arguing for the Nietzschean quality of the novel, that there is also a connection between Nietzsche and entropy. According to Moroney, Nietzsche felt that the law of entropy was false, because if it were true the world would have exhausted itself.[264] Canetti's position is a modification of Nietzsche's. Canetti proves the truth of entropy only by showing by example how its inverse, form, depends on the threat posed by disorder for its own internal momentum and drive.

O'Neill also argues about the relative status of tragedy and comedy in relation to entropy. If tragedy was originally privileged over comedy in terms of the history of literature, the distinction between tragedy and comedy is now extremely blurred. But entropy is clearly the preferred mode in contemporary literature now, O'Neill argues, and there are some very ambitious reasons for this. Contemporary thinking, loosely referred to as the thinking of postmodernism, whether philosophical or literary, works with the assumption that we have already seen the demise of Truth and Man. This is most clear in contemporary philosophy, where metaphysics and epistemology, which in classical philosophy were by far the most significant branches of the discipline, have been jettisoned altogether for all sorts of reasons.[265]

In their stress on fixed and single notions of Truth and fixed and single notions of Man as concepts, classical metaphysics and epistemology have produced a variety of systems of thought, which have been able to provide people with systematic frameworks, and points of reference which have given life meaning. In a climate of opinion where metaphysics and epistemology, and their two legitimate offspring, Truth and Man, have both lost their appeal and sanction, it follows, quite naturally, that a plurality of languages and a plurality of discourses be granted equal status, and a general kind of open-endedness. Since Nietzsche proclaimed that "God is dead," we have seen a rise in philosophy of the fragment, the form that symbolizes non-recognition of absolute fixity and a rejection of system building with which the originators of Continental thought, like Kant, are associated. It became central to Wittgenstein's project. It is almost symbolic, in this respect, that the "character" who appears to be the central character of *Die Blendung* is himself a parody of a certain kind of philosopher/scholar, for the scholar is arguably one who appears to symbolize ideal man in those systems of thinking that privilege Truth and Man. From the very beginning of *Die Blendung*, Kien appears to be associated with the systematic pursuit of knowledge and truth, and thus to conform to the pattern set by the scholar Faust in literature, with his extreme "metaphysical" and epistemological pretensions and desire to discover, and keep, Truth, intuitively felt to be single and absolute. Kien, like Faust, is apparently willing to pursue both Truth and Man to their logical conclusion, irrespective of the human cost.

But the treatment of the scholar figure in *Die Blendung* positively disrespects scholarship in the traditional sense, since virtually no narrative space is dedicated to showing how Kien thinks qualitatively, whether as an intellectual or not, as Edward Timms has pointed out.[266] We have already had an early indicator of Kien's difference, in terms of the traditional Faust type. He consulted Confucius before he went to ask Therese whether she would marry him. Quotations from Confucius (46–47) look as if they are not genuine, a trick of Stendhal's in *Le Rouge et Le Noir* that Canetti may well be imitating. So Kien allows himself to interpret what comes across as dubiously attributed material, according to his own wishes. No respect is shown for the image of Confucius promoted by, say, *The Analects*, in which a virtue is made of following a particular Way, of applying practical wisdom to one's life, of being virtuous and being a gentleman.[267] Allusions to names such as Eratosthenes (21), Arai Hakuseki (36), Mong Tse (23), Plato (37), and Antisthenes (37), to Kant and Schiller (231) are frequently made, but without substantial clarification concerning their importance or relevance to Kien as an intellectual. Indeed, allusions to scholarly works, and allusions to scholarly conferences, are littered throughout the novel, but are not supplemented by primary evidence of their "meaning" to Kien. We thus *withhold* our judgment of Kien as an intellectual, rather than find ourselves obliged to condemn him as a fraud. We are being denied access to the kind of material that ordinarily allows us to luxuriate in the power of standing in judgment on people. The book on Kien's desk with which he is more positively associated in an active, literal sense, one which he is producing himself, is one that contains evidence of Kien's experiences of man's follies: it is called "Dummheiten":

> Auf dem Titelblatt stand in hohen, eckingen Buchstaben:
> *Dummheiten.* Sein Auge verweilte erst hier. Dann blätterte er um, mehr als die Hälfte des Notizbuches war beschrieben. Alles, was er vergessen wollte, trug er da ein. Mit Datum, Stunde und Ort begann er. Es folgte die Begebenheit, welche wieder die Dummheit der Menschen illustrieren sollte. Ein angewandtes Zitat, immer ein neues, bildete den Beschluß. Die gesammelten Dummheiten las er nie; ein Blick auf das Titelblatt genügte. In späteren Jahren dachte er sie herauszugeben, als "Spaziergänge eines Sinologen." (*DB*, 19)[268]

This is funny in its own right because it is so stupid, yet it does not entitle us to dismiss Kien as a fraud. At the end of the novel, when Kien is watching people go in and out of the block of flats through a keyhole, he thinks of compiling a book with information on the kinds of trousers people wear:

> Eine systematische Bearbeitung, die Bestimmung von Menschen nach Hosen, schien ihm durchaus möglich. Er versprach sich eine kleine Abhandlung darüber, in drei Tagen war sie spielend fertig. Halb im Scherz erhob er Vorwürfe gegen einen gewissen Gelehrten, der ein Schneidergebiet bearbeite. Aber die Zeit hier unten war nun einmal verloren, gleichgültig, was er trieb. Er wußte sehr gut, warum er sich dem Guckloch ergab. Gestern war vorüber, gestern *mußte* vorüber. Und die wissenschaftliche Konzentration tat ihm unendlich wohl. (*DB*, 422)[269]

Further serious concessions to the willingness of the Faust type to abandon himself wholeheartedly to the pursuit of knowledge and truth are also positively not made, inasmuch as the bulk of the novel concentrates on how Kien gets sidetracked by a variety of different human beings and, indeed, how he lives with them. All we can say here, in conclusion, is that there is no positive proof of Kien's scholarly/intellectual skills throughout the novel. He "does" books, is the only thing one can say, and the neutrality of the verb "do" here is very important, since it implies no value judgment.[270] It is, therefore, possible to call into question the stream in criticism that sees him as a variation on the type, scholar. Scholarship in *Die Blendung* is a pretext for Peter Kien's life in the first instance, but for life generally, given what the narrative does with it. It has existential value, and Canetti understands the business of life's needing illusions very well indeed, both in the local sense (which is to say in the way in which all his figures have a vision), and in the grand sense (which is to say in the way in which the narrative as a whole is constructed along Nietzschean lines). Kien cannot be associated with either the affectionately satirical portraits of scholars in literature, like, say, *le bourgeois gentilhomme*, or the aggressively satirical portrait of a pseudo-scholar, like Pangloss. We cannot extract from Canetti's text any wantonly certifiable view, provided by Kien, about scholarship, its nature and function, because Kien nowhere consciously recognizes that the discipline has any intrinsic meaning or essence. He has no conceptual view about its status relative to other choices one might have, as he has few conceptual views, except about his right to "do" scholarship to the exclusion of all else. He does it, with a considerable amount of energy.

Kien is not a serious intellectual like Stephen Dedalaus, or Hans Castorp. Joyce and Thomas Mann allow their intellectually alive characters to explore their ideas, without either interventions from a judgmental narrator or substantial modifications to their pronouncements effected by the arrangement of the plot. Finally, if Kien had been like Pangloss and been the author of a statement like "Tout est pour le mieux dans ce meilleur des mondes possibles," and if that statement had been undermined by plot and character in the novel as a whole, one would be in a position to assess him both by "normative" standards concerning the nature of scholarship and by "normative" standards concerning the nature of man.

If Kien never produces any original thoughts of his own, and relies on name dropping and allusion/reference, he does make an appearance at the end of the novel as a thinker: he becomes a ruthless apologist for all those thinkers in history who have theories about the inferiority of woman. The misogyny, which is the single topic of the conversation between the two brothers at the end of the novel, is problematic, and will be discussed in a later chapter. Suffice to say here that when Kien appears to be endorsing views which he quotes from a variety of sources, there is evidence to suggest that the narrator, who is exemplary throughout the novel in imitating the "voice" of any given speaker (the contagion of which Darby spoke), is noticeably reticent, refrains from, and withdraws from, the "speeches" made by Peter to George(s) and by George(s) to Peter. The narrative perspective is substantially different in the latter sections of the novel, and the change in the mode of presentation of the material alerts the reader to the manifestly certifiable statements both express. The change in narrative perspective allows the theories to collapse themselves, as it were.

Darby argues, not that Kien is a parody of a scholar, but that there is a gap between what is said about Kien's interests and what Kien does to prove that he is worthy of the reputation the text maintains he has. There is no independent evidence in the text to endorse Kien's avowed scholarly skills. This leaves the reader ontologically insecure, according to Darby. One cannot disagree with Darby that there is a gap, merely that it is productive of humor, precisely because it is such a gaping one. This humor has ideological implications to which Darby is not sensitive, namely those that suggest that "essence" and "meaning" as such are not all that interesting, whether to do with human nature or the type, scholar. A space is left open, the extravagance of which is compelling in itself, which suggests that the spirit of Dionysus is very much alive in this text, actively destroying its rival, the spirit of gravity, and its supporters, fixity and form. The non-coincidence of signifier and signified is intentional in these terms.

Just as the agonistic spirit of Carnival and play deconstructs the type, scholar, so it deconstructs the specific attributes of megalomania, which appear to pertain to another type, the Jewish, dwarf chess player Fischerle. Again, one could start by comparing him to other chess players in literature. Zweig's *Schachnovelle* (1942) takes the business of playing chess in a particular way, and competing to win, very seriously, together with the personality disorders that may occur as a result of a singleminded dedication to a single goal. They form the substance of the narrative as a whole. Fischerle, whose dominance of the middle section of the novel is substantial, is a chess player, by contrast, in name only. In this, he would appear to be like Peter Kien, who is a scholar in name only. Once again, the lack of independent evidence to endorse the information that Fischerle provides us about his interests does not constitute proof that he is a fraud, in the same way that the lack of independent evidence to endorse the information that Peter Kien provides us does not constitute proof that Peter Kien is a fraud.

Fischerle is also often classified as a criminal, a ringleader in the underworld, at the center of which is the location, "Zum idealen Himmel," into which Peter Kien walks after Therese has apparently banished him from the flat. He is thought of as modelled on the picaro type by the critic Richard Lawson.[271] My response to the view that he is deceitful, intent on extracting money from Kien for his own benefit, is comparable to my response to the claim that he is a fraud as a chess player. My view is that the spirit of love speaks through him. He is an affectionate companion to both Peter Kien and the four who appear to work for him as a gang of thieves, who make themselves known to us in the section, "Vier und ihre Zukunft." His exuberance is infectious. He is modelled on Sancho Pansa, whose function in *Don Quixote* is clearly to sustain Don Quixote in his illusions. Sancho Pansa does this because he loves Don Quixote, not because he gets a kick out of misleading him. By the same token, Fischerle plays up to Kien's love of books. He does not destroy the illusion on which Peter Kien's life is based, he enriches it by pandering to it, and he enjoys doing this as an end in itself, gratuitously. The spirit of theatrical animation which inflates the long speeches Fischerle makes to his mates is compelling. The first example comes from the section in the novel where Fischerle comes across Peter Kien for the first time:

> "Ein Mensch, was ka Schach spielt, is ka Mensch. Im Schach sitzt die Intelligenz, sag' ich. Da kann einer vier Meter lang sein, Schach muß er spielen, sonst is er ein Tepp. Ich kann Schach. Ich bin auch kein Tepp. Jetzt frag' ich Sie; wenn Sie wollen, antworten Sie mir. Wenn Sie nicht wollen, antworten Sie nicht. Wozu hat ein Mensch den Kopf? Ich sag's Ihnen selbst, sonst zerbrechen S' Ihnen noch den Kopf, es wär' schad' drum. Zum

> Schach hat er den Kopf. Verstehn Sie mich? Sagen Sie ja, dann is alles gut. Sagen Sie nein, dann sag' ich's Ihnen nochmal, weil Sie's sind. Für die Buchbranche hab' ich ein Herz. Ich mach' Sie aufmerksam, ich hab's allein gelernt, nicht aus dem Buch. Was glauben S', wer hier der Meister is, vom ganzen Lokal? Ich wett', Sie kommen nicht drauf. Ich werde Ihnen den Namen verraten. Der Meister heißt Fischerle und sitzt am selben Tisch wie Sie. Und warum hat er sich hergesetzt? Weil Sie ein mieser Mensch sind. Jetzt glauben Sie vielleicht, ich flieg' auf die miesen Menschen. Falsch, Blödheit, stimmt nicht! Was glauben S', wie schön meine Frau is. So was Apartes haben Sie noch nicht geseh'n! Aber, frag' ich, wer hat die Intelligenz? Der miese Mensch hat sie, sag' ich. Wozu braucht der Feschak die Intelligenz? Verdienen tut sei Frau für ihn, Schach spielen mag er nicht, weil er sich bucken muß dabei, es kunnt' der Schönheit was schaden, und was kommt heraus dabei? Der miese Mensch hat die ganze Intelligenz für sich gepachtet. Nehmen Sie die Schachmeister—alle mies. Sehn's S', wenn ich in der Illustrierten einen berühmten Menschen seh', der was schön ist, da sag' ich gleich zu mir: Fischerle, da stimmt was nicht. Da haben s' ein falsches Bild erwischt. Ja, was glauben Sie, bei die vielen, vielen Bilder und jeder will ein berühmter Mensch sein—wo kommt so eine Zeitung hin? Die Illustrierte is auch nur ein Mensch. Wissen S', aber, was ein Wunder ist, daß Sie kein Schach spielen. Die ganze Buchbranche spielt Schach. Ist das a Kunst bei der Buchbranche? Der Mann nimmt sei Schachbüchel her und lernt die Partie auswendig. Aber glauben Sie, mir hat einer darum geschlagen? Von der Buchbranche keiner, so wahr Sie dazugehören, wenn's wahr is!" (*DB*, 191–92)[272]

The substance of this outburst, is, like all "actions" in the novel, not generated by any concrete cause. It is thus fully gratuitous and a mere reaction to an arbitrary stimulus. It also makes some hilarious equations. To play chess constitutes the only possibility of proving that one is fully human. It is the only possibility man has of using the intelligence with which he is born. Thereafter the speech reads like an enthusiastic endorsement of chess as a way of life. Instead of allowing Peter Kien to respond in kind to the above outburst, which is addressed to Peter Kien, the narrative concentrates on endorsing Fischerle's presentation of himself as crazy about chess, by stating how deeply committed he is to the game. Canetti has not created an opportunity for Peter Kien to respond to any one of the series of rhetorical questions asked by Fischerle. Instead, more opportunities are created to endorse the idea we might have constructed of Fischerle from the above, either in terms of straight narrative to the effect that Fischerle is actually playing a game, or by simply allowing Fischerle to carry on with his presentation of himself in monologue form, addressed to Peter Kien, the seemingly blank, non-responsive audience. One has to deduce from this that Canetti is *collaborating* with Fischerle, at a very deep level. Let's look at this diegetic material, for instance:

> Gehorchen und Horchen war hier für Kien eins. Seitdem der Kleine vom Schach sprach, war er der harmloseste Jud von der Welt. Er unterbrach sich nie, seine Fragen waren rhetorisch, aber er beantwortete sie sich doch. Das Wort "Schach" klang in seinem Mund wie ein Befehl, so, als ob es nur von seiner Gnade abhinge, das tödliche "Matt" hinzuzusetzen. Kiens Schweigsamkeit, die ihn anfangs gereizt hatte, erschien ihm jetzt als Aufmerksamkeit, und sie schmeichelte ihm.
>
> Während des Spiels fürchteten ihn seine Partner viel zu sehr, um ihn durch Einwürfe zu stören. Denn er rächte sich furchtbar und gab die Unbedachtheit ihrer Züge dem allgemeinen Gelächter preis. In den Pausen zwischen den Partien—sein halbes Leben verbrachte er am Brett—behandelte man ihn, wie es seiner Figur entsprach. Er hätte am liebsten ununterbrochen gespielt. Er träumte von einem Leben, wo man Essen und Schlafen während der Züge des Gegners erledigt. Hatte er sechs Stunden lang spielend gesiegt und fand sich zufällig ein weiterer Anwärter auf Niederlagen, so legte sich die Frau ins Mittel und zwang ihn aufzuhören, er wurde ihr sonst zu frech. Sie war ihm gleichgültig wie ein Stein. (*DB*, 192)[273]

What happens thereafter is that we focus on how Peter Kien reacts internally to the phenomenon, Fischerle. In other words, the narrative is a chain reaction in motion. Dionysus is pushing forward with the spinning of the illusion and not waiting or pausing to allow one to assume that there are any constructs on which to focus to balance oneself:

> Noch nie hatte sich Kien so tief in einen Menschen eingefühlt. Ihm war es geglückt sich von Therese zu befreien. Er hatte sie mit ihren Waffen geschlagen, sie überlistet und eingesperrt. Da saß sie nun auf einmal an seinem Tisch, forderte wie früher, keifte wie früher und hatte es, das einzige, was neu an ihr war, zu einem passenden Beruf gebracht. Doch ihr zerstörendes Treiben galt nicht ihm, ihn beachtete sie wenig, es galt dem

> Manne gegenüber, den die Natur durch eine traurige Etymologie ohnehin schon zum Krüppel geschlagen hatte. Kien stand tief in der Schuld dieses Menschen. Er mußte etwas für ihn tun. Er achtete ihn. Wäre Herr Fischerle nicht so fein geartet, er würde ihm geradezu Geld anbieten. Sicher könnte er es brauchen. Doch wünschte er ihn auf keinen Fall zu beleidigen. Vielleicht, wenn man auf jenes Gespräch zurückkäme, das von Therese mit weiblicher Unverschämtheit unterbrochen worden war?
>
> Er zog seine Brieftasche hervor, die noch immer von hohen Scheinen strotzte. Er entnahm ihr, die er ganz gegen seine Gewohnheit lange in der Hand hielt, sämtliche Banknoten und zählte sie friedlich nach. Herr Fischerle sollte sich durch den Anblick selbst davon überzeugen, daß der Antrag, den man ihm jetzt zu stellen gedachte, durchaus kein großes Opfer war. Beim dreißigsten Hundertschillingschein angelangt, blickte Kien auf den Kleinen hinunter. Vielleicht war er so weit besänftigt, daß man die Schenkung schon wagen konnte, wer zählt gern Geld? Fischerle sah sich verstohlen nach allen Seiten um; nur um den Zählenden schien er sich nicht im mindesten zu kümmern, sicher aus Feingefühl und Abneigung gegen gewöhnliches Geld. (*DB*, 202)[274]

Kien believes that the woman he has seen in "Zum idealen Himmel" is Therese, because he assumes she is the only woman in the world. She is, in fact, Fischerle's wife, and is billed as a prostitute, as Kien is billed a scholar and Fischerle a chess player: as stated above, all we can say is that Fischerle's wife does sex, Kien does books, and Fischerle does chess. One is not invited to pass judgment on their fitness for their chosen "careers" because the narrative refuses to allow us to stand in judgment on the quality of their skills. It fails to give us positive examples of their skills. Significantly, however, it does give us positive proof of the energy that can be injected into what creates the illusion that life has purpose and meaning. So one is wrong to say that Fischerle is a megalomaniac with an *idée fixe* about himself as the world champion of chess, an example of the type, megalomaniac.

Kien assumes, in the above, that Fischerle has helped him, and feels full of gratitude for him. He thinks of marking his gratitude by a token sum of money, although he feels embarrassed about this idea because he assumes that Fischerle has fine feelings and that he will think money a bit of an insult, because it is intrinsically vulgar. Mainstream criticism responds to both Fischerle's presentation of himself to Kien and Kien's responses to Fischerle in a negative way. Kien is condemned as deluded (causes posited range from his social isolation to his rank intellectualism, both of which have prevented him from being able to assess what is *really* happening in his life) and Fischerle is a deceitful megalomaniac, anxious to exploit an innocent abroad like Peter Kien. Once again, it is possible to sense the influence of *Don Quixote* in the above passage. Just as Don Quixote rides out in search of his loved one and "reads" everything and every encounter according to the substance of the vision he has derived from literary texts (the barber's washbasin is Mambrino's helmet, the windmills are the girls he is to rescue), so Peter Kien assumes that the only woman in the world is the woman he married, and that all people share his assumption that money is dirty and vulgar. Judged by the purely empirical evidence of the text, Kien cannot be condemned as wrong. He thinks, subjectively, that he has been helped. The narrative does exclude primary evidence that he has been helped, yet it succeeds in making us believe what Kien believes, because it is always sustained by a forward-moving drive, not the kind of irony, for instance, that inevitably interrupts and slows down narrative dynamism, usually to alert the reader to certain discrepancies, which it wants the reader to accept.

If Kien has found his own way to "Zum idealen Himmel," and there is no proof that Fischerle deserves the above kind of benevolence, the point has to be made that all the "actions" here are reactions. Thus, none of them has any claim to absolute causality. This arrangement of the narrative material—an arrangement that sees contribution follow contribution in strict linear progression—can be interpreted in terms of Canetti's formidable control of his material, a control that is exercised to privilege the reader's pleasure. In the above example, this pleasure is not induced and guaranteed by virtue of the fact that it is so obvious that Peter is injecting his own views of the world into what he thinks and says. It is induced and guaranteed when and as the reader realizes that no one figure is being privileged over any other. *They all excel, in equal measure, in the art of being/believing things, in accepting, in Nietzschean fashion, to live in the "as if" mode.* One is wrong to privilege individual figures, as mainstream criticism has done, consistently with respect to this novel, either in the form of condemning them as wrong for believing certain things, or in the form of condemning them for not being able to relate "productively" to others. The narrative is an active attack on this human and critical tendency to abstract individual characters from a competitive engagement and/or commitment to living life in the present. It is also an attack on those who want to attribute to them an "essence" or "essences," or some kind of "character." It is an active attack on this tendency in that the diegetic material endorses the contents of the verbal contributions made by characters, those stories that tend to furnish some critics with the material with which to condemn characters out of existence by pointing to the way in which they are wrong not to be able to make their actions express their words, *in that it positively refuses to refute those contents critically.*

Kien proposes, at a later date, that Fischerle work for him. There is no evidence in the text to suggest that Fischerle has put him up to it, as there is no evidence in the text to show that Fischerle encouraged Kien to part with cash. The proposition is born *ex nihilo*, as most actions/events/words are in this novel. It forms part of a chain reaction not held together by any kind of logic. Once again, this could be expressed as Canetti's wilful *exclusion of motive*. The exclusion of *causes* is expressed in a particular *effect*, that of the elegant level of playfulness that is sustained throughout this section of the novel, as it concentrates on the joy with which Kien demands that Fischerle work for him, a feeling the narrative privileges, in the way in which it carefully renders rather inferior the whole dirty business of what the job might entail (something material), by refusing to invent and take seriously actual scenes that might illustrate what it means to work, what it is like to work, etc.: "Kien fühlte sich verpflichtet, diesem Menschen, dem ersten, dem er in seinem Leben begegnet war, zu einer neuen und würdigen Existenz zu verhelfen. 'Ich bin kein Kaufmann, ich bin Gelehrter und Bibliothekar!' sagte er und beugte sich entgegenkommend zum Zwerg hinunter. 'Treten Sie in meine Dienste und ich werde für Sie sorgen'" (*DB*, 207).[275]

This becomes a parody of a business deal at one level, as we later learn that Fischerle is merely to help Kien unload books of an evening (207). The emphasis on Kien's desires and the comparative indifference to the effects of those desires, shows that Canetti is primarily interested in using his narrative to make certain compelling existential/ideological points. Namely, that confidence in one's desires is charming, beautiful, endearing, funny, in part because to take them so seriously is to relieve oneself from the strain of being passively determined, as it is also a statement of a belief that one is free to determine one's own destiny.

The above can also be read as a maliciously funny, if quiet, invocation of the Faust theme. The pact/wager in *Faust I,* which causes critics such trouble, is being affectionately parodied here, its demonic overtones thoroughly exploded by the hilarity of somebody suddenly deciding to employ someone, without having formulated any plan as to the use to which the person employed might be put. The contract Faust and Mephistopheles sign, with Faust signing his name in blood, just to make the "demonic" nature of the pact thoroughly obvious, together with all its "metaphysical" and secular pretentions, is parodied at a later date when Fischerle enlists four men into his troop, which appears to be a band of thieves working for a pimp in an underworld of crime. He first tells his men, joyfully, that he is in a position to offer them twenty Schilling per day (243). One of the four, "der schlaflose Hausierer," thinks about this and is pleased that the sum will get him eight kilos of toilet soap. If this were not sign enough that the whole setup is not to be taken seriously as a "normative" study of crime in the underworld, his address thereafter to the gang surely is. His four "men" have to agree that all earnings be returned to him: "'Ich hab' nämlich eine eigene Firma aufgemacht. Unterschreibt's, daß ihr alles dem Chef, der bin ich, abführt, und ich nehm' euch auf!'" (*DB*, 243–44) The idea that people will agree to do something for nothing is not really being stood on its head here, rather it is being taken for a beautiful ride. The insight here is that genuinely gratuitous ideas lend themselves to being taken for a ride, which can only be beautiful because there is absolutely no way that the idea can be forced to make any kind of alliance with any kind of identifiable institution or person. It is free, and if used freely will be capable of inciting us to freedom from causality which is the beginning of the challenge of freedom, the freedom to be as an end in itself.

Canetti cannot be credited with believing in the Fagan type here, because there is none of the air of intimidation which forces people to do things for nothing, returning all earnings to a pimp who, in return, might provide some kind of security. No concessions are made to this kind of scenario, at any level. Once again, it defies logic, amongst other things, that certain critics seriously believe that Canetti is seriously looking into the business of *evil.* My final example, to prove that this is a loving *parody* of the literary and extra-textual topos, "crime," is this piece of blissful nonsense: "'Der Unterzeichnete verpflichtet sich und verrechnet sofort bar jeden Groschen im Auftrag der Firma Siegfried Fischer einkassiert. Der Unterzeichnete frißt die volle Haftpflicht für eventuelle Schäden'" (*DB*, 244).[276] This can only be interpreted as yet more evidence of the huge premium placed on gratuitousness, on which the narrative relies as a whole. It is a wonderfully meaningless piece of weightlessness, delivered with a graceful flourish, which releases one from the pressures of existence, as does all humor.

Kien is here not so much *motivated* by love as animated by the spirit of love. He wants to take care of someone whom he thinks is nice and who needs a little guidance. We had an earlier example of this when he was on the tram with Therese. He is going to give Fischerle a salary but ask for nothing in return. It is a parody of the conservative idea that all actions have to have a motive in terms of gain, whether material or not. The effect of this kind of an incident in the novel is not to turn Peter into a kind of martyr/hero figure, but to raise the principle of gratuitousness to dazzling heights. The spirit of life and of play is put above individual lives and individual players.

The next passage, which has Fischerle at its center, would commonly be interpreted as evidence of Fischerle's so-called evil nature:

> "Das sag' ich doch," Fischerle löste ihn ab, "das Ganze kommt vom Schwindeln. Warum müssen die Menschen schwindeln? Soll einer sagen, ich hab' heut keinen Groschen, lieber Herr, morgen kriegen Sie dafür zwei. Aber nein, so ein Großmaul schwindelt lieber und Sie können den Knopf schlucken. Sie müssen sich einen anderen Beruf aussuchen, mein lieber Herr! Ich denke schon die längste Zeit darüber nach, was ich für Sie tun könnte. Ich werd' Ihnen was sagen, wenn Sie sich die drei Tage gut halten, stell' ich Sie für länger bei mir ein. Den anderen dürfen Sie nichts sagen, strengstes Geheimnis, die entlass' ich alle, unter uns gesagt, die nehm' ich jetzt nur aus Mitleid für die paar Tage. Bei Ihnen ist das was anderes. *Sie* können das Schwindeln nicht leiden, *ich* kann das Schwindeln nicht leiden, *Sie* sind ein besserer Mensch, *ich* bin ein besserer Mensch, Sie werden zugeben, wir passen zusammen. Und damit Sie sehen, welche Hochachtung ich vor Ihnen habe, gebe ich Ihnen das ganze Honorar für heute voraus. Die andern kriegen nichts." (*DB*, 247–48)[277]

The jokes in the next part of the text concern one of Fischerle's men, "der Blinde," or "Blinder," who is, in fact, quite capable of seeing. He always looks out for the effect he has on women, in particular the way his moustache is cut (247). Once again, Canetti relies on the alertness of his readers, on their capacity to be receptive to the absurd, the unexpected, the surprise. We laugh and do not condemn the blind man who uses the obvious *disguise* of blindness when it suits him, because he is an opportunist dedicated to making his own way in life. The gap between the name and what the name "means" or "represents" is productive of humor and deconstructs the human reliance on preconceived ideas. The implications of this small detail are ideological once again. The above passage derives its drive from the way in which it is winking, in an extrovert fashion, at the reader. Having protested that he is not blind and that he can see that people are taking him for a ride when they throw buttons into his cap instead of cash when he is "begging," Fischerle comes sympathetically to the "blindman's" rescue, consoling him in his need for the illusion that he is a good guy, suggesting that they are sister souls in their common hatred of deceit. This, on its own, renders redundant the conventional category of the beggar, whose status, socially and economically, is supposed to be nil in a capitalist society. It also deconstructs the category of the socially and economically privileged patron, that representative of capitalist society, who has status only because he is making a contribution to the free movement of goods, which is the hallmark of the free market in capitalist society. After all, the "blindman" has protested, not that the passers-by are vile for patronizing him in a way he finds demeaning (giving him buttons instead of cash), but that they don't assume he is clever enough to be able to know how they tick. He is protesting that he is an equal, not a subordinate. Fischerle does not get this "human" point and the narrative, being the chain reaction it is, sees him react. He starts out from his own assumption, which is that the blind man is protesting at the way in which he has been swindled. Intra-textually, this is not the case since the narrative did not include scenes in which "we" saw such an incident take place. To put a button in someone's cap (not cash) hardly constitutes, even in terms of extra-textual "norms," swindling, anyway. The chain reaction here makes a mockery of teleology, which is being taken for a beautiful ride, yet not at the expense of individual human beings, since the "blindman" and Fischerle remain unscathed, in our eyes, by the strategy. Their status does not diminish in our eyes.

Fischerle's response to what he assumes is the insult he feels the blindman has suffered at the hands of anonymous passers-by is fascinating in itself. Before we look at it, it is important to conclude again that we know the incident was nothing more, in the blindman's opinion, than disappointment that the passers-by did not credit him with much intelligence. Fischerle does not see this, and proceeds to shower the blindman with love, sympathy, and solidarity. He promises that the blindman will get the day's earnings, and not the others in the cartel. This cannot be read as evidence of his capacity for deceit, evil, or malice, but as evidence of the text's desire for yet further examples of gratuitousness, inspired by the idea of love of love, which wants to know absolutely nothing about gain. It is of minor importance, but the point needs to be made, because this idea is so "whimsical" by the standards of criticism that relate to this character, that the text excludes examples of scenes or actions when filthy lucre is actually handed over. This exclusion of the "evidence" or "proof" that the "intent" was really there is ideological again. Instead of "following through" what strikes me as Fischerle's sentiment of harmless indulgence to its "logical" conclusion, the text simply moves on. It neglects (wilfully) to translate the sentiment into the material (money), and thus lends prominence to the sentiment and demotes motive altogether. Although Fischerle appears to say that his love will manifest itself in terms of hard cash, no cash is handed over. We must conclude here that the promise is hereby given prominence as a beautiful, and beautiful because fully gratuitous, sentiment, or the spirit of love which wants no gain.

Fischerle and Kien then live in hotel bedrooms and spend the day wandering about town, like a pair of strays or social outcasts, yet a pair of strays or social outcasts in name only, since they do not behave as if they regarded themselves as rejects, an important point. They are exceptionally animated and full of beans. Once again, this is part and parcel of Canetti's attempt to deconstruct fixed categories, which, when lodged in the human imagination, actively prevent receptivity to the *imprévu*. In this part of the text, the categories loosely called up by scenes concern those of the criminal, crime, the social and economic outcast, and the violence and evil that the media like to think are features of the so-called "underworld." As it happens, events endorsing any of this are absent, in any primary sense, from the narrative proper. Fischerle's band of men has in fact been instructed to track down Kien and hand over a parcel of books to him. This is evidence that Fischerle is happily sustaining Kien in his personal illusion that books constitute the stuff of life. He is, like Sancho Pansa, collaborating with his master in an attempt to preserve his illusion. Fischerle's motive, therefore, is not a real motive. His actions testify to the fact that he loves Kien already and is committed to him. His actions cannot be interpreted as evidence of his desire to deceive Peter Kien and rob him of all his cash, which is what mainstream criticism makes of Fischerle. He has the critical reputation of being a criminal, capable of the inverse of love, namely evil.

However, neither Fischerle nor his gang is inspired by love in an overt sene, that is why this novel is riotously funny and this is not a melancholic romance, as the novel *Don Quixote* obviously is. As the above scenes should have made clear, it only appears, therefore, that we are dealing with a band of criminals. Yet they are not even criminals in name only, since they are not criminals at all. They are, however, criminals in terms of the kind of entrenched extra-textual assumption that "orderly" behavior, the kind of behavior that draws least attention to itself, which reduces the possibility of individuality and increases the possibility of amorphous, anonymous conformism, is socially acceptable. The behavior of Fischerle and his gang is subversive in these terms. They are doing something subversive, in the sense that they are daring to live for and by love, daring to use the kind of power that resists institutions and all established forms of power, and makes people into individuals with character and personality.

So one can conclude here that scenes, if looked at in detail, "show" that this is a parody of the underworld. More importantly, they show that the spirit of inflation which animates them is a subversive power capable of dissolving the distinction between primary and secondary worlds altogether, a distinction that orderly people tend to believe is meaningful. Extra-textually, for instance, the primary world, the so-called establishment, is commonly thought to consist in the authority vested by the state/nation in certain institutions, which are thought capable of preserving law and order. The secondary world is commonly thought to be that of the so called non-establishment, that world (underworld, bohemia, alternative scene/culture) that exists, with varying degrees of self-consciousness, independently of the main stream. Not only does Canetti not recognize the distinction, he implies that, in deciding to chose between the two, to become a member of either one world or the other, one is not being radical enough.

He implies that the real power of subversion lies in ways of thinking that can be described as subversive in metaphysical terms only, not social terms, only because they rely on wit, not Big Ideas. Groups or group thinking or group activity, by contrast, even if it is the group thinking of a culture that regards itself as outside the main stream, is vulnerable to fossilization in terms of the subversive power of genuine wit, because it still makes the mistake of vesting interest in Big Ideas and institutions. Genuine wit does not necessarily subvert the power and authority of social norms, institutions, or powerful people. It is subversive as an end in itself, because if used as an end in itself it enlarges the imaginative powers of the individual, and thus guarantees what liberals on the Left would term, following Foucault and others, the capacity of the individual to resist absorption into those legitimizing plots and ploys of institutions in particular.[278] Wit is the non-violent form of resistance as a mode of existence, capable of giving painless benefits to the individual who lives according to his/her wits. The display of wit by the individual is possibly a positive threat to institutionalizing pressures on the one hand, yes, but Canetti's emphasis in *Die Blendung* is not primarily on the vulnerability of the modern individual to mass worship of "embodiments" of Big Ideas, whether of people, such as Hitler and Stalin, or institutions ranging from the relatively banal, such as golf clubs, to the relatively powerful, such as political parties.

By example, the narrative of *Die Blendung* enacts the delight at what, from the individual's point of view, is the pleasure s/he may derive from displaying wit in public. Canetti is an aristocrat in this respect, in the best sense, in the high premium he places on a demanding kind of social interaction in conversation, which he probably inherited in part from the school out of which his hero Stendhal grew (La Rochefoucauld and others), and in part from the individuals who populated his own world, such formidable personalities as his mother and others, who stressed talk, and high-level talk, as a major ritual in life. He rejects the aristocracy of the blood in favor, less of the possible aristocracy of the soul, than of the Greek notion of the strong, self-sufficient human being, the measurer of all things, who rejects any kind of dependence on anything and always defines herself/himself actively. *Die Blendung* is Julien Sorel, for instance, in this very specific sense and *Die Blendung* is *Le Rouge et Le Noir* in its exploitation of a kind of prose that elevates aggressive, agonistic wit. Like Stendhal, Canetti is motivated by the desire to be "toujours sec." Canetti is also close to Nietzsche, who, in drawing his own genealogical tree, stressed his debt to what he felt were the great French psychologists (La Rochefoucauld and Stendhal), whose knowledge of human behaviour was also expressed linguistically in a particular kind of dry, abrupt, sharp, powerful prose. Stendhal, Nietzsche, and Canetti all exploit the sentence as a short, witty unit of energy and they all do so for the same reason.

So we are not really in the underworld at all. Finally, even if one is not responsive to the elegantly clumsy "hints" to this effect looked at above, one need only look at the "logic" that links individual "actions." It is the logic of absolute non-logic. Nothing leads to anything in any causal sense, because motive has been demoted altogether. One moves from one moment to another without realizing that the sequence makes it *impossible* to construct logic or motive. The arrangement of the narrative is such as to resist the pressure that readers bring to texts, as they presumably bring to life, to make something yield something that might give them the power to believe that the game has already been won. Of course, it is important here to comment on the charm with which all these ideological points are delivered to readers. They are not given any kind of ugly prominence, because the mood of theatrical inflation is so demanding and compelling in itself. It is, indeed, quite easy to be taken in by the brilliant construct the narrative of *Die Blendung* is, without being even remotely aware of the ideology that actively sustains it. In another example, when all we know is that what the gang is doing is running around town sustaining Kien in his illusion that books are what makes life living, Fischerle comes across the man, Kien, who the text implied, at an earlier stage, was his master. After all, in the above example, we saw that Kien asked Fischerle to work for him. The narrative seductively deconstructs the master/slave hierarchy that that scene loosely raised as an idea in the reader's mind, since, in scenes subsequent to the "deal," Fischerle clearly acts as an autonomous agent and takes no orders from his boss: he is the real boss. This is not because

Canetti has not created any scenes in which Peter Kien delivers orders to Fischerle. Nor does the effect of our realizing that Fischerle is really calling the shots make us reflect, as critics tend to do, on the way in which the "evil" Fischerle is intent on taking Peter Kien for a ride. In abandoning the expectations raised by the master/slave idea, Canetti goes on to something entirely different: he allows his narrative to be sustained by the absurdity of its own absurdity, where all "actions" are executed with an amazing flourish, "inspired" by the idea of the love of love as an end in itself.

One can sense Canetti laughing throughout this section of the novel at the grossness of the terms on which Faust, the scholar who had enjoyed such extreme autonomy in his life, submits to his new master, Mephistopheles. This mischief is arguably directed not only at the master/slave scenario, but at the play *Faust I* as a whole, for this next example makes another mischievous allusion to one of the more famous lines from *Faust I*: here, however, the grossness of Goethe's notions of salvation and redemption and their relationship to an authoritarian notion of secular Law, as they are "investigated" at the end of *Faust I*, is exploded by a near-lyrical moment of helpless laughter.

In the scene quoted below, Fischerle is calling the shots. He is the master of the situation. In the story or fairy tale that Fischerle tells Kien, all the sorts of actions one would call absolutely innocent (like eating, coming to someone's assistance, etc.) are categorized by Fischerle as criminal:

> Endlich hatte ihn Fischerle kraft seines Willens bis auf den Platz hinter der Kirche und unters Vordach gezogen. "Gerettet!" höhnte er. Kien staunte über die Größe der Gefahr, in der er eben noch geschwebt hatte. Dann umarmte er den Kleinen und sagte mit weicher, zärtlicher Stimme: "Wenn ich Sie nicht hätte . . ."—"Wären Sie schon längst eingesperrt!" ergänzte Fischerle. "Meine Handlungsweise verstößt also gegen das Gesetz?" "Alles verstößt gegen das Gesetz. Sie gehen was essen, weil Sie Hunger haben, und schon haben Sie wieder gestohlen. Sie helfen einem armen Teufel und schenken ihm ein Paar Schuh', er läuft in den Schuhen davon, und Sie haben Vorschub geleistet. Sie schlafen auf einer Bank ein, zehn Jahr' lang träumen Sie da, und schon werden Sie aufgeweckt! weggeschleppt werden Sie! Sie wollen ein paar einfachen Büchern helfen und schon ist das ganze Theresianum von Polizei umstellt, in jeder Ecke verkriecht sich einer, die neuen Revolver hätten Sie sehen

> sollen! Ein Major leitet die Operation, dem hab' ich unter die Beine geschaut. Was glauben Sie, hält er so tief, damit keiner von den großen Menschen, die vorübergehen, was merkt? Einen Verhaftbefehl! Der Polizeipräsident hat einen besonderen Verhaftbefehl ausgestellt, weil Sie ein höherer Mensch sind. Sie wissen selbst, wer Sie sind, was brauch ich Ihnen da weiter zu sagen! Um Punkt elf Uhr werden Sie in den Räumen des Theresianums tot oder lebendig verhaftet. Sind Sie draußen, so darf Ihnen nichts geschehen. Draußen sind Sie kein Verbrecher. Um Punkt elf Uhr. Und wie spät haben wir jetzt? Drei Minuten vor elf. Überzeugen Sie sich selbst!" (*DB*, 263)[279]

We have no independent evidence whatsoever of any of the things Fischerle maintains is going on. The whole idea that Peter Kien is a criminal has no referential value within the text itself, since primary scenes in which he might have acted as a criminal are missing. Fischerle is telling a story that is compelling in its own right, because it is being delivered, as everything in this novel is delivered, with absolute, irrevocable, and unconditional confidence, and with such authority and force that readers may be forgiven for not realizing that it is a fairy tale. If examined in detail, Fischerle's speech is a parody of logic and truth. Everything is a moveable feast. The absurdity of the speech comes to its climax when Fischerle says that Kien is to be arrested, either dead or alive. However, they are not on the run, they have not committed any crimes, the police are not in evidence, Kien's actions are not certifiable in terms of the Law. It is all a red herring.

Another example of the riot that is this whole section of the novel can be found in the following, only apparently more minor, detail: "Aber Fischerle gab keine Ruhe. Kiens Nase geriet in Fluß und nachdem er es längere Zeit, ohne sich zu bewegen, geschehen ließ, beschloß er, aus Ordnungsliebe, gegen den großen, schweren Tropfen an der Spitze einzuschreiten. Er zog ein Taschentuch hervor und wollte sich auch gleich schneuzen. Da stöhnte Fischerle laut auf. 'Halt, halt, warten Sie, bis ich komm'!' Er riß ihm das Taschentuch aus der Hand, selber hatte er kein's, näherte sich vorsichtig der Nase und fing den Tropfen wie eine kostbare Perle auf" (*DB*, 272–73).[280] As when Therese was pacing around the flat thinking that a crime had taken place there, the pace of the above makes no concessions to the emotions to which specific words in the passage actually refer. The pace of the narration is masterful. It flies in the face of the speed with which snot tends to fall out of the nose, thus creating yet another of the gaping spaces in which this novel abounds, which itself produces humor. It has a part to play in the exceptionally slick facetiousness sustained here. If this were a serious novel about crime and evil, the above kind of scene would have absolutely no place. It is fascinating that critics who have stressed the novel's concern with crime and evil have been able to suppress their memory of this incident. But perhaps they are too serious by nature to be sensitive to riotous humor.

In what appears to be a momentary concession to the idea that Fischerle is a criminal, intent on deceiving Kien and robbing him of his money, Fischerle is depicted advising the blind man how to make Kien unsteady. As he has just heard about the existence of Therese, Fischerle advises the blind man to step on Kien's toes first and then mention that she has died. The following passage tends to be used by those critics who believe that Kien is radically disturbed in psychological terms:

> Kien verfärbte sich. Er sah sie kommen. Sie ist ausgebrochen. Der blaue Rock glänzt. Die Irrsinnige, sie hat ihn gebläut und gestärkt, gebläut und gestärkt. Kien ist zerbläut und geschwächt. Sie sucht ihn, sie braucht ihn, sie braucht neue Kräfte für ihren Rock. Wo ist die Polizei? Man muß sie einsperren, sofort, sie ist gemeingefährlich, sie hat die Bibliothek allein gelassen, Polizei, Polizei, warum ist keine Polizei da, ach die Polizei kommt erst um 10.40, welch ein Unglück, wenn Fischerle da wär', wenigstens Fischerle, der fürchtet sich nicht, der hat ihre Zwillingsschwester zur Frau, der kennt sich aus, der hat sie erledigt, der vernichtet sie, der blaue Rock, entsetzlich, entsetzlich, warum stirbt sie nicht, warum stirbt sie nicht, sie soll doch sterben, diesen Augenblick, in der Glastür, bevor sie ihn erreicht, bevor sie ihn schlägt, bevor sie den Mund auftut, zehn Bücher, wenn sie stirbt, hundert, tausend, die halbe Bibliothek, die ganze, die in Fischerles Kopf, dann muß sie tot sein, für immer, das ist viel, er schwört es, die ganze Bibliothek gibt er her, nur tot muß sie sein, tot, tot vollkommen tot! "Sie ist leider gestorben" erklärt der Blinde mit aufrichtiger Trauer, "und läßt schön grüßen." (*DB*, 280)[281]

The above takes place after the blindman has stepped on Kien's toes. He has not mentioned Therese. In other words, in terms of strict logic, there is no justification for what the above appears to be, namely an intensely well orchestrated outburst of anxiety and fear, a depiction of Kien's vulnerability to fear at the possibility that he is going to suffer the presence of Therese again. Of course, critics would counter my view and dismiss it as a stubborn refusal to acknowledge that the above is evidence of Kien's suffering, which does not have to be stimulated logically by an external stimulus, precisely because he is supposed to "be" psychologically disturbed. My view is that this is another extrovert wink to the reader, since the above can be read as absurd in itself, and as a link in a chain reaction, which appears to link all the other moments of absurdity together. It comes after an absurd enough wink to the reader, that advice Fischerle gave the blindman on how to extort cash from Kien. After all, how would stepping on somebody's toes constitute a serious attempt to extort cash? That Kien also then "sees" Therese even before she has been mentioned, strikes me as proof, not that Kien is psychologically beyond salvation, but that the narrative is having a good time. It is obvious that Canetti is being facetious here, inasmuch as the whole of the passage, yes, does appear to make concessions to anxiety in terms of its pace. Yet the last line, and we have already had occasion to point out this technique of Canetti's, this virtual hallmark of his facetiousness, undercuts the apparent melodrama altogether. In its own right it is absolutely silly, and wonderfully so. It not only has the function of releasing us from the anxiety and near-seriousness of what preceded it, but of "arguing" that there are risks that go with looking for seriousness in life. The danger is that one runs a severe risk of losing one's wits.

6

Parody, Postmodernism, Careerism

To many, the claim that the narrative of *Die Blendung* resembles a dance will seem heretical in principle. It will also seem particularly heretical for the implicit view that *Die Blendung* praises the physical, the body. Yet it does this only because the body is never assumed to be merely physical, unlike so many "descendants" of Nietzsche. If the body is filled with agility and gaiety by the spirit of play, the body is really animated by the spirit of love. It celebrates the body, in a secondary sense, when the novel makes the reader laugh, which is to say makes the reader do something physical. It never does this in the popular way of drawing attention to the body in a literal sense. As already mentioned, when the body features literally in *Die Blendung* it is winking at the reader. The Western fascination with dualisms between mind and body has no resonance in the novel, because the body is never fully detached from the mind. I propose, in the next chapter, using the chapter "Privateigentum," that delight, the delight that is the reader's, and that comes from the need to laugh physically as one listens to the talking out loud of the narrative, is expressive in *Die Blendung*. It is in keeping with William Blake's cry in "The Marriage of Heaven and Hell" that the doors of perception be opened. Delight is born *ex nihilo* and created out of the sociable desire to enjoy displaying one's wit in public. This display takes the place of conventional intellectual exchanges with some pretence to rational analysis, where an emphasis might be placed on competing only to win. Rather the display perpetuates the competitive mode as an end in itself.

In "Privateigentum," a paradigm for "understanding" the world is absent, and with a vengeance. In other words, that chapter is particularly assertive with respect to the novel's consistently cavalier attitude toward Truth in the first place, and referential Truth in the second. Further, it is the experience, for the reader, of the liberating feelings induced by the dance. Quite simply, what the chapter makes clear is that the dance, if it is to be a dance *and* a feeling of liberation, *depends* (non-causally and non-logically, of course) on the absence of the pressure one associates with the desire to understand the world in the literal or material sense.

In the chapter as a whole, concessions appear once again to be made to an empirically verifiable "world." "Privateigentum" is set in a police station, and, since the interrogation conducted there is itself brought about by an arrest, we have every reason to believe that Canetti is making concessions to the "real" world. There appears to be a focus on Law and Order, on the procedures that supposedly protect innocent citizens and bring those guilty of crimes and evil to book, once and for all. There is an encounter between those suspected of some kind of crime (characters) and those beyond crime themselves (the police). The latter emerge as real characters or personalities in the story—they are not merely present for functional purposes, the means by which the ends of Law and Order are achieved, because they verify whether those arrested are guilty of the charges brought against them. The chapter is further concentrated by a relatively large number of literary references. In this chapter, we shall reflect on whether or not Canetti's manner of referring to literary texts entitles Canetti to be classified as a parodist.

We have already talked about *Don Quixote, Faust I, Le Rouge et Le Noir*, and have commented in such a way as to imply that the apparent pleasure of *Die Blendung* at its ability to invoke literary texts from the past was an innocent pleasure, that of respecting, preserving, and paying homage to a literary source in an overtly ahistorical kind of way. The references were made in such a way as to further the imaginative exhilaration of the reader in the present, as s/he reads. This was obvious, inasmuch as the reference was not reproduced to affirm character or scene in the narrative but to further the cause of hilarity and the *imprévu*. Peter Kien behaves, for instance, as Don Quixote did, and Fischerle behaves as Sancho Pansa had done. The echoing of Don Quixote and Sancho Pansa, we can conclude, was a charming way of inducing the light feeling of intoxication associated with the dance of one who is happy to be free.

We noticed that the literary reference to *Faust I* was positively modified, by contrast, in the sense that the novel seemed to want to make a virtue of ridding the original of its components of melodrama or tragedy. The logic behind such a strategy can be understood in terms of my theory of the dance. After all, melodrama and tragedy induce emotions that positively inhibit free dancing. When Fischerle referred to the Law to Kien, for instance, in the incident examined in the last chapter, he was referring to a banal representative of the secular world, the police, and in a context that was manifestly absurd: Fischerle was presented to us in the throes of telling a story *as if* it were true, when we as readers knew it referred to nothing objectively true, either intra-textually or extra-textually. Subsequent diegetic material neither confirmed nor rejected his theory that Kien was technically guilty of breaking the Law. When Kien is arrested, as we shall soon see, another manifestly inappropriate story is invented. Once again, this does not serve some intra-textual purpose, for its place in the narrative is such as to suggest it is not there to legitimize the arrest in logical terms for the reader, as if to prove to the reader that it has every reason to be there in the plot, etc. The material that emerges in the narrative is, once again, absurd enough to indicate to the reader that this is not a true story but a way of entertaining an audience. Narrative material is overtly put forward to the reader as the illusion it really is, which is to say nothing more or less than a theatrically invented and theatrically sustained performance with no claims to truth of any kind. Law and Order are not taken seriously in their own right. They are the pretext for the spinning out of the aesthetic illusion which is the work of *Die Blendung*.

The clash between the manifestation of divine/extra-terrestrial Law (Gretchen's own psyche) and an aberrant deviant or representative of lawlessness (Faust) in *Faust I* actually takes place, and is justified as an event in the narrative of Goethe's play in terms of emotional and intellectual logic, two kinds of "logic" on which Canetti never relies. The actual clash in *Faust I* has extraordinary consequences, inasmuch as it leads to Gretchen's surrendering herself to human representatives of Law and Order in society, who "execute her wishes" and execute her. Law and Order are taken seriously, and human beings are measured according to the Old Testament notions of Good and Evil on which Law and Order in the play are based. Needless to say, in keeping with Goethe's anti-feminism, these privilege men only, as they prevent them from the bother of having to accept responsibility for their actions. Woman not only pays for crimes that are not hers, but finds herself sentenced either to forms of living death or to death itself.[282]

When Fischerle told Kien the story examined in the last chapter, in which he insisted that Kien's behavior was technically illegal, we certainly do remember *Faust I* by association. Canetti's contextualization, however, indicates that Canetti shares none of Goethe's assumptions about the relationship between Law and Order and Good and Evil, and none of Goethe's "feeling" for the way human beings can fall short of standards of Good and Evil. The melodrama, "gravitas," or tragedy of *Faust I* is not there in *Die Blendung,* despite their common interest in the law, in breaking the law, and in the trial. These have been excluded, to the extent that the original has been remodelled or parodied. It has been taken for a ride in such a way as to show up some of its possible "limitations" and as a way of drawing attention to the differences between Canetti as thinker and writer and Goethe as thinker and writer. Importantly, however, it does not do this in a violent way, through satire or travesty, because Canetti does not resort to ridicule. He merely makes clear, in a nonviolent way, his detachment from some of Goethe's first principles.

We can say, on balance, that in the case of *Don Quixote* and *Faust I,* references ultimately have the function of affirming the reader. S/he is assumed to be as literary as the author of *Die Blendung,* and s/he is assumed also to enjoy the pleasure of creating a literary echo or allusion, of acknowledging in public the pleasure of having read certain literary works found imaginatively exhilarating. Given the form, the abrupt, brittle, violent sentences so characteristic of *Die Blendung,* in and through which the references were made visible, we can also say that the references were modified in such a way as to preserve the competitive wit of the reader. In other words, Canetti's love of literature manifests itself in what are obviously literary references, some of which are parodied *lovingly,* not aggressively. Yet the references are primarily all part of Canetti's particular kind of love of life—the idea, from Nietzsche, of the exhilarating task of affirming the potential for life in the present.

Linda Hutcheon, in her study of parody, *A Theory of Parody,* never cites Canetti as an example of a parodist, despite the fact that the references to *Faust I* are clearly parodic.[283] This is partly because Canetti cannot be classified as a parodist in the conceptual sense. Parody appears locally in *Die Blendung,* and it is not the dominant mode. We have already indicated in earlier chapters that Canetti sometimes parodies Weininger. We can now expand upon a comment made in Chapter Two on Canetti's attitude toward Freud's *Traumdeutung,* with a view to assessing Canetti's use of parody in the novel as a whole and to see whether it fits Hutcheon's model of parody, specifically her claims that it can undermine the socio-political "status quo."

In "Konfuzius, ein Ehestifter," the modulation of the narrative into a dream sequence is achieved without any recourse to those mimetic techniques capable of imitating what it is really like to dream. Canetti refuses to let his dream modulate into the real nightmare it could have become, given the references to tigers, sacrifice, fire, and the last judgement. He does this by deflating the potential for melodrama: "Der Himmel war schwarz und eng und hatte seine Sterne in der Tasche versteckt" (DB, 38).[284] Further, the narrative is absolutely resistant to the psychological theories Freud developed about repression and so on, because the narrator, who is not Peter Kien, insists on supplying his own commentary on the dream. This commentary plays down the melodrama, at an analytical level, by saying that the dream had been stimulated by a match seen on the street and by Michaelangelo's "Last Judgement." The refusal to participate in the earnestness of Freud's attempts to inject meaning into dreams is quite clear from the facetious and laconic final sentence, which reflects on the small things that had stimulated the dream: "Aus alledem hatte der Schlaf einen Traum gebraut" (DB, 41).[285]

Roisin O'Neill has also suggested that the whole of Part One of the novel is a *loving* and facetious parody of *Die Verwandlung*.[286] Gregor Samsa, like Peter Kien, is a prisoner in an urban flat, administered to by a woman, for whom objects in the room take on an amazing significance. O'Neill has also discovered, in the chapter "Prügel," for instance, when Canetti describes the movements of Kien's body, that there are more than just echoes of Gregor Samsa's painful attempts to negotiate the room, his prison: Canetti has virtually lifted sections of *Die Verwandlung* and quoted them verbatim, unacknowledged. Whereas *Die Verwandlung* raises any number of rhetorically charged questions about the human condition, Canetti's reworking of his raw material demonstrates his rejection of rhetoric as a way of living in the world. This position remains consistent throughout the novel, both when Canetti invokes his other favorite authors, Gogol and Stendhal, and when he does not.

Linda Hutcheon is interested in conceptual parodists who make parody a dominant mode, unlike Canetti, who is incidentally parodic. She is also not interested in parody throughout the ages, only as a form across the arts in the late twentieth century. This concentration allows her to draw certain pseudo-political conclusions about the relationship between the arts and the "dominant ideology" or the "status quo," terms that appear to have been popularized by Catherine Belsey and are used very freely and meaningfully now by loosely leftist critics.[287] I shall keep both in quotation marks in this chapter for reasons that will become apparent. Parody, like pastiche, is one of the major forms of postmodern self-reflexivity, according to Hutcheon. According to Fredric Jameson, in his essay "The cultural logic of late capitalism," both are neutral in an era of the simulacrum, where all is mere imitation in an ahistorical context, and where parody and pastiche display a "random cannibalization of all the styles of the past."[288] To Hutcheon, the overt turning of parody to other art forms implicitly contests Romantic singularity and its concept of originality. She argues that parody is a form of *imitation* characterized by ironic inversion, not always at the expense of the parodied text, since repetition with critical distance apparently marks difference rather than similarity. It is a productive-creative approach to tradition. It is capable of paying oblique homage. It can be used to satirize the reception or even the creation of certain kinds of art. It has transformative powers in creating new syntheses. Parody betrays through this, however, a tendency towards conservatism, as it overtly imitates art more than life. Further, parody's transgressions ultimately remain authorized by the very norm they seek to subvert. Even in mocking, parody reinforces. In formal terms, it inscribes the mocked conventions onto itself, thereby guaranteeing their continued existence. It is in this sense that parody is the custodian of the artistic legacy, defining not only where art is, but where it has come from.

Historians of parody apparently agree, according to Hutcheon, that parody prospers in periods of cultural sophistication, when parodists can rely on the competence of the reader, who must of course be in a position to recognize what is being parodied. Hutcheon's assessment of parody is a positive one, in that she claims it also has a capacity to historicize, by placing art within the history of art; others, like Jameson, see it as ahistorical, and more worrying for this reason.[289] To Hutcheon, parody's inclusion of the entire enunciative act and its paradoxical transgression of norms allow for certain ideological assumptions, namely a preference for the kinds of ideologies that celebrate, not repress, "difference," my final term to remain in inverted commas, for reasons that will also become apparent. In drawing this conclusion, we see a problem at the heart of postmodernism, to which Canetti has an extraordinarily challenging answer. Like so many writers, critics and thinkers currently at the forefront of the postmodernism industry, Hutcheon's work starts from the assumption, in the "high" tradition of Adorno and Jameson, if not in the apocalyptic tradition of Baudrillard and Kroker, that there is only such a thing as the "culture industry" out there. In a confusing way, all leftist critics like Hutcheon, Adorno, Kroker, and Jameson, are actually hostage to the macroeconomic truth that it is "late capitalism" which has made possible the high culture benefits of which parody is an excellent example. Late capitalism can provide a certain kind of writer with material security, on the condition that that writer restrict himself/herself to writing according to a mass market brief, that of entertaining and instructing the relatively large number of people who have the time and leisure for reading. Late capitalism guarantees the same kind of career for theoreticians of parody, whose jobs in the academy allow them the material access to multiple discourses, together with the imaginative time needed to formulate and publish findings based on the volume of discourses they have encountered, who are destined to "do well" if they decide to make a professional alliance with contemporary art and restrict themselves to commentary on what is available on the upmarket mass market.

In restricting themselves to commentary on what is *currently* being produced by the contemporary, postmodern market, however, both Jameson and Hutcheon show their real hatred of a sense of history, let alone of the past, in spite of their protcstations to the contrary. Concentration on the contemporary often doubles up as an unacknowledged refusal to think comparatively. It is also inseparable from an interest in types of literature, and a non-interest in the qualities that create absolute uniqueness and originality. It can also double up as a refusal to acknowledge the existence of the *range* and *variety* there is of literature, painting, music, sculpture, and architecture, if one thinks about each of the disciplines in terms of the past as well as the present. For an insistence on the present means a denial of the stretches of time and the multiplicity of not just "art forms" but of *individual works of art*. The often narrow focus of people like Hutcheon and Jameson, particularly in his last book on the supposed cultural logic of late capitalism is concerned, has serious implications in terms of their arguments, which we will be discussing. For the moment, it is important to note that neither

Jameson nor Hutcheon is prepared to admit that either the theory and practice of contemporary parody or the theory and practice of contemporary art forms might in fact be an expression of a formal complicity with financial success and professional opportunism.

Hutcheon's work is also hostage to another assumption, this time socio-political in kind. In *The Politics of Postmodernism*, her often unstated view is that there is a discrepancy between the present culture industry's apparent celebration of "difference," in the sheer multiplicity and variety of "things" available, and the actuality of people's everyday lives, where there is still injustice or lack of tolerance of "difference."[290] I say that her view that there is injustice is a socio-political one only because she implies that the liberal ideal of tolerance of "difference" is one that can be induced by certain kinds of political parties, either at the micro- or macro-political level. By "difference," she tends to mean the idea in late Foucault of self-invention, the individual's right to self-expression, whatever that might mean in terms of life styles. As a leftist, she believes that there are institutionalized obstacles to this goal, such as attitudes at the level of the imaginary, to class, sex, race, and religion. Legal and imaginative destruction of these barriers would result in our feeling free to express ourselves without fear of condemnation. Hutcheon is not writing a political pamphlet, but the implication of her arguments is that right-wing political ideologies are inimical to "difference," in that they tend to take a hard line on sexuality in particular, hate homosexuality and abortion, like the class system because it already serves their purposes, are racist and intolerant of non-Christian religions. Left-wing political ideologies apparently promote "difference," by contrast, because they are soft on sexuality, want to abolish the class system, believe in ethnic and racial diversity, and are tolerant of non-Christian religions. The leftist understanding of "difference" has its origins in a love of and support for the supposed empowerment of types of people deemed *historically oppressed*, like women, homosexuals, non-whites, non-Christians.

Terry Eagleton disapproves of the liberal stance of the few loosely leftist academics/intellectuals he is prepared to acknowledge, because he sees a lot of the above as phony and dishonest, as doing nothing more than endorsing the ruthless individualism of the already privileged. Eagleton is like Jameson here, who thinks the interest in "difference" is "simply liberal tolerance, a position whose offensive complacencies are well known"—although Jameson nowhere makes clear what these might be.[291] For Eagleton, Hutcheon's kind of position is all politically correct but empty, in his terms. Such lack of intellectual passion, coupled with such love of the purely subjective rights of some individuals, offends Eagleton's socialist goal of community. He sees the above as soft leftism, for stress on mere life styles does nothing to change the power structures at an infrastructural level in society, which, in the opinion of the hard Left, have an economic basis. Of course, he nowhere indicates how this goal might be achieved in practical terms, since he never mentions the presumably economic strategies necessary to effect change at the infrastructural level. He is actually very content, meanwhile, with the posture of melancholy, which allows him to get off the hook with the occasional wistful, yet thoroughly unsubstantiated, reference to the superiority in human terms of the trade union or condemnation of the public school as den of inhumanity. Neither does he indicate why his goal is necessary. This is, of course, because he is not a political ideologue, and because he is a literary critic with a vested interest in producing books that justify his having a career in the academy, and not in a trade union.

Since parody is currently in favor amongst theoreticians and practitioners of postmodernism for all the reasons (aesthetic, or socio-political) Hutcheon gives above,[292] the refusal of theoreticians of parody and postmodernism to take Canetti seriously, despite his occasional use of parody, needs to be accounted for. Canetti's novel has something provocative to say about Hutcheon's and postmodernism's repeated references to the relationship between the three elements that make up its holy trinity, namely "difference," the "status quo," and the "dominant ideology," because it exposes the intellectual confusions from which these terms spring.

How does Canetti use his and our literary inheritance? It is not the primary substance with which certain points are made about literature as process and not product, the "relativity" of all visions and/or the relative validity of all visions, as it is for those postmodernist writers of fiction with whom Hutcheon is concerned in *A Theory of Parody* and *Narcissistic Narrative*,[293] Patricia Waugh in *Metafiction*,[294] Brian McHale in *Postmodernist Fiction*,[295] and Edmund J. Smyth in *Postmodernism and Contemporary Fiction*.[296] To the postmodernists, art objects are never beyond ideological implication. They always mediate certain ideological positions, and ideology according to their interpretation has to mean a certain kind of socio-political agenda. Since all works of art always embody certain ideological premises, whether they like it or not, there are only art objects that are ideologically acceptable and art objects that are not ideologically acceptable. The criteria used to establish what constitutes an ideologically sound art object, and what not, seem to be varied. There is a particular sympathy for works that use themselves, as it were, to overtly deconstruct theories of art that actually believe in the absolute illusion, since absolute illusions apparently bespeak a love of preserving the "status quo" and are, therefore, conservative and more than likely, it is often implied, anti-homosexual, anti-abortion, and so on. They are inimical to "difference," but only if "difference" is defined in socio-political terms.

This sympathy for the ideological strategy of self-reflexivity is apparently a sympathy for the view that change is always possible, since in the overtly self-conscious worlds of the self-reflexive work, there is a repeated insistence on the fact that reality is made, is constructed, is mediated by the subjective imagination. Reality is not found in some pristine state. If it is made, then it can be remade, in the extra-textual world, it is argued. Works of art, therefore, that deconstruct the idea that the arts, generally speaking, are there to construct illusions are taken seriously and privileged as politically and aesthetically correct, since they apparently bespeak the *possibility* of changing a "status quo" assumed to be unfair, even if there is huge reluctance at the practical level to supply any practical program for change. Ideologically sound works apparently also achieve this polemical aim by overtly reminding us that they have *origins* and sources devised by others or forerunners. They enjoy telling us they are not original. Thus, the parody of particular characters or character per se, the parody of particular plots or plot per se, the parody of certain styles of writing.

It could also be argued, however, that what such practitioners are doing when they draw attention to the fact that they are depending, in some very substantial way, on ideas and techniques acquired from other works is to deny originality altogether. Of course, it goes without saying, all artists throughout history have borrowed, and some have done so without acknowledging their sources. It is, therefore, correct to to say that artists do rely on a body of inherited knowledge for inspiration. And it is true that so many critical commentators have failed to pay heed to the intertextuality in literature, preferring to believe that all art objects are absolutely solitary and owe nothing to the past, to a community of inheritance. In my terms, however, if borrowing is selective, and, crucially, *if the borrowing itself gives birth to a new constellation of ideas*, the achievement is worthy of being endorsed in terms that stress originality, both as a virtue and as an achievement.

When parody becomes the dominant mode, and when critics endorse parody as ideologically pure, the limitations of the achievement of parody are often obscured entirely. They are not discussed in Hutcheon's work, for instance, as it is simply assumed that the achievement is self-evident. One could claim, after all, that conceptual parodists are merely admitting that they enjoy borrowing. What they could be doing, in making a narrative that is only and primarily a performance of perpetual self-deconstruction, is *failing* to rise to a different and more demanding challenge, namely that of assuming that absolute originality is a possibility. Self-reflexivity might be a synonym for self-love. Parody might be a vehicle destined only to fulfill some self-congratulatory function, whereby the reader's chief imaginative experience concerns his mere ability to *recognize* that parody is taking place. It is not surprising that the title of one of Hutcheon's studies of postmodernist fiction is *Narcissistic Narrative*. She nowhere interrogates the problem raised by an art that loves only to imitate the already imitated, to stare at itself in the mirror, in terms of what this says about the refusal of *dialogue* between equals, and all that that implies in terms of freedom of the individual, his/her potential for creativity and agency, his/her being unique in absolute terms. One could claim that parody does not have a theory about real people, because it does not love real people, because it practises self-love.

The limitations of conceptual parody are overtly evident if we examine parody's attitude toward time. Those works of art that are only overtly deconstructing themselves also inevitably make positive points in favor of the ephemeral, the momentary, the illusory. Self-conscious self-reflexivity is about destroying the ontological basis for linear temporal development into the future, and it destroys that potential basis at regular intervals. So, yes, we know about the moment, but this is the moment in the weakest sense, not in the strong sense credited it by Nietzsche, and as it is enacted in *Die Blendung*.

The moments in parody in postmodernist fiction do not have any body. Each is exactly the same in kind as both the preceeding one and the following one, unlike in *Die Blendung*, where each moment has teleological strength, is absolutely new, original, and different each time, and depends on the collaboration of the reader and his/her emotional and intellectual strength. In postmodern parody we are invited to be lethargically analytical. There is, unlike in *Die Blendung*, where Small Ideas and Big Ideas are virtually banned, a small and very modest conceptual point, which a reader can understand very quickly. The point is always the same point. A parody by x is no different then, than a parody by y, even though its material may well be different. In getting the point so quickly, a limitation is placed on the emotional, imaginative, or intellectual satisfaction to be derived from the exercise of reading. Why? Because there has been only a limited exercise of those faculties. Going to see an exhibition of Stella's "installations" is nothing like as memorable, at the level of experience, as an exhibition of Wotruba's sculptures. What the postmodernists think is the really progressive achievement of having destroyed the supposedly archaic, and divisive, strength of the illusion, is in fact the poisonous gift of knowing that there is nothing, of admitting absolute defeat in the face of the world.

The moment, as it is celebrated in *Die Blendung* is injected with muscular strength, precisely because stamina is needed to bring it into existence, stamina of an emotional, imaginative, and intellectual kind. It is injected with strength that has body because Canetti is working according to the Nietzschean brief, whereby the construction of illusions is the only creative response to the challenge posed by existence. Parody, as it is currently being celebrated by postmodernism, has none of *Die Blendung*'s belief either in existence or the future, at the level of emotional, imaginative, and intellectual commitment. It thus cannot hope, amongst other things, to initiate change. Importantly, the self-reflexivity of postmodernist works simultaneously raises the status of rehearsal. "Practitioners," as opposed to named individuals, rehearse what has already been done. We come to the impasse of repetition and monotonous sameness. We come to the view that there are no longer named, individual artists or creators, but a mere series of equally competent "practitioners" who, like their consumers, can luxuriate in the monotonous, self-congratulatory mode which is ideology. Anyone can do it. There are no standards by which to judge whether anything is better than anything else, because parody and pastiche do not require critical engagement. They only ask to be accepted, silently and in passivity.

In making self-reflexivity crucial to art forms, Hutcheon is, therefore, demoting the individual in many serious ways. For in her celebration and endorsement of the mode of parody, it is assumed, wrongly, if one is prepared to take the long view on the history of literature and the arts generally, that there are no alternative possibilities or imaginative ways of doing things. If there really is only one way of doing things "correctly," comparative analysis and comparative judgment are not just redundant. An interest in the practice of self-reflexivity, whether one is writing a parody or talking about parody, is tantamount to a rejection of the pragmatic mode, which requires comparative analysis and judgment, dialogue and discussion. The pragmatic mode is rejected in favor of the dogmatic mode, which rules such activities out of court. Self-reflexivity stands for advocating a blank neutrality and anonymity in the face of everything. So when Hutcheon sees postmodernist writers of fiction as parodists, above all, one cannot take issue with what she says parody is, neither can one argue with her that it is a very popular mode at this particular time in history. But one can take issue with what she says it stands for in ideological terms. My view is that the practitioners of parody whom one could call conceptual parodists actively display a non-interest in something we might tentatively call *absolute difference*.

Since "difference" is something of a fashionable word at the moment, it is important to begin by saying what is meant by qualifying the noun "difference" with the adjective absolute. We have already seen how the space between the sentences in *Die Blendung* celebrates boundaries between individuals as absolute, binding, and sacred, for no violence is done to what lies behind them. This was guaranteed by the agonistic nature of narrative, where sentences follow one another chronologically but do not relate to one another semantically. In the further refusal to comment on or criticize what has already been produced, and in the delight expressed in going on and thinking up something entirely new, Canetti has something profound and wonderful to say about that climate that guarantees the imaginative space necessary to make absolute "difference" in my terms something by which we live.

Absolute "difference" has to be a purely *imaginative* space, animated by a spirit of love, for it is this emotion and attitude above all that maintain the security which creates respect *between* individuals, enshrines it as indestructible. This imaginative space knows that everyone is unique. It respects that uniqueness because its characteristic voice, facetiousness, does no violence at the emotional, intellectual, or imaginative level. Sentences in Canetti's narrative acknowledged one another in the way that is necessary in order for a chain reaction such as a particular kind of dance to take place. The novel, given the particular relationship between the diegetic material and the mimetic material, was also a respectful refusal to enter into the private worlds of speakers without permission. By implication, we also have the idea that speakers accept in principle the right of other speakers to speak, as well as their right to believe in an opinion, whatever that might be, as well as the redundancy of critical appraisal of that opinon, precisely because the listener has the courtesy and respect to assume that any speaker always invests faith and confidence in whatever it is s/he says. Canetti's writing already practises a vision of life based on the notion that communities can only exist where there is a strong, natural, and spontaneous sense of respect for the individual as a unique being. The Left, by contrast, tends to assume that communites can be created artificially, by bringing individuals together who are primarily representatives, or types, and who see lowest common denominators as the basis of human solidarity, like sex, class, or religion.

The stress on "difference," common amongst leftist liberals in academia who, like Hutcheon, are obssessed with the politically correct in terms of some vague idea of allowing everybody to be who they are, is thoroughly misconceived. My contention is that the current, fashionable definition of "difference" is dangerous because it is a material one. "Difference" seems to consist of my having to *be* lesbian, gay, black, brown, man, woman, yellow, Catholic, Protestant, Jew, or whatever in order to "qualify" for the "privilege" of "difference." Yet this is dangerous because it is a form of violence against the individual at a very fundamental level indeed. It concentrates on lowest common denominators.

Since, according to the definition proposed by this chapter, absolute "difference" is something that depends on *intersubjective* attitudes, it is highly unlikely that law or laws will be capable of inducing it. This is a view President Mary Robinson of Ireland, a trained constitutional lawyer and ex-Professor of Law at Trinity College Dublin, is excellent at propagating in her new high-profile position as a public servant. It is a pity that other influential public figures, like academics, are not intelligent enough to realize the crassness of their material definition of "difference." Their power in terms of influence over other people's imaginations is wildly excessive, and it is being deployed at the moment to indoctrinate people in ways that are socially divisive. After all, as Mary Robinson knows, "difference" should consist in my being a particular kind of agent, in my acting as if I knew how to sustain an imaginative space between myself and any other self. It is a *practice* above all. Further, the practice depends on cooperation between two *consenting* parties. It is absolutely nothing if it is only a theory. As something plastic, it will only be created by people who are interested in the benefits that can be derived from what sustains its existence. The benefits, a gay and happy kind of intimacy, Nietzsche's Greek "Heiterkeit," which he felt Christianity had managed to destroy, can only be entertained, furthermore, by certain types of individuals, namely those who are prepared to be dangerous and take a risk, to play an overtly theatrical game, the kind of game that always knows that that imaginative space between individuals referred to above is indestructible. Since the benefits of recognizing the space by playing the game are a sense of intimacy and well-being, it is highly unlikely that theatrical game playing can be of interest to people who do not already have a spontaneous or natural rapport with one another, who are not already friends, as it were. Consent cannot be induced, since what makes people trust one another or feel close to one another is beyond the intervention of the will or force. There is such a thing as Darwin's notion of natural selection, after all, as the postmodernists should know, given the huge numbers there are of them, and the way in which they stick together. It is for these reasons that one can be suspicious of the superficially attractive, utopian stress on a community of multiple discourses and multicultural societies, a sentiment both fashionable and popular within the postmodernist debate generally. For it is impossible to force people to respect one another.

Derrida's emphasis on "difference" as "différance," as his use of key words like trace, dissemination, spacing, alterity, and supplement, which are metaphors for "différance," has provoked a huge series of publications.[297] In the intense focus now also placed on sexual difference, it is easy to lose sight of the interpretation of "difference" just given.[298] In the current intense focus on how individual works are not what they seem, the view espoused by deconstructionists descending from Derrida and Paul de Man, such as Barbara Johnson, and in the current high-profile lobby given to loosely political left-wing liberals in the academy, it is obvious that more and more people are assuming that "difference" is something material.[299] "Difference" has, problematically, been greeted by feminist critics, too, as if it were some kind of panacea to the evils meeted against women in the past, and there is agonistic fighting about whether it is "difference" "within,"[300] "from," or "in," that is best thought to provide empowerment, as can be seen in the influential set of essays published in 1980 called *The Future of Difference.*[301]

Stephen Heath, in *The Sexual Fix*, has suggested that to lay the emphasis on "difference" and the specificity of women, as of men, in the paradigm male/female, is a damaging gesture within the terms of the existing system, for which, precisely, women are different from men. Patriarchy has always said that women are different, they are not men.[302] Luce Irigaray, in her book *Ethique de la Différence Sexuelle*, by contrast, wants to recognize sexual "difference."[303] She warns there and elsewhere against displacing the male-female binary model before the female side has acceeded to identity and subjectivity, concluding, hysterically, with the warning that if we try to suppress sexual "difference," we invite a genocide more radical than any destruction that has ever existed in history. She justifies the view by saying that the gender-neutral terms "justice" and "equality" have stood, historically, for culture's desire that woman merely become a man in order to exist. By contrast, Irigaray wants to start with the fact that men and women are different. She justifies the title of her book by saying that Descartes preached wonder. This should be the basis of what she calls an ethics of sexual "difference," for wonder cannot seize, possess, or subdue an object. Heath's estimate of the "value" of the word "difference" is an important one. Insisting on a revolution of values that would install the "feminine" in place of the "masculine" is hardly going to bring about productive change. But even though Irigaray's utopian views about wonder are appealing, none of her wishes is accompanied by any kind of strategy for practice. After all, whilst wonder is, of course, productive of autonomy, it is highly questionable whether the basis for wonder can be secured by a hanging on to sexual "difference" as she perceives it, which is to say,

"I as a woman am different from you as a man." This is deeply mindless. Use of the word "difference" often obscures, even trivializes, then, the *artistry* involved in bringing about absolute "difference" as outlined above. It obscures artistry, by actively privileging ideological points about class, race, religion, and sex, by assuming that people are merely "types" or "classes" of people, not unique individuals. The clear implication of the above material definition of "difference," and of the position of many leftist academics at the moment, is that it would also be preferable if the political Left were in power, for the Left would empower the oppressed by giving "them" not just complete social, economic, legal, and political "rights" "they" deserve, but other forms of power or authority which might compensate for the denial of power or authority "they" have experienced in the past.

This kind of "political" thinking is also problematic, since it is a version of the colonialism against which Edward Said seems to argue so passionately in *Orientalism*.[304] It sounds imperial, for merely to empower those considered to be "underprivileged" by giving "them" complete legal, economic, social, and political rights they might not have can easily become a substitute for the real task, that of getting the contented majority, those who are already materially privileged and who already have access to power, to accept those they have supposedly excluded from power sharing. If both the contented majority and the discontented exiles from power do not both make changes in their outlook, all we do when we instate change at the level of the law is to invite separatism, which can take the form of mutual indifference or actual hostility—which is no progress.

A final point that needs to be examined here is the issue of voice. Eagleton and Said, whilst, yes, male, white, and middle-class, as the slogan would have it, are themselves not members of the "categories" or "types" of persons mentioned above. They are not those who have firsthand experience of what it is like to live in those deeply hostile societies where, if one is going to play the material game, "my" particular "kind" of "difference" is not respected, and where it gives rise to abuse. Of course, Said is a Palestinian by birth. Said makes it known that he is in exile from his Palestinian homeland. He uses his position of influence to put pressure on the U.N. to do something about the persecuted Palestinians who live in the country where he grew up. Eagleton makes it known that he has working-class origins in Ireland, a country he has left. Gayatri Spivak is another internationally known public speaker who also makes use of her ethnic origins as a representative in the First World of the Third World, the state of Bengal, which she has also left.

As it happens, therefore, all three left their "origins" a long time ago and are not now, nor have been, direct victims of persecution because of their ethnic origins. They live and are making their careers amongst the professionally secure, integrated as they obviously are into the established, professional classes of Columbia and Oxford Universities respectively. All three also enjoy adulation on an international scale and are widely read, not just because of their books but because of their comparatively frequent contributions to the daily papers. Yet they do claim, because of their tenuous "personal" associations with the oppressed, to speak on behalf of those who have been historically oppressed. Ironically, in the critical work of all three writers, the oppressor, whether it is a colonial power in the case of Said and Spivak, or the upper classes in the case of Eagleton, is endorsed in the name of the very idea of hierarchy. All three writers approach the historically oppressed as if they assumed that their status, ontologically speaking, was that of the archetypal victim trapped permanently in a system from which there is no escape. In *Orientalism* we learn about how the West (the rich and privileged who could travel to the Orient) imagined orientals. We see orientals, therefore, as fictions of the subjective imagination of the materially privileged. Of course, Said's insights are revealing in terms of the way in which we imagine people as victims, but it is, curiously enough, much more significant that real, live, material orientals are not even present in *Orientalism*. Their experiences in the face of imperialism/colonialism are not even chronicled. They and their achievements have been erased from history within the confines of *Orientalism*.

Timothy Brennan, in an essay entitled "The national longing for form," published in a collection *Nation and Narration*, makes the same point about Eagleton's *Exiles and Emigrés*. Eagleton is accused of not including any reference to colonial subjects, despite their "screaming relevance to his theme."[305] The point about Brennan's rider is that it is unique in a high-profile and fashionable publication that otherwise seems ignorant of the internal contradictions in the arguments of a series of writers who dwell with such enthusiasm on the so-called crime of colonialism.

Meanwhile, it is amusing to note that the academy is much less interested in the culture produced by the subjects of a so-called colonial power. The notion that there is such a thing as an indigenous culture to countries like India is rarely entertained! The paradigm is so set up as to cast "natives" only as objects of colonial power or victims of that power, to the extent that their own culture is not given a voice, except as a footnote. At the conference in Galway, Ireland called "Colonialism and Gender," in May 1992, which had a huge international attendance, the literature and culture of the indigenous population of India, Canada, and Ireland were only present if they appeared to examine colonialism in the terms of the paradigm outlined above: Margaret Atwood's dystopias, for instance, became definitively representative of Canada. Alternatively, only the aspects of those writings of "blow-ins" that lend themselves to examination within the paradigm of victim/oppressor were the focus, such as Rudyard Kipling and Elizabeth Bowen (*The Last September*), or Kate O'Brien. Their outsider status, as a white man in colored India and Anglo-Irish women in Catholic Ireland, was repeatedly taken to be of central importance. It meant, not necessarily that they participated in the creation of a two-tier system of colonials and their subjects, but that their work was primarily of significance in terms of such a two-tier system.

The writings of Joseph Conrad, born in Poland but resident in Britain, of Derek Wallcott, born in the West Indies but resident in the USA, Salman Rushdie, of Indian descent but resident in the UK, Patrick White, born in Australia, sent to public school in Britain but resident before his death in Australia, V.S. Naipaul, from Trinidad but resident in the UK, Milosz, from Lithuania but resident in California, Joseph Brodsky, from the former USSR but resident in the USA—the writings of these (male) writers have all been taken very seriously by the academy. It is not insignificant that this list features a very large number of Nobel Prize winners or near-Nobel Prize winners. All of these writers, to a large extent, have turned their "origins" into a central thematic concern.

It is arguable, however, that the adopted country's enthusiasm for these writers (the London/New York cultural axis, in general) has been commercial and exploitative, a reflection of that adopted culture's need to romanticize countries of which they are unlikely to have any direct experience. The above writers have in part pandered to the ignorance of their audiences, by producing writing that centers on the quest on foreign soil. In their writings there is also a fair amount of romanticization about the historical and geographical past, whether that past is India, Lithuania, or the West Indies. There is no attempt to inform audiences as to what life is like, generally speaking, in those countries, which is to say from the point of view of one, if not two or more, of its permanent residents, except as these are "seen" by an outsider. The voices of permanent residents are not really taken seriously. Instead, we deal with the attitude of an exile to a country with which he has, for the most part, a tenuous link. This link is exploited for purely subjective reasons, either in absolute terms, where the solitary individual returns to a lost home only to be confronted with his own existential homelessness, or in relative terms, which is to say when the exiled traveller returns to an original "home" felt to be more "natural" than the home he has in his adopted country. Writers thus seem to agonize over the subjective issue of being alone, either in an absolute sense or relatively, which is to say as an outsider in a foreign culture. Alternatively, the past is created in an evasively melancholic or nostalgic manner, where it is implied that that past is better, relative to the uncivilized standards in the present of an adopted home. Finally, there is the role such writers adopt, a role offered them by the Western world, which appears to think that they are, *as exiles*, endowed with the authority, and apparently uniquely well-positioned, to pontificate on, as commentator, present-day culture throughout the world, no less.

The latter role has been fully exploited by V.S. Naipaul, who apparently regards himself as an authority on a huge number of countries throughout the world: contemporary India, in the 1964 publication, *An Area of Darkness*, contemporary India again, in his 1977 *India: A wounded Civilization* and in his 1990 *India: A Million Mutinies Now*. In 1980, he instated himself as an authority on Trinidad, in *The Return of Eva Peron, with the Killings in Trinidad*, and on Africa, with his *A Congo Diary*. In 1981, he toured parts of the Islamic Far East to produce *Among the Believers*, and in 1984, he produced an account of his experience in the Ivory Coast, *Finding the Centre*. Thereafter, in 1987, *The Enigma of Arrival*, and in 1989, *A Turn in the South*, in which he pronounces on America. V. S. Naipaul's books on India, to name but three, were rejected by native Indians, with good reason, given their boundless patronizing attitudes towards the country, India. They were read avidly by Westerns ignorant of India except as an imaginative construct, who believed that because Naipaul has Indian origins he was uniquely positioned to provide an assessment of India now, in the present. Western readers are then uniquely positioned, given their lack of experience of India as a country, or their ignorance of India as a culture and country, to neutralize the implications of what Indians felt were Naipaul's highly personalized and highly offensive fantasies. This is because they are programmed by their culture to worship the personal quest, and to turn the quester into a reason to launch the personality cult again.[306] The point that needs to be made is that Naipaul has no more and no less authority to pronounce so generally on India than either you or I do. His books were, after all, written after fleeting visits to the country. He is not a native resident in India, he merely visited India as a guest and as a traveller making a brief visit.

Joseph Conrad fell for and into exactly the same traps earlier in this century. His terrifying accounts of rootless isolation, either in Africa—*The Heart of Darkness*—or in the series of novels set in the Malaysian Archipelago, exploit Western ignorance of the Congo and Malaysia respectively, as they supply a series of fantasies about those countries that are based on a racist paradigm, whereby white, Western values are implicitly better and more civilized than colored, foreign values. This underlying racism is rarely talked about. Why? Because the racist background is severely neutralized by the stress both V. S. Naipaul and Conrad place on the quest by the individual for identity. This is never over, and it is more often than not unrequited. Imagined as such, the quest implicitly believes both that the Western male has a right to pursue his identity on his terms and that he has a right to his racism. For both Naipaul and Conrad cast, in racist terms, either their own adopted culture or the adopted culture of their fictionalized questing heroes. It is, reading between the lines, that which fails to provide the solitary questing individual with permanent identity in the shape of a home free from foreign natives. Why does it fail? Because of the civilization/barbarism paradigm on which their fictions or "travelogues" are based, where civilization is what whites inherit by birth, as barbarism is that which colored people inherit by birth. To complicate matters further, both the natives of the Congo and the natives of India constitute a threat to decent standards of civilized behavior, they are an offense to civilization because they have been contaminated by the evil of colonialism, by the whites who exported standards to their countries which they were then foolish enough to ape.

This seems to be a mere foul and pathetic cry for a golden age that has never existed. It seems to be a lament at what colonialism has, it is assumed, done. Yet it is really plain misanthropy, a hatred of anybody except the self. What Conrad and Naipaul do is export their own misanthropy and project it onto foreign races, pandering thereby to the racist prejudice of the audiences most likely to consume their stories, namely the culture industry on the London/New York axis, yet hiding the prejudice by dressing it up in terms with which that audience sympathizes, namely the quest by the solitary male individual for identity. More importantly, of course, it is a cry that is disrespectful of, and violent about, the indigenous cultures of both the Congo and India, the "culture" there that resisted influence from colonialism, and the "culture" there that cooperated with colonialism. Representation refuses to be discriminating, preferring the sensational posture instead. The solitary individual does not want to know that life exists beyond his quest for purely personal fulfillment. He does not want to know that there is happiness either, in any form. Thus, it invents the shallow view that colored natives are corrupt by the standards of Western "civilization."

The point about the widespread academic and lay appreciation of writers like Brodsky, Naipaul, and Milosz is largely a reflection of the real insularity of the audiences who consume their writings. Brodsky et al. are the acceptable face of the countries with which such writers have an extraordinarily tenuous association. Their central interest in the notion of an open-ended quest for identity, which culture appears to deny them, flatters the solitary, reading individual. It does so because it mimics his/her own situation, and fulfills that general audience's desire for racist-based, armchair cosmopolitanism. This effectively takes the place of firsthand experience of countries like Trinidad, Lithuania, the former USSR, and so on. As if to thank the writers for this service, a service that allows a Western readership to continue not to have to make any real effort of imagination with respect to the lives of the indigenous populations of the countries with which they only have some "literary" association, powerful individuals in the Establishment in the West get together to ensure that the above writers are nominated for, and then get, the highest possible accolade an insulated, sedentary culture can grant, namely the Nobel Prize itself.

Said's *Orientalism* can be looked at in the light of the above problem. His failure to represent the indigenous populations of the countries that make up that amorphous bloc, the Orient, his failure to grant them a voice, together with his enthusiasm for the ways in which solitary travellers create Orientals in their own imaginations, is, if not exactly blaming the victims, almost blaming the victims. Said certainly believes in the victim, but his project is, less complicatedly, the idea that the misfortune that is yours, because you are foreign, is for sure going to be put to my professional advantage! The story I can tell about you is going to get me a lot of jobs and a lot of publishing contracts! Why? Because it is mindless enough, in terms of its first principles, to flatter the herd instincts prevalent in Universities and outside them. Even in *The Question of Palestine* and *Blaming the Victims*, Said only expresses *sentiment* about a future in which Palestinians will not be victims.[307] Neither book contains a *concrete agenda* with specific policies concerning the future. Otherwise, both books are exclusively interested in identifying how the past created the present, and, in the case of the second book, merely marvelling at the "ideological" gaffes, with respect to the truth about the victim status of Palestinians, of colleagues in the field of historical/academic studies of Palestine: *Blaming the Victims* is about the pure pleasure of reprimanding his colleagues in "public," which certainly, from an aesthetic and ethical point of view, has to be one of the more grotesque pleasures enjoyed by people who actually think they are critics. It is, of course, also straight evidence of the practice of victimization within the academy.

Terry Eagleton, for whom the only decent and real people are trade unionists and the only attractive people are exuberant female feminists, has dedicated his career to approving of other male intellectuals who, like him, are dedicated to "opposition" in some vague form. This is true of his book on Walter Benjamin, for instance. He has also dedicated his career to deconstructing only the kinds of philosophers of aesthetics tainted by his version of corruption, that of endorsing some kind of vague socio-political "status quo." This is true of his book on *The Ideology of the Aesthetic*.[308] He takes a selective interest in literature and responds only when it can be forced to lend itself to his general model of oppressor and oppressed, which is the case in his book on Richardson, *The Rape of Clarissa*,[309] where the aristocrat Lovelace rapes the middle-class Clarissa—although of course Eagleton knows that it is patriarchy that has forced woman to treat herself as a sexual object in order to avoid becoming one for others![310] The same diminishing attitude colors his book on Shakespeare, all of whose works are apparently informed by the ubiquitous presence of desire, which is apparently the great leveller, making individuals mere vessels of impersonal forces.[311] Equally, his assessment of the history of English literary criticism is really only an interest in perpetuating class politics, whereby if you are a critic but had the misfortune to go to Eton, you are necessarily a careless liberal humanist with a vested interest in refusing to destabilize the "status quo." This is in fact another way of rejecting all of someone's insights without even assessing whether they have any independent value. His deeply prejudiced view is that one cannot be critical if one comes from a "materially privileged socio-economic background." Said's and Eagleton's term "oppositional criticism" is a deeply confused term, which merely privileges those who are on the intellectual Left, turning them into an alternative elite, only because they hold hard and fast views about the corruption of the "status quo."[312] This is really about paralysis, of all kinds.

Eagleton participates in a system, the University, that does not, in any way, represent the real interests of any historically oppressed people. Neither do his writings chronicle the history of the oppressed as a basis either for analysis or for action. The time spent reading the complete works of Kant and Hegel, hardly constitutes commitment to the causes Eagleton would like to think he espouses. One might think, by contrast, of what Sheila Rowbotham has done in *Hidden from History*, Germaine Greer in her study of female painters, *The Obstacle Race*, Elaine Showalter in *A Literature of Their Own*, and Dale Spender in *Women of Ideas and what men have done to them: From Aphra Behn to Adrienne Rich*. These critics have used their careers for the purposes of retrieval, to repair the damage done to those whose achievements have not been represented, who have apparently been erased from history.[313]

Eagleton's work assumes that his audience already shares his few Big Ideas. His work is merely addressed to the kind of "critic" most likely to share his firmly entrenched, and extraordinarily unsubtle, binary opposition about oppressor and oppressed. Most importantly, his interest is loaded firmly in favor of perpetuating an interest in the workings of the oppressor. Gayatri Spivak's work suffers from the same commitment to facile binary oppositions, as is clear from her formal sponsoring of so called "Subaltern Studies," a study of the various ways in which Indians under the British Raj were granted minority status.[314] Her study of the First World's exploitation of the Third, in *In Other Worlds: Essays in Cultural Politics*, likewise endorses persecution, in its commitment to the same model.[315]

It is arguable that the only real cultural politics today, which so many academics firmly believe are going on "out there," are those that are currently going on in the academy. The academy has possibly invented two ideas: the idea that the only politics are cultural politics, and the idea that all cultural politics can be explained by simple paradigms. The paradigm is naive enough to think that there are only absolute criminals and absolutely innocent victims of criminals in history. Of course the utility function of the paradigm in terms of one's career options is obvious. Its crassness as an instrument for interpreting the complexities of the world is not so obvious, and its wilful delight in erasing from discussion any of the moments in, say, Kipling or Elizabeth Bowen or whoever that possibly contradict or undermine the paradigm espoused by some of their interpreters, is more than just careless scholarship. It is evidence of the way in which literary texts are being exploited for the purposes of promoting ideology, whereby the reductive drive that maintains that everything is mere ideology, is also a way of denying the uniqueness of each literary text. It is also a very serious form of violence.

The simple and simplistic paradigm can perhaps be traced back to the politics of the survival of the academy in the community and the politicization in crass terms of teaching in the academy. The phenomenon of postmodernism, the banner under which the above battles are being fought out, can perhaps be traced back to the economic vulnerability of an institution that does not, for the most part and in most cases, justify itself economically, because it is structured so as to depend on public subsidies. In an era of world-wide recession, the nervousness of the academy can be detected in its desperate attempt to invent new ways of justifying itself. It does this by developing a resistance to the kinds of authorities most likely to call it to economic account. It has invented theory, colonialism, and feminism over the last twenty years for these purposes, and because these are now running out of steam, it has recently invented After Theory, post-feminism, and post-colonialism. It often, but not always, discusses its ideas in language that is stubbornly dense and resistant to access, unless you have already been initiated in postmodern speak by the academy.

The crass depersonalized form of the paradigm paraded by Eagleton, Spivak, and Said thus represents violence, yet there are only a few, lone voices on the intellectual Left who have challenged their views. Callinicos has argued, in one of the few books to dress down and expose the extraordinary shallow and shabby "principles" at the heart of the loud and vociferous spokesepeople of postmodernism, that what they all lack is a firm belief in rationality, resistance, and the subject.[316] What they all love talking about are systems that are already in the process of merely consuming a series of anonymous, and amorphous, human beings. They do not even acknowledge that there are subjects out there, let alone subjects already endowed with reasoning powers, with the moral energy necessary for resistance, or with pride and self-respect. This is obvious from the declamatory style of the writing of many apologists of postmodernism, as it is obvious from the generally high ideological content of the writing, and the hatred of what Stendhal felt was the truth of detail. The paradigm used by Said, Eagleton, and Spivak is not sophisticated enough to do justice to individuality, for it prefers to play the game of the personality cult, with all its trappings and with its firm belief in the existence of anonymous masses of unnamed, inarticulate, comotose, and spiritually miserable people out there who are victims of the actions of a few, named individuals. There are apparently only big, prestigious examples of criminals against humanity, and then a series of anonymous victims. This set of assumptions, based on violence itself anyway, is often accompanied by a further, uneasy desire for change by violent means. It is often implied that only revolutions can bring to an end the reign of apparent injustice. Where the end justifies the means, it does not matter how many anonymous corpses pile up; they were never named individuals anyway.

But to conclude: there is a strong case for reserving one's passion and not espousing with too much fervor the goal of equal social, economic, and political rights enshrined in law. The commentary on the enthusiasm for "difference" amongst academics in this chapter is an attempt to draw attention to a sounder notion of what creates the conditions that allow individuals to flourish. But it is also intended to draw attention to the violence being done to the individual that is going on in the debates like those outlined above, violence of which the participants appear to have not the slightest inkling, and which is far more insidious than the kinds of violence "in society" they maintain they are the first to uncover. A point also clearly needs to be made about the self-seeking function of the agendas of the critics outlined above. In a thoroughly petty kind of way, many academics participating in the public debate about postmodernism are obviously not jostling just for power but for the higher ground in moral terms, and feminism is often no exception here. The interest is a mere function of the need to give one's job a public profile.[317] As Bourdieu has shown in his book *Homo Academicus*, academics are not just reluctant to accept that power struggles are as much a feature of the professional life of the academic as they are of the lives of politicians, economists, and so on.[318] They live in a state of bad faith, for their vanity makes them convinced that power struggles are only things the sensitive intellectual observes "out there." In spite of the widespread acceptance of Foucault, then, the academic Left has failed to apply Foucault's insights to its own practices, continuing to believe that it is innocent when in fact it is very deeply implicated in the business of self-interest and self-promotion.

Paul Hollander, in his book *Political Pilgrims*, makes similar points about the intellectual community generally, but his argument also includes accounts of politically engaged activities of creative artists.[319] Intellectuals are as prone to mindless, zealous affirmation of political ideas, and as prone to double standards, as any one else, he maintains. The only difference is that they have a higher profile and are influential in a way most citizens are not. As Hollander's title indicates, the idea of socialism or communism, for instance, toward which large sections of the intellectual/artistic community have inclined historically, has often held sway in spite of empirical proof that the practice of a given socialism or communism has infringed upon basic human rights and more. Hollander's point is that we should notice how intellectuals project hopes or invest sympathies in existing political systems in *foreign* countries: the examples of the former USSR, Cuba, and China are given, when in the early part of this century the many high-profile intellectuals on tours of the USSR as invited guests failed to acknowledge they were being given a publicity-acceptable version of life in the USSR. They returned home to endorse communism as a more "human" system. The projection of hopes onto systems *away* from home more often fulfills the purely subjective need of the observer to have hope; it is an example of the sway of sentiment. More importantly, it often doubles up as a refusal to engage with political or social realities at the pragmatic level, both abroad and at home. Given what has been revealed recently about the quality of life in the former East Bloc generally, for instance, Hollander also notes the reluctance of intellectuals to acknowledge their mistakes in public, in the light of truth.

As we saw with the way the "deutsch-deutsch Literaturstreit" was conducted after the fall of the Berlin wall, where everyone was jostling for the higher ground, there was a veritable love amongst West German intellectuals of persecution of the individual: *Die Zeit* and the *FAZ* ran article after article on the issue of whether or not Christa Wolf and those who stayed should have collaborated as they did. Why weren't they brave like Wolf Biermann and Sarah Kirsch, who left earlier because they knew it was all wrong? There is even corruption written into the very questions themselves. Salvation is only physical escape from a source of danger to the intellectual's and creative artist's passionate conviction that the right to freedom of thinking should take precedence over everything else. Further, salvation is the individual's escape from what might contaminate him/her intellectually. Even if these creative artists or intellectuals helped to provide some kind of nourishment for the citizens of the GDR by daring to write in such a way as to assume there is such a thing as resistance to ideology, they still, in the wake of the collapse of the former GDR, seem to prefer to defend their special relationship with their special readership, rather than address the kinds of issues that concern the whole community. They are not, for instance, openly speaking out about the wider issue of the right of regimes to impose ideology and psychological persecution on generations of human beings. Christa Wolf has remained largely silent both about this wider issue and about the accusations levelled against her. Hermann Kant publishes his autobiography! Hollander's point is that this package of assumptions must be understood as a rejection of the community, a rejection based on the supposedly superior status of the lone intellectual, a status intellectuals would prefer to defend rather than confront broader moral, intellectual, and political issues of general concern to the majority.

The academic community should perhaps unite to reject the superficially uptopian call for a society composed of multiple discourses with respect for all citizens *as individuals*, irrespective of their orientation, color, or creed as it should reject the need to carry on discussing situations in society in terms of an aggressor and his victim for the above reasons. The two points of view are vulnerable, primarily because of the very terms of the debate, namely a binary opposition or paradigm in one form or another heavily weighted in favor of the aggressor. Both assumptions are vulnerable, in turn, because of the primacy of this matrix, to two further evils, of which Bourdieu has written with such beautiful cynicism. They are prone to the evil of exploitation by the superficially "innocent" "free" "thinker," who is already in a position of influence because of a job at a University. S/he is in a position to make purely personal profit in career and financial terms from being associated with what a minority of professional intellectuals has recently invented as fashionable, namely postmodernism with its claim to intellectual purity and emotive appeal to radicalism.

They are prone to the evil of paralysis at the practical level because of their insistence on people as representatives of the group, women, the group, gay. Asserting that the only issues worth taking seriously in the academy are issues to do with reflecting either on how those groups have been denied material power in the past or on the theory of instating groups in material terms is also a way of shifting the responsibility for change to the future. The long-term and highly debilitating effect of this package of ideas is the truth that in insisting on the political, one can very easily end up withholding one's personal commitment to the everday task of instating tolerance as an atmosphere in the home and the work place. In this respect, the slogan "the personal is the political" is as confused and misleading as the call for a society of multiple discourses is misleading. The slogans are self-serving, and nothing more.

"Difference" needs to be redefined as a respect and a belief in the power of the individual, a view which I have argued is enshrined in the narrative of *Die Blendung* as an imaginative attitude which is ideal, and, as such, something that completely bypasses politics, government, and the law. This respect and belief is something people can always practice, wherever they are and whatever their circumstances, precisely because it refuses absolutely to make a virtue of the material, either in terms of sex, religion, class, or color, those material goods that are endowed with such mystique by the Left. For life, according to *Die Blendung*, should be seen as an art that requires a certain agility of the imagination; an art that presupposes a sociable interest in others; an art that requires, above all, love, a gift that one cannot will into existence or induce in any way, shape, or form.

Postmodernist fiction, by showing through and in imitation that everything is relative to the past, that we all are thought by discourses, rather than create them, consitutes a refusal to engage with and negotiate life in the present, not just in the above, ideal terms, but in any terms. In refusing absolute uniqueness, absolute otherness, absolute originality, and absolute respect and belief in the power of the individual, it also refuses the empowerment of the individual for it bespeaks a "love" of interchangeability and anonymity, monotony, and absolute sameness. So although, in theory, as good readers of Foucault, the loosely socio-political agenda of postmodernism is to destroy monolithic structures, to eradicate the currents of power that speak through us because they are inimical to the "liberal" value of multiple discourses, postmodernism is, in effect, devoid of any kind of confidence in the individual as *creator and source of power.* It does not imagine the individual as someone free and/or capable of resistance in spite of his/her circumstances.

In addition to this major weakness, the loose political agenda of postmodernism suggests that the responsibility for change rests with others, out there, with new political parties and so on. But the agenda is also functional. It provides a focus for the herd instinct, as Nietzsche would see it, for it believes in group mentality and group thinking, which is why it dominated the MLA conference in 1991 and 1992, attended by over 10,000 academics each year. It is not a serious belief in the empowerment of the individual. The real appeal of postmodernism to high-profile academics, whether those academics are in favor of it or against it, lies in the fact that its premises are both simple and unsubtle, simple and unsubtle enough to make it practically possible to deliver a paper in public at an international conference before rushing off to give another paper on the same subject at another conference. It satisfies not those who like to think, but those who merely like to *think they think or to think of themselves* as sensitive, whether it is to the sufferings of others, such as the historically underprivileged, or whatever. This is really the vile and ghastly love of *sentiment*, or self-love. This stands for an entrenched refusal to cooperate or negotiate with others because of an assured sense of personal superiority, which in turn results in a lack of compassion, concern, or sympathy for the concrete needs of others.

Postmodernism is, therefore, primarily an invention of the academy for the academy. It is discussed strictly by those who are privileged enough not to suffer too overtly from vicious forms of discrimination, or who only have experience of the highly glamorous forms of discrimination that appear in literature. It appeals to those who have time and money to *reflect* on theories. The academy has a vested interest in theory, especially in a time when the threat of cuts is acute, which is presumably why it and its offspring are flourishing at the present time. It is both an expression of the insecurity of the academic, whose cultural capital is impotent in the face of a world in recession, and the formal refusal of any kind of commitment to change that requires practice, not theory. Whether or not the academy is seriously concerned with forming an alliance with political parties to effect change in society, whether or not it is seriously concerned with fighting outside the arena of the academy, or outside of the seminar room, tend to be the practical issues that are rarely discussed in pragmatic detail. They are not discussed in pragmatic detail because to do so would be to run the risk of facing up to the lack of anything resembling integrity, credibility, or honesty. The only attempt at self-analysis is the pathetic kind, that of the wistful melancholic who is upset things did not turn out the way he wanted. Such is the view of an apparently eminent scholar of Literary Theory and apologist of Derrida's contribution to the practice of literary criticism, Christopher Norris, who laments in one of his more recent books, *What's Wrong with Postmodernism*, that theory has merely served as an escape route from pressing political questions and a pretext for avoiding any serious engagement with real-world historical events.[320] Its theory of agency has been seen to be lacking.

It has often been said, and very predictably, that any nonpolitical or apolitical person or thinker is in effect endorsing the "status quo." There is everything to be said, however, about the thoroughly apolitical act of countering the evils of intolerance on a daily basis, in the way one lives one's life, in one's commitment to singling out persecution, and in one's appreciation of and enjoyment of individuality and individuals, especially those who do not take ideology seriously! Canetti's "ideology" here is thoroughly apolitical in *Die Blendung* in precisely this sense. The novel is overt in its defiance of the relevance of the political, economic, and historical world. The heretical view of this study is that it is not characterized by an analytical, or interrogative, "dialogue" with recognizable political, economic, and historical realities, as these exist outside the parameters of any novel. *Die Blendung* acknowledges certain customary forms of *social* life like scholarship, chess playing, "love," marriage, the police, and so on. In terms of narrative techniques used, there is no "playing" with the tricks of the trade at a novelist's disposal, like the narrator for instance, none of the kind of self-reflexivity practised by those who feel that attention must be drawn to the artifice of the novel in order to reduce its status or for the sake of play as an end in itself. Canetti is, in fact, thoroughly "conservative" by the "standards" of postmodern writing of today, in his unquestioning commitment to the use of dialogue, monologue, "erlebte Rede," the narrator, psycho-narration, and so on. All these techniques are only deployed as a means to a particular, affirmative end, that of achieving certain liberating effects on a reader's imagination, for they are all exploited to help construct the absolute illusion.

His way of writing is non-self-reflexive, precisely because his commitment is to what the tools of the trade can produce, and for which they are absolutely vital, namely the construction of the aesthetic illusion. As already implied, illusion is precisely that which postmodernist practitioners of fiction and postmodernists generally wish to do away with. Canetti subscribes, very positively, to the idea of the work of art as ideally suited to sustaining a particular idea in the imaginations of all his readers. As a symbol, *Die Blendung* tells us that we must keep on fighting to sustain the tension on which respect, in terms of sustained imaginative or intersubjective space, depends, as well as respect in a more concrete sense, as in the particular features which make me into a very different person from you and from him and from her. The work of art not only has to draw attention to the link between respect and personhood by making thoroughly original connections, but can already embody and apply these values by drawing attention to the internal dynamism and strength—that issue of tension just mentioned—or the creative power that is necessary if these values are to be affirmed in public. The function of the work of art is not to alert the reader to its relative similarity to that which already is (whether in art or in life), for those who do this could be accused of wishing to reduce the possibility of promoting humane values by refusing to show that respect for a person in "life" requires artistic skills.

As Canetti does not integrate repressive social and political ideology at a primary or secondary level in his text, in terms of either plot or character, he could, however, be accused of failing to acknowledge the existence of ideology as a powerful force and agent of repression. This exclusion, together with the exclusion of internal self-reflexivity, draws attention to itself. Yet if self-reflexivity likes to think it is capable of deconstructing a reader's confidence or faith in any of the traditional metanarratives associated with the so-called "dominant ideology," it also demotes the created work of art as a vessel of charisma and aura. What is created is presented for evaluation as if the purpose of evaluation were purely that of detecting what kind of ideology lies at the "heart" of any created work, as if the purpose of writing had been reduced to playing with a limited variety of ideological themes. It is, thus, not surprising that what is most improper to the ideologists in a created object is, above all, evidence of absolute originality. Relative originality is tolerable and saluted, such as parody as discussed by Linda Hutcheon. Absolute originality is not tolerable. Why? Because the confidence that is inseparable from originality is actually capable of upstaging socio-political ideology. Why? Because it is capable of proving, by example, that socio-political ideology is redundant. Yet for critics like Terry Eagleton, it is all quite simple: all aesthetics imply ideology and there are only two kinds of ideology anyway, acceptable ideology and unacceptable ideology: thus *The Ideology of the Aesthetic*. But his position does not exhaust the options by any means.

Canetti's exploitation of the wits of his readers proves, for instance, that he believes, quite ferociously and positively, in nurturing a particular kind of strength of character or agility of the wits in his reader. The hatred of Big Ideas and Small Ideas actually makes vulnerability to particular, defined ideologies with particular, defined political agendas unlikely and/or redundant. Canetti achieves this end by using means that are, in today's terms, rather unfashionable, but that are destined to induce a positive resistance to any kind of ideology, in the first place, and to create a positive or critical openness in the second. Canetti's position is radical in absolute terms, not in relative terms, inasmuch as he assumes he is talking to a particular individual, the kind who is naturally unavailable for legitimizing plots of any variety, reminding him/her that resistance is not passive, but active. It consists in particular and above all in a certain kind of practice: it is inseparable from that practice. It practices a certain kind of intellectual openness by example, and it practices a love and respect for people and a love and respect for their absolute uniqueness as individuals, precisely because it never assumes that people and things are of purely ideological interest, therefore interchangeable, therefore vulnerable to exploitation, therefore disposable.

The important conclusion to the involved ideas developed in this chapter concerns the view that *love and ideology are mutually exclusive.* Canetti tells us this with grandeur and overwhelming confidence, for the former thrives on variety and the latter thrives on monotonous, repetitive sameness. Love is the ethic, finally, that knows at its heart that if you do not start out with the assumption that each individual is unique and absolute, you can rapidly find reasons for exploiting that individual or disposing of him/her, or doing violence to him/her in other terms, such as refusing to take them seriously if they do not cooperate and repeat to your face the ideology you espouse. Ideology cannot and does not have this knowledge because people are only representatives, not individuals.

To this delight in the death of the imagination, the death of originality, and the refusal to be creative, Canetti has a profoundly cynical and highly demanding set of counter-positions. Cynicism about the desire of the self-conscious radical and his/her serious belief that an agenda for change/action can only be implemented by political parties, and only when they are in office. Canetti clearly rates the personal over and above the political and to the exclusion of the political, since the position implied by a narrative such as *Die Blendung* is that any kind of radicalism that makes a virtue of specific agendas is necessarily vulnerable to fossilization, necessarily runs the risk of being reified, of turning itself into another version of the "dominant ideology," precisely because in wanting to subvert the "dominant ideology" it merely wants to colonize it, to reinvent in its place another ideology, which in its turn will become dominant one day, no doubt.

In addition to this, all socio-political radicalisms are necessarily exclusive, for to advocate radical progress in the area of, say, homosexual rights, without at the same time advocating progress in areas at least as worthy of public time and public money, such as poverty in urban areas, not to mention poverty in rural areas, is to make a value judgment in favour of sexuality, which simultaneously makes a value judgment about nothing less than everything else. It is, of course, not possible to be radical in socio-political terms, in purely practical terms, without being exclusive. This practical problem apart, however, it nevertheless holds that any particular agenda is bound to be repressive, in absolute terms, of the value so paraded by those who classify themselves as liberal postmodernists descending (loosely) from Marx, namely that of absolute "difference." For every time I speak up for one lobby, I am also not speaking up for another lobby. Finally, it seems obvious that no single political party ever "manages" to give equal attention to all those issues and areas in need of assistance. Historically, it has always been those parties left of center that have been most consistently vocal about the desire to fight forms of oppression. Their vaunting of their "caring" commitment to the "underdog" is not necessarily matched by achievements or credits that outclass those made by the Right on behalf of the oppressed. When the Left does make progress on behalf of the oppressed, achievements are no doubt matched by new forms of oppression, directed against the perceived enemy, the Right, just as when gains made by the Right on behalf of the oppressed are no doubt matched by new forms of oppression, directed against the perceived enemy, the Left: this is the institutionalized game of party politics which Huizinga also lamented in *Homo Ludens*, comparing present-day infighting in the House of Commons and its European counterparts unfavorably to high-level, agonistic exchanges, which he maintains were the order of the day in the eighteenth century.

The popularity of the terms assumes that something called the "dominant ideology" and the "status quo" exist in the first place and that both can be fully characterized in the second. It suggests that life can be summarized in terms that make it fully homogenous. As such, then, right from the start, the term helps to obliterate the idea of the uniqueness of each person, for to admit that not everything in the world can be accounted for by such a reductive term would be to delay the (urgent) possibility of imposing a replacement ideology. The term assumes that whatever I do and say can only be understood in party-political or macro-political terms. I am either Labour or Conservative, either Marxist or Capitalist. In short, it is evidence of the dominance of that thinking in terms of binary oppositions, those very oppositions that postmodernists (inspired by Derrida), especially the overtly pious kind, maintain have been so destructive and that it is the business of postmodernist revisionism to expose and deconstruct forever. It is a view that is often supplemented by two other (usually uncontested) theories. The theory on the one hand that those associated with overt forms of power (governments and their agencies) have all the power there is in society and are unanimously hostile to programs for action likely to bring about change and "empower" those who have been oppressed. It is based on the theory that those not associated with overt forms of power are themselves innocent of repression and unanimously sympathetic to working in concert to help bring about a utopian society in which all will have equal rights. This package of assumptions tends, finally, to be accompanied by an unexplained belief that only some of those sympathetic to the idea of working together to bring about change are in a position to lead: a minority (the intellectuals) will lead the majority (non-intellectuals or merely potential intellectuals), whose "case" the minority can best represent by talking about it in theoretical terms. Again we have another binary opposition which hides an unacceptable piece of terrorism. The minority group (leaders) lead the majority group (the group who can only be led); yet that majority group has been theorized into an amorphous group or position. It has been constructed and theorized as consisting of a number of individuals, yes, but all of whom are made to want to share a common agenda. In all sorts of ways, then, the assumption that the personal is the political, that slogan used by the feminists in the 1970s, is one that actively hates *real* "difference," for vital is the idea of absolute sameness. It goes without saying, finally, that what this really is is yet another version of an age-old problem, the one created by certain members of the middle-class intelligentsia, to justify the removal, by terrorist or revolutionary means, either of those who are already in government or of those who prop up what they perceive to be the class system. In its place, of course, it merely installs another kind of class system, the two-tier one composed of intellectuals and the masses—and who are they? Merely the non-intellectual. In substance, therefore, the act of theorizing the non-intellectual, who is usually either the victim of popular culture or the victim of colonialism, is imperial by nature.

Canetti does not participate in a requiem for the evil deeds of the past. He faces the future squarely and expresses violent confidence in wit as a form of perpetual resistance. And confidence in wits is a vote of confidence in the power of the individual to effect change. Individuals can be agents of change, and only powerful individuals have what it takes, anyway, to be in a position to influence political parties to make changes, or to make changes in non-political ways. Power here is power of personality, not power as something that can only be exercised by those associated with the establishment, as the Left loves to believe. It is not really Schumacher's idea, developed in *Small is Beautiful*, that change on a small level is the only kind likely to make a practical impact.[321] It is the idea that you need will power to be effective as an agent. One certainly needs very little will power, by contrast, to run a seminar on the "dominant ideology" and discuss or even write about those more glamorous forms of oppression to be found in literature.

And thus Canetti fails to practise the skill of demystifying art in his particular practice of writing fiction. He still believes, *contra* postmodernist writers of fiction and their apologists, that there is something to be said for the great internal strength of the art object and for its capacity to be something mysterious, charismatic, and other, qualitatively different from, say, the computer on which this book is being written. He does not believe in the work of art as something self-contained, self-regarding, carelessly indifferent to anything except itself. He is not reviving the myth of Narcissus and Echo, for the unique feature of *Die Blendung*, and, indeed, all the works of art that Canetti himself loved—by Stendhal, Cervantes, Gogol, by Grünewald, Michaelangelo, Wotruba, and so on—is the belief in will as a form of exemplary resistance to the forces that might quell its drive. Canetti's novel, like those works of art that he loved, is not in the business of resisting the "dominant ideology," whatever that might be. All are asserting their absolute independence from anything that already exists, by showing up the heroic powers of will as a form of resistance into the future. For will is pure energy, and in *Die Blendung* it is already contained in sentences where energy is already perpetually being mobilized. It is not latent but patent. As such, the novel resists the tendency toward reification which is *arguably* inherent in a theory of fiction that can be accused of being apolitical in the worst sense of the word, where being apolitical really stands for a positive obssession with the purely private, with self-love as opposed to love.

Parody, as practised by Canetti, is not a self-conscious means of drawing attention to writing as a process, where process has to mean, hello look at me, look at what I am doing! Haven't you seen this somewhere before! Have a nice day! Parody is one of a wide variety of means Canetti uses for the purposes of reinstating the art object as unique and original as product. He does this in a Nietzschean sense, which is to say, in terms of a particular theory of existence: life is *only* an aesthetic illusion. *Die Blendung* as a whole is, according to this idea, a process in the sense that *each moment of the text reenacts Nietzsche's existential theory by acting it out as a performance.* The narrative of the novel is Nietzsche's philosophy of the future: it wants to have little or nothing to do with the past. References to a past that includes the reader are purely literary and do not, in themselves, acknowledge history as a process, for the references are ahistorical: *they say that I can remember in the present, not that I have remembered the past.*

Paul de Man has talked about the annihilation of the past in the above terms, undoubtedly under the influence of Nietzsche. In his essay "The Rhetoric of Blindness: Jacques Derrida's Reading of Rousseau," he has also discussed the difference between the diachronic art forms like music (which are temporal and aural) and the synchronic art forms like painting (which are spatial and visual).[322] Music represents nothing. It is hollow to the core because it means the negation of all presence.[323] The meaning of music is nothing more than knowledge of the existence of the void and a counter to it, for music can never rest for a moment in the stability of its own existence. It steadily has to repeat itself in a movement that is bound to remain endless. This movement persists regardless of any illusion of presence, regardless of the manner in which the subject interprets its intentionality. Music is the diachronic version of the pattern of non-coincidence within the moment. Interestingly, Paul de Man's theories are themselves a reworking of Nietzsche's ideas concerning the various art forms and preference for music because of its existential potential in Nietzschean terms: they are useful here inasmuch as Canetti's use of literary references and parody in the novel affirms his notion of the temporal experience of the present. His sense of temporality is too sophisticated and intense to be fully understood or appreciated by Beckett and his postmodern descendants, such as Pynchon, Vonnegut, Barthelme. Canetti's literary references are not an embellishment. The important thing about them when they occur in *Die Blendung* is that they are already implicated in a process, that of spinning out the aesthetic illusion: they are inconsistently present and show that Canetti did not wish to exploit parody systematically. They are thoroughly useless, both in terms of plot and character: they are irrelevant. But when they occur, they are consistently funny. Why? Because to laugh is to be in the present.

7

Pure Comic Alogism or the Music that is Non-Sense: "Frohlockender Wahnsinn" in "Privateigentum" and Thereafter

Let us return to the text now and examine the scene of the arrest in *Die Blendung.* What gets Peter Kien into the police station is his arrest by Benedikt Pfaff:

> Er kam herunter und wiederholte dumpf: "Sie haben gestohlen!" Einen anderen Ausweg aus dieser fatalen Lage sah er nicht. Den Diebstahl nahm er für bare Notlüge der Therese. Er legte Kien die schwere Hand auf die Schulter und erklärte, als sei er wieder aktiv: "Im Namen des Gesetzes, Sie sind verhaftet! Folgen Sie mir, ohne Aufsehen zu erregen!" Das Paket hing am kleinen Finger seiner Linken. Er blickte Kien gebieterisch ins Gesicht und zuckte die Achseln. Seine Pflicht gestattete ihm keine Ausnahme. Die Vergangenheit war vorbei. Damals konnten sie sich schmecken. Jetzt mußte er ihn verhaften. Wie gern hätte er ihm "Erinnern Sie sich noch?" gesagt. Kien knickte zusammen, nicht nur unter der Hand, und murmelte: "Ich hab's gewußt." Der Hausbesorger mißtraute dieser Äußerung. Friedliche Verbrecher sind falsch. Sie stellen sich so und machen dann einen Fluchtversuch. Drum wendet ein Mensch den Polizeigriff an. Kien ließ sich gefallen. Er versuchte sich geradezuhalten, seine Größe zwang ihn, sich zu bücken. Der Hausbesorger wurde zärtlich. Seit Jahren hatte er keinen Menschen mehr verhaftet. Er hatte Schwierigkeiten befürchtet. Delinquenten sind renitent. Sind sie es nicht, dann laufen sie davon. Trägt man die Uniform, dann verlangen sie die Nummer. Trägt man keine, dann wollen sie eine Marke. Hier war einer, der wenig Arbeit machte. Er ließ sich ausfragen, er folgte einem, er beteuerte nicht seine Unschuld, er machte kein Aufsehen, zu so einem Verbrecher konnte man sich gratulieren. Knapp vor der Glastür wandte er sich an Therese und sagte: "*So* macht man das!" Er wußte, daß ein Weib zusah. Doch war er nicht sicher, ob sie die Details seiner Arbeit zu schätzen verstand. "Ein anderer tut

> gleich prügeln. Bei mir geht das Verhaften von selbst. Ein Aufseh'n darf nicht sein. Stümpfer erregen Aufsehen. Was ein Kenner ist, dem folgt der Verbrecher von selbst. Haustiere tut man zähmen. Die Katzen haben eine wilde Natur. Dressierte Löwen sieht man im Zirkus. Die Tiger springen durch einen Feuerreifen. Der Mensch hat eine Seele. Das Organ packt ihn bei der Seele und er folgt wie ein Lamm." Er sprach seine Worte nur in Gedanken, sosehr es ihn brannte, sie laut hinauszubrüllen. (*DB*, 310–11)[324]

This in itself is another loving parody, this time of Kafka's *Der Prozeß*, where the arrest, melodramatic in itself, is an act/moment that condemns one man's life forever. It stands for the curse that is the gift of life in Kafka's terms. It is inescapable. The attempt to escape the impersonal authority which has named an individual, who is arrested without trial by absent powers, and without concrete evidence of crimes before the law, merely prolongs terror, and is the enactment in psychological terms of the wound already inflicted. Canetti takes Kafka's incident/scene, the imaginative moment of the arrest, with all its ambitious metaphysical resonance, rids it of melodrama and gravitas, and makes it creative of humor in the present for the reader. Further, Canetti's moment is a moment in a chain reaction. The "origins" of the chain reaction cannot be established precisely, because a chain refuses to acknowledge ends and beginnings. In this respect, Canetti could not be further removed from Kafka. For the Kafka of *Der Prozeß*, as for all those writers who believe in Objective Truth and Causality and Origins, it is possible to locate a beginning in time and space. For Kafka, however, the beginning is the beginning of the end. For Canetti, by contrast, a chain reaction is already already in motion. Further, the theatricality of the chain reaction in motion is imaginatively compelling enough to make it difficult to take the necessary time off to construct Objective Truth, Causality, and Origins. What is enacted in the passage quoted above is Benedikt Pfaff's pleasure at being able to act out the part played by a police officer, the part he had once played when he was still in service. Attention is thus focused on what he is doing, rather than why he is doing it. This is a sentimental scene. Pfaff does not want to arrest Kien, his old mate. He is delighted that Kien does not behave as if he were guilty. He wants to be watched, since he thinks he is rather stylish, acting out his part: because he draws no attention to himself and does not make a scene, he is puffed up with pride.

Of course, the humor is produced by the straight contradiction between Pfaff's assumption of quiet, slick stylishness and the loquaciousness and assertiveness of the sentences that "tell" us about what is not going on. And the passage concludes with that hallmark of Canetti's facetiousness, the parting thought that retrospectively inflates what was already inflated enough anyway. The style of style is now the subject of what started out as a brief and (as it has transpired) meaningless gesture toward the notion of law and order. We are as far away as ever from establishing whether a crime has really taken place and what kind of crime has taken place. This is a statement of Canetti's metaphysical facetiousness, that something he has in common with the Gogol who wrote short stories. For to take such a scenario as crime, a *topos* of extreme concrete and tangible dimensions which tends, in society, to be invested with powerful notions of causality and purpose, and refuse categorically to take it seriously is to parade one's carelessness about Truth, Origins, Purpose.

Those involved in the arrest are presented as if they were delightful patrons. Their interviewing technique is exemplary in terms of respect for those interviewed, and totally "disrespectful" of the substance of verbal exchanges. We already know that high facetiousness is in the air because a retired policeman has taken it upon himself to pretend he still has the authority to put people under arrest. This mood is extended here, when not who has stolen what but what has been stolen becomes *a charming matter of opinion*, where everybody has the chance to say what s/he wants, to make a couple of knowingly incompetent suggestions as to who it might have been. In short, the spirit of the passage is the absolute inverse of the kind of mood one would expect to dominate this kind of scene in our extra-textual world: as Gerald Stieg says about the chapter as a whole, it is a "kakophonische Opernszene."[325] Let's look at more of it:

> Fast alle Menschen hatten sich verlaufen. Teils saßen sie wieder hinter Schaltern, teils hielten sie mit flehenden oder trotzigen Mienen Pfänder hin. Doch ließen sich die Beamten dazu herab, selbst mit armen Teufeln einige Worte über die Ereignisse zu wechseln. Sie nahmen Meinungen von Menschen entgegen, denen das Ohr zu verschließen ihre heiligste Pflicht war. Über das Objekt des Verbrechens wurde keine Einigung erzielt. Wertsachen, rieten die einen, sonst wäre der Auflauf kaum der Mühe wert gewesen. Bücher, behaupteten andere, die Lokalität

> spreche dafür. Gesetztere Herren verwiesen auf die Abendblätter. Von den Parteien neigten die meisten zu Geld. Die Beamten verwiesen es ihnen, milder als üblich: wer soviel Geld habe, pflege nicht aufs Versatzamt zu gehen. Vielleicht hatten sie aber schon versetzt. Auch das schien ausgeschlossen, jeder Betreffende hätte sie erkannt, und es gab keinen Beamten, der sich nicht für den Betreffenden hielt. Einige bedauerten ihren roten Helden, den meisten war er gleichgültig geworden. Um Herz zu haben, fanden sie seine Frau bedauernswerter, wenn es auch eine alte Frau sei. Geheiratet hätte sie keiner. Um die verlorene Zeit sei es schade, doch war sie angeregt verbracht. (*DB*, 324)[326]

David Darby's article on the interview in the police station is entitled "A Fiction of Detection."[327] He believes, *contra* the argument here, that a crime has already been authenticated by the narrator's discourse: Fischerle "is" a criminal, even before proceedings start. He also argues that the chapter is full of character-motivated analepses, which aim to pass off non-authoritative meanings as definitive meanings. These collapse because analepsis after analepsis is interrupted rather than compeleted, making the information contained therein neither authenticated nor ordered. Their function is, therefore, to show how characters "are" disintegrating before our eyes. His conclusion is that Canetti's parodic subversion of the formal elements of the fiction of forensic detection foregrounds the problematic status of knowledge, by bringing together mutually exclusive narrative models of reality. In the absence of a legitimate pattern of reality, the evidence constitutes only a labyrinthine accumulation of contradictory, polysemous signifiers.

This is absolutely accurate, but once again it does not do justice to the spirit of the writing, inasmuch as it does not respond to its high-level, and highly self-conscious, theatricality. The theatricality is proof that Canetti is more than just subversive of the rules of forensic detection: it is proof of his delight in subversion as an end in itself. In short, I part company with Darby's slightly melancholic conclusion that all we have is an "open" text, Eco style.[328]

One of the first signs that we are dealing with a world in which all barriers are dissolved, in which there is an intoxicating level of divinely controlled mobility, comes when we realize that the man who is conducting the cross-examination of Peter Kien is as much a protagonist as any one of the many characters in this episode, in which each takes it in turn to speak. "Der Kommandant" is obviously not there as a representative of law and order. He is a character in his own right, who is as indifferent to Truth as anyone in this episode:

> Der Kommandant sah seine Gelegenheit gekommen, das übergescheite Weib eines männlichen zu belehren. Heftig griff er sich an die sehr kleine Nase, seinen großen Kummer. (Außer Dienst, im Dienst, zu allen unbeschäftigten Stunden besah und beseufzte er sie im Taschenspiegel. An Schwierigkeiten pflegte sie zu wachsen. Bevor er an deren Bewältigung ging, überzeugte er sich rasch von ihr, weil es so schön war, sie drei Augenblicke darauf total vergessen zu haben.) Jetzt beschloß er, den Verbrecher erst recht ausziehen zu lassen. "Ihr seid alle blöd," begann er. Den Nachsatz, der sich auf ihn selbst bezog, dachte er sich nur. "Bei einem Toten gehen die Augen auf, sonst tät' man sie ihm nicht zudrücken. Ein Simulant kann sich das nicht leisten. Öffnet er die Augen, so fehlt die Glasur. Schließt er die Augen, so glaub' ich ihm den Tod nicht, weil, wie gesagt, gehen bei einem Toten die Augen auf. Ein Tod ohne Glasur und ohne offene Augen ist einen Schmarr'n wert. Da ist er nocht nicht eingetreten. Mir macht keiner was vor. Merken Sie sich das, meine Herren! Ich fordere Sie auf, sich bezüglich des Häftlings die Augen anzuschauen!" (*DB*, 326–27)[329]

The first thing about this passage is that it is a tribute to Gogol's story *The Nose*. It is a parody of Gogol's story because it rids Gogol's intense study of the power of the police state, the irresponsibility of the police, the indifference of the police to the welfare of citizens of all its rhetoric. Whereas Gogol's commandant figure is a satirical set-piece, presented as a moral, social, and political problem, as proof of the decadence of St. Petersburg society, Canetti's commandant is an endearing, sentimental, vain, and rather charming aesthete, whose function is to charm the reader, not to compel him to take up an analytical response to the world, as Gogol's portrait functions. The whole of the chapter "Privateigentum" is also not just proof of how much Canetti enjoyed reading *The Nose*, but proof of how appreciative he was of Gogol's underlying first principles. He does this by giving the commandant a nose, which Kovalyov, the central figure in Gogol's story does not have, and integrating this into a narrative that works according to exactly the same principles as Gogol's. The title of Gogol's story refers to something that does not exist in his story, namely a nose; yet to say the story is about a nose is to miss the point, for the story refutes the physical world, what the eye can see. In truth, the story is what Donald Fanger has called a manifesto.[330] The story mocks a serious attitude toward plot (the accepted notion of significant form); mocks ordinary assumptions about intentionality (the very notion of language as the purveyor of messages); insists openly on this mockery, and gives the reader no access to paradigmatic meanings. The story triumphantly proclaims its existence as pure instrumentality. What it has done is enrich the reader by cheating her/him of meaning, yes, but also by enriching his/her own linguistic and imaginative experience. The delight with which Gogol makes comic connections at will is proof of the way in which vitality can hold its own in the world. It is the objectification of a faith it communicates as intuition. The helplessness of Gogol's sense of comedy has given rise to the best-known cliché about his work, namely that his art is "laughter through tears."[331] My claim for Canetti is that there is laughter, but with no tears.

The "vain" preoccupation of the commandant with his nose in Canetti's novel, silly enough in its own right, must also be something of a sendup of meaningful nose theories in psychology. Sterne had a field day with noses, probably for the same reason. Of course, Freud had some very serious things to say about them. Gogol's story has suffered from interpretations that maintain that it is a substitute penis, proof of anal eroticism which manifests itself in secondary characteristics like capriciousness, stinginess, and the love of orderliness.[332] Predictably, Curtius says the commandant in *Die Blendung* touches his nose because he is unsure of his potency.[333] Clearly, what Canetti is saying is something to the effect . . . do you really have to be so boring? Here, as elsewhere, then, Canetti reveals his radical distrust of theory, of Big Ideas, and sees them as inimical to the celebration of life. The nose is "detached" from any kind of meaningful framework. It is a nose. The commandant touches it for no reason other than that he is aware it is too short—the origins of his actions are therefore aesthetic only. The purpose of the action is to tickle the reader into understanding the art that is gratuitousness.

Canetti and Gogol are linked by what has been called Gogol's *comic alogism.*[334] Gogol raised non-sense, as opposed to nonsense, to dazzling heights, by positively enjoying destroying logical and causal connections with the tools of absurd deductions, disconnectedness, arbitrary associations, all of which are paraded in "Privateigentum," although they also propelled the narrative that preceded it. There are very few serious semantic interrelations between sentences in the novel generally, and in the chapter "Privateigentum" Canetti brings off a tour de force of a performance of this view, and with consummate skill. The final, important, general link with Gogol concerns the way in which Gogol, like Canetti, very much enjoyed performing his work, or reading it out loud. We have already mentioned that the sentences of *Die Blendung* are sentences that sound as if they are being spoken out loud. According to sources quoted by Eichenbaum, Gogol was an inimitable reader who could articulate each word distinctly and perform with a high degree of theatricality.[335] Gerald Stieg testifies to the oral vivacity of Canetti in an article that includes an interview with Canetti, as we can too if we listen to the few recordings Canetti has also made of some his works.[336] Raymond Furness also makes the point that Canetti had a histrionic talent àpropos of readings he heard in Manchester, commenting on his "Selbstinszenierung."[337]

To date, references to the Canetti-Gogol link have been fairly superficial. The exception here is Noel Thomas, who looks at the similarities at the level of first principles between the two writers, taking Gogol's *The Overcoat* as his example. Thomas is the only critic so far to read *Die Blendung* in the spirit in which it is written. He says that the narration of *Die Blendung* proceeds by a series of associations, he uses the word, "alogicality," and he feels the narrative is attempting to destroy logical and causal connections. He has taken his lead from the Gogol critics already mentioned.[338] In spite of this appreciation of the waywardness of *Die Blendung*, Thomas still partially adheres to the idea that Canetti is committed to a notion of "reality."

To return to the text: the commandant is, throughout the investigation, not motivated by or even remotely interested in ethics. His interests are aesthetic, as has already been made clear by his concern about how his nose looks. Instead of investigating whether Kien is guilty of something, and of what he is guilty, he is concerned to establish whether or not Kien is alive or dead. His performance with respect to his audience on this matter is as polished as his private performances are, when he is busy feeling his nose. In the next passage, his aesthetic concerns are projected onto Kien, the man who has to undergo a partial strip search for reasons the narrative refuses to make clear:

> Der Kommandant verachtete das Gestell noch ein wenig, dann begann er es eigenhändig auszuziehen. Er warf den Rock auf den Tisch hinüber. Die Weste folgte. Das Hemd war alt, aber anständig. Er knöpfte es auf und äugte scharf zwischen die Rippen. Da war wirklich nichts. Ekel stieg in ihm auf. Er hatte vieles erlebt. Sein Beruf brachte ihn mit allen möglichen Existenzen in Berührung. So eine magere war ihm noch nie vorgekommen. Das gehörte in ein Raritätskabinett und in keine Wachstube. Ja, war er denn ein Schaubudenbesitzer oder was? "Die Schuh' und die Hosen überlasse ich euch," sagte er zu den anderen. Sehr gedemütigt trat er zurück. Seine Nase fiel ihm ein. Er griff nach ihr. Sie war zu kurz. Wer sie vergessen könnte! Mißmutig setzt er sich hinter seinen Tisch. Der stand wieder falsch. Jemand hatte ihn verschoben. "Könntet ihr meinen Tisch nicht grad stehenlassen, ich sag das zum hundersten Male! Bagage!" Wer mit den Schuhen und Hosen des Diebes beschäftigt war, grinste in sich hinein, sonst stand man stramm. Ja, dachte er, solche Individuen sind abzuschaffen. Sie erregen öffentliches Ärgernis. Es wird einem schlecht, wenn man das sieht. Der schönste Appetit vergeht einem. Wo kommt man hin ohne Appetit? Da soll einer die Geduld bewahren. Für solche Fälle müßte es die Folter geben. Im Mittelalter war das Leben der Polizei schöner. Wenn einer so ausschaut, ist Selbstmord das beste. Die Statistik verträgt's, der fällt nicht ins Gewicht. Statt sich umzubringen, spielt er den Scheintoten. Keine Scham kennt so ein Geschöpf. Einer schämt sich schon wegen der Nase, weil sie um eine Kleinigkeit zu kurz ist. (*DB*, 328)[339]

The logic here is that Kien should be removed from public life because he is a joke, from an aesthetic point of view: he is thin and bony like Don Quixote. Kien should have known that the best thing he could have done was to commit suicide. Instead of acting out this logic, he is playing at being dead, and the commandant finds this behavior shameless. Should it be taken literally, as a "study" of a man? Curtius appropriates the above for a metanarrative, this time to prove that Canetti was anticipating Fascist eugenics.[340] This kind of response is fair enough, but only if you take the passage literally and are not sensitive to the spirit of fun that seems to animate it. Another interesting point about the above, and it affects many of the passages shortly to be analyzed, concerns the way in which the passage is laid out on the page. Canetti never indicates that there is a logic to when spoken thought begins (which is to say the thought expressed vocally to an audience) and when a voice in one's head takes over. Canetti does not separate each voice and give it a discrete, independent paragraph. In not doing so, he implies that there is a dynamic process going on the whole time. One voice, the voice that speaks out loud, effectively usurps the other, the voice that speaks in my head. Canetti does not privilege speaking out loud over thinking, because he believes a voice is at work in both cases. He in part acknowledges that both are equally powerful when he refuses to separate dialogue from narrated monologue at a *visual* level on the page, a habit that can become confusing if you are approaching the text in the mimetic mode.

In doing so, Canetti is encouraging us to think more *holistically* about life, in particular about the so-called distinction between the life of the imagination and the life we lead as social beings. In this, he is operating in a way different from other exploiters of narrated monologue, such as Flaubert in *Madame Bovary*. There, when Emma Bovary thinks to herself, one has a strong feeling that she is very private and that her conversation with herself is a kind of dialogue with herself only and for personal consumption only. Further, the frequency of her reliance on the internal monologue is much more limited than critics would have us believe. In fact, her internal life is rather limited, not, as we are told, because she is so dim, but in terms of narrative space dedicated to it by Flaubert in the novel. In *Die Blendung*, not only is narrated monologue used extensively throughout the novel, but the diegetic material impersonates the voice that speaks out loud in dialogue, thereby creating that sense we have that the narrative is one, that a person is the same "in private" as s/he is in public. Further, in *Die Blendung* everything sounds as if it could be spoken out loud anyway. Given the polish and amusing quality of everything in the text, one is hard put to argue, on those occasions when narrated monologue takes over, that: a. we as readers have access to a language intrinsically different from the language used in public; and b. we as readers have access to genuine privacy. Everything in the novel is always excitably sociable: "talking to oneself" is to act out the talk one would vocalize in "real" conversation. In this, Canetti also works in a totally different way from Thomas Bernhard in *Gehen*, where the refusal to give the reader paragraphs, and the refusal to break ideas down into beautifully tailored constitutent parts, is a major feature of the text. There is no predictability to the way paragraphs begin and end in *Gehen*: it is there, though, as a way of imitating the ontological problem which is existence to Bernhard: life is aimless.[341]

Instead of taking up a position with respect to what people feel he has done (namely, rob somebody of something), Kien does not begin a "defense." He makes an admission that he is partially guilty of either the death of Therese and/or her murder. Interestingly, he is only partially guilty. How can one be partially guilty of murder and how can one be partially guilty of somebody's death? This confession, then, is, in itself, a direct reference to Julien Sorel's winning admission, in court, of the fact he had murdered Madame de Rênal in *Le Rouge et Le Noir*. As such, it reads like a tribute to that work, another affectionate parody since allusions are sanitized of some of the earnestness of the arguments in that novel, especially the earnestness of Julien Sorel's attempt to be an être supérieur, to be a master of life at all times and to be the archetypal romantic hero, prepared to die for love.[342] When Kien introduces the idea of Therese's own guilt in her death, when he suggests she has consumed her own body, we might be tempted to say this is not parody but satire. Once again the narrative both refuses to tolerate the heroic/epic vision promoted by Stendhal, as it continues to seduce us by its facetiousness, teasing us not to accept the words on the page as literally true, rather as pretexts for the generation of originality, as for instance: "'Ich bekenne mich schuldig. Einen Teil der Schuld trägt sie selbst. Ich habe sie eingesperrt, aber mußte sie ihren eigenen Leib verzehren? Sie hat ihren Tod verdient. Um eines möchte ich Sie bitten, ich fühle mich etwas verwirrt. Wie erklären Sie es, daß die Ermorderte hier steht? Ich erkenne sie am Rock!'" (*DB*, 330)[343]

This latter example Darby has called an instance of character-motivated analepsis, which dominates the chapter as a whole. Kien begins to tell a story that has absolutely no resonance in intra-textual terms, since the narrative up to this point has not included any information concerning Therese's death or murder, nor any information on the specific details of that death or murder. In terms of Objective Truth, therefore, the statements are meaningless to readers. Further, we cannot interpret the story in terms of Subjective Truth, in the sense that Kien is clearly not inventing his story for some motive like gain, such as a desire to try and get off the hook or win over an audience. Psychology is redundant here. Clearly, when Kien admits that he is guilty of something like murder, Canetti is winking at us and giving us a sign that we are specifically not dealing with character in the traditional, conservative sense, where characters have to have motives in order to be plausible to readers. Since the story is dissociated from Objective Truth and Subjective Truth, and since its contents are anyway riotously stupid and theatrical enough in their own right, we can conclude that the above is not proof that Kien is dissociated from a reality to which he cannot relate (as critics would tend to have us believe), but an invitation that we as readers continue to play the carnivalesque game which is the mood of the novel as a whole.

Traditional critics would argue against attributing this degree of ironic self-consciousness to Canetti, by saying that Canetti is interested, in psychological terms, in how characters delude themselves and live in absolute isolation from "reality."[344] A different view is that the inflated theatricality and manifest stupidity of what is going on guarantees that readers stand well back and just enjoy the wild dancing that is the chain reaction of storytelling as an end in itself, which is the chapter as a whole. Kien's analepsis is absolutely charming. He believes Therese is dead, and finds empirical evidence, such as the fact that she is standing beside him, rather difficult to stomach. So instead of establishing whether or not Kien is guilty of a crime (stealing), which was already something of a "digression" in its own right, the narrative moves on to another "digression." What is unique about the technique of digression as it is exploited by Canetti is that it is not undertaken as a means of delaying something that is inevitable. Neither is it a means of distracting the reader by giving him/her an analytical issue to ponder. In Swift, Sterne, and Voltaire, digression has these functions. In Canetti a digression is credited absolute status. It is not relative to some overall conceptual argument. Neither is it an obvious "end in itself" with a self-contained truth, a mini-parable for instance. It never descends to the banality of having to serve some higher cause, such as that of wisdom. There is no distinction between a primary plot and a secondary plot.

Since in "Privateigentum" everyone takes his/her turn at speaking and producing a story which no one subsequently attempts to either refute or endorse, and which the "plot" of the novel also fails to either refute or endorse, we can conclude that Canetti is *instating* storytelling as a way of life. He is not instating storytelling as a means of establishing Objective Truth. The form is endorsed and the content, one assumes and deduces, is whatever happens to tickle your fancy. In this dissociation of storytelling from truth telling, *Die Blendung* is different from *The Life and Opinions of Tristram Shandy, Gentleman*, which is full of stories about human nature and the quality of the imagination. In spirit, though, there is some similarity, since in both novels the chain reaction dominates, even if in Sterne the thinking by association is always logical at some level. The point about what appears to be digression in *Die Blendung* is that the contents of the stories that are told are left totally exposed. If each of the stories had been positively refuted or positively endorsed, in terms of their contents, by the "plot" of the narrative, one would have to argue something different altogether. The stories told do not furnish us with arguments about Objective Truth. They do not help to affirm some overall vision of the world. As there is nothing "behind" them, as there is nothing from which they derive and to which they lead, we have to conclude that plot *is* storytelling.

Hence, rather than prove that Kien is either right or wrong about his worry that he can actually see Therese standing beside him, the narrative rises to the occasion of the fun of the stupidity of such a scenario, by spinning it out yet further. Words continue not to mean anything, not because Kien is mad, but because we can see that there is something positive to be said, in terms of the reader's pleasure, for sustaining a certain principle. This principle is the principle of the non-coincidence of words and concepts (truth and the like). In spite of this, Canetti still adheres to a notion of meaning, yet his notion of meaning is idiosyncratic, since meaning is equated with the appreciation of what it takes to play and sustain a game as a game. Ludic skills and artistry are elevated, requiring that one remain perpetually vigilant about the risk of descending into the serious, by remaining ever ready to transform everything into the gratuitous. Ludic skills are rated higher than analytical skills.

In another passage, Kien is admitting that he is "alright Jack," having just about recovered from the news that his wife has died. This news is news to the reader. It is also news that a trial lies ahead. The gap between these two thoroughly fictional events (which have no place in time or space) is filled productively by the spirit of theatre which infuses every single one of the sentences. Then there is the sense of theatre generally that comes with our realizing that this scene, as a scene, loosely calls up the extra-textual *topos* of the interview in the police station. In these terms, this scene is a riotous travesty of the emotions of fear, despair, guilt, and gravitas which might "usually" infuse interviews in police stations. Peter Kien is a model of charm and respect and human kindness and dignity:

> "Sie glauben wohl, daß ich an Halluzinationen leide. Im allgemeinen nicht. Meine Wissenschaft gebietet Klarheit, ich lasse mir kein X für ein U, noch sonst einen Buchstaben für einen anderen vormachen. Doch habe ich in letzter Zeit viel erlebt; gestern erhielt ich die Nachricht vom Tode meiner Frau. Sie wissen, worum es sich handelt. Ihretwegen habe ich die Ehre, mich unter Ihnen zu befinden. Der Gedanke an meinen Prozeß beschäftigt mich seither ununterbrochen. Als ich heute ins Theresianum ging, begegnete ich meiner ermordeten Frau. Sie war in Begleitung unseres Hausbesorgers, eines treuen Freundes von mir. Er hatte ihr an meiner Stelle das letzte Geleit gegeben, ich war damals verhindert. Halten Sie mich nicht für herzlos. Es gibt Frauen, die man nie vergißt. Ich will Ihnen die volle Wahrheit sagen: ich habe ihr Leichenbegängnis absichtlich gemieden, es wäre mir zuviel geworden. Sie begreifen mich doch, waren Sie nie verheiratet? Den Rock hat damals ein Fleischerhund in Stücke gebrochen und gefressen. Vielleicht besaß sie deren zwei. Auf der Treppe stieß sie mich an. Sie trug ein Paket, in dem ich meine eigenen Bücher vermutete. Ich liebe meine Bibliothek. Es handelt sich um die größte Privatbibliothek der Stadt. Seit einiger Zeit mußte ich sie vernachlässigen. Ich war mit barmherzigen Werken beschäftigt. Die Ermordung meiner Frau hielt mich vom Hause fern, wieviel Wochen mögen es her sein, daß ich die Wohnung verließ? Die Zeit hab' ich gut benützt, Zeit ist Wissenschaft, Wissenschaft ist Ordnung. Neben der Erwerbung einer kleinen Kopfbibliothek wandte ich mich, wie ich bereits oben bemerkte, barmherzigen Werken zu, ich erlöse Bücher vom Feuertode. Ich kenne ein Schwein, das sich von Büchern ernährt, aber schweigen wir darüber. Ich verweise Sie auf meine Rede vor Gericht, dort gedenke ich der Öffentlichkeit einige Enthüllungen zu machen. Helfen Sie mir! Sie rührt sich nicht von der Stelle. Befreien Sie mich von dieser Halluzination! Ich leide sonst nie daran. Sie geht mir nach, ich fürchte, schon über eine Stunde. Stellen wir den Tatbestand fest, ich will Ihnen die Hilfe erleichtern. Ich sehe Sie alle, Sie sehen mich. Genau so steht die Ermordete neben mir. Alle meine Sinne habe mich verlassen, nicht nur die Augen. Ich kann tun, was ich will, ich höre den Rock, ich fühle ihn, er riecht nach Stärke, sie selbst bewegt den Kopf, das war ihre Art, als sie noch lebte, sie spricht sogar,

> vor wenigen Augenblicken sagte sie "ich bitt' Sie," Sie müssen wissen, daß ihr Sprachschatz aus fünfzig Worten bestand, trotzdem sprach sie nicht weniger als andere Menschen, helfen Sie mir! Beweisen Sie mir, daß sie tot ist!" (*DB*, 331–32)[345]

This is a brilliant deconstruction of those notions of truth that depend on what the human subject knows through his senses. It is a refutation of empiricism and pragmatism, and an affirmation of the view that the only truth(s) are poetic, to do with the free play of the imagination, which Kien is already practising by example. At first sight, his statement appears to raise a straight question. Is the person standing beside me alive or dead? Clearly, however, we as readers cannot take this premise seriously, because we know that Therese is standing beside him. The narrative is unambiguous about this. So the terms of the question and the question itself are, to us, irrelevant. So when Kien appears to be playing the game of empirical truth by asking his audience to help establish for him, not that he is suffering from a hallucination, but that Therese is already dead, he is not manipulating his audience to enter his so-called damaged vision of the world, as critics would have us believe. Because Therese is to us readers not only not dead but alive, and not only not a hallucination but an empirical reality, *the narrative* is collaborating not with Kien the person but with the spirit of theatricality that speaks through him. It does so to create the carnivalesque, where all things coexist non-sensically, but meaningfully, in the sense that the mood is quite self-consciously aware of, and delighted that, Objective Truth is neither an active goal in the first place nor an active pursuit in the second.

If Kien is therefore in part charming "as a person" because his questions and attitude are divinely absurd, the commandant continues to be charming "as a person" in terms of his stress on aesthetic form, on performance according to certain strict rules, whether it be the way a cross-examination is conducted, or whether it be the position of his cravat and of the cushion he sits on, where the word private property is inscribed:

> "Wer sind Sie eigentlich, Herr?" rief der Kommandant. "Lassen Sie das Schweigen lieber bleiben!" Mit zwei Fingern berührte er Kien am Hemdärmel. Er hatte Lust, ihn zwischen den Nägeln zu zerquetschen. Was ist das für eine Bildung, die nur ein paar Sätze reden kann und auf vernünftige Fragen schweigt? Die wahre Bildung liegt im Benehmen, in der Tadellosigkeit und in

> der richtigen Kunst des Verhörs. Ernst und seiner Überlegenheit wieder bewußter, trat der Kommandant hinter den Tisch. Der Holzboden des Sessels, den er zu benützen pflegte, war von einem weichen Kissen, dem einzigen dieser Wachstube, bedeckt, auf dem man in rot gestickten Buchstaben *Privateigentum* las. Dieses Wort sollte den Untergebenen in Erinnerung bringen, daß ihnen—auch in seiner Abwesenheit—kein Recht darauf zustand. Die Leute hatten eine verdächtige Neigung, sich das Kissen unterzuschieben. Er rückte es mit wenigen sicheren Bewegungen zurecht: bevor er sich setzte, mußte das *Privateigentum* parallel zu seinen Augen liegen, die nie versäumten, sich an einem solchen Wort zu stärken. Er drehte dem Stuhl den Rücken. Schwer war es, sich vom Anblick des Kissens loszureißen, noch schwerer, sich so zu setzten, daß es nicht verschoben wurde. Langsam ließ er sich nieder; einige Augenblicke hielt er mit dem Hintern an sich. Erst wenn er auch von dieser Seite her das *Privateigentum* am Platz fand, erlaubte er sich, darauf zu drücken. Sobald er saß, war ihm von keinem Dieb, und habe er selbst mehr als Matura, die leiseste Achtung abzugewinnen. Rasch warf er einen letzten Blick auf sein Spiegelchen. Die Krawatte saß, wie er, breit und nicht ohne Eleganz. Das zurückgebürstete Haar lag in Fett erstarrt, kein Härchen regte sich. Die Nase war zu kurz. Sie gab ihm den Anstoß, das einzige, was noch fehlte, und er warf sich ins Verhör. (*DB*, 339)[346]

Curtius sees the above as proof of the way we can, in Freudian fashion, be driven by fetishistic needs.[347] We can begin by showing that the word "Privateigentum" has been borrowed from Gogol's story *The Nose*: "He turned round to tell the nose in uniform straight out that it was only masquerading as a state councillor, that it was an impostor and a scoundrel, and really nothing else than his own private property, *his* nose . . ." (51).[348] The investigation in Canetti's novel fails to correspond to any notions we readers might have about the function and purpose of investigations. Rather than attempt to establish anything, the narrative keeps "going back to basics." Has something happened? When? Where did something happen? What happened? This is not a source of farce but of high theatricality, as the enactment of the narrative of the commandant's performance spins out the performance with an air of studied pace, studied style, and studied rhythm. Presenting Kien with a skirt, for instance, the commandant merely finds that he has to "prove" to Kien that the skirt is a piece of evidence:

> "Der Rock ist am Tatort gefunden worden!" erklärte er mit fester Stimme.
>
> "Tatort? Dieses Wort in Ihrem Mund wiegt schwer!" Ein Nicken ging durch die versammelten Beamten. "Ich halte Sie für einen gebildeten Menschen. Geben Sie zu, daß zu einem Tatort eine Tat gehört? Es steht Ihnen frei, Ihre Äußerung zurückzuziehen. Doch muß ich Sie auf den ungünstigen Eindruck aufmerksam machen. Ich meine es gut mit Ihnen. Sie sind besser dran, wenn Sie gestehen. Also gestehen wir, lieber Freund! Gestehen Sie, wir wissen alles! Das Leugnen nützt Ihnen nicht mehr. Der Tatort ist herausgerutscht. Gestehen Sie und ich werde ein warmes Wort für Sie einlegen! Erzählen Sie alles der Reihe nach! Wir haben unsere Nachforschungen angestellt. Was können Sie da tun? Sie haben sich selbst hereingelegt! Zu einem Tatort gehört eine Tat. Ich hab' doch recht, meine Herren?"
>
> Wenn er "meine Herren" sagt, wissen die Herren, daß er den Sieg in Händen hält und überschüttern ihn mit bewundernden Blicken. Einer beeilt sich, dem anderen zuvorzukommen. Der Gedächtniskünstler sieht ein, daß für ihn nichts herausspringt und stößt seinen alten Plan um. Er schnellt vor, ergreift die glückliche Hand des Kommandanten und ruft: "Herr Kommandant, Sie erlauben, daß ich gratuliere!" (*DB*, 343–44)[349]

The following character-motivated analepsis by Kien is introduced as a defense, a "Verteidigungsrede":

> "Wochenlang hab' ich sie allein gelassen. Fest überzeugt, daß sie an Hunger eingehen müsse, verbrachte ich Nacht für Nacht im Hotel. Meine Bibliothek ging mir bitter ab, glauben Sie mir; ich begnügte mich mit einer kleinen Ersatzbibliothek, die ich für dringende Fälle gleich bei der Hand hatte. Das Schloß meiner Wohnung ist sicher—von der Furcht, Einbrecher könnten sie befreien, war ich nie geplagt. Stellen Sie sich ihre Lage vor: alle Vorräte sind aufgezehrt. Entkräftet und haßerfüllt liegt sie auf dem Boden, vor demselben Schreibtisch, in dem sie nach Geld zu suchen pflegte. Ihr einziger Gedanke galt dem Geld. Sie war wie keine Blume. Auf was für Gedanken ich vor diesem Schreibtisch kam, als ich die Wohnung noch mit ihr teilte, will ich Ihnen heute nicht erzählen. Wochenlang mußte ich, aus Furcht vor einer Plünderung meiner Manuskripte, zur Wächterstatue erstarrt, dahinleben. Es war die Zeit meiner tiefsten Erniedrigung. Wenn mein Kopf nach Arbeit brannte, sagte ich mir: du bist von Stein, und um stillzuhalten, glaubte ich daran. Wer von Ihnen schon Schätze zu hüten hatte, wird sich nicht zu

> helfen gewußt. Es fehlte ihr an Selbstbeherrschung. Sie fraß sich auf. Stück für Stück von ihrem Körper fiel der Gier anheim. Von Tag zu Tag magerte sie mehr ab. Sie war zu schwach, sich zu erheben und blieb im eigenen Kot liegen. Ich erscheine Ihnen vielleicht mager. Gegen mich gehalten war sie der Schatten eines Menschen, kläglich und verächtlich, wäre sie aufgestanden, ein Windhauch hätte sie umgeworfen, wie ein Zündholz war sie, jeder Schwächling hätte sie zerbrochen, ich glaube selbst ein Kind. Genaues läßt sich darüber nicht sagen. Der blaue Rock, den sie immer trug, deckte ihr Skelett. Er war gestärkt und hielt dank dieser Eigenschaft die widerwärtigen Reste ihres Leibes zusammen. Eines Tages hauchte sie aus. Auch dieser Ausdruck erscheint mir als Fälschung; wahrscheinlich besaß sie keine Lunge mehr. Niemand stand ihr in dieser letzten Stunde bei, wer hätte es wochenlang neben einem Gerippe ausgehalten? Sie troff von Schmutz. Das offene Fleisch, wie sie es in Fetzten vom Körper riß, stank zum Himmel. Die Verwesung begann bei lebendigem Leibe. (*DB*, 345–46)[350]

In theory, what Kien is talking about is disgusting, and enough to make one's blood run cold. It reminds us vaguely of the Dionysian rituals of disembowling people alive. In practice, what Kien appears to be describing as if it were incontrovertibly true is clearly, to us, in literal terms, impossible, and if not impossible, unlikely to a degree. Once again, what is loosely raised by the narrative as a topic is remodelled to the extent that whatever we summon up in our imaginations is denied. The particular constellation of details is a challenge to us not to believe in the existence of barbarism. The authority of the text, Canetti is saying, exceeds your authority and my authority. Whilst you are reading this novel you don't need any of your own ideas, and you can abandon any theories you have about the world and how it works. Just abandon yourself to the carnival world I am creating. In the above, after all, there is a quite beautiful mingling of the inverse of civilization, the idea that someone would want to consume herself because she was consumed by her own greed, with quite a charming form of social civilization, namely the modesty with which Kien talks about himself and Therese. And once again, the principle in Expressionist texts of the reduction of a character to one particular characteristic is refuted. For through Kien, who talks about Therese as a mere skeleton, possibly without a lung, "clothed" in her blue skirt, a cheeky voice is speaking, saying something like, come on, can't you see that it is possible to be knowingly amusing? Here, one is tempted to refer to the section called "Schnee" in *Der Zauberberg*, when Hans Castorp recalls a dream he had that encouraged him to appreciate the close proximity of barbarism to civilization. For Thomas Mann, in contrast to the willful idealist Canetti, barbarism is always quite a serious existential option.

The scene concludes with those who had heard the various stories and had not commented on their contributions surrounding Kien to *sympathize* with him about his situation, which situation to them (a gang of men, it has to be noted) is the misfortune of being married to Therese, who has just escaped. They sympathize with his personal circumstances and do not take up a position with respect to his apparent status as criminal. So the scene concludes with platitudes like "Man soll nur bessere Menschen heiraten!" (355), and "Jeder ist seines Glückes Schmied" (355), which in all senses are absolutely useless statements. The issues of Law and Order and Good and Evil have, therefore, not only not interested all protagonists, but are also of no interest to the narrative. The last words of the chapter see Benedikt Pfaff offering Kien a bed for the night until his flat has been cleaned up.

We will now return to yet another of the wondrous figures in this novel, the chess player Siegfried Fischerle. According to Caillois, chess is another form of play in culture, different from play motivated by the spirit of agon, in that the terms on which you play are partly already determined. Fischerle is never shown to us in terms of what he maintains are his skills as a chess player, which is to say actually playing a game of chess and having to negotiate a partner and her/his skills. Neither is he convincing in terms of plausibility as a man who really desires success in the future. Collapsing the pressure on the future supplied by genuine motive, Canetti infuses Fischerle's every statement in the present with an alarming degree of assertive and affirmative energy. Our first passage is an account of Fischerle's preparations for his trip to Paris and New York:

> "Ich bin der Schachmeister Doktor Siegfried Fischer. Sie haben mich sowieso nach der Zeitung erkannt. Was ich brauche, ist ein Maßanzug, bis heute abend fertig. Zahle allerhöchste Preise. Die Hälfte bekommen Sie voraus, die zweite Rate beim Empfang. Ich fahre mit dem Nachtzug nach Paris, man erwartet mich beim New Yorker Turnier. Meine ganze Garderobe ist im

> Hotel gestohlen worden. Sie verstehen, meine Zeit ist Platin wert. Ich wach auf und alles ist weg. Die Einbrecher kommen bei Nacht. Stellen Sie sich den Schreck der Hoteldirektion vor! Wie soll ich auf die Straße? Ich bin abnormal gewachsen, was kann ich dafür; wo findet man schon einen passenden Anzug für mich? Kein Hemd, keine Strümpfe, keine Schuhe, ein Mensch wie ich, der soviel auf Eleganz gibt! Nehmen Sie derweil Maß, ich will Sie nicht aufhalten! Zum Glück haben die in einer Spelunke ein gewisses Individuum aufgetrieben, einen buckligen Krüppel, so was haben Sie noch nicht geseh'n; der hat mir mit seinem besten Anzug ausgeholfen. Und was glauben Sie, was sein bester Anzug war? Der da! So verkrüppelt wie der Anzug bin ich nämlich noch lange nicht. Bei meinen englischen Anzügen merkt niemand was. Klein bin ich, gut, was soll ich mir tun? Aber die englischen Schneider sind Genies, sag' ich, alle Genies, einer wie der andere. Ohne Anzug hab' ich einen Buckel. Ich gehe zum englischen Schneider und der Buckel ist weg. Ein Talent macht den Buckel kleiner, ein Genie schneidert ihn weg. Schad' um die schönen Anzüge! Versichert bin ich natürlich. Dabei kann ich dem Verbrecher noch dankbar sein. Den frischen Paß, gestern ausgestellt, legt er mir auf den Nachttisch. Alles andere nimmt er mit. Da, seh'n Sie—Sie zweifeln an meiner Identität, wissen Sie, bei dem Anzug glaub' ich manchmal selbst, ich bin es nicht. Ich würde gleich drei auf einmal bestellen, aber weiß ich, wie Sie arbeiten? Im Herbst komm' ich wieder nach Europa. Ist Ihr Anzug gut, da werden Sie was erleben. Ganz Amerika schick' ich Ihnen her! Und Sie machen mir einen anständigen Preis, als gutes Vorzeichen. Sie müssen wissen, ich rechne auf die Weltmeisterschaft. Spielen Sie Schach?" (*DB*, 382–83)[351]

The above is full of alogism, of a particularly charming variety. Fischerle jumps from his reputation ("meine Zeit ist Platin wert"), to the fact that he has had his clothes stolen ("Ich wach auf und alles ist weg."), to the irrelevance of the shock reaction of the Hotel staff at the theft on the premises ("Stellen Sie sich den Schreck der Hoteldirektion vor!"). The passage moves from a tribute to Kien's generosity at having helped him out when he was in a tight corner, to an appreciation of the talent and genius of tailors, in particular of their capacity to disguise what is aesthetically disturbing, namely his hunchback, to a sense of relief that he can get money back for what has been stolen because he is insured. This excitement intensifies to end with one of Canetti's hallmarks, a final sentence that retrospectively undercuts the momentum sustained.

In preparation for his stay in the States, Fischerle learns English. There is no method in his madness, and his skills are simply superb:

> Es war nine o'clock, die große Uhr vor dem Bahnhof ging Englisch. Um zehn werden die Haustore gesperrt. Eine Begegnung mit dem Hausbesorger war am besten zu vermeiden. Der Weg bis zur verfallenen Kaserne, in der Fischerle leider zwanzig Jahre bei einer Hure verschwendet hatte, dauerte vierzig Minuten, forty minutes. Ohne sich zu übereilen, nahm er ihn unter die gelben Schuhe. Hier und da blieb er stehen und schlug unter einer Gaslaterne die Worte, die er sich Englisch dachte, in seinem Buche nach. Sie stimmten immer. Er benannte die Dinge und sprach zu den Menschen, die ihm begegneten, aber leise, damit sie ihn nicht aufhielten. Er wußte noch mehr, als er sich eingebildet hatte. Als er nach zwanzig Minuten nichts Neues traf, ließ er Häuser, Straßen, Laternen und Hunde laufen und setzte sich an eine englische Partie Schach. Diese zog er bis zur dreckigen Kaserne hinaus. Vor dem Haustor gewann er sie und trat in den Flur. Seine ehemalige Frau ging ihm auf die Nerven, aber schon stark. Um ihr nicht in den Schoß zu fallen, versteckte er sich hinter der Treppe. Da hatte er angenehm Platz. Mit den Augen durchbohrte er das Geländer. Von selbst besaß es großartige Löcher. Wenn er wollte, konnte er mit seiner Nase die Treppe verbarrikadieren. Bis zehn Uhr hielt er sich mäuschenstill. Der Hausbesorger, ein lumpiger Schuster, verschloß das Tor und löschte mit wackligen Händen die Treppenbeleuchtung aus. Als er in seine schäbige Wohnung verschwand, sie war kaum doppelt so geräumig wie Fischerles Frau, krähte dieser leise: "How do you do?" (*DB*, 395)[352]

Fischerle's wife, "die Hur," and pal hunt Fischerle down at home and, in the well-known scene, Fischerle finds himself having his hunchback cut off:

> Der Blinde schleudert ihn zu Boden und holt vom Tisch in der Ecke des Kabinetts ein Brotmesser. Mit diesem zerfetzt er Anzug und Mantel und schneidet Fischerle den Buckel herunter. Bei der schweren Arbeit ächzt er, das Messer ist ihm zu stumpf und Licht will er keines machen. Die Pensionistin sieht ihm zu und zieht sich indessen aus. Sie legt sich aufs Bett und sagt: "Komm!" Aber er ist noch nicht fertig. Er wickelt den Buckel in die Fetzen des Mantels, spuckt ein paarmal drauf und läßt das Paket so liegen. Die Leiche schiebt er unters Bett. Dann wirft er

> sich auf die Frau. "Kein Mensch hat was gehört," sagt er und lacht. Er ist müde, aber die Frau ist dick. Er liebt sie die ganze Nacht. (*DB*, 398)[353]

This passage qualifies, according to some commentators, as black humor. W. G. Sebald, for instance, says of the scene: "Ohnmächtig, entsetzlich komisch und desolat ist diese rêverie."[354] To some, it is difficult to take because the scene enacts evil. It can be shown, by contrast, that it is a brilliant deconstruction of evil and crime, and of romanticism's coupling of love and death in melodrama. Nowhere does Canetti show that he is actually taking evil or murder seriously as a serious desire, intention, or act. This is, after all, no psychodrama, and it is certainly no melodrama. It is none of these things, because the narration is purposefully laconic. It reads as a challenge to us to refuse to take evil and crime seriously. Rather than concentrate on the "object" of the "murder," Canetti willfully takes the "point of view" of the murderer, not in the sense that he makes us feel what it is like to be driven by a desire to murder, but to reduce the murder to nothing in particular. Not because he is indifferent to what murder might mean in terms of effects on loved ones in an extra-textual world. But because he understands that a culture, for as long as it professes a passionate delight in murder, whether literally or imaginatively (as does the gutter press, for instance) is a culture that inevitably has already set up a framework that makes murder likely. By contrast, if we forget the idea, in Nietzschean fashion annihilate it, we are already resistant to it. To the conservative fans of tradition and the like, this will sound wild, but it is the idea behind this strategic deconstruction of this particularly sensitive holy cow. Thus, "der Blinde" groans as he cuts off Fischerle's hunchback, not Fischerle; "der Blinde" is annoyed that his knife is rather blunt and that there is not enough light (of course there are still all the jokes that go with the name he has . . . how could he see anyway if he is supposed to be blind?). One can see how removed the narrative is from any kind of realism if one compares it to the celebrated scene in *Madame Bovary* when Charles Bovary carries out an operation. The minute description of the muscles busting under the knife is harrowing. Flaubert is a materialist. Canetti is always an idealist.

Simultaneously, Fischerle's wife is undressing to get into bed. Is this a truly demonic melodrama with the usual depraved combining of sex and death we associate with certain writers in Romanticism? The answer is no. It is something of a tribute to *Woyzeck* (one of Canetti's favorite plays, although he claims he had not read it when he wrote *Die Blendung*), and a sanitization of that play's melodrama surrounding the murdering of a woman with a knife. It is also a rewriting of the end of *Der Prozeß* where K. is murdered, again with the melodrama written out altogether. And finally, it is a reference to the murder scene in *Die Schlafwandler*. If one thinks of more psychological explorations into depravity, like Elfriede Jelinek's *Die Klavierspielerin*, where Jelinek explores Erika's sado-masochism from a supposedly feminist perspective, the difference between the two accounts is obvious. Canetti is something of a frivolous playboy, whose first principles are very idealistic.

The beginning of the third part of the novel, "Welt im Kopf," sees us settle into the life of Benedikt Pfaff, in the chapter entitled "Der gute Vater," a chapter that Canetti often chose for his public readings:

> Die Wohnung des Hausbesorgers Benedikt Pfaff bestand aus einer mittelgroßen, dunklen Küche und einem kleinen, weißen Kabinett, in das man vom Hausflur aus zuerst gelangte. Ursprünglich schlief die Familie, die fünf Mitglieder zählte, im größeren Raum, Frau, Tochter und dreimal er selbst, er, der Polizeibeamte, er, der Ehemann, er, der Vater. Die Ehebetten waren, zu seiner häufigen Entrüstung, gleich groß. Dafür zwang er Tochter und Frau zusammen in einem zu schlafen, das andere gehörte ihm allein. Sich selbst legte er eine Roßhaarmatratze unter, nicht aus Verweichlichung, Langschläfer und Weiber haßte er, sondern aus Prinzip. Das Geld brachte *er* nach Hause. Die Reinigung sämtlicher Treppen oblag der Frau, das Aufsperren des Haustores, nachts, wenn jemand läutete, seit ihrem zehnten Lebensjahr der Tochter, damit sie die Feigheit verlerne. Was an Einnahmen für beiderlei Leistungen einging, behielt er, denn er war der Hausbesorger. Hie und da gestattete er ihnen, eine Kleinigkeit auswärts zu verdienen, durch Bedienung oder Waschen. So spürten sie wenigstens am eigenen Leib, wie hart ein Vater arbeiten muß, von dem die Familie lebt. Beim Essen nannte er sich einen Anhänger des Familienlebens, bei Nacht verhöhnte er die ältliche Frau. Sein Züchtigungsrecht übte er aus, sobald er aus dem Dienst kam. An der Tochter rieb er seine rothaarigen Fäuste mit wirklicher Liebe, von der Frau machte er weniger Gebrauch. Sein ganzes Geld ließ er zu Hause; es stimmte immer genau, auch ohne daß er nachzählte,

denn als es einmal nicht gestimmt hatte, mußten Frau und Tochter auf der Straße übernachten. Alles in allem war er glücklich. (*DB*, 401)[355]

In the first instance, this introduction shows just how Canetti loves literature, for it calls up memories of the character Moosbrugger in *Der Mann ohne Eigenschaften*. As always, Canetti expresses his love of literature by affectionately recording his knowledge of works he has read and found imaginatively exhilarating. His difference as a writer, however, is not dependent on what he has already read. His difference as a writer concerns the way in which what he produces is absolutely original relative to all other novels, no less. What sustains his narrative are the connections that inflate it, connections that are thoroughly inimitable because they do not rely on the kinds of logic we all have to use or misuse in daily life. In this respect he is not, say, like T.S. Eliot in "Prufrock," whose use of quotations shows how much of a parasite he is: without the many references, some of his poems would be very feeble indeed, because they are often not supplemented by original material of Eliot's own. Canetti has no tolerance for non-originality, as is evident from his withering comment in *Die Provinz des Menschen*: "Alle geistigen Menschen leben auch von Diebstahl und sind sich dessen bewußt," before going on to distinguish between those who protest their borrowings and those who hide them.[356] The literary references in *Die Blendung* are not "subordinated" to the "higher" purpose of indicating that one is derivative by using parody. What makes Canetti unique is his desire to record his homage to writers he has enjoyed, and this is recorded in the way in which he invests the reference with his own spirit of play, the same spirit of play that is animating his "own" details.

If Pfaff reminds us of Moosbrugger, it is only in a relative sense. After all, Musil takes sex criminals very seriously, as he takes sexuality very seriously generally throughout the novel. Pfaff, by contrast, who is guilty of incest and sadism, and for whom sex is, if we take the words on the page literally, inseparable from violence, seems to be more of a send-up of bourgeois respectability, in particular the kind of bourgeois respectability espoused by the father figure. He earns the money, *ergo* all the rest of them should do what he says. The above can be read as a deconstruction of another sensitive holy cow as far as conservative traditionalists are concerned, namely a deconstruction of authority and authority figures. The references to violence and sex are the means by which Canetti achieves this—always, as usual, winking at the reader along the way. In the above, for instance, Benedikt Pfaff's treating everybody as a threat to his authority, his manipulation of the women, and his reducing all people to material is transformed into a transparent riot by words such as "von der Frau machte er weniger Gebrauch" and the final, parting thought, "alles in allem war er glücklich." A more common argument would take all the above literally and at its face value and maintain, as Dissinger does, that this is what "goes" on in capitalist societies where everything has to be thought of in terms of what it gets you on the open market.

That this is also an affectionate dig at bourgeois pride, at the bourgeois delight in self-sacrifice, and at the bourgeois belief that the world is degenerating and that standards are not what they were, is quite obvious. This is all apparent in Benedikt Pfaff's "relationship" to his daughter, when her rebellion causes Pfaff sadness and disappointment, causes him to stop enjoying life:

> Er verstand. Sie bedrohte ihn mit einer Anzeige. Seine Leibesfrucht wollte ihn verleumden. Für wen lebte er? Für wen war er ein solider Mensch geblieben? Da zog er an seinem Busen ein Schlangenelement heran. Sie gehörte aufs Schafott. Er richtet ihr die Erfindung ein, damit sie was lernt, jetzt, wo ihm die Welt und die Weiber offenstehen, er bleibt bei ihr, aus Erbarmen und weil er seelengut ist. Und sie will behaupten, daß er was Unrechtes tut! Das ist nicht seine Tochter! Die Alte hat ihn betrogen. Er war nicht dumm, wie er sie gezüchtigt hat. Ein Riecher war immer in seiner Nase. Sechzehn Jahre hat er sein Geld für eine falsche Tochter hinausgeworfen. Ein Haus kostet nicht mehr. Von Jahr zu Jahr wird die Menschheit schlechter. Bald wird man die Polizei abschaffen und die Verbrecher haben die Macht. Der Staat sagt: Ich zahl' die Pensionen nicht und die Welt geht unter! Der Mensch hat eine Natur. Der Verbrecher greift um sich und der Herrgott wird schauen!
>
> Bis zum Herrgott verstieg er sich selten. Er hatte Respekt vor der allerhöchsten Stelle, die ihm zukam. Der Herrgott war mehr als ein Polizeipräsident. Um so mehr ergriff ihn die Gefahr, in der heute Gott selbst schwebte. Wohl nahm er seine Stieftochter vom Bett herunter und prügelte sie blutig. Aber seine rechte Freude spürte er nicht dabei. Er arbeitete mechanisch, was er sprach, war voller Wehmut und inniger Trauer. Seine Schläge widersprachen der Stimme. Zum Brüllen war

> ihm alle Lust vergangen. Irrtümlich erwähnte er einmal eine gewisse Poli. Seine Muskeln machten den Fehler sofort wieder gut. Der Name der Weibsperson, die er züchtigte, lautete auf Anna. Sie behauptete mit einer Tochter von ihm identisch zu sein. Er schenkte ihr keinen Glauben. Die Haare fielen ihr aus, und da sie sich wehrte, zerbrachen zwei Finger. Sie maulte von seinem Kopf wie ein ganz gemeiner Schlächter. Sie beschimpfte die Polizei. Man sah, wie die beste Erziehung gegen eine böse Anlage nicht aufkommt. Die Mutter war nichts wert. Sie war krank und arbeitsscheu. Er konnte jetzt die Tochter zur Mutter befördern, da gehörte sie hin. Aber er war nicht so. Er verzichtete und ging ins Gasthaus essen. (*DB*, 411–12)[357]

Again, one could invoke more psychologically plausible accounts of what the above appears to be, namely ruthless sadism. One could refer to Barbara Frischmuth's *Die Klosterschule* and Waltraud Anna Mitgutsch's *Die Züchtigung*. In those works, as in any work that really wishes to acknowledge that sadism is more than an activity executed by certain agents, both writers explore the consequences to victims of physical violence. My point here, as elsewhere, is that Canetti's refusal to accept that sadism has consequences is not a ruthless siding with those who enjoy sadism, neither is it a gratuitous enjoyment of sadism. The contextualization in Canetti reads as a sign that we need to deny those impulses which undermine faith, hope, and confidence. Not because, as the Romantics would have it, life really is tragic, but because the alternative position is a highly defensible moral position in terms of self-preservation, self-affirmation, and, above all, resistance to legitimizing plots and institutions. It stands for a principled resistance, in Nietzschean terms, to everything potentially reductive or trivializing. As usual, Canetti relies on a certain kind of shock treatment to make these points.

In both this chapter and the last, we have argued that the Nietzschean theory of the relationship between art forms and life is enacted by Canetti's narrative. As a final rider, it would be appropriate to indicate that I *do* think a kind of madness lies at the heart of the novel, thus my choice of title for this chapter, a reference to Hölderlin's wonderful poem "Brot und Wein." The madness in *Die Blendung* is not the literal kind of madness invoked by those critics who think that all the characters in *Die Blendung* are deranged, irrational, schizophrenic. It is the wild madness of exhilaration which is in Nietzsche, the often semi-desperate attempt to keep on keeping on affirming life in its most general sense, as a potential. Thus the evasion of particulars, those things with which traditional criticism insists the novel is concerned, in a mimetic sense. The idealism of the novel is therefore the spirit of idealism; it is not the specific kind of idealism that we associate with Jesus Christ or Marx or Kant.

Lillian Feder in her book *Madness in Literature* looks at madness, not as a psychological complaint requiring scientific treatment but as a state that is imaginatively revealing. She traces its presence in myth and literature (203).[358] Dionysus in myth has always symbolized the breaking up of the repressive and restrictive forces exerted on the self by society. Nietzsche, who was of course not the first to draw attention to the significance of Dionysus (Haman, Winckelmann, and Herder and the German Romantics generally had already done so), is original because he was the first to formulate an aesthetic psychology that challenged the ego as being (205). The appeal, for Nietzsche, of the cult, lay in its dissolving ego boundaries, in its dissolving the principle of individuation. He endorsed the cult unconditionally, seemingly unaware of the problem of irrationalism with which it was necessarily associated (279, 285–86).

In the current, loosely agonistic debate between Derrida and Jürgen Habermas, the latter accuses Derrida and his followers of espousing the irrationalism of Nietzsche as Feder describes it above. It is amusing that neither Derrida nor Habermas appears to really believe in dialogism. They do not practise it as far as this "debate" is concerned, since Derrida's reply to the accusations of Habermas occupies a footnote in one of his vague works, namely *Mémoires pour Paul de Man.*[359] And Derrida is only intermittently present in what apparently counts as Habermas's attack, namely *Der philosophische Diskurs der Moderne.*[360] For Habermas, there are simply two poles in philosophy. On the one hand there is reason, in which Habermas has confidence, and which is used and useful in terms of the desire to bring about a socialist kind of utopia on earth, where a certain kind of consensus about the value and functioning of dialogue—as discussed in *Die Theorie des kommunikativen Handelns*—will make it possible for a community to live together as a community, as it will apparently guarantee that a plurality of discourses flourish in a non-violent atmosphere. On the other hand, there is irrationalism, which is attractive to overexcited and largely irresponsible writers and/or academics, for whom thinking is "just" playing about with ideas. Nietzsche's irrationalism is for Habermas, therefore not really dangerous in itself. Habermas's vision of philosophy is at the root of his rejection of Derrida and his followers. He simply has no time for skepticism, or the kind of thinking most likely to raise questions (other than those related to social order), as opposed to the kind of thinking that wants to provide enduring answers, the kind practised by Habermas. My point here is to suggest that Habermas is narrow, and to suggest that there is something nervous at the heart of his apparently utopian thinking. His clinging to the project of the Enlightenment and to the belief that reason is still pure, together with the belief that reason has to be applied to the way we think our society as an organization, is, at the very least, vulnerable to exploitation, even if it is not a covert attempt to promote ideology, because thinking is, in Habermas's terms, only what supports a kind of status quo, what guarantees the homogeneity of community. Free, still less individual, thinking is not really looked upon with any enthusiasm, because Habermas is more concerned to argue a very vague case for the terms that will allow a kind of basic consensus within the community. He wants to believe that we all have instincts for this anyway—but of course he is at something of a loss as to how this is going to be achieved by non-authoritarian means. And his concern with the way institutions can order and regulate society, makes one wonder whether he might not really enjoy coercion as a means of establishing consensus.

The example set by Canetti in *Die Blendung* is interesting here. In its overwhelming rejection of, for instance, the kind of Big Ideas with which Habermas and his ancestors in philosophy such as Kant and Hegel, have always been concerned, Canetti's libertarianism is responsible, not irresponsible. It paradoxically symbolizes *freedom from* irrationalism. The novel is not an active embodiment of irrationalism. It is always, in terms of its internal dynamism, stronger than any single idea or group of ideas. It is not even remotely vulnerable to theory, because of its stress on performance as a practice. It is already doing something, as opposed to thinking about what *might be* done or creating the void which *will be* filled. It is violent in its rejection of two roles adored by professional artists and intellectuals, the role of the prophet of doom and failure and the role of the secular Messiah, who can lead us to a promised land of truth and beauty, away from the assumed awfulness of the present.

We can also close with a reminder. It is historically proven that Big Ideas lend themselves, in the long run, to the kinds of perversions with which we associate genuine irrationalism, 1794 and 1939–1945, for instance. Inflexible, dogmatic faith in Small Ideas or Big Ideas is always dangerous, Canetti seems to be saying. With the exception of faith in the possibility of the future's being as enjoyable as the present already is. *Die Blendung* never lets itself go. It is always vigilant, and it always knows precisely where it is and where it is going. In other words, it has absolute control over even the potential for a small idea, let alone a Big Idea. In this sense Apollo is always already married to Dionysus in *Die Blendung*. Both never pause to invest faith in anything concrete, except the spirit of faith itself. The alliance of a self-conscious sense of plastic form to the drive that is dynamism is resolute. The binary oppositions which we are told by so many lie at the problematic heart of Western civilization are solved. Until, that is, the character of George(s) is introduced into the narrative, when this brilliant marriage is rent asunder.

8

The Breakdown of Agon: Degeneration of Play and the Rise of the Big Idea

According to Peter Russell, *Die Blendung* as a whole is not only flawed as a human document, it is artistically flawed. He cites as proof that the novel is artistically flawed the example of the chapter in Part Three called "Ein Irrenhaus," in which we meet George(s) Kien for the first time. Russell justifies his view by arguing that the change in place from a setting that is clearly Vienna to Paris, the change in narrative stance away from the centrality granted Peter Kien to the life of George(s), Peter's brother, and his success as a psychiatrist and as an original researcher into the behavioral habits of schizophrenics, interrupts the momentum of the plot. The change in focus contributes nothing to that plot.[361] Another critic whose attention has been caught by "Ein Irrenhaus" is Edward Thomson. His view, however, is that the chapter is only interesting in that it provides an alternative madness to the madness embodied by Peter Kien. He also maintains that it draws attention to itself as a chapter on the grounds that it has an objectivity and restraint about it more typical of the classical Novelle.[362] More ambitiously, Richard Lawson, in *Understanding Canetti*, talks of Canetti's loss of narrative control, early signs of which he maintains are there in Part Two.[363] This loss of control is, however, particularly noticeable in Part Three, where we have: "a frequently unmotivated accumulation of material that is not strictly relevant to the narrative or is relevant only tenuously, such as Canetti's theoretical and doctrinaire interpolations about crowds or madmen" (41).

Of course, these views have been heavily contested, indirectly, if not directly, by those who believe that in the last section of the novel there is a logical development toward the inevitable, as set up by the very terms of the first two sections of the novel. They argue that Peter Kien was always mad and demented in the ordinary sense, and in the final section this just becomes acutely obvious. Alternatively, they see in the change that comes over Peter Kien evidence of a theory promoted by Canetti himself, namely that of "Verwandlung" whereby change is change in terms of that which already is. Klaus-Peter Zepp argues this point with particular fervor.[364]

Such critics have also welcomed, in the same mimetic mode, the focus on George(s). His entrance is equal to an assertion of the normality they found to be so utterly lacking in all the other characters. David Turner, for instance, argues that George(s) Kien is normal, relatively speaking. He is more sympathetic and humane than other characters.[365] Turner's interpretation of George(s), together with others, will be looked at later in this chapter, as will the view that the end of the novel offers some sort of resolution to what they perceive to be "the problem studied by" the novel. Not all take the view that George(s) represents something new and better, however. Dagmar Barnouw, for instance, maintains that both Peter's world and George(s)' world are horrible.[366] Günter Blöcker, by contrast, maintains that not one character is sympathetic in the whole of the novel.[367]

What is interesting here, however, is the comparatively unusual idea raised by Russell, Thomson, and Lawson, that there is something artistically flawed about this novel, where artistically flawed clearly means, in their terms, inconsistency of narrative voice and/or the addition of information that does not seem to have any relevance to ideas already raised by the novel. Whereas, however, Russell is frustrated because the novel is both damaging as a human document and internally flawed as a work of art, this chapter will argue that the novel breaks down abruptly, in terms of its spirit and character, at a point before "Ein Irrenhaus" begins, namely at the beginning of Part Three, in the chapter called "Der gute Vater." It remains consistently broken thereafter. Whether this breakdown is equal to artistic failure is difficult to say, since the criteria invoked by Russell, Thomson, and Lawson are relatively phony. Perfection is equated with something that could arguably be considered to be rather monotonous, namely consistency of intellectual purpose. As this chapter sees it, the breakdown or collapse consists in the way the narrative positively *inverts* the premises that underlined all the chapters this study has considered so far. This only has implications in terms of what we have been maintaining is "the character of the novel." This position is not the mimetic one, whereby what happens throughout the last part is merely a grim inevitability already set up by the figures who apparently peopled the universe of *Die Blendung* in the two earlier sections. *The character* of the novel changes altogether after the beginning of Part Three. There is an abrupt decline in its brilliance and verve, a turning away from the drive of Dionysus tamed so beautifully by an Apollonian notion of form. In place of this marriage, we have the reign, not of Apollo as plasticity, but Apollo in terms of reified ideas.

The novel turns from dialogism to monologism. It turns from facetiousness to bored, even malignant, gravity. It does this in the way it invents, and then instates very Big Ideas, many of which are idiosyncratic in themselves and not original in an absolute sense, since they have a strong theoretical basis and a history in terms of the history of ideas. Big Ideas like Benedikt Pfaff's sadism, like the gorilla as schizophrenic, like the idea of a new kind of private language, like madness, like misogyny, like the theory of the masses. The Big Ideas, are, moreover, presented to us in a form that resembles the essay. In fact, essayism arguably becomes typical of the latter sections of the novel. The novel also invents emotions that are alien to the mood of the sections already examined, emotions and interpersonal experiences like misanthropy, jealousy, hatred, ambition, sex, and violence.

We noticed that in the first two sections of the novel that any idea with any pretention to weight and authority was lovingly deconstructed *because* such ideas are a suitable vehicle for the spirit of facetiousness: thus the frequency of a particular kind of parody, and parody directed exclusively at bourgeois conventions, on the one hand, and at characters and situations from literature on the other. None of the Big Ideas Canetti introduces into the end of the novel, mentioned above, receive this kind of user-friendly treatment. Nothing is lovingly deconstructed and nothing becomes the pretext for an elegant parody. What underlines both the theoretical ideas and the emotions of hatred and ambition is a level of uncomplicated seriousness and intellectual intent, not encountered before in the novel, and not undermined by anything, least of all irony or satire. The effect of this change in attitude is most clearly felt if we look immediately at the relationship between the mimetic and diegetic sections in the final part of the novel. The most obvious point about this relationship, central to the change in character of the novel, is that it ceases to be a happy relationship between equals. The narrator or "Geist der Erzählung" is transformed entirely. His ludic skills and his skill at stylistic contagion desert him, and are not replaced by any really individual skills, ethical or otherwise. He becomes relatively detached and, for the most part, refuses absolutely to respond to or comment on anything provided in the mimetic sections, at any level. He refuses to be an independent player or voice and, instead, tends to endorse, by default, what is being said in the mimetic sections, by assuming without further debate that the Big Ideas do not need to be subject to scrutiny of any kind. Alternatively, the ideas are left to collapse themselves, since they are so well exposed in all their clumsiness and ugliness.

The former view, the idea of complicity by default, represents a position we have not encountered in our analysis of the narrator's positive response, in the earlier part of the novel, to the subject matter of conversations. This is complicity of a different order, and it is important that we understand how different it is from the complicity of the narrator analyzed in the preceding six chapters. The complicity by default we encounter in the closing sections of the novel is complicity at the level of the letter of the law, as far as what is said is concerned. It is not complicity with the spirit of theatricality. As it happens, the diegetic material cannot, in the latter parts of the novel, invent fun, let alone enter into the spirit of fun by mimicry and stylistic contagion, that fun which had animated the mimetic sections of the earlier part of the novel. The new mimetic material, with its stress on serious Big Ideas, is superbly resistant to play. The narrative is no longer a theatrical performance requiring the cooperation and consent of the reader as an equal. It no longer wants to play, and it is resolute in its refusal of play. The narrative appears to lecture the reader, as if s/he were a subordinate. Further, actual readers often feel estranged from the narrative, estranged both by the tone of comparative superiority of the speakers, the clearly idiosyncratic Big Ideas discussed in highly extended dialogues between the characters, and by the relative silence of the narrator or "Geist der Erzählung" in the face of these Big Ideas. This silence is particularly surprising given the high-profile vocal and loquacious quality of that narrator or spirit in earlier parts of the novel. We have none of the deep commitment to fun, but rather the silence of tolerance without faith. Equally, and the two are inextricably linked, both George(s) and Kien take on a much more readily identifiable character as people; they become characters, yet are not flexible either as people or as thinkers. They are, by contrast, reified only because of the fixities of their often violently held intellectual ideas.

The book suddenly embraces the more traditional idea of character and motive associated with the novel, but with a difference. Characters suddenly begin to perform theatrically to each other. They do not even collaborate with one another in an amusing theatrical manner. Characters perform with a degree of hostility and intent to audiences within their own worlds. The name Peter Kien is no longer a pretext for the spirit of gratuitousness, and a pretext for the reign of play, which was the extent of the adherence to character in earlier chapters, but an individualized person. Kien, like others, is suddenly a spokesperson, with a keen desire to implement the rhetoric of cognition and persuasion with respect to his audiences. We return to an old-fashioned notion of the idea of a character's being identified with certain views or values and the idea of the importance of communication of analytical and/or intellectual material. Instead of destroying what Nietzsche perceived to be the evil of individuation, therefore, the narrative begins to invent and experience individuation.

The narrative suddenly becomes a fixed stage with a set and actors whom we as readers watch, and, as will become clear, to whom we often have no real access at any level. Actors, further, do not act in concert, for there is a widespread atmosphere of mistrust. Big Ideas, whilst actively constructed as subjects/objects of conversation by both George(s) and Peter, which is to say in the mimetic sections of the novel, refuse to be the pretext for any level of play in the diegetic sections of the novel in Part Three. The character of the diegetic sections of the novel changes accordingly; the narrator's profile virtually disappears altogether. What else must we make of this? The reader is asked, albeit obliquely, to position herself/himself in terms of an extra-textual world of people with ideas, strange as some of them may seem, which yet still touch on the issue of how to live. If there are references to an extra-textual reality, these are not made in the name of any kind of normality, let alone a consoling kind of normality. Nevertheless, the narrative asks us, as a result, to believe that art is a means to the end of social commentary of some kind—for now the narrative refers to a world beyond its own parameters, and one it believes has a prior claim on the reader's imagination.

The narrative suddenly instates the principles of mimesis, therefore. The idea of the Nietzschean value of art as something which silences the demands placed on the imagination by the extra-textual world, as something which demonstrates by example that that world need not make claims on our imagination, is dropped abruptly. The narrative is no longer proving by example that it is self-sufficient. It has lost its self-confidence, can no longer sustain the recklessly maintained festive spirit of the dance as a collaborative process between high-spirited voices. It refuses to construct and invent the new, the original, the *imprévu*, as a way of sustaining life as an aesthetic illusion which continually needs to be constructed *ex nihilo*. It has turned away from itself to imagine a world that must *already* have resonance in some way in terms of what readers already know about, and of which they already have some experience: namely family feuds, ambition, greed, money, sex, violence, despair, and, finally, that ultimate act of denial of the value of life, suicide. We move, abruptly, in the first instance, away from an exuberant dionysian proclamation of the joy of living life in the affirmative mode to a slow, then finally inevitable, deterioration, to the moment of death and anonymity itself.

In examining the new Big Ideas themselves, we will discover that they also read like a fascination with the inverse of difference, as it has been defined in earlier chapters. The Big Ideas all speak quite enthusiastically of what it is that can destroy the inviolable autonomy of the other. For instance, in the famous discussion about "die Masse" in the chapter, "Listenereicher Odysseus," Peter Kien proclaims the joy of the abandonment of the agile imagination and the vibrant emotions in favor of something quite anonymous, namely instinct. This is seen as something that successfully destroys what is felt to be the evil of individuation. Further, whereas the "world" in which "characters" lived in the earlier chapters was one in which money was always a bit of a joke, where figures were always absurdly exaggerated, we suddenly enter a world in which money has actual material power. This is the case when, for instance, George(s) pays off Benedikt Pfaff and Therese, at the end of "Listenreicher Odysseus." We also suddenly enter a world in which conversations are deeply colored by the view that sex has power, whereas it had more or less hypothetical status up until that point. George(s) works, for instance, with the intra-textually false assumption that Peter is upset because he has caught Benedikt

Pfaff and Therese in flagrante; we know that Benedikt Pfaff "took" Therese at the end of "Die Erfüllung," but we do not know that Peter Kien has this information.[368]

Something of an informal contest also begins between George(s), the symbol of secular success in terms of both his public career and his success with women, and Peter, the symbol of the rejection of "cheap" ways of being successful, the scholar who has not bothered with success with women or with his career in a public sense. This contest infuses the mood of hostility characteristic of the closing sections of the novel. This contest is not an *agonistic* one. It is not the gratuitous love of teasing out the other's genius. On the contrary, we encounter one-upmanship of a fairly hostile kind, in which each is motivated to see his point of view vindicated in an absolute sense. In this contest neither wins ultimately. The novel suddenly raises, therefore, the very concrete and material issue of how to live in the secular world, where how to live is very much a question of how you conduct yourself with respect to women and with respect to your career. This contest is not solved, not only in the sense that neither George(s) nor Peter wins, but in the sense that the ideas advanced by both George(s) and Peter seem to us to be questionable, whether these be about women or about "values" and career goals.

Crucial to the whole argument in the preceding chapters of this book was the idea of the sentence as an autonomous unit, of narrative as linear progression without semantic interrelations between those autonomous sentences, and of the idea of mimicry or contagion as the central act of the creative imagination, with sentences imitating the spirit, not the letter, of what is said. This was the reign of agon. Another way of putting what has just been said about the change in character of the novel is to say that the mood of competitive wit or the reign of agon, guaranteed by abrupt, brittle, bright sentences refusing to allow themselves to be integrated into intellectual power blocs, gives way to a mood of seriousness, where a much more extended, relaxed prose uses its constitutent part—the sentence—for entirely different purposes. No longer is the sentence gratuitous. It plays a part in an argument. Each sentence has a role to play in the construction of meaning at the semantic level. There are distinct semantic interrelations between sentences, and these do end up constructing monolithic power blocs in terms of apparently incontrovertible ideas.

So the prose of the first two sections of the novel, where words were an end in themselves and part of a never-ending game, gives way to a world in and through which words have referential meaning in an obvious sense. They are the means by which Big Ideas are constructed, ideas like the theory of the masses and so on, with which an intellectual reader will already be familiar in some way. Gone is the loving parody altogether. Absent is an attitude of irony or satire with respect to the new Big Ideas. In its place, clear signs of a highly idiosyncratic and highly unattractive life from our extra-textual world filter through. The implications of this concern the status of the reader. The terms on which Canetti's implied reader now lives, as s/he reads, are totally different from those implied by the first two sections of the novel. The terms implied by the major part of the novel considered so far were creatively imaginative and founded on an understanding of a highly human notion of the love of difference as a practice—they had to do with the dynamism of the imagination and the intellectual horsepower that can be injected into a particular kind of very sophisticated conversing in public. These terms suddenly become *material* in Part Three.

These clear signs of life from the extra-textual world are embedded in the narrative in idiosyncratic forms. They take the form of personal misanthropy and misogyny or boredom in characters like Peter or George(s). They also serve to construct the author Canetti, for the first time, as an individualized person. For they imply a negative attitude on the part of the author, Canetti, with respect to the extra-textual world. This secular world is thought of as narrow, as one in which actual relationships and actual survival are difficult, problematic, and dangerous, in which there is pressure to have a career and be successful in material terms, in which there is no evidence of that spirit of love which was the mystery at the heart of the first two sections of the novel. There is positive proof of the inverse of love, namely jealousy, rivalry, and vanity: there is even something like an aggressive spirit of hatred of all others except the self.

The reader's status from "Der gute Vater" onward is limited, as has already been indicated in the analysis in the preceding chapter of Benedikt Pfaff's so-called sadism. From being an equal and a dynamic producer of pleasure and laughter, the reader is passive, intellectually, imaginatively, and emotionally. S/he can only, as it were, watch with varying degrees of wonder/surprise/horror at what is said and done. S/he feels excluded. Finally, this is further complicated by an abrupt and very final change in the last few pages of the novel. The momentum of the closing stages of the novel constitutes a further change of character. The mood of the final pages can be generally characterized as that of emotional panic, collapse, and fear. This is not just important because it is the extreme inverse of those emotions of buoyancy, happiness, fun, facetiousness, and frivolity which had sustained the narrative for the most part of the novel. It might be a formal recognition of the cost of living in the Nietzschean mode, a recognition that the construction of the aesthetic illusion over the void of chaos is vulnerable and fragile, because the effort involves a risk and a danger, but because any failure, even momentary, of intellectual horsepower at the level of energy and imaginative agility has to mean collapse in an absolute sense. Outside the aesthetic illusion there is nothing but the void. It is not insignificant that both Hölderlin and Nietzsche, worshippers of the kind of flamboyant madness at the heart of most of Canetti's novel ("frohlockender Wahnsinn"), died "mad" in a conventional sense. To date, John Bayley seems to be unique in having put his finger on the problematic spirit of the novel taken as a whole, when he admits of the tedium of the novel: ". . . its fierce abstractness, its almost paralysing intelligence, are wholly at home: even the tedium which it by no means lacks seems, as it were, a wholly genuine and necessary tedium, as essential and even dynamic part of its massive mental specification" (185).[369]

To begin: George(s)' attitudes to those who are in psychiatric institutions, as his views concerning the reason why these people are in psychiatric institutions, when they are introduced for the first time, strike us as frivolous in a wanton and dangerous sense, as was already apparent in the discussion in the first chapter of this study, of Canetti's response to the mental institution opposite which he lived when he came to write his novel, namely Steinhof. On the one hand, George(s) is a confidence trickster who always tells his patients that he knows everything, and openly tries to enlist their trust. On the other, he tells his wives that madness (here in the ordinary sense, which is to say as decreed by society or its representatives, in this instance doctors) is a punishment for egoism. He does not publish these views, but he secretly believes in them. He continues to use patients in institutions, purely to facilitate his promotion within the profession and to acquire a reputation as a scholar in the field. He is, therefore, from the very beginning, something of a fraud. Lawson argues, in this context, that he is a vehicle for another parody—he is a send-up of Freudian psychiatry.[370]

George(s)' attitude to women is as unsophisticated. He is already on his third wife, having put the first two into the institution where he works. The third wife is introduced, by the narrator, in purely utilitarian terms:

> Ihr verdankte er seine rasche Karriere. Er war groß, stark, feurig und sicher; in seinen Zügen lag etwas von jener Weichheit, die Frauen benötigen, um sich bei einem Mann heimisch zu fühlen. Wer ihn ansah, nannte ihn den Adam des Michelangelo. Er verstand es sehr gut, Intelligenz mit Eleganz zu verbinden. Seine glänzende Begabung wurde durch die Politik seiner Geliebten zu genialer Wirksamkeit gesteigert. Als sie sicher war, daß niemand anderer Nachfolger ihres Mannes in der Anstaltsleitung werden könne als eben Georges, ging sie für ihn durch einen Giftmord, über den sie sogar schwieg. Seit Jahren hatte sie ihn bedacht und vorbereitet; er gelang. Der Mann starb unauffällig. Georges wurde sofort zum Direktor ernannt und heiratete sie aus Dankbarkeit für ihre früheren Dienste; vom letzten hatte er keine Ahnung. (*DB*, 433–34)[371]

The narrator, in the above, talks dispassionately about what it is that has made George(s) successful. In many respects, one could classify the above as a kind of facetiousness, different in kind from the facetiousness of the earlier parts of the novel, but facetiousness nonetheless. The narrator's angle seems, however, to be colored by a kind of bored jealousy of the success George(s) Kien has been, despite the fact that there is, generally speaking, a complete absence of anything resembling an ethical basis to either his professional or private life. The woman, too, comes across negatively inasmuch as she is exclusively dedicated to her man and willing to compromise herself in order to secure him.

The portrait of George(s) Kien that develops is one that stresses the sense in which George(s) Kien knowingly plays a part as he works: he is a conscious actor. His relationship to his patients is depicted in terms of its personality content. He is an actor and they form his audience:

> Mit der Zeit entwickelte er sich zu einem großen Schauspieler. Seine Gesichtsmuskeln, von seltener Beweglichkeit, paßten sich

> im Laufe eines Tages den verschiedensten Situationen an. Da er täglich mindestens drei, trotz seiner Gründlichkeit meist mehr Patienten zu sich lud, hatte er ebenso viele Rollen zu erschöpfen; die flüchtigen, aber treffenden Winke und Worte auf seinen Rundgängen nicht gerechnet, denn diese zählten zu Hunderten. Heftig umstritten war in der gelehrten Welt seine Behandlung von Bewußtseinsspaltung der verschiedensten Art. Gebärdete sich zum Beispiel ein Kranker als zwei Menschen, die nichts miteinander gemein hatten oder sich bekämpften, so wandte Georges Kien eine Methode an, die ihm anfang selbst gefährlich erschien: er befreundete sich mit beiden Parteien. Fanatische Zähigkeit war die Voraussetzung zu diesem Spiel. Um das wirkliche Wesen beider zu erforschen, stützte er jede mit Argumenten, aus deren Wirkung er seine Schlüsse zog. Schlüsse verbaute er zu Hypothesen und erdachte zarte Experimente, um sie zu beweisen. Dann ging er an die Heilung heran. In seinem eigenen Bewußtsein näherte er die getrennten Teile des Kranken, wie er sie verkörperte, und fügte sie langsam aneinander. Er fühlte, an welchen Punkten sie sich vertrügen, und lenkte die Aufmerksamkeit beider Teile durch starke, eindringliche Bilder immer wieder auf diese Punkte, bis sie hier haftenblieb und selbsttätig weiterkittete. Plötzliche Krisen, heftiges Abreißen, gewaltsame Trennungen, wo man schon eine endgültige Vereinigung erhofft hatte, geschahen oft und waren unvermeidlich. Nicht seltener gelang die Heilung. Mißerfolge führte er auf seine Oberflächlichkeit zurück. Irgendein verborgenes Glied hatte er übersehen, er war ein Stümper, er machte sich die Arbeit zu leicht, er opferte lebende Menschen seinen toten Überzeugungen, er war wie sein Vorgänger—da begann er von neuem, mit einem Schub neuer Kautelen und Experimente. Denn an die Richtigkeit seiner Methode glaubte er. (*DB*, 434–35)[372]

This sounds like gratuitous acting, of dubious professional and medical status. For instance, what does the patient (here the schizophrenic) gain from having a psychiatrist merely mimic his/her behavioral patterns? If one is to take the above seriously, the point seems to be that George(s) is pragmatic by nature, that he invents healing processes that respond to each individual patient's needs and that he relies heavily on his capacity to *empathize* with his patients. Although the narrator is categorical in his statement that George(s) is sometimes successful in healing his patients, the above information is couched in terms that show that George(s) is experimental and that his successes and failures are something of a hit and miss affair. To a certain extent, therefore, patients are victims of one man's unquestioning faith in himself and in his right to experiment with human beings.

Thereafter, George(s) is said to be in awe of the qualities of intensity and power of his patients. They are geniuses in a way that challenges the conventional notion of genius. He has given up reading and literature as a result. As a young man, by contrast, he had been heavily dependent on literature and books, as he had been heavily dependent on women, who had fallen into his lap. But that era had been brought to a close by his accidental encounter with a gorilla, an encounter brought about as a result of his activity as a gynaecologist. He had visited a woman patient in her home who was always ill when her husband, a banker, was away from home. Her brother-in-law was mad, and was kept in the home, guarded by a housekeeper, a young widow, who was to do anything he asked of her:

> Die Türe, die zum Schwager führte, war verschlossen. Dr. Georges läutete. Man hörte einen wuchtig schleppenden Schritt. Dann wurde es totenstill. Hinter dem Guckloch erschien ein schwarzes Auge. Madame legte den Finger an den Mund und grinste zärtlich. Das Auge verharrte regungslos. Die beiden warteten geduldig. Der Arzt bedauerte seine Höflichkeit und den empfindlichen Zeitverlust. Plötzlich ging die Türe lautlos auf. Ein angekleideter Gorilla trat vor, streckte die langen Arme aus, legte sie auf die Schultern des Arztes und begrüßte ihn in einer fremden Sprache. Die Frau beachtete er nicht. Seine Gäste gingen ihm nach. An einem runden Tische hieß er sie Platz nehmen. Seine Gebärden waren roh, aber verständlich und einladend. Über die Sprache zerbrach sich der Arzt den Kopf. Am ehesten erinnerte sie ihn noch an einen Negerdialekt. Der Gorilla holte seine Sekretärin. Sie war notdürftig bekleidet und sichtlich verlegen. Als sie sich gesetzt hatte, wies ihr Herr auf ein Bild an der Wand und klatschte ihr eine über den Rücken. Sie schmiegte sich frech an ihn an. Ihre Scheu verschwand. Das Bild stellte die Vereinigung zweier affenartiger Menschen dar. Madame hob sich und besah es aus verschiedenen Entfernungen, von allen möglichen Seiten. Der Gorilla hielt den männlichen Besuch fest, er hatte ihm wohl viel zu erklären. Georges war jedes Wort neu. Nur eines begriff er: das Paar am Tisch stand in enger Verwandtschaft zu dem Paar auf dem Bild. Die Sekretärin verstand ihren Herrn. Sie antwortete ihm in ähnlichen Worten. Er sprach stärker, mehr aus der Tiefe, hinter seinen Lauten lauerten Affekte. Sie warf manchmal ein franzö-

> sisches Wort hin, vielleicht um anzudeuten, was gemeint sei. "Sprechen Sie nicht Französisch?" fragte Georges. "Aber natürlich, mein Herr!" entgegnete sie heftig, "was denken Sie von mir? Ich bin Pariserin!" Sie überschüttete ihn mit einem eiligen Schwall von Worten, die schlecht ausgesprochen und noch schlechter zusammengefügt waren, wie wenn sie die Sprache schon halb verlernt hätte. Der Gorilla brüllte sie an, sofort schwieg sie. Seine Augen funkelten. Sie legte den Arm auf seine Brust. Da weinte er wie ein kleines Kind. "Er haßt die französische Sprache," flüsterte sie zum Besuch. "Er arbeitet schon seit Jahren an einer eigenen. Er ist noch nicht ganz fertig." (*DB*, 437–38)[373]

The gorilla, therefore, is not a domesticated animal but a schizophrenic man, dressed as a gorilla and capable of human gestures, such as inviting in his guests and bidding them sit down and talking to them in a nigger dialect. He is joined by his guardian, the secretary, who is introduced as if she were embarrassed because she had been caught *in flagrante*. The gorilla points to an image of two monkey-like human beings having sex. We understand that the secretary's relation to the gorilla is a sexual one. The issue is then raised of the kind of language the gorilla is speaking. He hates French and is working on his own language: it will be totally unique and original.

George(s) becomes fascinated by the language the gorilla uses:

> Madame hing beharrlich am Bild. Georges war ihr dankbar dafür. Ein Wort von ihr hätte ihn um seine Höflichkeit gebracht. Er selbst fand keines. Wenn der Gorilla nur wieder sprach! Vor diesem einen Wunsch verschwanden alle Gedanken an Zeitknappheit, Verpflichtungen, Frauen, Erfolge als hätte er von Geburt an den Menschen oder Gorilla gesucht, der seine eigene Sprache besaß. Das Weinen fesselte ihn weniger. Plötzlich stand er auf und verbeugte sich tief und andächtig vor dem Gorilla. Französische Laute vermied er, doch drückte sein Gesicht die größte Hochachtung aus. Die Sekretärin nahm diese Anerkennung für ihren Herrn mit einem freundlichen Nicken entgegen. Da hörte der Gorilla zu weinen auf, verfiel in seine Sprache und erlaubte sich die alte Gewalttätigkeit. Jeder Silbe, die er hervorstieß, entsprach eine bestimmte Bewegung. Für Gegenstände schienen die Bezeichnungen zu wechseln. Das Bild meinte er hundertmal und nannte es jedesmal verschieden; die Namen hingen von der Gebärde ab, mit der er hinwies. Vom

> ganzen Körper erzeugt und begleitet, tönte kein Laut gleichgültig. Wenn er lachte, breitete er die Arme weit aus. Seine Stirn schien er am Hinterkopf zu tragen. Die Haare waren dort weggerieben, als führe er in den Stunden seiner schöpferischen Tätigkeit unaufhörlich darüber.
>
> Plötzlich sprang er auf und warf sich mit Leidenschaft über den Boden. Georges bemerkte, daß dieser mit Erde belegt war, einer sicher sehr dicken Schicht. Die Sekretärin zerrte am Rock des Liegenden, er war ihr zu schwer. Flehentlich bat sie den Besuch um Hilfe. Sie sei eifersüchtig, sagte sie, so eifersüchtig! Zusammen hoben sie den Gorilla hoch. Kaum saß er, als er von seinem Erlebnis da unten zu erzählen begann. In wenigen gewaltigen Worten, die wie angeschnittene lebende Baumstämme ins Zimmer geschleudert wurden, vernahm Georges ein mythisches Liebesabenteuer, das ihn bis zum tiefsten Zweifel an sich selbst erschütterte. Er sah sich als Wanze neben einem Menschen. Er fragte sich, wie er begreifen könne, was von tausend Klaftern tiefer kam, als er je hinabzusteigen gewagt hatte. Welche Anmaßung mit einem solchen Geschöpf an einem Tisch zu sitzen, gesittet, gönnerhaft, an allen Poren der Seele von Fett und täglich frischem Fett verstopft, ein Halbmensch für den praktischen Gebrauch, ohne den Mut zum Sein, weil Sein in unserer Welt ein Anders-Sein bedeutet, eine Schablone für sich, eine aufgezogene Schneiderreklame, durch einen gnädigen Zufall in Bewegung oder in Ruhestand versetzt, je nach dem Zufall eben, ohne den leisesten Einfluß, ohne einen Funken Macht, immer dieselben leeren Sätze leiernd, immer aus gleicher Entfernung verstanden. Denn wo lebt der Normalmensch, der einen Nächsten bestimmt, verändert, gestaltet? Die Frauen, die Georges mit Liebe bestürmen und ihm zuliebe ihr Leben hergäben, besonders wenn er sie gerade umarmt, sind nachher genau dasselbe, was sie vorher waren, glattgepflegte Hauttierchen, mit Kosmetik oder Männern beschäftigt. Diese Sekretärin aber, von Haus aus ein gewöhnliches Weib, nicht anders als andere, ist unter dem mächtigen Willen des Gorillas zu einem eigenartigen Wesen geworden: stärker, erregter, hingebender. Während er sein Abenteuer mit der Erde besingt, packt sie die Unruhe. Sie wirft eifersüchtige Blicke und Bemerkungen in seine Erzählung, rutscht hilflos auf ihren Stuhl hin und her, zwickt ihn, lächelt, streckt die Zunge; er beachtet sie nicht. (*DB*, 438–40)[374]

The gorilla's language is, therefore, primarily a language of the body. The range does not seem very extensive, and the gorilla is primarily characterized by his emotional responses. This body language is accompanied by the sounds we associate with the formation of words, but these are not intelligible to George(s). What the experience precipitates in George(s) is a realization of the relativity of man to the schizophrenic, in terms of the superior capacity of the gorilla for powerful feeling and powerful expression. This is in contrast to what George(s) sees as the boring complacency of life, where life is nothing more than a series of mechanically repeated clichés. The schizophrenic represents an existential challenge to him.

To this reader, this passage is problematic. Extravagant claims are made about the superior expressivity of the schizophrenic vis à vis man. George(s) sees the gorilla writhe about on the floor. This stimulates an avalanche of highly negative criticism of life per se, which the narrator presents as if it were a general narrative statement, to which we all naturally consented. The demarcation lines between George(s)' psyche and the narrator's are not sustained. They collapse, and one has the impression that the narrator is extrapolating to affirm a general statement about the nature of life per se. Yet the view is reductive and negative in the extreme. This stance is partially undermined as we return to George(s) proper and to the plausible view that, relative to his experience of bored "promiscuity" or easy sex, the gorilla is a symbol of passion. Woman again is characterized in the worst possible terms, and, consistent with the general view of her throughout the closing sections of the novel, she is characterized exclusively in terms of sexuality. Whereas George(s)' women are discarded as useless after sex, he implies that there is something almost moving about the superior powers of devotion of the gorilla's woman. But this is undercut by the last sentence. Even if to George(s), she is attractive in her unconditional devotion, the gorilla does not notice her.

George(s) develops an attachment to the gorilla:

> Einige Monate hindurch kam er täglich. Seine Bewunderung für den Gorilla wuchs von Besuch zu Besuch. Mit unendlicher Mühe erlernte er seine Sprache. Die Sekretärin half ihm nur wenig; wenn sie zu oft in ihr Französisch heimkehrte, kam sie sich verstoßen vor. Für den Verrat am Mann, dem sie bedingungslos anhing, verdiente sie Strafe. Um den Gorilla bei guter Laune zu erhalten, verzichtete Georges auf den Umweg über gleichgültig welche andere Sprache. Er gab sich wie ein Kind, dem man mit den Worten auch die Beziehungen der Dinge zueinander nahebringt. Hier waren die Beziehungen das

> Ursprüngliche, beide Zimmer und was sie enthielten, lösten sich in ein Kraftfeld von Affekten auf. Die Gegenstände hatten, darin behielt der erste Eindruck recht, keine eigentlichen Namen. Je nach der Empfindung, in der sie trieben, hießen sie. Ihr Gesicht wechselte für den Gorilla, der ein wildes, gespanntes, gewitterreiches Leben führte. Sein Leben ging auf sie über, sie hatten aktiven Teil daran. Er bevölkerte zwei Zimmer mit einer ganzen Welt. Er schuf, was er brauchte, und fand sich nach seinen sechs Tagen am siebenten darin zurecht. Statt zu ruhen, schenkte er der Schöpfung eine Sprache. Was um ihn war, entstammte ihm. Denn die Einrichtung, die er hier gefunden, und das Gerümpel, das man nach und nach zu ihm hinübergeschafft hatte, trug längst die Spuren seiner Wirkung. Den Fremden, der plötzlich auf seinem Planeten gelandet war, behandelte er mit Geduld. Rückfälle des Gastes in die Sprache einer überwundenen, blassen Zeit verzieh er, weil er selbst einmal zu den Menschen gehört hatte. Auch bemerkte er wohl, welche Fortschritte der Fremde machte. Anfangs weniger als sein Schatten, wuchs er zu einem ebenbürtigen Freund heran. (*DB*, 440)[375]

So George(s) learns the language of the gorilla to enter his private world. This private language is one of speech, but it is accompanied by the language of feeling. The gorilla is able to endow everything with emotional intensity. The two become equals, become friends. It is interesting to remember at this point that Canetti, in an interview with Durzak, admitted to having enjoyed listening to a record of individual sounds made by animals in an African jungle, in particular the noise of a lion hunting for prey and the sounds of all the animals who join in once the zebra has been killed.[376] In that interview, he maintained that all the noises of the jungle represented for him what it was that he wanted to recreate in his plays. If the dramatic quality of the aggressivity of the sounds made by animals in search of prey was what stimulated him whilst he wrote his plays, it is still curious that he should be actually attracted to the sounds emitted by animals.

Canetti does not seem to acknowledge that what is being investigated by George(s) is a series of hypotheses as to the superiority of the schizophrenic vis à vis the non-schizophrenic. The objective value of George(s)' assumptions and interests is not endorsed. It is glossed over, to the extent that we merely see the schizophrenic in George(s)' own, subjective terms. Lovett, in her thesis, does not take this view. She maintains that the portrait of the gorilla is an *idyllic* portrait of a schizophrenic, in the tradition of Deleuze, Lacan, and Foucault, all of whom feel that the conduct of the schizophrenic is exemplary in that it is not permeated by the traditional binary oppositions. It is a symbol of a more pure form of existence in the stress on the fluency of desire. Although feminists have not taken *Die Blendung* seriously, it is interesting, given their vested interest in the apparently subversive aspects of hysterical behaviour, in terms of the symbolic order, that they have not responded to Canetti's portrait of an original: Cixous and Clément, for instance, dedicate part of a chapter in their celebrated *The Newly Born Woman* to "Sorceress and Hysteric."[377] Clearly, the portrait lends itself to such radical theories. The point about the schizophrenic in the novel is, however, that he is difficult to take seriously. Any claim to absolute status is undercut by the dubious character of the man George(s). His interest in the schizophrenic is limited. The schizophrenic is a pretext. George(s)' interests rapidly become material, since the experience with the gorilla is what brings George(s) more than secular success. He gets a reputation as a scholar after he publishes his findings. More importantly, perhaps, the experience is also crucial as an existential challenge.

George(s) leaves gynaecology and goes into psychiatry, not with the messianic intention of converting the mad back to health, of healing them from what would conventionally be thought of as an illness, but with the intention of sustaining them in their worlds. It seems from the above that George(s) has simply been converted to the view that it is only the mad who are really human. His entry into the profession is motivated by a desire to sustain an imaginative adventure already started, which is clearly enjoyable to the man George(s) but which continues to have ambiguous status, as a professional adventure:

> Georges war Gelehrter genug, um eine Abhandlung über die Sprache dieses Irren zu veröffentlichen. Auf die Psychologie der Laute fiel neues Licht. Heftig umstrittene Probleme der Wissenschaft löste ein Gorilla. Die Freundschaft mit ihm brachte Ruhm über einen jungen Arzt, der bisher nur Erfolg gekannt hatte. Aus Dankbarkeit beließ er ihn dort, wo es ihm gefiel. Er verzichtete auf einen Heilungsversuch. Die Fähigkeit, ihn von einem Gorilla in den betrogenen Bruder eines Bankiers zurückzuverwandeln, traute er sich, seit er sich seiner Sprache bemächtigt hatte, wohl zu. Doch er hütete sich vor einem Verbrechen, zu dem ihm nur das Gefühl einer über

> Nacht erworbenen Macht anreizte, und ging zur Psychiatrie über, aus Bewunderung für die Großartigkeit der Irren, die er sich seinem Freund verwandt vorstellte, mit dem festen Vorsatz, von ihnen zu lernen und keinen zu heilen. Von der schönen Literatur hatte er genug. (*DB*, 441)[378]

The narrative appears to be complicit with George(s)' professional principles, as it moves on to describe how George(s) is greeted by those who have left the institution after having been healed from their illnesses:

> Wenn Georges durch die Straßen von Paris ging, kam es vor, daß er einem seiner Geheilten begegnete. Er wurde umarmt und beinahe zu Boden geworfen, als wäre er der Herr eines großen Hundes und kehrte nach langer Abwesenheit heim. Hinter seinen freundschaftlichen Fragen verbarg er eine leise Hoffnung. Er sprach von Wohlergehen, Beruf, Zukunftsplänen und wartete auf kleine Bemerkungen, wie: "Damals war es schöner!" oder "Wie leer und dumm mein Leben jetzt ist!" "Ich wäre wieder krank!" "Warum haben Sie mich gesund gemacht?" "Die Menschen wissen nicht, was für Herrlichkeiten in einem Kopf stecken." "Geistesgesundheit ist eine Art Stumpfsinn." "Man müßte Ihnen das Handwerk legen! Sie haben mir meinen kostbarsten Besitz geraubt." "Ich schätze Sie nur als Freund. Ihr Beruf ist ein Verbrechen an der Menschlichkeit." "Schämen Sie sich, Sie Seelenschuster!" "Geben Sie mir meine Krankeit wieder!" "Ich werde Sie belangen!" "Gesund reimt sich auf zugrund!"
>
> Statt dessen regnete es Komplimente und Einladungen. Die Leute sahen dick, gesund und gewöhnlich aus. (*DB*, 442)[379]

As the last two sentences show, however, the narrative is being facetious about George(s)' idea that those healed from their illnesses might one day regret the loss of imaginative power their illnesses had given them. The reader is, as a result, in the difficult position of not knowing how to respond to George(s)' theories in themselves, or how to respond to George(s).

This difficulty, with respect to George(s) as a person and George(s) as a psychiatrist, is compounded when we learn more of the way he conducts himself on a day-to-day basis in the institution:

> Dreimal täglich, bei seinen Rundgängen durch die Säle, wurden ihm Ovationen dargebracht. Er hatte sich daran gewöhnt; je

> heftiger man ihm entgegenlief, je stürmischer man ihn bedrängte, um so sicherer fielen ihm Worte und Mienen ein, wie er sie brauchte. Die Kranken waren sein Publikum. Schon vor dem ersten Pavillon hörte er auf das vertraute Stimmengewirr. Kaum hatte ihn einer durchs Fenster erblickt, als Richtung und Ordnung in den Lärm kam. Auf diesen Umschlag wartete er. Es war, als fingen alle plötzlich zu klatschen an. Unwillkürlich lächelte er. Zahllose Rollen waren ihm in Fleisch und Blut übergangen. Sein Geist hungerte nach den Verwandlungen des Augenblicks. Ein gutes Dutzend Assistenten folgte ihm, um zu lernen. Manche waren älter, die meisten länger als er bei dem Beruf. Sie betrachteten die Psychiatrie als ein Spezialgebiet der Medizin, sich selbst als Verwaltungsbeamte für Irre. Was in ihr Fach einschlug, hatten sie sich mit Fleiß und Hoffnung angeeignet. Sie gingen mitunter mal auch auf die verrückten Behauptungen der Kranken ein, wie es die Lehrbücher, aus denen sie ihre Wissenschaft bezogen, empfahlen. Vom ersten bis zum letzten haßten sie den jungen Direktor, der ihnen täglich einschärfte, daß sie die Diener und nicht die Nutznießer der Kranken seien. (*DB*, 443)[380]

So on the one hand, the passage emphasizes the challenge felt by George(s) of acting out parts to his patients. He depends, intellectually, on this challenge, to sustain himself. His patients are also chronically dependent on him, as if he were a kind of savior. So are his students. But whereas the patients depend on him in sympathy, the students are hostile to his theory that they are there to serve the patients, not to use them. A point-of-view account of what it might be like to be a recipient of the treatment meted out to patients by George(s) is absent. This makes it difficult for the reader to assess the theory objectively. Given the absence of such proof, the reader is left in the awkward position of seeing the theories exclusively in George(s)' subjective terms.

Thereafter, the narrative does introduce us to an individual patient, Jean Préval, a village blacksmith who is deserted by his wife because of the poverty of their life style, brought about by modernization, and who goes in search of his wife, Jeanne. Like Jude the Obscure, he sets fire to his cousin's house, and throttles the four children when he learns that people think that his wife has gone off with another man. In prison, a teacher tells him that his situation is like that of Venus and Mars. Venus is Jeanne, Mars is the man she makes off with, and Jean is the vulcan who makes a net to catch the couple *in flagrante*. Jean is in George(s)' institution and George(s) too applies this formula, teasing Jean to think that he can catch his wife with her new lover. Jean remains "unheilbar." George(s)' trick only wins him the scorn of his students. The narrative does not follow through on his tactics, and once again the reader finds himself/herself exposed, unable to decide whether George(s) is successful as a psychiatrist.

The narrative's scornful characterization of these students as skeptical of George(s) reads as an indictment of the Western stress on formal logic, formal reasoning, and on the view that what drives mankind is the desire for pleasure and/or happiness. The inference is that they are unable to appreciate George(s)' unconventional theories, because they are at the mercy of modes of thinking that do not allow for the "illogical." This turns into another statement, essayistic in content, like the statements concerning life per se that were stimulated by George(s)' understanding of the gorilla, which is not attached to any particular individual in the text. This movement toward the essayistic form is problematic again from the reader's point of view.[381] The issue concerns an alternative to the theory of existence acted out by George(s)' students: "Von der viel tieferen und eigentlichsten Triebkraft der Geschichte, dem Drang des Menschen, in eine höhere Tiergattung, die Masse, aufzugehen und sich darin so vollkommen zu verlieren, als hätte es nie *einen* Menschen gegeben, ahnten sie nichts. Denn sie waren gebildet und Bildung ist ein Festungsgürtel des Individuums gegen die Masse in ihm selbst" (*DB*, 449).[382] This reads as a paean to the abandonment of individuation, which is endorsed as a higher form of existence than the form of existence or the pursuit of pleasure acted out by George(s)' students. The authoritative stance of the narrative here is unmistakeable. What prevents the birth, expression, or release of natural instinct, which can abolish differences between individuals, is the pressure placed on it by education. It represses or keeps suppressed the instinct that will change individuals and society, by abolishing difference altogether. This is presented as an ideal.

It is at this point that the essayistic stance takes over. The issue of the mass, not as a group of individuals acting together in concert but as an instinct within each individual, is set in a context which makes confused allusions to both Darwin and Freud. Incidentally, Canetti mentions, in his essay on the composition of the novel, "Das erste Buch: *Die Blendung*," that he was reading Darwin at the time of writing.[383] In *Die Blendung*, Darwinism seems to be present in the following passage:

> Den sogenannten Lebenskampf führen wir, nicht weniger als um Hunger und Liebe, um die Ertötung der Masse in uns. Unter Umständen wird sie so stark, daß sie den einzelnen zu selbstlosen oder gar gegen sein Interesse laufenden Handlungen zwingt. "Die Menschheit" bestand schon lange, bevor sie begrifflich erfunden und verwässert wurde, als Masse. Sie brodelt, ein ungeheures, wildes, saftstrotzendes und heißes Tier in uns allen, sehr tief, viel tiefer als die Mütter. Sie ist trotz ihres Alters das jüngste Tier, das wesentliche Geschöpf der Erde, ihr Ziel und ihre Zukunft. Wir wissen von ihr nichts; noch leben wir als vermeintliche Individuen. Manchmal kommt die Masse über uns, ein brüllendes Gewitter, ein einziger tosender Ozean, in dem jeder Tropfen lebt und dasselbe will. Noch pflegt sie bald zu zerfallen und wir sind dann wieder wir, arme, einsame Teufel. In der Erinnerung fassen wir es nicht, daß wir je so viel und so groß und so eins waren. "Krankheit," erklärt ein mit Verstand Geschlagener hier, "die Bestie im Menschen," beschwichtigt das Lamm der Demut dort und ahnt nicht, wie nah der Wahrheit es danebenrät. Indessen rüstet sich die Masse in uns zu einem neuen Angriff. Einmal wird sie nicht zerfallen, vielleicht in einem Land erst, und von diesem aus um sich fressen, bis niemand an ihr zweifeln kann, weil es kein Ich, Du, Er mehr gibt, sondern nur noch sie, die Masse. (*DB*, 449–50)[384]

So we move away from the view expressed essayistically earlier, that people resemble clichés and are powerless, to a totally different idea. The above insists that we should be aiming to abolish individuation altogether by abandoning ourselves to the impulse within which destroys our sense of being individuals. Surely this is an inversion of Darwin, since we are not talking about the survival of the fittest, we are not talking about life as a struggle and a competition where the strong "win" and the weak "lose." The view is much more radical, since we are talking about the abandonment of the drive that makes struggle possible in the first place. The individual has no social context—he merely abandons the struggle to be a social animal and surrenders to his own anonymous drives. As such, this is perhaps closer to Freud's idea of instinctual drives (perhaps a facetious rewriting of Freud's *Das Unbehagen in der Kultur*).

It is important to note here, for instance, that the gorilla and George(s)' patients were thought of positively by George(s) because they had reached a pinnacle of inimitable *individuality*, which it was his privilege to appreciate. The above abandons any appreciation of human uniqueness. In its place, we have the revolutionary view, by any standards, that it is possible for the individual to tune into the instinct that has been obscured or suppressed by the legacy of culture or education inspired by its antagonistic opposite, humanity. The framework is very much that of the classic binary opposition nature/culture, with both at war with one another. The messianic tone takes over at the end. The voice of this essayistic piece then assumes, without discussion, an identity with its readership ("wir"), and predicts a future in which instinct will prevail throughout society as a whole.

Without becoming in any way historically specific, George(s) is then credited with the view that the social phenomenon, "Masse," or the reign of instinct within the individual personality, is a phenomenon that has been creatively influential in history and in individual lives, in that it has challenged not intellect itself but certain intellectual views. He then points, however, to those who are the victims of the failure of instinct to challenge intellect successfully and to bring about a new order in the personality. His view is that those whom he deals with, those who are mad, are mad because instinct did not modify itself into something homogenous. It destroyed a potential balance:

> Auf *eine* Entdeckung tat sich Georges etwas zugute, auf eben diese: die Wirksamkeit der Masse in der Geschichte und im Leben des einzelnen; ihr Einfluß auf bestimmte Veränderungen des Geistes. Bei seinen Kranken war es ihm geglückt, sie nachzuweisen. Zahllose Menschen werden verrückt, weil die Masse in ihnen besonders stark ist und keine Befriedigung findet. Nicht anders erklärte er sich selbst und seine Tätigkeit. Früher hatte er persönlichen Neigungen, seinem Ehrgeiz und den Frauen gelebt; jetzt lag ihm nur daran, sich unaufhörlich zu verlieren. In dieser Tätigkeit kam er Wünschen und Sinnen der Masse näher, als die übrigen einzelnen, von denen er umgeben war. (*DB*, 450)[385]

The view that those whom he tends are *victims* of instinct then modulates into self-analysis. George(s) is in the business of dissolving the opposition intellect-instinct, and in the business of converting himself into instinct pure and simple, or advancing the process of deindividuation.

Against a background of growing frustration and boredom with both his patients and wife, George(s) receives a telegram, devised by Fischerle and written in "Wienerisch," which reads, "Bin total meschugge. Dein Bruder" (453). ("I'm totally crazy.

Your brother.") Thereafter, he takes the train to Vienna and meets Therese. Therese's story is that she is Peter Kien's second wife, that Peter murdered his first wife. This has only some intratextual resonance, in as much as Therese was present in the scene where Peter was interviewed by the police and told his story that Therese had devoured herself. That Therese has misunderstood Peter is evident: she is his first wife, after all. It is part of the chain reaction to which we have adapted ourselves. The difference here, however, is significant. Therese's statement is given an *objectivity* in the narrative. It becomes a statement of incontrovertible fact and a piece of truth when, thereafter, it becomes clear that George(s) invests faith in her views and acts on the basis of what they are supposed to mean or represent. This contextualization never took place in the earlier part of the novel, where all statements died as soon as they were born, never to be integrated meaningfully into plot or character, because of the theatrical spirit of fun which animated them. George(s) believes Therese here, however. He believes that his brother is a murderer and thinks about the consequences of this fact in terms of his own reputation:

> Peter ein Mörder. Der stille, magere Peter, den seine Schulkameraden immer verprügelt haben. Die Stiege schwankt. Die Decke stürzt ein. Ein Mensch von peinlicher Sauberkeit, Georg, läßt seinen Hut fallen und hebt ihn nicht auf. Peter verheiratet. Wer wußte davon. Die zweite Frau, über 50 alt, häßlich, beschränkt, gemein, kein menschliches Wort bringt sie hervor, vorgestern einem Überfall entronnen. Die erste hat er zerstückelt. Seine Bücher liebt er und benützt sie als Versteck. Peter und die Wahrheit. Hätte er doch gelogen, seine Jugend blind und blau gelogen! Dazu hat man Georg berufen. Das Telegramm ist fingiert, von der Frau oder von der Polizei. Das Märchen von Peters Geschlechtslosigkeit. Ein schönes Märchen wie alle Märchen, aus der leeren Luft gegriffen, dumm. Georg der Bruder eines Lustmörders. Schlagzeilen in allen Zeitungen. Der größte lebende Sinologe! Der beste Kenner Ostasiens! Doppelleben! Rücktritt von der Leitung einer Irrenanstalt. Fehltritt. Scheidung. Assistenten als Nachfolger. Die Kranken, die Kranken, man wird sie quälen, man wird sie behandeln! Achthundert! Sie lieben ihn, sie brauchen ihn, er darf sie nicht verlassen, ein Rücktritt ist unmöglich. Von allen Seiten zerren sie an ihm, du darfst nicht weg, wir gehen mit, bleib' da, wir sind ganz allein, die verstehen unsere Sprache nicht, du hörst uns, du verstehst uns, du lachst zu uns, seine schönen raren

> Vögel, sie sind da ganz fremd, jeder aus einer anderen Heimat, keiner versteht den Nächsten, sie beschimpfen einander und wissen es nicht einmal, ihretwegen lebt er, er verläßt sie nicht, er *bleibt*. Peters Affäre muß geregelt werden. Sein Unglück ist erträglich. *Er* war für chinesische Schriftzeichen da, Georg für Menschen. Peter gehört in eine geschlossene Anstalt. Er hat zu lange enthaltsam gelebt. Bei der ersten Frau sind seine Sinne mit ihm durchgegangen. Wie hätte er den plötzlichen Übergang meistern sollen? Die Polizei wird ihn herausgeben. Vielleicht gelingt die Überführung nach Paris. Seine Unzurechnungsfähigkeit läßt sich beweisen. Auf keinen Fall tritt Georg von der Leitung seiner Anstalt zurück. (*DB*, 460–61)[386]

So here the chain reaction works in a conventionally *logical* way, in terms of the so-called cardinal truth that we all have a supposed essence of character. George(s) feels professionally threatened, and thus personally threatenend, by what material power the information he has just received might have. The use of the present tense in the above draws attention to this struggle within George(s)' own mind. One of the sentences is particularly revealing. Given that George(s) is supposed to have a capacity to empathize with those who are unusual, his statement, "Peter gehört in eine geschlossene Anstalt," reads as a repressive one, which can be traced back to the unsympathetic view that there simply are some people who deserve to be banished from society altogether. It further diminishes the likelihood that we as readers are going to consent to any of George(s)' idiosyncratic views generally, even when they appear relatively harmless.

When George(s) is reunited with his brother, in "Listenreicher Odysseus," he begins by flattering him in a lengthy monologue that acknowledges Peter's scholarship and achievements. This is countered, aggressively, by Peter, in an ad hominem way. What begins to emerge is the idea that Peter simply hates his brother, on account of his success with women. George(s) maintains he has stopped pursuing women and now believes in the intellect, following the example of his brother. George(s)' tactics of flattering Peter could, at this stage, given the fact we know that George(s) actually hates "Bildung" and "Geist" and that he has long discarded them, be interpreted as proof of his own belief in his professional skills, designed to sustain each individual in his chosen imaginative world. If this is the case, we can judge his skills by their effects. Having flattered Peter into thinking he admires him, Peter replies:

> "Deine Erfolge beruhen auf schamloser Schmeichelei. Jetzt begreife ich den Lärm, den man um dich schlägt. Du bist ein abgefeimter Lügner. Das erste Wort, das du sprechen gelernt hast, war eine Lüge. Aus Vergnügen am Lügen bist du Irrenarzt geworden. Warum nicht Schauspieler? Schäm dich vor deinen Kranken! Bittere Wahrheit ist denen ihr Elend, sie klagen, wenn sie sich keinen Rat mehr wissen. Ich kann mir einen solchen armen Teufel vorstellen, der an Halluzinationen in einer bestimmten Farbe leidet. 'Ich hab' immer Grün vor den Augen', klagt er. Vielleicht weint er. Vielleicht hat er sich schon monatelang mit seinem lächerlichen Grün abgeplagt. Was tust du? Ich weiß, was du tust. Du schmeichelst ihm, du packst ihn bei seinen Achillesfersen, wo hätte er keine, ein Mensch ist aus schwachen Punkten zusammengesetzt, du redest ihn mit 'guter Freund' und 'mein Lieber' an, er wird weich, erst achtet er dich, dann achtet er sich. Er mag der letzte ärmste Teufel auf Gottes Erdboden sein: du überschüttest ihn mit Hochachtung. Kaum kommt er sich als der Mitdirektor deiner Irrenanstalt vor, den nur ein ungerechter Zufall von der alleinigen Leitung ausgeschlossen hat, als du mit deiner wahren Sprache herausrückst. 'Lieber Freund', sagst du ihm, 'die Farbe, die Sie sehen, ist gar nicht grün. Sie ist—sie ist—sagen wir blau!'" Peters Stimme schnappte über. "Hast du ihn damit geheilt? Nein! Seine Frau zu Hause wird ihn genauso quälen wie früher, sie wird ihn quälen bis zu seinem Tode. 'Wenn Leute krank und am Tode sind, dann gleichen sie sehr den Irren', sagt Wang-Chung, ein scharfer Kopf, er lebte im ersten Jahrhundert dieser Zeitrechnung, von 27 bis 98 im China der späteren Han, und wußte mehr von Schlaf, Irrsinn und Tod als ihr mit eurer angeblich exakten Wissenschaft. Heile deinen Kranken von seiner Frau! Solange er sie hat, ist er irrsinnig und am Tode—nach Wang-Chung zwei verwandte Zustände. Entferne die Frau, wenn du kannst! Das kannst du nicht, weil du sie nicht hast. Hättest du sie, du würdest sie für dich behalten, weil du ein Röckejäger bist. Sperr alle Frauen in deine Anstalt, treib mit ihnen was du willst, leb dich aus, stirb verbraucht und verblödet mit vierzig, wenigstens hast du die kranken Männer geheilt und weißt, wofür du Ruhm und Ehren einstreichst!" (*DB*, 472–73)[387]

George(s) has unwittingly unleashed a flow of misogyny in Peter. Individual women are the source of all evil. Peter hates George(s) personally on account of his preoccupation with women.

George(s) rises to the occasion by appearing to endorse Peter's cardinal principle. The narrator indicates, briefly, that George(s) is trying to empathize or flatter:

"Ich glaube," sagte Georg und legte reizendes Mitleid auf, wer hätte es nicht auf sich bezogen, "daß du die Bedeutung der Frauen stark überschätzt. Du nimmst sie zu ernst, du hältst sie für Menschen wie wir. Ich sehe in den Frauen ein nur vorläufig notwendiges Übel. Manche Insekten schon haben es besser als wir. Eine oder einige wenige Mütter bringen den ganzen Stock zur Welt. Die übrigen Tiere sind zurückgebildet. Kann man enger beisammenleben, als die Termiten es gewohnt sind? Welche furchtbare Summe geschlechtlicher Reizungen müßte ein solcher Stock vorstellen—besäßen die Tiere noch ihr Geschlecht! Sie besitzen es nicht, und die dazugehörigen Instinkte nur in geringem Maße. Selbst dieses Wenige fürchten sie. Im Schwarm, bei dem Tausende und Abertausende von Tieren scheinbar sinnlos zugrunde gehen, sehe ich eine Befreiung von der gespeicherten Geschlechtlichkeit des Stockes. Sie opfern einen kleinen Teil ihrer Masse, um den größeren von Liebeswirrungen freizuhalten. Der Stock würde an Liebe, wäre sie einmal erlaubt, zugrunde gehen. Ich weiß keine großartige Vorstellung als die einer Orgie im Termitenstock. Die Tiere vergessen—eine ungeheuerliche Erinnerung hat sie gepackt—was sie sind, blinde Zellen eines fanatischen Ganzen. Jedes will für sich sein, bei hundert oder tausend von ihnen fängt es an, der Wahn greift um sich, *ihr* Wahn, ein Massenwahn, die Soldaten verlassen die Eingänge, der Stock brennt vor unglücklicher Liebe, sie können sich ja nicht paaren, sie haben kein Geschlecht, der Lärm, die Erregung, alles Gewohnte überbietend, lockt ein Ameisengewitter an, durch die unbewachten Tore dringen die Todfeinde ein, welcher Krieger denkt an Verteidigung, jeder will Liebe, der Stock, der vielleicht Ewigkeiten gelebt hätte, die Ewigkeiten, nach denen wir uns sehnen, stirbt, stirbt an Liebe, an dem Trieb, durch den wir, eine Menschheit, unser Weiterleben fristen! Eine plötzliche Verkehrung des Sinnreichsten ins Sinnloseste. Es ist—man kann das mit nichts vergleichen, ja, es ist, als ob du dich eines hellichten Tages, bei gesunden Augen und voller Vernunft, mitsamt deinen Büchern in Brand setzten würdest. Niemand bedroht dich, du hast Geld, soviel du brauchst und willst, deine Arbeiten werden von Tag zu Tag umfassender und eigenartiger, seltene alte Bücher fallen dir in die Hände, du erwirbst wunderbare Manuskripte, keine Frau betritt deine Schwelle, du fühlst dich frei und behütet, durch deine Arbeit, von deinen Büchern—da legst du, ohne Anlaß, in diesem gesegneten und unerschöpflichen Zustand, Feuer an deine Bücher und läßt sie um dich ganz verbrennen. Das wäre ein Geschehen, das entfernt an jenes im Termitenstock heranreichte, ein Hervorbrechen des Sinnlosen, wie dort, nur nicht in so großartigen Maßen. Ob wir das

> Geschlecht einmal überwinden werden, wie die Termiten? Ich glaube an die Wissenschaft, täglich mehr, und täglich weniger an die Unersetzbarkeit der Liebe!"
>
> "Es gibt keine Liebe! Was es nicht gibt, kann weder ersetzbar noch unersetzbar sein. Mit derselben Sicherheit wünschte ich zu sagen: es gibt keine Frauen. Die Termiten gehen uns nichts an. Wer leidet dort an den Frauen? Hic mulier, hic salta! Bleib bei den Menschen! Daß die Spinnenweiber den Männchen ihre Köpfe abbeißen, nachdem sie die Schwächlinge mißbraucht haben, daß nur weibliche Mücken Blut saugen, gehört nicht hierher. Die Drohnenschlacht bei den Bienen ist eine Barbarei. Braucht man die Drohnen nicht, warum züchtet man sie, sind sie von Nutzen, warum schlachtet man sie? In der Spinne, dem grausamsten und häßlichsten aller Tiere, sehe ich die verkörperte Weiblichkeit. Ihr Netz schillert in der Sonne giftig und blau!" (*DB*, 473–75)[388]

George(s)' extended monologue affirms the principle that woman is the source of all evil, that love is an illusion, and that the sexual drive is something that, in an ideal world, could one day be abolished altogether, so that human beings reproduce or have sex not for pleasure, but merely to ensure the continuation of the species, like the termites. Indeed, Dissinger, in his full-length study of the novel, equates the world of the novel with the above image of a large number of termites, where all are subject to "Wahnsinn" and "Massenwahn."[389] He assumes from the above that Peter has become a termite himself by banishing sexuality altogether. Canetti, in the letter that prefaces Dissinger's book, endorses Dissinger's interpretation of the novel in this way. Both are assuming that the negative implications, in human terms, of the above theory are embodied by plot and character. If the novel is as facetious as this study suggests, this interpretation becomes redundant. The function of the above passage is then restricted to the argument that is being made about the change in characters of the novel. It is part of the uneven contest going on between the brothers for supremacy over each other. The ideas themselves do not appear to have any other function, except in these psychological terms. If one does reflect on them as ideas in their own right, their ridiculousness and crudity as a metaphor for human life is self-evident. The ideas are strange, idiosyncratic, and repellent.

Peter does not react analytically to his brother's theories. He extracts an idea that has resonance in his own terms and enthusiastically responds to the status credited the principle of misogyny by George(s). Confucius, the Buddha, and various characters from Greek mythology are cited to support the view that woman is inferior. George(s) interprets this all in a logical way. He attributes it all to a cause, the idea that Therese had sex with Benedikt Pfaff and was discovered *in flagrante* by Peter, who has been in a state of shock ever since: "Als er die beiden ertappte, denkt Georg, schlich sich der Hausbesorger, damals noch bescheiden, verlegen davon und vergaß seine Fäuste, angesichts des reichen Gelehrten. Sie aber setzte, einziger Schutz der Ertappten, eine freche Miene auf, nahm ihre Kleider ins nächste Zimmer mit und zog sich dort an. Jean wo bist du?" (*DB*, 483)[390]

So, once again, the narrative is lapsing into the habit of endorsing what have been mere hypotheses, by allowing individual characters to assume them to be literally true. George(s) thinks Peter has seen Therese and Benedikt Pfaff together, and he thinks this is the reason for Peter's passionate hatred of women. But the narrative itself had not made the connection obvious or central. Although it is said *en passant* that they had sex, this was not a scene in the empirical narrative. George(s)' view is a supposition with little serious intra-textual resonance.

In "Privateigentum," the non-referentiality of described scenes, what Darby called the character-motivated analepsis, had a comic effect largely because no one character was ever able to invest faith in the contents of any one story. One could argue here, however, that the arrangement of the narrative is entirely different. One character expresses one set of views, which are not explicitly countered by the other. Yet the other takes those views at face value. There is also no resolution of what now lies behind words. We had had, in the first two books in the novel, a love of the surface, yet now words have to mean things and have an uneasy kind of depth. In this instance there is an underlying issue somewhere that the novel does not want to face. Both George(s) and Peter work with mutually exclusive theories as to why the other is behaving as he is: Peter thinks George(s) is just patronizing him as he patronizes his patients, George(s) thinks that Peter is in need of a cure because he has been so upset by his wife's adultery. There is no mutual understanding, just privately held suppositions. The reader is more inclined to side with Peter, on the grounds that George(s) is positively unattractive, and on the grounds that he is indifferently patronizing. Further, George(s)' view that his brother's wife has committed adultery and that Peter is suffering as a result, is, in the narrative's terms, a connection that has not been given any serious weight, which makes it difficult for us to enter into his strategy with respect to his brother.

This substantial problem is compounded by the way in which material is presented. Whereas the relationship between the diegetic material and the mimetic material in the first two books guaranteed the chain reaction that was the dance, we now have a narrative in which there is very little diegetic material. In its place we have a narrative that, at this stage, now appears almost to deconstruct itself, at the expense of both individuals in question. After all, what is noticeable in all of the above kind of passages, is the almost-complete absence of the narrator, a point made earlier when it was stated that the narrative begins to collapse itself in this last section. Whereas in earlier sections of the novel, the narrator had imitated the "voice" of the voices in actual dialogue, the narrator has now withdrawn, to all intents and purposes, leaving the theory of misogyny very well exposed for what it is, useless, hopeless, meaningless, yet instated nonetheless as an institutionalized and readily recognizable Big Idea.

George(s) continues to apply his theory of empathy, teasing Peter to express what it is George(s) assumes he really feels. He teases him, encouraging him to reach an intensity of hatred that is frightening:

> "Ja, und genauso ein Wunder wie der Leibesaufruhr im Termitenstock, und der Brand meiner Bibliothek, der unmöglich ist, ganz ausgeschlossen, undenkbar, ein heller Wahnsinn, eine Verräterei ohnegleichen an Kostbarkeiten, wie sie sont nirgends beisammen sind, pure Gemeinheit und eine Schmutzerei, wie du sie vor mir nicht einmal zum Scherz aussprechen, geschweige denn annehmen dürftest, du siehst doch, daß ich nicht verrückt bin, ich bin nicht einmal verstört, ich hab' viel mitgemacht, Aufregung ist keine Schande, warum verhöhnst du mich, mein Gedächtnis ist intakt, ich weiß alles, was ich will, ich hab' mich in der Gewalt, warum, weil ich einmal geheiratet habe, ich habe keine einzige Liebschaft hinter mir, was hast du schon für Liebe getrieben, Liebe ist ein Aussatz, eine Krankheit, von den Einzellern an weitervererbt, andere heiraten zwei- und dreimal, ich hatte nichts mit ihr zu tun, du beleidigst mich, das hättest du nicht sagen dürfen, Wahnsinnige tun das vielleicht, *ich* zünde meine Bibliothek nicht an, pack' dich, wenn du darauf bestehst, fahr' in deine Idiotenanstalt zurück, wo hast du deinen Kopf, auf alles, was ich

> sage, antwortest du mit Ja und Amen! Ich hab' noch keinen eigenen Gedanken von dir gehört, du Schwätzer, du glaubst, du weißt alles! Ich rieche deine höhnischen Gedanken. Sie stinken. Er ist verrückt, denkst du, weil er auf die Frauen schimpft. Ich bin nicht der Einzige! Das werde ich dir beweisen! Nimm deine schmutzigen Gedanken zurück! Von mir hast du lesen gelernt, du Lausbub. Du kannst ja nicht einmal chinesisch. Ich lasse mich eben nachträglich scheiden. Ich muß meine Ehre rehabilitieren. Die Frau ist zu einer Scheidung nicht notwendig. Sie soll sich im Grab umdrehn. Sie steckt ja gar nicht im Grab. Nicht einmal ein Grab verdient sie. Die Hölle verdient sie! Warum gibt es keine Hölle? Man muß eine einrichten. Für Weiber und Röckejäger, wie du einer bist. Ich sage die Wahrheit! Ich bin ein ernster Mensch. Du wirst jetzt wegfahren und dich nicht um mich kümmern. Ich bin ganz allein. Ich habe meinen Kopf. Ich kann für mich selbst sorgen. (*DB*, 487–88)[391]

In the above, Peter's anxiety is real. For the first time in the novel, there is intellectual and emotional *intensity* of delivery which is taken seriously in a weak sense (it is left stranded). Further, it is not undercut in a savagely witty way—that characteristic facetious gesture so common in the first two books. What George(s) deduces from the above is that Therese must be removed without trace; that Peter's affairs should be put back in order; that he should be calmed down, so that an ordinary life may be resumed. George(s)' main assumption is that Therese is the cause of Peter's hatred. His concern for Peter appears altruistic. When he takes Peter out to dinner, he appears to endorse the view that there is nothing wrong with murdering women. He makes an eloquent plea that murder be legalized. In other words, his tactics are still those of the flatterer. He goes on to visit both Therese and Benedikt Pfaff with a view to paying them both off, where we see the skills of flattery in operation again:

> Er sprach mit Leidenschaft. Jedes Wort hatte die berechnete Wirkung. Sie verfärbte sich. Nach manchen Sätzen wartete er. So viel Schmierenpathos hatt er noch nie gewagt. Sie sagte nichts. Er begriff, daß er es war, der sie mit Stummheit schlug. Er sprach ihr so schön. Sie fürchtete, sie könnte ein Wort verlieren. Die Augen traten ihr aus den Höhlen, erst vor Angst, dann vor Liebe. Die Ohren hatte sie, keine Hündin, doch gespitzt. Aus ihrem Mund floß Speichel. Der Stuhl, auf dem sie saß, knarrte glücklich einen Gassenhauer. Die Hände hielt sie, zu einem Becher geschlossen, ihm entgegen. Sie trank mit

> Lippen und Händen. Als er diese küßte, verlor der Becher seine Form und ihre Lippen hauchten, er hörte es: bitte noch. Da überwand er seinen Ekel und küßte die Hände wieder. Sie zitterte; bis in die Haare pflanzte sich ihre Erregung fort. Hätte er sie umarmt, sie wäre in Ohnmacht gefallen. (*DB*, 497)[392]

George(s)' knowing flattery of a woman he assumes to be sexually aroused by his attentions further lowers the tone of the closing sections of the novel. He then manages to reach a material settlement with Benedikt Pfaff and Therese:

> Die Frau bedang sich aus, nicht geschlagen und nicht gezwickt zu werden, außerdem dürfe sie die Besuche des Herrn Bruders empfangen, wann der wolle. Pfaff willigte geschmeichelt ein. Gegen das Zwickverbot hatte er Bedenken. Er sei auch nur ein Mensch. Außer der Liebe, zu der sie sich verpflichteten, hatten sie einander zu überwachen. Verirrte sich der eine Teil in die Nähe der Ehrlichstraße, so meldete es der andere sofort nach Paris. Geschäft und Freiheit gingen dann unbarmehrzig verloren. Auf die erste Nachricht erfolgte telegraphisch ein Haftbefehl. Der Angeber habe Anspruch auf Belohnung. Pfaff schiß auf die Ehrlichstraße, wenn er unter lauter Kanarienvögeln wohne. Therese beschwerte sich: bitte, er scheißt schon wieder. Er soll nicht immer scheißen. Georg redete ihm zu, sich auszudrücken, wie es einem besseren Geschäftsmann gezieme. (*DB*, 498–99)[393]

David Darby's theory about George(s) Kien is that he is yet another example of the novel's capacity to turn everything into an open issue. Just as "Privateigentum" was a fiction of detection because it made a mockery of detection, George(s) Kien is a fiction of deliverance.[394] He appears to offer us the possibility of a meaningful resolution to the problem raised by the novel, but turns out not to be a deus ex machina. I would agree with this. George(s) Kien goes off back to Paris and leaves his brother, having made a deal with Benedikt Pfaff and Therese. He believes that he has solved what he has felt to be Peter's dilemma. That Peter then goes on to commit suicide in a frightening scene effectively shows up the weakness of Georg(e)s' hypotheses about schizophrenics or psychologically disturbed people. His tactics, aimed at seducing the subject into believing that he empathizes with his feeling about the world, if they are to be measured by the real effects they have on Jean Préval and Peter, his only two patients, are nothing more, on reflection, than near-totalitarian experiments in endorsing the law of repression, ruthless in their absolute non-interest in the long-term welfare of patients, who have really become victims.

It seems, therefore, that Lovett is absolutely wrong to assume that George(s)' fascination with the schizophrenic gorilla is unproblematic. Deleuze and Guattari, in *Capitalisme et Schizophrénie: L'Anti-Oedipe* and *Capitalisme et Schizophrénie: Mille Plateaux*, together with Lacan and Foucault have all talked excitedly about people as machines of desire, and yes, the gorilla is an embodiment of an alternative mode of existence that might be liberating in the emphasis placed on the expression of passion. Needless to say, the awkwardness of the portrait has to be taken into consideration. But Lovett's view puts a gloss on what George(s) is doing to those who are not already embodiments of pure desire, like the schizophrenic gorilla man. George(s) is guilty of precisely what Deleuze and Guattari maintained was the establishment's capacity to keep human beings in a state of fear, a pressure the establishment is able to exert through authority, such as that exercised by the state and the church. In an era of capitalism, when the wellsprings of desire are supposedly dammed up by the stress placed on competition and the struggle for survival, the psychiatrist has a particularly powerful role to play. S/he becomes necessary. S/he finds herself/himself called on to account for the experience of failure in individual lives, which Deleuze and Guattari trace back to capitalism. But the myths or theories which s/he propagates, rather than liberating the individual in any meaningful way, are themselves means of furthering the power of the establishment. Myths such as the Oedipus myth encourage patients to believe that the causes for suffering in the present lie in the past. They are the way of continuing the curse, not a practical way of liberating people from the curse.

George(s) is surely an example of precisely this kind of false subversive. For all his theories, he fails in practice. Neither Jean nor Peter Kien finds new ways of integrating the chaos within; they do not synthesize the disparate impulses of their personality into some kind of fluent desire. Indeed, George(s) does not seem seriously interested in liberating either. Yet he does regard himself as seriously concerned with sustaining both in their imaginative worlds. Lovett deflects attention away from a serious assessment of George(s) the man by making an appealing distinction between the gorilla as an idyllic portrait of a schizophrenic and Peter as a truly mad psychotic, suffering from paranoia. For her, Peter Kien always was a pure embodiment of the crisis of the epistemological and psychological subject who has been deluded into a belief in the power of consciousness and in the power of the mind to construct a fixed vision of the world. She, like many, sees the eruption of hatred and suicide at the end of the novel in terms of the cost to the individual of sustaining what she sees as the totalitarian model of the mind. She, along with J. M.Ritchie and David Roberts, sees the burning of the books in the fire in the library in historical terms, in terms of 10th May 1933, as already indicated. All maintain that the model provided by Kien is the model for fascism: his is a portrait of the so-called "totalitarian personality." In this, their theories are consistent with those expressed by psychologists of fascism like Fromm and Bettelheim and by philosophers of the Frankfurter Schule like Horkheimer and Adorno.

It is possible to query these extravagant claims because such interpretations have to fly in the face of what sustains the majority of *Die Blendung*, namely facetiousness of a particularly compelling variety, rich in ideological implication of a kind not even dreamed of by the likes of Lovett, Roberts, Horkheimer, and Adorno. Their claims are not convincing, simply because they depend on taking *Die Blendung* at face value. The monologues by Peter and George(s) analyzed above contain ideas, which whilst repellent in their own right, are certainly relativized by the spirit of facetiousness which sustained Parts One and Two of the novel. Ruth Kennedy has argued that if readers really took them seriously, they would be compelled to question the very basis of their own lives, and criticism does not suggest that this is the effect the conversations have generated.[395] On the contrary, critics have talked about the theories as if they were mere intellectual constructs about which one can argue intellectually without feeling personally undermined.

We have maintained that the ludic premises underlying Parts One and Two are inverted quite nicely at the beginning of "Der gute Vater" and thereafter. I would not want to stress the moment of Kien's suicide, one in which he yells out with a frantic laugh, on the grounds that it does not lend itself to the kind of symbolic interpretation attempted by Canetti and followers like W. E. Stewart and Dissinger. These critics maintain that Kien reaches a unity within himself or with his books. Such interpretations of the suicide are clearly ventured within the framework of the theory that literature is mimetic. Yet this is not the theory that sustains the vast majority of *Die Blendung*. Even when, from "Der gute Vater" onward, we seem closer to a theory of imitation or representation of an already-known extra-textual reality, this rarely has referential status except in the sense that in normative terms it would be the kind of world one would wish to avoid. The form of the Big Ideas raised, and their contextualization within the narrative, is such as to undermine, rather weakly, any confidence a reader might have in the wish to match these up with his/her own experience.

But more importantly, the narrative from "Der gute Vater" onward throws out the Nietzschean view that life is an aesthetic phenomenon which has to be created by will power, by wit, by each individual's aesthetic sense, the sense that revels in love and respect for others, that believes that it is imagination that keeps the world alive and going. Not only does it throw it out in terms of the new relationship it develops between diegetic and mimetic material and between character and motive. It does it by constructing Big Ideas, which it can then only partially deconstruct, leaving us with an unpleasant aftertaste; a cynical doubt concerning the value of such primitive energies as instinct; a sense that we are no longer as free, individual, unique, and different as the narrative with which we collaborated earlier on for the purposes of producing and experiencing pleasure. We become passive spectators, obliged to make something of "material" that then refuses to synthesize itself. That material is riddled with misogyny, obsequiousness, fear, panic, and hatred, that knows nothing any more about the spirit of love and its power.

Conclusion. Finished and Unfinished Business: The Place of the Novel in the Works as a Whole

In a speech made in Munich in 1976, entitled "Der Beruf des Dichters," Canetti stressed that the modern writer has a responsibility to the larger community in terms of his profession. He is, as "Dichter" (a word virtually impossible to translate into English), "der Hüter der Verwandlungen." This means that Canetti sees himself both as an heir to the riches of literatures, and a new creator in the tradition of literature. The task has a moral dimension to it, in that Canetti is a guardian of his inheritance of "Weltliteratur." The task takes on another dimension, Canetti implies, in the late twentieth century, given the increasing tendency toward specialization evident in the community as a whole. This tendency Canetti has always talked about with great contempt, regularly classifying Aristotle in his notebooks as an enemy, because of his apparently boring desire to compartmentalize everything. The "real" thinker, by contrast, has the capacity to be flexible, to feel free to use his inheritance and to develop his inheritance, by imagining and inventing. This is something Canetti insists on as a duty, and it is the duty of each professional thinker and writer. The wider purpose of this task becomes clear later when Canetti suggests the possibility of creating a more humane civilization. "Sie sollten, dank einer Gabe, die eine allgemeine war, die jetzt zur Atrophie verurteilt ist, die sie sich aber mit allen Mitteln erhalten müßten, die Zugänge *zwischen* den Menschen offenhalten" (*GW*, 286).[396]

The value of literature, then, has to do with its impact on the very way in which we live with one another in the community, in particular whether we are open to one another. This develops into a further statement about the general value of being receptive to the world. This project is then contextualized, in what reads as an account of the state of the world in 1976.

The world is in a state of irreparable decline, because of the tendency to specialization, the tendency to atrophy, which has compromised a magical gift for transforming the community into a more human community, and, finally, the threat to the work of the intellectual and thinker/writer posed by mass illiteracy at large. Canetti claims that the majority's reliance on a kind of language that is not real language is worrying, for language has been debased and is, in the majority's hands, a mere composite of clichés taken from the newspapers. It seems here as if Canetti is merely restating the claim made by Karl Kraus more than fifty years earlier in *Die letzten Tage der Menschheit* (1920–1921).

Canetti's argument contains something of a negative prognosis, since it insists on the idea that society is in a state of decline. The central claim is that the poet's responsibility to the community is being made difficult by the illiterate or semiliterate members of that community. Canetti refuses specificity of any kind, and soon neutralizes the problem that he has just raised, a social problem, to draw our attention to the inner world of individual thinkers. This inner world is characterized by the existence of chaos: the thinker has internalized the general chaos of the world out there, and this is the real material with which he has to cope (*GW*, 288). As such, Canetti assumes that there is a war going on within the mind and body of the individual writer. The writer/thinker develops a relationship with the chaos within, not with the wider community. He is consumed by the necessity of defying chaos by insisting on its inverse, hope. As the essay goes on, it becomes abundantly clear that the battle being fought out within the mind and body of the individual writer has become an end in itself. Gone is the idea of the writer as an individual within the community, with a possible responsibility to that community. Indeed, in the last two paragraphs of the essay, Canetti seems to embrace the idea of the writer as a law unto his own, unaccountable to the rest of society, someone uniquely positioned to start a witch hunt aimed at flushing the literary scene clean of those thinkers whose project is dedicated to death or nihilism, not life. Canetti is this self-appointed juror and murderer, as he is also the shepherd capable of guiding lost souls back to the path from which they have strayed (*GW*, 290). What started out as a concern for society became an acknowledgment of the trial of being a writer, then a statement both of Canetti's vision of himself as Big Brother, arbiter of all values, someone preoccupied with the credentials of other members of a small élite of writers.

"Der Beruf des Dichters" reveals a dimension to Canetti's work, project, and thinking that was not present in any of the first two sections of *Die Blendung*, and that only vaguely enters into the material in the final section of the novel. The essay accepts that the shadow of the apocalypse has already been cast over the world. If we relate the preoccupation with the writer to the opening statements about the state of society, the sense of doom is justified only because Canetti assures that the world is committed to non-aesthetic and non-intellectual values. However, we should be alert to the way in which this two-tier system is divisive. On the one hand, Canetti casts the intellectual/writer/thinker as pure, because he is dedicated to literature, because he is highly educated. On the other hand, the masses out there are cast as impure, because they are not highly educated, not sensitive to the literary aspects of language, and likely to take the mass media more seriously than literature. It is implied that this amorphous mass of anonymous people is likely to be leading less human lives as a result of their aesthetic and intellectual deficiencies.

These principles are turned into veritable laws of existence in Canetti's three plays, *Hochzeit*, *Komödie der Eitelkeit*, and *Die Befristeten*, all of which have no pretentions to intellectual complexity, in the sense that psychology worthy of the name does not get taken seriously. Instead, characters are figures, and all figures in all the plays are equally straightforward. They are not intellectuals; they are not dedicated to the pursuit of aesthetic values. It is part of the achievement that, despite this, the three plays are compelling. Certainly not compelling drama or melodrama, since there is no suspense and very little plot to speak of. But compelling in their ruthless unsentimentality, a feature of *Die Blendung*. The mixture of "hochdeutsch" and "wienerisch" is a compelling linguistic achievement in its own right. This, combined with the dazzling way in which figures are ignorant of themselves and of each other, and of the nature and quality of the purely material goals they set themselves, is productive in ways reminiscent of *Die Blendung*. The plays induce a state of tension in the audience, a sense of having to be open to the world, of being able to look out at the world with unflinching, muscular strength, which is intellectual in origin. Canetti achieves this without demolishing figures on stage, and this is both the artistry and the intellectual beauty of the project. In all of the plays Canetti expresses his love of pure theatricality as an end in itself. Yet this is without the momentum of the theatricality of *Die Blendung*, since our responses to what is going on on stage are conditioned in advance by the feeling we have from the very beginning that figures are intellectually and imaginatively predictable. A special case can be made for *Die Befristeten*, which is a more serious investigation of the state of fear, what it is like to live in a state of fear. In it there is evidence of Canetti's obsession with death, where death is something very obvious, the knowledge that we all have that we are mortal. On balance, in spite of the fact the capsules contain the proof of when it is I die, the play is more interesting as a study of fear. Its mood is more somber than that of either *Hochzeit* or *Komödie der Eitelkeit*. In all three, finally, is a complete absence of any sign from a better, happier, more sophisticated kind of world. This is the wholehearted commitment to the idea of the world as paralyzed. The sense of paralysis is merely neutralized by the inflated theatricality of the plays.[397]

Between 1942 and 1960, Canetti published his first *Aufzeichnungen*. These accompanied him as he researched and wrote *Masse und Macht*, itself published in 1960, the project that had preoccupied him ever since *Die Blendung*. Reading the notebooks makes it possible to talk of Canetti's affiliation to the Western idea of the status of the author as authority, as "philosopher king" within the community, to whom reverence is due, as it were, because of this exalted position. At first sight, too, Canetti also makes a much more personal appearance in the *Aufzeichnungen* and in *Masse und Macht* than was the case either in the three plays or in *Die Blendung*. He expresses his own personal ideas, which are often very idiosyncratic, and he expresses these very directly.

One of the central points about *Die Blendung* has been that the first two sections destroyed the idea of the author altogether. They were written in such a way as to imply that the novel worshipped and practised certain skills to do with inventiveness and originality and a sense, above all, of play. The novel worshipped players, not named individuals. There was, in the appeal to our playful skills made by the novel, the democratic assumption that we all are players, patent if not latent ones. The text did not make any serious investment in ideas, still less authors of ideas. Both the *Aufzeichnungen* generally, and *Masse und Macht* in a more intense way, imply that Canetti believes not only in the institution of the author, but in the author as someone uniqely positioned to pronounce authoritatively on nothing less than the contributions made to culture by the whole world. Canetti freely ranges in *Masse und Macht* between cultures, countries, religions, and races in what appears, at first sight, to be a work that resists categorization altogether. It would be useful to remember at this point that whilst *Masse und Macht* is undoubtedly Canetti's "baggy monster," Canetti is convinced it is his most significant work. He is its staunch and stubborn defender, protective of its assumed genius. In spite of the sheer volume of material used, he assures us in 1973, in an entry in the notebooks on the writing of *Masse und Macht*: "ich aber ruderte steuerlos in meinem Meer und ließ mich nicht beirren."[398] He has also protested on a number of occasions that in *Masse und Macht* he wanted to do justice to something as massive as the twentieth century as a whole, as he says in a letter.[399]

Canetti has also written a very robust defense of his notebooks in the foreword to *Die Provinz des Menschen*. They were embarked upon, he argues, to provide some relief whilst working on the all-consuming project of *Masse und Macht*, and their value was purely subjective. They were a form of salvation, a way of preventing mental paralysis, and served no purpose, since they were not embellished later. Canetti parades his irresponsibility with respect to his material. He does not need to feel any responsibility to that material because it is subordinate to their real purpose, which is to provide Canetti with subjective relief, a form of salvation whilst a more intellectually prestigious project proceeded apace.[400]

It is not possible here to do more than merely indicate the range of material that forms the substance of the *Aufzeichnungen*. The notebooks are, above all, dominated by intellectual conversations with the self, and the reflections tend mostly toward a worshipping of single, solitary intellectual giants, most of them male. These come either from Ancient Chinese philosophy, like Confucius, and Ancient Greek philosophy—Heraclitus, Democritus, Aristotle, and Plato—and go up to modern philosophy—Hobbes and Nietzsche in particular—but only as far as Wittgenstein. The interest in literature takes the same form of adulation of writers like Aristophanes, Quevedo, Montaigne, Joubert, Lichtenberg, Swift, Stendhal, Büchner, Kafka, Kraus, Broch, Musil, and Robert Walser. But yet again there is no interest in literature, as there was no interest in philosophy, after about 1930. Alternatively, Canetti insists, with equal passion, that he *hates* philosophers like De Maistre and Nietzsche—analytical reasons for the hatred are not really given. All these observations are linked, in the sense that they have something to say about Canetti's own observations on his own writings. They have a relative function, therefore, in terms of the light they help or helped shed on his own, subjective preoccupations. The other areas covered by the notebooks are themselves miscellaneous, as they are covered in a miscellaneous kind of way. There are very occasional references to present-day realities, to the war, the atom bomb, the conquest of space, the arms race, the possibility of a third world war. There is absolutely no interest in current affairs, except in the examples just mentioned. These arguably say more about Canetti's attraction to eschatology than anything else. There is a general hostility to established religions, which get very dismissive and reductive treatment at the hands of Canetti's theories about death and the crowd. There is no respect for, nor appreciation of, religious feeling. There are miscellaneous thoughts on his favourite hobby-horses, death, power, and survival, as there are aphorisms, which one critic has aptly called his "phantastic" aphorisms, many of which are thoroughly abstract and often impenetrable.[401] Finally, if rather insignificantly, there are a very few indications that Canetti has some kind of life apart from his intellectual life: there are occasional references to love and goodness.[402]

In the notebooks a self-appointed intellectual ranges subjectively through material of his own choosing, and in a context that makes a virtue of the refusal to incorporate that material into any kind of system. This has not been commented on in terms of its methodology, either by those who have written about the notebooks or those who have written about *Masse und Macht*. Stendhal had preached the vileness of system building, but this was justified in terms of the love of pragmatic detail, of the concrete fact. We have already quoted what appears to be a statement written in the spirit of Stendhal's refusal of system building, namely the sentence with which Canetti opens the essay "Macht und Überleben": "Zu den unheimlichsten Phänomenen menschlicher Geistesgeschiche gehört das Ausweichen vor dem Konkreten." The point here is to suggest that Canetti does not live up to this duty, either in the *Aufzeichnungen* or in *Masse und Macht*. This is all the more surprising, given his published opinions on the responsibility of the writer to the community, and to the published pretension cited above, about his conviction that in *Masse und Macht* he had summed up the spirit of the century as a whole. Indeed, it is interesting, in this general context, that, on the day after the manuscript of *Masse und Macht* was sent to the publisher in 1959, the entry in his notebooks is a triumphant statement that this project has been achieved: "Jetzt sage ich mir, daß es mir gelungen ist, dieses Jahrhundert an der Gurgel zu packen."[403]

Yet whilst it is immediately obvious that there is no system-building in *Masse und Macht*, it is *not* immediately obvious that Canetti positively avoids the concrete in *Masse und Macht*. We can say this, not because, in a prescriptive way, Canetti should be building systems, or that there should be either a single or a number of underlying theses systematically developed and implicit in all his observations. We can say this because his self-appointed right to range freely without constraint through time and place is a right that arguably doubles up as a *failure* to do justice to time and place. This is most obvious in the *Aufzeichnungen*, where Canetti deals with his favourite hobby-horses. Rarely is the phenomenon of power, of death, or of survival linked up with an example. This has the effect of making one feel that death, power, and survival have taken on, as mere abstract ideas, a life of their own. Canetti's obsessions, properly speaking, highlight nothing, apart from his personal conviction that death, power, and survival are anonymous facts about the human condition. Death, power, and survival are reified ideas, invested with the apparent dignity of absolute truth. They are not dynamic energies that cause or achieve anything in time or place, neither are they part of a wider project of life, still less are they used in good faith by named individuals, and even less do they actually have an effect upon named individuals. Indeed, death, power, and survival are not susceptible to form, let alone myriad forms, since there is no acknowledgment of the myriad forms death, power, and survival might take in practice.

The above thematic concerns are presented in a timeless way, which is to say in the form of autonomous units, either as single sentences or as reflections composed of a couple of sentences. Some are also aphorisms, properly speaking, because of their opaqueness and the sense that their meaning is rich, if elusive. In writing like this, in choosing and then relying so heavily on the single sentence, Canetti's very form elevates the assumption on which the "ideas" of the notebooks are based, namely the assumption that the rights of the subjective imagination to range freely within a timeless, ahistorical imaginative space, take precedence over any rights or claims his objective sources, whether these were historical or anthropological (one does not know), might have themselves. The idea of responsibility to objective truth is nowhere present.

The case of *Masse und Macht* is slightly different here. Canetti's bibliography indicates precisely on what objective material the project was based, and Canetti has obviously read very widely. The adventure into theory sees Canetti, as in the *Aufzeichnungen*, range freely through world history. This time, however, Canetti appears to be in a state of veritable dazzlement and extremely naive amazement at the existence of "Masse" and "Macht." His material is lifted, however, from different cultures and different countries, and transformed by Canetti himself as he sees fit and as befits his preordained purpose, which is to tell a story about the mere existence of crowds and power. No constraints are placed on Canetti's freedom to roam freely, and this is most obvious in the way in which his material is not placed in any kind of chronological order. It is also obvious in the way the material refuses to make clear distinctions between cultures. Yet presentation of material in this way is never justified formally. Canetti refuses to justify his non-recognition of historical, ethnic, religious, racial, or cultural boundaries.

These formal problems apart, it is obvious, after a while, that Canetti makes his material tell a relatively monotonous story about the mere existence of the phenomeneon of "Masse" and "Macht" in world history. In so doing, Canetti commits the crime of failing *to distinguish between* the relative function of rituals within geographically and historically specific cultures. He is not a critic in this respect, still less is he a responsible critic, in the sense he mentioned in the essay mentioned above, "Der Beruf des Dichters." There is actually no respect for the way in which community manifests itself in different cultures. One cannot use anthropological material from non-Western cultures, for instance, without acknowledging the different cultural status of rituals within different cultures. This is true of the comments on the bushmen of Australia, as it is true of his comments on African tribes. To do so is to trivialize. Canetti becomes imperialist and colonial in the way he exploits exotic cultures, and he does so not to develop his own theory but to tell his own *story* about the existence of "Masse" and "Macht" in world history.

When he becomes specific about his own Western culture, in the case of Schreber, for instance, his case study does nothing apart from illuminate the rather obvious psychological truth that there have been paranoid leaders in world history. This investigation into the private life of the public man also does nothing to undermine the status of the public leader as such. On the contrary, the idea that certain men are invested with authority to provide leadership by the culture in which they happen to exist is left untouched; it is not even questioned. This is also true of the way in which Canetti copes with Hitler in the essay, "Hitler, nach Speer," published in *Das Gewissen der Worte*, where Canetti only dwells on the way in which Hitler set out to build an empire to rival Napoleon's, and on how he used architecture for this purpose.[404] One cannot disagree with his view that the architectural projects designed by Speer were about Hitler's grandiose attempt to identify himself with status symbols. One might wish to ask why it is that in Canetti's account of Hitler, Hitler is not the author of any named crimes against humanity. Given the claim that Canetti is not reluctant to publicize, namely his desire to characterize the twentieth century, it is interesting here that he is capable of erasing from discussion so much European history that warrants comment on its own terms. Instead, Hitler merely emerges as a man capable of wielding power, a man who was successful in his manipulation of power. It is worthwhile asking why critics have not really taken Canetti to task for his extreme relativization and trivialization of the Hitler phenomenon. The tide is beginning to turn, to judge by some of the contributions made in a recently published Hanser critical volume on *Masse* and *Macht*.[405]

One could thus argue that the refusal to situate Hitler in terms of the community, and the refusal to situate Schreber in terms of the community, together with Canetti's positive desire to see both as isolated individuals, reads as a fairly gross and callous act. This allows Canetti to parade his admiration for public figures with status and power irrespective of how those individuals use that power, how it is executed, and to what ends and purposes, and with what effect. It is also very compromising of the promise inherent in the desire to characterize the twentieth century, because *his comments offer no point of entry* into our own, contemporary problems of power and its use and abuse. Canetti's attitude to history is that it is dead, and irrelevant to his present in 1960 and our present whenever we read *Masse und*

Macht. The comments on Hitler, on Schreber, or on the rituals described by Canetti do not provide a basis for *a critique of contemporary life.* Presentation insulates Canetti's reader from the presumably tiresome business of having to accept that the dynamics of life and death continued after the demise of Hitler, after the demise of Schreber and so on. So it is not just that Hitler is treated, in fact, as if he were insulated from community, but from history altogether. Canetti does not seem to think his readers live within a community, still less within history, which is why it seems appropriate to criticize him for not having fulfilled the promise raised by the essay "Der Beruf des Dichters" about the whole notion of responsibility.

The point about *Masse und Macht* is that its apparent freedom from systems is also problematic in more and rather devious ways. The project of *Masse und Macht* as a whole endorses a two-tier system. There are either single, solitary male leaders who have power or there are large numbers of undifferentiated individuals who are only significant when they form an anonymous and amorophous unit, "die Masse." In *Masse und Macht* crowds are for the most part kept separate from leaders with power, treated as if the dynamics of interaction in terms of motivation or legitimation were irrelevant, as if time always stood still.

The vast number of critics who have written on *Masse und Macht* are trained in literary criticism and are, arguably, not best positioned to comment on the achievement.[406] Only one contemporary political scientist seems to have taken Canetti's project seriously, and his view is that Canetti is original in terms of crowd theory, by writing the demagogues out of crowd theory and by denying that they do in fact command the crowd. Apparently a crowd without a demagogue is either a contradiction in terms or nothing in crowd theory before Canetti.[407] Yet to assume that crowds do not have or do not need leaders is to fly in the face of some of the most obvious facts about Western twentieth-century history above all. It is very telling, in this respect, that *Masse und Macht*, despite its appearance fifteen years after the suicide of Hitler, does not even want to investigate recent European history, Hitler's formidable exploitation of crowds as a way of gaining power and holding on to it in particular. This exclusion has not been taken very seriously, but it probably says the whole truth about Canetti's non-interest in power as a reality in the contemporary world, as his non-interest in the dynamics of power as these are experienced by its victims. This exclusion, in a work that tells the story of the existence of two separate phenomena, is a failure to provide a critique of power structures as they enter our daily life. *Masse und Macht* is, then, a narrative, with few pretensions to analysis that stand up to scrutiny. Compared to Foucault, for instance, Canetti seems to have no knowledge or experience or appreciation of how power creates victims, and this is possibly because he is so in awe, without knowing it, of the magic of power. As Blake said of Milton, he is on the side of the devil without knowing it.

This claim can be corroborated by the way in which Canetti plays into the hands of the personality cult, that institution that inevitably goes hand in hand with the creation of victims, that institution that depends on the assumed value of the magic, mystique, and charisma apparently exceptional individuals have at their disposal. By turning his attention to an examination of prestigious rulers in world history, such as the Emperor of Byzantine, and the Sultan of Delhi, Canetti alienates his readership from contemporary reality. His preoccupation with leaders who are remote and removed enough from the realm of experience of his readership prevents the reader from learning anything from history, and from applying any lessons to his/her own experience.

This is because power is, in Canetti's hands, equated with public status. It is not exercised as such. Alternatively, Canetti is interested in how power can be internalized. It is a mere psychological problem for individuals, like Schreber. Again, this is to play the ethically rather dubious trick of endorsing the personality cult, for shorn of context the Emperor of Byzantine, the Sultan of Delhi, and the individual Schreber stand only as individuals. They do not live in the community in Canetti's narratives and therefore are not evaluated in terms of their abuse or use of power with respect to that community. This suggests that, on balance, the *Aufzeichnungen* and *Masse und Macht* are marked by what we might want to call Canetti's failure, his failure to come to terms with the issue of both leading and following. This failure is itself a result of Canetti's secret and unacknowledged love of powerful individuals, as it is a result of the secret and unacknowledged love of participating in the rituals associated with the life of the crowd.

For if comments on power occupy a small overall position in the notebooks, the general observations themselves seem predicated on

Canetti's view that he, as a powerful intellectual leader, can provide intellectual nourishment, on his idiosyncratic and subjective terms, for a needy reading public, a crowd of relatively desperate individuals who are parasitic upon his comparative intellectual superiority. This two-tier system of undifferentiated crowds on the one hand and named powerful individuals associated with, if not executing, power, on the other, is already in place in *Masse und Macht*. It is never foregrounded as a problem, but it is permanently in the foreground. The patronizing attitude is further implied by the reliance the reader has on Canetti's insights, and these turn out to be mostly only interesting in terms of Canetti's own highly idiosyncratic story or agenda about the intellectual history of the world, in the *Aufzeichnungen*, and the cultural history of the world, in *Masse und Macht*.

I have argued that *Die Blendung* is dazzling in the confidence and authority with which, by contrast, it both denies and rejects the existence of leaders and followers. It relies on no *idées reçues*, because it knows that popular ideology and theory, generally speaking, is what destroys *originality*, that quality that is free of origins altogether. It knows that ideology and theory turn the individual from a player into a predictable source—a named character—of the kind of material—ideology—that then makes playing impossible, that compromizes play. *Die Blendung* implies there is only one class of person, a player. Both *Masse und Macht* and the *Aufzeichnungen* imply that there are two classes, leaders who have authority or status, either because they are intellectual or because they already inherit power by virtue of the positions they occupy, and crowds, non-intellectuals, who are merely led because they need leading. Appeals to popular thinking and ideology create the two-tier system whereby a named leader leads a crowd. Although Canetti is obviously hardly populist, the ideas marketed in the *Aufzeichnungen* and *Masse und Macht* lend themselves very easily to what underlines any kind of popular idea, namely a relatively simple theory. Canetti's ideas about crowds and power, when one has sifted through the wealth of material in which they are clothed, are actually quite simple, and certainly quite naive. They have convinced a number of literary critics, who, as David Darby has pointed out, have fallen on them as easy interpretative keys with which to open up *Die Blendung*. *Die Blendung* is, by contrast, in Nietzschean fashion, defiant in its passionate resistance to the herd instinct. It does this by making a democratic appeal to a capacity for play, a skill it worships and assumes everybody possesses.

Judged by the standards of *Die Blendung*, therefore, and by the occasional aphorism, like this one of 1955, "Der stolzeste Mensch wäre der, der jeden Führer haßt; der selbst vorangeht, ohne daß man ihm folgt. Der niedrige Mensch, weil er folgt, schafft sich selber eine Gefolgschaft,"[408] *Masse und Macht* and the *Aufzeichnungen* instate the two-tier system. I have argued how they do this in terms of material and formal presentation of that material, and I shall briefly comment now, on how this is also achieved by the kind of attitude toward the reader implied by both form and content of the two works.

The reader of *Die Blendung* was an equal collaborator in the production of the text, whose wits, stamina, and intellectual horsepower were tested from sentence to sentence, and by each sentence. There was a violent hatred of thinking and reflection, of analytic and synthetic reason where these end up producing the already recognizable. There was a veritable worshipping of what we can all create *ex nihilo* through individual acts of imagination. The *Aufzeichnungen* and *Masse und Macht* make appeals, by contrast, to our reflective skills, above all, but in a way that is problematic. Most readers of the two works, because of the highly personal and highly idiosyncratic nature of the ideas presented, will only be able to see them "in and on Canetti's own terms." They make sense in terms of some of Canetti's well-publicized general themes, in terms of his other works. Many of them imply an assumed sympathy or prior disposition of sympathy to the ideas themselves on the part of the reader. The reader feels under pressure, for many of the ideas are insinuating. The lack of context makes one absolutely dependent on the hand that is feeding. The reader cannot, for the most part, call on his/her own experience, since the range of topics covered is so alien, for the most part, to the experience of the reader. One senses something of a secret desire on Canetti's part to school or train a potential following to accept ideas dreamed up by a leader assumed superior by that following. Instead of dialogism, then, the facetiousness and delight in jousting so typical of *Die Blendung*, we have monologism. The reader of the *Aufzeichnungen* or *Masse und Macht* is refused the privilege of utter originality, for a reader is left, after reading, to merely paraphrase what someone else has produced: to repeat it verbatim, to quote its sources, to live like a parasite.

This brings us back to a point raised earlier in this study, namely the self-serving interest of much of the theory and ideology that dominate the academy, and which currently have such a high profile. What follows is not an attempt to argue that that theory and that ideology are definitive of academic life, nor do I deny that they have some value. It is an attempt to cast the net wider, and to ask a rather compelling question, one raised by the works by Canetti discussed so far in this chapter. How do we understand the value of reading, writing, researching, and thinking, generally speaking, in our culture?

From what has already been said about Canetti's essay "Der Beruf des Dichters," it is quite obvious that Canetti regards himself as at the center of the mainly right-wing position concerning the value of "Bildung" in our culture generally speaking. "Bildung," it is assumed, is both a valuable and noble end in itself, as it is a yard stick against which individuals in the community can be measured. Yet in social terms, this habit of using the assumed value of "Bildung" as a measuring stick is divisive, for it is creative of a two-tier system. Using such a measuring stick is the means, broadly speaking, by which two classes, the educated and the uneducated, are created in society. This right-wing position is quite obviously different from the socio-economic position on class adopted by the Left.

For many Canetti fans, Canetti is not just a symbol of the pursuit of purely aesthetic values; his career as a whole, particularly the latter stages, is personal proof of his commitment to the struggle against the assumed contaminating influence of a world that no longer values culture, as it is socially significant of the general attempt by the educated classes to resist the assumed vulgarity of the non-educated classes. The belief in and support of Canetti's personal struggle can be traced to the story of his life, his autobiography, published in 1977, 1980, and 1985. The belief in and support of Canetti's struggle as part of a social struggle can be traced to the publication of the *Aufzeichnungen* and *Masse und Macht* in particular. The timing of the publication of these theories must have played a part in the timing of the award of the Nobel Prize for Literature to Canetti in 1981 at the very end of his life, when Canetti was seventy-six years old.

Official culture, as symbolized by award-giving institutions generally and in particular by the unique institution of the Nobel Prize, continues to wish to believe in the literary author as someone uniquely capable of being entrusted with the apparently ethical task of resistance. To what? Official culture, or high culture, identifies evil, in a secular world, with low culture. This is a threat to high culture. Since low culture poses that threat, bestowing a Nobel Prize for Literature is more than just a personal accolade for named individuals. It is part of a loosely political game, for it is a public ritual which sends out messages to the educated classes, stating that, at least officially, high culture is still committed to high culture, given the threat apparently posed by low culture. The publication of certain types of books is important, given the dynamics of the battle which it is assumed is going on at large, for they carry on the task of keeping the torch of high culture alight.

Heine said, memorably, in "Almansor": "Dort wo man Bücher verbrennt/verbrennt man auch am Ende Menschen." *Die Blendung* ends with a fire in a library, in which one individual, the intellectual Peter Kien, volunteers to end his life on a bonfire of books he did not write, but which he had collected. In both the Spanish Inquisition and on May 10, 1933, to name but two obvious examples from human history, books were ceremoniously burned in public as part of a staged, theatrical attempt of new, and self-appointed, authorities to terrify people into general submission and consent to new, authoritarian ideology. It was also an attempt to indicate quite particularly how people should position themselves carefully with respect to the written word. In times of repression writers always fall, quite literally, into only two categories. There are ideologically acceptable writers and writers who are not ideologically acceptable. It is assumed that the written word is dangerous because it is capable of training the mind into certain established patterns of thought likely to make submission to a single ideology impossible. In both of the historical cases cited, the ritual of burning the books was, of course, followed very literally by the ritual of burning human bodies, again justified on ideological grounds.

Die Blendung has often been exploited to tell the story of pre-1945 German and European history. To many critics, Canetti is a prophet in his capacity to anticipate reality. The fire stands for the failure of the Third Reich, and its human consequences. We should remember, again, that this is history with a capital H, properly speaking, on the one hand, as we should also remember that this interpretation makes Canetti into a prophet of doom, a messenger preaching the imminence of the apocalypse, and as such complicit with that apocalypse. Whilst it is tempting, because of the precedent set by the Spanish Inquisition and May 10, 1933, to appropriate *Die Blendung* for the view that it is inevitable that ritual murder follow ritual burning of books, I propose caution. The real fear expressed by intellectuals/critics when they refer to Heine's quotation (and it has been cited in *Die Blendung* criticism[409]), or when they comment on May 10, 1933, is on balance less a fear about the possibility of millions, or even thousands of people losing their lives at the hands of ideology, and more a self-interested protest directed at society by a relatively small community of people who are dependent on books for their economic survival. Why else did Karl Kraus fall absolutely silent when faced with the concrete facts of Hitler's success?

The protest directed at society is based on the view that society does not take the writen word in its more complex manifestations as seriously as it should. The implicit view is that we should never burn the works of Thomas Mann because they are self-evidently great literature, a view which begs questions. The protest is also based on the intellectual's view that he be granted status and authority as a commentator on culture, a position in the community often justified by the idea that s/he can act as that community's moral conscience. It is a protest about the desire for power in the public arena. These views have a long yet little discussed history, but it can be argued that they are limited in their claim to morality. Indeed, history seems to teach us that writers and critics, whilst they may think they are uniqely positioned to act as a community's moral conscience have always been reluctant to use their power and position to make a direct impact on conflicts of the day implicating society as a whole. Instead they prefer the safety and security of "dealing" with history of the past, at a distance, afforded them by reading, writing, publishing, and communicating with select audiences. This failure has often been referred to as "la trahison des clercs."

The reference to corpses in Heine's quotation is, properly speaking, the rhetoric ("blendende Rhetorik") you need to dazzle people, to get them to consent by force to the above set of assumptions. You have to believe, emotionally and intellectually, that the ritual burning of corpses will follow the ritual burning of books only if you believe in and want to hold to the illusion that books have power to limit the number of theaters of human conflict in the world, to prevent them or to cure us from them. Yet, if one thinks about the interests, pursuits, and achievements of writers and intellectuals who rely so heavily on books, it is quite obvious that these are rather limited. Writers and intellectuals tend to limit their interest to comparatively small communities, if there is interest in the community at all. Thomas Mann's novels will never become popular classics like *Little Women* because the issues they discuss do not touch on the experiences of the majority.

Certainly, the witheringly contemptuous attitudes of Heine, and later Karl Kraus, generally speaking, to their contemporary world—a world found pitiful for its total lack of intellectuality and culture—has its root in this desire to create an intellectual elite, to appeal to a minority, and to discuss the majority as worthless because its interests are not intellectual. The uncontested assumption about the value of intellectual culture lies at the heart of that series of writers writing in German who associate themselves with "Bildung," from Goethe to Thomas Mann and beyond. Two things need to be underlined here. The package of assumptions holds that what intellectuals do is intrinsically superior, that is, read, research, think, teach, and write. This is a package that also holds that all non-intellectuals are rather irrelevant or worthy of one's contempt, because they are not intellectuals. This tends to add up to a refusal of engagement, at the negotiating table or elsewhere, with the community outside the intellectual community. The intellectual community, which professes to believe in humanism, and which often discusses intellectuals and writers in history in terms of their contribution to humanism, is often deeply ignorant of the extent and the cause of its alienation from the experience of life in the widest sense, let alone the experience of life in a contemporary world. It is often dishonest with itself about the nature of its commitment to life and so-called human values, because it operates with a repellent assumption, whereby to be fully human is only to be intellectual.

This phenomenal insularity lies behind three controversies in England in the late 1980s and early 1990s and the "Literaturstreit" in Germany which followed the fall of the Berlin wall, all of which have concentrated the minds of many intellectuals, within the academy and outside. The academic community at Oxford University refused to grant Margaret Thatcher an honorary degree in the 1980s. The academic and creative community rallied around in support of Salman Rushdie after the publication of *The Satanic Verses*. Cambridge University was deeply divided over the issue of whether to award Jacques Derrida an honorary degree in 1992. These responses were responses of the academic community as a community. Few people outside the academic community felt particularly strongly about these issues. So what was at stake, and why did the academic community suddenly mobilize itself as a community?

In the case of Margaret Thatcher, the community justified its abandoning of the tradition of awarding public servants with an honorary degree because it claimed that Margaret Thatcher was hostile to the value of intellectual culture. It responded, not to the letter of the law of Thatcher's recommendations for greater accountability of the academic community to the wider community, nor to the spirit of the law of Thatcher's recommendations for change within the Universities and outside. It neither accepted the principle of the issue, namely that accountability is a good thing and vital in a democracy, nor did it wish to negotiate with the specific agenda laid down on the negotiating table as a basis for reform of the system as a whole. It merely protested because the accountability issue was assumed to express hostility to the value of intellectual culture. The view put about was that the Conservative government preferred only money-spinning enterprises, and thus money-spinning subjects within the academy. The government was supposedly hostile to any subject unlikely to generate direct economic capital, like Latin and Greek. Many of the proposals made by the government were certainly clumsy, but the early reluctance of the academy to enter into negotiations, and the near-hysterical way in which some academics kept up a protest based on a simple piece of ideology, whereby the Conservative government was simply hostile to "Bildung," said more. The early protest was not just about the reluctance of the academy to become a genuinely accountable institution. The protest was based on its assumption that being intellectual is *ipso facto* indicative of one's superiority as a human being and superiority to be indulged by the wider community in the form of the right to non-accountability to that wider community, the right to withhold its practices from scrutiny and leave them as they already are. This all said most, therefore, about the insularity of the community from the wider community, and its lack of a sense of proportion, regarding how its contribution fits into the life of the community as a whole.

Margaret Thatcher was burnt alive, so to speak, by the academic community. It made her into a sacrificial victim, punishing her for presuming to question the insulated livelihoods of those in the academy, their reliance on such indefensible "rights" as the right to tenure for life irrespective of the quality of their teaching or publications. It refused to acknowledge that Oxford University's tradition of awarding public figures honorary degrees was a tradition that had carried on irrespective of the general balance sheet of achievements and failures of any given public figure. This is now a tradition, of course, that the University is willing to perpetuate since it is now in its interests to use it as an instrument of survival. The universities capitulated to the Conservatives, who won on the principle of opening up the Universities to scrutiny, and to greater self-financing. The Campaign for Oxford has since 1988 raised over 238 million pounds from corporations, trusts, foundations and individuals. Oxford University is now quite happy to award the Sultan of Brunei an honorary degree only because he is going to endow a Chair, one of the very straightforward reforming policies suggested, it should be remembered, by the Conservatives. His "record" in the community, generally speaking, is conveniently set aside so this pragmatic goal can be achieved.

Salman Rushdie lived in fear of his life, because he published a work which was disrespectful of Islamic tradition, *The Satanic Verses*. His books were ceremoniously burned in certain quarters, and he risked death himself. It is in the tradition of the Islamic community to resort to ritual forms of punishment, and it is not, therefore, in cultural terms, surprising that the Islamic community responded to the book as it did. Blasphemy is simply punished in an extreme way in Islamic culture. Rushdie either took a calculated risk or he was culturally ignorant. Yet the point here is to comment on the nature of the response of the academic and creative community to the whole affair. The academic community has rallied around in support of Rushdie, protesting that he has, as an individual, a right to express his own opinion, a right which it was necessary for the academic and creative communities and governments to defend in public.

Part of the reason the academic/intellectual community support for Salman Rushdie was so strong has to do with the fact that he is socially and/or culturally prestigious as an individual because he is a published author. Our society worships published authors, as it worships the personality cult in all its forms, and it is the personality cult that is at the heart of our two-tier system. The support for Salman Rushdie, in spite of the widescale, world-wide upset he has caused, in spite of the fact that people have lost their lives as a result of his book, has been cast aside as irrelevant by those who defend him. The justification for their support has to do with the liberal principle of free speech, "his" right to say what he wants, and his right to publish what he wants, irrespective of the consequences. Yet this justification is based on a number of unacceptable views, views that have little integrity. The support is based on the view that only some people have rights; that only some rights are worth making a fuss about; that all the world should support the Western definition of rights; that those who do not support the Western definition of rights should be punished by means of the removal by force of rights they might have within the international community.

The Islamic community punished Salman Rushdie for daring not to show respect for the religion of Islam. One could argue that no one has a right to live in the wider international community without being sensitive to the differences there are in cultural expression across the globe. For Britain and other countries to come to Salman Rushdie's defense and impose sanctions or threaten punishment is a statement on the part of the Western community, and is evidence of its refusal to acknowledge the meaning and practice of cultural difference. It is evidence of its imperialism, for it is based on the view that our standards are the only standards. It asks that Islam capitulate to the Western definition of cultural expression or civilization as embodied by the right to freedom of speech relatively well established in the so-called "free" West. Since postmodernism vaunts the delights of the multicultural society, this is particularly fascinating, for official culture is still punishing those who do not have "our" standards. The implication of these points is not that Islamic countries should be allowed to win the day in terms of what is right. On the contrary. A pragmatic attitude has to intervene, whereby the knee-jerk resort to violence of the Islamic world has to be recognized for what it is: a very powerful social lever, which it is not in the wider interests of the international community to see indulged further, which is why we should not provide that world with further opportunities to resort to intimidation. In short, there are no rights without responsibilities, and in the case of the Salman Rushdie affair, the West, for pragmatic reasons, should be able to recognize the long-term value of compromising its unconditional belief in freedom of speech for the greater common good. Yet the academy thinks that intellectual creativity is a right *tout court*, and that it brings with it no set of reciprocal responsibilities in the wider community.

The academy was deeply divided about Jacques Derrida. Does he represent a threat to the humanist tradition of the academy? Is he a charlatan? Is he a fraud? Is he a proper philosopher, a proper literary critic? These were the questions the academy raised when Cambridge University floated the idea of awarding him an honorary degree. In this instance, we had the high-profile, apparently fashionable academics, who have sympathy for postmodernism because they are "in" theory and ideology. These took on the quieter sections of the academic community, those who probably mind their own business and believe that literary criticism is perfectly acceptable in its non-theoretical, non-ideological form. Again, my point is not to pass judgment on Derrida, but to look at the lineup. What was at stake, what was symbolized by the fact that the name, Derrida, seemed capable of concentrating the minds of the community of Cambridge University as a whole? The commentaries one could read in *The Higher*, *The Times Literary Supplement*, and elsewhere showed that the community was unsure whether to sanction Derrida's project. They also revealed that the only terms that are capable of igniting the intellectual imagination are ones that recognize the status attached to being an intellectual within the community. The question, whether this particular intellectual is ideologically acceptable to the community, is a secondary issue here. The issues of the drought in Somalia or the civil war in former Yugoslavia are issues, for instance, that would never ignite the imagination of the intellectual community as a whole. Intellectuals recognizable to the West and on Western terms are not, for the most part, in peril in either Somalia or former Yugoslavia. Engagement in Somalia or Yugoslavia would, quite frankly, not advance the interests of the academy.

Finally, the "Literaturstreit" in Germany followed precisely the trajectory outlined above. What might be regarded as the wider issues of how large numbers of people lived in fear in the former East German Republic, and of the role of the intellectual community in "supporting" the regime, albeit passively and not passionately, are not the issues that are being foregrounded by the debate. On the contrary, those who were defending themselves, East German intellectuals, or those who for the most part were attacking, West German intellectuals, were primarily motivated by the desire to salvage the idea of intellectual purity, not to prove that the intellect might be able to make a productive alliance with the concrete, and limit the power of evil. The terms within which intellectual purity are imagined are straightforward. If you want to be intellectually pure you have to insulate yourself from the world. Being intellectual is being insular. You also have to think salvation in terms of physical movement from the physical source of contamination. The idea of negotiating with the source of corruption is one that is not even entertained, because of the sway of vanity and self-love that arguably lie at the heart of the intellectual.

The self-interest in the debate takes other forms. Whether you are attacking or defending, the unquestioned idea is the assumed status and role of the intellectual per se. This has to be salvaged from the social, economic, and political ruins of a whole country, and, more importantly, in spite of the social and economic ruins of that country. It could be countered here that the work of Christa Wolf *is* evidence of the role moral conscience can play as a subversive force within an ideologically strict system. Any pretension to the power of critique within an existing society, can, however, easily be exposed as limited, if not shallow. Any social or political critique ventured by intellectuals in literature, whether this is published and read in a repressive or non-repressive society, is ventured firmly within a tradition that guarantees, despite appearances to the contrary, the absolute insularity of literature from present-day realities. Arguably, literature prefers to see its responsibility to literature, not to life; which is why it goes to considerable trouble to cultivate in language an atmosphere of otherness, so that it is "higher," and so that it can be separated both from its enemy, low culture, and from the complexity of life as we have to confront it on a daily basis.

This tradition is cemented by the book, by the private experience of writing and the private experience of reading. It is one that individual readers and individual writers can exploit, so that they can experience the special relationship of refined, rareified subjectivity, the intense experience, the thrill that momentarily makes me think I am intellectual and imaginative precisely because I am not peeling potatoes or scrubbing the floor. It is this special relationship that, in practice, tends, by virtue of its inherent appeal to one's vanity, to both absolve the reader from any responsibility to the wider community of non-readers, non-thinkers, and ensure that the reader is only likely to take intellectuals and books seriously. If one accepts this contention, then the special relationship developed between reader and book is one that takes place in a historical, social, economic, and moral vacuum, where self-love gives rise to self-love, not love. Even if the subject of the writing seeks to be provocative in some form, the provocation is limited to the way in which it merely provides material to think about on one's own or discuss with others. It is flattering to one's vanity to *think* about society. And this can so easily take precedence over any kind of concrete commitment to that society, where commitment is a practice and a way of life.

So to dedicate oneself to writing, reading, thinking, and researching is to participate, not in the romance of literature, but in what might properly be called the corrupt romance of literature. There is, therefore, a political significance to the institution of literature in the community, rarely recognized even by those who regard themselves as politically engaged. Literature insulates the individual from a sense of community, and it does this, by and large, because its notions of life are literary enough not to be recognizable in terms of life outside literature. Yet it hides and disguises this by appealing to our vanity that literature is a prestigious acitivity, that there is something virtuous about being a solitary intellectual. The fact that thousands of people lost their lives because of the ideology of the countries that made up the former East Bloc, is, as far as the "Literaturstreit" in Germany is concerned, actually considered to be rather a piffling and trivial matter. Nobody really wants to negotiate this one, which is why it so rapidly degenerated into an in fight amongst people who were desperate to prove that *their* actions and words were worthy, in terms of the low standards of morality associated with the profession of the writer.

The only kind of ideology the academic community can respond to is the kind unlikely to affect human lives, the kind with which this study began. Factions spring up à propos of ideas, whose intellectual credentials are fought over. This frequently tends to eclipse the interest in human values, to the extent that it frequently seems that matters relating to humanity and morality in the widest sense are only raised when they can be helpful in perpetuating the life of the academy. The academy and, indeed, large sections of society do not like the kind of ideology that makes people lose their lives, and they would prefer to ignore it. The academy, and society, wants to be consoled in its vanity, and it turns to literature and its many supporting institutions to provide this service, to free it from the need to have to negotiate the fabric of the community as a whole. It wants to carry on the romance of literature, a romance that is not based on community in a meaningful sense, nor leads to community in a meaningful sense, because of the many ways in which it is predicated on the dubious value of insularity.

The whole of this book is, amongst other things, an attempt to put some of these interesting issues on the agenda, using the example of *Die Blendung* because it is absolutely unique and absolutely original in literature, in terms of its violent commitment to living life in the present, where this is a commitment to and in a fully democratic community. It is one where there are no distinctions made between people, and where players are already always collaborating with one another. It knows theory and ideology are inimical to community, yet it does not escape the challenge posed by them, because its formidable agility, its tenaciousness, its violent engagement, and its sustained patience suggest a great capacity to negotiate with the given, whatever form the given might take. The novel is not evasive, but a lively challenge to our powers to negotiate: it does not lay down an agenda or prescribe the issues that should arise on that agenda, but its tenaciousness, the spirit of the novel itself, suggests that dialogue will never be abandoned. *Die Blendung* does not know about insularity because it is so vocal and so busily vocal, because it is so enjoys life, because it loves life, because it is exuberant enough to parade its lust for life, because it is sociable, because it likes and enjoys direct encounters with real people. It does not offer vicarious living as a form of life. It cannot abide the self-complacency of solipsistic pleasures. It is very keen to return readers straight to the community after the lively experience of reading in private has come to the end, and it returns one to the community in more confident and exuberant form and style.

Die Blendung is thus singular, even by Canetti's standards, in that life in the *Aufzeichnungen*, as in *Masse und Macht*, is defined very differently from the way in which it is defined in *Die Blendung*. In the other works life is equated with those activities more common to the corpus of literature as a whole, namely, thinking and reflecting in private and particularly in intellectual terms. This is elitist, not democratic, it is life in the head, not life in the community. Even where communities were present in an obvious sense in *Masse und Macht*, they were shrouded in mystique and ritual, and offered no kind of blueprint for life as

Canetti's readership might be able to recognize it, let alone live it. Its preoccupation with the distant, archaic past and its worshipping of solitary individuals was a form of deeply problematic insularity, which offers the reader no point of access to the larger community in which s/he might live in the present.

These problems do not surface in Canetti's 1967 *Die Stimmen von Marrakesch: Aufzeichnungen nach einer Reise*, in which Canetti's trip to Marrakech sees him wandering around as a solitary individual making highly successful attempts at contact with the inhabitants of the city. This bespeaks his conviction that human beings accept their responsibilities, and that they benefit from seeing themselves as members of a community, not as individualists.[410] Canetti wrote the book in 1954 and waited thirteen years to publish it, on the grounds that he did not consider it very significant.[411] Göpfert has argued that the pieces are expressions of epiphanies.[412] The case of his 1974 *Der Ohrenzeuge: Fünfzig Charaktere* is, however, different, for in this latter work there is the love of words, of originality, and of sound, the same skill at invention so typical of *Die Blendung*. In *Das Gewissen der Worte: Essays*, of 1975, Canetti goes on to parade his love of literature. Here, one can single out two essays for special comment: the essay to which I have already referred in this study, namely "Karl Kraus, Schule des Widerstands," and then "Der andere Prozeß: Kafkas Briefe an Felice."

In the former, quite apart from the essay's autobiographical significance at the level of information about the role of Karl Kraus in Canetti's own intellectual development, Canetti pays tribute to Karl Kraus, even in spite of the damning comments he makes about him. He does so, by imitating Kraus's own style, a trick we saw was typical of Canetti in *Die Blendung* in the way in which Canetti approached and exploited parody. The sculptural quality of the language in Canetti's essay, its extreme and violent hardness, seems unparalleled. The same quality of tenaciousness in the pursuit of an idea colors the whole of another tribute in love, this time to the life and literary career of Franz Kafka. To paraphrase the essay would be to make it seem banal, for in truth Canetti's idea is quite simple, that the whole of Kafka's correspondence with Felice was a trial, like the trial of the novel of the same name, but based on Kafka's acute sense of his own inferiority as a man, and his sense or conviction that life in any ordinary sense might compromise his unconditional dedication to literature. The essay makes no appeals to any kind of banal psychology; it is a sustained act of approval of another human being. One cannot say that all the essays are as powerful or of the same standard. In this chapter alone, I have indicated some of the problematic shortcomings of "Hitler, nach Speer" and "Der Beruf des Dichters," for instance. But the question now is, what of the overall title of the collection? What about the so-called conscience of words?

I have already mentioned how little understood the link is between Canetti and the plastic arts, in particular sculpture, so it would be appropriate now to think about the little-discussed and little-known monograph on Fritz Wotruba, published in 1955. Quite apart from what this says about the existential value of creation in Nietzschean terms, the violent engagement with chaos to defy chaos by parading the existence of form, this monograph represents a genuine contribution to our understanding of the work of Fritz Wotruba, and it has been quoted often in exhibition catalogues of Wotruba. Since it has been out of print for a very long time, it is to be hoped that Hanser will include it in their new hardcover issue of the complete works, both to acknowledge Canetti's contribution to the history of art criticism, to encourage further debate on the common bond between the two men, and to encourage the comparative thinking across the arts practised by Canetti himself. This would have the effect of defying the tendency to specialization, of which Canetti was so contemptuous. Finally, such research would complement the sections of *Das Augenspiel* that concentrate on the personal relationship between the two men. As a piece of writing, it displays the same violence of language as that used by Canetti in "Karl Kraus, Schule des Widerstands," and merits investigation, even on purely literary terms.

Research might usefully be done on violence in Canetti's work as a whole. I do not mean violence as critics think it is depicted in Benedikt Pfaff in *Die Blendung*, nor do I mean the kind of violence that one might think is being commented on obliquely in Canetti's essay "Dr. Hachiyas Tagebuch aus Hiroshima," which is to say violence as a physical reality. I am interested in the unacknowledged atavistic instincts of this apparently so mental author. I have already indicated how I see Canetti as naively complicit with violence, naively in awe of some of the violent rituals of exotic cultures, as described in *Masse und Macht*. I am talking now about violence in terms of the sculptural quality of some of his most powerful writing, the writing of *Die*

Blendung, *Fritz Wotruba*, and "Karl Kraus: Schule des Widerstands," the writing that *enacts* power which is often so sustained, it seems close to violence. To unearth this might force us to reconsider the parameters within which Canetti's contributions to the power debate have been placed hitherto. It would be appropriate to see Canetti less as an opponent of power and violence and more as a wily, masterful, cunning ally, of both power and violence as sources of magical life. Power is often the power of individual words to invade the imagination theatrically, power in the artistic sense, where words can make one aware of one's powers as a creator, as a shaper of the world. Another area that still needs to be investigated more thoroughly, concerns the level of intertextuality present in the novel. Clearly, I have looked at this in some detail, but it seems to me that a book is needed on world literature and its uses in *Die Blendung*. And there is ample scope for looking at Canetti's novel more closely in a comparative context. It would be fascinating to set *Die Blendung* alongside *Tristram Shandy*, for instance, to look at the similarities and differences in writing, in particular the love of the *imprévu* and the love of comic alogism.

If in *Das Gewissen der Worte* Canetti parades his love of words, if in *Fritz Wotruba* he parades his love of Art, in the autobiography as a whole Canetti parades his love of, *and* hatred of, individual people.[413] The story of his life as we have it, from 1905 to 1937, is one in which the author Canetti shapes his account of his life at every step of the way.[414] The experience of moving in and out of different cities and countries within Europe has not made Canetti an apostle of the cult of melancholy or nostalgia, neither has he carved a place for himself in the state of permanent exile. Although born in Rustschuk, which is now in Bulgaria but was, in 1905, still in the Austro-Hungarian Empire, and although he also grew up in Manchester, Zürich, Frankfurt, and Vienna, Canetti's account of his life shows that he is genuinely cosmopolitan, genuinely at home in the world wherever he goes. This is primarily because of his talent for friendship, his love of close friends and associates, an experience he clearly developed as a young child, considering the highly intense association he had with his mother, especially after the trauma of his father's death. The story of his life moves forward with a grandeur and a dignity of pace, and nowhere is Canetti in the throes of a crisis of identity. His identity remains not just constant but intact, from beginning to end. Apart from its value as a symbol of the individual's capacity to retain integrity at this basic level, the autobiography indicates that this was always achieved in, and through, a critical distance from the outside world, that imaginative space that both protects one and produces autonomy and strength. But the autobiography is also a symbol of resistance and survival, where resistance is the priority one puts on oneself as an individual, the responsibility one has to oneself as an individual. Compared to, say, *Dichtung und Wahrheit*, Canetti's account of his life shows that the author took considerable pride in his life, and that he took pleasure in his life as an adventure. It is the emotional intensity of the seriousness of this commitment to life as an adventure that marks this autobiography: for Canetti's seriousness is not paraded, nor does it ever generate into earnestness, it is the sense of commitment he is able to communicate, as if, he seems to be saying, life is worthwhile simply if you assume it is worthwhile. Susan Sontag has talked about the autobiography in terms of what she has called his "policy of triumphalism . . . his staunchless capacity for admiration and enthusiasm, and his civilized contempt for complaining."[415]

Although Canetti embarked on the autobiography when he was seventy years old, and although he only told us about the first thirty-two years of his life, he does here what he does in *Die Blendung*: the past is not remembered as if it were past, it is dignified by the sense that it is still part of the present; indeed, in Nietzschean fashion, there is only the world of an eternal present, where all moments have equal validity and everything is held in a state of tension, the tension that indicates that one is committed. Dionysus and Apollo are married in and through *Die gerettete Zunge*, *Die Fackel im Ohr*, and *Das Augenspiel*. As in *Die Blendung*, there is the same drive and the same capacity to endow with form. Yet the mood is slightly more sombre in the autobiography, for there is none of the exuberant hilarity and facetious noisiness of the earlier work, the novel.

I see *Die Blendung*, in conclusion, when set alongside Canetti's other works, as a bright and dazzling meteor dashing speedily across the horizon. I see it as a brief moment in Canetti's career, and as a force whose influence and principles recur in problematic form, for the most part, in the other works. Its dionysian aesthetics are not a *statement about* life, but an *enactment of* life where, specifically, the playful skills, those that endorse fun, frivolity and facetiousness, are proven to create the liveliest kind of life. Appeals are not made to our analytical skills; all rhetorical questioning, theory, and ideology is denied because it is anti-life. This refusal to make literature separate from life is entirely original in terms of literature, generally speaking. The terms of the novel are particularly challenging to the academic community and its problematic insularity from the wider community. The novel challenges us to investigate the truth about our parasitic dependence on literature and criticism, to acknowledge the terms on which we work on and with it and the terms on which we defend our activities if challenged. The institution of literature, as the institutions that support it in society, is often founded on self-love and vanity, for many of the practitioners or apologists of literature work with the assumption that the act of reading literature and the act of reflecting on literature are intellectual acts, and *as such* both truly superior and truly human. This is more than just socially divisive. *Die Blendung* challenges us to face up to this prejudice, challenges us to live life fully, to resist by example, not just this set of theories, but *any* theory and *any* ideology. For resistance is resistance only if it is performance. It is the intellect that prevents us from living as if we were performers and players of life. Intelligence, by contrast, is what makes it possible for us to interact socially in the community on competitive and enjoyable terms. A belief in the intellect, by contrast, necessarily tends to paralyze the natural intelligence of such life-giving qualities as fun, frivolity, and facetiousness. The vital intelligence of *Die Blendung* demands that we accept that the task of life is the task of creativity, where to create new connections *ex nihilo*, at every single moment, is the task of love. It is this attitude that creates community and responsibility, as it turns both the experience of community and the experience of responsibility into a pleasure, not a duty.

NOTES

1. "Upton Sinclair wird 50 Jahre alt," *Der Querschnitt* 10 (1928): 736.

2. Hanna Wallinger, "Elias Canettis Übersetzungen von Upton Sinclair," in *Österreichische Dichter als Übersetzer*, ed. Wolfgang Pöckl (Wien: Verlag der österreichischen Akademie der Wissenschaften, 1991), 103–12.

3. Elias Canetti, *Die Fackel im Ohr: Lebensgeschichte 1921–1931*, reprinted (Frankfurt: Fischer, 1986), (hereafter referred to as *FO*).

4. Elias Canetti, "Karl Kraus, Schule des Widerstands," in *Das Gewissen der Worte*, zweite, erweiterte Auflage, reprinted (Frankfurt: Fischer, 1982), 42–53, (hereafter referred to as *GW*), and Elias Canetti, "Der neue Karl Kraus," in *GW*, 254–78. See also Werner Kraft, "Canetti pour et contre Karl Kraus," *Austriaca* 11 (1980): 81–88, Manfred Schneider, "Augen- und Ohrenzeuge des Todes: Elias Canetti und Karl Kraus," *Austriaca* 11 (1980): 89–101, and Gerald Stieg, "Elias Canetti und Karl Kraus: Ein Versuch," *MAL* 16 (1983): 197–210.

5. Georg Grosz, *Ein kleines Ja und Ein großes Nein: Sein Leben von ihm selbst erzählt. Mit siebzehn Tafel- und fünfundvierzig Textabbildungen* (Hamburg: Rowohlt, 1955).

6. See Alma Mahler-Werfel, *Mein Leben*, reprinted (Frankfurt: Fischer, 1985).

7. See Elias Canetti, *Masse und Macht*, reprinted (München: Hanser, 1986), 249–311.

8. Elias Canetti, "Macht und Überleben," in *GW*, 25–41.

9. "The true pull of things was a *centrifugal* pull; they strove apart, leaving one another at top speed. Reality was not at the center, holding everything together as if with reins; there were many realities, and they were all outside. They were wide apart from one another, they were

unconnected; anyone attempting to harmonize them was a falsifier. Way, way out, in a circle, almost at the edge of the world, the new realities I was heading toward stood like crystals. As spotlights, these realities were to be turned inward, toward our world, in order to illuminate it." Elias Canetti, *The Torch in my Ear*, trans. Joachim Neugroschel (London: Picador, 1982), 318–19 (hereafter referred to as *TE*).

10. Elias Canetti, *Die Provinz des Menschen: Aufzeichnungen 1942–1972*, reprinted (Frankfurt: Fischer, 1984) (hereafter referred to as *PM*).

11. Other accounts of the writing of the novel, written by Canetti, also use exactly the same metaphors and vocabulary. See "Gespräch mit Horst Bienek: 1965," in *Die gespaltene Zukunft: Aufsätze und Gespräche* (München: Hanser, 1972), 93–103, "Realismus und neue Wirklichkeit," *Neue Rundschau* 77 (1966): 87–91, "Unsichtbarer Kristall: Aus der Rede anläßlich der Verleihung des Großen österreichischen Staatspreises am 25. Jänner 1968," *Literatur und Kritik* 22 (1968): 65–67, and "Das erste Buch: *Die Blendung*," *GW*, 241–53.

12. Friedrich Nietzsche, "Die dionysische Weltanschauung," in *Friedrich Nietzsche: Sämtliche Werke: Kritische Studienausgabe in 15 Bänden*, I, ed. Giorgio Colli and Mazzino Montinari (Berlin: De Gruyter, 1980).

13. "These spotlights were the true means of knowledge: with them, one could penetrate the chaos one was filled with. If there were enough such spotlights, if they were properly conceived, then the chaos could be *taken apart*. Nothing must be left out. One must drop nothing. All the usual tricks of harmonizing caused nausea." (*TE*, 319)

14. "In reality, everything had a direction and everything increased; *expansion* was a chief characteristic of people and things; to understand any of this, one had to take things apart. It was a bit as if you had to disentangle a jungle in which everything was ensnarled; you had to detach every plant from another without damaging or destroying it; you had to view it in its own tension and let it keep growing without losing sight of it." (*TE*, 319)

15. See Edward Hussey, *The Presocratics* (London: Duckworth, 1972), G. S. Kirk, J. E. Raven and M. Schofield, *The Presocratic Philosophers: A critical history with a selection of texts*, second edition (Cambridge: Cambridge University Press, 1983), and Patrick Moroney, *Nietzsche's Dionysian Aristocratic Culture: The influence of Ancient Greco-Roman Thought on Nietzsche's Philosophy* (Maynooth: Kairos, 1986).

16. Humbert Fink, "In diesem Gehirn siedelt die Epoche," *Deutsche Zeitung*, 09.10.1963, opens his review of the novel with a statement that links Canetti's novel with Heraclitus: "Ein Haufen aufs Geratewohl

hingeschütteter Dinge sei die schönste Weltordnung, meinte schon der Grieche Heraklit . . ."

17. David Roberts seems to be alone amongst critics in making the connection. He mentions this aspect of *Die Blendung* briefly in *Kopf und Welt: Elias Canettis Roman Die Blendung*, trans. Fred und Helga Wagner (München: Hanser, 1975): "Die Theorien der Vorsokratiker über das elementare Wesen der Wirklichkeit—der Weltfluß des Heraklit, die Atome des Demokrit, die kosmischen Elemente Feuer, Erde, Wasser und Luft—haben offensichtliche Bedeutung für Canettis Weltbild in der *Blendung*" (207). Idris Parry makes a connection between the biographical details of Democritus and the life of Peter Kien. A legend says that Democritus blinded himself to prevent his desiring women. Kien was always afraid of literally going blind: see Idris Parry, "Attitudes to power," in I.P., *Hand to Mouth and other Essays* (Manchester: Manchester University Press 1981), 151–73 (159).

18. For mention of Democritus see E.C., *PM*, 208, 258 and 270. For mention of Heraclitus see E.C., *PM*, 215 and 218, and Elias Canetti, *Das Geheimherz der Uhr: Aufzeichnungen 1973–1985* (Frankfurt: Fischer, 1990), (hereafter referred to as *GU*), 49.

19. Ruprecht Slavko Baur, "Gespräch mit Elias Canetti," *Literatur und Kritik* 65 (1972): 272–79 (275).

20. Elias Canetti, "Das erste Buch: *Die Blendung*," in *GW*, 246.

21. Elias Canetti, *GU*, 182.

22. "I was reluctant to give them names; they weren't like individuals one knew: each was invented in terms of his main preoccupation, the very thing that kept driving and driving him, away from the others. Each was to have a completely personal view of things, the dominant feature of his world, not to be likened to anything else. It was important that everything was kept in terms of that view. The rigor with which everything was excluded from each figure's world may have been the most important aspect. It was a strand that I pulled out of the tangle. I wanted the strand to be pure and unforgettable. It had to lodge in people's mind like a Don Quixote. The strand should think and say things that no one else could have thought or said. It should express some aspect of the world so thoroughly that the world would be poorer without that strand, poorer, but also more mendacious." (*TE*, 321–22)

23. "An entire year was filled with sketches of these eight, it was the richest, the most unbridled year of my life. I felt as if I were struggling with a *Comédie Humaine*; and since the characters were intensified to an utmost extreme and closed off against one another, I called it a *Human Comedy of Madmen*." (*TE*, 323)

24. Dieter Dissinger, *Vereinzelung und Massenwahn: Elias Canettis Roman Die Blendung* (Bonn: Bouvier, 1971), viii.

25. Elias Canetti, "Das erste Buch: *Die Blendung*," in *GW*, 241.

26. "The ending I had in mind was that they would talk to one another. In their individual isolation, they would find sentences for one another, and these peculiar sentences would have a tremendous *meaning*. It struck me as demeaning them to think of their recovering. None of them was to find his way back to the triviality of everyday life. Any adjustment to us would be tantamount to diminishing them; they were too precious for this because of their unique experiences. On the other hand, their reactions to one another struck me as sublimely, inexhaustibly valuable. If the speakers of these individual languages had anything to say to one another, anything meaningful for them, then there was still hope for us ordinary people, who lacked the dignity of madness." (*TE*, 324)

27. "During my year of dissipation, Gogol, whom I so greatly admired, had been my master. In his school, I had devoted myself to the freedom of invention. I never lost my joy in this freedom, not even later, when I strove for other things. Now, however, in my year of concentration, when I was after clarity and density, a transparency without residue, as in amber, I stuck to a model that I admired no less than I did Gogol: Stendhal's *The Red and the Black*. Every day, before starting to write, I read a few pages of this novel, thus repeating what the author himself had done with a different model, the renowned new book of laws in his day." (*TE*, 370–71)

28. Ingeborg Brandt, "'Stendhal war meine Bibel': Gespräch mit Elias Canetti, dem Autor der *Blendung*," *Welt am Sonntag*, 08.11.1963.

29. Elias Canetti, "Dialog mit dem grausamen Partner," in *GW*, 54–71 (69).

30. Elias Canetti, *GU*, 18–19.

31. Elias Canetti, *GU*, 143. See also *GU*, 19 and 141, for Canetti's appreciation of the European/cosmopolitan dimension to Stendhal.

32. Elias Canetti, *PM*, 79.

33. Elias Canetti, *GU*, 107.

34. "Kant became Kien: the ignitability of the world, a threat that I felt, was maintained in the name of the chief character. However, the pain intensified into the title *Die Blendung*. This title preserved (recognizable to no one else) the memory of Samson's blinding, a memory that I dare not abjure even today." (*TE*, 371–72)

35. In another context, his speech made on January 25, 1968, on the occasion of his receiving a prize in Vienna, entitled "Unsichtbarer Kristall," talks of the institution for the mad in Steinhof as "die abgeschlossene Welt der Irren, die für mich zum Bild der Verwirrung und Bedrohung unserer eigenen Welt wurde . . ." (66).

36. See Ann Jefferson, *Reading Realism in Stendhal* (Cambridge: Cambridge University Press, 1988), and Roger Pearson, *Stendhal's Violin: A novelist and his reader* (Oxford: Oxford University Press, 1988).

37. See John Bayley, "Canetti and Power," in *Selected Essays* (Cambridge: Cambridge University Press), 176–91 (182).

38. The correspondence has now been published independently. Elias Canetti to Thomas Mann, *Blätter der Thomas Mann Gesellschaft Zürich* 14 (1974): 22–23, and Elias Canetti to Thomas Mann, *Blätter der Thomas Mann Gesellschaft Zürich* 15 (1975): 11–12.

39. This becomes the title of another account given of how he began to write, which was published by Hans Daiber: Elias Canetti, "Jede Absage bestärkte mich," in *Wie ich anfing . . . 24 Autoren berichten von ihren Anfängen*, ed. by Hans Daiber (Düsseldorf: 1979), 122–34.

40. See Dieter Dissinger, "Erster Versuch einer Rezeptionsgeschichte Canettis am Beispiel seiner Werke *Die Blendung* und *Masse und Macht*," in Herbert G. Göpfert. ed., *Canetti lesen: Erfahrungen mit seinen Büchern* (München: Hanser, 1975), 90–101, and Herbert G. Göpfert, "Vorbemerkung zur Publikationsgeschichte des Romans," in *Hüter der Verwandlung: Beiträge zum Werk von Elias Canetti* (München: Hanser, 1985), 277–84, for a history of the reception of this work.

41. Walter Bensel, ed., *Elias Canetti: Eine Personalbibliographie* (Bremerhaven: Dux, 1989), 22–24.

42. See David Darby, ""Esse Percipi," "Sein ist Wahrgenommenwerden": perception and perspective in Berkeley and Canetti," *Neophilologus* 75 (1991): 425–32.

43. Raymond Furness, *The Twentieth Century: 1890–1945* (London: Croom Helm, 1978), 243.

44. Salman Rushdie, "Die Schlange der Gelehrsamkeit windet sich, verschlingt ihren Schwanz und beißt sich selbst entzwei," in *Hüter der Verwandlung*, 85–89.

45. Siegfried Lenz, "Krieg zwischen Küche und Kopf. Zu Canettis Roman *Die Blendung*," in *Elfenbeinturm und Barrikade* (Hamburg: Hoffmann und Campe, 1983), 146–51.

46. Ph.D diss., Indiana University, 1981.

47. See Lothar Hennighaus, *Tod und Verwandlung: Elias Canettis poetische Anthropologie aus der Kritik der Psychoanalyse* (Frankfurt am Main: Peter Lang, 1984) in particular.

48. Roman Karst, "Elias Canetti's *Die Blendung*: A study in insanity," *MAL* 16 (1983): 133–45.

49. J. M. Paul, "Rationalität in Canetti's Roman *Die Blendung*," *MAL* 16 (1983): 111–31.

50. Edward A. Thomson, "Elias Canetti's *Die Blendung* and the changing image of madness," *GLL* 26 (1972–1973): 38–47.

51. Walter H. Sokel, "The ambiguity of madness: Elias Canetti's Novel *Die Blendung*," in K. S.Weimar, ed., *Views and Reviews: Festschrift für Adolf D. Klarmann* (München: Delp, 1974), 181–87.

52. For more on the involved response to Freud, see Ritchie Robertson, "Between Freud and Nietzsche: Canetti's *Crowds and Power*," *Austrian Studies* 3 (1991): 109–24.

53. See Claudio Magris, "Die rasenden Elektronen," in *Canetti lesen*, 35–47 (40).

54. See Mary O'Donnell, "The theme of death in Elias Canetti's novel, *Die Blendung*," M.A. diss., St. Patrick's College, Maynooth, Ireland, 1979.

55. Kristie A. Foell, "Absence as Presence: Sigmund Freud in the Works of Elias Canetti," in Terry Prewitt et al., eds., *Semiotics 1988* (London: University Press of America, 1990), 350–55.

56. See Bernd Widdig, *Männerbünde und Massen: Zur Krise männlicher Identität in der Literatur der Moderne* (Opladen: Westdeutscher Verlag, 1992).

57. See Carl E. Schorske, *Fin de Siècle Vienna: Politics and Culture* (New York: Vintage, 1981), Nike Wagner, *Geist und Geschlecht: Karl Kraus und die Erotik der Wiener Moderne* (Frankfurt: Suhrkamp, 1982), Jacques le Rider, *Der Fall Otto Weininger: Wurzeln des Antifeminismus und Antisemitismus* (Wien: Löcker, 1985), and Jacques le Rider, *Modernité Viennoise* (Paris: PUF, 1990).

58. *FO*, 75 and 115.

59. See Elfriede Pöder, "Spurensicherung: Otto Weininger in der *Blendung*," in Friedbert Aspetsberger und Gerald Stieg, eds., *Elias Canetti: Blendung als Lebensform* (Königstein/Taunus: Athenäum, 1985), 57–79.

60. Johannes Pankau, "Körper und Geist: Das Geschlechterverhältnis in Elias Canettis Roman *Die Blendung*," *Colloquia Germanica* 23 (1990): 146–70.

61. Jacques le Rider, *Der Fall Otto Weininger*, 243.

62. Kristie A. Foell, *Blind Reflections: Gender in Elias Canetti's Die Blendung* (Riverside, Calif.: Ariadne, 1994).

63. See here W. E. Stewart, "The role of the crowd in Elias Canetti's novel *Die Blendung*," M.A. diss., University of Manchester, 1968.

64. David Darby, *Structures of Disintegration: Narrative Strategies in Elias Canetti's Die Blendung* (Riverside: Ariadne, 1991), 1–16.

65. Canetti/Baur, 275.

66. Canetti/Baur, 276.

67. Canetti/Baur, 276.

68. George Steiner, *Extraterritorial: Papers on Literature and the Language Revolution* (London: Faber and Faber, 1972), 58–101.

69. Ph.D diss., Indiana University, 1974.

70. For more ideas on the problem of dialogue and communication in the novel, see Harriet Murphy, *The Rhetoric of the Spoken Word in Die Wahlverwandtschaften* (Frankfurt: Peter Lang, 1990).

71. Peter Jansen, "Die Komik des Sprechens: Zur sprachlich-ästhetischen Erfahrung des Komischen am Beispiel von Canettis Roman *Die Blendung*," *Sprache im technischen Zeitalter* 76 (1980): 312–26.

72. See also Manfred Durzak, "Versuch über Elias Canetti," *Akzente* 17 (1970): 169–91, and David Roberts, *Kopf und Welt*, 209.

73. It seems most prominent in W. E. Stewart's thesis.

74. Gretzky, for instance, argues this line about George(s) in the thesis as a whole.

75. Elias Canetti, *Literatur und Kritik* 165/166 (1982): 53.

76. *FO*, 339.

77. Martin Bollacher, "Chaos und Verwandlung—Bemerkungen zu Canettis 'Poetik des Widerstands,'" *Euphorion* 73 (1979): 169–85.

78. Canetti/Adorno, in Elias Canetti, *GZ*, 66–92 (67–68).

79. See Paul Connerton, *The Tragedy of Enlightenment: an Essay on the Frankfurt School* (Cambridge: Cambridge University Press, 1980),

David Held, *An Introduction to Critical Theory: Horkheimer to Habermas* (Berkeley: University of California Press, 1980), Martin Jay, *Adorno* (Cambridge, Mass.: Harvard University Press, 1984), and Frederic Jameson, *Late Marxism: Adorno, or the persistence of the Dialectic* (London: Verso, 1990).

80. Stefan Kaszynski, "Canetti und Hitler," in Adrian Stevens and Fred Wagner, eds., *Elias Canetti: Londoner Symposium* (Stuttgart: H. D. Heinz, 1991), 148–57 (155).

81. Richard Lawson, *Understanding Canetti* (Columbia: University of South Carolina Press, 1991), 32.

82. Walter Sokel, "The ambiguity of madness . . . ," 186–87. See also J. M. Ritchie, "The Nazi Book-Burning," *MLR* 83 (1988): 627–43. Also see Ulrich Walberer, ed., *10. Mai 1933: Bücherverbrennung in Deutschland und die Folgen* (Frankfurt: Fischer, 1983).

83. Mechthild Curtius, *Kritik der Verdinglichung in Canettis Roman Die Blendung* (Bonn: Bouvier, 1973), 9, 67–80 and 125–32.

84. Max von Brück, "Die unfreiwillige Monade," *Die Gegenwart* 4 (1949): 20. Canetti, was, after publication of the novel in 1935, actually privileged enough to escape the fate that awaited many of the Jews of Europe at the time. He was able to escape Vienna in 1938 and eventually moved to the relative comfort and security of England.

85. Gerald Stieg, *Frucht des Feuers: Canetti, Doderer, Kraus und der Justizpalastbrand* (Wien: Edition Falter, 1990).

86. Stieg, *Frucht*, 108.

87. Urs Jenny, "Von Vätern und Göttern—Elias Canetti," *Merkur* 216 (1966): 285–88.

88. See David Roberts, "The sense of an Ending: Apocalyptic Perspectives in the twentieth century German Novel," *Orbis Litterarum* 32 (1977): 140–58, and Hugo Schmidt, "Narrative Attitudes in Canetti's *Die Blendung*," *MAL* 16 (1983): 93–109 (108).

89. Annemarie Auer, "Ein Genie und sein Sonderling—Elias Canetti und *Die Blendung*," *Sinn und Form* 21 (1969): 963–83.

90. Annemarie Auer, "Nachwort zu *Die Blendung*," in *Die Blendung* (Berlin: Volk und Welt, 1969), 515–34.

91. Thomas Docherty, *After Theory: Postmodernism/postmarxism* (London and New York: Routledge, 1990).

92. See Terence Cave, *Recognitions: A Study in Poetics* (Oxford: Oxford University Press, 1988).

93. "Rudolf Hartung und Elias Canetti," in Werner Koch, ed., *Selbstanzeige: Schriftsteller im Gespräch*, (Frankfurt: Fischer, 1971), 27–38 (33).

94. See J. Isaacs, *An Assessment of twentieth-century Literature: Six lectures delivered in the BBC Third Programme* (London: University of London, 1951), 61 for instance.

95. Thomas Docherty, *Reading (Absent) Character: Towards a Theory of Characterization in Fiction* (Oxford: Oxford University Press, 1983).

96. Nancy Miller, *Subject to Change: Reading Feminist Writing* (New York: Columbia University Press, 1988), 102–21.

97. Jutta Paal, *Die Figurenkonstellation in Elias Canettis Roman Die Blendung* (Würzburg: Königshausen und Neumann, 1991).

98. See Judith Ryan, *The Vanishing Subject: Early Psychology and Literary Modernism* (Chicago: University of Chicago Press, 1991).

99. Ph.D diss., Queens University, Kingston, Ontario, 1988. The book is published with the same title by Ariadne Press (Riverside, California, 1991).

100. Others who have raised the issue of narratology, besides Darby, are Dieter Liewerscheidt, "Ein Widerspruch in der Erzählkonzeption von Elias Canetti's Roman *Die Blendung*," *Wirkendes Wort* 28 (1978): 356–64, and David Turner, "Elias Canetti: The intellectual as King Canute," in Alan Best and Hans Wolfschütz, eds., *Modern Austrian Writing: Literature and Society after 1945* (London: O. Wolff, 1980), 79–96 (84), and Hugo Schmidt, "Narrative attitudes in Canetti's *Die Blendung*," *MAL* 16 (1983): 93–109.

101. Ph.D diss., Stanford University, 1988.

102. Herbert G. Göpfert, "Die Lesbarkeit der Welt," in Stefan H. Kaszynski, ed., *Elias Canettis Anthropologie und Poetik* (München: Hanser, 1984), 148.

103. Isaacs, 62.

104. Walter Allan, "New Novels," *New Statesman*, 07.06.1947.

105. Anthony Thwaite, "Burning bibliomania," *Observer Review*, 17.01.1982.

106. David Turner, "Elias Canetti: the Intellectual as King Canute," 79–96 (83).

107. Marcel Brion, "Elias Canetti et *La Tour de Babel*," *Le Monde*, 13.12.1949.

108. Dagmar Barnouw, "Elias Canetti—Poet and Intellectual," in Donald G. Daviau, ed., *Major Figures of Contemporary Austrian Literature* (New York: Peter Lang, 1987), 117–41 (129).

109. Josef Mühlberger, "Welt ohne Kopf—Kopf ohne Welt," *Welt und Wort* 18 (1963): 363.

110. Idris Parry, "Elias Canetti's Novel *Die Blendung*," in Idris Parry, *Essays in German Literature I* (London: London University, 1965), 145–66 (166).

111. Peter Russell, "The vision of man in Elias Canetti's *Die Blendung*," *GLL* 28 (1974–1975): 24–35 (34).

112. Dieter Dissinger, "Erster Versuch . . . ," 99.

113. Urs Jenny, "Ein Menetekel der ewigen Dummheit," *Du* 23 (1963): 51–52 (52).

114. W. G. Sebald, "Gedanken zu Elias Canetti," *Literatur und Kritik* 65 (1972): 280–85 (281).

115. David Roberts, *Kopf und Welt*, 64.

116. Curtius, *Kritik*, 150.

117. Edgar Piel, "'Herr seiner Schicksals ist der Mensch allein': Elias Canettis *Blendung*," *Literatur und Kritik* 157/158 (1981): 444–61 (449).

118. Christian Ferber, "Keine Angst vor Canetti," *Frankfurter Hefte* 6 (1951): 66.

119. Hermann Hesse, "Erzählende Literatur: *Die Blendung* von Elias Canetti," *Neue Zürcher Zeitung*, 12.1.1936.

120. Ernst Waldinger, "Comédie humaine an Irren," *Das Silberboot* 1 (1935): 143–44 (144).

121. Mühlberger, "Welt ohne Kopf . . . ," 363.

122. Thomas Mann, "Brief an Elias Canetti," in *Canetti lesen*, 122–23 (123).

123. Hermann Broch, "Einleitung zu einer Lesung von Elias Canetti in der Volkshochschule Leopoldstadt am 23. Januar 1933," in *Canetti lesen*, 119–21 (119–20).

124. This study as a whole is indebted to thinking on the subject by Norman N. Holland, *Laughing: A Psychology of Humor* (Ithaca: Cornell University Press, 1982), and Rosemary Jackson, *Fantasy and Mimesis: The Literature of Subversion* (London: Routledge, 1984).

125. Plato, *The Republic*, trans. Desmond Lee (Harmondsworth: Penguin, 1986), 436–39.

126. Aristotle, *Poetics*, trans. W. Hamilton Fyfe, (London: Dent, 1982), 19.

127. Plato, *The Statesman: Philebus: Ion*, trans. Harold N. Fowler and W. R. M. Lamb (London: Dent, 1975), 331–40.

128. Hobbes, *Leviathan*, ed. John Plamenatz (London: Fount, 1974), 93.

129. See Michele Hannoush, *Baudelaire and Caricature: From the Comic to an Art of Modernity* (University Park: 1992).

130. Charles Baudelaire, *Oeuvres complètes*, ed. C. Pichois, 2 volumes (Paris: Gallimard, 1975–1976).

131. Paul de Man, *Blindness and Insight: Essays in the rhetoric of contemporary criticism*, second edition, revised introduction by Wlad Godzich, reprinted (London: Methuen, 1989).

132. De Man, *Blindness*, 228.

133. Neil Schaffer, *The Art of Laughter* (New York: Columbia University Press, 1981).

134. Arthur Koestler, *The Act of Creation*, reprinted (Harmondsworth: Penguin, 1989).

135. Stendhal, *Racine et Shakespeare: Etudes sur le Romantisme*, reprinted (Paris: Garnier, 1970).

136. Roger Hillman, "Der Wiener Karneval—Elias Canettis *Die Blendung*," in Kurt Bartsch und Gerhard Melzer, eds., *Experte der Macht: Elias Canetti* (Graz: Droschl, 1985), 91–101.

137. See Kurt Bartsch, "Dialog mit Antike und Mythos: Christoph Ransmayrs Ovid-Roman: *Die letzte Welt*," *MAL* 23 (1990): 121–33 (133). Bartsch refers to Michael Bachtin, *Literatur und Karneval: Zur Romantheorie und Lachkultur* (München: Hanser, 1969).

138. Richard Sheppard, "Upstairs-Downstairs—Some Reflections on German literature in the light of Bakhtin's theory of Carnival," in Richard Sheppard, ed., *New Ways in Germanistik* (Oxford: Berg, 1990), 278–315.

139. Friedrich Schiller, *Werke*, XX, *Philosophische Schriften I* (Weimar: Böhlaus Nachfolger, 1962), 353.

140. Irmgard Kowatzki, *Der Begriff des Spiels als ästhetisches Phänomen von Schiller bis Benn* (Bern: Herbert Lang, 1973).

141. Mikhail Bakhtin, *Rabelais and His World*, trans. Helene Iswolsky (Bloomington: Indiana University Press, 1984).

142. Juliet Mitchell, "Femininity, Narrative and Psychoanalysis," in Mary Eagleton, ed., *Feminist Literary Theory: A Reader* (Oxford: Blackwell, 1986), 100–3.

143. Patricia Yaeger, *Honey-Mad Women: Emancipatory Strategies in Women's Writing* (New York: Columbia University Press, 1988), 207–38.

144. Quoted by T. G. A. Nelson, *Comedy: The Theory of Comedy in Literature, Drama and Cinema* (Oxford: Oxford University Press, 1990), 178.

145. T. J. Reiss, *The Uncertainty of Analysis: Problems in Truth, Meaning and Culture* (Ithaca: Cornell University Press, 1988), 135–52.

146. See Allon White and Peter Stallybrass, *The Politics and Poetics of Transgression* (London: Methuen, 1986).

147. J. Huizinga, *Homo Ludens: A Study of the Play-Element in Culture* (London: Routledge, Keegan and Paul, 1949).

148. Plato, *The Laws*, trans. A. E. Taylor, reprinted (London: Dent, 1969), 187–88.

149. Harold Bloom, *Agon: Towards a Theory of Revisionism* (Oxford: Oxford University Press, 1982).

150. William Fitzgerald, *Agonistic Poetry: The Pindaric Mode in Pindar, Horace, Hölderlin, and the English Ode* (Berkeley: University of California Press, 1987).

151. Michael Lloyd, *The Agon in Euripides* (Oxford: Oxford University Press, 1992).

152. Jean-Francois Lyotard, *La Condition Postmoderne: Rapport sur le Savoir* (Paris: Editions de Minuit, 1979), *Le Différend* (Paris: Editions de Minuit, 1983), and Lyotard and Jean-Loup Thébaud *Just Gaming*, trans. Wlad Godzich and Brian Massumi (Minneapolis: University of Minnesota Press, 1985).

153. See Nietzsche, "Homers Wettkampf," in F. N., *Sämtliche Werke: Kritische Studienausgabe in 15 Bänden*, Band I, 783–92.

154. See Renata von Scheliha, *Vom Wettkampf der Dichter. Der musische Agon bei den Griechen* (Amsterdam: Castrum Peregrini Presse, 1987).

155. Moroney, 41–44.

156. Mihai Spariosu, *Literature, Mimesis and Play: Essays in Literary Theory* (Tübingen: Narr, 1982).

157. Spariosu, 14.

158. Spariosu, 16.

159. Roger Caillois, *Man, Play and Games*, trans. Meyer Barash (New York: Schocken, 1961).

160. For more on games etc., see Jacques Ehrmann, ed., *Game, Play Literature* (New Haven: Yale University Press, 1968).

161. Elias Canetti, "Schule des Widerstands," in *GW*, 42–53 (44).

162. Elias Canetti, *GW*, 50.

163. Elias Canetti, *Die gerettete Zunge: Geschichte einer Jugend*, reprinted (München: Hanser, 1984), (hereafter referred to as *GZ*).

164. Elias Canetti, *Das Augenspiel: Lebensgeschichte 1931–1937*, reprinted (München: Hanser, 1988), (hereafter referred to as *AS*).

165. See Kathleen Thorpe, "Notes on *Die Blendung* by Elias Canetti," *Theoria* 67 (1986): 61–77, for the view (64) that this could easily be an affectionate sendup of that piece of intellectual history which has it that Kant went on a daily walk at the same time every day in Königsberg.

166. All quotations in German are taken from *Die Blendung* (München: Hanser, 1993), and remain in the main body of the text. All quotations in English will be found in footnotes. "A man of learning who owns an exceptionally large library wants a responsibly-minded housekeeper. Only applicants of the highest character need apply. Unsuitable persons will be shown the door. Money no object." Elias Canetti, *Auto-da-Fé*, translated from the German under the personal supervision of the author by C. V. Wedgewood (New York: Seabury Press, 1979), (hereafter referred to as *AdF*) (*AdF*, 26).

167. "The tone impressed her: here was a man. It flattered her to think of herslf as an applicant of the highest character. She saw the unsuitable persons being shown the door and took a righteous pleasure in their fate. Not for one second did it occur to her that she herself might be treated as an unsuitable person." (*AdF*, 26)

168. Mikhail Bakhtin, *The Dialogic Imagination: Four Essays*, ed. Michael Holquist and trans. Caryl Emerson and Michael Holquist (Houston: University of Austin Press, 1981), Tzvetan Todorov, *Mikhail Bakhtin: The Dialogical Principle*, trans. Wlad Godzich (Manchester: Manchester University Press, 1984), Michael Holquist, *Dialogism* (London: Methuen,

1990), and Dale M. Bauer, ed., *Feminism, Bakhtin, and the Dialogic* (Albany: State University of New York Press, 1991).

169. Henry James, "The Art of Fiction," in H.J., *Henry James: Literary Criticism: Essays on Literature: American Writers: English Writers*, notes and selection of texts by Leon Edel with the assistance of Mark Wilson (Cambridge: Cambridge University Press, 1984), 44–65.

170. Adrian Stevens, "Creating Figures: Narrative, Discourse and Character in *Die Blendung*," in *Elias Canetti: Londoner Symposium*, 106–17.

171. A. D. Nuttall, *A New Mimesis: Shakespeare and the Representation of Reality* (London: Methuen, 1983), Christopher Prendergast, *The Order of Mimesis: Balzac, Stendhal, Nerval, Flaubert* (Cambridge: Cambridge University Press, 1986), and Raymond Tallis, *Not Saussure: A Critique of post-Saussurean Literary Theory* (Basingstoke: Macmillan, 1988).

172. Prendergast, 249–52.

173. Curtius uses the clichés in the novel to make the point that they are a means of sham communication, 150.

174. Erich Fromm, *To Have or To Be* (London: Abacus, 1979).

175. "Therese was in the very act of finding her way into the starched skirt which completed her attire, when the screeching had broken loose. Terrified out of her wits, she fastened her skirt provisionally and glided fast to the door of the study. 'For Heaven's sake', she wailed, flute-like, 'What has happened?' She knocked, discreetly at first, then louder. Receiving no answer, she tried the door, in vain. She glided from door to door. In the last room she heard him, shouting angrily. Here she hammered on the door with all her strength. 'Quiet!' he shouted in a rage, in such a rage as she had never heard him. Half indignant, half resigned, she let her hard hands drop against her hard skirt, and stood stiff as a wooden doll. 'What a calamity!' she murmured, 'what a calamity!' and was still standing here, out of mere habit, when he opened the door." (*AdF*, 32)

176. "If he fell and hurt himself, there'd be an end of this wickedness. Therese's arm could be controlled no longer; it reached for her ear and tugged vigorously at it. Both eyes were fixed, gloating, on her imperilled employer. When his feet at length reached the thick carpet, she could breathe again. So the books were a fraud. Now for the truth. She knew every inch of the library, but secret vices are crafty. There's opium, there's morphia, there's cocaine—who could remember them all? You couldn't fool her. Behind the books, that's it. Why for instance did he never walk straight across the room? He stood by the ladder and what

he wanted was on the shelf exactly opposite. He could fetch it as easy as anything, but no, he must always go creeping round by the wall. Carrying that great heavy thing under his arm, he goes all the way round by the wall. Behind the books, that's it. Murderers are drawn to the scene of the crime. Now the briefcase is full. He can't get anything more into it; she knows the briefcase, she dusts it out every day. Now something must happen. It can't be seven yet. It it's seven he'll go out. Where is it seven? It shan't be seven.

Shameless and sure of herself, she stooped forward, pressed her arm to her side, pricked her two large ears and opened her little eyes greedily. He took the briefcase by both ends and laid it firmly on the carpet. His face looked proud. He stooped down and remained stooping. She was running with sweat and trembling in every limb. Tears came into her eyes, under the carpet then, that's it. She'd cracked his joints and spat. Or did he only say 'There!' He took up the briefcase, extracted a volume and slowly replaced it on the shelves. He did the same with all the others." (*AdF*, 33–34)

177. See Toril Moi, ed., *The Kristeva Reader* (Oxford: Blackwell, 1986), 24–33.

178. See Elias Canetti, "Dialog mit dem grausamen Partner,"in *GW*, 54–71.

179. Stefan Kaszynski, "Dialog und Poetik," in *Hüter der Verwandlung: Beiträge zum Werk von Elias Canetti* (München: Hanser, 1985), 205–16.

180. "'You're a good creature.'

'I must have a look what you've chosen for me,' she said and the corners of her mouth seemed to reach out almost to her ears. She opened the book and read aloud, 'The Trousers'—she interrupted herself but did not blush. Her face was bedewed with a light sweat.

'Excuse me, Professor,' she exclaimed, and glided away, swiftly triumphant, towards her kitchen.

During the ensuing days Kien exerted himself to recover his old power of concentration. He too knew moments when he was tired of his services to the written word and felt a secret desire for more of the company of human kind than his strength of character normally permitted." (*AdF*, 43–44)

181. See Friedbert Aspetsberger, "Weltmeister der Verachtung. Zur *Blendung*," in F.A. and Gerald Stieg, eds., *Blendung als Lebensform* (Königstein/Taunus: Athenäum, 1985), 101–25.

182. "Kien had no time to thank him for this last encouragement. He flung himself towards the kitchen, and seized violently upon the door. The handle came off in his hand. Therese was seated in front of the

cushion and made as if she were reading. When she sensed that he was already behind her, she got up, so that he could see what she had been reading. The impression of his last conversation had not been lost on her. She had gone back to page 3. He hesitated a moment, did not know what to say, and looked down at his hands. Then he saw the broken door handle; in a rage he threw it to the ground. He took his place stiffly in front of her and said: 'Give me your hand!' 'Excuse me,' breathed Therese and stretched it out to him. Now for the seduction, she thought and began to sweat all over. 'No,' said Kien; he had not meant her hand in that sense. 'I want to marry you!' So sudden a decision had been beyond Therese's expectations. She twisted her astonished head round in the opposite direction and replied proudly, though with an effort not to stammer: 'I make so bold!' (*AdF*, 48)

183. Gerald Stieg, *Frucht*, maintains the title of the chapter is a reference to the female sex organs and that the character Peter Kien is a case study of the Freudian theory of repression and of the castration complex.

184. "The wedding took place quietly. The witnesses were an oddman who could still strike a few last sparks from his tottering frame, and a worthy cobbler who, having cunningly evaded marriage himself, for the drink-sodden life of him, enjoyed watching other people's. Superior clients he would urgently press to have sons and daughters who would marry soon. He had convincing arguments in favour of early marriage. 'Settle your children properly, you'll have grand-children in no time. Look sharp and get your grand-children settled, and you'll have great-grandchildren!' In conclusion he would point to his good suit which could mix with anybody. Before grand weddings he had it pressed at the cleaners, for ordinary ones he ironed it himself at home. Only one thing he begged leave to ask, and that was reasonable notice. When his services had not been in request for some time, he would offer—slow worker though he was by temperament—repairs while-you-wait for nothing. Usually unreliable, in this sphere he was a man of his word, did the shoes on the spot and charged really very little. Children—mostly young girls—so lost to their duty as to marry without their parents' knowledge, but not so lost as to dispense with marriage altogether, sometimes made use of him. Indiscretion incarnate, he was in these matters silent as the grave. Not by a flicker did he betray his clients, even though he recounted in pompous detail the tale of her daughter's wedding to her own unsuspecting mother. Before setting off for his 'little bit of heaven'—as he called it—he would fix to the door of this workshop an enormous notice. On it could be read in writhing, soot-black letters the message: 'Out on my business. Back sooner or later. The undersigned: Hubert Beredinger.'" (*AdF*, 49)

185. "He was the first to learn Therese's luck and doubted the truth of her story until, offended, she invited him to the registry office. When

all was over, the witnesses followed the happy pair into the street. The oddman received his tip bowed down with gratitude. Muttering his congratulations he made his way off. '. . . at your service any other time . . .' echoed in the ears of Mr and Mrs Kien. Ten paces off, his empty mouth was still mumbling with zeal. But Hubert Beredinger was bitterly disappointed. He did not hold with this sort of wedding. He had sent his suit out to be pressed; the bridegroom was in his working clothes, his shoes trodden over, his suit threadbare; without love or joy, instead of looking at the bride, he had been reading the words in the book. He said 'I will' no different from 'thank you'; then never even gave his arm to the old stick, and as for the kiss, the kiss on which the cobbler lived for weeks—a kiss by proxy was worth twenty of his own—the kiss which he'd have paid good money for, the kiss which was the 'business' hung up on his workshop door; the public kiss under official eyes; the bridal kiss; the kiss for all eternity; that kiss, that kiss had never happened at all. When they parted the cobbler refused his hand. He disguised his resentment under a hideous grin. 'Just a moment please,' he giggled; like a photographer, while the Kiens hesitated. Suddenly he bent down towards a woman, chucked her under the chin, smacked his lips loudly and with eager gestures outlined her opulent figure." (*AdF*, 49–50)

186. Mechthild Curtius, *Kritik der Verdinglichung*, 68.

187. Dieter Liewerscheidt, "Ein Widerspruch in der Erzählkonzeption von Elias Canettis Roman *Die Blendung*."

188. "What was the right way to treat this timid, reserved creature? She was no longer young and took life very seriously. The woman who sat opposite was certainly a great deal younger, but she aleady had four children; Therese had none. 'Children last'. That sounded straightforward enough, but what did she really mean by it? She probably wanted no children; neither did he. He had never thought about children. For what purpose had she said that? Perhaps she took him for a person of no morals. But she knew his life. For eight years she had been aware of all his habits. She knew that he was a man of character. Did he ever go out at night? Had a woman ever called on him, even for a quarter of an hour? When she had first taken up her post with him, he had most emphatically explained to her that he received no visitors on principle, male or female, of whatever age, from infants in arms to octogenarians. She was to send everyone away. 'I have no time!' Those had been his very words. What devil had got into her? That shameless cobbler, perhaps? She was an innocent ingenuous creature; how otherwise, uneducated as she was, could she have acquired so great a love for books? But what dirty fellow's pantomime had been all too obvious. His gestures were self-explanatory; a child, without even knowing the reasons for his movements, would have understood that he had a woman in his arms. People of that kind, capable of losing control of

themselves in the open street, ought to be segregated in asylums. They induce ugly thoughts in hard-working people. She was a hard-working woman. The cobbler had insinuated ideas into her head. Why else should children have occurred to her? It was not impossible that she might have heard something about such things. Women talk among themselves. She had perhaps been present at a birth, when she was in some other service. What did it signify if she did indeed know all there was to know? Better perhaps than if he had to explain it to her himself. There was a certain bashfulness in her expression; at her age it was faintly comic." (*AdF*, 52)

189. According to Gerald Stieg, *Frucht*, (127), both Peter Kien and Benedikt Pfaff are brutally anti-feminist. Richard Lawson, *Understanding Canetti*, (20–23), makes a lot of Canetti's misogyny, which he maintains is patent in the autobiography in Canetti's accounts of men friends and their relations with women.

190. Philip Brady et al, eds., *Günter Grass' Der Butt: Sexual Politics and the Male Myth of History* (Oxford: Oxford University Press, 1990).

191. See Kate Millett, *Sexual Politics* (London: Hart Davis, 1971).

192. "At last they were inside the flat. Therese opened the door to the room in which he slept and signed him to go in. 'I shall be back at once,' she said, and left him there alone.

He looked round and breathed deeply, a man set free.

Yes, this was his home. Here no harm could come to him. He smiled at the mere idea that any harm could come to him here. He avoided looking at the divan on which he slept. Every human creature needed a home, not a home of the kind understood by crude knock-you-down patriots, not a religion either, a mere insipid foretaste of a heavenly home: no, a real home, in which space, work, friends, recreation, and the scope of a man's ideas came together into an orderly whole, into—so to speak—a personal cosmos. The best definition of a home was a library. It was wisest to keep women out of the home. Should the decision however be made to take in a woman, it was essential to assimilate her first fully into the home, as he had done. For eight long, quiet, patient years the books had seen to the subjugation of this woman for him. He himself had not so much as lifted a finger. His friends had conquered the woman in his name. Certainly there is much to be said against women, only a fool would marry without a certain testing time. He had been clever enough to put off the event until his fortieth year. Let others seeks to emulate his eight years of testing! Gradually the inevitable had borne fruit. Man alone was master of his fate. When he came to think it over carefully, he saw that a wife was the only thing he had lacked. He was not a man of the world—at the word 'man of the world' he saw his brother George the gynaecologist before his eyes—he was everything else, but not a man of the world. Yet the bad dreams of these last days were doubtless connected with the exaggerated austerity of his life. Everything would be different now." (*AdF*, 56–57)

193. Curtius, *Kritik*, 17.

194. Edgar Piel, "'Herr seines Schicksals ist der Mensch allein': Elias Canettis *Blendung*," *Literatur und Kritik* 157/158 (1981): 444–61.

195. "'Here I am.'

He turned round. She was standing on the threshold of the neighbouring room, in a dazzling white petticoat with white lace insertions. He had looked first for the blue, the danger. Horrified, his eyes travelled up her figure; she had kept on her blouse.

Thank God. No skirt. Now there would be no need to crush anything. Was this respectable? But how fortunate. I would have been ashamed. How could she bring herself to do it? I should have said: Take it off. I couldn't have done it. So naturally she stood there. As though we had known each other for a long time. Naturally, my wife. In every marriage. How did she know? She was in service. With a married couple. She must have seen things. Like animals. They know what to do by nature. She had no books in her head.

Therese approached swinging her hips. She did not glide, she waddled. The gliding was simply the effect of the starched skirt. She said gaily: 'So thoughtful? Ah, men!' She held up her little finger, crooked it menacingly and pointed down at the divan. I must go to her, he thought, and did not know how but found himself standing at her side. What was he to do now—lie down on the books? He was shaking with fear, he prayed to the books, the last stockade. Therese caught his eye, she bent down and, with one all-embracing stroke of her left arm, swept the books on to the floor. He made a helpless gesture towards them, he longed to cry out, but horror choked him, he swallowed and could not utter a sound. A terrible hatred swelled up slowly within him. This she had dared. The books!

Therese took off her petticoat, folded it up carefully and laid it on the floor on top of the books. Then she made herself comfortable on the divan, crooked her little finger, grinned and said 'There!'

Kien plunged out of the room in long strides, bolted himself into the lavatory, the only room in the whole house where there were no books, automatically let his trousers down, took his place on the seat and cried like a child." (*AdF*, 58–59)

196. Laurence Arthur Gretsky, "Sprachverzerrung," 130.

197. "'No better than a step-mother, that's what you are!' I screamed. To her dying day she thought he'd done me wrong. He never did. I'm a respectable woman and never had anything to do with men. If a girl doesn't look out for herself, she'd have ten at every finger's end.

And what would you do then? Prices going up every day. Potatoes cost double already. Where'll it end? You don't catch me that way. I'm a married woman with nothing to look forward to but a lonely old age . . ." (*AdF*, 64)

198. "She directed her steps towards the superior salesman. As it was already one o'clock she hurried so as to get there before they closed for lunch. She created quite a sensation; among all the men in trousers and the women in short skirts, she was the only one whose legs, concealed under the starched blue skirt which reached to her feet, functioned in secret. It was clear to every passer-by that gliding was as good as walking. It was even better, for she overtook them all. Therese felt all eyes upon her. Like thirty, she thought and began to perspire with haste and pleasure. It gave her some difficulty to keep her head still. She put on an adored smile. Uplifted by her ears, broad wings, her eyes flew up to heaven and settled in a cheap bedroom suite. Therese, a lace-trimmed angel, made herself comfortable in it. Yet she did not seem to have fallen from the clouds when all of a sudden she fetched up in front of the shop she knew. Her proud smile was transformed into a joyful grin. She stepped inside and glided over towards the superior young man, swinging her hips with such vigour that her wide skirt billowed about her.

'Here I am again!' she said coyly.

'At your service, dear lady, what an unexpected honour! What brings you back to us, dear lady, if I may ask?'

'A bedroom suite. You know how it is.'

'I thought it must be that, dear lady. A double-bed, naturally, if I am permitted to use the expression.'

'Excuse me, everything is permitted you.' He shook his head, sadly.

'Oh no, not to me, dear lady. Am I the happy man? You would never have married me, dear lady. A poor shop assistant.'

'Why not? You never can tell. Poor people are human too. I don't hold with pride.'

'That's because you have a heart of gold, dear lady. I hope the gentleman you've made happy knows how fortunate he is.'

'I ask you, what are men like these days?'

'You surely don't mean, dear lady . . .' The superior young man raised his eyebrows in astonishment. His two eyes were the moist adoring nose of a dog; he nuzzled her gently.

'They take you for a servant. But they pay you nothing at all. A servant gets wages.'

'So you are going to choose yourself a handsome bedroom suite instead, dear lady. This way please! Excellent, first class quality, I knew that you'd be coming again, dear lady, and I specially kept this on one side for you. We could have sold it six times over, honour bright! Your husband will be delighted with it. When you get home, dear lady, welcome home, darling, he'll say. Good afternoon, darling, you'll say, dear lady. I've got a bedroom suite for us both, darling—you follow me, dear lady, that is what you will say, and perch yourself on the gentleman's knee. Excuse me, dear lady, I say what is in my mind, no man could resist that, not a single man in the world, not even a husband. If I were married, I won't say if I were married to you, dear lady, a poor shop assistant like me, how could I dream of such a thing, but if I were married, even to an elderly lady, say to a lady of forty—but there, you couldn't even imagine that, dear lady!'" (*AdF*, 78–79)

199. H. Vaihinger, *The Philosophy of "as if": A system of the Theoretical, Practical and Religious Fictions of Mankind*, trans. C. K. Ogden, second edition (London: Routledge, Keegan and Paul, 1935).

200. Elias Canetti, *PM*, 153.

201. See Jefferson, *Reading Realism in Stendhal*, 112.

202. Gilles Deleuze and Félix Guattari, *Capitalisme et Schizophrénie: Mille Plateaux* (Paris: Editions de Minuit, 1980).

203. See Tania Hindenberger-Burton, "Elias Canetti: *Die Blendung*: Eine Analyse," Ph.D diss., State University of New York at Stony Brook, 1982, and her article (based on the thesis), "The Quixotic in Canetti's *Die Blendung*," *MAL* 16 (1983): 165–76.

204. See Piet van Meeuwen, *Elias Canetti und die bildende Kunst. Von Breughel bis Goya* (Frankfurt: Peter Lang, 1988).

205. David Roberts, *Kopf und Welt*, 53.

206. Ritchie Robertson, "'Jewish Self-Hatred?' The Cases of Schnitzler and Canetti," in Robert S. Wistrich, ed., *Austrians and Jews in the Twentieth Century* (Basingstoke: Macmillan, 1992), 82–96.

207. See *Die Blendung*, 193–94.

208. For the opposing view, see Manfred Schneider, "Die Krüppel und ihr symbolischer Leib," in *Hüter der Verwandlung*, 22–41.

209. Mechthild Curtius, *Kritik der Verdinglichung*, 84.

210. "'I implore you, dear lady, don't forget the most important thing of all! As madam's husband's bed is made, so madam's husband does. Give him a good bed, you can do what you like with him. Believe me, dear lady. Married bliss doesn't only flow from the stomach, married bliss flows just as much from furniture, pre-eminently from bedroom furniture, and I should like to say, most preeminently from beds; the marriage bed if I may use the phrase. You follow me, dear lady, husbands are human beings. A husband may have the most charming lady

wife, a lady wife in the bloom of her years; what use is she to him if he sleeps badly? If he sleeps badly, he'll be bad tempered; if he sleeps properly, well, he'll come a bit closer. I can tell you something, dear lady, you can rely on what I say, dear lady, I know something about business, I've been in the trade twelve years, eight in the same shop, what good are hips when a bed is bad? A man will disregard even the loveliest hips. Even madam's husband. You can tempt him with oriental stomach-dancing, you can display your beauty in all its charm, unveil it in front of him, nude as it were—but I take my oath on it, nothing will help, if the gentleman is in a bad mood, not even if it were you, my dear lady, and that's saying something! Do you know what gentlemen have been known to do, supposing, dear lady, a worn-out old thing—the bed I mean—gentlemen have been known to fly out and find more comfortable beds. And what sort of beds, do you think? Beds made by this firm. I could show you testimonials, dear lady, written by ladies like yourself. You would be astonished if you knew how many happy marriages we carry with pride on our clear conscience. No divorces with us. We know nothing about divorces. We do our part, and our customers are satisfied. This is the one I particularly recommend, dear lady. All are of the best quality, guaranteed, dear lady, but this one I do most particularly recommend to your heart of gold, my dear lady!'" (*AdF*, 80)

211. "She had taken the fellow out to lunch and in return he had been impertinent. She didn't want anything of him, did she? She'd no need to run after every man she saw. A married woman like her. She wasn't a servant girl to pick up just anyone.

At the restaurant first of all he took the menu and asked, what should he order for us. Like a fool, she said: 'Oh, but I'm going to pay.' The things he ordered! Now, she'd have been ashamed before all the people. He swore he was a better-class gentleman. Never had he dreamed he'd have to be a poor employee. She comforted him." (*AdF*, 98)

212. "Before he begins on his second cutlet he's taking her hand and saying: 'This is the hand which will make my fortune.'

Then he tickles her. He could tickle beautifully. Nobody ever called her his little fortune before. And does she want to take shares in his business?

But where has the money come from all of a sudden?

Then he laughs and says: my sweetheart will give me the money.

She feels the blood rush to her head with rage. What does he want a sweetheart for when she's there, she's human too.

How old is your sweetheart? she asks.

Thirty, he says.

Is she pretty, she asks.

Pretty as a picture, says he.

Then she asks, couldn't she see a photo of her.

At your service, this very moment if you please. And all at once he sticks his finger into her mouth, such a handsome thick finger as he has too, and says: 'Here she is!'

When she doesn't answer, he chucks her under the chin, such a very forward young man—what can he be up to under the table with his foot, squeezing close up to her, who ever heard of such a thing—stares hard at her mouth and says: he's all on fire with love, if he could only sample those magnificent hips? She can rely on him. He understands business inside out. She'll miss nothing with him." (*AdF*, 98–99)

213. Aspetsberger, "Zur *Blendung*," (114), makes a case for the scurrilous undertones of the novel, with which I do not disagree. They are quite obvious and not hidden: I merely see them as part of the theatrical spirit of play. He sees them mimetically as proof of the extent to which the characters in question are diseased. One of his examples is the assonance of the word Therese uses privately for Herr Grob, namely Puda. It is close in sound to a vulgar word for having sex in Austria, namely "pudern."

214. Mechthild Curtius, *Kritik der Verdinglichung*, 98.

215. Michel-François Demet, "The Theme of Blood in Elias Canetti's *Die Blendung*," *MAL* 16 (1983): 147–53.

216. Timms, 91, for instance.

217. Wagner, 149, for instance.

218. Frank Field, *The Last Days of Mankind: Karl Kraus and His Vienna* (London: Macmillan, 1967), 6 and 57–8, for instance.

219. Jacques le Rider, *Modernité Viennoise* (Paris: PUF,1990), for instance.

220. Bram Dijkstra, *Idols of Perversity: Fantasies of Feminine Evil in Fin-de-Siècle Culture* (Oxford: Oxford University Press, 1986).

221. *FO*, 143.

222. Denis de Rougemont, *L'Amour et l'Occident* (Paris: Plon, 1939), and I. Singer, *The Nature of Love*, two volumes (Chicago: University of Chicago Press, 1984).

223. Stephen Heath, *The Sexual Fix* (London: Macmillan, 1982).

224. Hélène Cixous, "The Laugh of the Medusa," *Signs*, 7 (1), (1976): 41–55.

225. Hélène Cixous, *Le livre de Promethea* (Paris: Gallimard, 1983).

226. Monique Wittig, *Les Guérillères* (Paris: Editions de Minuit, 1969).

227. Werner Helwig, "Der Hausdrache oder die Macht in ihrer Trivialgestalt," *Der Tagesspiegel*, 06.10.1963.

228. See Joachim Schickel, "Aspekte der Masse, Elemente der Macht: Versuch über Elias Canetti," *Text und Kritik* 28 (1970): 9–23 (18).

229. John Berger, *Ways of Seeing* (London: BBC, 1972).

230. Luce Irigaray, *Speculum de l'autre femme* (Paris: Editions de Minuit, 1974).

231. E. Ann Kaplan, *Women and Film: Both Sides of the Camera* (London: Routledge, 1983), 23–35. See also Norman Bryson, *Vision and Painting: The Logic of the Gaze* (London: Macmillan, 1983).

232. Fredric Jameson, *Signatures of the Visible* (London: Routledge, 1992), 1.

233. Fredric Jameson, *Postmodernism, or, the Cultural Logic of Late Capitalism* (London: Verso, 1991).

234. Susan Sontag, "Geist als Leidenschaft," in *Hüter der Verwandlung*, 90–110 (103).

235. Docherty, *After Theory*, 28–30, for instance.

236. Barbara Meili, *Erinnerung und Vision: Der lebensgeschichtliche Hintergrund von Elias Canettis Roman Die Blendung* (Bonn: Bouvier, 1985).

237. See Ann Rosalind Jones, "Writing the Body: Towards an Understanding of l'Ecriture féminine," in Elaine Showalter, ed., *The New Feminist Criticism* (London: Virago, 1986), 361–77.

238. Elias Canetti, "Macht und Überleben," 25.

239. Claudio Magris, "Ein Schriftsteller, der aus vielen Personen besteht," in *Hüter der Verwandlung*, 260–73.

240. Marcel Brion, "La Tour de Babel," *Le Monde*, 13.12.1949.

241. John Bayley, "Canetti and Power," in *Selected Essays*, 179.

242. Aspetsberger, "Zur *Blendung*," 113 for instance, together with the books of Curtius and Dissinger.

243. See Dorit Cohn, *Transparent Minds: Narrative Modes for Presenting Consciousness in Fiction* (Princeton: Princeton University Press,

1978), David Lodge, "Mimesis and diegesis in modern fiction," in David Lodge, *After Bakhtin, Essays on Fiction and Criticism* (London, 1990), 25–44, and Gerald Prince, *A Dictionary of Narratology* (Aldershot: Scolar, 1991).

244. See John McGowan, *Post-modernism and its Critics* (Ithaca: Cornell University Press, 1991), for his theory that what postmodernism has failed to acknowledge is its tragic view of freedom, since freedom, although much discussed, is a negative freedom.

245. See Gilles Deleuze, *Nietzsche et la Philosophie* (Paris: PUF, 1962), Paul de Man, *Allegories of Reading: Figural Language in Rousseau, Nietzsche, Rilke and Proust* (New Haven: Yale University Press, 1979), 79–131, and Julian Roberts, *German Philosophy: An Introduction* (Oxford: Blackwell, 1988). For a detailed commentary on Nietzsche on Art see Julian Young, *Nietzsche's Philosophy of Art* (Cambridge: Cambridge University Press, 1992).

246. Tarmo Kunnas, *Nietzsches Lachen: Eine Studie über das Komische in Nietzsches Werken* (München:, 1982).

247. Harold Alderman, *Nietzsche's Gift* (Athens: Ohio University Press, 1977).

248. For the theatricality of Nietzsche, see Peter Sloterdijk, *Der Denker auf der Bühne: Nietzsches Materialismus* (Frankfurt: Suhrkamp, 1986).

249. See C. A. Macartney, *The Habsburg Empire: 1790–1918* second edition (London: Weidenfeld and Nicholson, 1971), Hellmut Andics, *Das österreichische Jahrhundert: Die Donaumonarchie 1804–1918* (Wien: Kremayr und Scheriau, 1986), Winfried R. Garscha and Barry McLoughlin, *Wien 1927: Menetekel für die Republik* (Berlin: Dieter Verlag, 1987), Erich Zöllner, *Geschichte Österreichs: Von den Anfängen bis zur Gegenwart*, achte Auflage (Wien: Verlag für Geschichte und Politik, 1990), and William Carr, *A History of Germany 1815–1990*, fourth edition (London: Arnold, 1991).

250. Georg Stauth and Bryan S. Turner, *Nietzsche's Dance: Resentment, Reciprocity and Resistance in Social Life* (Oxford: Blackwell, 1988).

251. See Jean-Philippe Faure, "*Die Blendung*—Roman Casse-Portes: Canetti et Breton," *Austriaca* 11 (1980): 103–13, and Gerald Stieg, "Questions à Elias Canetti," *Austriaca* 11 (1980): 17–30 (27–28).

252. Elias Canetti, *Fritz Wotruba* (Wien: Rosenbaum, 1955). See also Harriet Murphy, "Fritz Wotruba: The neglected master of stone," *The European*, 12.10.1990.

253. See Michael Lewin, *Alfred Hrdlicka. Das Gesamtwerk. Druckgraphik* 2 volumes (Wien: Europa Verlag, 1989) for illustrations to *Die Blendung, Masse und Macht,* and *Hochzeit* (Volume I, 233–55), E.C., "Das Chaos des Fleisches. Alfred Hrdlickas Radierungen zu *Masse und Macht,*" in *Alfred Hrdlicka: Acht Radierungen zu Elias Canetti Masse und Macht,* with an introduction by Karl Diemer (Stuttgart: Galerie Valentin, 1973), 19–35, for Canetti's view on Hrdlicka's obsession with flesh, and E.C., "Kleiner Dialog über die Plastik," *Akzente* 3 (1980): 193–94. See also Jean-Pierre Hammer, "Canetti et Hrdlicka," *Austriaca* 11 (1980): 115–20, and Harriet Murphy, "Alfred Hrdlicka: a careless and cynical art," *The European,* 09.11.1990.

254. See Anna Mahler, *Her Work,* introduced by Ernst Gombrich with an essay, "The Human Figure in Art," by Anna Mahler (Stuttgart: 1975).

255. See Mechthild Curtius, "Einkreisung der Wirklichkeit: Die Rolle der extremen Charaktere für Canettis Dichtung," *Literatur und Kritik* 93 (1975): 176–82, Gretsky, *Sprachverzerrung,* and Gitta Honegger, "Acoustic Masks: Strategies of language in the theatre of Canetti, Bernhard and Handke," *MAL* 18 (1985): 57–66.

256. Manfred Durzak, "Die Welt ist nicht mehr so darzustellen wie in früheren Romanen. Gespräch mit Elias Canetti," in *Gespräche über den Roman mit Joseph Breitbach, Elias Canetti, Heinrich Böll, Siegfried Lenz, Hermann Lenz, Wolfgang Hildesheimer, Peter Handke, Hans Erich Nossack, Uwe Johnson, Walter Höllerer: Formbestimmungen und Analysen* (Frankfurt: Suhrkamp, 1976), 86–127.

257. Elias Canetti, "Der neue Karl Kraus: Vortrag, gehalten in der Berliner Akademie der Künste," in E.C., *GW,* 254–78 (256).

258. Pat Rogers, *The Augustan Vision* (London: Methuen, 1974).

259. Gilbert Highet, *The Anatomy of Satire* (Princeton: Princeton University Press, 1957).

260. Michael Seidel, *Satiric Inheritance: Rabelais to Sterne* (Princeton: Princeton University Press, 1979).

261. Peter Petro, *Modern Satire: Four Studies* (Berlin: Mouton, 1982).

262. Frank Palmeri, *Satire in Narrative: Petronius, Swift, Gibbon, Melville and Pynchon* (Austin: University of Texas Press, 1988).

263. Patrick O'Neill, *The Comedy of Entropy: Humour, Narrative, Reading* (Toronto: University of Toronto Press, 1990).

264. Moroney, 83.

265. See Richard Kearney, *Dialogues with Contemporary Continental thinkers: The Phenomenological Heritage: Paul Ricoeur, Emmanuel Levinas, Herbert Marcuse, Stanislas Breton, Jacques Derrida* (Manchester: Manchester University Press, 1984), and R.K., *Modern Movements in European Philosophy* (Manchester: Manchester University Press, 1986).

266. Edward Timms, "Canetti, Kraus and China," in *Elias Canetti: Londoner Symposium*, 21–31.

267. See Reinhard Düßel, "Aspects of Confucianism in Elias Canetti's Notes and Essays," *Tamkang Review* 18 (1987): 333–41.

268. "On the title page, in tall, angular letters was written the word: STUPIDITIES. His eyes rested at first on this. Then he turned over the pages; more than half the notebook was full. Everything he would have preferred to forget he put down in this book. Date, time and place came first. Then followed the incident which was supposed to illustrate the stupidity of mankind. An apt quotation, a new one for each occasion, formed the conclusion. He never read these collected examples of stupidity; a glance at the title page sufficed. Later on he thought of publishing them under the title 'Morning Walks of a Sinologist.'" (*AdF*, 21)

269. "A systematic study of the classification of men by trousers seemed to him abundantly possible. He promised himself a small thesis on the subject; it would be completed easily in three days. Half joking he uttered a reproach against a certain scholar who was pursuing researches in the tailor's department. But the time he spent down there was lost; it was of no consequence what he did with it. He knew well why he had become so devoted to the peep-hole. Yesterday was over, yesterday had to be over. And this scholarly concentration was doing him infinite good." (*AdF*, 386)

270. See Henry Sussman, *Afterimages of Modernity: Structure and Indifference in Twentieth-Century Literature* (Baltimore: John Hopkins Press, 1990), for what he implies is the poverty-stricken aspect of doing in postmodern fiction in particular. In an era in which all mystique has been removed because it has been found to be sham, people in fiction are left to merely do things, as if indifferent to themselves and to goals, generally speaking.

271. Richard Lawson, *Understanding Canetti*, 35.

272. "A person who can't play chess isn't a person. Chess is a matter of brain, I always say. A person may be twelve foot tall, but if he doesn't play chess, he's a fool. I play chess. I'm not a fool. Now I'm asking you; answer me if you like. If you don't, don't answer me. What's a man got brains for? I'll tell you, or you'll be worrying your head about it,

wouldn't that be a shame? He's got brains to play chess with. Do you get me? Say yes, then that's that. Say no, I'll explain it all over again, for you. I've always liked the book racket. May I point out to you that I learnt it on my own, not out of a book. What do you think, who's the champion in this place? I bet you don't know that one. I'll tell you who it is. The champion's called Fischerle and sitting at the same table as you are. And why do you think he came to sit here? Because you look such a misery. Now maybe you'll be thinking I always make for the miseries. Wrong rubbish, not a bit of it. Have you any idea what a beauty my wife is! Such a rare creature as you don't often see! But, say I, who's got the brains? The miseries have got brains, that's what I say. What's the good of brains to a handsome fellow? Earning? His wife works for him. He wouldn't play chess because he'd have to stoop, might spoil his figure; now what's the conclusion? The miseries get all the brains there are. Look at chess champions—all miseries. Look here, when I see a famous man in the picture paper and he's anything to look at, Fischerle, I say to myself, there's someting fishy. They've got the wrong picture. Well, what do you expect, piles and piles of photos, every one supposed to be someone famous. What's a picture paper to do? Picture papers are only human. Tell you what, it's queer you don't play chess. Everyone in the book racket plays chess. No wonder, considering the racket. They just open the book and learn the moves by heart. But do you think one of them's ever got me beaten? No man in the book racket ever beat me. As true as you're in it yourself, if you are.'" (*AdF*, 176)

273. "To obey and to listen was the same for Kien. Since the manikin had got on to the subject of chess he was the most harmless little Jew in the world. He never paused, his questions were rhetorical but he answered them himself. The word chess rang in his mouth like a command, as though it depended on his gracious mercy, whether he would not add the mortal 'check-mate'. Kien's silence, which had irritated him at first, now appeared to him as attentiveness and flattered him.

During games his partners were far too much afraid of him to interrupt him with objections. For he took a terrible vengeance and would hold up the foolishness of their moves to the general derision. In the intervals between games—he passed half his life at the chessboard—people treated him as his shape and size warranted. He would have preferred to go on playing for ever. He dreamed of a life in which eating and sleeping would be got through while his opponent was making his moves. When he had won uninterrupted for six hours and managed to find yet another victim, his wife interfered and forced him to stop, otherwise he would get above himself. He was as indifferent to her as if she were made of stone." (*AdF*, 176–77)

274. "Never before had Kien felt himself enter so deeply into the mind of another man. He had been successful in freeing himself from

Therese. He had struck at her with her own weapons, outwitted her and locked her in. Here she was again, sitting at his very table, making the same demands as before, nagging as before, and—the only alteration in her—had this time adopted a suitable profession. But her destructive activity was not directed at him, she took little notice of him, all her attention was directed at the man opposite, whom nature by a mistaken etymology had, moreover, fashioned as a cripple. Kien felt himself deeply indebted to this man. He must do something for him. He respected him. Had Mr Fischerle not been of so delicate a sensibility he would have offered him money direct. No doubt he could make use of it. But he was as anxious not on any account to hurt his feelings, as he was anxious not to hurt his own. Possibly he might steer the conversation back to that point at which, with a woman's shamelessness, Therese had interrupted them?

He drew out his wallet, still crammed full of valuable banknotes. Holding it unusually long in his hand, he extracted from it all the banknotes and placidly counted them all over. Mr Fischerle was to be persuaded by this that the offer about to be made to him was by no means a great sacrifice. When he reached the thirtieth-hundred schilling note Kien looked down at the little fellow. Possibly he was already mellowed enough for the offer to be dared, for who enjoys counting money? Fischerle was looking stealthily all about him; the only person for whom he had no eyes at all was Kien counting his money, surely out of the delicacy of his feelings and his repulsion from filthy lucre." (*AdF*, 185–86)

275. "Kien felt obliged to help this person, the first worthy object he had found in his life, to a better and more dignified existence. 'I am not a tradesman, I am a man of learning and a librarian,' he said and bowed condescendingly to the dwarf. 'You may enter my service and I will look after you.'" (*AdF*, 190)

276. "'The undersigned guarantees and immediately pays cash down every penny taken to the firm of Siegfried Fischer. The undersigned agrees to keep mum and take the consequences in the event of a misfortune.'" (*AdF*, 223–24)

277. "'Just what I say,' Fischerle finished for him, 'it all comes of swindling. Why must people do each other? They might say "I haven't a penny to-day, my dear sir, to-morrow I'll give you two." But no, they'd sooner do you, and you have to swallow a button. You ought to try another trade, my dear sir! For a long time I've been thinking over what I might do for you. Tell you what, if you do well these three days, I'll take you on for longer. Don't say a word to the others, strictly confidential, I'll sack the lot; between ourselves I only took them on out of charity for a day or two. You're different, you can't stand cheating, I can't stand cheating, you're a better class of person, I'm a better class of person, you'll admit, we suit each other all right. Just to show you how highly I

respect you, I'll give you your whole commission for to-day in advance. The others won't get a penny.'" (*AdF*, 227)

278. According to Leo Bersani, *The Culture of Redemption* (Cambridge, Mass.: Harvard University Press, 1990), it is the practice of sexuality that ensures that we are not available for the legitimizing plots of cultural authority.

279. "'Saved!' he mocked. Kien was astounded at the magnitude of the danger in which he had been. Then he embraced the dwarf and said in a soft, caressing voice: 'If it were not for you . . .' 'You'd be in clink long ago!' Fischerle completed the sentence. 'Are my actions then such as to bring me into collision with the law?' 'Everything brings you into collision with the law. You get yourself a meal because you're hungry and they take you up for stealing again. You help a poor devil to a pair of shoes, he goes off in the shoes and you've aided and abetted. You go to sleep on a bench, dream away for ten years, and they wake you up because you did something ten years ago—wake you up, indeed! Take you up, more like! You try to help a few poor innocent books and they put a cordon right round the Theresianum, one of them in every corner, you ought to have seen their new revolvers! There's a major in charge of them, I ran right between his legs. What d'you think he's got down there, so low that none of the tall people walking by should notice—a warrant. The president of the police has drawn up a special warrant because you're sort of high up. You know yourself who you are, I don't need to tell you! Eleven o'clock sharp you're to be taken, alive or dead, inside the *Theresianum*. Once you're outside nothing's allowed to happen to you. Outside you're not a criminal any more. Eleven o'clock sharp. And how late is it now? Three minutes to eleven. Look for yourself!'" (*AdF*, 240–41)

280. "But Fischerle gave him no peace. Kien's nose began to run; after he had left it a while to its own devices, he determined, out of his love for order, to take steps to deal with the large, heavy drop at its tip. He drew out his handkerchief and made to wipe it. But Fischerle gasped aloud: 'Stop! Stop! Wait till I come!' He tore the handkerchief out of his hand—he had none himself—cautiously approached the nose and gathered the drop as though it had been a pearl of great price." (*AdF*, 249)

281. "Kien changed colour. He saw her coming. She has broken out. Her blue skirt gleams. The mad woman, she blued it and starched it, starched it and blued it, Kien himself goes blue and limp. She's looking for him, she wants him, she wants new starch for her skirt. Where are the police? She must be shut up at once, she's a public danger, she's left the library unguarded, police, police, where are the police, ah, the police don't come till 10.40, what a disaster, if only Fischerle were there, Fischerle at least, he wouldn't be afraid, her twin sister's his wife, he knows

what to do, he's dealt with her, he'll destroy her, the blue skirt—appalling, appalling, why doesn't she die, why doesn't she die, she ought to die, this very moment, in the glass door, before she gets to him, before she strikes him, before she can open her mouth, ten books for her death, a hundred, a thousand, half the library, all of it, the ones in Fischerle's head, then surely she must be dead, for ever, it's a lot, but he swears it, he'll hand over the whole library, but she must be dead, dead, dead, absolutely dead! 'I'm sorry to say she's dead,' said the blind man with genuine regret,' and sends you her kind regards.'" (*AdF*, 255–56)

282. See Harriet Murphy, *The Rhetoric of the Spoken Word in Die Wahlverwandtschaften*, for more on Goethe's anti-feminism.

283. Linda Hutcheon, *A Theory of Parody: The Teachings of Twentieth Century Art Forms* (London and New York: Methuen, 1985).

284. "The sky was black and narrow, and had hidden his stars in his pocket." (*AdF*, 39)

285. "From all these recollections sleep had concocted a dream." (*AdF*, 42)

286. Roisin O'Neill in conversation with the author at UCD in February 1992.

287. Catherine Belsey, *Critical Practice* (London: Routledge, 1980), 69 for instance.

288. Jameson, *Postmodernism*, 1–54.

289. Jameson, *Postmodernism*, 18.

290. Linda Hutcheon, *The Politics of Postmodernism* (London: Routledge, 1989).

291. Jameson, *Postmodernism*, 341.

292. See Hilary Lawson, *Reflexivity: The post-modern predicament* (London: Hutchinson, 1985), Linda Hutcheon, *A Poetics of Postmodernism: History, Theory, Fiction* (London:Routledge, 1988), and E. Ann Kaplan, *Postmodernism and its Discontents: Theories, Practices* (London: Verso, 1988).

293. Linda Hutcheon, *Narcissistic Narrative: The Metafictional Paradox* (Waterloo: Wilfrid Laurier, 1980).

294. Patricia Waugh, *Metafiction: The Theory and Practice of Self-Conscious Fiction* (London: Methuen, 1984).

295. Brian McHale, *Postmodernist Fiction* (New York: Routledge, 1987).

296. Edmund J. Smyth, *Postmodernism and Contemporary Fiction* (London: Batsford, 1991).

297. See Jacques Derrida, *L'Ecriture et la Différence* (Paris: Editions du Seuil, 1967), J.D., "Differance at the Origin," and "Sexual Difference in Philosophy," in Peggy Kamuf, ed., *A Derrida Reader: Between The Blinds* (New York: Columbia University Press, 1991), 3–139 and 313–456.

298. See Elizabeth Abel, ed., *Writing and Sexual Difference* (Brighton: Harvester, 1982).

299. Barbara Johnson, *The Critical Difference: Essays in the Contemporary Rhetoric of Reading* (Baltimore: Johns Hopkins Press, 1980) and B.J., *A World of Difference* (Baltimore: Johns Hopkins Press, 1987).

300. See Elizabeth Messe, ed., *The Difference Within: Feminism and Critical Theory* (Amsterdam: John Benjamins, 1989).

301. Hester Eisenstein, ed., *The Future of Difference* (Boston: G. K. Hall, 1980).

302. Stephen Heath, *The Sexual Fix*, 117.

303. Luce Irigaray, *Ethique de la Différence Sexuelle* (Paris: Editions de Minuit, 1984).

304. See Edward Said, *Orientalism*, reprinted (Harmondsworth: Penguin, 1985).

305. Timothy Brennan, "The national longing for form," in Homi Bhabha, ed., *Nation and Narration* (London: Routledge, 1990), 44–70 (62).

306. See Rob Nixon, *London Calling: V. S. Naipaul, Postcolonial Mandarin* (Oxford: Oxford University Press, 1992) for an example of how Naipaul is being reinvented.

307. Edward Said, *The Question of Palestine* (London: Vintage, 1979), and Edward Said and Christopher Hitchens, eds., *Blaming the Victims: Spurious Scholarship and the Palestinian Question* (London: Verso, 1988).

308. Terry Eagleton, *The Ideology of the Aesthetic* (Oxford: Blackwell, 1990).

309. Terry Eagleton, *The Rape of Clarissa: Writing, Sexuality and Class Struggle in Richardson* (Oxford: Blackwell, 1982).

310. Eagleton, *Rape*, 34.

311. Terry Eagleton, *William Shakespeare* (Oxford: Blackwell, 1987).

312. Terry Eagleton, *Literary Theory: An Introduction* (Oxford: Blackwell, 1983).

313. Sheila Rowbotham, *Hidden From History* (London: Pluto, 1973), Germaine Greer, *The Obstacle Race: The Fortunes of Women Painters and their Work* (London: Pan, 1979), Elaine Showalter, *A Literature of Their Own: British Women Novelists from Bronte to Lessing* (Princeton: Princeton University Press, 1977) and Dale Spender, *Women of Ideas and What Men Have Done to Them: From Aphra Behn to Adrienne Rich*, reprinted (London: Ark, 1983).

314. Gayatri Chakravorty Spivak, ed., *Selected Subaltern Studies* (Oxford: Oxford University Press, 1988).

315. Gayatri Chakravorty Spivak, *In Other Worlds: Essays in Cultural Politics* (London: Routledge, 1988).

316. Alex Callinicos, *Against Postmodernism: A Marxist Critique* (Cambridge: Polity, 1989), 73.

317. See K. K. Ruthven, *Feminist Literary Studies: An Introduction* (Cambridge: Cambridge University Press, 1984), and Alice A. Jardine, ed., *Men in Feminism* (New York: Methuen, 1987), for instance.

318. Pierre Bourdieu, *Homo Academicus*, trans. Peter Collier (Oxford: Oxford University Press, 1988).

319. Paul Hollander, *Political Pilgrims: Travels of Western Intellectuals to the Soviet Union, China and Cuba 1928–1978* (Oxford: Oxford University Press, 1981).

320. Christopher Norris, *What's Wrong with Postmodernism: Critical Theory and the Ends of Philosophy* (New York: Harvester Wheatsheaf, 1990), and C.N., *Spinoza and the Origins of Modern Critical Theory* (Oxford: Blackwell, 1991).

321. E. F. Schumacher, *Small is Beautiful: A Study of Economics As If People Mattered* (London: Blond and Briggs, 1973).

322. Paul de Man, *Blindness and Insight*, 102–41.

323. See Kevin Barry, *Language, Music and The Sign* (Cambridge: Cambridge University Press, 1985).

324. "He came down and repeated dully: 'You're a thief!' He saw no other egress from this disastrous situation. The theft was obviously a lie in self-defence on Therese's part. He laid a heavy hand on Kien's shoulder and declared, as though once again he were on active service:

'In the name of the law, you are under arrest! You come along with me, and come quiet!' The parcel dangled from the little finger of his left hand. He stared commandingly in Kien's face and shrugged his shoulders. His duty allowed him to make no exceptions. The past was the past. Then they'd got on well enough. Now he had to arrest him. How gladly he would have said 'Do you remember . . . ?' Kien crumpled up, not alone under the pressure of the hand, and muttered: 'I knew it.' The caretaker distrusted this answer. Peaceable criminals are artful. They make themselves out to be like that and then try for a getaway. That's why the come-along was invented. Kien submitted to it. He tried to stand upright, his height forced him to stoop. The caretaker grew affectionate. He hadn't arrested a soul for years. He had anticipated difficulties. Delinquents offer resistance. If they don't they'll make a getaway. If you're in uniform they want to know your number. If you're not, they want a warrant. But here was one who made no trouble. He allowed himself to be questioned, he came quiet, he didn't protest his innocence, he made no disturbance, he was a criminal anybody could be proud of. Immediately in front of the glass door he turned to Therese and said: '*That's* how it's done!' He was well aware a woman was watching him. But he was uncertain whether she fully appreciated the details of his work. 'Anyone else would have knocked him out straight away. With me, taking a man up's a simple matter. Come quiet, that's the rule. An amateur couldn't make 'em come quiet. If you're an expert a criminal will come quiet of his own free will. Domestic animals have to be tamed. Cats have a wild nature. At the circus you see performing lions. You can make tigers jump through a burning hoop. But a man's got a soul. The organ of the law grabs his soul, and he'll come quiet as a lamb.' He spoke these words only in thought, although he was burning to bellow them out loud." (*AdF*, 283–84)

325. Gerald Stieg, "Die Masse als dramatische Person," in Stefan Kaszynski, *Elias Canetti Anthropologie und Poetik* (München: Hanser, 1984), 87–115 (99).

326. "Almost all the crowd had dispersed. Some of them had gone back behind their counters, others were offering goods with imploring or defiant countenances. But the officials unbent so far as to exchange, even with these poor devils, a word or two on the event. They accepted the opinions of people towards whom it was their highest duty to turn a deaf ear. As to the object of the crime, no united opinion was reached. Some said it was jewellery, or else what was all the fuss about? Books, said others, for it happened in the book section. More respectable gentlemen referred to the evening papers. Of the conflicting views, the majority leant towards money. The officials pointed out, more gently than usual, that people with so much money rarely came to the public pawnbroking establishment. But perhaps they were coming away after

completing a transaction. This too had to be ruled out, for every official was sure he would have recognized them if he had dealt with them. Some still regretted the redheaded hero, most of them had forgotten him already. To prove their finer feelings, they were sorrier for his wife, even though she was no chicken. Not one of them would have married her. It had all been a waste of time, but pleasant while it lasted." (*AdF*, 296)

327. David Darby, "A Fiction of Detection: The Police Enquiry in Elias Canetti's *Auto-Da-Fé*," in *Semiotics 1988*, 343–49.

328. Umberto Eco, *The Open Work*, trans. Anna Cancogni, with an introduction by David Robey (Cambridge, Mass.: Harvard University Press, 1989).

329. "The Inspector saw an opportunity at hand to teach this presumptuous woman that here a man was master. Violently he plucked at his minuscule nose, his great grief. (On duty and off duty, at every free moment he would contemplate and sigh over it in his pocket mirror. When he was in difficulties it would swell. Before he set himself to overcome them, he would convince himself quickly of his nose's existence, because it was so delightful, three minutes later, to have forgotten all about it.) Now he decided to have the criminal properly stripped. 'Idiots, all of you,' he began. The next sentence, which referred only to himself, he merely thought. 'Dead men's eyes are open. Otherwise why do you have to close them? You can't sham dead. Open your eyes, they don't glaze. Close your eyes, you don't look dead, because, just as I say, dead men's eyes are open. A corpse without glazed eyes and without open eyes isn't worth a song. It simply means death has not supervened. I'd like to see anyone take me in. Watch carefully gentlemen! I put it to you, with regard to the prisoner, direct your attention to his eyes!" (*AdF*, 298–99)

330. See Donald Fanger, *The Creation of Nikolai Gogol* (Cambridge, Mass.: Harvard University Press, 1979), 121–22.

331. See Richard Pearce, *The Enigma of Gogol: An Examination of the Writings of N. V. Gogol and their Place in the Russian Literary Tradition* (Cambridge: Cambridge University Press, 1981), 8.

332. See Ivan Yermakov, "The Nose," in Robert A. Maguire, ed., *Gogol from the Twentieth Century: Eleven Essays* (Princeton: Princeton University Press, 1974), 155–98.

333. Curtius, 69.

334. See Alexander Slonimsky, "The Technique of the Comic in Gogol," in Robert A. Maguire, ed. *Gogol from the Twentieth Century: Eleven Essays*, 323–73 (345).

335. Boris Eichenbaum, "How Gogol's *Overcoat* is made," in Maguire, 267–91 (271).

336. Gerald Stieg, "Questions à Elias Canetti," *Austriaca* 11 (1980): 17–30 (17).

337. Raymond Furness, "Canetti the Dramatist," in *Elias Canetti: Londoner Symposium*, 76 and 84.

338. Noel Thomas, "'My great Russian': Reflections on Reality and Unreality in Canetti's *Die Blendung* and Gogol's *The Overcoat*," in *Elias Canetti: Ein Londoner Symposium*, 119–30.

339. "The Inspector was still a little repelled by the object before him, then he began to pull its clothes off himself. He tossed the jacket on to the table. The waistcoat followed. The shirt was old, but of good material. He unbuttoned it and directed a piercing eye between the creature's ribs. There was really nothing there. Disgust rose within him. He had had much experience. His profession brought him into contact with every form of human life. He had never come across anything so thin before. Its place was in a show, not a police station. Did they take him for a Barnum, or what? 'Shoes and trousers I leave to you,' he said to the others. Crestfallen he withdrew. His nose occured to him. He clutched at it. It was too short. If only he could forget it! Sullenly he sat down behind his table. It was in the wrong position again. Someone had pushed it. 'Can't you leave my table straight, for the hundredth time! Idiots!' The policemen busied over the shoes and trousers of the thief grinned to themselves, the others stood to attention. Yes, he thought, creatures like that ought to be put away. They're a public nuisance. They make you ill to look at. The healthiest stomach would be turned. And where would you be without a stomach. There's no patience with them. This was a case for torture. In the middle ages the police had a better time. A creature like that ought to drown itself. It wouldn't affect the suicide rate; it wouldn't weigh enough to count. Instead of making away with itself it shams dead. Shameless, creature like him. Some people are ashamed of their noses, only because they're a wee bit on the short side." (*AdF*, 299–300)

340. Curtius, 70.

341. See Bernhard Fischer, *Gehen von Thomas Bernhard: Eine Studie zum Problem der Moderne* (Bonn: Bouvier, 1985).

342. See Barbara Surowska, "Nur aus der Gesinnung heraus schreiben," in *Hüter der Verwandlung*, 167–81.

343. "'I confess my guilt. Yet part of the blame must redound to her. It is true, I locked her in. But was it necessary for her to devour her own body? She merited her death. One point I would beg you to clarify, for I

feel a certain confusion. How do you explain the presence here of the murdered woman? I know her by her skirt.'" (*AdF*, 301)

344. See Erika Tunner, "Das Verhör: Zu einem Kapitel aus Canetti's Roman *Die Blendung*," *MAL* 16 (1983): 155–63.

345. "'You may well believe that I am the victim of an hallucination. I am not generally subject to them. Scholarship demands a clear head, I would not read an X for U, or take any other letter for its fellow. But recently I have been through much; yesterday I had news of my wife's death. You are aware of the circumstances. On her account I have the honour to find myself among you. Since then thoughts of my trial have ceaselessly occupied my mind. To-day, when I went to the Theresianum, I encountered my murdered wife. She was accompanied by our caretaker, a very good friend of mine. He had followed her, as my representative, to her last resting place; I was myself unable to attend. Do not regard me as unduly hard-hearted. There are women whom it is impossible to forget. I will admit the whole truth to you: I deliberately avoided her funeral, it would have been too much for me. I trust you understand me; were you never yourself married? Her skirt was torn in pieces and devoured by a bloodhound. It is however conceivable that she possessed two. Ascending the stairs, she brushed against me. She was carrying a parcel which I presumed to contain my two books. I love my library. You must understand. I am speaking of the largest privately-owned library in the town. For some time I have been compelled to neglect it. I was occupied with errands of mercy. My wife's murder kept me away from home; how many weeks it is I cannot precisely calculate since I left the house. But I have made good use of the time; time is knowledge, knowledge is order. Besides the accumulation of a small head-library I turned my attention, as above mentioned, to errands of mercy. I redeem books from the stake. I know of a hog who lives on books, but do not let us speak of him. I refer you to the speech I shall make in my own defence, on which occasion I propose to make certain public revelations. I ask for your help! She does not move from her place. Liberate me from this hallucination! I am not generally subject to them. She has been following me, I fear, for more than an hour. Let us first be clear in our facts; I will make your task of helping me the easier. I see you all, you see me. Even so clearly, the murdered woman stands at my side. All my senses have betrayed me, not my eyes alone. Do as I will, I hear the crackling of her skirt, I can feel it, it smells of starch; she moves her head in the very manner in which she moved it living, she even speaks; a few moments ago she said, "I ask you"; you must know that her vocabulary contained not above fifty words, in spite of which she talked no less than most people. I implore your help! Prove to me that she is dead.'" (*AdF*, 302–3)

346. "'Who are you then, sir?' shouted the Inspector. 'Speak up if you please!' With two fingers he pulled at Kien's shirt-sleeve. He would

have liked to squash him between two finger-nails. What kind of an education is this, which can only produce a couple of sentences and then not a word in answer to a reasonable question? True education reveals itself in a man's bearing, in his immaculate appearance and in the art of interrogation. Gravely, and ever more confident of his superiority, the Inspector retired behind his table. The wooden seat of the chair on which he usually sat was covered by a soft cushion, the only one in the sub-station, on which, in letters of scarlet embroidery, was clearly to be read: PRIVATE PROPERTY. These words were intended to remind his inferiors that—even in his absence—they had no right to it. The fellows had a reprehensible tendency to slide the cushion under their own bodies. With a few deft movements he set it to rights; before he seated himself the words PRIVATE PROPERTY must be precisely parallel with his eyes, which overlooked no opportunity of drawing strength from the phrase. He turned his back on the chair. It was hard to tear himself from contemplation of the cushion, even harder so to seat himself that the cushion should not be disturbed. Slowly he lowered himself; for a few seconds he restrained his backside. Only when this part of his person had PRIVATE PROPERTY in its proper place he allowed himself to put pressure on it. As soon as he was sitting, no thief in the world—even if he had passed Matric and more—could have imposed on him. Swiftly he took a last peep at his little mirror. His tie, like himself, sat firmly but with elegance. His hair, brushed back, was disciplined with grease, not a hair out of place. His nose was too short. It gave him the spur he needed; he flung himself into the inquiry." (*AdF*, 309–10)

347. Curtius, 32.

348. Nikolai Gogol, "The Nose," in *Diary of a Madman and Other Stories*, trans. with an introduction by Ronald Wilks, reprinted (Harmondsworth: Penguin, 1987).

349. "'The skirt was found at the scene of the crime!' he asserted in a firm voice.

'The scene of the crime? You recognize what you are admitting?'

A confirmatory nod passed through the surrounding police. 'I take you for an educated man. You admit, presumably, that a scene of a crime presupposes a crime? You are at liberty to withdraw your statement. But it is my duty to call your attention to the unfortunate impression it would make. I am advising you for your own good. You will do better to admit everything. Let's admit everything, my good man! Confess. We know all! Denying will do you no good. You've let the scene of the crime slip out. Admit everything and I'll put in a good word for you! Admit everything in order! We have made our own investigations. How can you hope to escape? You walked into the trap yourself! The scene of the crime presupposes a crime. I take it I am right, gentlemen?'

When he said 'gentlemen' the gentlemen knew that he had victory in the palm of his hand, and overwhelmed him with admiring glances. Each hastened to do better than the other. The man with a memory saw that there was going to be nothing for him, and abandoned his old plan. He darted forward, seized the lucky hand of the Inspector and shouted: 'Inspector, permit me to congratulate you!'" (*AdF*, 313–14)

350. "'For weeks I left her alone. Convinced that she must die of hunger, I passed night after night at hotels. Bitterly did I miss my library, believe me; I had to content myself with a small substitute library, which, for essential needs, I kept always at hand. The locks on my door are strong—I was not tormented by the fear that burglars might release her. Imagine for yourselves her condition: all provisions are consumed. Enfeebled and full of hatred she lies on the floor, in front of that very desk in which she had so often looked for money. Her only thoughts were of money. In nothing did she resemble a flower. Of the thoughts which came into my head when I sat at that writing desk, at the time when I still shared my dwelling with her, I will not tell you to-day. For weeks I had to live, for fear that she should steal my manuscripts, petrified into a guardian-statue. This was the period of my deepest humiliation. When my head glowed for work, I had to say to myself: you are made of stone, and to remain motionless, I believed it myself. Those of you who have ever had to watch over a treasure, will readily be able to put yourselves in my place. I do not believe in fate; but she hastened towards hers. Instead of me—for by many a secret assault she brought me near to death—she now lay there, devoured by her own mad hunger. She did not know how to help herself. She had not sufficient self-control. She devoured herself. Piece by piece of her body fell a prey to her greed. Day by day she grew thinner. She was too weak to stand, but lay there in her own filth. Perhaps I seem thin to you. Compared to me she was the shadow of a being, pitiful and despicable; had she stood up a breath of wind could have snapped her in two, I verily believe even a child. I cannot particularize further. The blue skirt, which she always wore, covered her skeleton. It was starched, and thanks to this peculiarity held the repulsive remains of her body together. One day she breathed her last. Even this expression appears to me corrupt, for very probably she had no lungs left. No one was with her in her last hour; who could have remained week in, week out, with that skeleton? She was deep in filth. The flesh which she had torn off in strips from her body stank to heaven. Corruption set in before she was dead." (*AdF*, 315–16)

351. "'I am Dr. Siegfried Fischer, the chess champion. You've recognized me, doubtless, from my photographs in the papers. What I need is a suit made-to-measure, ready by to-night. I'll pay top prices. Half immediately, the other half on receipt. I'm going on the night train to

Paris, I'm expected at the tournament in New York. My entire wardrobe has been stolen at my hotel. You will understand, my time is platinum. I wake up, and everything has gone. The burglars came at night. Only think of the shock to the management! How am I even to venture into the street? I am an abnormal shape, how can I help it: where are they to find a suit to fit me? No shirt, no socks, no shoes, for a man like me, to whom elegance is meat and drink? Take my measurements please; I won't delay you! By the merest chance they routed out a certain individual in a café, a hunchbacked cripple, you never saw such an object; he helped me out with his best suit. And what do you think his best suit was? This one! Such a deformity as this suit makes me, I am not by a long way, I assure you. In one of my English suits now, nobody would notice anything. Small, I grant you, can I help it? But the English tailors are geniuses, all of them, geniuses every one. Without a suit, I have a hump. I go to an Engish tailor, and no hump. A tailor of talent may make the hump look smaller, a genius tailors it right away. A tragedy—all my beautiful suits! Of course I'm insured. All the same, I must be grateful to the burglar. My new passport, issued yesterday, he left on the night-table. Everything else he took. There, have a look—you doubt my identity; tell you what, in this suit I often doubt it myself. I'd order three suits at once, but do I know what your work is like? In the autumn I'll be back again in Europe. If your suit's a success, you'll see things. I'll send all America to you! Charge me a reasonable price, for goodwill. You must know, I count on winning the world championship. Do you play chess?" (*AdF*, 350)

352. "'It was *nine o'clock*, the great clock in front of the station spoke English. At ten o'clock the house doors would be locked. It would be best to avoid meeting the porter. The way to the tumble-down barracks, in which Fischerle had unfortunately wasted twenty years with a whore, lasted forty minutes. Without hurrying too much he took it in the stride of his yellow shoes. Now and again he stood still under a street lamp and checked up in his book the words which he was saying in English. He was always right. He named the objects and spoke to the people whom he met, but quietly so that they should not interrupt him. He knew even more than he had imagined. When, after twenty minutes he could find nothing new, he dismissed houses, streets, street lamps and dogs and set himself to play a game of chess in English. This lasted him to the door of the filthy barracks. Just on the threshold he won the game and stepped into the hall. His quondam wife got on his nerves, very much on his nerves. So as not to run straight into her he hid himself behind the stairs. There was comfortable room. His eyes bored the banisters. There were plenty of holes in them on their own account. Had he wished he could have barricaded the stairs with his nose. Until ten o'clock he was as still as a mouse. The caretaker, a ragged shoemaker, closed the doors and with a quivering hand extin-

guished the staircase light. When he had disappeared into his shabby dwelling place, which was hardly twice as capacious as Fischerle's wife, Fischerle crowed softly: 'How do you do!'" (*AdF*, 361–62)

353. "The blind man hurled him to the ground and fetched from the table in the corner of the little room a bread knife. With this he slit coat and suit to shreds and cut off Fischerle's hump. He panted over the laborious work, the knife was too blunt for him and he wouldn't strike a light. The woman watched him, undressing meanwhile. She lay down on the bed and said: 'Ready!' But he wasn't yet ready. He wrapped the hump in the strips of the coat, spat on it once or twice and left the parcel where it was. The corpse he shoved under the bed. Then he threw himself on the woman. 'Not a soul heard anything.' he said and laughed. He was tired, but the woman was fat. He loved her all night long." (*AdF*, 365)

354. W. G. Sebald, "Gedanken zu Elias Canetti," *Literatur und Kritik* 65 (1972): 280–85 (281).

355. "The dwelling of the caretaker Benedikt Pfaff consisted of a middle-sized dark kitchen and a small white closet which gave on to the entrance hall of the house. Originally the family, which numbered five members, slept in the larger room; there were his wife, his daughter and three times over himself; himself as policeman, himself as husband, himself as father. The twin beds were, to his frequent indignation, the same size. For that reason he forced his daughter and wife to sleep together in one, the other belonged to him alone. Under himself he put a horsehair mattress, not because he was soft—he hated sluggards and women—but on principle. *He* it was who brought the money home. Washing all the stairs was his wife's duty, opening the street door at nights when anyone rang had since her tenth year been his daughter's, so that she should get over her timidity. Whatever return either of them received for their services he kept, for he was the caretaker. Now and again he permitted them to earn a little something on the side, by cleaning or washing. Thus they learned by their own experience how hard a father has to work when he had a family to support. At meals he proclaimed himself in favour of family life, at night he derided his enfeebled wife. He exercised his rights of discipline as soon as he came home from work. He polished his red-haired fists on his daughter with real pleasure, he made less use of his wife. He left all his money at home; the sum was always perfectly correct, even without his checking it over, for the only time he had found an error his wife and daughter had had to spend the night in the street. Taken for all in all he was a happy man." (*AdF*, 367)

356. Elias Canetti, *PM*, 171.

357. "He understood. She was threatening to inform against him. His offspring wanted to slander him. For whom did he live then? For

whom had he kept himself respectable? He'd nourished a viper in his bosom. She belonged on the gallows. *He* had made a special invention for her so that she should learn something; now, when the world and women were open to him, *he* stayed with her, out of kindness and because he had a heart of gold. And *she* pretended he'd done something wrong. She was no daughter of his! The old woman had tricked him. He was no fool to discipline her like he had. He'd had a fishy smell in his nose. Sixteen years he'd thrown money away on someone else's daughter. He could have bought a house for less. From year to year humanity deteriorated. Soon they'd abolish the police and criminals would have it all their own way. The State will say: No more pensions: and the whole world goes under! Human nature! Criminals spreading day by day, what'll happen to God Almighty!

Rarely did he rise to the height of God Almighty. He had respect for the all-highest position which belonged to him. God Almighty was greater even than the head of the police. All the more was he struck by the danger in which God found himself to-day. It was all very well to lift his step-daughter off the bed and beat her bloody. He took no real pleasure in it. He worked mechanically and what he said was full of grief and deep regret. His blows belied his voice. He had lost all desire to bellow. By mistake he referred once to a certain Polly. But his muscles made up for the mistake immediately. The name of the female he was disciplining was Anna. She claimed to be identical with a daughter of his. He did not believe her. Her hair came out in handfuls and when she defended herself two of her fingers got broken. She mouthed someting about his head, like a common butcher. She abused the police. It was plain that the best education could not prevail against a corrupt nature. Her mother was no good. She was ill and work-shy. He could send the daughter to join her mother, where she belonged. But he wasn't that kind. He stayed his hand, and went out to eat at a café." (*AdF*, 376–77)

358. Lillian Feder, *Madness in Literature* (Princeton: Princeton University Press, 1980).

359. Jacques Derrida, *Mémoires pour Paul de Man* (Paris: Galilée, 1988), 225–28.

360. See Jürgen Habermas, *Der philosophische Diskurs der Moderne: Zwölf Vorlesungen* (Frankfurt: Suhrkamp, 1985).

361. See Peter Russell, "The Vision of Man in Elias Canetti's *Die Blendung*," *GLL* 28 (1974–1975): 24–35.

362. See Edward Thomson, "Elias Canetti's *Die Blendung* and the changing image of madness . . . ," (44).

363. Richard Lawson, *Understanding Canetti*, 40.

364. Klaus-Peter Zepp, *Privatmythos und Wahn: Das mythopoetische Konzept im Werk Elias Canettis* (Frankfurt: Peter Lang, 1990), 214.

365. See David Turner, "Elias Canetti: The Intellectual as King Canute . . . ," (86).

366. See Dagmar Barnouw, "Elias Canetti—Poet and Intellectual . . . ," (129).

367. Günter Blöcker, "Die Masse in uns selbst," *FAZ*, 24.08.1963.

368. See *Die Blendung*, 304–305: Pöder, "Spurensicherung," (72), takes this sentence as more proof that Canetti is sending up Weininger. According to Weininger, policemen "take" servants, and here Benedikt Pfaff is the former and Therese the latter.

369. John Bayley, "Canetti and Power," in *Selected Essays*.

370. Lawson, *Understanding*, 56.

371. "To her he owed his rapid rise. He was tall, strong, fiery, and sure of himself; in his features there was something of that gentleness which women need before they can feel at home with a man. Those who saw him compared him to Michelangelo's Adam. He understood very well how intelligence and elegance could be combined. His brilliant gifts had been brought to fruitful effectiveness by the policy of his beloved. When she was sure that no one would follow her husband as the head of the institute but George himself, the director suddenly died without provoking any comment. George was at once nominated his successor and married her as a reward for her earlier services; of her last one he had no suspicion." (*AdF*, 396)

372. "In time he developed into a remarkable actor. The muscles of his face, of exceptional mobility, would fit themselves in the course of a day to the most various situations Since he would daily invite at least three patients, in spite of his thoroughness sometimes even more, he must play at least so many parts; not to count the fugitive but significant hints and words thrown out in the course of his rounds, which ran into hundreds. The scientific world argued vigorously over his treatment of a few chosen cases of alternating personalities. If a patient, for instance, imagined himself to be two people who had nothing in common or who were in conflict with each other, George Kien adopted a method which had at first seemed very dangerous even to him: he made friends with both parties. A fanatical pertinacity was the postulate for this ruse. So as to discover the true inwardness of both characters, he would support each with arguments from whose effects he would draw his own conclusions. He built up the conclusions into hypotheses and thought of delicate experiments to prove them. Then he would proceed to the cure. In his own consciousness he would gradually draw the sepa-

rate halves of the patient—as he embodied them—closer to each other, and thus gradually would rejoin them. He sensed the points of contact between them, and directed the attention of the separate personalities by striking and impressive images always back to these points until they remained there and of their own accord grew together. Sudden crises, violent partings, just when a final unanimity seemed to be achieved, happened often and were inevitable. But no less often did the cure succeed. Failures he ascribed to his own superficiality. He must have overlooked some hidden element, he was a botcher, he didn't take his work seriously enough, he was sacrificing living creatures to his own dead convictions, he was no better than his predecessor—then he would begin all over again, with a store of new curatives and experiments. For he believed in the soundness of his method." (*AdF*, 397–98)

373. "The doors which led to her brother-in-law's rooms were locked. Dr. George rang the bell. They heard a heavy dragging step. Then all grew still. Behind a peep-hole appeared a black eye. Madame put her finger to her lip and grinned tenderly. The eye stayed there, motionless. The two waited patiently. The doctor was regretting his politeness and the serious waste of his time. Suddenly the door swung silently open. A gorilla in human clothes stepped out, stretched forth its long arms, laid them on the shoulders of the doctor and greeted him in a foreign language. He took no notice of the woman. His gestures were crude, but comprehensible and inviting. The doctor racked his brains to follow his language. It seemed on the whole to recall an African dialect. The gorilla fetched his secretary. She was scantily dressed and evidently embarrassed. When she had seated herself her master pointed to a picture on the wall and clapped her on the back. She nestled up against him, unashamed. Her timidity disappeared. The picture represented the marriage of two ape-like creatures. Madame rose to her feet and looked at it from different angles and from all sides. The gorilla kept tight hold of his male visitor; he evidently had much to say to him. To George every word was strange. He grasped only one thing: the couple seated at the table were in some way closely connected with the couple in the picture. The secretary understood her master. She answered him in a similar language. He spoke louder, in a deeper voice, behind his tones there seemed to be passion. Occasionally she threw in a word in French, perhaps to indicate what was really meant. 'Don't you speak French?' George asked. 'Naturally, monsieur!' she countered emphatically, 'what do you take me for? I am a Parisian!' She flooded him with a hasty gush of words, badly pronounced and even worse strung together, as though she had already half forgotten the language. The gorilla bellowed at her, and she was quiet at once. His eyes shone. She put her arm across his chest. He cried like a child. 'He hates the French language,' she whispered to the visitor. 'He's been working for years on one of his own. It's not quiet finished yet.'" (*AdF*, 400–1)

374. "Madame was for ever gazing at the picture. George was grateful to her for this. One word from her would have broken down his politeness at last. He himself could find no words. If only the gorilla would speak again! Before this single wish all his thoughts of time-wasting, duties, women, success had vanished, as if from the day of his birth he had only been seeking for that man, or that gorilla, who had made up his own language. His crying interested him less. Suddenly he stood up and bowed low and reverently to the gorilla. He avoided French sounds, but his face expressed the greatest respect. The secretary accepted this recognition of her lord with a friendly nod. Then the gorilla stopped crying, fell back to his talking and permitted himself his original vehement gestures. Each syllable which he uttered corresponded to a special gesture. The words for objects seemed to change. He meant the picture a hundred times and called it each time something different; the names seemed to depend on the gesture with which he demonstrated them. Expressed and accompanied by his whole body no sound appeared indifferent. When he laughed he spread his arms out wide. He seemed to have a forehead at the back of his head. His hair had been rubbed away there as though, in the hours of his creative labour, he was for ever passing his hands over it.

Suddenly he sprang up and threw himself with passion on the floor. George noticed that it was strewn with earth, probably a thick layer. The secretary caught at his clothes as he lay there, but he was too heavy for her. Imploringly, she asked the visitor to help. She was jealous, she said, so very jealous! Together they raised the gorilla. Hardly was he seated again when he began to recount his experiences down below. From a few powerful words, hurled into the room like living tree trunks, George guessed at some mythical tale of passion, which shattered him with fearful doubts of himself. He saw himself as an insect in the presence of a man. He asked himself, how could he understand things which came from depths a thousand feet deeper than any he had ever dared to plumb. How could he measure himself, sitting at the same table with a creature such as this, he a creature of custom, of favours, with every pore of his soul stopped with fat, every day more fat, a half-man in all practical uses, without the courage to be, since to be in our world means to be different, a plaster cast, a tailor's dummy, set in motion or put to rest by gracious chance, entirely dependent on chance, without the slightest influence over it, without a spark of power, strumming always the same empty phrases, always understood at the same safe distance. For where is there a normal man, a man who determines, alters and forms his neighbour? The women, who had stormed George with love and who would give their lives for him, especially when he was making love to them, were afterwards just the same as they had been before, smoothly groomed skin-worshippers, busied about cosmetics or men. But this secretary, in her origin doubtless an ordinary woman, just the same as any other, had grown under the powerful will of the gorilla into an original creature, stronger, more passionate, more devoted. While he was singing his adventures with the earth, she grew restive. She threw jealous glances and words into the midst of his story, fidgeted helplessly hither and thither on her chair, pinched him, smiled, put out her tongue; he took no notice." (*AdF*, 401–2)

375. "For some months he came every day. His admiration for the gorilla grew from visit to visit. With infinite pains he learnt his language. The secretary did not help much; if she dropped back too often into her native French, she felt discarded. For her treachery to the man, to whom she clung without reservations, she deserved punishment. To keep the gorilla in a good temper George renounced the short cut of learning through any other language. He learnt like a child, who is being taught by words the relation of things to each other. Here their relation was the essential; the two rooms and their contents were dissolved in a magnetic field of passions. Objects—in this his first impressions had been correct—had no special names. They were called according to the mood in which they floated. Their faces altered for the gorilla, who lived a wild, tense, stormy life. His life communicated itself to them, they had an active part in it. He had peopled two rooms with a whole world. He created what he wanted, and after the six days of creation, on the seventh took up his abode therein. Instead of resting, he gave his creation speech. All that was round him proceeded from him. For the furniture which he had found here and the rubbish which little by little had been passed on to him, had long since carried the marks of his activities. The foreigner, who had suddenly descended on to his planet, he treated with patience. He could forgive back-slidings of his guest into the language of a worn-out and faded past, because he had himself once been a man. And he noticed clearly the progress the stranger was making. At first little more than his shadow, he grew in time to be his equal and friend." (*AdF*, 403)

376. Elias Canetti/Manfred Durzak, "Akustische Maske und Maskensprung: Materialien zu einer Theorie des Dramas. Ein Gespräch," *Neue Deutsche Hefte* 147 (1975): 497–516.

377. Hélène Cixous and Catherine Clément, *The Newly Born Woman*, trans. Betsy Wing, foreword by Sandra M. Gilbert (Minneapolis: University of Minnesota Press, 1986), 3–39.

378. "George was learned enough to publish a thesis on the speech of this madman. A new light was thrown on the psychology of sounds. Vigorously disputed problems of learning were solved by a gorilla. His friendship with him brought fame to the young doctor who had known hitherto only success. Out of gratitude he left him in the condition which made him happy. He renounced any attempt at a cure. He believed indeed, since he had learnt his language, that he had the skill

to change him back from a gorilla into the disinherited brother of a banker. But he resisted the temptation to commit a crime, a temptation provoked alone by the sense of a power which he had gained over night, and instead became a psychiatrist out of admiration for the greatness of the distracted to whom his friend was so closely akin, and with the firm principle that he would learn from them but would heal none. He had had enough of polite literature." (*AdF*, 403)

379. "When George walked along the streets of Paris it sometimes happened that he met one of his cures. He would be embraced and almost knocked down, like the master of some enormous dog coming home after a long absence. Under his friendly questions he concealed a timid hope. He spoke of general health, profession, plans for the future and waited for just one such little comment as '*Then* it was nicer!' or 'How empty and stupid my life is now!' 'I wish I were ill again!' 'Why did you cure me?' 'People don't realize what wonderful things there are in their heads!' 'Being sane is a kind of retarded development!' 'You ought to be put out of business! You've robbed me of my most priceless possession!' 'I value you as my friend. But your profession is a crime against humanity.' 'Be ashamed, you cobbler of souls!' 'Give me back my madness!' 'I'll have the law on you!' 'Sane rhymes with bane!'

Instead, compliments and invitations rained on him. His ex-patients looked plump, well and common." (*AdF*, 404)

380. "Three times a day when he went on his rounds through the rooms he received an ovation. He had grown accustomed to it; the more enthusiastically they ran to greet him, the more violently they crowded about him, the more certainly did he find the words and actions which he needed. The sick were his public. Before he came into the first room he was listening for the familiar hum of voices. Scarcely had one of them seen him from the window than the noise gained direction and order. He waited for this revolution. It was as if they had all begun to applaud. Involuntarily he smiled. Countless parts had become second nature to him. His spirit hungered for rapid transformations. A round dozen assistants followed him, to learn. Some were older, most of them had been in the profession longer than he. They regarded psychiatry as a special field of medicine, and themselves as the administrators of the mentally diseased. Whatever touched on their subject they had acquired with industry and hope. Sometimes they even pretended to agree with the crazy ideas of the patients, just as it said they should in the text books from which they drew their knowledge. One and all they hated the young director, who impressed on them daily that they were the servants and not the beneficiaries of the patients." (*AdF*, 405)

381. See Thomas Harrison, *Essayism: Conrad, Musil and Pirandello* (Baltimore: Johns Hopkins University Press, 1992).

382. "Of that far deeper and most special motive force of history, the desire of men to rise into a higher type of animal, in to the mass, and to lose themselves in it so completely as to forget that one man ever existed, they had no idea. For they were educated men, and education is in itself a cordon sanitaire for the individual against the mass in his own soul." (*AdF*, 410–11)

383. Elias Canetti, "Das erste Buch . . . ," 246.

384. "We wage the so-called war of existence for the destruction of the mass-soul in ourselves, no less than for hunger and love. In certain circumstances it can become so strong as to force the individual to selfless acts or even acts contrary to their own interests. 'Mankind' has existed as a mass for long before it was conceived of and watered down into an idea. It foams, a huge, wild, full-blooded, warm animal in all of us, very deep, far deeper than the maternal. In spite of its age it is the youngest of the beasts, the essential creation of the earth, its goal and its future. We know nothing of it; we live still, supposedly as individuals. Sometimes the masses pour over us, one single flood, one ocean, in which each drop is alive, and each drop wants the same thing. But it soon scatters again, and leaves us once more to be ourselves, poor solitary devils. In memory we can hardly conceive that we were ever so great, so many and so much one. 'Disease', says one overburdened intelligence; 'the beast in man' soothes the lamb of humility, and does not guess how near to the truth is its mistake. In the meantime the mass within ourselves is arming for a new attack. There will come a time when it will not be scattered again, possibly in a single country at first, eating its way out from there, until no one can doubt any more, for there will be no I, you, he but only it, the mass." (*AdF*, 411)

385. "For one discovery alone George flattered himself, and it was precisely this: the effects of the mass on history in general and on the life of individuals; its influence on certain changes in the human mind. He had succeeded in proving it in the case of some of his patients. Countless people go mad because the mass in them is particularly strongly developed and can get no satisfaction. In no other way did he explain himself and his own activity. Once he had lived for his private tastes, his ambition and women; now his one desire was perpetually to lose himself. In this activity he came nearer to the thoughts and wishes of the mass, than did those other single people among who he lived." (*AdF*, 411)

386. "Peter a murderer. Quiet, lanky Peter, whom all the other boys at school bullied. The stairs swayed. The roof fell in. And George, a person of the utmost fastidiousness, dropped his hat and did not pick it up. Peter married . . . Who would have believed it? The second wife, more than fifty years old, ugly freakish, common, not able to utter a single

human sentence, escaped an assault the day before yesterday. He cut the first one into pieces. He loves his books, and uses them as a hiding place. Peter and truth! If only he had lied, all his childhood lied, black and blue! So this was why George had been sent for. The telegram was a forgery, either of his wife or of the police. That legend of Peter's sexlessness. A pretty legend like all legends, made out of thin air, idiotic. George the brother of a blue-beard. Headlines in all the papers. The greatest living sinologist! The highest authority on eastern Asia! A double life! His retirement from the direction of the institute. Aberration. Divorce. His assistants to succeed him. The patients, the patients, they will be tormented, they will be ill-used! Eight hundred! They love him, they need him, he cannot leave them. Resignation is impossible. They cling to him on all sides, you mustn't leave us, we'll come too, stay with us, we've no one else, they don't talk our language, you listen to us, you understand us, you laugh with us; his beautiful, rare birds; they are all of them strangers there, each one from a different land, not one understands his neighbour, they accuse each other and do not even know it; he lives for them, he can't forsake them, he *will* stay. Peter's affairs must be seen to. His catastrophe is bearable. He was all for Chinese characters, George for human beings. Peter must be put in a home. He lived alone too long. His senses broke loose with his first wife. How could he control this sudden change? The police will give him up. Possibly he will be allowed to take him to Paris. It is evident that he is not responsible for his actions. In no circumstances will George retire from the direction of the institute." (*AdF*, 420–21)

387. "Your successes depend on shameless flattery. Now I understand why you are so famous. You are a consummate liar. The first word you learnt to speak was a lie. Because you delighted in lies you became a mental specialist. Why not an actor? You ought to be ashamed to confront your patients! Their suffering is the bitter truth, they suffer because they have no help left in the world. I can imagine just such a poor devil, suffering from hallucinations about a particular colour. "I can see nothing but green," he complains. He may even cry. Perhaps for months already he's been tormenting himself with this ridiculous green. What do you do? I know what you do. You flatter him, you grasp him by his Achilles heel—and how would he not have one, human beings are made up of weaknesses—you talk to him with your "my friend" and your "my dear fellow," he weakens, first he respects you, then he respects himself. He may be the wretchedest poor devil on God's earth; you overwhelm him with respect. Hardly has he begun to think of himself as co-director of your lunatic asylum, merely kept out of the general directorship by an unjust accident, then you come along with your true speech. "My dear fellow," you say to him, "the colour you keep seeing is not green. It is—it is—let us say blue!" Peter's voice grew sharp. 'Have you cured him? No! His wife at home will torment him just as she did

before, she will torment him to his dying day. "When men are ill and at the gates of death, they become as men out of their minds," said Wang-Chung, a penetrating thinker; he lived in the first century of our era, from 27 to 98, in China under the later Han dynasty, and knew more about sleep, madness and death than you with all your supposedly accurate science. Cure your lunatic of his wife! As long as he has her he will be both mad and dead—which according to Wang-Chung are closely related conditions. Send his wife away if you can! You cannot do it, because you have not got her. If you had her you'd keep her for yourself because you like a skirt. Shut up all women in your institute, do what you like with them, wear yourself out, die exhausted and stupefied at forty, at least you'll have healed many sick men and will know for what you have received so much fame and honour!'" (*AdF*, 431)

388. "'I believe,' said George, and put on his most charming air of sympathy—who would not have been touched by it—'that you overestimate the importance of women. You take them too seriously, you think they are human beings like us. I see in women merely a passing necessary evil. Many insects even have these things better arranged. One or a very few mothers bring into being the entire race. The rest remain undeveloped. Is it possible to live at closer quarters than the termites do? What a terrifying accumulation of sexual stimuli would not such a stock produce—if the creatures were still divided as to sex? They are not so divided, and the instincts inherent in that division are much reduced among them. Even what little they have, they fear. When they swarm, at which period thousands, nay millions, are destroyed apparently without reason, I see in this a release of the amassed sexuality of the stock. They sacrifice a part of their number, in order to preserve the rest from the aberrations of love. The whole stock would run aground on this question of love, were it once to be permitted. I can imagine nothing more poignant than an orgy in a colony of termites. The creatures forget—a colossal recollection has seized hold of them—what they really are, the blind cells of a fanatic whole. Each will be himself, it begins with a hundred or a thousand of them, the madness spreads, *their* madness, a mass madness, the soldiers abandon the gates, the whole mound burns with unsatisfied love, they cannot find their partners, they have no sex, the noise, the excitement far greater than anything usual, attracts a storm of real ants; through the unguarded gates their deadly enemies press in, what soldier thinks of defending himself, they want only love; and the colony which might have lived for all eternity—that eternity for which we all long—dies, dies of love, dies of that urge through which we, mankind, prolong our existence! It is a sudden transformation of the wisest into the most foolish. It is—no, it can't be compared with anything—yes, it is as if by broad daylight, with healthy eyes and in full possession of your understanding, you were to set fire to yourself and all your books. No one threatens you, you have as much

money as you need and want, your work is growing every day more comprehensive and more individual, rare old books fall into your lap, you are acquiring superb manuscripts, not a woman crosses your threshold, you feel yourself free through your work and protected by your books—and then, without provocation, in this blissful and creative condition, you set fire to your books and let them and yourself burn together without a protest. That would be an event which would have a remote relation to the one I have described among the termites, an outbreak of utter senselessness, as with them, but not in so astounding a form. Shall we too one day, like the termites, dispense with sex? I believe in learning more firmly every day, and every day less firmly in the indispensability of love!'

'There is no love! A thing which does not exist can be neither indispensable nor dispensable. I would like to say with the same assurance: there are no women. What have the termites to do with us? Who among them has suffered anything from a woman? *Hic mulier, hic salta.* Let us confine ourselves to human beings! That female spiders eat their husbands after they have made use of the poor weaklings; that female gnats alone feed on blood, this has nothing to do with us. The slaughter of the drones among bees, is totally barbarous. If they do not need drones, why do they breed them, if they do need them why do they kill them? In the spider, the most cruel and ugly of all creatures, I see an embodiment of woman. Her web shimmers in the sunlight, poisonous and blue.'" (*AdF*, 432–33)

389. Dissinger, *Massenwahn*, 98–99.

390. "When he found the two of them, thought George, the caretaker, still humble in those days, must have taken himself off, embarrassed, forgetting his fists at the sight of the wealthy man of learning. She, however, put on an impertinent air—the one defence of the discovered—took her clothes into the next room and dressed herself there. Jean, where are you?" (*AdF*, 441)

391. "'Yes, and just such another miracle as the love riot in the termite hill and the burning of my library, which is impossible, out of the question, inconceivable, stark madness, treason unparalleled to priceless treasures such as no one else has gathered together, sheer scandal, an obscenity, something you must not even mention to me in jest, let alone presume, you can see now, I'm not mad. I'm not even a little unbalanced, I've gone through a lot, there's nothing wrong in getting excited, why do you sneer at me, my memory is perfect, I know everything I want to know, I am master of myself, why?—even if I married once I never had a single love affair, and you, what haven't you done in love, love is a leprosy, a disease, inherited from the first living organisms, others marry twice, three times, I had nothing to do with her, you insult me, you've no right to say it, a madman might do such a thing but I

shan't set my library on fire, clear out, if you insist on it, go back to your Bedlam, where are your wits, you answer everything I say with yes, or Amen! So far I've heard not one personal expression of thought from you, you rattle, you think you know everything! I can smell your contemptuous thoughts. They stink. He's mad, you think, because he abuses women! I'm not the only one! I'll prove that to you! Take away your filthy ideas! You even learnt to read from me, you squirt. You don't even know Chinese. Very well, I'll have my divorce later. I must rehabilitate my honour. A wife isn't necessary for a divorce. Let her turn in her grave. She's not even in a grave. She doesn't deserve a grave. She deserves hell! Why is there no Hell? One must be founded. For women and womanizers, like you. What I say is the truth! I am a serious person. You are going away now and won't bother with me any more. I am alone. I have a head. I can look after myself." (*AdF*, 444–45)

392. "He spoke with passion. Each word had the calculated effect. She changed colour. He paused after some sentences. Never before had he dared so much melodrama. She said nothing. He grasped that it was his presence which struck her dumb. He spoke so beautifully. She was afraid of missing a single word. Her eyes started out of their sockets, first with fear, then with love: she pricked her ears; water ran out of her mouth. The chair on which she sat creaked a popular tune. She held out her hands to him, folded into a cup. She drank with lips and hands. When he kissed her hands, the cup lost its shape and her lips breathed—he could hear it: more please. So he overcame his revulsion and kissed her hands again. She trembled: her emotion extended even to the roots of her hair. Had he embraced her she would have fainted." (*AdF*, 453)

393. "The woman made her own terms: she was not to be pinched or knocked about and she was to be allowed to receive the Professor's brother whenever he wanted. Pfaff agreed, flattered. He had his doubts about the prohibition on pinching. He was only human after all. But as well as committing themselves to mutual love, they were each to watch the other. If one or the other were to go wandering off in the direction of Ehrlich Strasse the other was immediately to inform Paris. In which case both shop and liberty would be ruthlessly removed. The very first information would be followed by arrest by telegraph. The informer could reclaim a reward. Pfaff didn't give a sh— for Ehrlich Strasse if he could live among a crowd of canary birds. Therese complained: Please he's doing it again. He mustn't always sh—. George spoke to him seriously about using the sort of language which was more suited to a better-class business man." (*AdF*, 454)

394. David Darby, *Studies of Disintegration*, 124–46.

395. Ruth Kennedy in conversation with the author at Univeristy College Dublin, May 1992.

396. Elias Canetti, "Der Beruf des Dichters," in *GW*, 279–90.

397. Hans Feth, *Elias Canettis Dramen* (Frankfurt, 1980).

398. Elias Canetti, *GU*, 9.

399. Elias Canetti to Fräulein Gorgosch, in *Butzbacher Autorenbefragung: Briefe zur Deutschstunde*, ed. Hans-Joachim Müller (München: Ehrenkirth, 1973), 201–2 (202).

400. Elias Canetti, "Vorbemerkung," in *PM*, 7.

401. Peter von Matt, "Der phantastische Aphorismus bei Elias Canetti," in *Elias Canetti: Ein Londoner Symposium*, 9–19.

402. See Thomas Lappe, *Canettis Aufzeichnungen* (Aachen: Alano, 1989) and Ingo Seidler, "'Bruchstücke einer großen Konfession': Zur Bedeutung von Canettis 'Sudelbüchern,'" *MAL* 16 (1983): 1–21.

403. Elias Canetti, *PM*, 204.

404. Elias Canetti, "Hitler, nach Speer," in *GW*, 175–204.

405. See Michael Krüger, ed., *Einladung zur Verwandlung* (München: Hanser, 1995).

406. J. Pattillo-Hess, ed., *Masse und Macht oder die Aufgabe des gegenwärtigen Denkens* (Wien: Löcker, 1988), Pattillo-Hess, ed., *Tod und Verwandlung in Canettis Masse und Macht* (Wien: Löcker, 1990), Pattillo-Hess, Ed., *Verwandlungsverbote und Befreiungsversuche in Canettis Masse und Macht* (Wien: Löcker, 1991), Pattillo-Hess, ed., *Der Stachel des Befehls* (Wien: Löcker, 1992), and Pattillo-Hess and Mario Smole, eds., *Nationen* (Wien: Löcker, 1994).

407. J. S. McClelland, *The Crowd and the Mob: From Plato to Canetti* (London: Unwin Hyman, 1989).

408. Elias Canetti, *PM*, 169.

409. Adrian Stevens, "Creating Figures," in *Elias Canetti: Ein Londoner Symposium*, 106–17 (116).

410. See Caren Jane Caplan, *The Poetics of Displacement: Exile, Immigration, and Travel in Contemporary Autobiographical Writing*, unpublished Ph.D, University of California, Santa Cruz, 1987, and Cecile Zorach, "The outsider Abroad: Canetti in Marrakesh," *MAL* 16 (1983): 47–64.

411. Herbert Göpfert, "Zu den Stimmen von Marrakesch," in *Elias Canettis Anthropologie und Poetik*, 135–50 (135–36).

412. Göpfert, "Zu den Stimmen," 143.

413. See Harriet Murphy, "A Passion for People: Elias Canetti's Autobiography and its Implications for Exile Studies," *Austrian Studies* 6 (1995): 134–46, and Harriet Murphy "The Art of Autobiography," forthcoming.

414. See Barbara Meili, *Erinnerung und Vision*, Barbara Saunders, *Contemporary German Autobiography: Literary Approaches to the Problem of Identity* (London: Institute of Germanic Studies, 1985), Friederike Eigler, *Das autobiographische Werk von Elias Canetti: Verwandlung—Identität—Machtausübung* (Tübingen: Stauffenburg, 1988), and Madeleine Salzmann, *Die Kommunikationsstruktur der Autobiographie mit kommunikationsorientierten Analysen der Autobiographien von Max Frisch, Helga M. Novak und Elias Canetti* (Bern: Peter Lang, 1988).

415. Susan Sontag, "Mind as Passion," in *Under the Sign of Saturn* (New York: Farrar, Straus and Giroux, 1980), 181–204.

BIBLIOGRAPHY: General Sources Consulted

Abel, Elizabeth, ed. *Writing and Sexual Difference*. Brighton: Harvester, 1982.

Adam, Ian, and Hellen Tiffin, eds. *Past The Last Post: Theorizing Post-colonialism and Post-modernism*. London: Harvester Wheatsheaf, 1991.

Alderman, Harold. *Nietzsche's Gift*. Athens: Ohio University Press, 1977.

Arendt, Hannah. *The Origins of Totalitarianism*. London: Allen and Unwin, 1967.

Arens, Katherine. *Functionalism and Fin de siècle: Fritz Mauthner's Critique of Language*. New York: Peter Lang, 1984.

Aristotle. *Poetics*. Translated by W. Hamilton Fyfe. London: Dent, 1982.

Armstrong, Nancy. *The Violence of Representation: Literature and the History of Violence*. New York: Routledge, 1989.

Auerbach, Erich. *Mimesis*. Bern: Francke, 1946.

Bachelard, Gaston. *La Psychanalyse du Feu*. Paris: Gallimard, 1949.

Bakhtin, Mikhail. *The Dialogic Imagination: Four Essays*. Translated by Michael Holquist. Edited by Caryl Emerson and Michael Holquist. Austin: University of Texas Press, 1981.

———. *Rabelais and His World*. Translated by Hélène Iswolsky. Bloomington: Indiana University Press, 1984.

Bal, Mieke. *Narratology*. Toronto: University of Toronto Press, 1985.

Barry, Kevin. *Language, Music and the Sign*. Cambridge: Cambridge University Press, 1985.

Baruch, Elaine. *Women, Love, Power*. New York: New York University Press, 1991.

Basil, Otto, et al. *Das grosse Erbe: Aufsätze zur österreichischen Literatur*. Graz und Wien: Stiasny Verlag, 1962.

Baudelaire, Charles, *Oeuvres complètes*. Edited by C. Pichois. 2 volumes. Paris: Gallimard, 1975–1976.

Baudrillard, Jean. *Selected Writings*. Edited by Mark Poster. Cambridge: Polity, 1988.

Bauer, Dale M., and Susan Janet McKinstry, eds. *Feminism, Bakhtin and the Dialogic*. Albany: State University Of New York Press, 1991.

Bayley, John. *Selected Essays*. Cambridge: Cambridge University Press, 1984.

Behler, Ernst. *Irony and the Discourse of Modernity*. Seattle: University of Washington Press, 1990.

Belsey, Catherine. *Critical Practice*. London: Routledge, 1980.

Belsey, Catherine, and Jane Moore, eds. *The Feminist Reader: Essays in Gender and the Politics of Literary Criticism*. Basingstoke: Macmillan, 1989.

Berger, John. *Ways of Seeing*. London: BBC, 1972.

Berman, Russell. *The Rise of the Modern German Novel: Crisis and Charisma*. Cambridge, Mass.: Harvard University Press, 1986.

Bernstein, Jay. *The Fate of Art: Aesthetic Alienation from Kant to Derrida and Adorno*. Cambridge: Polity, 1992.

Bersani, Leo. *The Freudian Body: Psychoanalysis and Art*. New York: Columbia University Press, 1986.

———. *The Culture of Redemption*. Cambridge, Mass.: Harvard University Press, 1990.

Best, Steven, and Douglas Kellner. *Postmodern Theory Critical Interrogations*. Basingstoke: Macmillan, 1991.

Bhabha, Homi, ed. *Nation and Narration*. London: Routledge, 1990.

Blondel, Eric. *Nietzsche: The Body and Culture*. Translated by Sean Hand. London: Athlone, 1991.

Bloom, Harold. *A Map of Misreading*. Oxford: Oxford University Press, 1975.

———. *Deconstruction and Criticism*. London: Routledge, Keegan and Paul, 1979.

———. *Agon: Towards a Theory of Revisionism*. Oxford: Oxford University Press, 1982.

———. *Ruin The Sacred Truths: Poetry and Belief from the Bible to the Present.* Cambridge, Mass.: Harvard University Press, 1989.

———. *The Anxiety of Influence: A Theory of Poetry.* New York: Oxford University Press, 1973.

Boa, Elizabeth, and J.H.Reid. *Critical Strategies: German Fiction in the Twentieth Century.* London: Edwin Arnold, 1972.

Boone, Joseph Allen. *Tradition Counter Tradition: Love and the Form of Fiction.* Chicago: University of Chicago Press, 1987.

Booth, Wayne. *The Company We Keep: An Ethics of Fiction.* Berkeley and Los Angeles: University of California Press, 1988.

Bourdieu, Pierre. *Homo Academicus.* Cambridge: Polity, 1988.

Bovenschen, Silvia. *Die imaginierte Weiblichkeit: Exemplarische Untersuchungen zu kulturgeschichtlichen und literarischen Präsentationsformen des Weiblichen.* Frankfurt: Suhrkamp, 1979.

Brady, Philip, et al., eds. *Günter Grass' Der Butt: Sexual Politics and The Male Myth of History.* Oxford: Oxford University Press, 1990.

Breicha, Otto, and Gerhard Fritsch, eds. *Aufforderung zum Misstrauen: Literatur: Bildende Kunst: Musik in Österreich seit 1945.* Salzburg: Residenz, 1967.

Breicha, Otto, ed. *Wotruba: Figur als Widerstand: Bilder und Schriften zu Leben und Werk.* Salzburg: Galerie Welz, 1977.

Broch, Hermann, *Massenwahntheorie: Beiträge zu einer Psychologie der Politik.* Edited by Paul Michael Lützeler. Frankfurt: Suhrkamp, 1979.

Bryson, Norman. *Vision and Painting: The Logic of the Gaze.* London: Macmillan, 1983.

Cadava, Eduardo, ed. *Who comes after the Subject.* London: Routledge, 1991.

Caillois, Roger. *Man, Play and Games.* Translated by Meyer Barash. New York: Free Press of Glencoe, 1961.

Callinicos, Alex. *Against Postmodernism: A Marxist Critique.* Cambridge: Polity, 1989.

Canetti, Veza. *Die gelbe Straße.* München: Hanser, 1990.

———. *Der Oger.* München: Hanser, 1991.

———. *Geduld bringt Rosen.* München: Hanser, 1992.

Carey, John. *The Intellectuals and the Masses: Pride and Prejudice among the Literary Intelligentsia.* London: Faber, 1992.

Cixous, Hélène, and Catherine Clément. *The Newly Born Woman*, Translated by Betsy Wing. Minneapolis: University of Minnesota Press, 1986.

———. "The Laugh of the Medusa," *Signs* 7 (1), 1976: 41–55.

———. *Le Livre de Promethea.* Paris: Gallimard, 1983.

Coffey, M. *Roman Satire.* London: Methuen, 1976.

Cohn, Dorrit. *Transparent Minds: Narrative Modes for presenting Consciousness in Fiction.* Princeton: Princeton University Press, 1978.

Coward, Rosalind, and John Ellis. *Language and Materialism.* London: Routledge, Keegan and Paul, 1977.

Culler, Jonathan. *Structuralist Poetics: Structuralism, Linguistics and the Study of Literature.* London: Routledge, Keegan and Paul, 1975.

De Man, Paul. *Allegories of Reading: Figural Language in Rousseau, Nietzsche, Rilke and Proust.* New Haven: Yale University Press, 1979.

———. *The Resistance to Theory.* Minneapolis: University of Minnesota Press, 1986.

———. *Blindness and Insight: Essays in the Rhetoric of Contemporary Criticism.* London: Methuen, 1989.

Deiritz, Karl, and Hannes Krauss. *Der deutsch-deutsche Literaturstreit oder "Freunde, es spricht sich schlecht mit gebundener Zunge."* Hamburg: Luchterhand, 1991.

Del Caro, Adrian. *Dionysian Aesthetics.* Frankfurt: Peter Lang, 1981.

Deleuze, Gilles. *Nietzsche et la Philosophie.* Paris: PUF, 1962.

Deleuze, Gilles, and Félix Guattari. *Capitalisme et Schizophrénie: L'Anti-Oedipe.* Paris: Editions de Minuit, 1972.

———. *Kafka: Pour une littérature mineure.* Paris: Editions de Minuit, 1975.

———. *Capitalisme et Schizophrénie: Mille Plateaux.* Paris: Editions de Minuit, 1980.

Demetz, Peter. *After the Fires: Recent Writing in the Germanies, Austria and Switzerland.* London: Harcourt, Brace Jovanovich, 1986.

Derrida, Jacques. *L'Ecriture et la Différence.* Paris: Editions du Seuil, 1967.

———. *De la Grammatologie*. Paris: Editions de Minuit, 1967.

———. *L'Archéologie du Frivole: Lire Condillac*. Paris: Denoel Gonthier, 1976.

———. *Mémoires pour Paul de Man*. Paris: Editions de Minuit, 1988.

———. *A Derrida Reader: Between The Blinds*. Edited by Peggy Kamuf. Hemel Hempstead: Harvester Wheatsheaf, 1991.

Doane, Janice, and Devon Hodges. *Nostalgia and Sexual Difference: The Resistance to Contemporary Feminism*. New York: Methuen, 1987.

Docherty, Thomas. *Reading (Absent) Character: Towards a Theory of Characterization in Fiction*. Oxford: Oxford University Press, 1983.

———. *On Modern Authority*. Brighton: Harvester, 1987.

———. *After Theory: Postmodernism/Postmarxism*. London: Routledge, 1990.

Eagleton, Mary, ed. *Feminist Literary Theory: A Reader*. Oxford: Blackwell, 1986.

Eagleton, Terry. *Criticism and Ideology: A Study in Marxist Literary Theory*. London: Verso, 1976.

———. *The Rape of Clarissa: Writing, Sexuality and Class Struggle in Samuel Richardson*. Oxford: Blackwell, 1982.

———. *Literary Theory: An Introduction*. Oxford: Blackwell, 1983.

———. *Against the Grain*. London: Verso, 1986.

———. *The Ideology of the Aesthetic*. Oxford: Blackwell, 1990.

———. *The Significance of Theory*. Oxford: Blackwell, 1990.

———. *Ideology: An Introduction*. London: Verso, 1991.

Ehrmann, Jacques, ed. *Game, Play, Literature*. New Haven: Yale University Press, 1968.

Elliott, Robert C. *The Power of Satire*. Princeton: Princeton University Press, 1960.

Ellmann, Mary. *Thinking about Women*. London: Virago, 1979.

Fanger, Donald. *The Creation of Nikolai Gogol*. Cambridge, Mass.: Harvard University Press, 1979.

Feder, Lillian. *Madness in Literature*. Princeton: Princeton University Press, 1980.

Felman, Shoshana. *La Folie et la Chose littéraire*. Paris: Editions du Seuil, 1978.

Field, Frank. *The Last Days of Mankind: Karl Kraus and his Vienna.* London: Macmillan, 1967.

Fish, Stanley. *Literature and Psychoanalysis*. Baltimore: Johns Hopkins University Press, 1982.

Fitzgerald, William. *Agonistic Poetry: The Pindaric Mode in Pindar, Horace, Hölderlin, and the English Ode*. Berkeley: University of California Press, 1987.

Flieger, Jerry Aline. *The Purloined Punch Line: Freud's Comic Theory and the Postmodern Text*. Baltimore: Johns Hopkins University Press, 1990.

Foster, John Burt. *Heirs To Dionisus: A Nietzschean Current in Literary Modernism*. Princeton: Princeton University Press, 1981.

Foucault, Michel. *The Foucault Reader: An Introduction to Foucault's Thought*. Edited by Paul Rainbow. Harmondsworth: Penguin, 1991.

Fox-Genovese, Elizabeth. *Feminism without Illusions: A Critique of Individualism*. Chapel Hill: University of North Carolina Press, 1991.

Freud, Sigmund, *Abriß der Psychoanalyse. Das Unbehagen in der Kultur.* Frankfurt: Fischer, 1953.

———. *Massenpsychologie und Ich-analyse: Die Zukunft einer Illusion.* Frankfurt: Fischer, 1967.

———. *Die Traumdeutung*. Frankfurt: Fischer, 1972.

———. *Der Witz und seine Beziehung zum Unbewußten*. Frankfurt: Fischer, 1978.

———. *Drei Abhandlungen zur Sexualtheorie und verwandte Schriften.* Frankfurt: Fischer, 1970.

———. *Bildende Kunst und Literatur*. Frankfurt: Fischer, 1969.

Fromm, Erich. *The Anatomy of Human Destructiveness*. Harmondsworth: Penguin, 1977.

———. *To Have or To be*. London: Abacus, 1979.

Fuchs, Albert. *Geistige Strömungen in Österreich: 1867–1918*. Wien: Löcker, 1984.

Furness, Raymond. *The Twentieth Century 1890–1945*. London: Croom Helm, 1978.

Gilbert, Sandra, and Susan Gubar. *No Man's Land: The Place of the Woman Writer in the Twentieth Century: The War of the Words.* New Haven: Yale University Press, 1988.

———. *No Man's Land: The Place of the Woman Writer in the Twentieth Century: Sexchanges.* New Haven: Yale University Press, 1989.

Gilman, Sander. *Jewish Self-Hatred: Anti-Semitism and the Hidden Language of the Jews.* Baltimore: Johns Hopkins University Press, 1986.

———. *Inscribing the Other.* Lincoln: University of Nebraska Press, 1992.

Graddol, David, and Joan Swann. *Gender Voices.* Oxford: Blackwell, 1989.

Greer, Germaine. *The Obstacle Race: The Fortunes of Women Painters and Their Work.* London: Pan, 1979.

Grimstad, Kari. *Masks of the Prophet: The Theatrical World of Karl Kraus.* Toronto: University of Toronto Press, 1982.

Grosz, Georg. *Ein kleines Ja und Ein großes Nein: Sein Leben von ihm selbst erzählt: Mit siebzehn Tafel- und fünfundvierzig Textabbildungen.* Hamburg: Rowohlt, 1955.

Hannoush, Michele. *Baudelaire and Caricature: From the Comic to an Art of Modernity.* University Park: Pennsylvania State University Press, 1992.

Harrison, Thomas. *Essayism: Conrad, Musil and Pirandello.* Baltimore: Johns Hopkins University Press, 1992.

Hart, Kevin. *The Trespass of the Sign.* Cambridge: Cambridge University Press, 1989.

Harvey, Irene. *Derrida and the Economy of Différance.* Bloomington: Indiana University Press, 1986.

Hassan, Ihab. *The Postmodern Turn: Essays in Postmodern Theory and Culture.* Columbus: Ohio State University Press, 1978.

Hatfield, Henry. *Crisis and Continuity in Modern German Fiction: Ten Essays.* Ithaca: Cornell University Press, 1969.

Heath, Stephen. *The Sexual Fix.* London: Macmillan, 1982.

Heilbrun, Carolyn G., ed. *The Representation of Women in Fiction.* Baltimore: Johns Hopkins University Press, 1983.

Held, David. *Introduction to Critical Theory: Horkheimer to Habermas.* Berkeley: University of California Press, 1980.

Higgins, Lynn A. and Brenda R. Silver, eds. *Rape and Representation.* New York: Columbia University Press, 1991.

Highet, Gilbert. *The Anatomy of Satire.* Princeton: Princeton University Press, 1957.

Hinton, Thomas R., and Wilfred van der Will. *The German Novel and the Affluent Society.* Manchester: Manchester University Press, 1968.

Hobbes, Thomas. *Leviathan.* Edited by John Plamenatz. London: Fount, 1974.

Hoesterey, Ingeborg, ed. *Zeitgeist in Babel: The Postmodernist Controversy.* Bloomington: Indiana University Press, 1991.

Holland, Norman N. *Laughing: A Psychology of Humor.* Ithaca: Cornell University Press, 1982.

Hollander, Paul. *Political Pilgrims: Travels of Western Intellectuals to the Soviet Union, China and Cuba 1928–1978.* Oxford: Oxford University Press, 1981.

Holquist, M. "How to play Utopia: Some Brief notes on the Distinctiveness of Utopian Fiction," in *Game, Play, Literature.* Edited by Jacques Ehrmann. New Haven: Yale University Press, 1968.

———. *Dialogism: Bakhtin and his World.* London: Methuen, 1990.

Holub, Robert C. *Reception Theory: A Critical Introduction.* London: Methuen, 1984.

Holzner, Johann, Michael Klein, and Wolfgang Wiesmüller, eds. *Studien zur Literatur des 19. und 20. Jahrhunderts in Österreich.* Innsbruck: Institut für Germanistik, 1981.

Huizinga, J. *Homo Ludens: A Study of the Play Element in Culture.* London: Routledge, Keegan and Paul, 1949.

Hume, Kathryn. *Fantasy and Mimesis: Responses to Reality in Western Literature.* New York: Methuen, 1984.

Hunt, Lester H. *Nietzsche and the Origin of Virtue.* London: Routledge, 1991.

Hussey, Edward. *The Presocratics.* London: Duckworth, 1972.

Hutcheon, Linda. *Narcissistic Narrative: The Metafictional Paradox.* Waterloo: Wilfrid Laurier University Press, 1980.

———. *A Theory of Parody: The Teachings of Twentieth-Century Art Forms.* London: Methuen, 1985.

———. *A Poetics of Postmodernism: History, Theory, Fiction.* London: Routledge, 1988.

———. *The Politics of Postmodernism.* London: Routledge, 1989.

Huyssen, Andreas. *After the Great Divide: Modernism, Mass Culture and Postmodernism.* Basingstoke: Macmillan, 1986.

Huyssen, Andreas, and David Bathrick, eds. *Modernity and the Text: Revisions of German Modernism.* New York: Columbia University Press, 1989.

Irigaray, Luce. *Speculum de l'Autre Femme.* Paris: Editions de Minuit, 1974.

———. *Ce Sexe Qui N'en Est Pas Un.* Paris: Editions de Minuit, 1977.

———. *Amante Marine.* Paris: Editions de Minuit, 1980.

———. *Ethique de la Différence Sexuelle.* Paris: Editions de Minuit, 1984.

———. *Je, Tu, Nous: Pour Une Culture De La Différence.* Paris: B. Grasset, 1990.

———. *The Irigaray Reader.* Edited by Margaret Whitford. Oxford: Blackwell, 1991.

Iser, Wolfgang. *Sterne: Tristram Shandy.* Cambridge: Cambridge University Press, 1988.

Jackson, Rosemary. *Fantasy and Mimesis: The Literature of Subversion.* London: Routledge, 1984.

Jameson, Fredric. *The Political Unconscious: Narration as Socially Symbolic Act.* London: Methuen, 1981.

———. *The Ideologies of Theory: Essays 1971–1986: Volume I: Situations of Theory.* London: Routledge, 1988.

———. *Late Marxism: Adorno, or, the Persistence of the Dialectic.* London: Verso, 1990.

———. *Signatures of the Visible.* London: Routledge, 1990.

———. *Postmodernism, or, The Cultural Logic of Late Capitalism.* London: Verso, 1991.

Janik, Allan, and Stephen Toulmin. *Wittgenstein's Vienna.* New York: Simon and Schuster, 1973.

Jardine, Alice, and Hester Eisenstein, eds. *The Future of Difference.* Boston: G. K. Hall, 1980.

Jardine, Alice A. *Gynesis: Configurations of Woman and Modernity.* Ithaca: Cornell University Press, 1985.

———, ed. *Men In Feminism.* London: Methuen, 1987.

Jay, Martin. *Adorno.* Cambridge, Mass.: Harvard University Press, 1984.

Jefferson, Ann. *Reading Realism in Stendhal.* Cambridge: Cambridge University Press, 1988.

Johnson, Barbara. *The Critical Difference: Essays in the Contemporary Rhetoric of Reading.* Baltimore: Johns Hopkins University Press, 1980.

———. *A World of Difference.* Baltimore: Johns Hopkins University Press, 1987.

Johnston, William M. *The Austrian Mind.* Berkeley: University of California Press, 1972.

Kaplan, E. Ann, ed. *Postmodernism and its Discontents: Theories, Practices.* London: Verso, 1988.

Kauffman, Linda, ed. *Gender and Theory: Dialogues on Feminist Criticism.* Oxford: Blackwell, 1988.

———, ed. *Feminism and Institutions: Dialogues on Feminist Theory.* Oxford: Blackwell, 1989.

Kayser, Wolfgang. *Das Groteske: Seine Gestaltung in Malerei und Dichtung.* Oldenburg: G. Stalling, 1957.

Kearney, Richard. *Dialogues with Contemporary Continental Thinkers: The Phenomenological Heritage: Paul Ricoeur, Emmanuel Levinas, Herbert Marcuse, Stanislas Breton, Jacques Derrida.* Manchester: Manchester University Press, 1984.

———. *Modern Movements in European Philosophy.* Manchester: Manchester University Press, 1986.

———. *Poetics of Imagining: From Husserl to Lyotard.* London: Harper Collins Academic, 1991.

Kirk, G. S., J. E. Raven, and M. Schofield. *The Presocratic Philosophers: A Critical History with a Selection of Texts.* Cambridge: Cambridge University Press, 1983.

Koestler, Arthur. *The Act of Creation.* London: Arkana, 1989.

Kofman, Sarah. *Nietzsche et La Métaphore.* Paris: Payot, 1972.

———. *Nietzsche et La Scène Philosophique.* Paris: Union générale d'Editions, 1979.

———. *Pourquoi Rit On? Freud et Le Mot d'Esprit*. Paris: Union générale d'Editions, 1985.

Kowatzki, Irmgard. *Der Begriff des Spiels als ästhetisches Phänomen von Schiller bis Benn*. Bern: Herbert Lang, 1973.

Kristeva, Julia. *The Kristeva Reader*. Edited by Toril Moi. Oxford: Blackwell, 1989.

———. *Desire in Language: A Semiotic Approach to Literature and Art*. Edited by Leon S. Roudiez. Translated by Thomas Gora et al. New York: Columbia University Press, 1980.

Kroker, Arthur, and David Cook. *The Postmodern Scene: Excremental Culture and Hyper-Aesthetics*. Basingstoke: Macmillan, 1988.

Kunnas, Tarmo. *Nietzsches Lachen: Eine Studies über das Komische bei Nietzsche*. München: Edition Wissenschaft und Literatur, 1982.

Lacan, Jacques. *Écrits: A Selection*. Translated by Alan Sheridan. London: Tavistok Publications, 1977.

Lacoue-Labarthe, Philippe. *Typography. Mimesis, Philosophy, Politics*. Cambridge, Mass.: Harvard University Press, 1989.

Lamb, Johnathan. *Sterne's Fiction and the Double Principle*. Cambridge: Cambridge University Press, 1989.

Lauretis, Teresa de. *Technologies of Gender*. Bloomington: Indiana University Press, 1987.

———, ed. *Feminist Studies/Critical Studies*. Basingstoke: Macmillan, 1988.

Lawson, Hilary. *Reflexivity: The Post-modern Predicament*. London: Hutchinson, 1985.

Le Bon, Gustave. *The Crowd: A Study of the Popular Mind*. London: Benn, 1947.

Le Rider, Jacques. *Der Fall Otto Weininger*. Wien: Löcker, 1985.

———. *Modernité Viennoise*. Paris: PUF, 1990.

Lloyd, Michael. *The Agon in Euripides*. Oxford: Oxford University Press, 1992.

Lodge, David. *After Bakhtin: Essays on Fiction and Criticism*. London: Routledge, 1990.

Loveridge, Mark. *Laurence Sterne and the Argument about Design*. Basingstoke: Macmillan, 1982.

Lyotard, Jean-François. *La Condition Postmoderne: Rapport sur le Savoir.* Paris: Editions de Minuit, 1979.

———. *Le Différend.* Paris: Editions de Minuit, 1983.

———. *The Lyotard Reader.* Edited by Andrew Benjamin. Oxford: Blackwell, 1989.

Lyotard, Jean-Francois, and Jean-Loup Thébaud. *Just Gaming.* Translated by Wlad Godzich and Brian Massumi. Minneapolis: University of Minnesota Press, 1985.

MacCannell, J. F., ed. *The Other Perspective in Gender and Culture: Rewriting Woman and the Symbolic.* New York: Columbia University Press, 1992.

McClelland, J. S. *The Crowd and the Mob: From Plato to Canetti.* London: Unwin Hyman, 1989.

McGowan, John. *Post-Modernism and its Critics.* Ithaca: Cornell University Press, 1991.

McGuinness, Brian, ed. *Wittgenstein And His Times.* Oxford: Basil Blackwell, 1982.

Mc Hale, Brian. *Postmodernist Fiction.* New York: Routledge, 1987.

Maguire, Robert A. *Gogol from the Twentieth Century.* Edited and translated by Robert A. Maguire. Princeton: Princeton University Press, 1974.

———. *Exploring Gogol.* Stanford: Stanford University Press, 1994.

Mahler, Anna. *Her Work.* Introduced by Ernst Gombrich with an essay "The Human Figure in Art" by Anna Mahler. Stuttgart: Belser, 1975.

Mahler-Werfel, Alma. *Mein Leben.* Frankfurt: Fischer, 1985.

Meese, Elizabeth, and Alice Parker, eds. *The Difference Within: Feminism and Critical Theory.* Amsterdam: John Benjamins Publishing Co., 1989.

Meltzer, Françoise. *Salomé and the Dance of Writing: Portraits of Mimesis in Literature.* Chicago: University of Chicago Press, 1987.

Miller, Nancy, ed. *Poetics of Gender.* New York: Columbia University Press, 1986.

———. *Subject to Change: Reading Feminist Writing.* New York: Columbia University Press, 1988.

Mitchell, Juliet, and Jacqueline Rose. *Feminine Sexuality: Jacques Lacan and the Ecole Freudienne.* Basingstoke: Macmillan, 1982.

Modleski, Tani. *Feminism without Women.* London: Routledge, 1991.

Moi, Toril, ed. *French Feminist Thought: A Reader.* Oxford: Blackwell, 1987.

———. *Sexual/Textual Politics.* London: Methuen, 1985.

Moroney, Patrick. *Nietzsche's Dionysian Aristocratic Culture: The Influence of Ancient Greco-Roman Thought on Nietzsche's Philosophy.* Maynooth: Kairos Publications, 1986.

Morson, Gary Saul, and Caryl Emerson. *Rethinking Bakhtin: Extensions and Challenges.* Evanston: Northwestern University Press, 1989.

———. *Mikhail Bakhtin: Creation of a Prosaics.* Stanford: Stanford University Press, 1990.

Morson, Gary Saul. *Mikhail Bakhtin: Essays and Dialogues on his Work.* Chicago: University of Chicago Press, 1986.

Moscovici, Serge. *The Age of the Crowd: A Historical Treatise on Mass Psychology.* Translated by J. C. Whitehouse. Cambridge: Cambridge University Press, 1985.

Murdoch, Iris. *Metaphysics as a Guide to Morals.* London: Chatto and Windus, 1992.

Murphy, Harriet. *The Rhetoric of the Spoken Word in Die Wahlverwandtschaften.* Frankfurt: Peter Lang, 1990.

Nardo, Anna K. *The Ludic Self in Seventeenth Century English Literature.* Albany: State University of New York Press, 1991.

Nash, Cristopher. *World Games: The Tradition of Anti-Realist Revolt.* London: Methuen, 1987.

Naumann, Michael. *Der Abbau einer verkehrten Welt.* München: List, 1969.

Nemoianu, Virgil, and Robert Royal, eds. *Play, Literature, Religion: Essays in Cultural Intertextuality.* Albany: State University of New York Press, 1992.

Neumann, Michael. *Unterwegs zu den Inseln des Scheins: Kunstbegriff und literarische Form in der Romantik von Novalis bis Nietzsche.* Frankfurt: Klostermann, 1991.

Nelson, T. G. A. *Comedy: The Theory of Comedy in Literature, Drama and Cinema.* Oxford: Oxford University Press, 1990.

Nicholson, Linda J., ed. *Feminism/Postmodernism.* New York: Routledge, 1990.

Nixon, Rob. *London Calling: V. S. Naipaul: Post-colonial Mandarin.* New York: Oxford University Press, 1991.

Norris, Christopher. *The Contest of Faculties: Philosophy and Theory after Deconstruction.* New York: Methuen, 1985.

———. *Derrida.* Cambridge, Mass.: Harvard University Press, 1987.

———. *What's Wrong with Postmodernism: Critical Theory and the Ends of Philosophy.* New York: Harvester Wheatsheaf, 1990.

———. *Spinoza and the Origins of Modern Critical Theory.* Oxford: Blackwell, 1991.

Nussbaum, Martha. *Love's Knowledge: Essays on Philosophy and Literature.* New York: Oxford University Press, 1990.

———. "The Transfigurations of Intoxication: Nietzsche, Schopenhauer, and Dionysus," *Arion* 1 (1991): 75–111.

Nuttall, A. D. *A New Mimesis: Shakespeare and the Representation of Reality.* London: Methuen, 1983.

Nye, Andrea. *Words of Power: A Feminist Reading of the History of Logic.* London: Routledge, 1990.

O'Neill, Patrick. *The Comedy of Entropy: Humour, Narrative, Reading.* Toronto: University of Toronto Press, 1990.

Ortega y Gasset, José. *The Revolt of the Masses.* London: Allen and Unwin, 1969.

Palmeri, Frank. *Satire in Narrative: Petronius, Swift, Gibbon, Melville and Pynchon.* Austin: University of Texas Press, 1990.

Pasley, Malcolm, ed. *Nietzsche: Imagery and Thought.* London: Methuen, 1978.

Paulsen, Wolfgang. *Das Ich im Spiegel der Sprache: Autobiographisches Schreiben in der deutschen Literatur des 20. Jahrhunderts.* Tübingen: Niemeyer, 1991.

Pearce, Richard. *The Enigma of Gogol: An Examination of the Writings of N. V. Gogol and their Place in the Russian Literary Tradition.* Cambridge: Cambridge University Press, 1981.

Pearson, Roger. *Stendhal's Violin: A Novelist and his Reader.* Oxford: Oxford University Press, 1988.

Petro, Peter. *Modern Satire: Four Studies.* Berlin: Mouton, 1982.

Plato. *The Laws.* Translated by A. E. Taylor. London: Dent, 1960.

Prendergast, Christopher. *The Order of Mimesis: Balzac, Stendhal, Nerval, Flaubert.* Cambridge: Cambridge University Press, 1986.

Prince, Gerald. *A Dictionary of Narratology.* Aldershot: Scolar, 1991.

Raine, Kathleen. *Autobiographies.* London: Skoob, 1991.

Rasch, Wolfdietrich. *Die literarische Décadence um 1900.* München: C. H. Beck, 1986.

Reich, Wilhelm. *The Mass Psychology of Fascism.* Translated by Vincent R. Carfagno. Harmondsworth: Penguin, 1972.

Reich-Ranicki, Marcel. *Entgegnung zur deutschen Literatur der 70er Jahre.* Stuttgart: Deutsche Verlagsanstalt, 1979.

Reichert, Herbert. *Friedrich Nietzsche's Impact on Modern German Literature.* Chapel Hill: University of North Carolina Press, 1975.

Reik, T. *Jewish Literature.* New York, 1962.

Reiss, Timothy J. *The Discourse of Modernism.* Ithaca: Cornell University Press, 1982.

———. *The Uncertainty of Analysis: Problems in Truth, Meaning and Culture.* Ithaca: Cornell University Press, 1988.

———. *The Meaning of Literature.* Ithaca: Cornell University Press, 1992.

Ricoeur, Paul. *A Ricoeur Reader: Reflection and Imagination.* Edited by Mario J. Valdes. London: Harvester Wheatsheaf, 1991.

Rieder, Heinz. *Österreichische Moderne: Studien zum Weltbild und Menschenbild in ihrer Epik und Lyrik.* Bonn: Bouvier, 1968.

Roberts, David, ed. *Comic Relations: Studies in the Comic, Satire and Parody.* Frankfurt: Peter Lang, 1985.

———. *Art and Enlightenment: Aesthetic Theory after Adorno.* Lincoln: University of Nebraska Press, 1991.

Roberts, Julian. *German Philosophy: An Introduction.* Oxford: Blackwell, 1988.

Robertson, Ritchie. *Kafka: Judaism, Politics and Literature.* Oxford: Oxford University Press, 1988.

Rogers, Pat. *The Augustan Vision.* London: Methuen, 1974.

Ruthven, K. K. *Feminist Literary Studies: An Introduction.* Cambridge: Cambridge University Press, 1984.

Ruthven, Malise. *A Satanic Affair: Salman Rushdie and the Wrath of Islam.* London: Hogarth Press, 1991.

Ryan, Judith. *The Vanishing Subject: Early Psychology and Literary Modernism.* Chicago: University of Chicago Press, 1991.

Said, Edward. *Beginnings: Intention and Method.* Baltimore: Johns Hopkins University Press, 1975.

———. *The Question of Palestine.* London: Vintage, 1980.

———. *The World, The Text, The Critic.* Cambridge, Mass.: Harvard University Press, 1983.

———. *Orientalism.* Harmondsworth: Penguin, 1985.

———. *Culture and Imperialism.* London: Verso, 1993.

Said, Edward, and Christopher Hitchens, eds. *Blaming the Victims: Spurious Scholarship and the Palestinian Question.* London: Verso, 1988.

Saunders, Barbara. *Contemporary German Autobiography: Literary Approaches to the Problem of Identity.* London: Institute of Germanic Studies, 1985.

Schaeffer, Neil. *The Art of Laughter.* New York: Columbia University Press, 1981.

Scheichl, Sigurd Paul, and Gerald Stieg, eds. *Österreichishce Literatur des 20. Jahrhunderts: Französische und österreichische Beiträge.* Innsbruck: Institut für Germanistik, 1986.

Schorske, Carl E., *Fin de Siècle Vienna: Politics and Culture.* New York: Vintage Books, 1981.

Schumacher, E. F. *Small is Beautiful: A Study of Economics As If People Mattered.* London: Blond and Briggs, 1973.

Screech, M. A. *The Rabelaisian Marriage: Aspects of Rabelais's Religion, Ethics and Comic Philosophy.* London: Arnold, 1958.

———. *Rabelais.* London: Duckworth, 1979.

———. *Erasmus: Ecstasy and the Praise of Folly.* Harmondsworth: Penguin, 1988.

Seidel, Michael. *Satiric Inheritance: Rabelais to Sterne.* Princeton: Princeton University Press, 1979.

Sellers, Susan, ed. *Writing Differences: Readings from the Seminar of Hélène Cixous.* New York: St. Martin's Press, 1988.

———. *Language and Sexual Difference in Feminist Writing in France.* Basingstoke: Macmillan, 1991.

Shapiro, Gary. *Nietzschean Narratives.* Bloomington: University of Indiana Press, 1989.

———. *Nietzsche on Gifts, Noise and Women.* Albany: State University of New York Press, 1992.

Sherman, Nancy. *The Fabric of Character: Aristotle's Theory of Virtue.* Oxford: Oxford University Press, 1989.

Sloterdijk, Peter. *Der Denker auf der Bühne: Nietzsches Materialismus.* Frankfurt: Suhrkamp, 1986.

Smith, Paul. *Discerning the Subject.* Minneapolis: University of Minnesota Press, 1988.

Smyth, Edmund J. *Postmodernism and Contemporary Fiction.* London: Batsford, 1991.

Sontag, Susan. *Under the Sign of Saturn.* New York: Farrar, Straus and Giroux, 1980.

Spacks, Patricia. *The Female Imagination.* London: Allen and Unwin, 1976.

Spariosu, Mihai. *Literature, Mimesis and Play: Essays in Literary Theory.* Tübingen: Narr, 1982.

———, ed. *Mimesis in Contemporary Theory: An Interdisciplinary Approach.* Philadelphia: J. Benjamins Publishing Co., 1984.

———. *Dionysus Reborn: Play and the Aesthetic Dimension in Modern Philosophical and Scientific Discourse.* Ithaca: Cornell University Press, 1989.

———. *God of Many Names: Play, Poetry and Power in Hellenic Thought from Homer to Aristotle.* Durham: Duke University Press, 1991.

Spivak, Gayatri Chakravorty. *In Other Worlds: Essays in Cultural Politics.* New York: Routledge, 1988.

———. *Selected Subaltern Studies.* New York: Oxford University Press, 1988.

Stauth, Georg. *Nietzsche's Dance : Resentment, Reciprocity and Resistance in Social Life.* Oxford: Blackwell, 1988.

Steiner, George. *Language and Silence: Essays 1958–1966.* London: Faber, 1967.

———. *Extraterritorial: Papers on Literature and the Language Revolution.* London: Faber and Faber, 1971.

———. *Real Presences: Is There Anything In What We Say?* London: Faber and Faber, 1989.

Stern, J. P., *The Heart of Europe: Essays on Literature and Ideology.* Oxford: Blackwell, 1992.

Strelka, Joseph P., et al., eds. *Protest—Form—Tradition: Essays on German Exile Literature.* Alabama: University of Alabama Press, 1979.

Sturrock, J., *Structuralism and Since.* Oxford: Oxford University Press, 1979.

Suleiman, Susan Rubin, and Inge Crosman, eds. *The Reader in the Text: Essays on Audience and Interpretation.* Princeton: Princeton University Press, 1980.

Suleiman, Susan Rubin, ed. *The Female Body in Western Culture: Contemporary Perspectives.* Cambridge, Mass.: Harvard University Press, 198.

———. *Subversive Intent: Gender, Politics and the Avant Garde.* Cambridge, Mass.: Harvard University Press, 1990.

Sussman, Henry. *Afterimages of Modernity: Structure and Indifference in Twentieth-Century Literature.* Baltimore: Johns Hopkins University Press, 1990.

Tallis, Raymond. *In Defence of Realism.* London: Edward Arnold, 1988.

———. *Not Saussure: A Critique of Post-Saussurean Literary Theory.* Basingstoke: Macmillan, 1988.

Tejera, V. *Nietzsche and Greek Thought.* Dordrecht: Nijhoff, 1987.

Thiele, Leslie Paul. *Friedrich Nietzsche and the Politics of the Soul: A Study of Heroic Individualism.* Princeton: Princeton University Press, 1990.

Thomson, Philip. *The Grotesque.* London: Methuen, 1972.

Timms, Edward. *Karl Kraus: Apocalyptic Satirist: Culture and Catastrophe in Habsburg Vienna.* New Haven: Yale University Press, 1986.

Tomlinson, John. *Cultural Imperialism.* Baltimore: Johns Hopkins University Press, 1991.

Tong, Rosemarie. *Feminist Thought: A Comprehensive Introduction.* London: Routledge, 1989.

Vaihinger, H., *The Philosophy of "As If": A System of the Theoretical, Practical and Religious Fictions of Mankind.* Translated by C. K. Ogden. London: Routledge, Keegan and Paul, 1935.

Vattimo, Gianni. *The End of Modernity: Nihilism and Hermeneutics in Post-modern Culture.* Translated by Jon R. Snyder. Baltimore: Johns Hopkins University Press, 1988.

Von Scheliha, Renata. *Vom Wettkampf der Dichter: Der musische Agon bei den Griechen.* Amsterdam: Castrum Peregrini Presse, 1987.

Wagner, Nike. *Geist und Geschlecht: Karl Kraus und die Erotik der Wiener Moderne.* Frankfurt: Suhrkamp, 1982.

Walton, Kendall L. *Mimesis as Make-Believe: On the Foundations of the Representational Arts.* Cambridge, Mass.: Harvard University Press, 1990.

Waugh, Patricia. *Metafiction: The Theory and Practice of Self-Conscious Fiction.* London: Methuen, 1984.

Weedon, Chris. *Feminist Practice and Poststructuralist Theory.* Oxford: Basil Blackwell, 1987.

Weinbrot, Howard. D. *Eighteenth Century Satire: Essays on Text and Context From Dryden to Peter Pindar.* Cambridge: Cambridge University Press, 1988.

Weininger, Otto. *Geschlecht und Charakter.* Leipzig: Braumüller, 1922.

Weiss, Walter, and Eduard Beutner, eds. *Literatur und Sprache im Österreich der Zwischenkriegszeit.* Stuttgart: H.D.Heinz, 1985.

Wellberry, David E., T. C. Heller, and Morton Sosna, eds. *Reconstructing Individualism: Autonomy, Individuality and the Self in Western Thought.* Stanford: Stanford University Press, 1986.

White, Allon, and Peter Stallybrass. *The Politics and Poetics of Transgression.* London: Methuen, 1986.

White, Hayden. *Metahistory: The Historical Imagination in Nineteenth-Century Europe.* Baltimore: Johns Hopkins University Press, 1973.

White, J. J. *Mythology in the Modern Novel: A Study of Prefigurative Techniques.* Princeton: Princeton University Press, 1971.

Wisse, Ruth R. *The Schlemiel as Modern Hero.* Chicago: University of Chicago Press, 1971.

Wistrich, Robert, S. *The Jews of Vienna in the Age of Franz Joseph.* Oxford: Oxford University Press, 1989.

——— , ed. *Austrians and Jews in the Twentieth Century: From Franz Joseph to Waldheim.* Basingstoke: Macmillan, 1992.

Wittig, Monique. *Les Guérillères.* Paris: Editions de Minuit, 1969.

Wunberg, Gotthart, and Johannes J. Braakenburg, eds. *Die Wiener Moderne: Literatur, Kunst und Musik zwischen 1890 und 1910.* Stuttgart: Reclam, 1981.

Wyschogrod, Edith. *Saints and Postmodernism: Revisioning Moral Philosophy.* Chicago: University of Chicago Press, 1990.

Yeager, Patricia. *Honey-Mad Women: Emancipatory Strategies in Women's Writing.* New York: Columbia University Press, 1988.

Young, Julian. *Nietzsche's Philosophy of Art.* Cambridge: Cambridge University Press, 1992.

Ziolkowski, Theodor. *Dimensions of the Modern German Novel: German Texts and European Contexts.* Princeton: Princeton University Press, 1969.

Zweig, Stefan. *Die Welt von Gestern: Erinnerungen eines Europäers.* Stockholm: Bermann-Fischer Verlag, 1942

BIBLIOGRAPHY:
Specialist Sources Consulted

PRIMARY TEXTS

Canetti, Elias. *Werke.* München: Hanser, 1993–

Nietzsche, Friedrich. *Sämtliche Werke: Kritische Studienausgabe.* Edited by Giorgio Colli and Mazzino Montinari. Berlin: De Gruyter, 1967–1977.

Stendhal. *Oeuvres Complètes.* Edited by Victor Del Litto and Ernest Abravanel. 50 volumes. Genève: Slatkine reprints, 1986.

There is now a general bibliography available of secondary literature relating to Elias Canetti, to which readers are referred for detailed knowledge of critical work on the author:

Bensel, Walter, ed. *Elias Canetti: Eine Personalbibliographie.* Bremerhaven: Dux, 1989.

SELECTED SECONDARY LITERATURE

Works cited below are relevant to *Die Blendung* in particular.

Albers, Bernhard, ed. *Rudolf Hartung-Elias Canetti: Ein Rezipient und sein Autor.* Aachen: Rimbaud, 1992.

Andics, Hellmut. *Das österreichische Jahrhundert: Die Donaumonarchie 1804–1918.* Wien: Kremayr und Scheriau, 1986.

Aspetsberger, Friedbert, and Gerald Stieg, eds. *Elias Canetti: Blendung als Lebensform.* Königstein/Taunus: Athenäum, 1985.

Auer, Annemarie. "Ein Genie und sein Sonderling. Elias Canetti und *Die Blendung,*" *Sinn und Form* 21 (1969): 936–83.

Ayren, Armin. "Don Quijote Kien und Sancho Pansa Fischerle: über Elias Canetti," *Die Horen* 22 (1977): 111–15.

Barnouw, Dagmar. "Der Stachel des Zweifels," *Literatur und Kritik* 65 (1972): 285–93.

———. "Doubting Death: On Elias Canetti's Drama: The Deadlined," *Mosaic* 7 (1974): 1–23.

———. *Elias Canetti.* Stuttgart: Metzler, 1979.

———. "Mind and Myth in *Masse und Macht*," *Modern Austrian Literature* 16 (1983): 65–79.

———. "Elias Canetti—Poet and Intellectual." In *Major Figures of Contemporary Austrian Literature*. Edited by Donald G. Daviau, 117–41. New York: Peter Lang, 1987.

Bartsch, Kurt, and Gerhard Melzer, eds. *Experte der Macht: Elias Canetti.* Graz: Droschl, 1985.

Bartsch, Kurt, and Dietmar Goltschnigg, eds. *Für und wider eine österreichische Literatur.* Königstein/Taunus: Athenäum, 1982.

Bartsch, Kurt. "Dialog mit Antike und Mythos: Christoph Ransmayrs Ovid-Roman *Die letzte Welt*," *Modern Austrian Literature* 23 (1990): 121–33.

Baumann, Gerhart. "Die Weltoffenheit des Dichters Elias Canetti," *Neue Rundschau* 91 (1980): 5–14.

Baur, Ruprecht Slavko. "Gespräch mit Elias Canetti," *Literatur und Kritik* 65 (1972): 272–79.

Beller, Manfred. "The fire of Prometheus and the theme of progress in Goethe, Nietzsche, Kafka and Canetti," *Colloquia Germanica* 17 (1984): 1–13.

Bernhard, Thomas. "Die Komödie der Eitelkeit," *Die Zeit*, 27.2.1976.

Bienek, Horst. "Die Zeit entlässt uns nicht: Rede auf Elias Canetti," *Akzente* 7 (1972–1973): 557–64.

Bischoff, Alfons-M. *Elias Canetti: Stationen zum Werk.* Frankfurt am Main: Herbert Lang, 1973.

Blöcker, Günter. "Die Masse in uns selbst," *FAZ*, 24.8.1963.

Bollacher, Martin. "Chaos und Verwandlung—Bemerkungen zu Canettis 'Poetik des Widerstands,'" *Euphorion* 73 (1979): 169–85.

———. "Vom Gewissen der Worte: Elias Canetti und die Verantwortung des Dichters im Exil," in *Im Zeichen Hiobs: Jüdische Schriftsteller und deutsche Literatur im 20. Jahrhundert.* Edited by Gunter

E. Grimm and Hans-Peter Bayerdörfer, 326–37. Königstein/ Taunus: Athenäum, 1985.

Bonhage, Hans Joachim. "Ein Kopf ohne Welt—Welt im Kopf," *Westermann* 105 (1964): 82–83.

Brück, Max von. "Die unfreiwillige Monade," *Die Gegenwart* 4 (1949): 20.

Burgess, Anthony. "Elias Canetti: *Auto Da Fé*," *The Yorkshire Post*, 22.2.1962.

Canetti, Elias. "Zu Tibor Dery," *Wort in der Zeit* 12 (1965): 38–39.

———. "Realismus und neue Wirklichkeit," *Neue Rundschau* (1966): 87–91.

———. "Unsichtbarer Kristall," *Literatur und Kritik* 22 (1968): 65–67.

———. "Wir werden 300 Jahre leben," *Neues Forum* 17 (1970): 987–88.

———. Letter to Fräulein Gorgosch (London, 22.07.71) in *Butzbacher Autorenbefragung: Briefe zur Deutschstunde*, edited by Hans Joachim Müller, 201–2. Ehrenwirth: München, 1973.

———. "*Das Chaos des Fleisches. Alfred Hrdlicka: Acht Radierungen zu Masse und Macht*," in *Alfred Hrdlicka: Acht Radierungen zu Elias Canetti Masse und Macht*, with an introduction by Karl Diemer, 19–35. Stuttgart: Galerie Valentin, 1973.

———. "Akustische Maske und Maskensprung: Materialien zu einer Theories des Dramas: Ein Gespräch," *Neue Deutsche Hefte* 147 (1975): 497–516.

———. "Der neue Karl Kraus," *Neue Rundschau* 86 (1975): 1–21.

———. An Herrn Göpfert, gedruckt in hundert Exemplaren im Auftrag der Historischen Kommission des Börsenvereins des Deutschen Buchhandels und der Horst Kliemann Stiftung zum 70. Geburtstag von Herbert G. Göpfert am 22. September 1977.

———. "Jede Absage bestärkte mich," in *Wie ich anfing . . . 24 Autoren berichten von ihren Anfängen*. Edited by Hans Daiber, 122–34. Düsseldorf: Claasen, 1979.

———. "Kleiner Dialog über die Plastik," *Akzente*, 3 (1980): 193–94.

———. "Hebel und Kafka," *Bogen* 1 (1980): 3–5.

———. Letter to Herr Göpfert, *Bogen* 7 (1982): 13–14.

———. *Literatur und Kritik*, 165/166 (1982): 53.

Caplan, Caren Jane. "*The Poetics of Displacement: Exile, Immigration, and Travel in Contemporary Autobiographical Writing.*" Ph.D diss., University of California, Santa Cruz, 1987.

Carr, William. *A History of Germany 1815–1990.* London: Arnold, 1991.

Cohen, Yaier. "Elias Canetti: Exile and the German Language," *German Life and Letters* 42 (1988): 32–45.

Curtis, Anthony. "Elias Canetti: *Auto Da Fé*," *Sunday Telegraph*, 11.2.1962.

Curtius, Mechthild. *Kritik der Verdinglichung in Canettis Roman Die Blendung: Eine sozialpsychologische Literaturanalyse.* Bonn: Bouvier, 1973.

———. "Einkreisung der Wirklichkeit. Die Rolle der extremen Charaktere für Canettis Dichtung," *Literatur und Kritik* 93 (1975): 176–82.

Daiber, Hans. "Elias Canetti," *Wort in der Zeit* 7 (1957): 1–6.

———. "*Die Blendung*," *Neue Deutsche Hefte* 11 (1964): 133–35.

Darby, David Malcom. "*Studies of Disintegration: Narrative Strategies in Elias Canetti's Die Blendung.*" Ph.D diss., Queens University, Kingston, Ontario, 1988.

———. "A fiction of detection: The Police Enquiry in Elias Canetti's Auto-da-Fé," in *Semiotics 1988*, edited by Terry Prewitt et al., 343–49. London: University Press of America, 1990.

———. "'Esse Percipi,' Sein ist Wahrgenommenwerden": Perception and Perspective in Berkeley and Canetti," *Neophilologus* 75 (1991): 425–32.

———. *Studies of Disintegration: Narrative Strategies in Elias Canetti's Die Blendung.* Riverside: Ariadne, 1991.

———. "A literary life: the textuality of Elias Canetti's autobiography," *Modern Austrian Literature* 25 (1992): 37–49.

Demet, Michel-Francois. "The theme of Blood in Elias Canetti's *Die Blendung*," *Modern Austrian Literature* 16 (1983): 147–53.

Dissinger, Dieter. "Der Roman *Die Blendung*," *Text und Kritik*, 28 (1970): 30–38.

———. *Vereinzelung und Massenwahn: Elias Canettis Roman Die Blendung.* Bonn: Bouvier, 1971.

———. "Alptraum und Gegentraum. Zur Romanstruktur bei Canetti und Bernhard," *Literatur und Kritik* X (1975): 168–75.

Durzak, Manfred. "Versuch über Elias Canetti," *Akzente* 17 (1970): 169–91.

———. *Gespräche über den Roman mit Joseph Breitbach, Elias Canetti, Heinrich Böll, Siegfried Lenz, Hermann Lenz, Wolfgang Hildesheimer, Peter Handke, Hans Erich Nossack, Uwe Johnson, Walter Höllerer: Formbestimmungen und Analysen.* Frankfurt: Suhrkamp, 1976.

———, ed. *Zu Elias Canetti.* Stuttgart: Klett, 1983.

Dussel, Reinhard. "Aspects of Confucianism in Elias Canetti's Notes and Essays," *Tamkang Review* 18 (1987–1988): 333–41.

Ehlers, Swantje. "Stilmanier und Imaginationsbildung am Beispiel von Elias Canettis Roman *Die Blendung*," *Sprachkunst* 6 (1985): 18–24.

Eigler, Friederike. *Das autobiographische Werk von Elias Canetti. Verwandlung—Identität—Machtausübung.* Stauffenburg: Tübingen, 1988.

Enright, D. J. "*Auto Da Fé*," *Encounter* 18 (1962): 65–68.

Enzensberger, Hans Magnus. "Elias Canetti: *Die Blendung*," *Der Spiegel*, XVII/32 (1963): 48.

Falk, Thomas. *Elias Canetti.* New York: Twayne, 1993.

Ferber, Christian. "Keine Angst vor Canetti," *Frankfurter Hefte* 1 (1951): 66.

———. "Elias Canetti: *Die Blendung*," *Welt am Sonntag*, 8.9.1963.

———. "Ein Untergang, der kaltlässt," *Die Welt*, 5.11.1965.

Fiedler, Leslie A. "*The Tower of Babel*," *Partisan Review* (June 1947): 316–20.

Foell, Kristie A. "Absence as Presence: Sigmund Freud in the works of Elias Canetti," in *Semiotics 1988*, edited by Terry Prewitt et al., 350–55. London: University Press of America, 1990.

———. *Blind Reflections: Gender in Elias Canetti's Die Blendung.* Riverside, Calif.: Ariadne, 1994.

Fink, Humbert. "Elias Canetti: *Die Blendung*," *Deutsche Zeitung*, 9.10.1963.

Furbank, P. N. "Elias Canetti: *Auto Da Fé*," *The Spectator*, 16.2.1962.

Galli, Matteo. *Canetti: Invito alla lettura di Canetti.* Milano: Mursia, 1986.

Garscha, Winfried R. and Barry McLoughlin. *Wien 1927: Menetekel für die Republik*. Berlin: Dieter Verlag, 1987.

Göpfert, Herbert G., ed. *Canetti lesen*. München: Hanser, 1975.

Greiner, Bernhard. "Das Bild und die Schriften der *Blendung*: Über den biblischen Grund von Canettis Schreiben," in Link, Franz, ed. *Paradigmata: Literarische Typologie des Alten Testaments*, I: *Von den Anfängen bis zum 19. Jahrhundert*: II: *20. Jahrhundert*. Berlin: Duncker und Humblot, 1989.

Grenier, Roger. "La moustache de Nietzsche," *Le Nouvel Observateur*, 15.06.1966.

Gretsky, Laurence Arthur. "*Sprachverzerrung und Sprachüberwindung als Themen in Elias Canettis Roman Die Blendung*." Ph.D. diss., Indiana University, 1974.

Günther, Joachim. "Die moralische Quadratur des Zirkels. Das Todesproblem im Werk Elias Canettis," *Text und Kritik* 28 (1970): 24–29.

Hammer, Jean-Pierre. "Canetti and Hrdlicka," *Austriaca* 11 (1980): 115–20.

Hartung, Rudolf. "Elias Canetti: *Die Blendung*," *Literarische Revue* 3 (1948): 341–47.

———. "Hinweis auf Elias Canetti," *Neue Deutsche Hefte* 7 (1960–1961): 445–47.

Hennighaus, Lothar. *Tod und Verwandlung: Elias Canettis poetische Anthropologie aus der Kritik der Psychoanalyse*. Frankfurt: Peter Lang, 1984.

Hesse, Hermann. "Erzählende Literatur: *Die Blendung* von Elias Canetti," *Neue Zürcher Zeitung*, 12.1.1936.

Hinderberger-Burton, Tania. "*Elias Canetti: Die Blendung: Eine Analyse*." Ph.D. diss., State University of New York at Stony Brook, 1982.

———. "The Quixotic in Canetti's *Die Blendung*," *Modern Austrian Literature* 16 (1983): 165–67.

Hüter der Verwandlung. Beiträge zum Werk von Elias Canetti. München: Hanser, 1985.

Ishaghpour, Youssef. *Elias Canetti: Métamorphose et identité*. Paris: La Différence, 1990.

Isaacs, Jacob. *An Assessment of Twentieth-Century Literature: Six lectures delivered in the BBC Third Programme*. London: Secker and Warburg, 1951.

Jansen, Peter. "Die Komik des Sprechens. Zur sprachlich-ästhetischen Erfahrung des Komischen am Beispiel von Canettis Roman *Die Blendung," Sprache im technischen Zeitalter* 76 (1980): 312–26.

Jebb, Julian. "Elias Canetti: *Auto Da Fé*," *Time and Tide*, 1.3.1962.

Jenny, Urs. "Ein Menetekel der ewigen Dummheit," *Du* 23 (1963): 51–52.

———. "Von Vätern und Göttern—Elias Canetti," *Merkur* 216 (1966): 285–88.

Karst, Roman. "Elias Canetti's *Die Blendung*: A Study in insanity," *Modern Austrian Literature* 16 (1983): 133–45.

Kaszynski, Stefan H. *Elias Canettis Anthropolgie und Poetik*. München: Hanser, 1984.

Kaufholz, Elaine. "*Die Blendung*: un roman de la vie mutilée," *Austriaca* (11) 1980: 57–66.

Knoll, Heike. *Das System Canetti: Zur Rekonstruktion einer Wirklichkeitsentwurfes*. Stuttgart: Verlag für Wissenschaft und Forschung, 1993.

Kramberg, Karl Heinz. "Die verbrannte Bibliothek," *Süddeutsche Zeitung*, 19/20.10.1963.

Krüger, Michael, ed. *Finladung zur Verwandlung*. München: Hanser, 1995.

Krumme, Detlef. *Lesemodelle: Canetti, Grass, Höllerer*. München: Hanser, 1983.

Lappe, Thomas. *Canettis Aufzeichnungen*. Aachen: Alano, 1989.

Lawson, Richard, H. *Understanding Elias Canetti*. Columbia: University of South Carolina Press, 1991.

Lenz, Siegfried. "Krieg zwischen Küche und Kopf: Zu Elias Canettis *Die Blendung*," in S. L., *Elfenbeinturm und Barrikade: Erfahrungen am Schreibtisch*, 146–51. Hamburg: Hoffmann und Campe, 1983.

Lewis, Cecil Day. "Elias Canetti: *Auto Da Fé*," *The Listener*, 13.6.1946.

Liewerscheidt, Dieter. "Ein Widerspruch in der Erzählkonzeption von Elias Canettis Roman *Die Blendung," Wirkendes Wort* 28 (1978): 356–64.

Lorenz, Dagmar. "Elias Canetti: *Masse und Macht* und *Die Blendung*. Bezüge zwischen Roman und Massentheorie," *Modern Austrian Literature* 16 (1983): 81–92.

Lovett, Marilyn Smith. "*Fire in the Library: Paranoia and Schizophrenia as Models of Linguistic Crisis in Elias Canetti's Die Blendung.*" Ph.D diss., Indiana University, 1981.

Lützeler, P. M. *Deutsche Romane des 20. Jahrhunderts.* Königstein/Taunus: Athenäum, 1983.

Macartney, C. A. *The Habsburg Empire: 1790–1918.* London: Weidenfeld and Nicholson, 1971.

McFarlane, J. W., "The Tiresian Vision," *The Durham University Journal NS* 13 (1957): 109–15.

März, Eduard. "Erinnerungen," in *Vertriebene Vernunft I*, edited by F. Stadler, 499–512. Wien: Jugend und Volk, 1987.

Magris, Claudio. *Der habsburgische Mythos in der österreichischen Literatur.* Salzburg: Müller, 1966.

———. "Das geblendete Ich: Das Bild des Menschen in Elias Canetti," *Colloquia Germanica* 8 (1974): 344–75.

———. *Der unauffindbare Sinn: Zur österreichischen Literatur des 20. Jahrhunderts.* Klagenfurt: Carinthia Verlag, 1978.

———. "Der Schriftsteller, der sich versteckt," *Modern Austrian Literature* 16 (1983): 177–95.

Mankowitz, W. "*Auto Da Fé*," *The Critic* 1 (1950–51): 63–65.

Meili, Barbara. *Erinnerung und Vision.* Bonn: Bouvier, 1985.

Meyer, Christine. "La vie de Henry Brulard comme modèle pour l'autobiographie de Canetti," *Austriaca* 33 (1991): 89–107.

Michel, Karl Markus. "Der Intellektuelle und die Masse. Zu zwei Büchern von Elias Canetti," *Neue Rundschau* 75 (1964): 308–16.

Morgan, Peter. "Georges Kien and the 'diagnosis of delusion' in Elias Canetti's *Die Blendung*," *Neophilologus* 76 (1992): 77–89.

Moser, Manfred. "Zu Canettis *Blendung*," *Literatur und Kritik* 5 (1970): 591–609.

———. *Musil, Canetti, Eco, Calvino: Die überholte Philosophie.* Wien: Verband der wissenschaftlichen Gesellschaften Österreichs, 1986.

Mühlberger, Josef. "Welt ohne Kopf—Kopf ohne Welt," *Welt und Wort* 18 (1963): 353.

Murphy, Harriet. "Fritz Wotruba: The neglected master of stone," *The European*, 12.10.1990.

———. "Alfred Hrdlicka: a careless and cynical art," *The European*, 09.11.1990.

———. "A Passion for People: Elias Canetti's Autobiography and its Implications for Exile Studies," *Austrian Studies* 6 (1995): 134–46.

O'Donnell, Mary. "*The Theme of death in Elias Canetti's novel, Die Blendung.*" M.A. thesis, St. Patrick's College, Maynooth, Ireland, 1979.

Paal, Jutta. *Die Figurenkonstellation in Elias Canettis Roman Die Blendung.* Würzburg: Königshausen und Neumann, 1991.

Parry, Idris F. "Elias Canetti's Novel *Die Blendung*," in *Essays in German Literature I*, edited by F.Norman, 145–66. London: London University, 1965.

———. "Attitudes to Power," in Idris Parry, *Hand to Mouth and other Essays*, 151–73. Manchester: Carcanet, 1981.

Pattillo-Hess, J., ed. *Masse und Macht oder die Aufgabe des gegenwärtigen Denkens.* Wien: Löcker, 1988.

———, ed. *Tod und Verwandlung in Canettis Masse und Macht: Canetti Symposium.* Wien: Löcker, 1990.

———, ed. *Verwandlungsverbote und Befreieungsversuche in Canettis Masse und Macht: Canetti Symposium.* Wien: Löcker, 1991.

———, ed. *Der Stachel des Befehls.* Wien: Löcker, 1992.

Pattillo-Hess, J., and Mario Smole, eds. *Nationen.* Wien: Löcker, 1994.

Paul, J. M. "Rationalität und Wahnsinn in Canettis Roman *Die Blendung*," *Modern Austrian Literature* 16 (1983): 111–31.

Périsson-Waldmüller, Jutta and Gerald Stieg. "Elias Canetti en France," *Austriaca* 11 (1980): 121–64.

Peters, Carol. *Elias Canetti.* Berlin, 1990.

Piel, Edgar. "Herr seines Schicksals ist der Mensch allein. Elias Canettis *Blendung*," *Literatur und Kritik* 157/158 (1981): 444–61.

———. *Elias Canetti.* München: Beck, 1984.

Plard, Henri. "Elias Canetti, Prix Nobel de littérature," *Revue Générale* 12 (1981): 3–21.

Powe, B. W. *The Solitary Outlaw.* Toronto: Lester and Orpen Dennys, 1987.

Prewitt, Terry, et al., eds. *Semiotics 1988.* London: University Press of America, 1990.

Ritchie, J. M. "The Nazi Book-Burning," *Modern Language Review*, 83 (1988): 627–43.

Roberts, David. *Kopf und Welt: Elias Canettis Roman Die Blendung.* München: Hanser, 1975.

———. "The sense of an Ending: Apocalyptic Perspectives in the 20th Century German Novel," *Orbis Litterarum* 32 (1977): 140–58.

Rosen, Steven J. "Canettian and Freudian Approaches to Swift," in *Semiotics 1988*, edited by Terry Prewitt et al., 356–63. London: University Press of America, 1990.

Rosenfeld, Sidney. "1981 Nobel Laureate Elias Canetti: A Writer Apart," *World Literature Today* 56 (1982): 5–9.

Rüdiger, Horst. "Elias Canetti: *Die Blendung* 1948," *Wiener Literarisches Echo* 2 (1950): 38.

Russell, Peter. "The Vision of Man in *Die Blendung*," *German Life and Letters* I (1974): 24–35.

Sacharoff, Mark. "Grotesque Comedy in Canetti's *Auto da Fé*," *Critique* 14.1 (1972): 99–112.

Salzmann, Madeleine. *Die Kommunikationsstruktur der Autobiographie mit kommunikationsorientierten Analysen der Autobiographien von Max Frisch, Helga M. Novak und Elias Canetti.* Bern: Peter Lang, 1988.

Scheichl, Sigurd Paul. "Sprachreflexion in Canettis autobiographischen Büchern," *Modern Austrian Literature* 16 (1983): 23–46.

Schickel, Joachim. "Aspekte der Masse, Elemente der Macht. Versuch über Elias Canetti," *Text und Kritik* 28 (1970): 9–23.

Schmidt, Hugo. "Narrative attitudes in Canetti's *Die Blendung*," *Modern Austrian Literature* 16 (1983): 93–109.

Schottlaender, Rudolf. "Zur Rolle der Verehrung in Canettis Leben," *Sinn und Form* 40 (1988): 141–54.

Sebald, Winfried Georg. "Gedanken zu Elias Canetti," *Literatur und Kritik* 65 (1972): 280–85.

———. "Kurzer Versuch über System und Systemkritik bei Elias Canetti," *Etudes Germaniques* 39 (1984): 268–75.

Seidler, Ingo. "Who is Elias Canetti," in *Cross Currents: A Yearbook of Central European Culture*, edited by Ladislav Matejka and Benjamin Stolz, 107–23. Ann Arbor: Department of Slavic Languages and Literatures, University of Michigan, 1982.

———. "'Bruchstücke einer großen Konfession': Zur Bedeutung von Canettis 'Sudelbüchern,'" *Modern Austrian Literature* 16 (1983): 1–21.

Sheppard, Richard. "Upstairs-Downstairs—Some Reflections on German Literature in the light of Bakhtin's theory of Carnival," in *New Ways in Germanistik*, edited by Richard Sheppard, 278–315. Oxford: Berg, 1990.

Sokel, Walter H. "The Ambiguity of Madness: Elias Canetti's Novel *Die Blendung*," in *Views and Reviews of Modern German Literature. Festschrift für Adolf D. Klarmann*, edited by Karl S. Weimar, 181–87. München: Delp, 1974.

Soring, Jurgen. "Die Literatur als 'Provinz der Menschen': Zu Elias Canettis Aufzeichnungen," *Deutsche Vierteljahresschrift* 60 (1986): 645–66.

Stevens, Adrian, and Fred Wagner, eds. *Elias Canetti: Londoner Symposium*. Stuttgart: H. D. Heinz, 1991.

Stewart, William E. "The Role of the Crowd in Elias Canetti's Novel *Die Blendung*," M.A. diss., Manchester University, 1968.

Stieg, Gerald. "Canetti und Brecht oder 'es wird kein echter Chor daraus,'" *Austriaca* 2 (1976): 77–92.

———. "Questions à Elias Canetti," *Austriaca* (11) 1980: 17–30.

———. "Elias Canetti und Karl Kraus. Ein Versuch," *Modern Austrian Literature* 16 (1983): 197–210.

———. *Frucht des Feuers: Canetti, Doderer, Kraus und der Justizpalastbrand*. Wien: Edition Falter, 1990.

Stieg, Gerald, Uwe Dick, and Youssef Ishaghpour. "Drei Referate der Feier für Elias Canetti am österreichischen Kulturinstitut Paris," *Literatur und Kritik* 8 (1983): 382–93.

Strachey, Julia. "*Auto Da Fé*," *Horizon* 14 (July 1946): 60–63.

Sulzer, Dieter. "Canetti, Wotruba und die Erfahrung des Raumes," *Akzente* 3 (1980): 195–208.

Szell, Zsuzsa. "Verzicht auf Verständigung—Exkurs—Canetti: Blendende Möbel (*Die Blendung*)," in *Ichverlust und Scheingemeinschaft:*

Gesellschaftsbild in den Romanen von Franz Kafka, Robert Musil, Hermann Broch, Elias Canetti und George Saiko, 59–73. Budapest: Akadémiai Kiadó, 1979.

Taylor, Ronald. *Literature and Society in Germany 1918–1945*. Brighton: Harvester, 1980.

Thomas, Noel. "Elias Canetti's *Die Blendung* and Robert Musil's *Der Mann ohne Eigenschaften*: A Comparison," in *Robert Musil and the Literary Landscape of his Time: International Symposium 1990*, edited by Hannah Hickman. Salford: Department of Modern Languages, University of Salford, 1991.

Thomson, Edward A. "Elias Canetti's *Die Blendung* and the Changing Image of Madness," *German Life and Letters* 26 (1972): 38–47.

Thorpe, Kathleen. "Notes on *Die Blendung* by Elias Canetti," *Theoria* 67 (1986): 61–77.

Thwaite, Anthony. "Burning bibliomania," *Observer Review*, 17.1.1982.

Tunner, Erika. "Das Verhör. Zu einem Kapitel aus Canettis Roman *Die Blendung*," *Modern Austrian Literature* 16 (1983): 155–63.

Turner, David. "Elias Canetti: The Intellectual as King Canute," in *Modern Austrian Writing: Literature and Society after 1945*, edited by A. Best and H. Wolfschütz, 79–96. London: O. Wolff, 1980.

van Meeuwen, Piet. *Elias Canetti und die bildende Kunst. Von Breughel bis Goya*. Frankfurt: Peter Lang, 1988.

von Matt, Peter. "Der phantastische Aphorismus bei Elias Canetti," *Merkur* 445–95 (1990): 398–405.

Waldiger, Ernst. "Comédie humaine an Irren," *Das Silberboot* 1 (1935): 143–44.

Wallinger, Hanna. "Elias Canettis Übersetzungen von Upton Sinclair," in Wolfgang Pöckl, ed., *Österreichische Dichter als Übersetzer*, 103–22. Wien: Verlag der österreichischen Akademie der Wissenschaften, 1991.

Wallmann, J. P. "Zeitkritik im Roman: Elias Canetti: *Die Blendung*/ Günter Grass: *Hundejahre*," *Deutsche Rundschau* 89 (1963): 93–96.

Watt, R. H. "Der Einbruch von Unten: An Austrian syndrome of the inter-war years?" *German Life and Letters* 27 (1973–1974): 315–24.

Werlen, Hans-Jakob. "*Narrative Strategies in Elias Canetti's Die Blendung and Masse und Macht*," Ph.D. diss., Stanford University, 1988.

West, Anthony. "*The Tower of Babel*," *The New Yorker*, 11.4.1964, 172–74.

Widdig, Bernd. *Männerbünde und Massen: Zur Krise männlicher Identität in der Literatur der Moderne*. Opladen: Westdeutscher Verlag, 1992.

Wiethölter, Waltraud. "Sprechen—Lesen—Schreiben: Zur Funktion von Sprache und Schrift in Canettis Autobiographie," *Deutsche Vierteljahresschrift* 64 (1990): 149–71.

Williams, C. E. *The Broken Eagle: The Politics of Austrian Literature from Empire to Anschluss*. London: Paul Elek, 1974.

Zagari, L. "*Auto Da Fé*," in *Il Romanzo tedesco del Novecento*, 315–32. Torino: Edizio dell'albero, 1973.

Zepp, K. P. *Privatmythos und Wahn: Das mythopoetische Konzept im Werk Elias Canettis*. Frankfurt: Peter Lang, 1990.

Zöllner, Erich. *Geschichte Österreichs: Von den Anfängen bis zur Gegenwart*. Wien: Verlag für Geschichte und Politik, 1990.

INDEX